With best
regards,
from Charlie

A HANDBOOK FOR DATA ANALYSIS IN THE BEHAVIORAL SCIENCES: Statistical Issues

Edited by

Gideon Keren
Free University of Amsterdam

Charles Lewis
Educational Testing Service

LEA LAWRENCE ERLBAUM ASSOCIATES, PUBLISHERS
1993   Hillsdale, New Jersey   Hove & London

Lawrence Erlbaum Associates, Inc., Publishers
365 Broadway
Hillsdale, New Jersey 07642

Library of Congress Cataloging-in-Publication Data

A Handbook for data analysis in the behavioral sciences : statistical
issues / edited by Gideon Keren, Charles Lewis.
    p. cm.
  includes bibliographical references and index.
  ISBN 0-8058-1092-7 (cloth : alk. paper). — ISBN 0-8058-1093-5
(paper : alk. paper)
    1. Psychology—Statistical methods. 2. Social sciences—
Statistical methods. 3. Psychology—Research—Methodology.
4. Social sciences—Research—Methodology. I. Keren, Gideon.
II. Lewis, Charles, 1943– .
  [DNLM: 1. Behavioral Sciences. 2. Data Interpretation,
Statistical. 3. Models, Statistical. BF 39 H236]
BF39.H26437 1992
150'.72—dc20
DNLM/DLC
for Library of Congress   92-49442
                         CIP

Books published by Lawrence Erlbaum Associates are printed
on acid-free paper, and their bindings are chosen for strength
and durability.

Printed in the United States of America
10 9 8 7 6 5 4 3 2 1

Contents

Preface   ix

PART I: ANALYSIS OF VARIANCE AND MULTIPE REGRESSION

1. **Elements of the General Linear Model**
    Maurice Tatsuoka   **3**
    Introduction   3
    The Simplest Case of Two Groups: An Informal Treatment   4
    The Two-Group Case: Formal Treatment   10
    Matrix Formulation: Parameter Estimation   14
    Matrix Formulation: Significance Testing   26
    Higher-Order, Multivariate, and Covariance Designs   31

2. **Pairwise Comparison Procedures for One-Way Analysis**
    of Variance Designs
    Rebecca Zwick   **43**
    Type I Error and Power   43
    Comparing the Empirical Type I Error Rates and Powers
        of Competing MCPS   46
    The Independent-Sample Case   47
    One-Factor Repeated Measures Designs   64
    Conclusions   67

3. **Analyzing Means From Repeated Measures Data**
    Charles Lewis   **73**
    The Current State of Affairs   75
    Alternatives to Standard Repeated Measures Analysis of Variance   76
    A Numerical Illustration   89

*4. **A Balanced Approach to Unbalanced Designs**
     Gideon Keren   **95**
     Introduction   95
     Possible Sources of Unequal Designs   96
     The Regression Solution for the Balanced Design   97
     The Case of Unequal but Proportional Cell Frequencies   102
     Unequal Disproportionate Cell Frequencies   108
     Additional Considerations: Sample vs Population, Weighting and
        Coding   114
     Final Comments and a Brief Summary   120
     Appendix A: Construction and Proofs of a Coding System
        for the Case of Proportional N's Which Will Always
        Maintain Orthogonality   122

5.   **MANOVA and MANCOVA: An Overview**
     Neil M. Timm   **129**
     Introduction   129
     Fundamentals: Full Rank Model   130
     Fundamentals: Less Than Full Rank Models   141
     Geometry: ANCOVA Model   149
     Fundamentals: Restricted Full Rank Model   154
     The Multivariate Linear Model: Estimation   157
     The Multivariate Linear Model: Hypothesis Testing   158
     MANOVA and MANCOVA: Some General Principles   161

6.   **Set Correlation**
     Jacob Cohen   **165**
     Sets as Research Factors   165
     Partialling   166
     Canonical Analysis   167
     Elements of Set Correlation   168
     Hypothesis Testing, Estimation, and Statistical Power Testing
        the Null Hypothesis   174
     Computation   180
     Applications of Set Correlations   180
     Illustrative Examples   183
     A Hierarchical Analysis of a Quantitative Set and
        Its Unique Components   185

PART II: **BAYESIAN STATISTICS**

*7. **Bayesian Statistics: An Overview**
     Robert L. Winkler   **201**
     Introduction   201
     Bayes' Theorem   203
     Assessment of Likelihood Functions and Prior Distributions   216

Estimation and Hypothesis Testing   221
Prediction   225
Decision Making Under Uncertainty   228
Conclusions   229

*8. **Bayesian Methods for the Analysis of Variance**
  Charles Lewis   **233**
  Introduction   233
  Fixed Effect, Between Subject Designs   234
  Designs Having Repeated Measures   246
  Closing Remarks   254

PART III: CATAGORICAL DATA AND THE ANALYSIS OF FREQUENCIES

9. **Analysis of Categorical Data**
  Stephen S. Brier   **259**
  Introduction   259
  Generation of Contingency Tables   260
  Formulation and Interpretation of Log-Linear Models   262
  Estimation of Parameters in Log-Linear Models   269
  Goodness of Fit Tests   277
  Analyzing Incomplete Tables   281
  Path Analysis in Contingency Tables   285
  Other Applications of the Methodology of Log-Linear Models   288
  Further Readings References   291

10. **On the Use and Misuse of Chi-Square**
  Kevin L. Delucchi   **295**
  The Use of Chi-Square   296
  Supplementary and Alternative Procedures   304
  Conclusions   314

11. **Some Aspects of the Analysis of Categorical Data**
  B. S. Everitt   **321**
  Introduction   321
  The 2 × 2 Contingency Table   322
  Correspondence Analysis   332
  Logistic Regression   334
  Case-Control Studies   338
  Latent Class Models   342
  Conclusions   345

PART IV: OTHER TOPICS

12. **Exploratory Data Analysis**
  Albert F. Smith and Deborah A. Prentice   **349**
  Philosophy of Exploratory Data Analysis   353
  Nonparametric Procedures, Robust Statistics, and EDA   355

Techniques for the Examination of a Sample Measured
on One Variable   356
Techniques for the Comparison of Several Samples Measures
on One Variable   363
The Analysis of the Relationship Between Two Ordered Variables   370
Analysis of Two-Way Tables   379
Conclusion   388

13. **Graphical Data Analysis**
Howard Wainer and David Thissen   **391**
Introduction   391
History   393
Graphics for Data Analysis   395
Two-Way Displays of One-Way Data   399
Two-Way Displays of Multivariate Data   424
A Multivariate Example: The Worst American State Revisited   435
Everything Else   445
Conclusions   450

14. **Uses of Computers in Psychological Research**
Russell M. Church   **459**
Literature Search   460
Experimental Design   462
Experimental Control   462
Data Acquisition   465
Data Retention   465
Data Analysis   466
Development of Theory   468
Comparison of Theory to Data   470
Preparation of Manuscript   473
Communication   473
Conclusions and Speculations   474

15. **Computer Simulation: Some Remarks on Theory in Psychology**
Geoffrey R. Loftus   **477**
The Historical Approach   478
Psychology and Cosmology   485
Computer Simulation in the Social Sciences   487
Should Computers Be Banned   488
Conclusions   490

16. **Essentials in the Design and Analysis of Time-Series Experiments**
Regina H. Rushe and John M. Gottman   **493**
How to Design Time-Series Experiments   493
How to Describe Time-Series Data   502

How to Do a Time-Series Analysis   512
Recent Innovations in Time-Series Analysis   524
Resources for Time-Series Analysis   525

AUTHOR INDEX   529

SUBJECT INDEX   539

Preface

Science is supposed to be an ever *changing* enterprise. Yet "change is not made without inconvenience, even from worse to better" (quoted by Johnson in the preface to the *English Dictionary*). This inherent resistance to change may account (at least partly) for the recent claim made by Aiken, West, Sechrest, and Reno (1990) that statistical and methodological training of psychologists has barely advanced during the past 20 years. Their conclusions are based, among other things, on a survey conducted in close to 200 psychology departments in North America, and are further supported by examining the leading psychological journals from which it is apparent that the methodology and methods of data analysis have hardly changed. For instance, the conventional null hypothesis testing remains by far the most common and preferred method for analyzing empirical data. The continuous and growing number of articles that appeared in methodological- and statistical-oriented journals such as the *Psychological Bulletin* point out the pitfalls of null hypotheses testing (see chapter 16 of the *Methodological Issues* volume) and offer some remedies or alternative methods of data analysis, but apparently had little impact (see chapter 11 of *Methodological Issues* volume for a more elaborated discussion).

The lack of change is further accompanied by some misunderstandings of the use of statistical tools. Apparently, people are poor intuitive statisticians, (chapters 12 and 13 of the *Methodological Issues* volume), and even social scientists have been shown to possess some fundamental misunderstandings regarding statistical theory. Unfortunately, statistical methodology is often conceived by social scientists in a technical manner, and its utilization resembles a drunken man's use of lamp posts: for support rather than for illumination. There are several causes that have led to this state of affairs and a few of these are mentioned here.

As pointed out earlier, most graduate programs offer a rather narrow number of courses. Psychology departments usually require a single course that is mainly centered on hypothesis testing and analysis of variance. Other courses, which are usually considered as advanced, are not required and consequently have a low attendance.

Most of the methodology and statistical textbooks (particularly those for the social sciences) do not improve the situation. They are typically written in the technical style of a cookbook, and provide straightforward algorithms usually avoiding the controversial issues, confusions, and complexity that characterize our knowledge. In particular, they do not sufficiently introduce the uncertainties involved in the use and application of statistical tools. Consequently, many readers are led to believe that once they know and understand well the algorithm or procedure of a certain method, the major goal has been achieved. Statistical procedures are thus frequently performed mechanically by a "blind" process (Wertheimer, 1959), rather than in a genuine constructive mode. In fact, the use of statistical methodology often requires careful considerations (e.g., what is the appropriate tool for a given question, what are the underlying assumptions of a particular methodology) and several subjective decisions—even if one is not a Bayesian! It is especially the latter aspect that is often ignored or misunderstood: Any statistical tool may aid researchers in their scientific inquiry, but it cannot substitute for the subjective judgments and personal interpretations that have to be made by the researcher.

Another source of difficulty lies in the fact that many of the methodological and statistical developments appear in specialized journals, frequently in journals with little relation to the substantive area of the researcher (e.g., pure statistical journals). Moreover, such articles are frequently written in a highly technical language and include mathematical sophistication that social scientists often find difficult to follow. Finally, methodological and statistical methods constitute such a broad area that it is difficult to systematically follow the progress on so many different fronts.

The present two-volume book is an attempt to provide some partial remedy to the aforementioned problems. The first volume is devoted to methodological issues and related topics such as mathematical modeling, measurement, and scaling. The second volume focuses on statistical issues: In addition to covering traditional topics of classical statistics (e.g., hypothesis testing, analysis of variance, multiple regression), it also offers an extensive treatment of the Bayesian approach as well as some recent developments like Exploratory Data Analysis (EDA). Indeed, our choice of topics (for both volumes) was guided by including traditional issues as well as more novel and recent developments that we believe to be of growing importance of the social sciences. All the chapters were written under the assumption that potential readers have a limited acquaintance with the basics of statistical methodology and possess only elementary mathematical skills. Indeed, all authors were asked to follow three major guidelines: (a) Present the material in a simple and clear style (including intuitive explanations), avoiding complex mathematical formulations unless necessary; (b) emphasize applications by using as many examples as possible, explaining the rationale underlying each analysis and briefly summarizing potential difficulties associated with the application of a specific tool; and (c) provide as many references as possible so that the interested reader can refer to other sources for elaboration. It is our hope that, to the extent that we were able to follow these guidelines, these two volumes will enable the reader to overcome some of the aforementioned difficulties. In particular, our aim is to provide an updated survey on different aspects of empirical research and data analysis, facilitate the understanding of the internal logic underlying different methods, and provide novel and broader perspectives beyond what is usually covered in traditional curricula.

This book constitutes a considerable and elaborated revision of *Statistical and Methodological Issues in Psychology and Social Sciences Research* published in 1982. Some chapters from the previous book have been substantially revised (these are marked in the table of contents by an asterisk). A few chapters are based on journal articles that have been specifically revised to accommodate the book.[1] Most of the chapters, however, are original contributions to this edition.

The present edition departs from the previous book in several fundamental respects. According to the basic assumption of these volumes, philosophy of science, research methodology, and statistics are deeply interrelated in most applications. Consequently, we make an attempt to cover these different facets rather than to focus solely on statistical methodology. We also include several chapters dealing with descriptive data. A growing body of empirical psychological research indicates that people are not always good "intuitive statisticians." This research suggests that reasoning is sometimes guided by unwarranted heuristics and hampered by (logically) unjustified biases. Any scientific activity results from operations carried by the human's cognitive system, so it seems to us that the study of this cognitive system and its limitations are an integral part of the scientific endeavor. It is also our belief that realization of one's own weaknesses is a necessary condition for change.

Our emphasis on the cognitive facet has another aspect, namely the tendency of practitioners to view and apply methodological and statistical methods in a mechanical and technical manner. We believe that analysis and explanation of empirical data requires creativity as well as judgments (as is reflected explicitly in many chapters in this book). Data as well as results of statistical analysis can be interpreted in different ways. In fact, the initial decision of which particular method or statistical technique is most appropriate requires careful and meticulous considerations. We deliberately chose a broad spectrum of methods, some of which are known to be conflicting (e.g., Bayesian vs. classical statistics). We are also aware that the views expressed by different authors may occasionally be

---

[1]Only chapters 12 and 16 of the *Methodological Issues* volume have been reprinted without any modifications.

incompatible. The decision of which method to use, how, and when, is, in our opinion, part of the researcher's task. We believe there is not always one right approach or method, and the final choice depends on the particular question the researcher wants to address, the nature of the data, and the larger context in which it was collected. The choice of which method is the appropriate one under given circumstances is part of what constitutes the art of the scientific inquiry.

GIDEON KEREN

CHARLES LEWIS

REFERENCES

Aiken, L. S., West, S. G., Sechrest, L., & Reno, R. R. (1990). Graduate training in statistics, methodology, and measurement in psychology. *American Pscyhologist, 45,* 721–734.

Keren, G. (1982). *Statistical and methodological issues in psychology and social sciences research.* Hillsdale, NJ: Lawrence Erlbaum Associates.

Wertheimer, M. (1959). *Productive thinking.* New York: Harper & Row.

ANALYSIS OF VARIANCE AND MULTIPLE REGRESSION

Analysis of variance, multiple regression and other special cases of the general linear model enjoy great popularity in the social sciences. Chapter 1, by Tatsuoka, provides an accessible introduction to the subject. It takes the reader in careful detail through the problem of comparing the means of two independent groups, first showing informally how it can be recast as a regression problem and then spelling out the formal details. The setup for this case is re-expressed in matrix notation, thus allowing general expressions for the linear model to be introduced. The chapter concludes with a discussion of how factorial designs, multivariate problems and the analysis of covariance can all be expressed in the same framework.

In chapter 2, Zwick discusses the multiple comparisons problem in the context of one-way analysis of variance, focusing on the pairwise comparison of all treatment means for both the independent groups and repeated measures cases. She compares the best known procedures in terms of both power and Type I error probability, and describes alternatives that are available when there is concern about violation of the assumptions of normality and/or homogeneity of variance. Single-step methods of comparison are recommended because of their simplicity and the availability of associated simultaneous confidence intervals for the comparisons.

Several procedures for carrying out a repeated measures analysis of variance have been proposed. Chapter 3, by Lewis, emphasizes that the most commonly used method of analysis should, in fact, be avoided and describes in detail the properties of three satisfactory alternatives. One of these develops ideas introduced by Zwick regarding multiple comparisons for repeated measures. This approach appears to provide the best combination of power, robustness and interpretability.

When unequal numbers of observations have been obtained in the different cells of a factorial analysis of variance design, the result is referred to as unbalanced (or nonorthogonal). Such a situation presents difficulties in choosing a method of analysis and interpreting the results. Keren, in chapter 4, gives an introduction to a variety of issues associated with unbalanced designs, emphasizing the value of the framework provided by the general linear model and the importance of specifying clearly the questions that the researcher is trying to answer before selecting a method of analysis.

Chapter 5, by Timm, provides an overview of various approaches to the analysis of variance and covariance in the context of the general linear model. He shows correspondences among the approaches in terms of hypotheses tested or parameters estimated. In addition, he gives geometric interpretations of the analyses which are a valuable tool for developing intuitions when working with the linear model. Using the restricted full rank formulation, Timm extends the model to the multivariate case and again addresses the issues of hypothesis testing and estimation.

Since multiple regression and analysis of variance are both special cases of the general linear model, it is reasonable to consider whether approaches developed in one context may be usefully applied in the more general situation. In chapter 6, Cohen describes and illustrates the application of correlational tools to the multivariate linear model. He discusses measures of multivariate association (set correlations) between two sets of variables and gives special attention to the case when other sets of variables have been partialled from either or both of the original two sets. This provides a framework for testing hypotheses, assessing statistical power and estimating parameters, as well as describing degree of partial association. Several examples are analyzed in detail to illustrate the breadth and strength of this approach.

1

Elements of the General Linear Model

Maurice Tatsuoka
Educational Testing Service

INTRODUCTION

It has been commonplace at least since the mid-1960s to hear of the *general linear model* (or the general linear hypothesis) being used in computer programs for carrying out significance tests in the analysis of variance (ANOVA) or analysis of covariance (ANCOVA) and their multivariate counterparts (MANOVA and MANCOVA). This may seem to some readers like a major departure from the customary F ratio (MS_h/MS_e) approach to significance testing in this field. The two approaches are, however, very closely related. It might be more accurate to say that the general linear model is just an alternative, more general and more rational way to get to the significance-test F ratio than is the "traditional" way of partitioning the total sum of squares somewhat arbitrarily into various components.

The word "traditional" used in referring to the customary partitioning of sums of squares is placed in quotation marks because, in a way, the general linear model approach (or a precursor of it) is the older and hence the more traditional approach. This is because Fisher, the originator of ANOVA (and many other statistical techniques) initially used multiple regression analysis (which is basically what the general linear model is) to carry out multigroup significance testing. The multiple regression approach was feasible for the simplest cases (i.e., one-way design problems) of ANOVA, but for factorial and more complicated designs the computational difficulty proved to be insurmountable in the precomputer days. It was largely for this reason that Fisher invented what we now know as the traditional variance-partitioning approach to ANOVA. It may thus be said that the widespread availability of computers has restored multiple

3

regression analysis to its rightful position as the "truly traditional" (or neoclassical, if you will) approach to ANOVA, because computational difficulty no longer posed a problem. Of course, Fisher's original developments have undergone many refinements and extensions—to the point that virtually any conceivable ANOVA and ANCOVA design can be handled by a single general model (and hence a single computer program), with minor technical adjustments to accommodate the different designs.

In this chapter we describe in detail only the simplest cases of the general linear model. Applications to more complicated designs are only indicated, without their solutions being carried out. One of our goals is to show the equivalence of the results of significance tests based on the general linear model approach and those using the F ratios stemming from the familiar partitioning of sums of squares. Another goal is to provide the reader with sufficient background to be able to profit from reading more extensive, and necessarily more difficult, treatments of this subject, such as Searle (1971), Finn (1974), Arnold (1981), and McCullagh and Welder (1983). It should also enable readers to understand the theoretical underpinnings of computer programs for (or using) the general linear model such as those contained in the BMDP, SAS and SPSS^x packages.

THE SIMPLEST CASE OF TWO GROUPS: AN INFORMAL TREATMENT

It is well known that for testing the significance of the difference between two independent group means, a simple t-test with $n_1 + n_2 - 2$ degrees of freedom will suffice. However, the square of a t-variate with v degrees of freedom is an F-variate with one degree of freedom in the numerator and v degrees of freedom in the denominator (see, e.g., Hays, 1988, p. 337). Furthermore, it can be shown that the t-statistic for testing the H_0: $\mu_1 = \mu_2$, when squared, yields a quantity that is algebraically equivalent to $F = MS_b/MS_w$ as computed for the two-group case. Hence, the equivalence of the significance test in the general linear model for the two-group case and the ANOVA F test will have been established once we show the equivalence of the former with the customary t test.

The first step in our informal linear-model formulation is to define a group-membership indicator variable X, which takes on any two distinct values—most commonly 1 and 0—for members of the two groups, respectively. That is to say, every member of Group 1 gets one value (say 1) and everyone in Group 2 gets the other value (say 0) on this "dummy variable," X. This serves as the predictor variable in the simple linear regression equation

$$\hat{Y} = a + bX. \tag{1}$$

The criterion variable Y is, of course, the variable whose means $\bar{Y}_1$ and $\bar{Y}_2$ in the two groups we want to compare; that is, we want to test whether or not Y_1 and

Y_2 differ significantly from each other. It should be intuitively obvious that the question being asked is equivalent to the question, "Is the regression coefficient b in Equation 1 significantly different from zero?" For if this coefficient were not significantly different from zero, it would mean that Equation 1 offers only a chance prediction of Y from X. Hence the means of the *predicted* Y values in the two groups—which, it should be recalled, are equal respectively to the two *observed* group means on Y—differ only by chance, which is the same as saying that $\bar{Y}_1$ (= $\hat{Y}_1$) and $\bar{Y}_2$ (= $\hat{Y}_2$) are not significantly different from each other. (A mathematical proof of this equivalence is given in the appendix of this chapter, for the benefit of those who want something more than an argument based on "intuitive obviousness.")

Returning to Equation 1, we recall that, in the least-squares approach, the constants a (the intercept) and b (the slope) are determined by minimizing the sum of squared discrepancies between the actual and predicted Y scores in the total sample (i.e., Groups 1 and 2 combined). The quantity to be minimized as a function of a and b is:

$$Q = \Sigma(Y - \hat{Y})^2.$$

In our present context, we are interested only in the regression coefficient b, for it is this quantity whose nonnullity we want to test for significance. It is shown in most statistics texts (e.g., Hays, 1988, p. 563) that the optimal value of b is given by the expression

$$b = \frac{N\Sigma XY - (\Sigma X)(\Sigma Y)}{N\Sigma X^2 - (\Sigma X)^2}. \tag{2}$$

Three of the sums that occur in this expression, ΣX, ΣX^2 and ΣXY, take on special values because of the nature of the group-membership variable X. Let us consider the simplest case, letting $X = 1$ for Group 1 members and $X = 0$ for Group members. It should then be obvious that

$$\Sigma X = \Sigma X^2 = n_1$$

because for both these sums, only the members of Group 1 contribute nonzero summands, namely 1 for each member; hence the sum over the entire sample (both groups combined) will simply be the number of individuals in Group 1, or n_1.

Next, let us see what ΣXY reduces to when X takes the values 1 and 0. The product XY is just the Y value itself for each member of Group 1 and is 0 for every member of Group 2. It therefore follows that

$$\Sigma XY = \underset{\text{Gr1}}{\Sigma Y},$$

the sum of Y for Group 1. Equivalently, we may write

$$\Sigma XY = n_1\bar{Y}_1,$$

where n_1 is the size of Group 1, as before and $\bar{Y}_1$ is the mean of Y in Group 1. Upon substituting these special values for ΣX, ΣX^2 and ΣXY in Equation 2 and leaving ΣY as is for the time being, we obtain

$$b = \frac{N(n_1 \bar{Y}_1) - n_1(\Sigma Y)}{Nn_1 - n_1^2}$$

$$= \frac{N\bar{Y}_1 - \Sigma Y}{n_2} \tag{3}$$

(because $N - n_1 = n_2$, the size of Group 2).
Next, we rewrite ΣY as follows:

$$\Sigma Y = \Sigma Y_1 + \Sigma Y_2 = n_1 \bar{Y}_1 + n_2 \bar{Y}_2.$$

Substituting this in Equation 3 and simplifying, we get

$$b = \bar{Y}_1 - \bar{Y}_2. \tag{4}$$

It should be noted that if we had assigned two distinct nonzero values c_1 and c_2 as the X values for Group 1 and Group 2 members, respectively, instead of 1 and 0 as we did earlier, the algebra would have been slightly more tedious, and we would have got

$$b = (\bar{Y}_1 - \bar{Y}_2)/(c_1 - c_2), \tag{4a}$$

as interested readers may verify for themselves.

We thus see that the regression coefficient b given by Equation 1 is equal to the difference between the two group means of Y divided by the difference between the X value assigned to members of the two groups, respectively. An alternative (and geometrically more meaningful) way of putting this is to say that b is the ratio of the difference between the Y means and the difference between the X means of the two groups. (All members of each group have the same X scores, c_1 and c_2 respectively for Groups 1 and 2, so these values also are the X means for the two groups.) The regression line passes through the centroids of the two groups—that is, points with coordinates $(\bar{X}_1, \bar{Y}_1)$ and $(\bar{X}_2, \bar{Y}_2)$; hence the ratio $(\bar{Y}_1 - \bar{Y}_2)/(\bar{X}_1 - \bar{X}_2)$ is precisely the slope of this line, as shown in Fig. 1.1. When the X values are 1 and 0, this reduces to the difference $\bar{Y}_1 - \bar{Y}_2$ itself as in Equation 4, but if we assign two distinct nonzero values c_1 and c_2, we get the more general result of Equation 4a. In either case, it is clear that testing the significance of the difference $\bar{Y}_1 - \bar{Y}_2$ amounts to the same thing as testing whether or not b is significantly different from zero. However, "amounts to the same thing" might sound rather loose, and some readers may want to know if the two significance tests are actually *identical*. As mentioned earlier, the appendix to this chapter proves that this is indeed the case. Here we illustrate the point by means of a numerical example.

Example 1

Suppose that the subjects in two groups in an experiment got the following scores on Y, the criterion variable.

Group 1 ($n_1 = 12$)	Group 2 ($n_2 = 14$)		
16	4		
18	10		
6	9		
12	13		
11	11		
12	9		
23	13		
19	9		
7	5		
11	8		
14	7		
13	10		
	8	Total Sample	
	10	($N = 26$)	

$\sum Y_{Gr_j}$	162	126	288	$= \sum Y$
$\bar{Y}_j$	13.5	9.0	11.08	$= \bar{Y}$
$\sum Y^2_{Gr_j}$	2450	1220	3670	$= \sum Y^2$

We want to test the null hypothesis, H_0: $\mu_1 = \mu_2$, against the two-sided alternative, H_1: $\mu_1 = \mu_2$. The standard way to do this, of course, is to carry out a t test for two independent-group means. The intermediate quantities needed for this test are shown at the bottom of the data table. Substituting the appropriate quantities in the customary formula for s^2_w (or the MS_w of ANOVA), we get

$$s^2_w = \frac{[\sum_{Gr1} Y^2 - (\sum_{Gr1} Y)^2/n_1] + [\sum_{Gr2} Y^2 - (\sum_{Gr2} Y)^2/n_2]}{n_1 + n_2 - 2}$$

$$= \frac{[2450 - (162)^2/12 + [1220 - (126)^2/14]}{24}$$

$$= 14.5417.$$

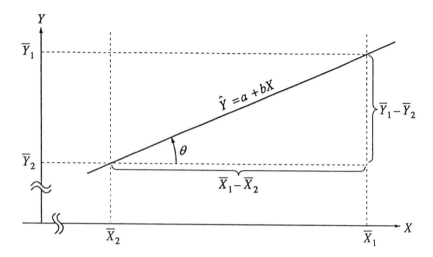

$$b = \tan \theta = \frac{\bar{Y}_1 - \bar{Y}_2}{\bar{X}_1 - \bar{X}_2}$$

FIG. 1.1. Regression line of Y on X when X is a dichotomous variable, showing that the regression coefficient b is equal to $(\bar{Y}_1 - \bar{Y}_2)/(\bar{X}_1 - \bar{Y}_2)$.

The required t statistic is then calculated as

$$t = \frac{\bar{Y}_1 - \bar{Y}_2}{\sqrt{s_w^2(1/n_1 + 1/n_2)}}$$

$$= \frac{13.5 - 9.0}{\sqrt{14.5417(1/12 + 1/14)}}$$

$$= 2.999666,$$

with $n_1 + n_2 - 2 = 24$ degrees of freedom. (Ordinarily, it would be ridiculous and spurious to calculate the t value to so many decimal places, but we have purposely kept seven significant digits here, in order to show the extent of agreement with the result later obtained by the regression-analysis approach.) The difference, 4.5, between the two group-means on Y is significant at the 1% level, because $t_{24;.995} = 2.797$.

Let us now use our "informal" general linear model approach (i.e., the plain regression-analysis method) by testing the significance of the coefficient b in the regression equation of Y on the dummy group-membership variable, X. Although we already know from Equation 4 that $b = Y_1 - Y_2$, we here compute b from scratch, using Equation 2, in order to confirm this relation numerically.

For this example, the relevant numerical values are

$$\Sigma X = \Sigma X^2 = 12,$$

$$\Sigma XY = \Sigma Y = 162,$$

$$\Sigma Y = 288 \text{ and } \Sigma Y^2 = 3670$$

as seen at the top and bottom of the data table. Upon substituting all but the last of these values, and $N = 26$, in Equation 2, we get

$$b = \frac{(26)\ (162) - (12)\ (288)}{(26)\ (12) - (12)^2}$$

$$= 4.5,$$

which agrees, as expected, with the value of $\bar{Y}_1 - \bar{Y}_2$.

The t statistic for testing the significance of b (i.e., the significance of its difference from zero) is readily derived from the more widely known t statistic for testing the significance of the correlation coefficient r, which is related to b as follows:

$$r = b\frac{\sqrt{\Sigma X^2 - (\Sigma X)^2/N}}{\sqrt{\Sigma Y^2 - (\Sigma Y)^2/N}}.$$

Substituting this expression in the formula

$$t = \frac{r\sqrt{N - 2}}{\sqrt{1 - r^2}}$$

we get

$$t = \frac{b\sqrt{(N - 2)\ [\Sigma X^2 - (\Sigma X)^2/N]}}{\sqrt{[\Sigma Y^2 - (\Sigma Y)^2/N] - b^2[\Sigma X^2 - (\Sigma X)^2/N]}}.$$

With the appropriate numerical substitutions, we obtain the following value

$$t = (4.5)\frac{\sqrt{(24)\ (12 - 144/26)}}{\sqrt{[3670 - (288)^2/26] - (4.5)^2\ (12 - 144/26)}}$$

$$= 2.999669.$$

This is clearly equal, within rounding error, to the value 2.999666 earlier obtained for the t statistic for testing the significance of the difference between the Y means of our two treatment groups. We have thus verified numerically both that $b = \bar{Y}_1 - \bar{Y}_2$ (when the dummy variable takes the values 1 and 0) and that the significance tests of b and of $\bar{Y}_1 - \bar{Y}_2$ by their respective t statistics yield identical results.

Even the most skeptical reader will probably have been convinced by the foregoing demonstration that, at least in the two-group case, testing the significance of the difference between independent group means can be done just as well by a linear regression model approach.

THE TWO-GROUP CASE: FORMAL TREATMENT

One problem with the "informal treatment" given in the preceding section is that it cannot easily be generalized to multigroup cases, much less to designs of higher order. In contrast, the formal treatment presented in this section, although more complicated at first glance, has the advantage that it can be readily generalized to any ANOVA design.

The first step of the formal treatment is to define the linear structural model for the design. For the two-group design, the simplest form in which to write the structural model is

$$Y_{ij} = \mu_j + \epsilon_{ij} \quad (i = 1, 2, \ldots, n_j; \, j = 1, 2),$$

which simply says that an individual's Y scores can be expressed as the sum of the mean μ_j of the subpopulation to which the person belongs and an error term specific to that individual. This is certainly an intuitively appealing expression, but it has the disadvantage of not being explicit in specifying whether the design is one-way or factorial or whatever. To make this distinction explicit we need to introduce what are called *effect parameters,* defined as the deviation of the jth subpopulation mean from the overall mean:

$$\alpha_j = \mu_j - \mu.$$

From this definition, it follows that

$$\mu_j = \mu + \alpha_j$$

so that the aforementioned structural equation can be rewritten as

$$Y_{ij} = \mu + \alpha_j + \epsilon_{ij} \quad (i = 1, 2, \ldots, n_j; \, j = 1, 2). \tag{5}$$

This form can be generalized to factorial and other designs by including further parameters like β_k for the effect of the kth level of the second factor, $(\alpha\beta)_{jk}$ for the effect of interaction of the jth level of the first factor and the kth level of the second factor, and so forth, as discussed later.

We now omit the error term ϵ_{ij} from the right-hand side of Equation 5 and denote the remaining expression by $\hat{Y}_{ij}$, which the *predicted Y* score, as against the *actual Y* score that was modeled by that equation. We then have the prediction equation,

$$\hat{Y}_{ij} = \mu + \alpha_j \quad (i = 1, 2, \ldots, n_j; \, j = 1, 2), \tag{6}$$

which is really a regression equation, as can be made explicit by introducing two group-membership indicator variables X_1 and X_2 taking the following values:

$$X_I = \begin{cases} 1 & \text{for Group 1 members} \\ 0 & \text{for Group 2 members} \end{cases}$$

$$X_2 = \begin{cases} 0 & \text{for Group 1 members} \\ 1 & \text{for Group 2 members} \end{cases}$$

and numbering the subjects in a single sequence from $i = 1$ through N, instead of from 1 through n_1 and 1 through n_2 in two cycles. The equation then becomes

$$\hat{Y}_i = \mu + \alpha_1 X_{1i} + \alpha_2 X_{2i} \qquad (i = 1, 2, \ldots, N) \qquad (7)$$

as the reader may readily verify. (The dummy variables X_1 and X_2 serve to select the appropriate one of the two effect parameters α_1 and α_2 depending on the group to which a given individual belongs.)

Equation 7 is a *multiple* regression equation, in contrast to the simple regression equation that was used in our earlier informal treatment. One reason for the greater generality of our present formal treatment may be explained as follows: When there are more groups than two (say J), it will not do to assign the values 0, 1, . . . , $J - 1$ to a single group-indicator variable X, for that would introduce an artificial *ordering* of the groups. We avoid this problem when we use as many indicator variables, $X_1, X_2, \ldots, X_J$, as there are groups, with each one taking just the values 0 and 1. The parameters μ, α_1, and α_2 can again be estimated by invoking the least-squares principle and minimizing the sum of squared discrepancies,

$$Q = \Sigma(Y_i - \hat{Y}_i)^2$$

between the observed and predicted scores, this time as a function of three unknowns, μ, α_1, α_2 (or $J + 1$ unknowns, μ, α_1, α_2, . . . , α_J, in the case of J groups). This is accomplished by taking the partial derivatives of Q (after substituting the right-hand side of equation 7 for $\hat{Y}_i$) with respect to μ, α_1, and α_2 and setting each of these equal to zero. Details may be found in most textbooks on multivariate analysis (e.g., Tatsuoka, 1988, pp. 39–40). The results are a set of *normal equations*

$$N\mu + (\Sigma X_{1i})\alpha_1 \quad + (\Sigma X_{2i})\alpha_2 \quad = \Sigma Y_i$$
$$(\Sigma X_{1i})\mu + (\Sigma X_{1i}^2)\alpha_1 \quad + (\Sigma X_{1i}X_{2i})\alpha_2 = \Sigma X_{1i}Y_i$$
$$(\Sigma X_{2i})\mu + (\Sigma X_{2i}X_{1i})\alpha_1 + (\Sigma X_{2i}^2)\alpha_2 \quad = \Sigma X_{2i}Y_i.$$

By the nature of the dummy variables X_1 and X_2 shown earlier, all the sums in this set of equations, except ΣY_i, simplify as follows:

$$\Sigma X_{1i} = \Sigma X_{1i}^2 = n_1$$
$$\Sigma X_{2i} + \Sigma X_{2i}^2 = n_2$$
$$\Sigma X_{1i}Y_i = \underset{\text{Gr}1}{\Sigma Y_i}, \qquad \Sigma X_{2i}Y = \underset{\text{Gi}2}{\Sigma Y_i}$$

and
$$\Sigma X_{1i}X_{2i} = 0.$$

(The last relation holds because one or the other of X_1 and X_2 must be zero for everyone in the entire sample.)

Upon substituting these special values and writing m, a_1 and a_2 in place of μ, α_1 and α_2 (because we are solving for *estimates* of these parameters), the set of normal equations simplify as follows:

$$Nm + n_1 a_1 + n_2 a_2 = T$$

$$n_1 m + n_1 a_1 \qquad = T_1$$

$$n_2 m \qquad + n_2 a_2 = T_2 \qquad (8)$$

where T, T_1 and T_2 are abbreviations for the sums of Y in the total sample, in Group 1 and in Group 2, respectively. Because there are three linear equations in three unknowns, it would seem that we could readily solve these simultaneously for m, a_1 and a_2 and thus get the sample estimate of the regression Equation 7. (With J groups, there will be $J + 1$ normal equations in as many unknowns, m, $a_1, a_2, \ldots, a_J$.) However, on closer examination, it turns out that only two (in general, only J) of these equations are independent. For if we add the last two (last J in general) equations, we get

$$(n_1 + n_2)m + n_1 a_1 + n_2 a_2 = T_1 + T_2,$$

which reduces to

$$Nm + n_1 a_1 + n_2 a_2 = T$$

(because, by definition, $n_1 + n_2 = N$ and $T_1 + T_2 = T$). But this is precisely the first equation of the set. So, in effect, we have only two equations in three unknowns; hence there is no unique solution to this set.

How do we surmount this impasse, which is technically known as the problem of *deficient rank?* Fortunately, there are several ways out, perhaps the simplest of which is to introduce a new constraint on the parameters and replace the first normal equation with this. One such constraint is

$$\alpha_1 + \alpha_2 = 0,$$

which, at least for fixed effect models, is a natural one; by definition

$$\alpha_1 + \alpha_2 = (\mu_1 - \mu) + (\mu_2 - \mu)$$

$$= (\mu_1 + \mu_2) - 2\mu = 0$$

because $\mu = (\mu_1 + \mu_2)/2$ when the subpopulation sizes are assumed to be equal. [If they are palpably not equal, but stand in the proportion $\pi_1{:}\pi_2$ (with $\pi_1 + \pi_2 = 1$), then $\mu = \pi_1\mu_1 + \pi_2\mu_2$, and the natural constraint on α_1 and α_2 would be $\pi_1\mu_1 + \pi_2\mu_2 = 0$.]

Replacing the first normal equation of Set 8 by the sample counterpart of the constraint on the parameters α_1 and α_2, we get

$$a_1 + a_2 = 0$$

$$n_1 m + n_1 a_1 = T_1$$

$$n_2 m + n_2 a_2 = T_2 \qquad (9)$$

as the new set of normal equations, which does not have the problem of deficient rank. That is to say, it comprises three *independent* equations in three unknowns, and hence yields a unique solution, which the reader may verify to be

$$m = (\bar{Y}_1 + \bar{Y}_2)/2$$

$$a_1 = (\bar{Y}_1 - \bar{Y}_2)/2$$

$$a_2 = (\bar{Y}_2 - \bar{Y}_1)/2.$$

Thus, we again see that a test of the significance of the difference between $\bar{Y}_1$ and $\bar{Y}_2$ can equivalently be carried out by testing the significance of a_1 (and, redundantly, of a_2)—just as we saw in the informal treatment of the preceding section.

For the numerical example of the previous section, the set of normal equations is

$$a_1 + a_2 = 0$$

$$12m + 12a_1 = 162$$

$$14m + 14a_2 = 126$$

whose solution is

$$m = (13.5 + 9.0)/2 = 11.25$$

$$a_1 = (13.5 - 9.0)/2 = 2.25$$

$$a_2 = (9.0 - 13.5)/2 = -2.25.$$

It should be noted that m is not the grand mean of the total sample, but the *unweighted mean* of the two group means. These will, of course, coincide when the two groups are of equal size. Alternatively, if we had taken the proportionate sample sizes $12/(12 + 14) = 6/13$ and $14/(12 + 14) = 7/13$ as though they were the subpopulation proportions π_1 and π_2 and had therefore used

$$(6/13)a_1 + (7/14)a_2 = 0$$

instead of

$$a_1 + a_2 = 0$$

as the constraint equation to replace the first equation of the normal set, the solutions would have been

$$m = 144/13 = 11.08 \qquad \text{(the grand mean of } Y\text{)}$$

$$a_1 = 189/78 = 2.42$$

$$a_2 = -27/13 = -2.08,$$

as the reader may verify. Note also that $a_1 - a_2 = 4.5 = \bar{Y}_1 - \bar{Y}_2$, regardless of which of the two constraint equations is used. This is important, because it means that the equivalence of the test of significance of the mean difference $\bar{Y}_1 - \bar{Y}_2$ and that of the nonnullity of a_1 and a_2 holds regardless of what constraint equation we introduce to cope with the deficient rank problem. That this should be the case follows from the fact that $a_1 - a_2$ is an estimate if the difference $\alpha_1 - \alpha_2$ between the two effect parameters, which in turn is by definition equal to $(\mu_1 - \mu) - (\mu_2 - \mu) = \mu_1 - \mu_2$. Interested readers may find it instructive also to show that the last two equations of the Set 9 of normal equations lead to

$$a_1 - a_2 = T_1/n_1 - T_2/n_2 = \bar{Y}_1 - \bar{Y}_2$$

without any resort to the first equation, which is the constraint.

MATRIX FORMULATION: PARAMETER ESTIMATION

In order to see that the formal treatment of this section—although more complicated than the informal one of the preceding section—generalizes more readily to multigroup and factorial designs, it is convenient (indeed, almost necessary) to recast it into matrix notation,[1] starting with Equation 5. The first step is to define an N dimensional vector of Y scores, which is called the *observation vector*, thus:

$$\mathbf{Y} = [Y_{11}, Y_{21}, \ldots, Y_{n_1 1} : Y_{12}, Y_{22}, \ldots, Y_{n_2 2}]'$$

We then equate this to the product of an $(N \times 3)$ *design matrix* (which specifies the particular ANOVA design being used),

$$\mathbf{X} = \begin{bmatrix} 1 & 1 & 0 \\ 1 & 1 & 0 \\ \cdot & \cdot & \cdot \\ \cdot & \cdot & \cdot \\ \cdot & \cdot & \cdot \\ 1 & 1 & 0 \\ \cdots & \cdots & \cdots \\ 1 & 0 & 1 \\ \cdot & \cdot & \cdot \\ \cdot & \cdot & \cdot \\ \cdot & \cdot & \cdot \\ 1 & 0 & 1 \end{bmatrix}$$

---

[1]Those who are not familiar with matrix algebra should refer to some source, such as Tatsuoka (1988, Appendix A), to learn its elementary aspects, at least through matrix multiplication, before proceeding. A conceptual knowledge of matrix inversion is also necessary, but the actual technique for calculating matrix inverses need not be mastered for understanding the following developments.

and the three-dimensional *parameter vector,*

$$\Theta = \begin{bmatrix} \mu \\ \alpha_1 \\ \alpha_2 \end{bmatrix},$$

plus an N-dimensional *error vector,*

$$\epsilon = \begin{bmatrix} \epsilon_{11} \\ \epsilon_{21} \\ \cdot \\ \cdot \\ \cdot \\ \epsilon_{n_1 1} \\ \cdots \\ \epsilon_{12} \\ \cdot \\ \cdot \\ \cdot \\ \epsilon_{n_2 2} \end{bmatrix}$$

Thus, in explicit matrix notation, the entire set of N equations (one for each subject) subsumed under Equation 5 takes the form

$$\begin{bmatrix} Y_{11} \\ Y_{21} \\ \cdot \\ \cdot \\ \cdot \\ Y_{n_{11}} \\ \cdots \\ Y_{12} \\ \cdot \\ \cdot \\ \cdot \\ Y_{n_{22}} \end{bmatrix} = \begin{bmatrix} 1 & 1 & 0 \\ 1 & 1 & 0 \\ \cdot & \cdot & \cdot \\ \cdot & \cdot & \cdot \\ \cdot & \cdot & \cdot \\ 1 & 1 & 0 \\ \cdots \\ 1 & 0 & 1 \\ \cdot & \cdot & \cdot \\ \cdot & \cdot & \cdot \\ \cdot & \cdot & \cdot \\ 1 & 0 & 1 \end{bmatrix} \begin{bmatrix} \mu \\ \alpha_1 \\ \alpha_2 \end{bmatrix} + \begin{bmatrix} \epsilon_{11} \\ \epsilon_{21} \\ \cdot \\ \cdot \\ \cdot \\ \epsilon_{n1} \\ \cdots \\ \epsilon_{12} \\ \cdot \\ \cdot \\ \cdot \\ \epsilon_{n2} \end{bmatrix}$$

$$\quad\quad \mathbf{Y} \quad\quad\quad\quad \mathbf{X} \quad\quad\quad\quad \mathbf{\Theta} \quad\quad\quad \mathbf{\epsilon} \quad\quad\quad (10)$$

The first column of the design matrix $\mathbf{X}$ always consists of N 1's. The second column for this example has n_1 1's followed by n_2 0's, whereas the third column contains n_1 0's trailed by n_2 1's. On carrying out the matrix multiplication $\mathbf{X\Theta}$ and adding the error vector $\mathbf{\epsilon}$ to this product, we get an N-dimensional column vector whose first n_1 elements are

$$\mu + \alpha_1 + \epsilon_{i1} \quad\quad (i = 1, 2, \ldots, n_1)$$

and the last n_2 elements are

$$\mu + \alpha_2 + \epsilon_{i2} \qquad (i = 1, 2, \ldots, n_2)$$

as the right-hand side of Equation 10. By definition of equality of two vectors (elementwise equality), we see that the matrix Equation 10 is equivalent to the set of N scalar equations

$$Y_{i1} = \mu + \alpha_1 + \epsilon i_1 \qquad (i = 1, 2, \ldots, n_1)$$

$$Y_{i2} = \mu + \alpha_2 + \epsilon i_2 \qquad (i = 1, 2, \ldots, n_2)$$

constituting Equation 5.

Writing Equation 10 in *symbolic* (as against *explicit*) matrix form, we have

$$\mathbf{Y} = \mathbf{X\Theta} + \boldsymbol{\epsilon}, \tag{11}$$

which is what we refer to as the general linear model. By approximately choosing the design matrix $\mathbf{X}$ and the parameter vector $\mathbf{\Theta}$, we can get Equation 11 to represent the structural equation for any ANOVA or ANCOVA design. (For the latter, the design matrix will have not only 1's and 0's as elements, but will have two or more columns that contain the subjects' scores on the covariates, as discussed later.) Hence, once we obtain the formal solution of this equation, the result can be used for the estimation of parameters for any design. Testing the significance of these estimated parameters, too, can be done by a general formula based on the solution of Equation 11 and differing only in the error mean-square appropriate to each design. This is the great economy that accrues to the use of the general linear model.

To get the least-squares estimate of the parameter vector $\mathbf{\Theta}$ in Equation 11, we need to minimize the quantity

$$Q = \sum_{j=1}^{J} \sum_{i=1}^{nj} \epsilon_{ij}^2,$$

which, in matrix notation, becomes

$$Q = \boldsymbol{\epsilon}'\boldsymbol{\epsilon}$$

$$= (\mathbf{Y} - \mathbf{X\Theta})'(\mathbf{Y} - \mathbf{X\Theta})$$

because $\boldsymbol{\epsilon} = \mathbf{Y} - \mathbf{X\Theta}$ from Equation 11. We then take the *symbolic vector derivative*[2] of Q with respect to $\mathbf{\Theta}$ and set the result equal to the three-dimensional null vector $\mathbf{0}_3$ to get the normal equations in symbolic matrix form.

---

[2]A symbolic vector derivative of a scalar function $f(v_2, \ldots, v_n)$ of the elements of a vector $\mathbf{v} = [v_1, v_2, \ldots, v_n]'$ is simply the vector, $[\partial f/\partial v_1, \partial f/\partial v_2, \ldots, \partial f/\partial v_n]'$, whose elements consist of the partial derivatives of f with respect to the successive elements of $\mathbf{v}$. (The vector of partial derivatives is written in the same form—row or column as the case may be—as the vector with respect to which the symbolic derivative is taken.) For further details and carried-out examples the reader may refer to Tatsuoka (1988, Appendix C).

Carrying out the multiplication in the right-hand side expression for Q, we get

$$Q = \mathbf{Y'Y} - 2(\mathbf{Y'X})\boldsymbol{\Theta} + \boldsymbol{\Theta}'(\mathbf{X'X})\boldsymbol{\Theta},$$

so the symbolic vector derivative $\partial Q/\partial\boldsymbol{\Theta}$ is

$$\partial Q/\partial\boldsymbol{\Theta} = -2(\mathbf{X'Y}) + 2(\mathbf{X'X})\boldsymbol{\Theta}.$$

Setting this equal to $\mathbf{0}_3$ and simplifying, we get

$$(\mathbf{X'X})\hat{\boldsymbol{\Theta}} = \mathbf{X'Y} \tag{12}$$

as the normal equations in matrix form. Here $\boldsymbol{\Theta}$ has been replaced by $\hat{\boldsymbol{\Theta}}$ to indicate that what we would get by solving this equation is not $\boldsymbol{\Theta}$ itself, of course, but an estimate thereof. The reader should verify, by carrying out the indicated multiplications on both sides of the equation and setting the corresponding elements equal to each other, that Equation 12 is equivalent to the set of Equations (8) in the preceding section.

At first glance, it may seem that Equation 12 can readily be solved for $\hat{\boldsymbol{\Theta}}$ by premultiplying both sides of the equation by $(\mathbf{X'X})^{-1}$ to get

$$\hat{\boldsymbol{\Theta}} = (\mathbf{X'X})^{-1}(\mathbf{X'Y}).$$

However, this assumes that $\mathbf{X'X}$ is *nonsingular* when, in point of fact, it is singular, as may be inferred from the fact that the columns of $\mathbf{X}$ are *linearly dependent*. More specifically, it can be seen from the definition of $\mathbf{X}$ that its first column is the sum of its other two columns. Equivalently, if we carry out the multiplicaiton $\mathbf{X'X}$, we find that

$$\mathbf{X'X} = \begin{bmatrix} N & n_1 & n_2 \\ n_1 & n_1 & 0 \\ n_2 & 0 & n_2 \end{bmatrix},$$

whose first row is the sum of the other two. The observant reader will have noticed that the elements of this matrix are precisely the coefficients of the right-hand sides of the normal equations (8). Thus, the fact that only two of the three normal equations are independent manifests itself here in there being only two linearly independent rows (and also columns) in the 3×3 coefficient matrix $\mathbf{X'X}$. The number of independent rows (or columns) in a square matrix is called its *rank,* and when this is smaller than the total number of rows or columns (i.e., the *order* of the matrix) the matrix is said to be of *deficient rank,* and it is singular so that it has no inverse. (It was this terminology that we transferred to the set of normal equations when we said, in the preceding section, that it had the problem of deficient rank.)

Thus, we encounter the same problem as before—which is as it should be, for Equation 12 is merely a rewriting of Equation 8 in symbolic matrix form. There is a difference because, whereas the replacement of one of the normal equations by a constraint equation was the method of choice in the previous context, we now have two other "natural" ways of coping with the deficient rank problem.

One of these is to define a new set of parameters, equal in number to the rank of $X'X$, in terms of linear combinations of the original parameters, and then transform the normal equations into an equivalent set for these new parameters. These new equations (or its coefficient matrix) will be of full rank (i.e., will not have deficient rank), and hence can be solved for the new parameters. This is called the method of *reparameterization*, and we use this method here.[3]

There are, of course, any number of ways in which we could reparameterize. However, in selecting an appropriate set of linear combinations to define the new parameters, we would consider, among other things, the meaningfulness of the resulting parameters. For example, it would be meaningful to choose an "overall level" parameter, $\lambda = \mu + (\alpha_1 + \alpha_2)/2$, and the difference, $\delta = \alpha_1 - \alpha_2$, of the two effect parameters. These are obviously linear combinations of the original parameters, for

$$\lambda = 1.\mu + (\tfrac{1}{2}).\alpha_1 + (\tfrac{1}{2}).\alpha_2$$

and

$$\delta = 0.\mu + 1.\alpha_1 + (-1).\alpha_2$$

or, in matrix notation,

$$\begin{bmatrix} \lambda \\ \delta \end{bmatrix} = \begin{bmatrix} 1 & \tfrac{1}{2} & \tfrac{1}{2} \\ 0 & 1 & -1 \end{bmatrix} \begin{bmatrix} \mu \\ \alpha_1 \\ \alpha_2 \end{bmatrix}.$$

The matrix of combining weights that define the new parameters is called the *contrast matrix*, because all except the first linear combination are usually *contrasts* of the original parameters. If the contrast matrix is denoted by C and the vector of the new parameters by Ψ, the transformation equation may be written as

$$\Psi = C\Theta. \tag{13}$$

With the new set of parameters thus defined, the linear model may be rewritten as

$$Y = K\Theta + \epsilon, \tag{14}$$

where K, which is called the *basis matrix*, is obtained as follows. From Equation 13, we write

$$K\Theta = K(C\Theta)$$

$$= (KC)\Theta.$$

---

[3]Another method is to utilize what is called a *generalized inverse* of $X'X$, which is a matrix $(X'X)^-$ that satisfies the relation

$$(X'X)(X'X)^-(X'X) = X'X$$

and exists even for singular matrices. It can then be shown (see Searle, 1971, p. 20) that

$$\hat{\Theta} = (X'X)^-(X'Y)$$

is a solution of Equation 12, *if* the equation has a solution at all.

Comparing the last member with Equation 11, we must have

$$\mathbf{KC} = \mathbf{X}$$

for Equations 11 and 14 to be equivalent. Hence

$$\mathbf{K(CC')} = \mathbf{(KC)C'} = \mathbf{XC'} \tag{15}$$

and, because $\mathbf{CC'}$ is nonsingular by definition, we get

$$\mathbf{K} = \mathbf{(XC')(CC')^{-1}}.$$

Next, following exactly the same steps as those that led from Equation 11 to Equation 12, we derive the normal equations for the new parameters,

$$\mathbf{(K'K)\Psi} = \mathbf{K'Y} \tag{16}$$

—which has the same form as Equation 12 with $\mathbf{K}$ taking the place of $\mathbf{X}$, and $\mathbf{\Psi}$ replacing $\mathbf{\Theta}$. The big difference is that, whereas the coefficient matrix $\mathbf{X'X}$ of Equation 12 was singular, the new coefficient matrix $\mathbf{K'K}$ is nonsingular, because the contrast matrix is so defined as to be of full row rank. (Actually, one more condition must be satisfied by $\mathbf{C}$, as is indicated later.) Therefore, Equation 16 has a unique solution,

$$\mathbf{\Psi} = \mathbf{(K'K)^{-1}(K'Y)}, \tag{17}$$

to obtain which was the whole purpose of reparameterization.

The reader may well ask what is accomplished by getting a solution for a different set of parameters from those we originally set out to estimate (namely, μ, α_1 and α_2). The answer is that although we cannot get estimates of the old parameters from those of the new ones (because there are fewer of these), the new parameters serve just as well for significance testing, which is our main purpose here anyway.

In particular, the second of the new parameters, δ, is equal by definition to

$$\alpha_1 - \alpha_2 = (\mu_1 - \mu) - (\mu_2 - \mu) = \mu_1 - \mu_2.$$

Hence, estimating δ is indeed related directly to testing the significance of $\bar{Y}_1 - \bar{Y}_2$. In the case when there are J groups, the single new parameter is superseded by a set of $J - 1$ new parameters

$$\delta_1 = \alpha_1 - \alpha_J = \mu_1 - \mu_J$$
$$\delta_2 = \alpha_2 - \alpha_J = \mu_2 - \mu_J.$$
$$.$$
$$.$$
$$.$$
$$\delta_{J-1} = \alpha_{J-1} - \alpha_J = \mu_{J-1} - \mu_J$$

representing the differences between each of the first $J - 1$ population means and the Jth. The foregoing should convince the reader not only that reparameterization does not lead us astray from our original purpose, but also that choosing a contrast matrix C that has full row rank poses no problem. This requirement may always be satisfied by taking the following $J \times (J + 1)$ matrix as the contrast matrix:

$$
C = \begin{bmatrix}
1 & \frac{1}{J} & \frac{1}{J} & \cdots & \frac{1}{J} & \frac{1}{J} \\
0 & 1 & 0 & \cdots & 0 & -1 \\
0 & 0 & 1 & \cdots & 0 & -1 \\
\vdots & & & & & \\
0 & 0 & 0 & \cdots & 1 & -1
\end{bmatrix}
$$

Only when researchers are interested in more complex contrasts than the differences represented by $\delta_1, \delta_2, \ldots, \delta_{J-1}$ above, do they need to be careful to have the contrast matrix be of full row rank. Even then, so long as the research questions being asked are nonredundant (i.e., so long as the answer to no question logically follows from those to the others), this requirement holds automatically, and the matrix C is acceptable provided one other condition—to be indicated later—is satisfied.

Example 2

We now apply the foregoing developments to the first numerical example. The design matrix is

$$
X = \begin{bmatrix}
1 & 1 & 0 \\
1 & 1 & 0 \\
\cdot & \cdot & \cdot \\
\cdot & \cdot & \cdot \\
1 & 1 & 0 \\
\cdots\cdots \\
1 & 0 & 1 \\
\cdot & \cdot & \cdot \\
\cdot & \cdot & \cdot \\
1 & 0 & 1
\end{bmatrix}
\begin{matrix}
\\ \\ \\ n_1(= 12) \text{ rows} \\ \\ \\ \\ \\ \\ n_2(= 14) \text{ rows} \\ \\
\end{matrix}
$$

The contrast matrix for defining the new parameters $\lambda = \mu + (\alpha_1 + \alpha_2)/2$ and $\delta = \alpha_1 - \alpha_2$ is

$$
C = \begin{bmatrix}
1 & \frac{1}{2} & \frac{1}{2} \\
0 & 1 & -1
\end{bmatrix}.
$$

To get the basis matrix K using Equation 15, the following intermediate results are needed:

$$
\mathbf{XC'} =
\begin{bmatrix}
1 & 1 & 0 \\
1 & 1 & 0 \\
\cdot & \cdot & \cdot \\
\cdot & \cdot & \cdot \\
\cdot & \cdot & \cdot \\
1 & 1 & 0 \\
\cdots\cdots \\
1 & 0 & 1 \\
\cdot & \cdot & \cdot \\
\cdot & \cdot & \cdot \\
\cdot & \cdot & \cdot \\
1 & 0 & 1
\end{bmatrix}
\begin{bmatrix}
1 & 0 \\
\frac{1}{2} & 1 \\
\frac{1}{2} & -1
\end{bmatrix}
=
\begin{bmatrix}
\frac{3}{2} & 1 \\
\frac{3}{2} & 1 \\
\cdot & \cdot \\
\cdot & \cdot \\
\cdot & \cdot \\
\frac{3}{2} & 1 \\
\cdots\cdots \\
\frac{3}{2} & -1 \\
\cdot & \cdot \\
\cdot & \cdot \\
\cdot & \cdot \\
\frac{3}{2} & -1
\end{bmatrix}
$$

and

$$
\mathbf{CC'} =
\begin{bmatrix}
1 & \frac{1}{2} & \frac{1}{2} \\
0 & 1 & -1
\end{bmatrix}
\begin{bmatrix}
1 & 0 \\
\frac{1}{2} & 1 \\
\frac{1}{2} & -1
\end{bmatrix}
=
\begin{bmatrix}
\frac{3}{2} & 0 \\
0 & 2
\end{bmatrix},
$$

whence

$$
(\mathbf{CC'})^{-1} =
\begin{bmatrix}
\frac{2}{3} & 0 \\
0 & \frac{1}{2}
\end{bmatrix},
$$

(because the inverse of a diagonal matrix is just a diagonal matrix with diagonal elements equal to the reciprocals of the corresponding elements of the original matrix).

Hence, from Equation 15, we get the basis matrix

$$
\mathbf{K} = (\mathbf{XC'})\,(\mathbf{CC'})^{-1} =
\begin{bmatrix}
\frac{3}{2} & 1 \\
\cdot & \cdot \\
\cdot & \cdot \\
\cdot & \cdot \\
\frac{3}{2} & 1 \\
\cdots\cdots \\
\frac{3}{2} & -1 \\
\cdot & \cdot \\
\cdot & \cdot \\
\cdot & \cdot \\
\frac{3}{2} & -1
\end{bmatrix}
\begin{bmatrix}
\frac{2}{3} & 0 \\
0 & \frac{1}{2}
\end{bmatrix}
=
\begin{bmatrix}
1 & \frac{1}{2} \\
1 & \frac{1}{2} \\
\cdot & \cdot \\
\cdot & \cdot \\
\cdot & \cdot \\
1 & \frac{1}{2} \\
\cdots\cdots \\
1 & \frac{1}{2} \\
\cdot & \cdot \\
\cdot & \cdot \\
\cdot & \cdot \\
1 & \frac{1}{2}
\end{bmatrix}
$$

From Equation 14, the structural equations in terms of the new parameters are

$$
Y_{i1} = \lambda + \delta/2 + \epsilon_{i1} \ (i = 1, 2, \ldots, n_1)
$$
$$
Y_{i2} = \lambda - \delta/2 + \epsilon_{i2} \ (i = 1, 2, \ldots, n_2).
$$

The reader may verify that these revert back to Equation 5 when the new parameters are expressed as linear combinations of the original ones.

Thus, as to be expected, the process of reparameterization has actually changed nothing; it is just a mathematical "trick" to make the normal equations uniquely solvable. To carry out the solution, the next step is to compute $\mathbf{K'K}$ and $\mathbf{K'Y}$. They are

$$
\mathbf{K'K} = \begin{bmatrix} 1 & 1 & \dots & 1 & 1 & \dots & & 1 \\ \frac{1}{2} & \frac{1}{2} & \dots & \frac{1}{2} & -\frac{1}{2} & \dots & & -\frac{1}{2} \end{bmatrix} \begin{bmatrix} 1 & \frac{1}{2} \\ 1 & \frac{1}{2} \\ \cdot & \cdot \\ \cdot & \cdot \\ \cdot & \cdot \\ 1 & -\frac{1}{2} \\ \dots & \dots \\ 1 & -\frac{1}{2} \\ \cdot & \cdot \\ \cdot & \cdot \\ 1 & -1.2 \end{bmatrix} = \begin{bmatrix} N & \dfrac{n_1 - n_2}{2} \\ \dfrac{n_1 - n_2}{2} & \dfrac{N}{4} \end{bmatrix}
$$

and

$$
\mathbf{K'Y} = \begin{bmatrix} 1 & 1 & \dots & 1 & \vdots & 1 & \dots & & 1 \\ \frac{1}{2} & \frac{1}{2} & \dots & \frac{1}{2} & \vdots & -\frac{1}{2} & \dots & & -\frac{1}{2} \end{bmatrix} \begin{bmatrix} Y_{11} \\ Y_{21} \\ \cdot \\ \cdot \\ \cdot \\ Y_{n_{1_1}} \\ \dots \\ Y_{12} \\ \cdot \\ \cdot \\ \cdot \\ Y_{n_{2_2}} \end{bmatrix} = \begin{bmatrix} T \\ \dfrac{T_1 - T_2}{2} \end{bmatrix}.
$$

For our numerical example, with $n_1 = 12$, $n_2 = 14$, $N = 26$, and the Y totals $T_1 = 162$, $T_2 = 126$, $T = 288$, these become

$$
\mathbf{K'K} = \begin{bmatrix} 26 & -1 \\ -1 & \frac{13}{2} \end{bmatrix}
$$

and

$$
\mathbf{K'Y} = \begin{bmatrix} 288 \\ 18 \end{bmatrix}.
$$

For using Equation 17 to get $\mathbf{\Psi}$, we further need

$$(\mathbf{K'K})^{-1} = (\tfrac{1}{168}) \begin{bmatrix} \tfrac{13}{2} & 1 \\ 1 & 26 \end{bmatrix}.$$

Making the appropriate substitutions, we finally obtain

$$\hat{\mathbf{\Psi}} = \begin{bmatrix} \hat{\lambda} \\ \hat{\delta} \end{bmatrix} = (\tfrac{1}{168}) \begin{bmatrix} \tfrac{13}{2} & 1 \\ 1 & 26 \end{bmatrix} \begin{bmatrix} 288 \\ 18 \end{bmatrix} = \begin{bmatrix} 11.25 \\ 4.50 \end{bmatrix}.$$

We note that $\delta = 4.5$ agrees with $\hat{\alpha}_1 - \hat{\alpha}_2 = a_1 - a_2 = 2.25 - (-2.25)$ as previously obtained by solving Equation 9. However, the fact that $\hat{\lambda} = \hat{\mu} + (\hat{\alpha}_1 + \hat{\alpha}_2)/2 = m + (a_1 \, a_2)/2 = 11.25$ agrees with the value of m itself as obtained from Equations 9 may seem contradictory—until it is recalled that the constraint equation (the first of Equations 9) sets $a_1 + a_2 = 0$.

We now address ourselves to the other condition besides being of full row-rank that must be satisfied by the contrast matrix $\mathbf{C}$—as forewarned earlier. This is the requirement that the rows of $\mathbf{C}$ must be expressible as linear combinations of those of the design matrix $\mathbf{X}$. Loosely speaking, this says that the process of forming new parameters from the old has to be compatible with the design of the experiment. That is, only questions that are "built into" the design can be answered by the data from the experiment. The reason this requirement did not seem to pose a problem in the foregoing developments was that we had "surreptitiously" made sure that it was satisfied. Let us verify that this is so.

The design matrix in our example was

$$\mathbf{X} = \begin{bmatrix} 1 & 1 & 0 \\ 1 & 1 & 0 \\ \cdot & \cdot & \cdot \\ \cdot & \cdot & \cdot \\ \cdot & \cdot & \cdot \\ \cdots & \cdots \\ 1 & 0 & 1 \\ \cdot & \cdot & \cdot \\ \cdot & \cdot & \cdot \\ \cdot & \cdot & \cdot \\ 1 & 0 & 1 \end{bmatrix}$$

The first row of $\mathbf{C}$ is the average of any one of the first n_1 rows of $\mathbf{X}$ and any of its last n_2 rows, for

$$\{[1, 1, 0] + [1, 0, 1]\}/2 = [2, 1, 1]/2$$
$$= [1, \tfrac{1}{2}, \tfrac{1}{2}].$$

The difference between any of the first n_1 rows of $\mathbf{X}$ and any of its last n_2 rows yields the second row of $\mathbf{C}$:

$$[1, 1, 0] - [1, 0, 1] = [0, 1, -1].$$

So the rows of $\mathbf{C}$ were indeed linear combinations of those of $\mathbf{X}$.

Be that as it may, just where in the foregoing development was this condition invoked without our knowledge, as it were? It was hidden in a tacit assumption made in going from the original structural equation to the reparameterized structural equation; that is, in getting from

$$\mathbf{Y} = \mathbf{X\Theta} + \boldsymbol{\epsilon} \quad \text{to} \quad \mathbf{Y} = \mathbf{K\Psi} + \boldsymbol{\epsilon}.$$

If readers review our earlier derivation of the basis matrix $\mathbf{K}$, they will find the clause "we must have $\mathbf{KC} = \mathbf{X}$" instead of the customary "it follows that $\mathbf{KC} = \mathbf{X}$." This was a sleight of hand—perpetrated to facilitate the flow of argument. In point of fact, the relation $\mathbf{KC} = \mathbf{X}$ does not mathematically follow from the preceding comparison. Rather, it merely implies that this could be the case, and suggests that it would be "nice" if this were the case; nice, because if so, the next two steps would follow logically. So we conveniently assumed that $\mathbf{KC} = \mathbf{X}$, which says that the rows of $\mathbf{X}$ are linear combinations of those of $\mathbf{C}$. Or, because $\mathbf{X}$ existed before the advent of $\mathbf{C}$, this amounts to requiring that, for $\mathbf{C}$ to be eligible, its rows must be linear combinations of those of $\mathbf{X}$. This is called the *estimability condition* on the new parameters $\mathbf{\Psi}$. Unless it is satisfied, the basis matrix $\mathbf{K}$ cannot be expressed as in Equation 15, and all subsequent developments would be but castles in the air.

To cinch the point, let us examine the consequences of trying to use a contrast matrix that satisfies the full-rank condition but not the estimability condition. One such matrix is

$$\mathbf{C} = \begin{bmatrix} 1 & 0 & 0 \\ 0 & 1 & -1 \end{bmatrix},$$

which represents the intention to estimate μ and $\alpha_1 - \alpha_2$. Its rows are linearly independent, so $\mathbf{C}$ does have full row-rank 2. But the estimability condition is not satisfied, because the first row of $\mathbf{C}$ is not expressible as a linear combination of the rows of $\mathbf{X}$. If we ignored this fact and proceeded to determine a purported basis matrix $\mathbf{K}$ (which we can, because $\mathbf{CC}'$ is nonsingular), we would find

$$\mathbf{XC}' = \begin{bmatrix} 1 & 1 & 0 \\ 1 & 1 & 0 \\ \cdot & \cdot & \cdot \\ \cdot & \cdot & \cdot \\ \cdot & \cdot & \cdot \\ 1 & 1 & 0 \\ \hline 1 & 0 & 1 \\ \cdot & \cdot & \cdot \\ \cdot & \cdot & \cdot \\ \cdot & \cdot & \cdot \\ 1 & 0 & 1 \end{bmatrix} \begin{bmatrix} 1 & 0 \\ 0 & 1 \\ 0 & -1 \end{bmatrix} = \begin{bmatrix} 1 & 1 \\ 1 & 1 \\ \cdot & \cdot \\ \cdot & \cdot \\ \cdot & \cdot \\ 1 & 1 \\ \hline 1 & -1 \\ \cdot & \cdot \\ \cdot & \cdot \\ \cdot & \cdot \\ 1 & -1 \end{bmatrix}$$

and

$$CC' = \begin{bmatrix} 1 & 0 & 0 \\ 0 & 1 & -1 \end{bmatrix} \begin{bmatrix} 1 & 0 \\ 0 & 1 \\ 0 & -1 \end{bmatrix} = \begin{bmatrix} 1 & 0 \\ 0 & 2 \end{bmatrix}.$$

Hence, by following Equation 15, we would get

$$K = \begin{bmatrix} 1 & 1 \\ 1 & 1 \\ \cdot & \cdot & \cdot \\ \cdot & \cdot & \cdot \\ \cdot & \cdot & \cdot \\ 1 & 1 \\ \cdots \cdots \\ 1 & -1 \\ \cdot & \cdot & \cdot \\ \cdot & \cdot & \cdot \\ \cdot & \cdot & \cdot \\ 1 & -1 \end{bmatrix} \begin{bmatrix} 1 & 0 \\ 0 & \frac{1}{2} \end{bmatrix} = \begin{bmatrix} 1 & 1 \\ 1 & \frac{1}{2} \\ 1 & \frac{1}{2} \\ \cdot & \cdot \\ \cdot & \cdot \\ 1 & \frac{1}{2} \\ \cdots \cdots \\ 1 & -\frac{1}{2} \\ \cdot & \cdot \\ \cdot & \cdot \\ 1 & -\frac{1}{2} \end{bmatrix}$$

It becomes evident that this is an unacceptable result when we try to recover **X** as the product **KC**, for

$$KC = \begin{bmatrix} 1 & \frac{1}{2} \\ 1 & \frac{1}{2} \\ \cdot & \cdot \\ \cdot & \cdot \\ \cdot & \cdot \\ 1 & \frac{1}{2} \\ \cdots \cdots \\ 1 & -\frac{1}{2} \\ \cdot & \cdot \\ \cdot & \cdot \\ 1 & -\frac{1}{2} \end{bmatrix} \begin{bmatrix} 1 & 0 & 0 \\ 0 & 1 & -1 \end{bmatrix} = \begin{bmatrix} 1 & \frac{1}{2} & -\frac{1}{2} \\ 1 & \frac{1}{2} & -\frac{1}{2} \\ \cdot & \cdot & \cdot \\ \cdot & \cdot & \cdot \\ \cdot & \cdot & \cdot \\ 1 & \frac{1}{2} & -\frac{1}{2} \\ \cdots \cdots \cdots \\ 1 & -\frac{1}{2} & \frac{1}{2} \\ \cdot & \cdot & \cdot \\ \cdot & \cdot & \cdot \\ 1 & -\frac{1}{2} & \frac{1}{2} \end{bmatrix}$$

which does not equal the design matrix **X**. Thus, the proposed **C** is ineligible as a contrast matrix. That is, a reparameterization using this as the transformation matrix would yield new parameters that simply cannot be estimated by an experiment whose design matrix is **X**.

The foregoing demonstration should not leave the reader in a mood of desperation, however. In fact, the estimability condition will always be satisfied by using a contrast matrix with the following characteristics: (a) The first row is the average of all (or of a linearly independent subset of) the rows of **X**. This will generate an "overall level" type of new parameter. (b) The remaining $J - 1$ rows are linearly independent contrasts of the effect parameters, where $J - 1$ can be more general than the number of groups minus one: It is the number of degrees of freedom between cells in the particular design.

MATRIX FORMULATION: SIGNIFICANCE TESTING

The parameter-estimation phase of ANOVA presented in the preceding section may have been new to some readers, for analysis of variance is associated primarily with the testing of null hypotheses concerning population means. However, a moment's reflection should suffice to reveal that, once the appropriate parameters have been estimated, they need only be supplemented with their estimated standard errors in order to carry out the relevant significance tests (as well as getting confidence intervals for the parameters if so desired). It is for this reason that, when ANOVA is carried out by the general linear hypothesis approach, it is done in two phases: first, the reparameterized parameters are estimated; second, these estimates are tested for significance, which requires us to get estimates of their standard errors—or, more inclusively, estimates of the covariance matrix of the joint sampling distribution of the parameter estimates. We now address this task.

First note that Equation 17 defines the estimates of the new parameters as linear combinations of the observed data:

$$\boldsymbol{\Psi} = (\mathbf{K'K})^{-1}(\mathbf{K'Y}). \tag{17}$$

This may be made more explicit by writing the right-hand side of the equation as $[(\mathbf{K'K})^{-1}\mathbf{K'}]\mathbf{Y}$ and denoting the matrix in brackets by $\mathbf{H}$ for short. Because $(\mathbf{K'K})^{-1}$ is a $J \times J$ matrix and $\mathbf{K'}$ is $J \times N$, $\mathbf{H}$ is a $J \times N$ matrix, where N is the total sample size and J is the number of new parameters. Hence each of the J elements of $\hat{\boldsymbol{\Psi}}$ (i.e., each of the new parameters) is a linear combination

$$\hat{\Psi}_j = h_{j1}Y_1 + h_{j2}Y_2 + \ldots + h_{jN}Y_N$$

of the observations $Y_1, Y_2, \ldots, Y_N$.

Consequently, in order to estimate the covariance matrix $\mathbf{V}(\boldsymbol{\Psi})$ of the estimated parameters, it is necessary first to express the expected values, variances, and covariances of the observations $Y_1, Y_2, \ldots, Y_N$ in terms of quantities that occur in the reparameterized structural equation

$$\mathbf{Y} = \mathbf{K\Psi} + \boldsymbol{\epsilon}. \tag{14'}$$

The expected value of $\mathbf{Y}$ (i.e., the vector whose elements are the expected values of $Y_1, Y_2, \ldots, Y_N$) is immediately obtainable from this equation; namely,

$$\mathbf{E}(\mathbf{Y}) = \mathbf{E}(\mathbf{K\Psi} + \boldsymbol{\epsilon}) = \mathbf{K\Psi}. \tag{18}$$

The second step follows from the facts that $E(\mathbf{K\Psi}) = \mathbf{K\Psi}$, because $\mathbf{K}$ and $\mathbf{\Psi}$ involve only fixed numbers and population values, respectively, and that $E(\boldsymbol{\epsilon}) = 0$ by definition of random errors. The covariance matrix of the joint distribution of the Y_i is obtained as

$$\begin{aligned} V(\mathbf{Y}) &= E[\mathbf{Y} - E(\mathbf{Y})][\mathbf{Y} - E(\mathbf{Y})]' \\ &= E[(\mathbf{Y} - \mathbf{K\Psi})(\mathbf{Y} - \mathbf{K\Psi})'] \\ &= E(\boldsymbol{\epsilon}\boldsymbol{\epsilon}') \\ &= \sigma^2 \mathbf{I}_N. \end{aligned} \tag{19}$$

In the last step, we have utilized the basic assumption of ANOVA, that the ϵ_i are independently and identically distributed (*iid*) with mean 0 and variance σ^2. The result of $\sigma^2 \mathbf{I}_N$ is a diagonal matrix of order N whose diagonal elements are all equal to σ^2. Since $\boldsymbol{\epsilon}$ is the only random variable in the structural Equation 14′, the variance of each Y_i is the same as that of the corresponding ϵ_i, so the Y_i all have a common variance σ^2. The covariance between Y_i and Y_k for any pair of individuals $i \neq k$ is equal to $\text{cov}(\epsilon_i, \epsilon_k) = 0$. Hence the covariance matrix of the Y_i is a diagonal matrix with identical diagonal elements σ^2, as indicated below:

$$\begin{bmatrix} \sigma^2 & 0 & 0 & \ldots & 0 \\ 0 & \sigma^2 & 0 & \ldots & 0 \\ 0 & 0 & \sigma^2 & \ldots & 0 \\ \cdot & & \cdot & & \\ \cdot & & & \cdot & \\ \cdot & & & & \cdot \\ 0 & 0 & 0 & \ldots & \sigma^2 \end{bmatrix}$$

Although our main purpose in this section is to determine the covariance matrix of $\hat{\mathbf{\Psi}}$, we must first make sure that $\hat{\mathbf{\Psi}}$ is an unbiased estimator of $\mathbf{\Psi}$; otherwise the significance tests of the $\hat{\Psi}_j$ would be meaningless. Invoking Equation 17 once again, we find

$$\begin{aligned} E(\hat{\mathbf{\Psi}}) &= E[(\mathbf{K'K})^{-1}\mathbf{K'Y}] \\ &= (\mathbf{K'K})^{-1}\mathbf{K'}E(\mathbf{Y}). \end{aligned}$$

[The second step follows because $(\mathbf{K'K})^{-1}\mathbf{K'}$ contains only fixed numbers.] Equation 18 allows us to replace $E(\mathbf{Y})$ by $\mathbf{K\Psi}$ in this expression, resulting in

$$\begin{aligned} E(\hat{\mathbf{\Psi}}) &= (\mathbf{K'K})^{-1}\mathbf{K'}(\mathbf{K\Psi}) \\ &= (\mathbf{K'K})^{-1}(\mathbf{K'K})\mathbf{\Psi} \\ &= \mathbf{\Psi}, \end{aligned} \tag{20}$$

thus verifying that $\hat{\mathbf{\Psi}}$ is an unbiased estimator of $\mathbf{\Psi}$.

We can now meaningfully compute the covariance matrix of $\hat{\Psi}$ which is a linear combination of the Y_i, with coefficient matrix $\mathbf{H}$. the result is a matrix of quadratic and bilinear forms,

$$V(\Psi) = \mathbf{H}V(\mathbf{Y})\mathbf{H}'.$$

Substituting the full expression for $\mathbf{H}$ and the last member of Equation 19 for $V(\mathbf{Y})$, this becomes

$$
\begin{aligned}
V(\hat{\Psi}) &= [(\mathbf{K'K})^{-1}\mathbf{K'}](\sigma^2)[(\mathbf{K'K})^{-1}\mathbf{K'}]' \\
&= \sigma^2[(\mathbf{K'K})^{-1}\mathbf{K'}][\mathbf{K}(\mathbf{K'K})^{-1}] \\
&= \sigma^2(\mathbf{K'K})^{-1}(\mathbf{K'K})(\mathbf{K'K})^{-1} \\
&= \sigma^2(\mathbf{K'K})^{-1}.
\end{aligned}
\tag{21}
$$

Although Equation 21 gives the *exact* covariance matrix of Ψ, we cannot use this expression in practice, because σ^2 is unknown. It must therefore be replaced by an unbiased estimate $\hat{\sigma}^2$ in order to get a usable formula. As the reader is no doubt aware, the pooled within-groups mean square, MS_w of ANOVA offers such an unbiased estimate. Its usual definitional formula is

$$MS_w = \frac{1}{N-J} \sum_{j=1}^{J} \sum_{i=1}^{n_j} (Y_{ij} - Y_j)^2$$

but we here compute it by a more circuitous route in order to get an expression that is easier to generalize to more complicated designs.

We first calculate the *raw total sum of squares* S_T, the sum of the squared criterion scores in the entire sample. In matrix notation, the formula is

$$S_T = \mathbf{Y'Y}. \tag{22}$$

Next we find the *raw model sum of squares* S_B, which reduces to the raw between-groups sum of squares for one-way designs. Its general formula in matrix notation is

$$
\begin{aligned}
S_B &= (\mathbf{K}\Psi)'(\mathbf{K}\Psi) \\
&= \Psi'(\mathbf{K'K})\Psi \\
&= \Psi'(\mathbf{K'Y}),
\end{aligned}
\tag{23}
$$

the last step following from Equation 16.

It should be noted that these are not the customary SS_t and SS_b of ANOVA, which are the sums of squared *deviation* scores. However, they are related in the following manner:

$$SS_t = S_T - T^2/N$$

and

$$SS_b = S_B - T^2/N,$$

where T is, as defined before, the sum of the Y scores over the total sample. Hence, the within-groups sum of squares SS_w of ANOVA, which generalizes to the error sum of squares in other designs, may be calculated either from the usual formula

$$SS_w = SS_t - SS_b$$

or from the more general

$$SS_e = S_T - S_B = S_E$$

because the term $-T^2/N$, common to both S_T and S_B will cancel out on subtraction; it is more general because S_B may be a raw-score model sum of squares that is more general than the raw-score between-groups sum of squares. Substituting expressions 22 and 23 in this equation, we have

$$S_E = \mathbf{Y'Y} - \mathbf{\Psi'(K'Y)}. \tag{24}$$

The final step for calculating σ^2 is to divide S_E by its degrees of freedom, $N - J$, which yields

$$\hat{\sigma}^2 = [\mathbf{Y'Y} - \mathbf{\Psi'(K'Y)}]/(N - J). \tag{25}$$

If $\mathbf{\Psi}$ has only I ($<J$) estimated parameters instead of the maximum possible J, S_E will have $N - I$ degrees of freedom, which will replace $N - J$ as the divisor in expression 25. Replacing the σ^2 in Equation 21 by the $\hat{\sigma}^2$ of Equation 25, we get the estimated covariance matrix $\mathbf{V(\Psi)}$, which has the usable formula

$$\mathbf{V(\Psi)} = [\mathbf{Y'Y} - \mathbf{\Psi(K'Y)}](\mathbf{K'K})^{-1}/(N - J). \tag{26}$$

The diagonal elements of this matrix give the estimated sampling variances of the successive elements of $\mathbf{\Psi}$, that is, the new parameters. Hence their square roots are the estimated standard errors that enable us to carry out the desired significance tests.

There is, however, one further complication: The off-diagonal elements of $\mathbf{V(\Psi)}$ are, in general, not zero. That is to say, even though the new parameters are linearly independent by definition, they are not necessarily *statistically* independent. This means, in intuitive terms, that although the research questions corresponding to the significance testing of the several new parameters are not *deterministically* redundant, they may (and generally will) be *probabilistically* redundant. For example, even though $\mu_1 = 0$ and $\mu_2 = 0$ will not *strictly* imply that μ_3 (say) is zero, the nullity of the first two parameters may increase the chances of the third being zero.

As the reader may be aware, the correlatedness of several quantities to be tested can wreak havoc on the probabilities of Type I errors. The ideal thing to do is to carry out a multivariate significance test, using Hotelling's T^2 statistic or Wilks's Λ. The latter of these (which includes the former as a special case) is discussed in chapter 5 of this volume. Here we describe the univariate test, which is adequate when only a few of the parameters are of interest, and the p-values are adjusted appropriately. For the two-group case, it reduces to the familiar t test of the sole new parameter, $\delta = \alpha_1 - \alpha_2$, of real interest. For multigroup and more complex designs, we may conduct a series of t tests, bearing the above caveat in mind.

Example 3

Let us test the null hypothesis, $\alpha_1 - \alpha_2 = 0$, in the context of the numerical example introduced earlier. All of the intermediate quantities involved in Equation 26 for $\mathbf{V}(\boldsymbol{\Psi})$ have already been computed in several places. Thus,

$$S_T = \mathbf{Y'Y} = 3670,$$

as shown at the bottom of the data table in Example 1.

The factors of

$$S_B = \boldsymbol{\Psi}'(\mathbf{K'Y})$$

have been computed in Example 2. That is,

$$\boldsymbol{\psi} = \begin{bmatrix} 11.25 \\ 4.50 \end{bmatrix}$$

and

$$\mathbf{K'Y} = \begin{bmatrix} 288 \\ 18 \end{bmatrix}.$$

From these, we get

$$S_B = [11.25,\ 4.50] \begin{bmatrix} 288 \\ 18 \end{bmatrix} = 3321.$$

Finally, $(\mathbf{K'K})^{-1}$ was obtained (as an intermediate quantity for computing $\hat{\boldsymbol{\Psi}}$) as

$$(\mathbf{K'K})^{-1} = (\tfrac{1}{168}) \begin{bmatrix} \tfrac{13}{2} & 1 \\ 1 & 26 \end{bmatrix}.$$

Putting these numerical results together and recalling that $N - J = 26 - 2 = 24$, the estimated covariance matrix $\mathbf{V}(\boldsymbol{\Psi})$ for our example is found, in accordance with Equation 26, to be

$$\mathbf{V}(\boldsymbol{\psi}) = (\tfrac{1}{24})\,[3670 - 3321]\,(\tfrac{1}{168}) \begin{bmatrix} \tfrac{13}{2} & 1 \\ 1 & 26 \end{bmatrix}$$

$$= \begin{bmatrix} .56262 & .08656 \\ .08656 & 2.25050 \end{bmatrix}.$$

Thus, the t ratio for testing H_0: $\alpha_1 = \alpha_2 = 0$ is

$$t = \frac{\hat\psi_2}{\sqrt{[\hat{V}(\psi)_{22}}} = \frac{4.5}{\sqrt{2.2505}}$$

$$= 2.999667,$$

which differs only by .000001 (obviously a rounding error) from the 2.999666 obtained earlier.

HIGHER-ORDER, MULTIVARIATE, AND COVARIANCE DESIGNS

As stated at the outset of this chapter, we have no intention of going into any detail with respect to more complex designs of ANOVA, let alone MANOVA and MANCOVA. All we plan to do in this section is to give a general idea of how the extensions to these designs are made. Actually, so far as the parameter-estimation phase is concerned, there is very little to add to the earlier discussion. However, the design matrix becomes more complicated here, and the observation and parameter vectors become longer. (For MANOVA they become matrices, with each dependent variable represented by a separate column.) Of course, the computations become much more complicated and virtually impossible without a computer. Nevertheless, the same set of formulas suffices for both the simplest and the most complex cases. Hence, in this section we merely present the design matrices, and in one case show how a contrast matrix can be constructed.

In the significance-testing phase, however, somewhat more drastic modifications are required—including a "second generation" transformation (a re-reparameterization, as it were) by means of *orthogonal* contrasts so that the new parameters will be pairwise uncorrelated. Nevertheless, all these modifications fall in the rubric of technical adjustments, and the basic method remains unchanged.

Higher-Order Designs

We use the simplest possible nontrivial higher-order design, the 2×3 factorial, to illustrate how the design matrix changes, and to construct a possible contrast matrix. The general principles for further extension to other higher-order designs are also given.

The structural equation for a two-factor design with two levels in one factor and three in the other, plus an interaction effect, is as follows:

$$Y_{ijk} = \mu + \alpha_j + \beta_k(\alpha\beta)_{jk} + \epsilon_{ijk} \; (i = 1, 2, \ldots, n_{jk};$$
$$j = 1, 2; k = 1, 2, 3). \qquad (27)$$

Writing separate equations for the n_{jk} members of each (j, k)-cell, this equation ramifies to

$$
\begin{array}{llllll}
Y_{i11} = \mu + \alpha_1 & + \beta_1 & + (\alpha\beta)_{11} & & + \epsilon_{i11} \\
Y_{i12} = \mu + \alpha_1 & + \beta_2 & + (\alpha\beta)_{12} & & + \epsilon_{i12} \\
Y_{i13} = \mu + \alpha_1 & + \beta_3 & + (\alpha\beta)_{13} & & + \epsilon_{i13} \\
Y_{i21} = \mu & + \alpha_2 + \beta_1 & & + (\alpha\beta)_{21} & + \epsilon_{i21} \\
Y_{i22} = \mu & + \alpha_2 + \beta_2 & & + (\alpha\beta)_{22} & + \epsilon_{i22} \\
Y_{i23} = \mu & + \alpha_2 + \beta_3 & & + (\alpha\beta)_{23} + \epsilon_{i23}
\end{array}
$$

The design matrix for this case has

$$N = \sum_{j=1}^{2} \sum_{k=1}^{3} n_{jk}$$

rows and 12 columns [one for the grand mean, one for each of the two levels of α, one for each of the three levels of β, and one for each of the six (α, β) combinations]. The N rows come in six sets of repeated rows, one set for each of the cells, containing $n_{11}, n_{12}, \ldots, n_{23}$ identical rows, respectively. In order to highlight the pattern (besides saving space), we write the design matrix $\mathbf{X}$ with six rows of column vectors (of successive dimensionality $n_{11}, n_{12}, \ldots, n_{23}$) instead of N rows of 1s and 0s, which it really has, thus:

$$
\mathbf{X} = \begin{bmatrix}
1 & 1 & 0 & 1 & 0 & 0 & 1 & 0 & 0 & 0 & 0 & 0 \\
1 & 1 & 0 & 0 & 1 & 0 & 0 & 1 & 0 & 0 & 0 & 0 \\
1 & 1 & 0 & 0 & 0 & 1 & 0 & 0 & 1 & 0 & 0 & 0 \\
1 & 0 & 1 & 1 & 0 & 0 & 0 & 0 & 0 & 1 & 0 & 0 \\
1 & 0 & 1 & 0 & 1 & 0 & 0 & 0 & 0 & 0 & 1 & 0 \\
1 & 0 & 1 & 0 & 0 & 1 & 0 & 0 & 0 & 0 & 0 & 1
\end{bmatrix}
\begin{array}{l}
(A_1 B_1) \\
(A_1 B_2) \\
(A_1 B_3) \\
(A_2 B_1) \\
(A_2 B_2) \\
(A_2 B_3)
\end{array}
$$

[The (A_j, B_k) to the right of each row of $\mathbf{X}$ identifies the cell to which it corresponds.] The parameter vector is now a 12-dimensional column vector,

$$\mathbf{\Theta} = [\mu, \alpha_1, \alpha_2, \beta_1, \beta_2, \beta_3, (\alpha\beta)_{11}, (\alpha\beta)_{12}, \ldots, (\alpha\beta)_{23}]'.$$

Given these definitions of the design matrix $\mathbf{X}$, the parameter vector $\mathbf{\Theta}$, and the obvious definitions of the observation vector $\mathbf{Y}$ and the error vector $\mathbf{\epsilon}$, it is easy to verify that the six distinct types of structural equations displayed after Equation 27 take on exactly the same form as Equation 11 for the two-group case, namely,

$$\mathbf{Y} = \mathbf{X\Theta} + \mathbf{\epsilon}. \qquad (11)$$

As before, the product $\mathbf{X\Theta}$ serves to pick out, for subjects in each cell, the appropriate ones of the 12 parameters for inclusion in the structural equation for their Y score. For instance, the score for any subject in the (A_1, B_3)-cell—that is, any element of Y from the $(n_{11} + n_{12} + 1)$th through the $(n_{11} + n_{12} + n_{13})$th— will be expressed as the sum of the four elements of $\mathbf{\Theta}$ that correspond to the four 1s in the third row of $\mathbf{X}$ [viz., μ, α_1, β_3 and $(\alpha\beta)_{13}$] plus the appropriate ϵ_{i13}.

The next step is to construct the contrast matrix $\mathbf{C}$ to define the new parameter vector $\mathbf{\Psi}$ in accordance with Equation 13, namely, $\mathbf{\Psi} = \mathbf{C\Theta}$. There are six cells in the design, thus there can be at most six rows in $\mathbf{C}$. One way to construct a suitable contrast matrix is as follows:

1. As the first row of a 6×12 matrix, use

$$[1, \tfrac{1}{2}, \tfrac{1}{2}, \tfrac{1}{3}, \tfrac{1}{3}, \tfrac{1}{3}, \tfrac{1}{6}, \tfrac{1}{6}, \tfrac{1}{6}, \tfrac{1}{6}, \tfrac{1}{6}, \tfrac{1}{6}],$$

which comprises the coefficients of a linear combination of the original parameters that defines the overall-level parameter.

2. Write the submatrix showing the actual contrast(s) in the contrast matrix for each factor separately. That is, write these contrast matrices each with its first row and first column deleted. To make the procedure clear, we show the entire contrast matrices with their first rows and first columns written and then stricken out. The remaining submatrices (not the entire matrices) are denoted by $\mathbf{C}_a$ and $\mathbf{C}_b$. Their orders are $(J - 1) \times J$ and $(K - 1) \times K$, where J and K are the numbers of levels in factors A and B, respectively, so that $J = 2$ and $K = 3$ in this example.

$$\mathbf{C}_a = \begin{bmatrix} 1 & \tfrac{1}{2} & -\tfrac{1}{2} \\ 0 & 1 & -1 \end{bmatrix}, \qquad \mathbf{C}_b = \begin{bmatrix} 1 & \tfrac{1}{3} & \tfrac{1}{3} & \tfrac{1}{3} \\ 0 & 1 & 0 & -1 \\ 0 & 0 & 1 & -1 \end{bmatrix}$$

3. Transcribe $\mathbf{C}_a$ and $\mathbf{C}_b$ as parts of the second row and the third through fourth rows of the 6×12 matrix. $\mathbf{C}_a$ should occupy the two columns in which the $\tfrac{1}{2}$'s stand in the first row, whereas $\mathbf{C}_b$ should come in the columns with the three $\tfrac{1}{3}$'s. The incomplete 6×12 matrix would now look like this:

$$\begin{bmatrix} 1 & \tfrac{1}{2} & \tfrac{1}{2} & \tfrac{1}{3} & \tfrac{1}{3} & \tfrac{1}{3} & \tfrac{1}{6} & \tfrac{1}{6} & \tfrac{1}{6} & \tfrac{1}{6} & \tfrac{1}{6} & \tfrac{1}{6} \\ & 1 & -1 & & & & & & & & & \\ & & & 1 & 0 & -1 & & & & & & \\ & & & 0 & 1 & -1 & & & & & & \end{bmatrix}$$

4. The 1 and -1 in the second row are now regarded as the results of having subtracted the average of the rows in the matrix $\mathbf{X}$ displayed at the beginning of this section that pertain to A_2 (i.e., rows 4 through 6) from the average of the rows relating to A_1 (rows 1 through 3). Imagining the entire second row to be generated in this way, the next three entries will be 0s, and the last six entries will be

$$\tfrac{1}{3}\ \tfrac{1}{3}\ \tfrac{1}{3}\ -\tfrac{1}{3}\ -\tfrac{1}{3}\ -\tfrac{1}{3}.$$

Similarly, the entries 1, 0, -1 of the third row of the contrast matrix being constructed may be regarded as having been obtained by subtracting the average of the β_3-row of $\mathbf{X}$ (rows 3 and 6) from the average of the B_1-rows (rows 1 and 4). Generating the entire third row in this manner will give us 0s in the preceding columns and the following in the last six columns:

$$\tfrac{1}{2}\ 0\ -\tfrac{1}{2}\ \tfrac{1}{2}\ 0\ -\tfrac{1}{2}.$$

Likewise, generating the entire fourth row in the way the second row of $\mathbf{C}$ (0, 1, -1) can be imagined as having been obtained, the last six columns will have the elements

$$0\ \tfrac{1}{2}\ -\tfrac{1}{2}\ 0\ \tfrac{1}{2}\ -\tfrac{1}{2}.$$

The partially completed matrix $\mathbf{C}$ now becomes

$$\begin{bmatrix}
1 & \tfrac{1}{2} & & \tfrac{1}{2} & \tfrac{1}{3} & \tfrac{1}{3} & & \tfrac{1}{3} & \tfrac{1}{6} & \tfrac{1}{6} & & \tfrac{1}{6} & \tfrac{1}{6} & \tfrac{1}{6} & \tfrac{1}{6} \\
 & 1 & -1 & & & & & \tfrac{1}{3} & \tfrac{1}{3} & & \tfrac{1}{3} & -\tfrac{1}{3} & -\tfrac{1}{3} & -\tfrac{1}{3} \\
 & & & 1 & 0 & -1 & \tfrac{1}{2} & 0 & -\tfrac{1}{2} & \tfrac{1}{2} & 0 & -\tfrac{1}{2} \\
 & & & 0 & 1 & -1 & 0 & \tfrac{1}{2} & -\tfrac{1}{2} & 0 & \tfrac{1}{2} & -\tfrac{1}{2}
\end{bmatrix},$$

where the remaining blank positions in rows 2 through 4 are understood to be 0s (deliberately not shown in order to highlight the pattern so far).

5. The first six elements of the last two rows also are 0s. The last six elements are obtained as follows:

(a) Multiply the first row of $\mathbf{C}_b$ by the first element of $\mathbf{C}_a$ (which is 1 in this example). To this result, tack on the product of the first row of $\mathbf{C}_b$ and the second element of $\mathbf{C}_a$ (-1 in this example). The combined result is the six-dimensional vector

$$[1,\ 0,\ -1,\ -1,\ 0,\ 1].$$

(b) Repeat the same operation as above on the second row of $\mathbf{C}_b$, to obtain

$$[0,\ 1,\ -1,\ 0,\ -1,\ 1].$$

Putting together the outcomes of (a) and (b), we get the lower right-hand 2 × 6 segment of $\mathbf{C}$, and the final result is

$$\begin{bmatrix}
1 & \tfrac{1}{2} & & \tfrac{1}{2} & \tfrac{1}{3} & \tfrac{1}{3} & & \tfrac{1}{3} & \tfrac{1}{6} & \tfrac{1}{6} & & \tfrac{1}{6} & \tfrac{1}{6} & \tfrac{1}{6} & \tfrac{1}{6} \\
 & 1 & -1 & & & & & \tfrac{1}{3} & \tfrac{1}{3} & & \tfrac{1}{3} & -\tfrac{1}{3} & -\tfrac{1}{3} & -\tfrac{1}{3} \\
 & & & 1 & 0 & -1 & \tfrac{1}{2} & 0 & -\tfrac{1}{2} & \tfrac{1}{2} & 0 & -\tfrac{1}{2} \\
 & & & 0 & 1 & -1 & 0 & \tfrac{1}{2} & -\tfrac{1}{2} & 0 & \tfrac{1}{2} & -\tfrac{1}{2} \\
 & & & & & & 1 & 0 & -1 & -1 & 0 & 1 \\
 & & & & & & 0 & 1 & -1 & 0 & -1 & 1
\end{bmatrix}.$$

(The reader who has more than passing familiarity with matrix algebra may find the instructions of Step 5 easier to follow when they are stated succinctly as follows: The lower right-hand 2×6 submatrix of C is the *Kronecker product* $C_a \otimes C_b$.)

The contrast matrix C, just constructed, is acceptable because its rows are linearly independent, and they also are expressible as linear combinations of the rows of the design matrix X, as is evident from the way in which they were generated. We may therefore define an estimable new parameter vector in accordance with Equation 13, as

$$\Psi = C\Theta.$$

The rest of the parameter-estimation phase follows exactly as described earlier. That is, the basis matrix is computed as

$$K = (XC')(CC')^{-1} \tag{15}$$

and the estimates of the new parameters are obtained as

$$\hat{\Psi} = (K'K)^{-1}(K'Y). \tag{17}$$

The significance-testing phase for all but the completely balanced design requires a further reparameterization, as stated at the outset of this section. Other than this complication, which we do not go into here (see Finn, 1974, pp. 297–304), everything follows as discussed in the preceding section.

Multivariate Designs

When more than one criterion variables are considered simultaneously, we have a multivariate design. For example, if the quality of performance is measured by both speed and accuracy, we are using a bivariate design. Any ANOVA design can be generalized into a MANOVA (multivariate analysis of variance) design with minor modifications so far as the parameter-estimation phase is concerned. The significance-testing phase requires further modifications besides the re-reparameterizing, due partly to the different test statistics that are involved. (See, e.g., Tatsuoka, 1988, pp. 285–288.)

Suppose that there is a set of p criterion variables to be used in an experiment with a one-way MANOVA design. We take $p = 2$ and confine ourselves to the two-group case to save space, but the discussions here hold for any p and any number of groups. The vector Y of observations and the error vector ϵ mentioned earlier become $N \times 2$ matrices, and the parameter vector Θ is expanded into a 3×2 matrix [a $(J + 1) \times p$ matrix in general]. The design matrix X remains unchanged, and the structural equation in explicit matrix form is quite analogous to Equation 10:

$$\begin{bmatrix} Y_{11}^{(1)} & Y_{11}^{(2)} \\ \cdot & \\ \cdot & \\ \cdot & \\ Y_{n_11}^{(1)} & Y_{n_11}^{(2)} \\ \cdots\cdots\cdots\cdots \\ Y_{12}^{(1)} & Y_{12}^{(2)} \\ \cdot & \\ \cdot & \\ \cdot & \\ Y_{n_22}^{(1)} & Y_{n_22}^{(2)} \end{bmatrix} = \begin{bmatrix} 1 & 1 & 0 \\ \cdot & \cdot & \cdot \\ \cdot & \cdot & \cdot \\ \cdot & \cdot & \cdot \\ 1 & 1 & 0 \\ \cdots\cdots \\ 1 & 0 & 1 \\ \cdot & \cdot & \cdot \\ \cdot & \cdot & \cdot \\ \cdot & \cdot & \cdot \\ 1 & 0 & 1 \end{bmatrix} \begin{bmatrix} \mu^{(1)} & \mu^{(2)} \\ \alpha_1^{(1)} & \alpha_1^{(2)} \\ \alpha_2^{(1)} & \alpha_{11}^{(2)} \end{bmatrix} + \begin{bmatrix} \epsilon_{11}^{(1)} & \epsilon_{11}^{(2)} \\ \cdot & \\ \cdot & \cdot \\ \cdot & \\ \epsilon_{n_11}^{(1)} & \epsilon_{n_11}^{(2)} \\ \cdots\cdots\cdots\cdots \\ \epsilon_{12}^{(1)} & \epsilon_{12}^{(2)} \\ \cdot & \\ \cdot & \\ \cdot & \\ \epsilon_{n_22}^{(1)} & \epsilon_{n_11}^{(2)} \end{bmatrix}$$

Here the superscripts in parentheses distinguish the two (or, more generally, p) criterion variables.

In symbolic matrix form, this looks exactly the same as Equation 11, namely,

$$\mathbf{Y} = \mathbf{\Theta X} + \mathbf{\epsilon},$$

except that $\mathbf{Y}$, $\mathbf{\Theta}$, and $\mathbf{\epsilon}$ are now matrices instead of vectors. Hence all of the developments discussed earlier continue to hold without any modifications other than those stemming from the changes already noted. The contrast matrix $\mathbf{C}$ is unchanged, and hence also the basis matrix $\mathbf{K}$ of Equation 15, which involves only the unchanged $\mathbf{X}$ and $\mathbf{C}$, thus:

$$\mathbf{K}(\mathbf{XC'})(\mathbf{CC'})^{-1}.$$

The estimated new parameter matrix is computed, as before, from Equation 17,

$$\hat{\mathbf{\Psi}} = (\mathbf{K'K})^{-1}(\mathbf{K'Y}),$$

but it is now a 2×2 (or, in general, a $J \times p$) matrix instead of a two-dimensional column vector.

The developments discussed in the preceding section for the significance-testing phase continue to hold with the modifications described later—up to but not including the actual tests—so long as the design is completely balanced. If the design is not completely balanced, a re-reparameterizing is needed to achieve orthogonality, just as in the univariate case. After the re-reparameterizing, the previously mentioned procedures may be used, but still stopping short of the actual tests themselves.

There is one essential difference from the univariate case. In lieu of the population variance σ^2 of the sole criterion variable Y there, we now have a population covariance matrix $\mathbf{\Sigma}$ of order $p \times p$. Therefore, the covariance matrix $\mathbf{V}(\mathbf{\Psi})$ of the new parameters is defined by a generalization of Equation 21 rather than that equation itself. Symbolizing the matrix $(\mathbf{K'K})^{-1}$ there by $\mathbf{G}$ the generalized form of Equation 21 for the two-group, two-variable case is

$$\mathbf{V}(\mathbf{\psi}) = \begin{bmatrix} g_{11}\mathbf{\Sigma} & g_{12}\mathbf{\Sigma} \\ g_{21}\mathbf{\Sigma} & g_{22}\mathbf{\Sigma} \end{bmatrix}, \tag{28}$$

which reduces back to

$$V(\Psi) = G\sigma^2 = (K'K)^{-1}\sigma^2 \tag{21}$$

when $p = 1$. The analogy between Equations 28 and 21 is accentuated by using the Kronecker product notation, which was introduced earlier in the discussion of the construction of a contrast matrix for two-factor designs. For Equation 28 may then be rewritten as

$$V(\Psi) = (K'K)^{-1} \otimes \Sigma. \tag{29}$$

As before, we must replace Σ by its sample estimate in order to get a usable formula. This is done by going through the steps of computing S_T and S_B, which now become the $p \times p$ matrices S_T and S_B instead of scalars. Other than this, Equations 22 and 23 remain intact. The final result is closely analogous to Equation 26 if the Kronecker product is used; namely,

$$V(\Psi) = (K'K)^{-1} \otimes [Y'Y - \Psi'(K'Y)]/(N - J). \tag{30}$$

The modifications up to this point—although quite extensive—have all been formal in nature, and the analogy with the univariate case was transparent. However, the actual test procedures now involve diagonal submatrices of $V(\Psi)$ instead of scalar diagonal elements. This makes for essential departures from the univariate tests. For one thing, there is no single "uniformly best test"—that is, a test that is most powerful against various ways in which the null hypothesis could be false. Studies comparing the relative efficiencies of four multivariate test statistics (Hotelling's trace criterion τ, the Pillai–Bartlett trace criterion V, Roy's largest-root criterion θ, and Wilks's likelihood-ratio criterion Λ) have been conducted by Olson (1976) and Stevens (1979); their (somewhat conflicting) results are briefly summarized in Tatsuoka (1988, pp. 285–289). Fortunately, all these tests are available in most widely used computer programs such as SAS PROC GLM and BMDP ANOVA 1V through 8V; if the conclusions differ, users may choose the one that is most consonant with their judgment of the relative seriousness of Type I versus Type II errors in their particular research context.

Covariance Analysis

In practice, it may sometimes happen that random assignment of subjects to treatment groups may be infeasible, thus violating one of the requirements of ANOVA. This will be the case, for instance, when intact classes are taught by two or more randomly assigned teaching methods in an experiment to compare their relative merits. In such situations, the several classes may differ significantly on some variable related to the criterion performance, such as IQ. In fact, the groups may differ significantly in mean IQ even if subjects had been assigned randomly to the treatment groups. It may then become doubtful whether an observed significant difference among group performances on the criterion variable is due to the differential effectiveness of the teaching methods or to the group discrepancies in IQ, or to a combination of both. The relevant but uncontrolled variable (such as IQ) is called a covariate or a "nuisance variable." It is the purpose of covariance analysis to test whether significant treatment differences continue to exist even after allowances are made for group differences on the covariate. (Or, alternatively, whether significant treatment differences might have been masked by differences on the covariate but might emerge if the latter had been controlled.)

The structural equation for a one-way covariance analysis is

$$Y_{ij} = \mu + \alpha_j + \gamma_j(X_{ij} - \mu_x) + \epsilon_{ij} \ (i = 1, 2, \ldots, n_i;$$
$$j = 1, 2, \ldots, J), \tag{31}$$

where γ_j is the coefficient of regression of Y on X in the jth group, and μ_x is the grand mean of X. For the two-group case Equation 31 may be written in explicit matrix form as

$$
\begin{bmatrix}
Y_{11} \\
\cdot \\
\cdot \\
\cdot \\
Y_{n_1 1} \\
\cdots \\
Y_{12} \\
\cdot \\
\cdot \\
\cdot \\
Y_{n_2 2}
\end{bmatrix}
=
\begin{bmatrix}
1 & 1 & 0 & x_{12} & 0 \\
\cdot & \cdot & \cdot & \cdot & \cdot \\
\cdot & \cdot & \cdot & \cdot & \cdot \\
\cdot & \cdot & \cdot & \cdot & \cdot \\
1 & 1 & 0 & x_{n_1 1} & 0 \\
\cdots & \cdots & \cdots & \cdots & \cdots \\
1 & 0 & 1 & 0 & x_{12} \\
\cdot & \cdot & \cdot & \cdot & \cdot \\
\cdot & \cdot & \cdot & \cdot & \cdot \\
\cdot & \cdot & \cdot & \cdot & \cdot \\
1 & 0 & 1 & 0 & x_{n_2 2}
\end{bmatrix}
\begin{bmatrix}
\mu \\
\alpha_1 \\
\alpha_2 \\
\gamma_1 \\
\gamma_2
\end{bmatrix}
+
\begin{bmatrix}
\epsilon_{11} \\
\cdot \\
\cdot \\
\cdot \\
\epsilon_{n_1 1} \\
\cdots \\
\epsilon_{12} \\
\cdot \\
\cdot \\
\cdot \\
\epsilon_{n_2 2}
\end{bmatrix},
$$

where $x_{ij} = X_{ij} - \bar{X}$ is the sample estimate of $X_{ij} - \mu_x$.

In symbolic matrix form, this again reduces to Equation 11:

$$\mathbf{Y} = \mathbf{X\Theta} + \boldsymbol{\epsilon},$$

but with an important difference from previous cases: The design matrix $\mathbf{X}$ here contains not only 1's and 0's as it did before, but also the observed covariate score (in deviation-score form) for each subject.

The rationale of ANCOVA dictates a slightly different procedure from ANOVA, not only in the significance-testing phase but also in parameter estimation. The two phases are more intertwined in ANCOVA, for we must first test the null hypothesis $\gamma_1 = \gamma_2$, using the contrast matrix (actually a row vector)

$$\mathbf{C} = [0, 0, 0, 1, -1].$$

Depending on the outcome of this test, the γ_js in the parameter vector of Equation 31 are either left as they are, or are both rewritten as γ without subscript.

The final step consists in testing whether H_0: $\alpha_1 = \alpha_2$ is tenable after the effect of γ (or of γ_1 and γ_2, as the case may be) has been accounted for, or "partialled out." In principle, this calls for constructing "residualized" matrices corresponding to $\mathbf{S}_T$ and $\mathbf{S}_B$ after the parameter vector excluding the regression coefficients has been transformed as in Section 4. This means that wherever $\mathbf{Y}$ appears in the formulas for $\mathbf{S}_T$ and $\mathbf{S}_B$ (either explicitly or through $\boldsymbol{\Psi}$), it has to be replaced by $\mathbf{Y} - \hat{\mathbf{Y}}$, the vector of residuals of Y from its regression on X. In practice, however, the process of residualizing the actual criterion scores is by-passed, and the adjustments are made directly on the sums of squares.

Appendix

Equivalence of t tests for Significance of the Difference Between Two Means and for Significance of Regression Weight of Criterion on Dummy Variate Indicating Group Membership

We have seen, in Equation 4, that the regression weight in question is given by

$$b = \bar{Y}_1 - \bar{Y}_2, \tag{1}$$

where $\bar{Y}_1$ is the criterion mean of the group for which $X = 1$, and $\bar{Y}_2$ is that of the group with $X = 0$.

The t statistic for testing the significance of b is easily derivable from the more familiar t statistic for the significance of the correlation coefficient r, namely,

$$t = \frac{r\sqrt{N - 2}}{\sqrt{1 - r^2}}.$$

We need only express r in terms of b by the relation

$$r = bs_x/s_y$$

which, substituted in the expression for t, yields

$$t = \frac{\dfrac{bs_x}{s_y}\sqrt{N - 2}}{\sqrt{1 - \dfrac{b^2 s_x^2}{s_y^2}}}$$

$$= \frac{bs_x\sqrt{N - 2}}{\sqrt{s_y^2 - b^2 s_x^2}}. \tag{2}$$

The variance s_x^2 (in the total sample) for the dummy variate X is

$$s_x{}^2 = \frac{\Sigma X^2 - (\Sigma X)^2/N}{N - 1}$$

$$= \frac{n_1 - n_1{}^2/N}{N - 1}$$

$$= \frac{n_1(N - n_1)}{N(N - 1)}$$

$$= \frac{n_1 n_2}{N(N - 1)}.$$

Substituting this and expression 1 for b in Equation 2 gives

$$t = \frac{(\bar{Y}_1 - \bar{Y}_2) \sqrt{\frac{n_1 n_2}{N(N - 1)}} \sqrt{N - 2}}{\sqrt{s_y^2 - (\bar{Y}_1 - \bar{Y}_2)^2 \frac{n_1 n_2}{N(N - 1)}}}$$

or

$$t = \frac{(\bar{Y}_1 - \bar{Y}_2) \sqrt{\frac{n_1 n_2 (N - 2)}{N}}}{\sqrt{(N - 1)s_y^2 - \frac{n_1 n_2}{N} (\bar{Y}_1 - \bar{Y}_2)^2}}. \tag{3}$$

The first term under the radical in the denominator of the right-hand expression is the total sum of squares (SS_t) for Y. The second term turns out to be the between-groups sum of squares for the two-group case. For, from the usual formula for SS_b, we know that

$$SS_b = \sum_{j=1}^{2} n_j (\bar{Y}_j - \bar{Y})^2$$

in which we may substitute the expression

$$\bar{Y} = \frac{n_1 \bar{Y}_1 + n_2 \bar{Y}_2}{N}$$

for the grand mean $\bar{Y}$, to obtain

$$SS_b = n_1 \left(\bar{Y}_1 - \frac{n_1 \bar{Y}_1 + n_2 \bar{Y}_2}{N} \right)^2 + n_2 \left(\bar{Y}_2 - \frac{n_1 \bar{Y}_1 + n_2 \bar{Y}_2}{N} \right)^2$$

$$= \frac{n_1}{N^2} (N\bar{Y}_1 - n_1 \bar{Y}_1 - n_2 \bar{Y}_2)^2 + \frac{n_2}{N^2} (N\bar{Y}_2 - n_1 \bar{Y}_1 - n_2 \bar{Y}_2)^2$$

$$= \frac{n_1 n_2^2}{N^2} (\bar{Y}_1 - \bar{Y}_2)^2 + \frac{n_2 n_1^2}{N^2} (\bar{Y}_2 - \bar{Y}_1)^2$$

$$= \frac{n_1 n_2}{N} (\bar{Y}_1 - \bar{Y}_2)^2.$$

Consequently, the expression under the radical in Equation 3 becomes

$$SS_t - SS_b = SS_w,$$

the within-groups sum-of-squares of $\bar{Y}$. Hence, the entire expression for t becomes

$$t = \frac{(\bar{Y}_1 - \bar{Y}_2)\sqrt{\dfrac{n_1 n_2 (N - 2)}{N}}}{\sqrt{SS_w}}$$

or

$$t = \frac{\bar{Y}_1 - \bar{Y}_2}{\sqrt{\dfrac{SS_w}{N - 2}\dfrac{N}{n_1 n_2}}}$$

$$= \frac{\bar{Y}_1 - \bar{Y}_2}{\sqrt{MS_w \left(\dfrac{1}{n_1} + \dfrac{1}{n_2}\right)}},$$

which is precisely the familiar expression for the t statistic for testing the significance of the difference between two independent means.

REFERENCES

Arnold, S. (1981). *The theory of linear models and multivariate analysis.* New York: Wiley.

Finn, J. D. (1974). *A general model for multivariate analysis.* New York: Holt, Rinehart & Winston.

Hays, W. L. (1988). *Statistics for psychologists* (4th ed.). New York: Wiley.

McCullagh, P., & Welder, J. A. (1983). *Generalized linear models.* New York: Chapman & Hall.

Olson, C. L. (1976). On choosing a test statistic in multivariate analysis of variance. *Psychological Bulletin, 83,* 579–586.

Searle, S. R. (1971). *Linear models.* New York: Wiley.

Stevens, J. P. (1979). Comment on Olson: Choosing a test statistic in multivariate analysis of variance. *Psychological Bulletin, 86,* 355–360.

Tatsuoka, M. M. (1988). *Multivariate analysis: Techniques for educational and psychological research* (2nd ed.). New York: Macmillan.

2 Pairwise Comparison Procedures for One-Way Analysis of Variance Designs

Rebecca Zwick
Educational Testing Service

Research in the behavioral and health sciences frequently involves the application of one-factor analysis of variance (ANOVA) models. The goal may be to compare several independent groups of subjects on a quantitative dependent variable or, alternatively, to compare measurements made on different occasions or under different conditions on a single group of subjects. If there is reason to believe there are differences among the groups (or occasions or conditions), the researcher frequently wishes to compare the means in a pairwise fashion. Although the procedures for conducting omnibus hypothesis tests for one-factor ANOVA models are familiar to most researchers, the issues that must be considered in choosing pairwise multiple comparison procedures (MCPs) are not as well-understood. In this chapter, the selection of pairwise MCPs for one-factor ANOVA models is considered, following a discussion of Type I error and power issues as they apply to the testing of multiple hypotheses. Although the focus is on the independent-sample case, repeated measures models are considered briefly as well.

TYPE I ERROR AND POWER

Any student who has taken an elementary statistics course can recite the definitions of Type I error and power: The Type I error rate is the probability of rejecting the null hypothesis when the null hypothesis is true and power is the probability of rejecting the null hypothesis when the null hypothesis is false. However, these concepts become much more complex when applied to multiple hypothesis tests, such as MCPs. In the multiple-comparison case, it is possible to define many varieties of Type I error rates (Bernhardson, 1975; Zwick & Marasciulo, 1984). Two of the most important (defined here in terms of *pairwise* MCPs only) are the comparisonwise error rate, α_C, which is the probability of making a Type I error on a particular comparison, and the experimentwise error rate, α_E, which is the probability of making at least one Type I error in conducting the entire set of pairwise comparisons associated with an experiment. (For an experiment with k means, there are $k(k - 1)/2$ distinct pairwise comparisons.). Some MCPs are designed to allow direct control of the comparisonwise error rate; that is, the researcher sets a nominal Type I error rate for each comparison. In other methods, the researcher determines a nominal value for the experimentwise error rate. If a method that allows direct control of α_C is chosen, probability inequalities such as the Bonferroni inequality can be used to calculate an upper bound for α_E. The Bonferroni inequality, as applied in this context, states that if $k(k - 1)/2$ pairwise comparisons are performed, each with a Type I error probability equal to α_C, then the experimentwise Type I error rate, α_E, will be less than or equal to $[k(k - 1)/2]\alpha_C$. That is, the experimentwise error rate is less than or equal to the sum of the comparisonwise error rates. (This upper bound can exceed 1, whereas α_E, of course, cannot.) Other probability inequalities, such as the Dunn-Šidák inequality (Dunn, 1958, 1959, 1974; Šidák, 1967) can be used to produce a more refined upper bound in certain cases. The Bonferroni inequality, however, has the advantage of simplicity and generality.

It is important to note that experimentwise and comparisonwise error rates are not simply interchangeable ways of evaluating Type I error. This can be illustrated with an example. Suppose we used computer simulation techniques to investigate the Type I error rates of two competing MCPs. In order to study Type I error in this way, random numbers are generated and assigned to groups. (There are no "population" differences among the groups, so all statistically significant comparisons will be Type I errors.) The test statistics of interest are then performed on the random data. Suppose that the results for 100 simulated experiments with $k = 3$ groups and a nominal α_E of .05 are as shown in Table 2.1. We can calculate an empirical estimate ($\hat{\alpha}_E$) of the experimentwise error rate for each of the two MCPs as follows:

$$\hat{\alpha}_E = \frac{\text{Number of experiments with at least one significant pairwise comparison}}{\text{Number of experiments}}. \tag{1}$$

In calculating $\hat{\alpha}_E$, the 100 experiments are divided into two classes: those that have no Type I errors and those that have one or more Type I errors. The value of $\hat{\alpha}_E$ is simply the proportion of experiments in the second class. For each of the MCPs, $\hat{\alpha}_E = .05$; that is, the estimated experimentwise error rate is equal to the nominal α_E. We therefore expect that when the null hypothesis is true, application of either of these MCPs will lead to at least one Type I error in 5% of the experiments performed. The value of $\hat{\alpha}_E$ tells us nothing about the likelihood of a

TABLE 2.1
Hypothetical Data on 100 Simulated Experiments with $k = 3$

Number of Significant Comparisons (Type 1 Errors)	Number of Experiments with the Indicated Number of Significant Comparisons	
	Multiple Comparison Procedure 1	Multiple Comparison Procedure 2
0	95	95
1	4	0
2	1	0
3	0	5
Total	100	100

Type I error on a particular comparison. The estimated comparisonwise error rate for this example can be calculated as follows:

$$\hat{\alpha}_C = \frac{\text{Number of significant pairwise comparisons}}{[k(k-1)/2] \cdot [\text{Number of experiments}]}. \tag{2}$$

Note that this is simply the overall proportion of pairwise comparisons that resulted in Type I errors. For MCP 1, $\hat{\alpha}_C = [1(4) + 2(1)]/3(100) = .02$; for MCP 2, $\hat{\alpha}_C = 3(5)/3(100) = .05$. Therefore, although the MCPs are identical in terms of $\hat{\alpha}_E$, they differ in terms of $\hat{\alpha}_C$. Which of these error rates is most useful to the applied researcher?

If, as in most cases, the research conclusions depend on the simultaneous correctness of the set of $k(k-1)/2$ inferences, experimentwise error control is appropriate; if the researcher is concerned instead about the correctness of individual inferences about pairs of means, an MCP that allows direct control of the comparisonwise error rate should be selected. An example of a case in which comparisonwise control might be preferable is as follows: Suppose researchers conduct a study in which three groups, A, B, and C, are compared with $\alpha_E = .05$. The researchers then conduct a similar study that includes two additional groups, D and E, although their primary interest is still in groups A, B, and C. If they again use $\alpha_E = .05$, their tests of the three pairwise differences among groups A, B, and C will be more conservative (i.e., less likely to lead to statistically significant results) than in the previous study because the experimental error rate of .05 will be allocated among a larger number of comparisons. Therefore, it might be considered desirable to hold the value of α_C, rather than α_E, constant across studies. Even if this rationale were applied, however, it would still be important for the researchers to be aware of the experimentwise error rate. That is, if the researchers decide to set α_C equal to .02, they should be prepared to accept an experimentwise error rate as large as $[k(k-1)/2](.02) = 10(.02) = .20$ for the five-group study, assuming all pairwise comparisons are to be conducted.

Just as there are several kinds of Type I error rates that are pertinent to the choice of MCPs, there are several definitions of power that may be useful as well. For instance, for a set of three means with population values 1, 2, and 10, we could consider the probability of detecting one or more of these differences (any-pair power) or the probability of detecting all three pairwise differences (all-pairs power). These definitions will not be explained in detail here; a good discussion is given by Ramsey (1981; see also Einot & Gabriel, 1975; Gabriel, 1978; Ramsey, 1978).

COMPARING THE EMPIRICAL
TYPE I ERROR RATES AND POWERS
OF COMPETING MCPS

Simulation studies like the previously described, hypothetical ones are often performed in order to compare empirical estimates of the true Type I error rates and powers associated with competing MCPs. Unfortunately, many published studies are misleading because they are flawed in design or interpretation. For example, investigators conducting simulation studies of competing MCPs have often failed to distinguish between procedures that provide comparisonwise error control and those that control Type I errors in an experimentwise fashion. It is not unusual to find an MCP with a nominal α_C of .05 being compared to a procedure with a nominal α_E of .05 (Einot & Gabriel, 1975; Zwick & Marascuilo, 1984). Comparisons of this kind provide no useful information about the relative performance of the MCPs. Even without performing a simulation study, it can be predicted that a procedure with a nominal α_C of .05 will produce more Type I errors than a procedure with a nominal α_E of .05. To achieve a more useful comparison of procedures that provide experimentwise control with those that provide comparisonwise control, MCPs with a nominal α_E of .05 should be compared with MCPs with a nominal α_C of $.05/[k(k-1)/2]$. The MCPs that controls α_C can then be regarded as having a nominal α_E of approximately .05.[1]

Similarly, power comparisons can be meaningfully interpreted only if the MCPs under evaluation have the same nominal α_E. This is because the probability of rejecting a false null hypothesis (power) can always be made larger by increasing α. Thus, a procedure with a nominal α_C of .05 is expected to lead to more rejections of false null hypotheses than a procedure with a nominal α_E of .05 because the former procedure is known to have a larger experimentwise error rate. This does not mean that the former procedure is more powerful in any

---

[1]According to the Bonferroni inequality, if $\alpha_c = .05/[k(k-1)/2]$, then α_E cannot exceed .05; that is, $\alpha_E \leq k(k-1)/2 \cdot \alpha_c = .05$. If α_c is small and the number of comparisons is not too large, the Bonferroni approach provides a surprisingly good upper bound, that is, the bound does not exceed the true error rate by a large amount (Miller, 1981).

practical sense. (If meaningful power increases could be achieved by increasing the Type I error rate, we could simply set the nominal α equal to 1.00. By always rejecting the null hypothesis, we would be assured of detecting any true differences!) A related point that is often overlooked is that in making power comparisons, it is important to consider whether the true Type I error rates for the procedures being compared depart substantially from the nominal α. That is, even if the nominal α_E is equal to .05 for two MCPs, it may be that the true error rate for one of the procedures is known to exceed the nominal α_E (as is the case with the protected t test procedure, discussed later), whereas the other MCP does, in fact, control the error rate at the nominal α_E. Here again, it would be a mistake to conclude that the former procedure was more powerful.

These points have important implications for the MCP user, who may be tempted to pick the MCP that tends to yield the largest number of statistically significant differences without determining whether the apparent power superiority is, in fact, achieved at the expense of an increased risk of Type I error.

THE INDEPENDENT-SAMPLE CASE

One of the most common ANOVA designs involves a comparison of k independent groups of subjects on a quantitative dependent variable. In this section, five of the most common MCPs that are applicable to this model are described and illustrated using a hypothetical example. Like the ANOVA F test, these methods require the assumption that observations are independent random samples from normal populations with equal variances. The inclusion of an MCP in the discussion does not constitute a recommendation. Some of the MCPs were selected to be representative of certain types of procedures or of particular philosophies of Type I error control. A detailed evaluation of these five methods is provided, followed by a discussion of MCPs for use when normality or variance equality are thought to be violated.

Example

Suppose we are interested in comparing different forms of psychiatric treatment for psychotic inpatients. We choose a random sample of 40 psychotics and then randomly assign them to one of four forms of treatment: pharmacologic therapy (P), which involves the administration of antipsychotic drugs; group psychotherapy (G); individual psychotherapy (I); and a combination of antipsychotic drugs and individual psychotherapy (C). After 1 month, we ask an experienced clinical researcher to rate each patient on a series of items pertaining to the patient's ability to perform everyday tasks, maintain personal relationships, and hold a job. The rating scale yields overall scores ranging from 0 to 100, with higher scores indicating greater ability to function. The scores, means, variances, and sample sizes are as shown in Table 2.2. These hypothetical data are used to illustrate the multiple comparison methods presented here.

MCPs for the Normal Equal-Variance Case

In this section, the following MCPs are discussed: (a) Scheffé's (1953) procedure, (b) Tukey's (1953) Studentized range test and the Tukey–Kramer (Kramer, 1956; Tukey, 1953) modification for unequal sample sizes, (c) the Dunn–Bonferroni method (Dunn, 1961), (d) Fisher's (1935) protected t test procedure, and (e) the Newman–Keuls (Keuls, 1952; Newman, 1939) test. All five of these procedures are described in Hochberg and Tamhane (1987), Kirk (1982), and Miller (1981). It is important to note that these five methods do not differ in terms of the formulation of the test statistics used to make pairwise comparisons. In each case the test statistic can be written as follows:

$$t_{ii'} = \frac{\bar{X}_i - \bar{X}_{i'}}{\sqrt{MSW \left(\frac{1}{n_i} + \frac{1}{n_{i'}} \right)}}, \tag{3}$$

where $\bar{X}_i$ and $\bar{X}_{i'}$ are the two means being compared, n_i and $n_{i'}$ are the sample sizes associated with these two means, and MSW is the mean square within groups for the entire k-sample study, defined as $\sum_{i=1}^{k} (n_i - 1)s_i^2/(N - k)$ where k is the number of groups, $N = \sum_{i=1}^{k} n_i$ is the overall sample size, and s_i^2 is the

TABLE 2.2
Hypothetical Data for Psychiatric Treatment Study[a]

	Pharmacologic Therapy (P)	Group Psychotherapy (G)	Individual Psychotherapy (I)	Combination of P and I (C)
	24	12	21	27
	29	13	25	28
	33	18	30	35
	36	20	32	37
	38	21	36	39
	42	29	37	44
	44	30	38	45
	47	30	42	46
	51	35	43	52
	56	42	56	57
$\bar{X}_i$	40	25	36	41
s_i^2	99.11	95.33	98.67	94.22
n_i	10	10	10	10

[a]$\bar{X} = 35.5$, $MSB = 536.67$, $MSW = 96.83$, $N = 40$, $t_{PG} = 3.41$, $t_{PI} = .91$, $t_{PC} = -.23$, $t_{GI} = -2.50$, $t_{GC} = -3.64$, and $t_{IC} = -1.14$.

variance in each sample. The example involves samples of equal size, so Equation 3 can be simplified as follows:

$$t_{ii'} = \frac{\bar{X}_i - \bar{X}_{i'}}{\sqrt{MSW\left(\dfrac{2}{n}\right)}}, \tag{4}$$

where $n = 10$ is the sample size in each of the $k = 4$ groups. For instance, the test statistic for comparing group therapy (G) to the combination of pharmacologic and individual therapy (C) is:

$$\frac{\bar{X}_G - \bar{X}_C}{\sqrt{MSW\left(\dfrac{2}{n}\right)}} = \frac{25 - 41}{\sqrt{96.83\left(\dfrac{2}{10}\right)}} = -3.64. \tag{5}$$

The values of $t_{ii'}$ for the remaining five pairwise comparisons are given in Table 2.2.

The difference among the five MCPs to be discussed here lies in (a) the rules, if any, used to determine whether a given comparison is to be performed and (b) the choice of critical values to which the t statistics are to be compared. These aspects of each of the five procedures are described next.

Scheffé's Procedure. Scheffé's comparisons are ordinarily performed after a significant ANOVA F test. That is, the statistic $F = MSB/MSW$ is first computed, where the mean square between groups MSB, is equal to $\Sigma_{i=1}^{k} n_i (\bar{X}_i - \bar{X})^2$, $\bar{X}$ is the grand mean, and MSW is as defined earlier. Then if the observed value of F exceeds $F_{k-1,N-k:1-\alpha_E}$, the critical value of F with $k - 1$ and $N - k$ degrees of freedom for the desired α_E level, pairwise t tests of the form shown in Equation 3 (or Equation 4) are performed, using as a critical value

$$S_{k-1,N-k:1-\alpha_E} = \sqrt{(k - 1)\, F_{k-1,N-k:1-\alpha_E}}. \tag{6}$$

The comparison is significant if $|t| > S$ (i.e., if $t < -S$ or $t > S$). The Scheffé method controls the experimentwise Type I error rate at α_E regardless of the number of pairwise comparisons performed. In fact, the method controls the experimentwise error rate at α_E for the set of all *contrasts*. A contrast is a linear combination of population means (μ_i) of the form $a_1\mu_1 + a_2\mu_2 + \ldots + a_k\mu_k$, where the a_i are weights chosen so that $\Sigma_{i=1}^{k} a_i = 0$. For example, we might want to test the hypothesis that $\mu_1 - \dfrac{\mu_2 + \mu_3}{2} = 0$; that is, the mean of group 1 is equal to the mean of groups 2 and 3 combined. This contrast would be estimated in the sample as $\bar{X}_1 - \dfrac{\bar{X}_2 + \bar{X}_3}{2} = (1)(\bar{X}_1) + (-\frac{1}{2})(\bar{X}_2) + (-\frac{1}{2})(\bar{X}_3)$. Here, $a_1 = 1$, $a_2 = -\frac{1}{2}$, and $a_3 = -\frac{1}{2}$. A *pairwise comparison* is a special case of a contrast, where the weights are $a_i = 1$ and $a_{i'} = -1$. Contrasts other than pairwise comparisons are called *complex contrasts*. Although the Scheffé method applies to all contrasts, it is often used even when only pairwise comparisons are of interest. It is important to understand the relationship between the overall F test and the pairwise comparisons performed via the Scheffé method. Although a significant F ratio implies the existence of at least one significant contrast, it does not imply the existence of a significant pairwise comparison. Therefore, the finding of a significant F test, but no significant pairwise t tests, is not inconsistent with theory. It should also be noted that no additional risk of Type I error is incurred if the prior F test is omitted. The F test can, however, be useful as a labor-saving device because, if the F test is not significant, no pairwise comparison (or other contrast) will be found significant using S as a critical value.

In the present example MSB $= 536.67$, the observed value of F is 5.54, and, for $\alpha_E = .05$, $F_{k-1,N-k:1-\alpha_E} = F_{3,36:.95} = 2.87$.[2] Therefore, the null hypothesis of no group differences is rejected. Comparisons of the form shown in Equation 4 can be performed, with $S_{k-1,N-k:1-\alpha_E} = \sqrt{3(2.87)} = 2.93$ as a critical value. The only statistically significant pairwise comparisons are those between the P and G groups and between the C and G groups. We would therefore conclude that, although pharmacologic therapy or a combination of pharmacologic and individual therapy differ from group psychotherapy in terms of their impact on the functioning of psychotic patients, no other distinctions can be made among the various modes of therapy.

Examination of the means for the G and C groups indicates that there is a 16-point difference in favor of the combined therapy group. Instead of merely concluding that these groups differ, we may wish to make an inference about the size of the difference between the G and C group means in the population. We can do this by constructing $100(1 - \alpha_E)\%$ simultaneous confidence intervals of the following form:

$$(\bar{X}_i - \bar{X}_{i'}) - S_{k-1,N-k:1-\alpha_E} \sqrt{\text{MSW}\left(\frac{2}{n}\right)} < (\mu_i - \mu_{i'})$$

$$< (\bar{X}_i - \bar{X}_{i'}) + S_{k-1,N-k:1-\alpha_E} \sqrt{\text{MSW}\left(\frac{2}{n}\right)}.$$

$$(7)$$

Substituting in the values from the example, we can write the 95% confidence interval for $\mu_G - \mu_C$ as follows:

$$(25 - 41) - 2.93 \sqrt{96.83\left(\frac{2}{10}\right)} < (\mu_G - \mu_C) < (25 - 41) + 2.93 \sqrt{96.83\left(\frac{2}{10}\right)}$$

$$-28.89 < (\mu_G - \mu_C) < -3.11.$$

Thus, we can state with 95% confidence, that in the population, the number of points by which the mean for the combined therapy group exceeds the mean for

---

[2]All critical values for 36 degrees of freedom were obtained by linear interpolation between values for 30 and 40 degrees of freedom.

the group therapy group is between about 3 and 29. The reason that the Scheffé intervals are called *simultaneous* confidence intervals is related to the type of error control that characterizes the Scheffé procedure. As stated earlier, the probability of at least one Type I error is controlled at α_E. This implies that, before the experiment is conducted, the probability of no Type I errors is $1 - \alpha_E$. Therefore, after performing the experiment, we can state with $100(1 - \alpha_E)\%$ confidence that *all* statements of the form shown in Equation 7 are true. In fact, the 95% confidence statement applies to all contrasts, not merely pairwise comparisons. In interpreting the results of a study, confidence intervals are usually more valuable than hypothesis tests alone. They can help the researcher to determine whether results that are statistically significant have any practical importance. For instance, in the present example, the researcher must take into consideration that the difference between the G and C groups may be as small as about three points, a quantity that may be insignificant from a clinical standpoint.

Tukey's Studentized Range Test and the Tukey–Kramer Modification. Tukey's Studentized range test, also called the Honestly Significant Difference (HSD) test or Wholly Significant Difference (WSD) test,[3] is usually described as follows: Find the largest and smallest sample means, compute

$$T = \frac{\bar{X}_{max} - \bar{X}_{min}}{\sqrt{\dfrac{MSW}{n}}} \tag{8}$$

and compare T to a critical value, denoted as $q_{k,N-k:1-\alpha_E}$ based on the distribution of the Studentized range. If this value is statistically significant (i.e., $|T| > q$), perform all other pairwise comparisons in the same fashion. The test statistic in Equation 8 differs from that shown in Equation 4 by a factor of $\sqrt{2}$ in the denominator. Therefore, comparing T to $q_{k,N-k:1-\alpha_E}$ is the same as comparing the largest value of $t_{ii'}$ to $q_{k,N-k:1-\alpha_E}/\sqrt{2}$. In order to find the appropriate critical value for the example, we must enter a table of the percentiles of the Studentized range (e.g., see Kirk, 1982; Miller, 1981) and find the critical value corresponding to the number of means in the overall experiment (k), the error degrees of freedom ($N - k$), and the desired level of α_E. For four means, 36 degrees of freedom, and $\alpha_E = .05$, the critical value of $q_{k,N-k:1-\alpha_E}$ is found by linear interpolation to be approximately 3.81. Therefore, if we want to use test statistics of the form shown in Equation 4, our critical value is $3.81/\sqrt{2} = 2.70$. The largest value of $t_{ii'}$, shown in Equation 5, exceeds the critical value; thus we conclude, as before, that combined and group therapy produce different results. Proceeding to the remaining five comparisons, we find that, as in the Scheffé

---

[3]"WSD" is sometimes used to refer to a different procedure developed by Tukey in which the critical values are obtained by averaging the critical values from the HSD and Newman–Keuls methods.

procedure, the only other statistically significant comparison is that between the P and G groups.

Like the Scheffé MCP (see Scheffé, 1953), the Tukey procedure controls the experimentwise error rate at a nominal value of α_E for the set of all contrasts (Hochberg & Tamhane, 1987), which, of course, includes all pairwise comparisons. (Although complex contrasts can be performed via the Tukey approach, however, this is rarely done because the Bonferroni and Scheffé methods are usually more powerful for this kind of test; Miller, 1981. A single procedure should be selected for all comparisons of interest, so a researcher who wanted to test a substantial number of complex contrasts would be wise to select the Scheffé method.)

For the Tukey MCP, the "prior" test shown in Equation 8 is simply an evaluation of the largest pairwise difference. There is no theoretical reason that this test need be performed before the other pairwise comparisons. It can save computational labor, however, because, if this comparison is not significant, no other pairwise comparisons will be found significant. For the significant comparisons, simultaneous confidence intervals of the form shown in Equation 7 can be constructed, with $q_{k,N-k:1-\alpha_E}/\sqrt{2}$ replacing $S_{k-1,N-k:1-\alpha_E}$.

Although the HSD method per se is applicable in the case of equal sample sizes only, the Tukey–Kramer modification for unequal sample sizes has been shown to have an experimentwise Type I error rate that does not exceed the nominal α (Hayter, 1984; see Hochberg & Tamhane, 1987, pp. 91–93). Applying the Tukey–Kramer method is equivalent to comparing t statistics of the form shown in Equation 3 to $q_{k,N-k:1-\alpha_E}/\sqrt{2}$. Note that the substitution of the harmonic mean of the sample sizes of all k groups for the n in the denominator of T in Equation 8, as recommended by Winer (1962), leads to a test with poor Type I error control (Hochberg & Tamhane, 1987).

Dunn–Bonferroni Method.   Dunn (1961) suggested the application of the Bonferroni inequality to multiple comparisons of means. To apply this method in its simplest form, we need only decide at what level we wish to control α_E and then set the nominal α_C for each pairwise comparison equal to $\alpha_E/[k(k-1)/2]$. (Fisher, 1935, also suggested this approach.) If, in our example, we do not want the experimentwise error rate to exceed .05, we set the nominal α_C equal to .05/6 = .0083. The easiest way to achieve this is to refer to a table of the Bonferroni t statistic (see Kirk, 1982; Miller, 1981). For $\alpha_E = .05$, $C = k(k-1)/2 = 6$ comparisons, and $N - k = 36$ degrees of freedom, we find by linear interpolation that the critical value for a two-sided test is $t^B_{C,N-k:1-\alpha_E} = t^B_{6,36:95} = 2.80$. Therefore, as was the case with the Scheffé and Tukey procedures, only the comparisons of the G and C groups and of the P and G groups are statistically significant. For significant comparisons, simultaneous $100(1 - \alpha_E)\%$ confidence intervals of the form shown in Equation 7 can be constructed, with $t^B_{C,N-k:1-\alpha_E}$ substituted for $S_{k-1,N-k:1-\alpha_E}$. In the case of the Bonferroni approach, each interval could also be interpreted as an individual (nonsimultaneous) $100(1 - \alpha_C)\%$ confidence interval for the mean difference in question.

The Bonferroni approach is extremely flexible. It can be applied to cases in which the researcher wishes to use an unequal allocation of error rates (i.e., a different value of α_C for each contrast) or to perform one-sided tests. For these more complicated applications, the best table of critical values is that of Dayton and Schafer (1973). The Bonferroni approach is not limited to pairwise comparisons, but can be applied to any contrasts of interest. Because this MCP controls α_E at a nominal value, there is no reason to precede Bonferroni t tests with an F test.

Fisher's Protected t *tests.*   The protected t test procedure, also called the Least Significant Difference (LSD) test, is unlike the procedures described previously in that it is a sequential or stagewise procedure. First, an F test is performed at the desired α_E level, say, .05. If it is found to be significant, all pairwise t tests are performed, each with $\alpha_C = \alpha_E = .05$. The determination of whether the t tests are to be conducted depends on the results of the prior F test. It is not permissible to omit the F test here, as is allowed in the Scheffé approach. (Note that the term *Least Significant Difference Test* is sometimes applied to multiple t tests performed without a prior F test as well.)

In the present example, the F test was found to be significant. Therefore, in accordance with the protected t approach, all six pairwise t tests are to be computed and compared to $t_{N-k:1-\alpha_E/2} = t_{36:.975} = 2.03$. We find that the P $-$ G, G $-$ I, and G $-$ C comparisons are statistically significant.

The protected t test procedure tends to lead to a larger number of statistically significant comparisons than many of its competitors; thus it has sometimes been recommended as a powerful MCP (e.g., Carmer & Swanson, 1973; Cohen & Cohen, 1975). In fact, its apparent power is, at least in part, a result of poor Type I error control: Although this MCP provides better Type I error control than multiple t tests without a prior F, use of the protected t procedure can still lead to excessive Type I error rates. Contrary to what is often believed, the policy of performing pairwise t tests only when the F test is significant does not, in general, ensure that the experimentwise error rate will be controlled at α_E, the Type I error rate for the F test. When there are more than $k = 3$ groups, the error rate will be controlled at α_E in the complete null case; that is, when all k means are identical in the population.

However, the true situation may be a partial null case: Some pairs of population means may differ, whereas others do not. Suppose, for instance, that we were conducting an experiment with $k = 5$ groups and the values of the five population means were as follows: 10, 3, 3, 3, 3. If we found the F test significant, this would not be a Type I error. We would then perform $k(k - 1)/2 = 10$ pairwise t tests, each at $\alpha_C = .05$. In doing so, we would have the opportunity to make Type I errors by falsely concluding that the identical means were different. In fact, the number of Type I errors could be as large as $(k - 1)(k - 2)/2 = 6$, the number of distinct pairwise comparisons among the $k - 1 = 4$ means with population values of 3. The occurrence of these second-stage Type I errors leads to an inflated experimentwise error rate for this procedure (see Ryan, 1959, 1980; Zwick & Marascuilo, 1984).[4] It should be mentioned, however, that despite the liberalized error control in the second stage, a significant F does not imply the existence of a significant *pairwise* comparison (see Games, 1971, p. 558).

Hayter (1986) derived an exact expression for the maximum experimentwise error rate that can be attained for Fisher's protected t procedure in the equal-n case. (The same quantity serves as an upper bound for the unequal-n case.) With a nominal α_E of .05 and infinite degrees of freedom, the maximum experiment-wise error rate is found to be .1222 for $k = 4$, .5715 for $k = 10$, and .9044 for $k = 20$. Some empirical evidence on the experimentwise error rates of the pro-tected t test procedure in partial null cases is provided by Carmer and Swanson (1973). Computer simulation techniques were used to estimate the experiment-wise error rates of the method in 14 partial null configurations said to be "some-what representative of situations found in actual experiments in the agricultural sciences" (p. 69). The number of means was 5, 10, or 20. With the nominal α_E set at .05, the $\hat{\alpha}_E$ values ranged from .023 to .455. Five of the 14 error rates were greater than .15. Thus, it can be demonstrated both theoretically and empirically that (for $k > 3$) the protected t method, unlike the Scheffé and Tukey procedures, is not assured to control the error rate in partial null cases.

This MCP is a sequential procedure, involving different levels of error control at each stage; consequently it is impossible to derive confidence intervals corre-sponding to the protected t procedure. The unavailability of confidence intervals is a property of all MCPs in which the performance of certain comparisons is contingent on the significance of other comparisons or of an omnibus test, such as the F test.

Newman–Keuls Test.   Another commonly used sequential procedure is the Newman–Keuls test. Like the Tukey MCP, this method involves rank-ordering the means and performing the test shown in Equation 8 (or the equivalent test based on Equation 4) to compare the largest and smallest means. If this initial range test is significant, further comparisons are made using reduced critical values: The closer two means are to each other in the ranking, the less stringent the criterion for significance. For testing the range of p means, where $p \leq k$, the critical value is $q_{p,N-k:1-\alpha_E}/\sqrt{2}$, assuming here that test statistics are of the form

---

[4]For $k = 3$, the protected t and Newman–Keuls MCPs are assured to control α_E even in partial null cases (see Hayter, 1986; Hochberg & Tamhane, 1987; Shaffer, 1979, 1986). Also see Hochberg and Tamhane (1987, p. 4 and elsewhere) for a detailed discussion of the power of the protected t method.

shown in Equation 4. That is, in determining the critical values for all tests that follow the first one, we simply ignore the fact that the experiment has k groups and use the same critical value we would use if we were performing Tukey's test with p groups.

For example, with four groups of 10 subjects as in the present study, the first step in performing the Newman–Keuls test is to rank-order the means from smallest to largest $(\bar{X}_1, \bar{X}_2, \bar{X}_3, \bar{X}_4)$. If we set the nominal α_E equal to .05, $\bar{X}_1$ is compared to $\bar{X}_4$ using a critical value of $q_{k,N-k:1-\alpha_E}/\sqrt{2} = q_{4,36:95}/\sqrt{2} = 3.81/\sqrt{2} = 2.70$. If this test is significant, the tests of $\bar{X}_2$ versus $\bar{X}_4$ and $\bar{X}_1$ versus $\bar{X}_3$ (ranges of $p = 3$ means) are performed using a critical value of $q_{p,N-k:1-\alpha_E}/\sqrt{2} = q_{3,36:95}/\sqrt{2} = 3.46/\sqrt{2} = 2.45$. Finally if all these tests prove to be significant, we test $\bar{X}_1$ versus $\bar{X}_2$, $\bar{X}_2$ versus $\bar{X}_3$, and $\bar{X}_3$ versus $\bar{X}_4$ with a critical value of $q_{2,36:95}/\sqrt{2} = 2.87/\sqrt{2} = 2.03$. If at any point, a range of p means is found to be nonsignificant, no comparisons of means within that range are performed. Thus, no range included in a nonsignificant range can be declared significant. In the case of unequal sample sizes, the Newman–Keuls MCP can be modified in the same manner as Tukey's test.

In the present example, the four means, from lowest to highest, are $\bar{X}_G = 25$, $\bar{X}_I = 36$, $\bar{X}_P = 40$, and $\bar{X}_C = 41$. The test of the range of all $k = 4$ means, shown in Equation 8, was statistically significant. We can therefore proceed to test the two ranges of $p = 3$ means with a critical value of 2.45, as already described. The P − G comparison is found to be significant, whereas the I − C comparison is not. The G − I comparison is then tested with a critical value of 2.03 and is found to be statistically significant. (The P − I and P − C comparisons are not tested because they fall within a nonsignificant range.)

As is the case with protected t tests, the Newman–Keuls test is often mistakenly believed to be a powerful procedure because it tends to produce a larger number of statistically significant differences than some of its competitors. However, because its error control becomes less stringent at each stage, the Newman–Keuls test, like the protected t procedure, does not maintain the experimentwise error rate at the nominal α_E for all possible configurations of true mean values (unless $k \leq 3$; see footnote 4). Some empirical evidence of its lack of error control in partial null cases is provided by Ramsey (1981), who found $\hat{\alpha}_E$ to range from about .13 to .15 for $k = 6$ and a nominal α_E of .05. Another popular stagewise MCP that is based on the Studentized range is Duncan's (1955) multiple range test. This procedure provides even less stringent error control than the Newman–Keuls test. For the same reason cited in connection with the protected t procedure, confidence intervals cannot be derived for the Newman–Keuls or Duncan tests.

Relation of MCPs to the ANOVA F test. It is important at this point to summarize the relation between pairwise MCPs and the ANOVA F test: If a researcher is interested only in pairwise comparisons between means, there is no need to perform an F test. In fact, an F test and an MCP may produce inconsistent results: The F test may be significant when there are no significant pairwise comparisons and, except in the case of the Scheffé MCP, a pairwise comparison may be significant when the F is not significant. It is often believed that a prior F test is necessary to achieve adequate Type I error control. However, the Tukey and Bonferroni MCPs, which have been recommended here as the most desirable procedures, provide experimentwise error control without a prior test. Requiring a significant F prior to the performance of these tests will cause an unnecessary reduction of their Type I error rates and a corresponding loss in power. In the case of the Scheffé MCP, a prior F serves only as a labor-saving device, but does not affect the comparisons found significant. The protected t procedure does rely on a prior F to maintain the experimentwise error control at the nominal level in the complete null case. Similarly, a Studentized range test of the largest versus the smallest means must precede all other tests in the Newman–Keuls MCP. However, as stated earlier, these two sequential procedures should be avoided because, for $k > 3$, they provide inadequate error control in partial null cases *despite* the use of prior overall tests.

In practice, most MCPs are now conducted using statistical software packages that perform MCPs only in conjunction with an ANOVA F test. However, the results of the F test need not be used as a criterion for consideration of MCP results; rather, the researcher can proceed directly to the MCP results, regardless of whether the F is significant.

Evaluation of the Five MCPs.   Five MCPs have been described for the case of k independent samples: (a) Scheffé's procedure, (b) Tukey's Studentized range test and the Tukey–Kramer modification, (c) the Dunn–Bonferroni approach, (d) Fisher's protected t tests, and (e) the Newman–Keuls test. A summary of the properties of these methods is given in Table 2.3. How can we choose among these procedures? Ideally, we would like to select a method that provides a powerful test while maintaining adequate Type I error control, requires few statistical assumptions, and is easy to apply. All five procedures can be performed by hand, although the Newman–Keuls becomes unwieldy for large k, and all can be conducted using software packages such as SPSS^x (SPSS, Inc., 1986), SAS (SAS Inc., 1988), and BMDP (Dixon, Brown, Engelman, Hill, & Jennrich, 1988). They all require the assumption that the observations are independent random samples from normal populations with equal variances.

One way in which the five MCPs can be distinguished is in terms of the number of statistically significant comparisons. Two of the MCPs—the protected t procedure and the Newman–Keuls—yielded three significant comparisons for the psychotherapy data, whereas the remaining MCPs found only two comparisons to be significant. However, this evidence alone is not sufficient to draw conclusions about the relative power of the methods. The Type I error rates of the MCPs must also be considered. The protected t tests and Newman–Keuls test can

TABLE 2.3
Properties of Pairwise Multiple Comparison Procedures for Independent Samples in the Normal Equal-Variance Case

	Scheffé	Tukey HSD	Dunn–Bonferroni	Fisher's protected t-tests	Newman–Keuls
Allows control of experimentwise Type I error rate at preassigned level	Yes	Yes	Yes	Error rate is not controlled at nominal α_E for all possible configurations of means	
Allows computation of confidence intervals	Yes	Yes	Yes	No	No
Allows efficient one-sided tests and unequal allocation of error rates	No	No	Yes	No	No
Can provide tests of complex contrasts	Yes	Yes	Yes	Yes, but Type I error control is inadequate	No
Power ranking for pairwise comparisons*	3	1	2	Not ranked because of inadequate Type I error control	
General critical value for t statistics of Equation 4	$\sqrt{(k-1)F_{k-1,N-k:1-\alpha_E}}$	$q_{k,N-k:1-\alpha_E}/\sqrt{2}$	$t^B_{C,N-k:1-\alpha_E}$	$t_{N-k:1-\alpha_E/2}$, t tests performed only if $F > F_{k-1,N-k:1-\alpha_E}$	$q_{p,N-k:1-\alpha_E}/\sqrt{2}, p \leq k$ No comparisons are performed within ranges declared nonsignificant
Type of table required	F	Studentized range	Bonferroni t	F, t	Studentized range
Critical value for example of Table 2.2 ($N = 40$, $k = 4$, $C = k(k-1)/2 = 6$, $\alpha_E = .05$)	2.93	2.70	2.80	2.03	2.70 for $p = 4$, 2.45 for $p = 3$, 2.03 for $p = 2$.

*This ranking holds in almost all cases. It is assumed that all $k(k-1)/2$ pairwise comparisons are of interest.

be ruled out as acceptable procedures because (for $k > 3$) they do not control the experimentwise Type I error rate at the nominal α_E for all possible configurations of true mean values. It should be stressed that there is no reason (other than tradition) that the Type I error rate need be controlled at .05. However, it is important to choose a procedure that allows the researcher to control the error rate at some prespecified level. The protected t test and Newman–Keuls procedures do not satisfy this criterion. In addition, the conditional nature of these MCPs makes the derivation of confidence intervals impossible.

The remaining three MCPs provide adequate Type I error control for pairwise contrasts. The test statistics for these MCPs are identical; thus we can compare their power for $k = 4$ groups, $N - k = 36$ degrees of freedom, and $\alpha_E = .05$ by comparing their critical values for the example. The Scheffé, Bonferroni, and Tukey critical values for test statistics of the form of Equation 3 or 4 were 2.93, 2.80, and 2.70, respectively, indicating that the Tukey method is the most powerful. For performing the set of all pairwise comparisons, the superiority in power of the Tukey (and Tukey–Kramer) methods to the Bonferroni and Scheffé methods holds in general (Miller, 1985; Stoline, 1981); the superiority of the Bonferroni to the Scheffé methods nearly always holds, with some exceptions occurring at small values of $N - k$. (For a fixed value of $N - k$, the discrepancies between the critical values increase with k. For instance, with $N - k = 36$ degrees of freedom and $k = 6$, the critical values for the Scheffé, Bonferroni, and Tukey methods are 3.52, 3.15, and 3.01, respectively; for $k = 10$, the values are 4.40, 3.55, and 3.37. For fixed values of k, the disparities between the critical values decrease slightly as the error degrees of freedom increase.) These three MCPs can also be applied to complex contrasts. In most practical, situations, the Bonferroni method will have the highest power for tests of this kind; followed in order by the Scheffé and Tukey methods (Miller, 1981). (The LSD test could be extended to apply to complex contrasts, but this would compound its lack of Type I error control. Extension of the Newman–Keuls test to complex contrasts would not be straightforward.)

The Tukey or Tukey–Kramer approach is therefore recommended as the best method, in general, for performing pairwise comparisons in the normal equal-variance case. There are, however, special circumstances in which the Bonferroni MCP may be preferred. If only a subset of all pairwise comparisons is to be performed, the Bonferroni approach may be more powerful than the Tukey method. For example, if only three of the six pairwise comparisons in the psychotherapy study had been of interest, the Bonferroni critical value would have been $t^B_{C,N-k:1-\alpha_E} = t^B_{3,36:95} = 2.52$, which is smaller than the Tukey critical value of 2.70. Furthermore, the Bonferroni approach, unlike the Tukey method, controls the Type I error rate in a comparisonwise fashion, which may be desirable if conclusions are to be based in the truth of individual statements. Also, the method can provide efficient tests of one-sided hypotheses and can accommodate unequal allocation of error rates, which may be useful in certain applications.

As a postscript to this evaluation of MCPs, it must be noted that there do exist stepwise MCPs that control the Type I error rate at a prespecified α_E and are more powerful than the Tukey and Bonferroni methods (see Hochberg & Tamhane, 1987; Shaffer, 1986). However, application of these methods may require more effort than most researchers are willing to invest. A more important drawback is that stepwise methods do not allow the construction of confidence intervals, which are extremely useful for the interpretation of results. For these reasons, single-step procedures are recommended here.

MCPs for Use Under Violation of the Equal-Variance and Normality Assumptions

The five MCPs described in the preceding sections are based on the assumptions of normality and equality of variances. If these assumptions are violated, neither the MCPs described nor the ANOVA F test are strictly valid. Alternative procedures that can be substituted in these cases are discussed in this section. In determining whether these alternative methods are required, it is important to consider that slight deviations from normality have been found to have little effect on the power and Type I error rates of normal theory ANOVA-based procedures, except when sample sizes are very small. On the other hand, relatively small departures from variance equality can have substantial effects, particularly when sample sizes are unequal.

MCPs for the Normal Unequal-Variance Case.   A number of MCPs have been proposed for the normal unequal-variance case (see Dunnett, 1980; Games, Keselman, & Rogan, 1981; Tamhane, 1979). Many of these are based in Welch's (1938) modification of the t test, which requires that a test statistic of the form

$$t_{ii'}^* = \frac{\bar{X}_i - \bar{X}_{i'}}{\sqrt{\dfrac{s_i^2}{n_i} + \dfrac{s_{i'}^2}{n_{i'}}}} \tag{9}$$

be compared to the desired percentile of the t distribution with $v_{ii'}$ degrees of freedom, where

$$v_{ii'} = \frac{(s_i^2/n_i + s_{i'}^2/n_{i'})^2}{s_i^4/[n_i^2(n_i - 1)] + s_{i'}^4/[n_{i'}^2(n_{i'} - 1)]}. \tag{10}$$

Noninteger values of $v_{ii'}$ are rounded to the nearest integer. A simple way to apply this procedure to the case of multiple comparisons is to perform all $k(k - 1)/2$ tests of this kind, controlling α_E via the Bonferroni inequality (Ury & Wiggins, 1971). The procedure is somewhat cumbersome to perform by hand because the degrees of freedom, $v_{ii'}$, must be recomputed, and a new critical value, $t_{C,v_{ii'}:1-\alpha_E}^B$, obtained for each comparison. In practice, however, the significance probabilities (*p* values) for Welch t tests can be obtained from packaged software, such as the SPSS^x T-TEST program (SPSS, Inc., 1986), the SAS

TTEST program (SAS Institute, Inc., 1988), or BMDP7D (Dixon et al., 1988). The Bonferroni inequality can then be applied by declaring significant those comparisons for which the p value is less than $\alpha_E/[k(k-1)/2]$.
For illustration, the procedure is applied to the data of Table 2.2. For the G − C comparison,

$$t^*_{GC} = \frac{25 - 41}{\sqrt{\dfrac{95.33}{10} + \dfrac{94.22}{10}}} = -3.68$$

$$\text{and } \nu_{GC} \quad \frac{(95.33^2/10 + 94.22^2/10)^2}{95.33^4/[10^2(9)] + 94.22^4/[10^2(9)]} = 17.97.$$

The appropriate critical value is $t^B_{C,\nu_{ii'}:1-\alpha_E} = t^B_{6,18:95} = 2.97$; therefore, the contrast is again found significant. The t^* values for the P − G, P − I, P − C, G − I, and I − C comparisons are 3.40, .90, −.23, −2.50, and −1.14, respectively. The value of $\nu_{ii'}$ is, in each case, 18 when rounded to the nearest integer, leading, once again, to a critical value of 2.97. Therefore, only the G − C and P − G comparisons are statistically significant. An alternative to the Bonferroni approach is the Tukey-type MCP developed by Games and Howell (1976). However, the Type I error rates for this MCP sometimes exceed their nominal levels to a small degree (Dunnett, 1980; Tamhane, 1979). A Scheffé-type MCP has been developed for the unequal-variance case as well (Brown & Forsythe, 1974), but its power is low for pairwise comparisons. (Also, Rubin, 1983, described some problems associated with the approximation proposed by

TABLE 2.4
Ranked Data for Psychiatric Treatment Study[a]

	Pharmacologic Therapy (P)	Group Psychotherapy (G)	Individual Psychotherapy (I)	Combination of P and I (C)
	7	1	5.5	9
	11.5	2	8	10
	17	3	14	18.5
	20.5	4	16	22.5
	24.5	5.5	20.5	26
	28	11.5	22.5	31.5
	31.5	14	24.5	33
	35	14	28	34
	36	18.5	30	37
	38.5	28	38.5	40
R_i	249.5	101.5	207.5	261.5
n_i	10	10	10	10

[a]$Z_{PG} = 2.83$, $Z_{PI} = .80$, $Z_{PC} = -.23$, $Z_{GI} = -2.03$, $Z_{GC} = -3.06$, and $Z_{IC} = -1.03$.

Brown & Forsythe.) Although the methods mentioned here do not require a prior test, it should be noted that overall hypothesis tests analogous to F test exist for the one-way ANOVA model in the unequal-variance case (e.g., Welch, 1951; see Rubin, 1983).

MCPs for the Nonnormal Case.   Nonparametric MCPs for the nonnormal case are described in this section. All the procedures in this section (Equations 11–14) are based on large-sample approximations. As a rule of thumb, it is suggested that they be used with caution for $N < 20$. If there is reason to believe that normality does not hold, one option is to use Scheffé-type MCPs based on the Kruskal–Wallis (1952) rank analogue to parametric ANOVA. This approach, which was presented by Nemenyi (1963) and is described in Marascuilo and McSweeney (1977) and Miller (1981), is illustrated for the data of Table 2.2. To perform a Kruskal–Wallis test, the observations must first be ranked from 1 to N, ignoring group membership. Midranks are assigned to ties. The ranked observations and the sums of the ranks for each group (R_i) are shown in Table 2.4. The Kruskal–Wallis statistic is computed as follows:

$$H = \frac{12}{N(N+1)} \sum_{i=1}^{k} \frac{1}{n_i} R_i^2 - 3(N+1)$$

$$= \frac{12}{40(41)} [249.5^2/10 + 101.5^2/10 + 207.5^2/10 + 261.5^2/10] - 3(41)$$

$$= 11.63. \tag{11}$$

The value of H exceeds $\chi^2_{k-1:1-\alpha_E} = \chi^2_{3;.95} = 7.81$, so the null hypothesis of no group differences is rejected at $\alpha_E = .05$. In order to compare groups i and i', the following test statistic is computed:

$$Z_{ii'} = \frac{\bar{R}_i - \bar{R}_{i'}}{\sqrt{\frac{N(N+1)}{12} \left(\frac{1}{n_i} + \frac{1}{n_{i'}} \right)}}, \tag{12}$$

where $\bar{R}_i$ and $\bar{R}_{i'}$ are the mean ranks for groups i and i', respectively. The critical value is

$$S' = \sqrt{\chi^2_{k-1:1-\alpha_E}}. \tag{13}$$

This is analogous to the use of S (Equation 6) as a critical value for parametric ANOVA. A comparison is statistically significant if $Z > S'$ or $Z < -S'$. The $Z_{ii'}$ statistic for comparing the G and C groups is

$$Z_{GC} = \frac{101.5 - 261.5}{\sqrt{\frac{40(41)}{12} \left(\frac{2}{10} \right)}} = -3.06,$$

which exceeds $S' = \sqrt{7.81} = 2.79$. Therefore, as in the previous analyses, it is concluded that the combined therapy and group therapy groups differ in ability to function. The $Z_{ii'}$ values for the P − G, P − I, P − C, G − I, and I − C comparisons are 2.83, .80, −.23, −2.03, and −1.03, respectively. Again, only the G − C and P − G comparisons are statistically significant. For a more precise test, a correction for ties should be used in the computation of both the H statistic and the Z statistics (see Marascuilo & McSweeney, 1977, pp. 302, 318). Use of the correction increases the likelihood of rejecting the null hypothesis. In the present example, the use of the correction would not have changed the conclusions.

As was true of the Scheffé approach in the parametric case, it is possible to find that the Kruskal–Wallis test is significant, but that no pairwise comparisons are significant. Another similarity to the parametric case is that no additional risk of Type I error is incurred if the Kruskal–Wallis test itself is omitted; the researcher can proceed directly to the performance of pairwise MCPs using S' as a critical value. However, if only pairwise comparisons are of interest, a more powerful test can be achieved by employing the Bonferroni critical value, $t^B_{C,\infty:1-\alpha_E}$, where ∞ indicates that the critical value for infinite degrees of freedom should be used (Dunn, 1964). The Bonferroni critical value for the example is $t^B_{6,\infty:95} = 2.64$, as compared to $S' = 2.79$. A still more powerful approach is the joint-ranking analog to Tukey's test, for which the critical value is $q_{k,\infty:1-\alpha_E}/\sqrt{2}$ $= q_{4\infty:95}/\sqrt{2} = 3.63 = 2.57$. This method was proposed for the equal-n case by Nemenyi (1963; also see Levy, 1979; Miller, 1981) but provides a good approximation in the case of unequal sample sizes (Miller, 1985; Zwick & Marascuilo, 1984).

The three MCPs described make use of ranks based on all k groups (joint ranking). This may be considered undesirable because it leads to a situation in which the hypothesis test for each pair of populations is conditional on the location of the other $k − 2$ populations in the study. (In addition, Oude Voshaar, 1980, showed that, because of this property, the experimentwise Type I error rate for the rank analog to Tukey's test can exceed the nominal α_E in partial null cases.) A related disadvantage of MCPs based on joint ranking is that it is nearly impossible to obtain confidence intervals in the original metric of the observations. The complexity of the calculations is a result of the dependence of each pairwise comparison on all observations in the study (Miller, 1981, pp. 168–169). Because of these properties, the researcher may prefer an MCP in which a separate ranking is performed for each comparison (pairwise ranking). For example, all pairwise independent-sample Wilcoxon tests could be performed, controlling α_E via the Bonferroni inequality (see Dunn, 1964). A Z statistic of the form shown in Equation 12 is then compared to $t^B_{C,\infty:1-\alpha_E}$. (Although the Z statistic in Equation 12 does not resemble a conventional Wilcoxon test, it is equivalent to the normal approximation to the Wilcoxon test when pairwise ranking is used.) There is only one difference between this MCP and the previously described rank-based Bonferroni approach: In this MCP, the ranks for a given comparison are based only on the groups included in that comparison. A more powerful test is the k-sample Steel–Dwass procedure, which is an analog to Tukey's test based on pairwise ranking (see Hochberg & Tamhane, 1987; Miller, 1981). The use of MCPs based on pairwise, rather than joint ranking, allows the construction of confidence intervals (Miller, 1981, pp. 145–146). It should be noted that joint and pairwise ranking procedures will not necessarily lead to the same conclusion (see Dunn, 1964, Hollander & Wolfe, 1973, and Hochberg & Tamhane, 1987 for further discussion of this issue).

Rank procedures are useful when there is reason to believe that normality does not hold. If normality is violated, rank tests can be substantially more powerful than parametric tests. (Under some circumstances, related nonparametric methods called *normal score procedures* are more powerful than rank tests; see Marascuilo and McSweeney, 1977.) Unfortunately, rank methods, like their parametric counterparts, do not provide adequate Type I error control if the equal-variance assumption is not met (e.g., see Van der Vaart, 1961). They are therefore not well-suited to the situation in which both the normality and equal-variance assumptions are violated. A procedure that may perform adequately in this situation is the MCP based on the all pairwise median tests. The first step is to find the median for the combined data for each pair of groups. Then the observations in each pair of groups are categorized according to whether they fall above or below the median for that pair. For example, if the data for the G and C groups in Table 2.2 are combined and ranked, the median is found to be 32.5. Two observations in the G group and eight observations in the C group are found to be above the median. For equal sample sizes, the appropriate test statistic is

$$Z'_{ii'} = \frac{\hat{p}_i - \hat{p}_{i'}}{\sqrt{1/2n}}, \tag{14}$$

where $\hat{p}_i$ and $\hat{p}_{i'}$ represent the proportion of cases in groups i and i' that are above the median. These $Z'_{ii'}$ values are compared to $q_{k,\infty:1-\alpha_E}/\sqrt{2}$. (Critical values based on the Scheffé or Bonferroni approach could be used but would lead to less powerful tests.)

The test statistic for the G − C comparison is

$$Z'_{GC} = \frac{.8 - .2}{\sqrt{1/20}} = 2.68.$$

Z'_{GC} exceeds $q_{k,\infty:95}/\sqrt{2} = q_{4,\infty:95}/\sqrt{2} = 2.57$, so it can be concluded once again that the G and C groups differ. Analogous computations show that the P − G comparison is also significant, but the remaining four comparisons are not. Further discussion of pairwise median test is given by Hochberg and Tamhane (1987). Another median-based MCP that has been proposed (see Miller, 1981) is conducted by obtaining the combined median for all k groups and then calculating what proportion of each group is above it. This procedure is subject to the problems associated with all joint ranking procedures and can also lead to nonsensical conclusions in some circumstances (see Hochberg & Tamhane, p. 269). As an alternative to the traditional nonparametric MCPs for the nonnormal case discussed in this section, it may be possible to transform the data and then apply standard MCPs. Another alternative is the application of robust MCPs, which involve t-like statistics based on estimators other than the sample mean and variance (Dunnett, 1982). Robust methods may be a good choice when both the normality and equal-variance assumptions are thought to be violated.

ONE-FACTOR REPEATED MEASURES DESIGNS

The example of Table 2.2 involved three independent groups, each of which was exposed to a different condition. Another commonly used design involves a single group of subjects examined under k different conditions or on k occasions. An analysis of variance can be performed to test the hypothesis that all k means are equal in the population. If an overall test of this kind is desired, the researcher must choose between two general analysis strategies: the multivariate approach and the univariate mixed-model approach. Useful discussions of the computational details of these analyses and of the issues involved in choosing between the two approaches are given by Lewis (chap. 3 in this vol.) and by Barcikowski and Robey (1984), Finn and Mattson (1978), McCall and Appelbaum (1973), and Vitaliano (1981). Only a brief description of the two methods is given here.

In the multivariate approach, the k original variables (one for each occasion or condition) are transformed to $k - 1$ new variables, each of which may represent a contrast of interest (see Morrison, 1976, pp. 145–146 for details). One possibility is to transform the k observations for each subject $(x_1, x_2, \ldots, x_k)$ to differences between successive observations $(x_1 - x_2, x_2 - x_3, \ldots, x_{k-1} - x_k)$. These $k - 1$ difference scores are then treated as a single multivariate observation and a one-sample Hotelling's (1931) T^2 is applied. In the univariate mixed-model approach, the analysis is treated as a Subjects × Conditions ANOVA. The appropriate F statistic is the mean square for subjects divided by the mean square for the Subjects × Conditions interaction.

Both the multivariate and mixed-model approaches require the assumption that the k observations for each subject are drawn from a multivariate normal distribution (Rouanet & Lépine, 1970) and subjects are independently sampled. A disadvantage of the mixed-model approach is that, in order for the analysis to be valid, the variance-covariance matrix of the repeated measures must satisfy a condition called *sphericity* or *circularity*. This property is equivalent to equality of the variances of difference scores for all possible pairs of the k conditions included in the experiment (Huynh & Feldt, 1970). The multivariate approach does not require this assumption, but will often be less powerful than the mixed-model analysis.

Fortunately, if a researcher is interested only in comparing pairs of conditions, it is not necessary to choose between the two analysis strategies or to be concerned about sphericity. The researcher need only perform all $k(k - 1)/2$ correlated-sample t tests (or any subset of these), using an error term based only on the two groups being compared, and controlling α_E via the Bonferroni equality (Myers, 1979). To illustrate this approach, assume that the data of Table 2.2 represent a series of four measurements (which, for ease of reference, will continue to be denoted as P, G, I, and C) on a single group of $n = 10$ subjects. A correlated-sample t test comparing conditions i and i' can be calculated according to the following formula

$$ t'_{ii'} = \frac{\bar{D}_{ii'}}{\sqrt{\dfrac{s_{\mathrm{D}_{ii'}}^2}{n}}}, \tag{15} $$

where $\bar{D}_{ii'} = \bar{X}_i - \bar{X}_{i'}$ is the mean difference between the two conditions and $s_{\mathrm{D}_{ii'}}^2$ the variance of the difference scores $(x_i - x_{i'})$. The appropriate critical value of $t_{\mathrm{C},n-1:1-\alpha_E}^{\mathrm{B}}$ can be obtained from a table of the Bonferroni t statistic. It can be shown that

$$ s_{\mathrm{D}_{ii'}}^2 = s_i^2 + s_{i'}^2 - 2r_{ii'}s_i s_{i'}, \tag{16} $$

where $r_{ii'}$ is the correlation between the two sets of observations. However, the simplest way to calculate $s_{\mathrm{D}_{ii'}}^2$ is to actually compute the difference scores and then calculate their variance. Table 2.5 shows all three sets of difference scores,

TABLE 2.5
Difference Scores for the Data of Table 2.2
Treated as a Repeated Measures Design with $n = 10$

	P-G	P-I	P-C	G-I	G-C	I-C
	12	3	-3	-9	-15	-6
	16	4	-1	-12	-15	-3
	15	3	-2	-12	-17	-5
	16	4	-1	-12	-17	-5
	17	2	-1	-15	-18	-3
	13	5	-2	-8	-15	-7
	14	6	-1	-8	-15	-7
	17	5	-1	-12	-16	-4
	16	8	-1	-8	-17	-9
	14	0	-1	-14	-15	-1
$\bar{D}_{ii'}$	15	4	-1.40	-11	-16	-5
$s^2_{\mathrm{D}_{ii'}}$	2.89	4.89	.70	6.67	1.15	2.36
$t_{ii'}$	27.90	5.72	-5.29	-13.47	-47.18	-10.29

along with their means and variances. A pairwise comparison of the G and C conditions can be conducted as follows:

$$t'_{GC} = \frac{\bar{D}_{GC}}{\sqrt{\dfrac{s^2_{D_{GC}}}{n}}} = \frac{-16}{\sqrt{\dfrac{1.15}{10}}} = -47.18.$$

For $n - 1 = 9$ degrees of freedom, $C = 6$ comparisons, and $\alpha_E = .05$, the critical value can be found by linear interpolation to be approximately 3.40. Therefore, we would conclude that there is a difference between the G and C conditions. The t statistics for the remaining five pairwise comparisons, given at the bottom of Table 2.5, are also statistically significant. Confidence intervals could be constructed for these mean differences as well. This example demonstrates that the inadvertent application of an MCP intended for independent samples to a repeated-measures design can lead to a substantial reduction in power: The Bonferroni approach led to two significant comparisons in the independent-sample case and six in the repeated measures analysis. Examination of Equation 16 reveals the reason for this: If an independent sample test is mistakenly applied, the square of the denominator of the test statistic will be

$$\text{MSW}\left(\frac{2}{n}\right) = \frac{(n - 1)s^2_i + (n - 1)s^2_{i'}}{2(n - 1)}\left(\frac{2}{n}\right) = \frac{s^2_i + s^2_{i'}}{n}$$

instead of

$$\frac{s^2_{D_{ii'}}}{n} = \frac{s^2_i + s^2_{i'} - 2r_{ii'}s_i s_{i'}}{n}.$$

The term $2r_{ii'}s_i s_{i'}$ will be positive whenever the correlation between the two sets of measurements is positive, which is the case in most applications. Therefore, by using an independent-sample MCP, the researcher is forfeiting the opportunity to subtract a positive term from the error estimate.

An important property of the correlated-sample t tests described earlier is that, unlike the sets of t tests conducted in the independent-sample, equal-variance case, they do not make use of a common error term. It is because there is no pooled error term that the sphericity assumption is not needed for these pairwise comparisons (see Boik, 1981).[5] The Bonferroni t tests require no prior F test; thus the best procedure to follow if only pairwise tests are of interest is to perform the t tests only. It should be noted that, in the multivariate approach to repeated measures ANOVA, pairwise comparisons of condition means performed via the Roy–Bose (1953) method reduce to correlated-sample t tests of

---

[5]Boik (1981) showed that if sphericity does not hold, use of a pooled error term will, in general, lead to unsatisfactory tests of individual contrasts even if one of the available corrections for nonsphericity is applied. Even under minimal departures from sphericity, these "corrected" tests can have poor power properties and Type I error rates that differ substantially from their nominal values.

the form shown in Equation 15. The critical value, however, is larger than that used in the Bonferroni approach, leading to a more conservative test.

Some empirical evidence on the performance of the Bonferroni approach with separate error terms is given by Maxwell (1980). He compared Tukey's Studentized range test (with a pooled error term based on the Subjects × Conditions interaction), two modifications of Tukey's test, both of which make use of separate error terms, the Roy–Bose method associated with the multivariate approach, and the Bonferroni method already described. For conditions in which sphericity held, both Tukey's test and the Bonferroni approach performed well. However, when sphericity was violated, the only procedure that provided adequate power while controlling the Type I error rate at the nominal level was the Bonferroni method.

When normality cannot be assumed, nonparametric procedures can be applied. For instance, multiple sign tests or multiple Wilcoxon signed-rank tests can be conducted, using the normal approximation (see Marasciulo & McSweeney, 1977) and controlling α_E via the Bonferroni inequality. Alternatively, the multiple comparison approach associated with the Friedman (1937) model can be applied (Levy, 1979; Marascuilo & McSweeney, 1977; Miller, 1981).

CONCLUSIONS

In order to select the appropriate pairwise MCP for use in a one-factor ANOVA model, the researcher should have a good understanding of experimentwise and comparisonwise Type I error rates. When testing multiple hypotheses, the experimentwise error rate is usually of primary interest, although there are occasions in which comparisonwise control is useful. These two methods of assessing error rates are related but not interchangeable.

Another important issue is the relationship between Type I error rate and power. The power of competing MCPs cannot be compared meaningfully unless the MCPs have equivalent experimentwise Type I error rates. Therefore, the selection of MCPs solely on the basis of the number of statistically significant results they produce is not well-founded. If a researcher wants to increase power, he should not attempt to do so by allowing the Type I error to exceed the desired level, but by increasing sample size, increasing the homogeneity of the sample, and improving the quality of measurement (see Cohen, 1982). There is, however, no reason that the experimentwise Type I error rate need be set to .05. A larger error rate certainly may be acceptable in some situations. But it is important that the researcher know and report the level at which the error has been controlled.

For the case of independent samples drawn from normal populations with equal variances, the Tukey method and, for unequal sample sizes, the Tukey–

Kramer modification, were recommended as the best procedures in most situations. For certain specialized applications, such as those requiring one-sided tests or unequal allocation of error rates, the Bonferroni method may be preferred. For the normal unequal-variance case, Welch t tests were recommended, with the Bonferroni approach used to control the experimentwise error rate. For the nonnormal case, a number of rank procedures were discussed. The performance of all pairwise Wilcoxon tests, with the experimentwise error rate controlled via the Bonferroni or Steel–Dwass approach, has certain advantages over the procedures based on joint ranking. For the case in which both normality and equality of variances are thought to be violated, the MCP based on all pairwise median tests may be a good choice. For one-factor repeated measures designs, dependent t tests with separate error terms were recommended, with error control achieved through the Bonferroni approach. Nonparametric MCPs for this design include multiple sign tests, multiple Wilcoson signed-rank tests, and MCPs based on the Friedman model. In all MCP applications, the computation of confidence intervals can provide a useful supplement to significance testing. For this reason, as well as simplicity of computation, single-step MCPs, rather than more powerful stepwise methods, were recommended.

This chapter was limited to the discussion of pairwise MCPs in one-factor designs. MCPs for complex contrasts, two-way ANOVA designs, and special situations, such as comparing experimental groups to a control group, are discussed by Hochberg and Tamhane (1987) and Miller (1981). Information about Bayesian, decision-theoretic, and robust MCPs, as well as extensive discussion of stepwise MCPs, is given in Hochberg and Tamhane (1987).

ACKNOWLEDGMENTS

This chapter is a revised version of an article, "Testing Pairwise Contrasts in One-Way Analysis of Variance Designs," that appeared in 1986 in *Psychoneuroendocrinology, 11*, 253–276. It appears here with the permission of Pergamon Press. The initial research was supported in part by a National Research Service Award (No. 5-T32-MH15745) from the National Institute of Mental Health to the University of North Carolina at Chapel Hill. Preparation of the current version was supported in part by Educational Testing Service. Special thanks are due to Juliet Shaffer for her valuable and detailed recommendations for improving this chapter. In addition, I would like to thank C. Clifford Attkisson, Henry Braun, and Peter Vitaliano for their comments on the original article, Charles Lewis and Jo-Ling Liang for comments on the current version, and Kay Tyberg for preparation of the manuscript.

REFERENCES

Barcikowski, R. S., & Robey, R. R. (1984). Decisions in single group repeated measures analysis: Statistical tests and three computer packages. *The American Statistician, 38*, 148–150.

Berhardson, C. S. (1975). Type I error rates when multiple comparison procedures follow a significant *F*-test of ANOVA. *Biometrics, 31*, 229–232.

Boik, R. J. (1981). A priori tests in repeated measures designs: Effects of nonsphericity. *Psychometrika, 46*, 241–255.

Brown, M. B., & Forsythe, A. B. (1974). The ANOVA and multiple comparisons for data with heterogeneous variances. *Biometrics, 30*, 719–724.

Carmer, S. G., & Swanson, M. R. (1973). An evaluation of ten pairwise multiple comparison procedures by Monte Carlo methods. *Journal of the American Statistical Association, 68*, 66–74.

Cohen, J., & Cohen, P. (1975). *Applied multiple regression/correlation analysis for the behavioral sciences.* Hillsdale, NJ: Lawrence Erlbaum Associates.

Cohen, P. (1982). To be or not to be: Control and balancing of Type I and Type II error. *Evaluation and Program Planning, 5*, 247–253.

Dayton, C. M., & Schafer, W. D. (1973). Extended tables of t and chi square for Bonferroni tests with unequal error allocation. *Journal of the American Statistical Association, 68*, 78–83.

Dixon, W. J., Brown, M. B., Engelman, L., Hill, M. A., & Jennrich, R. I. (Eds.). (1988). *BMDP statistical software manual.* Berkeley, CA: University of California Press.

Duncan, D. B. (1955). Multiple range and multiple *F*-tests. *Biometrics, 11*, 1–42.

Dunn, O. J. (1958). Estimation of the means of dependent variables. *Annals of Mathematical Statistics, 29*, 1095–1111.

Dunn, O. J. (1959). Confidence intervals for the means of dependent, normally distributed variables. *Journal of the American Statistical Association, 54*, 613–621.

Dunn, O. J. (1961). Multiple comparisons among means. *Journal of the American Statistical Association, 56*, 52–64.

Dunn, O. J. (1964). Multiple comparisons using rank sums. *Technometrics, 6*, 241–252.

Dunn, O. J. (1974). On multiple tests and confidence intervals. *Communications in Statistics, 3*, 101–103.

Dunnett, C. W. (1980). Pairwise multiple comparisons in the unequal variance case. *Journal of the American Statistical Association, 75*, 796–800.

Dunnett, C. W. (1982). Robust multiple comparisons. *Communications in Statistics: Theory and Methods, 22*, 2611–2629.

Einot, I., & Gabriel, K. R. (1975). A study of the powers of several methods of multiple comparisons. *Journal of the American Statistical Association, 70*, 574–583.

Finn, J. D., & Mattson, I. (1978). *Multivariate analysis in educational research: Applications of the MULTIVARIANCE program.* Chicago: National Educational Resources.

Fisher, R. A. (1935). *The design of experiments.* Edinburgh: Oliver & Boyd.

Friedman, M. (1937). The use of ranks to avoid the assumption of normality implicit in the analysis of variance. *Journal of the American Statistical Association, 32*, 675–701.

Gabriel, K. R. (1978). Comment: Multiple comparison power. *Journal of the American Statistical Association, 73*, 485–487.

Games, P. A. (1971). Multiple comparisons of means. *American Educational Research Journal, 8*, 531–565.

Games, P. A., & Howell, J. F. (1976). Pairwise multiple comparison procedures with unequal *N's* and/or variances: A Monte Carlo study. *Journal of Educational Statistics, 1*, 113–125.

Games, P. A., Keselman, H. J., & Rogan, J. C. (1981). Simultaneous pairwise multiple comparison procedures for means when sample sizes are unequal. *Psychological Bulletin, 90*, 594–598.

Hayter, A. J. (1984). A proof of the conjecture that the Tukey-Kramer multiple comparisons procedure is conservative. *Annals of Statistics, 12*, 61–75.

Hayter, A. J. (1986). The maximum familywise error rate of Fisher's Least Significant Difference test. *Journal of the American Statistical Association, 81*, 1000–1004.

Hochberg, Y., & Tamhane, A. (1987). *Multiple comparison procedures.* New York: Wiley.

Hollander, M., & Wolfe, D. A. (1973). *Nonparametric statistical methods.* New York: Wiley.

Hotelling, H. (1931). The generalization of Student's ratio. *Annals of Mathematical Statistics, 2*, 360–378.

Huynh, H., & Feldt, L. S. (1970). Conditions under which mean square ratios in repeated measurements designs have exact F-distributions. *Journal of the American Statistical Association, 65,* 1582–1589.

Keuls, M. (1952). The use of the 'Studentized range' in connection with an analysis of variance. *Euphytica, 1,* 112–122.

Kirk, R. E. (1982). *Experiment design* (2nd ed.). Monterey, CA: Brooks/Cole.

Kramer, C. Y. (1956). Extension of multiple range tests to group means with unequal numbers of replications. *Biometrics, 12,* 307–310.

Kruskal, W. H., & Wallis, W. A. (1952). Use of ranks in one-criterion variance analysis. *Journal of the American Statistical Association, 47,* 583–621.

Levy, K. J. (1979). Nonparametric large-sample pairwise comparisons. *Psychological Bulletin, 86,* 371–375.

Marascuilo, L. A., & McSweeney, M. (1977). *Nonparametric and distribution free methods for the social sciences.* Monterey, CA: Brooks/Cole.

Maxwell, S. E. (1980). Pairwise multiple comparisons in repeated measures designs. *Journal of Educational Statistics, 5,* 269–287.

McCall, R. B., & Appelbaum, M. I. (1973). Bias in the analysis of repeated measures designs: Some alternative approaches. *Child Development, 44,* 401–415.

Miller, R. G. (1981). *Simultaneous statistical inference* (2nd ed.). New York: Springer-Verlag.

Miller, R. G. (1985). Multiple comparisons. In S. Kotz & N. L. Johnson (Eds.), *Encyclopedia of statistical sciences* (Vol. 5, pp. 679–689). New York: Wiley.

Morrison, D. F. (1976). *Multivariate statistical methods* (2nd ed.). New York: McGraw-Hill.

Myers, J. L. (1979). *Fundamentals of Experimental Design* (3rd ed.). Boston: Allyn & Bacon.

Nemenyi, P. (1963). *Distribution-free multiple comparisons.* Unpublished doctoral dissertation, Princeton University.

Newman, D. (1939). The distribution of range in samples from the normal population, expressed in terms of an independent estimate of standard deviation. *Biometrika, 31,* 20–30.

Oude Voshaar, J. H. (1980). (k − 1) − mean significance levels of nonparametric multiple comparisons procedures. *The Annals of Statistics, 8,* 75–86.

Ramsey, P. H. (1978). Comment: Multiple Comparison power. *Journal of the American Statistical Association, 73,* 487.

Ramsey, P. H. (1981). Power of univariate pairwise multiple comparison procedures. *Psychological Bulletin, 90,* 352–366.

Rouanet, H., & Lepine, D. (1970). Comparison between treatments in repeated-measurement design: ANOVA and multivariate methods. *British Journal of Mathematical and Statistical Psychology, 23,* 147–163.

Rubin, A. S. (1983). The use of weighted contrasts in analysis of models with heterogeneity of variance. *Proceedings of the Business and Economics Section of the American Statistical Association.*

Roy, S. N., & Bose, R. C. (1953). Simultaneous confidence interval estimation. *Annals of Mathematical Statistics, 24,* 513–536.

Ryan, T. A. (1959). Multiple comparisons in psychological research. *Psychological Bulletin, 56,* 26–47.

Ryan, T. A. (1980). Comment on "Protecting the overall rate of Type I errors for pairwise comparisons with an omnibus test statistic." *Psychological Bulletin, 88,* 354–355.

SAS Institute, Inc. (1988). *SAS/STAT user's guide* (release 6.03 ed.). Cary, NC: Author.

Scheffé, H. (1953). A method for judging all contrasts in the analysis of variance. *Biometrika, 40,* 87–104.

Shaffer, J. P. (1979). Comparison of means: An F test followed by a modified multiple range procedure. *Journal of Educational Statistics, 4,* 14–23.

Shaffer, J. P. (1986). Modified sequentially rejective multiple test procedures. *Journal of the American Statistical Association, 81,* 826–831.

Šidák, Z. (1967). Rectangular confidence regions for the means of multivariate normal distributions. *Journal of the American Statistical Association, 62,* 626–633.

SPSS, Inc. (1986). *SPSS^x user's guide* (2nd ed.). Chicago: Author.

Stoline, M. R. (1981). The status of multiple comparisons: Simultaneous estimation of all pairwise comparisons in one-way ANOVA designs. The *American Statistician, 35,* 134–141.

Tamhane, A. C. (1979). A comparison of procedures for multiple comparisons of means with unequal variances. *Journal of the American Statistical Association, 74,* 471–480.

Tukey, J. W. (1953). *The problem of multiple comparisons.* Unpublished manuscript, Princeton University.

Ury, H. K., & Wiggins, A. D. (1971). Large sample and other multiple comparisons among means. *British Journal of Mathematical and Statistical Psychology, 24,* 174–194.

Van der Vaart, H. R. (1961). On the robustness of Wilcoxon's two-sample test. In H. de Jonge (Ed.), *Quantitative methods in pharmacology* (pp. 140–158). Amsterdam: North Holland.

Vitaliano, P. P. (1982). Parametric statistical analysis of repeated measures experiments. *Psychoneuroendocrinology, 7,* 3–13.

Welch, B. L. (1938). The significance of the difference between two means when the population variances are unequal. *Biometrika, 29,* 350–362.

Welch, B. L. (1951). On the comparison of several mean values: An alternative approach. *Biometrika, 38,* 330–336.

Winer, B. J. (1962). *Statistical principles in experimental design.* New York: McGraw-Hill.

Zwick, R., & Marascuilo, L. A. (1984). Selection of pairwise comparison procedures for parametric and nonparametric analysis of variance models. *Psychological Bulletin, 95,* 148–155.

3 Analyzing Means from Repeated Measures Data

Charles Lewis
Educational Testing Service

Suppose you were reading a journal article describing the results of a repeated measures experiment and you cam across statements such as "the main effect of Alternation Rate was marginally significant, $F(5, 115) = 2.06, p < .08$, and the Playing Speed $\times$ Alternation Rate interaction was reliable, $F(5, 115) = 3.48, p < .01. \ldots$ The main effect of Playing Speed [was not] significant $\ldots F(1, 23) = 2.56, ns$" (Samuel, 1991, p. 396).[1] Leaving aside any substantive interpretation of these effects, what would your reaction be to the statistical information that has been given? (For completeness, it should be noted that the 2×6 cell means that are being compared in the analysis are also plotted in an accompanying figure.)

To focus attention on the object of concern, suppose the reported p values were changed as follows: for Alternation Rate, from $<.08$ (actually .075) to .165; for the interaction, from $<.01$ (actually .006) to .075; and for Playing Speed, no change (current value .123). Would your reaction to the results change at all? The author would apparently now identify both main effects as *ns,* and the interaction as marginally significant. The same sort of changes could be made for the p values associated with any standard F test of a main effect or interaction involving a repeated measures factor with three or more levels. But wait a moment! Where did these new p values come from and what do they represent?

Almost 40 years ago, Box (1954) pointed out that correlated observations in the analysis of variance can have an impact on the probability of a Type I error for any F test used to test hypotheses about means. One place where correlated

---

[1]Here 24 subjects provided data (percent correct scores) for a matching task in each of the 12 conditions defined by the combinations of 2 levels of Playing Speed and 6 levels of Alternation Rate.

observations are almost certain to arise is in a repeated measures experiment. A few years later, Geisser and Greenhouse (1958) proposed a conservative test, based on Box's (1954) results, which represents a worst-case scenario as far as Type I error probabilities are concerned. Shortly thereafter, Imhof (1962) gave actual examples in which the true significance levels for repeated measures F tests depart dramatically from the chosen values (and closely approach the Geisser–Greenhouse limits). For instance, .01 becomes .078 and .05 becomes .140 in one situation with five subjects and five conditions. The numbers given in the preceding paragraph are the Geisser–Greenhouse conservative levels of significance for the results in our example. They represent, for this case, the degree to which the reported F tests, based on a standard repeated measures analysis of variance, could fail to control the probability of a Type I error at the desired level.

Before going any further, perhaps a comment should be made about the use of hypothesis testing in reporting the results of an experiment. (See chap. 6, Vol. I on the "good enough principle," chap. 16, Vol. I, on the prejudice against the null hypothesis, and chap. 17, Vol. I, on the significance of "significance" for a detailed treatment of this subject.) Obviously, no one takes seriously the null hypotheses that are typically tested: For example, there are really no main effects of Alternation Rate or Playing Speed and no interaction between the two in the population from which the data were sampled. Some sort of effects are certainly there, and a goal of the researcher should be to use the data from the experiment to correctly describe these effects. With this goal in mind, hypothesis testing might be thought of as a preliminary step.

Only if the observed patterns of sample means can be reliably distinguished from those that might have risen by chance when sampling from a population with no true differences, are they likely to provide useful information about the corresponding patterns of population means. To actually describe the effects themselves, other statistical tools are needed. (Chap. 18, Vol. I, on effect size, chap. 20, Vol. I, on cumulating evidence, chap. 2, this volume, on multiple comparisons, chap. 6, this volume, on set correlation, chaps. 7 and 8, this volume, on Bayesian methods, chap. 12, this volume, on exploratory data analysis, and chap. 13, this volume, on graphics discuss a variety of possibilities.)

Returning to our discussion, the basic point is that carrying out a standard analysis of variance of repeated measures data is not a good way to take the preliminary step represented by hypothesis testing. In particular, standard F tests involving repeated measures factors with more than two levels may identify patterns of means as worthy of further attention, which cannot be reliably distinguished from patterns arising due to sampling fluctuation. In the remainder of the chapter, we first briefly and selectively note the literature on the subject, concentrating on the references of most interest to researchers rather than statisticians, and consider the impact of this literature on practice. Then we discuss and compare alternative methods of analysis proposed. Finally, we look at an illustration of these methods.

THE CURRENT STATE OF AFFAIRS

Much has been written, in sources accessible to researchers, describing the problem with F tests for comparing means in repeated measures research and explaining how to carry out alternative analyses. Most of the standard references on experimental design (including Dayton, 1970; Edwards, 1985; Keppel, 1982; Kirk, 1982; Myers, 1979; Winer, Brown, & Michels, 1991) treat the topic in some detail. Moreover, a number of excellent review articles on the subject have appeared in nontechnical journals (including Hertzog & Rovine, 1985; Lana & Lubin, 1963; McCall & Appelbaum, 1973; O'Brien & Kaiser, 1985; Vasey & Thayer, 1987).

Statistical software packages (including MULTIVARIANCE, BMDP, SAS, and SPSS for mainframe computers and PCs, and SYSTAT for PCs and Macs) allow researchers to readily carry out the computations necessary for alternative analyses. References, as well as additional information about the use of software, are given in Hertzog and Rovine (1985), Jennings, Cohen, Ruchkin, and Fridlund (1987), O'Brien and Kaiser (1985), and Vasey and Thayer (1987). An extremely valuable resource to aid in the use of BMDP, SAS, and SPSS programs for alternative repeated measures analyses is Barcikowski (1983), which includes extensively annotated input and output for all three packages.

Unfortunately, the response of most researchers to all this information seems to be less than one might have hoped for. Vasey and Thayer (1987) reported that, in 1984 and 1985, fewer than 50% of the relevant articles appearing in *Psychophysiology* addressed the issue. Ekstrom, Quade, and Golden (1990) surveyed articles published in four psychiatry journals during the first 6 months of 1988. They found a total of 10 articles for which it could be ascertained that a standard repeated measures analysis of variance had been used, and 11 articles using an alternative analysis. (Perhaps most distressing was the fact that there were 22 articles reporting repeated measures data for which the method of analysis used could not be determined!)

To update and broaden this information, I reviewed the most recent issue available (almost all were from 1991) of a nonsystematic selection of psychology journals. There were 15 journals among those I examined whose latest issue contained at least one article where it was clear that the analysis of repeated measures data could present a problem, and a total of 58 such articles. Of these, only 3 (!) actually avoided the problem by carrying out an alternative analysis, whereas the remaining 55 reported at least one questionable repeated measures F test and gave no indication of an awareness of the issue of inflated significance

levels. For the record, the journals included in this survey were the *American Journal of Psychology; Child Development; Developmental Psychology; Journal of Comparative Psychology; Journal of Educational Psychology; Journal of Experimental Child Psychology; Journal of Experimental Psychology: Animal Behavior Processes, General, Human Perception and Performance,* and *Learning, Memory and Cognition; Journal of General Psychology; Journal of Personality and Social Psychology; Memory and Cognition; Organizational Behavior and Human Decision Processes;* and *Perception and Psychophysics.*
There is one bright spot in this gloomy picture. Simultaneously with the publication of Vasey and Thayer (1987), *Psychophysiology* adopted an editorial policy requiring articles reporting experiments with repeated measures data to use one of the alternatives to standard analysis of variance for analyzing these data (Jennings, Cohen, Ruchkin, & Fridlund, 1987). A check of their January 1991 issue confirmed that this policy is being followed: There were more alternative analyses than in the other 15 journals combined, and no clearly questionable uses of the standard analysis.

ALTERNATIVES TO STANDARD REPEATED MEASURES ANALYSIS OF VARIANCE

Two general approaches have been suggested to deal with the fact that the usual F test in the analysis of variance, when used to test hypotheses about main effects or interactions involving repeated measures with three or more levels, may not adequately control the probability of a Type I error. One of these strategies is to continue to work with the same F statistics as computed in the standard analysis, but to reduce the degrees of freedom used to obtain the associated p values. In other words, the sampling distribution of the usual F statistic under the null hypothesis being tested is approximated by an F distribution with reduced degrees of freedom.

The second general approach that has been advocated in the literature replaces the standard analysis of variance for experiments involving repeated measures by an alternate analysis so that, with some exceptions, the usual F statistics are not even computed. This more radical alternative identifies methods of testing hypotheses about repeated measures effects that take into account the correlations among observations, whatever they may be. The power of the tests used with this approach is definitely affected by the nature of these correlations, but the probability of a Type I error is not. In the remainder of this section, we discuss and compare two alternatives associated with each of the two strategies outlined here. The advantages and disadvantages of each alternative are mentioned.

The Geisser–Greenhouse Conservative F test

The first, and most straightforward, alternative to the standard repeated measures F test that should be considered is the Geisser–Greenhouse conservative test. It is also the easiest to carry out of any of the approaches proposed. Box (1954) showed that, under the null hypothesis of no mean differences among the repeated measures, the sampling distribution for the usual F statistic can be approximated by an F distribution, but with reduced degrees of freedom, the amount of the reduction depending on the pattern of the correlations among the repeated measures. Geisser and Greenhouse (1958) derived the lower bounds for the degrees of freedom in this approximation and used them as the basis for their proposed conservative test. The rule for computing these degrees of freedom is simple: Just pretend that all repeated measures factors have only two levels and then apply the usual formulas for the degrees of freedom.

In our example, Alternation Rate has six levels and Playing Speed has two. If we pretend there were only two Alternation Rates, then the F test for that main effect would have $(2 - 1) = 1$ and $(2 - 1)(24 - 1) = 23$ degrees of freedom. Playing Speed actually has only two levels, so the degrees of freedom for its F test $(1, 23)$ remain unchanged. For the interaction, we obtain $(2 - 1)(2 - 1) = 1$ and $(2 - 1)(2 - 1)(24 - 1) = 23$. From this illustration we can make a simple generalization: When the design consists exclusively of within-subjects factors, the conservative degrees of freedom for all tests are $(1, n - 1)$, where n is the number of subjects in the study.

As Geisser and Greenhouse (1958) showed, the rule can also be used for designs that include between-subjects factors. For instance, suppose the design in our example were expanded to include three Groups of 24 subjects each and every subject participated in all 12 combinations of the within-subjects factors. The degrees of freedom for the F test related to the main effect for Group would be unaffected by the rule: $(3 - 1) = 2$ and $(3)(24 - 1) = 69$. Similarly, the F test for the interaction of Group and Playing Speed would still have degrees of freedom $(3 - 1)(2 - 1) = 2$ and $(3)(2 - 1)(24 - 1) = 69$. However, the degrees of freedom of the F test for the interaction of Group with Alternation Rate, for instance, would change: $(3 - 1)(2 - 1) = 2$ instead of $(3 - 1)(6 - 1) = 10$, and $(3)(2 - 1)(24 - 1) = 69$ instead of $(3)(6 - 1)(24 - 1) = 345$.

Here we can observe the general principle that the Geisser–Greenhouse rule only affects F tests involving repeated measures factors with more than two levels. Perhaps the simplest way of explaining this fact is that assumptions for the F test involve *patterns* of correlations among observations at different levels.[2]

---

[2]The actual assumption here (for the F test of a repeated measures main effect) is that the variance–covariance matrix for the different levels be spherical (sometimes also called the circularity assumption, Kirk, 1982, p. 257). As Huynh and Feldt (1970) showed, this is equivalent to the

There need to be at least three levels in order to have more than one correlation between levels (and thus a pattern of correlations). Thus, for instance, a $2 \times 2 \times 2$ repeated measures design could be analyzed using a standard analysis of variance for all main effects and interactions without any danger of inflating Type I error probabilities due to correlations among observations at different levels. This is not to say that such a design is necessarily appropriate on substantive grounds. For instance, in the example with which we began, it was quite reasonable to use several levels of Alternation Rate.

The greatest advantage of the Geisser–Greenhouse conservative test is its simplicity. The greatest disadvantage is its (possible) conservatism. One reason researchers adopt repeated measures designs is the considerable power they often seem to provide with relatively few subjects, as compared to between-subjects designs. (See chap. 8, Vol. I, for a discussion of other issues involved in this choice.) It would appear that the conservative F test, reducing degrees of freedom in both numerator and denominator by at least a factor of two (five in our example), sacrifices much of that power out of concern for Type I errors.

Actually, the power of a test is a meaningless concept unless the probability of a Type I error is controlled at a specified level. (The same issue comes up in chap. 2, this volume, when different multiple comparisons procedures are considered.) The standard repeated measures F test will typically not provide this control, thus its apparent power is, to some degree at least, illusory. Nonetheless, researchers in statistics have been sufficiently concerned about the low power of the Geisser–Greenhouse conservative test to investigate a number of additional alternatives.

Other Degrees of Freedom Adjustments

Returning to Box's (1954) approximation of the null sampling distribution of the repeated measures F statistic with an F distribution having reduced degrees of freedom, the general expression multiplies both numerator and denominator degrees of freedom by an adjustment factor (usually denoted by ϵ), which is less than or equal to one. The maximum reduction in degrees of freedom possible with this adjustment produces the values used in the Geisser–Greenhouse conservative procedure. Greenhouse and Geisser (1959) gave an example where they estimated the actual amount of reduction, substituting sample variances and covariances for responses to the different levels in place of the corresponding population values that appear in Box's (1954) original formula for ϵ. Huynh and

---

assumption that the sampling variances for all pairwise differences among means are equal. Of course, this assumption will always be false (unless there are only two levels, in which case it is trivial) as will be the assumption of (multivariate) normality for the distribution of the observations. The difference is that the F test is relatively robust to violations of normality, but quite sensitive to departures from sphericity.

Feldt (1976) derived an alternative estimate for ϵ, designed to be an improvement in cases where the true value is not too far below one.

Not having the original data for our example, it is not possible to evaluate the adjustments in this case. It should be noted that, in general, a different adjustment will be found for each test, so that the reduced degrees of freedom needed for testing the main effect of Alternation Rate would probably be different than those for the interaction of Alternation Rate and Playing Speed. Just as with the conservative test, no adjustment is needed for testing the main effect of Playing Speed, because this factor has only two levels. Similarly, no adjustment would be needed for any test involving only between-subjects factors.

The adjustments of Greenhouse and Geisser (1959) and Huynh and Feldt (1976) are not quantities researchers would want to routinely calculate on their own, although several references on experimental design (for instance, Kirk, 1982, p. 262) provide worked out examples where they show how to do just that. Fortunately, the computer packages BMDP, SAS, and SPSS all include programs that carry out repeated measures F tests with adjusted degrees of freedom using both the Greenhouse–Geisser and Huynh–Feldt estimates for ϵ (Jennings, Cohen, Ruchkin, & Fridlund, 1987; Vasey & Thayer, 1987). Thus the computational hurdle that once existed with respect to this approach no longer exists for researchers with access to one of these packages.

The ϵ-adjusted tests share the advantage of the Geisser–Greenhouse conservative procedure that they work with familiar F statistics, thus making them conceptually accessible to researchers. Moreover, they are guaranteed to have at least the power of the conservative test and, in practice, undoubtedly have considerably more power. Their only disadvantage relative to the conservative procedure is that they require the full data set (and, realistically, a computer program) to evaluate. Thus they are not suitable for a quick check of a result or for a reanalysis of F statistics reported in a journal article (such as our example). The same point applies to the remaining alternative analyses discussed here.

Multivariate Analysis of Repeated Measures Data

Rao (1952, pp. 239–240) was apparently the first author to describe the application of a multivariate test (Hotelling's T^2) to a simple, "univariate," one-factor repeated measures design. To take this step, a conceptual shift was necessary. Instead of thinking of the design having subjects as a random factor crossed with the (fixed) repeated measures factor, responses to different levels of the repeated measures factor are viewed as different dependent variables, and subjects are considered to provide replications in a single-cell design. With a typical multivariate setup, each dependent variable is measured on a different scale. For repeated measures, however, all dependent variables are measured on the same scale, and the primary interest is in differences among the means of the different variables (levels). Rao's (1952) response to this problem was to define a new set of dependent variables based on the original ones.

Specifically, he defined new variables that provide a complete set of comparisons (or contrasts) among the levels. An example would be the difference scores comparing responses at each level of the repeated measures factor to responses at the last level. For simplicity, we may refer to the new variables in the general case as difference scores. The hypothesis of no population differences among the means of the original dependent variables is equivalent to the hypothesis that each of the new difference scores has a population mean of zero. He then applied Hotelling's T^2 to the set of difference scores to test this hypothesis. A parallel can be drawn with the paired observations t test, which can be thought of as testing the hypothesis of a zero mean in the population for a new variable formed by taking the difference between the paired responses. Indeed, this is exactly what Rao's procedure reduces to when the repeated measures factor has only two levels.

This multivariate approach can be extended to factorial repeated measures designs simply by computing more complex sets of difference scores (sometimes referred to as contrasts in the variables) and using subsets of them for testing the different main effects and interactions. In our example, with two levels of Playing Speed and six levels of Alternation Rate, one might proceed by first computing the average response for each subject at each of the two levels of Playing Speed and then finding the difference between these two averages. We would then have a new variable, "Average Playing Speed Difference," with a value for each of the 24 subjects. A t test of the hypothesis that this variable has a mean of zero in the population could then be carried out. In fact, this test is equivalent to the standard F test of the main effect for Playing Speed [$F(1, 23) = t^2(23)$]. Note that all methods considered so far agree with each other when there is only one degree of freedom for the repeated measures effect.

The main effect for Alternation Rate can be approached similarly. First obtain the average response for each subject at each of the six levels of Alternation Rate. Then take the differences between the average for each of the first five levels and the average for the sixth level. Now there are five new difference variables that express, for each subject, the average difference between the response at a given level of Alternation Rate and the last level. According to the appropriate hypothesis to be tested, all five of these variables have zero means in the population. Hotelling's T^2 can be used for this purpose and can be transformed to provide a statistic that, under the null hypothesis, has an F distribution with 5 and 19 degrees of freedom. It cannot be emphasized too strongly that this "multivariate F statistic" is essentially different from the standard F statistic associated with this hypothesis. The two may have very different values for the same data and, consequently, have very different p values as well, whether or not the degrees of freedom for the standard F test have been adjusted.

To deal with the Playing Speed × Alternation Rate interaction, we should remember that interaction has to do with differences between differences. Thus suppose we find the difference between responses at the two Playing Speeds for each level of Alternation Rate for each subject. Then we may take the difference between the Playing Speed difference at each of the first five levels of Alternation Rate and the Playing Speed difference at the sixth level. This gives us five new "difference of differences" variables, indicating for each subject how much the effect of Playing Speed differed at a given level of Alternation Rate from its effect at the last level. As with the main effect for Alternation Rate, the relevant null hypothesis here purports that all of these new variables have zero means in the population. Again, this hypothesis can be tested with Hotelling's T^2, yielding an F statistic with 5 and 19 degrees of freedom.

A multivariate analysis of any main effect or interaction in a pure repeated measures design would proceed in a similar manner. A set of new variables is identified that, together, describe the effect of interest. They take the form of contrasts among the original responses and give, for each subject, the size of that contrast. There should be as many new variables in the set as there were degrees of freedom for the effect in the standard repeated measures analysis of variance. Moreover, the contrasts should be linearly independent, which is to say there should be no redundancies in the set. To put it another way, it should not be possible to obtain any one of the new scores from the remaining scores in the set.

The computer programs referred to earlier, which can be used to carry out multivariate repeated measures analyses of variance, either choose the sets of new variables automatically or make it easy for users to specify the new variables with which they want to work. Actually, new sets of scores are not computed directly by these programs, because the sums of squares and cross products needed for the new variables can be obtained directly from the sums of squares and cross products of the original repeated measures. Nonetheless, it is convenient to think in terms of new scores, and we continue to discuss the multivariate approach in these terms.

Now consider designs that include between-subjects as well as within-subjects factors. One additional new variable is needed to carry out a multivariate analysis for such designs. This is simply the average response for each subject across all combinations of levels of the repeated measures factors. Returning to our example, extended to three Groups of 24 subjects each, we are talking about the score that is the average over all six repeated measures responses. The null hypothesis of no main effect for Group can be tested by carrying out a standard one-way between-subjects analysis of variance for our new average response variable. This is equivalent to the test for Group in the usual repeated measures analysis.

To look at the interaction between Group and Playing Speed, we would again perform a one-way between-subjects analysis of variance, but this time we would use the new variable created to test the main effect of Playing Speed, referred to earlier as the Average Playing Speed Difference. Here we would be testing the hypothesis of no differences among Groups in the mean effect of Playing Speed. Again, this test is equivalent to the standard test for this interaction. Things become more interesting when we consider the interaction between Group and Alternation Rate. Now we use the five variables representing Alternation Rate differences. The null hypothesis to be tested is that the pattern of population means for these five variables is the same for all three groups. This is a hypothesis appropriately dealt with via multivariate analysis of variance. (See chap. 5, this volume, for details.) Again, the programs referred to earlier will carry out such an analysis, automatically using the appropriate variables. The results will, in general, differ from those of the standard repeated measures analysis of variance, the conservative analysis, and the ϵ-adjusted analysis.

Similarly, for the three-way interaction of Group, Playing Speed, and Alternation Rate, we need to carry out a one-way multivariate analysis of variance to test the hypothesis of no differences among Groups for the population means of the five variables constructed to assess the Playing Speed $\times$ Alternation Rate interaction. In general, between-subjects analyses of variables constructed to measure within-subjects effects can be applied to any level of interaction involving both types of factors.

As long as only between-subjects factors are involved in the main effect or interaction to be tested, we would analyze only the average response variable. If the main effect or interaction includes only within-subjects factors, we would test the hypothesis that the population grand means over all levels of the between-subjects factors for the appropriate new variables are zero. Thus the population mean over the three Groups of our extended example for each of the five variables representing the Playing Speed $\times$ Alternation Rate interaction is hypothesized to be zero in the multivariate test of that interaction.

As suggested by this discussion, the multivariate approach can be applied to a wide variety of designs involving repeated measures. It has the advantage over the standard analysis that it makes no assumptions regrading the nature of the correlations among repeated measures. Consequently, the multivariate approach continues to be valid regardless of the pattern of these correlations. A traditionally cited disadvantage of a multivariate analysis of repeated measures designs is the complexity of the computations involved. For those with access to modern statistical software, this concern no longer applies.

There is an associated problem, namely that many researchers may not fully understand what takes place when repeated measures data are analyzed with multivariate procedures. Thinking in terms of new variables chosen to describe repeated measures effects, and understanding why analyses are performed on these new variables, may help this problem, though the general multivariate tests will probably remain somewhat mysterious for those more accustomed to standard F tests. This situation is not improved by the fact that there are a variety of competing multivariate tests and no unanimity among statisticians as to the most appropriate choice among them for the best combination of power and robustness to violations of the assumptions of multivariate normality and homogeneity of covariance matrices across groups.

Finally, there is a general concern about the power of multivariate tests applied to repeated measures hypotheses. The most extreme version of this concern occurs for designs having no more subjects than degrees of freedom for some repeated measures main effect or interaction. In this case, a multivariate test cannot even be carried out. For instance, in our original 2×6 design, suppose there had been only five subjects. Then the degrees of freedom for the multivariate F tests (based on Hotelling's T^2) for Alternation Rate and for the interaction would be five and zero! (The F statistic itself is not defined for this case.) If there were six subjects instead of five, the test statistics could be computed, with the denominator degrees of freedom equal to one, but the tests would have almost no power to detect effects of any reasonable size. The situation improves rapidly as the number of subjects increases. In fact, Davidson (1972), Imhof (1962), and Rogan, Keselman, and Mendoza (1979) described situations involving relatively few subjects where multivariate tests can actually have more power than the corresponding univariate tests with ϵ-adjusted degrees of freedom.

Multiple t Tests for Repeated Measures Data

The last general approach to repeated measures analysis of variance that we discuss is based on carrying out multiple t tests. This method of analysis is similar to the multivariate approach in that it does not involve the computation of standard repeated measures F statistics. The two are also similar in making use of new variables, constructed from the original repeated measures. Finally, neither makes any assumption about the nature of the correlations among responses, nor involves any adjustments based on these correlations.

The basic idea behind this method is simple. We carry out a series of t tests that, taken together, test the hypothesis of interest (main effect or interaction). To control the probability of a Type I error for all tests together, we may make use of the Bonferroni inequality, which says that the overall probability of a Type I error can never be larger than the sum of the Type I error probabilities for the individual tests. If any of the t tests rejects its null hypothesis, we can reject the overall null hypothesis. The only issue left to consider is the choice of t tests to carry out. The strategies we consider might be labeled "planned" and "unplanned." If specific comparisons are of interest, and can be identified before the experiment is carried out (i.e., planned), testing these comparisons is usually the most appropriate course of action. This approach provides maximum power to detect effects of interest, but runs the risk of missing unanticipated effects. For the unplanned approach, we may simply test all pairwise differences for a main effect, or all differences of differences for an interaction.

Using multiple t tests in place of F tests to test repeated measures effects has been advocated from time to time in the literature, though not nearly as often as the three alternatives already described. For instance, in his text on experimental design, Myers (1979) said, "In many cases it might be better to decide on a family of single df contrasts in advance of the data collection and to carry out those tests" (p. 482). Rogan, Keselman, and Mendoza (1979) pointed out: "Another data analytic strategy, therefore, is to forego omnibus testing . . . and rely upon one degree of freedom tests which are . . . appropriate to specific experimental questions" (p. 277). The Hertzog and Rovine (1985) review of repeated measures analysis alternatives advised: "Consider whether the omnibus testing procedure may be avoided in favor of the statistical evaluation of specific hypotheses in the form of planned comparisons" (p. 788).

In chapter 8 of this volume, the author illustrates the use of planned comparisons with the Bonferroni inequality for designs involving repeated measures as well as between-subject factors. Although this is done in the context of a Bayesian analysis, and emphasizes interval estimates of effects, rather than hypothesis testing, the principle is basically the same as in the current discussion. Most directly, Zwick (chap. 2) discusses multiple comparisons procedures for repeated measures designs and advises the Bonferroni controlled t tests for all pairs of means be substituted for an overall test. This is an example of the unplanned strategy referred to earlier. (More information regarding the Bonferroni inequality and its value for making multiple comparisons may also be found in chap. 2.)

Turning to our example, the test for the main effect of Playing Speed would proceed exactly as in the multivariate approach, using the new variable we referred to as Average Playing Speed Difference and carrying out a one sample t test with 23 degrees of freedom for the hypothesis that this new variable has a mean of zero in the population. In fact, the standard analysis and all four alternatives will produce the same test for any repeated measures hypothesis with one degree of freedom.

In testing the main effect of Alternation Rate, one possibility would be to proceed again with the new variables defined for the multivariate analysis. These were the differences between the average response to each of the first five levels of Alternation Rate and the average response to the sixth level. Suppose these comparisons had been identified beforehand as being of particular interest. We could test each of the new variables with a one sample t test. If our goal is to control the probability of a Type I error at .05, each of the five tests may be carried out at the .01 level. The Bonferroni inequality then guarantees that, regardless of the true pattern of means of the original repeated measures or of the pattern of correlations among these measures, the probability of committing one or more Type I errors with this set of tests will not exceed the sum of the individual levels, in this case .05.

Given the quantitative nature of the levels of the Alternation Rate factor, a more appropriate set of new variables than those just considered might be scores based on orthogonal polynomial contrasts, commonly used in trend analyses.

The computer packages mentioned earlier allow these contrasts to be specified as part of an analysis. Using this approach, five new variables could be constructed, representing a linear trend of the responses with Alternation Rate, a quadratic trend, a cubic trend, a quartic trend, and a quintic trend. Again, performing a one sample t test at the .01 level with each of these variables would test the main effect at the .05 level.

These two alternatives are examples of the planned approach to multiple t tests. For the unplanned approach, we would need a total of 15 new variables, representing differences between all pairs of levels of Alternation Rate (after first averaging over the two levels of Playing Speed). These would lead to 15 t tests, each at the $.05/15 = .0033$ level. If the null hypothesis could be rejected for any of these tests, then the hypothesis of no main effect for Alternation Rate would be rejected as well.

Before continuing with the t tests appropriate for testing the interaction in our example, it may be worthwhile to make an observation about the three alternatives just described, namely they may very well not yield the same conclusion. In other words, the set of variables the researcher chooses will generally have an effect on the outcome of the testing procedure. (Note that this is not true for the multivariate approach. The multivariate test could just as well be carried out using polynomial trend variables as the ones we actually discussed, and the test results would be identical in the two cases.)

One way to think about this is that the choice of variables to test with multiple t tests will result in the procedure having relatively high power to detect certain patterns of mean differences (corresponding to the contrasts chosen), but relatively low power to detect others (those not chosen). The unplanned strategy, by testing more variables, allows the detection of more different patterns of differences. However, it gives up power by testing each variable with a Type I error probability of .0033 rather than .01. With 23 degrees of freedom, the relevant critical values for the t test are 3.274 and 2.807, respectively. In other words, the absolute value of the t statistic for the variable representing the difference between the first and last levels of Alternation Rate would have to exceed 3.274 to result in a rejection as part of an unplanned analysis, but would only have to be greater than 2.807 when tested as part of the first planned analysis.

The author, together with many other writers on the subject, strongly advocates the use of planned comparisons in the analysis of variance. Nonetheless, in the present context of considering alternatives to standard F tests as tools for providing a preliminary analysis of the results of an experiment, the use of unplanned multiple t tests would seem to be more appropriate. Consequently, this is the strategy pursued in the remainder of the discussion.

For the Playing Speed × Alternation Rate interaction of our example, the unplanned strategy leads us to consider all differences of differences. To do this, we first make six new variables, representing the difference between the responses to the two levels of Playing Speed at each of the six levels of Alternation

Rate. From these six, we could then construct 15 additional new variables, taking the difference between the first and the second, the first and the third, the second and the third, and so on, until every pair of the six has been included. We would carry out a one sample t test on each of these 15 difference of differences variables, using, as with the main effect for Alternation Rate, a level of .0033 for each test. If any of these 15 tests rejected its null hypothesis, we would reject the overall hypothesis of no interaction at the .05 level.

How a researcher actually carries out the multiple t test approach to analyzing repeated measures data will depend on the computer software available. Any program designed to make multiple comparisons for repeated measures designs should be appropriate for the present purpose, with one qualification. Some programs may use a pooled standard error for all comparisons, based on the error term from the standard repeated measures analysis of variance. As Boik (1981) pointed out, this practice should be avoided. Even more than for the overall F test, the probabilities of Type I errors may be substantially inflated for individual comparisons using pooled standard errors. Thinking of the comparisons as one sample t tests on new variables leads directly to the use of the appropriate (i.e., unpooled) standard errors. If in doubt about what a program is doing, look at the degrees of freedom associated with the t tests. In our example, these would be 23 for the unpooled standard errors and 115 for the pooled value. In general, with a pure repeated measures design, the degrees of freedom for the multiple t tests we have been discussing (unpooled) are one less than the number of subjects.

Actually, all that is needed to carry out this procedure is a facility for creating new variables and a program to perform t tests for specified variables and groups. For instance, in the case of the interaction just discussed, suppose we use our software to construct the six Playing Speed difference variables. We may then ask for paired or dependent t tests for this set of variables, and many packages will then automatically test all pairs of these, thus saving us the work of constructing the 15 variables needed to test the interaction. The output of these tests typically includes a p value associated with each statistic. A simple rule for using these is to take the smallest p value and multiply it by the number of tests carried out (15 in this case). The resulting value may then be reported as the obtained p value for the set of tests.

For example, suppose the largest t statistic in our case were 3.14, with an associated p value of .0024. Multiplying by 15 gives .036. Thus we would be justified in writing $p = .036$ (or $p < .05$) when giving the results of the test for the interaction. One possible shorthand notation for the entire result could be: $Bt(15, 23) = 3.14$, $p = .036$. Here, Bt stands for "Bonferroni t," 15 is the number of tests carried out, 23 is the degrees of freedom for each test, and 3.14 is the value of the largest t statistic (in absolute value). The particular contrasts whose t statistics exceeded the critical value (earlier determined to be 3.274) need not be reported at this stage, although they would be available for further interpretation of the interaction being tested.

As with the other approaches, we must also consider what happens with designs that include between-subjects factors. For this purpose, it is convenient to refer to our extended example: three Groups of 24 subjects, with each subject responding to all conditions of the original 2 × 6 repeated measures design. For the main effect of Group as well as for the interaction of Group with Playing Speed, we may proceed just as in the multivariate approach, conducting one-way between-subjects analyses of variance on the new variables Average Response and Average Playing Speed Difference, respectively. These tests are identical to the standard ones.

For the interaction of Group with Alternation Rate, we need the 15 new "Average Alternation Rate Difference" variables used to test the Alternation Rate main effect. There is a difference now because instead of multiple *t* tests, we use multiple *F* tests. Specifically, we perform a one-way between-subjects analysis of variance on each of these variables and select the smallest *p* value from the results. Multiply it by 15, and take this as the effective *p* value for the test of no interaction. Here we make use of what are known as Bonferroni *F* tests, which have been proposed as an alternative to standard multivariate tests (for multivariate analysis of covariance by Huitema, 1980, pp. 238–252). One attraction of the Bonferroni inequality is that it can be applied to any set of tests, and is not restricted to use with *t* statistics.

For the three-way interaction of Group, Playing Speed, and Alternation Rate, we would again make use of Bonferroni *F* tests, this time with the 15 new difference of differences variables. If the *p* value for any of these tests is less than .0033, we may reject the null hypothesis of no three-way interaction at the .05 level.

Finally, what happens with the tests of repeated measures main effects and interactions in a design with between-subjects factors? As with the multivariate approach, our goal is to test the hypothesis that each of the appropriate new variables has a zero population mean when averaged over all Groups. Actually, we may obtain the results we desire as byproducts of the analyses of variance just described. For instance, in the case of the analysis of the Average Playing Speed Difference variable to test the Group × Playing Speed interaction, the test that the grand mean is zero is the test of the Playing Speed main effect that we want.

When more than one variable is analyzed, we again make use of the Bonferroni inequality to combine the results into a single test of the main effect or interaction of interest. Thus the main effect of Alternation Rate is dealt with by testing the hypothesis that the population grand mean for each of the 15 Average Alternation Rate Difference variables is zero, using individual .0033 levels for an overall .05 test.

Many analysis of variance programs provide tests that the grand mean is zero, either by default or as an option (sometimes in connection with model parameter estimates). They may be reported either as *t* tests or as *F* tests with one degree of freedom in the numerator (each being the square of the corresponding *t* value).

The t statistics used in these tests are formed by dividing each sample grand mean by an estimate of its standard error. In our example, the grand mean is the sum of the three Group means, divided by three. Its sampling variance may be estimated by taking the Mean Square within Groups and dividing by 72 (the total number of subjects).[3] The estimated standard error of the sample grand mean is the square root of this quantity. Thus, even if a computer program that tests grand means as part of an analysis of variance is not available, the evaluation of these statistics should present no serious problems.

Under the null hypothesis, together with the assumptions that the observations on the variable under consideration are independently normally distributed with the same variance and the same number of subjects in each Group, the statistic has a t distribution with, in our example, $3(24 - 1) = 69$ degrees of freedom. More importantly, these tests show reasonable robustness to the inevitable violations of the normality and homogeneity of variance assumptions, as long as sample sizes in the cells of the between-subjects part of the design are equal.

Keselman and Keselman (1988) showed that serious lack of robustness for these tests can occur when unequal cell sizes are coupled with unequal cell variances and the Mean Square within Cells is used in the estimate of the standard error for the grand mean. More recently, Keselman, Keselman, and Shaffer (1991) demonstrated that satisfactory control of Type I error probabilities in these circumstances is achieved if the "unpooled" estimates of sampling variance described in footnote 3 are used when the test statistics are computed.

To test hypotheses in this case, the sampling distribution of the statistics may be approximated by a t distribution with adjusted degrees of freedom (Satterthwaite, 1941). This is a generalization of the Welch (1938) adjustment for two groups described in Chapter 2. These adjusted degrees of freedom will not exceed the within cells degrees of freedom (total number of subjects minus total number of cells), but are at least as great as the smallest degrees of freedom for any cell in the design (number of subjects in that cell minus one). Keselman, Keselman, and Shaffer (1991) gave computational details, including a description of a setup for use in the SAS statistical package.

If we compare the use of multiple t tests to the other alternatives to standard repeated measures analysis of variance discussed, we see that it has both advantages and disadvantages. One major disadvantage is the lack of widespread acceptance, or even awareness of the approach. This is reflected in the fact that no major package of statistical programs offers straightforward procedures for carrying out multiple t or multiple F tests for repeated measures designs. As we

---

[3]This estimate is appropriate when all cells of the between-subjects design (in our example, the three Groups) contain the same number of subjects. With unequal cell sizes, the sampling variance of the (unweighted) grand mean should be estimated by dividing the sample variance for each cell by the number of subjects in that cell and adding all these ratios together. This sum should then be divided by the square of the total number of cells. For equal cell sizes, this estimate reduces to the Mean Square within Cells divided by the total number of subjects.

have tried to describe here, performing these analyses is not particularly difficult. Nonetheless, it would certainly be more convenient if one could provide a description of a design and directly obtain the appropriate information, as now occurs with the other approaches.

One major advantage of the multiple t test approach over the other alternatives is its conceptual simplicity. Many researchers may not understand either the logic of the degrees of freedom adjustments for standard repeated measures F tests or the rationale behind the various multivariate tests, and this may be an obstacle to their more widespread use. For the multiple t test approach, neither the individual tests themselves nor the use of the Bonferroni inequality to combine their results requires any extensive mathematical training to understand. Even researchers who routinely use statistical software to analyze their data should appreciate the value of a procedure all steps of which could easily be carried out with nothing more than a pocket calculator.

In general, the power of the multiple t test approach is comparable with that of the other alternatives. It is, however, important to note that multiple t tests can still be carried out in cases where the multivariate approach would not be possible, due to sample sizes being too small. The numerical illustration of the next section provides a case where the multiple t test approach is apparently the most powerful among the alternatives, but this should not be construed as typical.

A NUMERICAL ILLUSTRATION

For purposes of illustrating the points discussed so far, we now introduce an artificial example, having one within-subjects factor (A) with three levels and one between-subjects factor (B) with two levels. There are a total of eight subjects in this example, four at each level of B. The complete data set is reproduced in Table 3.1. The form of Table 3.1 shows how the data should be

TABLE 3.1
Artificial Data, Factor A Within Subjects
and Factor B Between Subjects

A1	A2	A3	B
17	25	24	1
16	22	16	1
18	16	12	1
25	21	20	1
16	25	19	2
17	19	13	2
21	17	15	2
30	31	25	2

input to a statistical package, namely as four variables measured on eight subjects. The first three variables represent the responses at the three levels of the repeated measures factor, A, and the fourth variable indicates for each subject which level of the between-subjects factor, B, they were assigned to in the hypothetical study.

Table 3.2 provides the mean (and standard deviation) for each cell in the design, together with row, column, and grand means. Looking at the pattern of means, we see that there is a suggestion of a main effect for factor A, with level A2 having the highest mean response and level A3 the lowest. Factor B appears to have a small effect, with level 2 having a slightly higher mean than level 1. Finally, there is an indication of a small interaction between A and B, with factor B showing some effect at A1 and A2, but no effect at A3. As regards the cell standard deviations, there is some suggestion that standard deviations associated with level 1 of factor B are smaller than those associated with level 2.

Of course, all these conclusions are based on only four observations per cell. Thus it is entirely reasonable to ask if the effects seen here are any greater than those that might simply be due to sampling fluctuations. As noted before, asking such a question does not imply that we seriously believe there are no population main effects or interactions for this setup. Instead, the concern is whether it is reasonable to interpret the sample results as observed in Table 3.2.

For purposes of comparison, let us begin to address this question by looking at a standard repeated measures analysis of variance. The usual table summarizing this analysis is presented as Table 3.3. The between-subjects factor (B) is tested using the Mean Square for Subjects nested within levels of B as an error term. It produces an F statistic (with 1 and 6 degrees of freedom) less than one and having a correspondingly high p value. This is the one result of the analysis that will not change for any of the alternative approaches. The main effect for A and the interaction of A and B are both tested using the Mean Square for the interaction of A and Subjects nested within B as error term. The F statistic for testing A has 2 and 12 degrees of freedom and a p value of .084, not quite significant at the .05 level. The interaction has an F statistic less than one.

The p values for the conservative F tests of these two effects are also given in Table 3.3. Note that the marginal .08 for the main effect of A increases to .13. There is no point to computing the adjusted degrees of freedom in this case,

TABLE 3.2
Means (and Standard Deviations)
for Artificial Data

A1	A2	A3	B
19 (4.1)	21 (3.7)	18 (5.2)	19.3
21 (6.4)	23 (6.3)	18 (5.3)	20.7
20	22	18	20

TABLE 3.3
Standard Analysis of Variance for Artificial Data

Source	SS	df	MS	F	p
B	10.7	1	10.7	0.172	.693
Subjects w. B	372.7	6	62.1		
A	64.0	2	32.0	3.064	.084
					(.130)[a]
A × B	5.3	2	2.7	0.255	.779
					(.631)[a]
A × S w. B	125.3	12	10.4		

[a]Conservative p values given in parentheses.

but—were we to do this—the resulting p value for A would lie somewhere between .08 and .13.

Preliminary to carrying out the multivariate analysis of these data, let us consider the new scores presented in Table 3.4. Here, all three pairwise differences have been obtained, together with a mean response for each subject. Table 3.5 gives the cell means (and standard deviations) for these new variables, together with their grand means. These values mainly confirm our observations regarding the means for the original responses in Table 3.2. One new point concerns the standard deviations of the differences. Note that the standard deviations for A2–A3 are less than half those for the other two differences. This suggests the possibility of a serious violation of the sphericity assumption necessary to the validity of the standard analysis.

Table 3.6 summarizes the results of a multivariate analysis of the artificial data. Unfortunately, few statistical packages provide such a table. Instead, the information it contains must typically be gleaned from several tables, not always clearly labeled, and giving a number of different test statistics. Comparison with Table 3.3 confirms that the test for B is identical in the two analyses. The test for

TABLE 3.4
Pairwise Difference Scores and Mean Score
Based on Artificial Data

A1–A2	A1–A3	A2–A3	$\bar{A}$	B
−8	−7	1	22	1
−6	0	6	18	1
2	6	4	15.3	1
4	5	1	22	1
−9	−3	6	20	2
−2	4	6	16.3	2
4	6	2	17.7	2
−1	5	6	28.7	2

TABLE 3.5
Means (and Standard Deviations)
for Pairwise Difference Scores
and Mean Score

A1–A2	A1–A3	A2–A3	$\bar{A}$
−2 (5.9)	1 (5.9)	3 (2.4)	19.3 (3.3)
−2 (5.4)	3 (4.1)	5 (2.0)	20.7 (5.5)
−2	2	4	20

A, however, is not only different from the standard result, but also gives a p value of .014, allowing us to reject the null hypothesis of no effect for the repeated measures factor at the .05 level. No claim is made that the direction of this discrepancy is typical, but Table 3.6 shows that it is possible for a multivariate test to reject a repeated measures hypothesis that has not been rejected with the standard test. The result for the interaction, although not identical to that in Table 3.3, leads to the same conclusion: failure to reject the hypothesis.

Finally, we turn to multiple t tests to analyze our artificial data. Table 3.7 presents seven t statistics used for this purpose. First, a two groups t test is performed on the mean scores to test the hypothesis of no main effect for factor B. If B had more than two levels, this would have been an F test on the mean score. The two-tailed p value associated with this test is identical to that reported in the other two analyses.

To test the main effect for the repeated measures factor A, we test the grand mean for each of our pairwise difference variables. These tests were obtained by feeding the difference variables, two at a time, into a multivariate analysis of variance and taking the results from the tables of univariate tests of the difference scores for the "Constant" factor. (The reason only two difference scores could be analyzed at one time is that the third is linearly dependent on the first two. Trying to perform a multivariate analysis of variance on a linearly dependent set of variables produces an error message from most packages.) The t statistics for the interaction of A and B are obtained in the same runs, and are taken from the tables of univariate tests of the difference scores for factor B.

The results for the interaction between A and B are consistent with those of

TABLE 3.6
Multivariate Analysis of Variance
for Artificial Data

Source	df_1	df_2	F	p
B	1	6	0.172	.693
A	2	5	11.326	.014
A × B	2	5	0.813	.495

TABLE 3.7
Multiple t Tests (and p values) for Mean and Difference Scores

Source	$\bar{A}$	A1–A2	A1–A3	A2–A3	Bonferroni p value
B	−0.414 (.693)				.693
A		−1.005 (.354)	1.109 (.310)	5.060 (.002)	.007
A × B		0.000 (1.000)	−0.555 (.599)	−1.265 (.253)	.758

Note: All t tests have six degrees of freedom.

the other analyses. However, as regards the main effect of A, the t statistic for A2–A3 is 5.06 with a two-tailed p value of .0023. When multiplied by three (the number of differences tested), this gives a Bonferroni p value of .0069. Thus, using the multiple t test approach allows us to reject the null hypothesis of no repeated measures effect at the .01 level. For this example, then, multiple t tests provide the most powerful alternative analysis available, with considerably more power than the standard, incorrect, F test.

REFERENCES

Barcikowski, R. S. (Ed.). (1983). *Computer packages and research design.* Lanham, MD: University Press of America.

Boik, R. J. (1981). A priori tests in repeated measures designs: Effects of nonsphericity. *Psychometrika, 46,* 241–255.

Box, G. E. P. (1954). Some theorems on quadratic forms applied in the study of analysis of variance problems, II. Effects of inequality of variance and of correlation between errors in the two-way classification. *The Annals of Mathematical Statistics, 25,* 484–498.

Davidson, M. L. (1972). Univariate versus multivariate tests in repeated measures experiments. *Psychological Bulletin, 77,* 446–452.

Dayton, C. M. (1970). *The design of educational experiments.* New York: McGraw-Hill.

Edwards, A. L. (1985). *Experimental design in psychological research* (5th ed.). New York: Harper & Row.

Ekstrom, D., Quade, D., & Golden, R. N. (1990). Statistical analysis of repeated measures in psychiatric research. *Archives of General Psychiatry, 47,* 770–772.

Geisser, S., & Greenhouse, S. W. (1958). An extension of Box's results on the use of the F distribution in multivariate analysis. *The Annals of Mathematical Statistics, 29,* 885–891.

Greenhouse, S. W., & Geisser, S. (1959). On methods in the analysis of profile data. *Psychometrika, 24,* 95–112.

Hertzog, C., & Rovine, M. (1985). Repeated-measures analysis of variance in developmental research: Selected issues. *Child Development, 56,* 787–809.

Huitema, B. E. (1980). *The analysis of covariance and alternatives.* New York: Wiley.

Huynh, H., & Feldt, L. S. (1970). Conditions under which mean square ratios in repeated measurements designs have exact F-distributions. *Journal of the American Statistical Association, 65,* 1582–1589.

Huynh, H., & Feldt, L. S. (1976). Estimation of the Box correction for degrees of freedom from sample data in randomized block and split-plot designs. *Journal of Educational Statistics, 1,* 69–82.

Imhof, J. P. (1962). Testing the hypothesis of no fixed main-effects in Scheffé's mixed model. *The Annals of Mathematical Statistics, 33,* 1085–1095.

Jennings, J. R., Cohen, M. J., Ruchkin, D. S., & Fridlund, A. J. (1987). Editorial policy on analyses of variance with repeated measures. *Psychophysiology, 24,* 474–478.

Keppel, G. (1982). *Design and analysis: A researcher's handbook* (2nd ed.). Englewood Cliffs, NJ Prentice-Hall.

Keselman, H. J., & Keselman, J. C. (1988). Comparing repeated measures means in factorial designs. *Psychophysiology, 25,* 612–618.

Keselman, H. J., Keselman, J. C., & Shaffer, J. P. (1991). Multiple pairwise comparisons of repeated measures means under violation of multisample sphericity. *Psychological Bulletin, 110,* 162–170.

Kirk, R. E. (1982). *Experimental design: Procedures for the behavioral sciences* (2nd ed.). Monterey, CA: Brooks/Cole.

Lana, R. E., & Lubin, A. (1963). The effect of correlation on the repeated measures design *Educational and Psychological Measurement, 23,* 729–739.

McCall, R. B., & Appelbaum, M. I. (1973). Bias in the analysis of repeated-measures designs Some alternative approaches. *Child Development, 44,* 401–415.

Myers, J. L. (1979). *Fundamentals of experimental design* (3rd ed.). Boston: Allyn & Bacon.

O'Brien, R. G., & Kaiser, M. K. (1985). MANOVA method for analyzing repeated measures designs: An extensive primer. *Psychological Bulletin, 97,* 316–333.

Rao, C. R. (1952). *Advanced statistical methods in biometric research.* New York: Wiley.

Rogan, J. C., Keselman, H. J., & Mendoza, J. L. (1979). Analysis of repeated measurements. *British Journal of Mathematical and Statistical Psychology, 32,* 269–286.

Samuel, A. G. (1991). Perceptual degradation due to signal alternation: Implications for auditory pattern processing. *Journal of Experimental Psychology: Human Perception and Performance, 17,* 392–403.

Satterthwaite, F. E. (1941). Synthesis of variance. *Psychometrika, 6,* 309–316.

Vasey, M. W., & Thayer, J. F. (1987). The continuing problem of false positives in repeated measures ANOVA in psychophysiology: A multivariate solution. *Psychophysiology, 24,* 479–486.

Welch, B. L. (1938). The significance of the difference between two means when the population variances are unequal. *Biometrika, 29,* 350–362.

Winer, B. J., Brown, D. R., & Michels, K. M. (1991). *Statistical principles in experimental design* (3rd ed.). New York: McGraw-Hill.

4 A Balanced Approach to Unbalanced Designs

Gideon Keren
Free University of Amsterdam

INTRODUCTION

A problem encountered by many researchers in psychology and other disciplines is the one of an "unbalanced design" (also referred to as "unequal frequencies" or "non-orthogonal" design). This is the case in which the number of observations in different cells of an experimental design are not necessarily equal. The question of how to treat such designs has become a major controversial issue in recent years (Appelbaum & Cramer, 1974; Cramer & Appelbaum, 1980; Herr & Gaebelein, 1978; Keren & Lewis, 1976, 1977; Overall & Spiegel, 1960; Overall, Spiegel, & Cohen, 1975; Speed & Hocking, 1976, to mention just a few). The purpose of the present chapter is to discuss briefly several methods that were recently proposed and to provide the reader with some guidelines of how to deal with a nonorthogonal design.

The approach presented in the chapter employs least square regression methods as a substitute for the traditional analysis of variance (ANOVA). Several investigators (Cohen, 1968; Cohen & Cohen, 1975; Darlington, 1968; Kerlinger & Pedhazur, 1973) have pointed out the equivalence of analysis of variance (ANOVA) and multiple regression (MR) and have advocated the use of the latter on grounds of greater flexibility. It is unfortunate that only a few researchers have indeed applied the MR approach and it is still the case that over 80% of the articles in psychological journals are employing the traditional ANOVA, even under circumstances where MR is the more appropriate tool at least in terms of flexibility and elegance. In the case of nonorthogonal designs it seems to the present author that the use of MR is almost unavoidable. The only treatment of unequal n's proposed within the traditional ANOVA is the so-called "unweighted means analysis" (see Glass & Stanley, 1970; Winer, 1971, for a description of the method). Despite its simplicity, this procedure is based on some strong assumptions and is to a great extent arbitrary. We will not discuss this procedure in any detail, and rather focus on the regression solutions to the problem of unequal n's. In one of the next sections we will briefly describe the use of MR as a substitute for the traditional ANOVA. The reader who is not sufficiently familiar with this approach is advised to consult a text like Cohen and Cohen (1975) Kerlinger and Pedhazur (1973), or Myers (1978). These texts provide excellent discussion and analysis of how to use MR for analyzing an experimental design

Possible Sources of Unequal Designs

An unbalanced design can occur for different reasons, and the decision as to how to treat a particular case should depend (among other things) on the reasons that have led to that particular design (Keren & Lewis, 1977). Let us consider a few examples:

1. An unbalanced design might reflect the experimenter's plan. Depending on the specific phenomena under examination, the researcher's interest, and limitations regarding collection of data, the experimenter may use more observations for certain cells, in order to gain precision in estimating the means of those cells. Notice that in this case the experimenter has control of determining the different cell frequencies. Often under such circumstances (though not necessarily) the experimenter might wish to construct a design with unequal but proportional cell frequencies. This case is the simplest to handle, because it is possible to maintain an orthogonal design by a procedure that is described in one of the following sections.

2. The experimenter might have sufficient evidence to assume that the population cells are not equal in size. Hence his unbalanced experimental design might simply reflect the state of affairs at the population level. It is important to note that an experimental design that is completely balanced (i.e., equal frequencies in all cells) actually assumes that the independent variables under investigation are orthogonal or uncorrelated. If on the other hand, the cell frequencies in the population are not equal, which implies that the variables are correlated (by virtue of different n's in different cells), then an orthogonal experimental design is not representative of the population. Following Humphreys and Fleishman (1974) such a design will be termed *pseudo-orthogonal*. Humphreys and Dachler (1969) and Humphreys and Fleishman (1974) have strongly advocated the use of sample sizes in different cells that would represent the population n's.

3. The unbalanced design might result from some randomly missing data (e.g., some subjects did not appear for the experiment or misunderstood the instructions and did not reply to all questions). The emphasis in this case is on the assumption that the missing observations result from a random process.

4. The unabalanced design might be a result of nonrandomly missing data, probably due to treatments (e.g., death of animals in a particular treatment, omission of responses to certain questions because they are embarrassing, etc.). Data might also be nonrandomly missing with respect to the dependent variable as, for example, reaction times that exceed a certain criterion might not be recorded.[1]

A basic assumption of the present chapter is that any unbalanced design will inherently be nonorthogonal. One has to keep in mind the nonexistence theorem stated by Cohen (1982), namely that there is *no* way to partition the Y variance unambiguously among two or more sets of *IV*s when the sets are nonorthogonal. The issue of nonorthogonal designs is therefore the following: Given the fact that we cannot get rid of nonorthogonality, what is the optimal way to treat non-orthogonal designs such that conceptually the interpretation of the analysis would be as similar as possible to the orthogonal case.[2] The answer to this question depends, according to the point of view presented in the present chapter, on the circumstances under which the unbalanced design occurred (some of which were mentioned earlier), and on the goals the researcher has set for himself.

The Regression Solution for the Balanced Design

For purposes of illustration and further comparisons, let us use the data presented in Table 4.1 which is adopted from Myers (1978, pp. 108–111). The data represent an experiment involving two independent variables, variable A with 2 levels, $i = 1, 2$ and variable B with 3 levels, $j = 1, 2, 3$. Each cell contains eight observations and thus we are dealing with a balanced or an equal n's design. The traditional analysis of this design by using ANOVA is presented by Myers, and the reader who is not sure that he is familiar with this solution should consult Myers (1978) who provides a detailed explanation. Here, we would like to present one (out of many) possible analysis that utilizes a least square regression method.

The first step in such an analysis involves a coding method that will specify the different treatment classifications and interactions. It is important to remember that there are many possible coding methods (see Cohen & Cohen, 1975, chap. 5, or Kerlinger & Pedhazur, 1973, chap. 7), each of which is carrying different implicit assumptions (Keren & Lewis, 1977). In the present example we

---

[1]We are referring here to what are usually called "outliers." Some possible ways of how to deal with outliers are discussed by H. Wainer (1982) in his chapter on robust statistics.

[2]In the orthogonal case the partitioning of variance is unambiguous and there is no overlapping variance for different sources. Hence the interpretation of significance tests and variance accounted for by different effects is straightforward in this respect.

TABLE 4.1
Raw Data for a Two-Way Design with Equal n's†

	A_1B_1		A_1B_2		A_1B_3
	7		6		9
	33		11		12
	26		11		6
G1	27	G3	18	G5	24
	21		14		7
	6		18		10
	14		19		1
	19		14		10
	153		111		79
	A_2B_1		A_2B_2		A_2B_3
	42		28		13
	25		6		18
	8		1		23
G2	28	G4	15	G6	1
	30		9		3
	22		15		4
	17		2		6
	32		37		2
	204		113		70

†This example is adopted from Myers (pp. 108–111).
The traditional solution of ANOVA is given there in detail
and will not be repeated here.

will use the 1, 0, −1 coding—often called *effect coding*—and defer the more
general discussion on coding for a later section.

Consider the familiar ANOVA model for the two-way case with interaction
where each observation is expressed as

$$Y = \mu + \alpha_i + \beta_j + \alpha\beta_{ij} + \epsilon_{ijk} \tag{1}$$

where μ is the grand mean, α_i are deviations of row means about μ, β_j are
deviations of column means about μ, $\alpha\beta_{ij}$ are deviations of cell means about row
and column effects (interactions), and ϵ_{ijk} is a random error distributed normally
with a mean zero and variance σ^2. Customary ANOVA restrictions on the parameters require that

$$\sum_i \alpha_i = \sum_j \beta_j = \sum_i \alpha\beta_{ij} = \sum_j \alpha\beta_{ij} = 0 \tag{1}$$

which implies $a - 1$ degrees of freedom available for variable A, $b - 1$ degrees
of freedom for variable B and $(a - 1)(b - 1)$ for the interaction AB.

We may now employ the effect coding method for estimating the previous
parameters by constructing a design matrix that will incorporate the restrictions

in Equation 2. The design matrix is formed to include $a - 1$ columns representing the first $a - 1$ levels of variable A, $b - 1$ columns for variable B, and $(a - 1)(b - 1)$ columns for the interaction. The last column is the dependent variable Y. Hence, each observation is coded according to the cell it belongs to in the following way: For a given level A_i a column is constructed such that each observation that belongs to this level is assigned a 1, and all other observations are assigned a 0 except observations belonging to the last level on A, which are assigned a -1.[3] In the same manner $b - 1$ columns are constructed for variable B, and $(a - 1)(b - 1)$ columns for the interaction. The interaction columns can be simply obtained as products of entries in the corresponding main effect columns. Notice that each column represents one degree of freedom for rows, columns, or interactions.

Applying this coding method to the data in Table 4.1 yields the design matrix which is presented in Table 4.2. The first five columns are categorical variables obtained from the coding of the independent variables, and the last column contains the scores of the actual observations, that is, the dependent variable. Based on the design matrix a correlation matrix is calculated. For our data this correlation matrix is presented in Table 4.3. Note that all the correlations among the different independent variables are zero, which is a basic requirement of ANOVA and is referred to as orthogonality. In our example levels B_1 and B_2, as well as AB_1 and AB_2 are correlated, but this fact is of no importance because it does not violate the ANOVA assumptions. Orthogonality only implies that the different independent variables be uncorrelated, not that levels within a given variable be uncorrelated. The last row (or column) contains the correlations between each of the categorical (independent) variables and the criterion (the dependent variable).

If all the coded vectors in the design matrix are completely uncorrelated (orthogonal), we can proceed by squaring the zero-order correlations of each coded vector with the dependent variable Y, which will indicate the proportion of variance, or the relative sum of squares, explained by that vector. To obtain the proportion of variance due to a given factor (independent variable) we would simply have to sum the proportions of variance accounted for by all the vectors which represent this factor. In our example, however, the vectors within both factor B and the interaction are correlated, which indicates that they are not orthogonal (again, they are not orthogonal within the factor, but are orthogonal to all vectors of other factors). Instead of adding the squared correlations for each vector, one may estimate the contribution (or proportion of variance) of each factor by calculating the multiple R^2 with any number of vectors (representing a given factor) as parameters in the model. The square of the multiple correlation

---

[3]The "last" level has no special significance and can be determined arbitrarily, but once chosen, all the variables (corresponding to the different levels) have to be constructed with the same "last" variable.

TABLE 4.2
Design Matrix Using Overall and Spiegel's Method

		A_1	B_1	B_2	A_1B_1	A_1B_2	Y†
(A_1B_1)	G1	1	1	0	1	0	•
(A_2B_1)	G2	−1	1	0	−1	0	•
(A_1B_2)	G3	1	0	1	0	1	•
(A_2B_2)	G4	−1	0	1	0	−1	•
(A_1B_3)	G5	1	−1	−1	−1	−1	•
(A_2B_3)	G6	−1	−1	−1	1	1	•

†A score is given for each individual (i.e., there are eight rows for (A_1B_1), eight rows for (A_2B_1), and so forth).

coefficient will represent the proportion of variance or sum of squares that is accounted for by the set of vectors.

By choosing each time a different set of vectors and by computing for each case the multiple R^2 for relating the criterion to these vectors (independent variables) we obtain the following results for our example:

$$R^2(\alpha_i) = .00809$$

$$R^2(\beta_j) = .27808$$

$$R^2(\alpha_i, \alpha\beta_{ij}) = .03366$$

$$R^2(\beta_j, \alpha\beta_{ij}) = .30364$$

$$R^2(\alpha_i, \beta_j) = .28617$$

$$R^2(\alpha\beta_{ij}) = .02557$$

$$R^2(\alpha_i, \beta_j, \alpha\beta_{ij}) = .31173$$

where $R^2(\alpha_i)$ is the multiple R^2 when only variable A is used as a predictor in equation (1), $R^2(\alpha_i, \alpha\beta_{ij})$ is the multiple R^2 when variable A and the interaction AB are used as predictors in Equation 1 and so forth.

As was noted by Overall and Spiegel (1969):

TABLE 4.3
Correlation Matrix for the Data Presented in Table 4.1

	A_1	B_1	B_2	A_1B_1	A_1B_2	Y
A_1	100					
B_1	0	1.00				
B_2	0	.50	1.00			
A_1B_1	0	0	0	1.00		
A_1B_2	0	0	0	.50	1.00	
Y	.0899	.5206	.1877	−.1502	−.0275	1.00

The square of the multiple correlation coefficient realting a criterion measure to several independent variates represents the proportion of the total sum of squares for the criterion that can be accounted for by regression on the set of independent variates. The independent contribution of each subset of independent variates (say α_i, $i = 1, 2 \ldots a - 1$) can be estimated by calculating the multiple R^2 with the α_i parameters disregarded. Similarly for β_j and $\alpha\beta_{ij}$ effects. (p. 315)

However, for the identity with ANOVA, the subsets must be orthogonal, and hence satisfy the following conditions in order to avoid overlapping variance:

$$R^2(\alpha_i, \beta_j, \alpha\beta_{ij}) = R^2(\alpha_i) + R^2(\beta_j) + R^2(\alpha\beta_{ij})$$
$$R^2(\alpha_i, \alpha\beta_{ij}) = R^2(\alpha_i) + R^2(\alpha\beta_{ij})$$
$$R^2(\beta_j, \alpha\beta_{ij}) = R^2(\beta_j) + R^2(\alpha\beta_{ij})$$
$$R(\alpha_i, \beta_j) = R^2(\alpha_i) + R + (\beta_j) \tag{3}$$

The reader can verity that the multiple R^2's computed for our example indeed satisfy these requirements.

Because the multiple R^2 can be interpreted as the amount of variance accounted for by the predictors that have been related to the criterion, we can now use the SS_T that is usually derived in ANOVA, and slice it into pieces according to the relative weight of each variable as dictated by the appropriate R^2.

The sum of squares total in our example is

$$SS_T = \sum_i^n \sum_j^a \sum_k^b Y^2 - \frac{(\sum_i^n \sum_j^a \sum_k^b Y)^2}{nab} = 4987.92 \tag{4}$$

The final question now is how to calculate the SS for each independent variable and the interaction, and it is indeed this question which is highly controversial.

Following Overall and Spiegel (1969) there are three different methods by which the SS for each variable can be calculated.

The *complete linear model analysis* (or method I in Overall & Spiegel) considers the independent effects of each factor in the context of the full model. The SS for our particular example, using this method, are as follows:

Source	df	SS
A	$a - 1 = 1$	$SS_T[R^2(\alpha_i,\beta_j,\alpha\beta_{ij}) - R^2(\beta_j,\alpha\beta_{ij})] =$ $(4987.92)(.31173 - .30364) = 40.35$
B	$b - 1 = 2$	$SS_T[R^2(\alpha_i,\beta_j,\alpha\beta_{ij}) - R^2(\alpha_i,\alpha\beta_{ij})] =$ $(4987.92)(.31173 - .03366) = 1386.99$
AB	$(a - 1)(b - 1) = 2$	$SS_T[R^2(\alpha_i,\beta_j,\alpha\beta_{ij}) - R^2(\alpha_i,\beta_j)] =$ $(4987.92)(.31173 - .28617) = 127.49$
Error	$N - ab = 42$	$SS_T[1 - R^2(\alpha_i,\beta_j,\alpha\beta_{ij})] =$ $(4987.92)(1 - .31173) = 3433.04$

An alternative approach to obtain the different SS is by the *experimenta* *design analysis* (method II of Overall & Spiegel). The main effects under thi method are obtained by:

Source	df	SS
A	$a - 1 = 1$	$SS_T[R^2(\alpha_i, \beta_j) - R^2(\beta_j)] =$ $(4987.92)(.28617 - .27808) = 40.35$
B	$b - 1 = 2$	$SS_T[R^2(\alpha_i, \beta_j) - R^2(\alpha_i)] =$ $(4987.92)(.28617 - .00809) = 1387.04$

The SS for interaction and the error term are calculated in the same way as i method I.

Finally, one can calculate the SS by using the *step down analysis* (method III) This procedure entails an initial ordering, followed by estimating each effec adjusted for those preceding it and ignoring those following it. Using our exam ple, the procedure is as follows:

Source	df	SS
A	$a - 1 = 1$	$SS_T[R^2(\alpha_i)] = (4987.92)(.00809) = 40.35$
B	$b - 1 = 2$	$SS_T[R^2(\alpha_i, \beta_j) - R^2(\alpha_i)] =$ $(4987.92)(.27808) = 1387.04$

Again, the SS for interaction and error are derived as in methods II & III.

The reader should notice that the SS for the different effects obtained by th three methods are identical (except for rounding error). This is actually a result o the conditions required in Equation 3. In the case of unequal and nonproportiona cell frequencies the requirements in Equation 3 are not met and as a result th three different methods will yield different values of the SS for the variou effects. After the SS have been obtained (by any of the three methods) th analysis proceeds as in the traditional ANOVA by calculating the MS for th different effects (and error term) and conducting the appropriate F tests.

The Case of Unequal But Proportional Cell Frequencies[4]

We now depart from the assumption of equal n's that has been used in th previous section. The case of unequal but proportional cell frequencies is deal with first because it is the simplest case and a noncontroversial one.

For purposes of demonstration we use the same data presented in Table 4.

---

[4]Parts of this section are based on an unpublished manuscript entitled "Least squares analysis fc proportional cell frequencies design," 1973, by G. Keren and C. Lewis.

except that some observations have been randomly eliminated. In case I we randomly eliminated two observations from each cell in level 2 of variable A. In case II one observation was eliminated from each cell in level $B2$ and two observations from each cell in level $B3$. Thus we have produced two sets of data with unequal but proportional cell frequencies that are presented in Table 4.4. In general, cell sizes are said to be proportional whenever

$$n_{ij} = (n_{i.})(n_{.j})/N \qquad (5)$$

where $n_{i.}$ is the sum of the cell sizes for the ith level of variable A, $n_{.j}$ is the sum of the cell sizes for the jth level of variable B, and N is the total number of observations in the design.

Let us first apply Overall and Spiegel's (1969) coding system and the three methods which were discussed in the previous section. The analysis is performed on both sets of data in Table 4.4. The design matrix for both cases is actually the same as the one presented in Table 4.2 except that some observations have been eliminated from certain conditions. Overall and Spiegel's method is based only on group membership and is independent of the size of cell frequencies. This is a crucial point, because (as will be shown later in the case of proportional n's) a design matrix which will produce orthogonal factors is dependent upon the relative sizes of the n's.

TABLE 4.4
Two Cases of Unequal But Proportional Cell Frequencies

	Case I				Case II		
	A_1B_1	A_1B_2	A_1B_3		A_1B_1	A_1B_2	A_1B_3
	7	6	9		7	6	9
	33	11	12		33	11	12
	26	11	6		26	11	6
G1	27	18 (G3)	24 (G5)	G1	27	18 (G3)	7 (G5)
	21	14	7		21	18	10
	6	18	10		6	19	1
	14	19	1		14	14	
	19	14	10		19		
	153	111	79		153	97	45

	A_2B_1	A_2B_2	A_2B_3		A_2B_1	A_2B_2	A_2B_3
	42	6	13		42	15	13
	25	1	1		25	6	1
	8	9	3		8	1	3
G2	30	15 (G4)	4 (G6)	G2	28	9 (G4)	4 (G6)
	22	2	6		30	15	6
	17	37	2		22	2	2
	144	70	29		17	37	29
					32		
					204	85	29

TABLE 4.5
Correlation Matrix Using Overall and Spiegel's Coding Method
For Two Cases of Unequal but Proportional Cell Frequencies
(non-zero correlations between variables have been underlined)

	A_1	B_1	B_2	A_1B_1	A_1B_2	Y
			Case I			
A_1	1.000					
B_1	0	1.000				
B_2	0	.500	1.000			
A_1B_1	0	.143	.071	1.000		
A_1B_2	0	.071	.143	.500	1.000	
Y	.039	.548	.212	−.119	−.026	1.000
			Case II			
	A_1	B_1	B_2	A_1B_1	A_1B_2	Y
A_1	1.000					
B_1	0	1.000				
B_2	0	.441	1.000			
A_1B_1	.116	0	0	1.000		
A_1B_2	.061	0	0	.445	1.000	
Y	−.052	.620	.227	−.186	−.016	1.000

Using the above coding system, the correlation matrix for each case was computed and the results are presented in Table 4.5. It is important to notice that the main effects and interaction are not uncorrelated. Unlike the case in the previous section, we have now obtained nonzero correlations both within and between the different variables, which is in violation of the requirements for orthogonality.

We also computed for both cases the different multiple R^2 values:

	Case I	Case II
$R^2(\alpha_i, \beta_j, \alpha\beta_{ij})$	.34947	.43817
$R^2(\alpha_i, \alpha\beta_{ij})$	.30579	.04190
$R^2(\beta_j, \alpha\beta_{ij})$	.34795	.43819
$R^2(\alpha_i, \beta_j)$	.01715	.39999
$R^2(\alpha\beta_{ij})$	.01563	.04090
$R^2(\alpha_i)$	.00152	.00272
$R^2(\beta_j)$	.30731	.39728

The reader can verify that the multiple correlations obtained by the 1, 0, −1 coding method will not necessarily satisfy the requirements for orthogonality stated in (3).

Table 4.6 presents the SS obtained by traditional ANOVA and by the three least squares methods based on the above coding. By now, the reader would not be surprised to find out that not all the results obtained by the three methods are

TABLE 4.6
SS Obtained by ANOVA and the Three Least Squares Methods

Source	ANOVA	Case I Method 1	Method 2	Method 3
A	6.44	6.45	6.45	6.45
B	1297.76	1410.33	1297.74	1297.74
AB	178.90	178.92	178.92	178.92
Error	2760.80	2760.78	2760.78	2760.78
(Sum)	4243.90	4356.48	4243.89	4243.89
Total	4243.90	4243.90	4243.90	4243.90

Source	ANOVA	Case II Method 1	Method 2	Method 3
A	12.60	4.54	12.56	12.56
B	1841.01	1840.99	1840.99	1840.99
AB	181.57	181.56	181.56	181.56
Error	2598.94	2598.95	2598.95	2598.95
(Sum)	4634.12	4626.04	4634.06	4634.95
Total	4634.12	4634.12	4634.12	4634.12

identical with those of ANOVA. Specifically, as Overall and Spiegel (1969, p. 317) observed, it is method I which differs from the others in both cases. In general any deviation from orthogonality will yield nonidentical results for the traditional ANOVA and the three least squares methods.

There is a procedure which will always maintain the requirement of orthogonality for the case of equal or proportional n's. This procedure simply employs an alternative coding system that makes explicit use of the proportionality of the sample sizes. The method is described in this section in brief and is applied to our example.[5] The reader who is interested in a detailed description of how the method has been derived as well as proof that it will always satisfy the orthogonality requirements is referred to Appendix A.

We start by constructing our design matrix as follows: As in the equal n's case a vector is assigned to each level of a variable (except the last level) and will be denoted with an * in order to be distinguished from the former case. Constructing A_1^*, for example, each observation at level i of factor A is assigned the score $(N - n_i.)$ whereas all other observations have a score of $-n_i.$. In our example (Table 4.4, case I), $n_1. = 24$ and $n_2. = 18$. Hence, vector A_1^* is constructed such that each observation from level A_1 is assigned $N - n_1. = 42 - 24 = 18$ and all observations from level A_2 are assigned $-n_1. = -24$. The B_j^* vectors are similarly constructed by assigning a score of $(N - n_{.j})$ to each observation belonging

---

[5]Gocka (1973) has proposed a coding method for proportional n's that also takes into account cell sizes. The approach presented here is similar to Gocka's but is believed to be more general.

to level j of factor B and $-n_{\cdot j}$ to all other scores. Using our example again, $n_{\cdot 1} = n_{\cdot 2} = n_{\cdot 3} = 14$. To construct B_1^* each observation belonging to level B_1 is assigned $N - n_{\cdot 1} = 42 - 14 = 28$ and all other observations are assigned $-n_{\cdot 1} = -14$. Vector β_2^* is constructed in a similar manner.

Finally, to construct the interaction vectors, each observation in cell ij is assigned $N + n_{ij} - Nn_{ij}\left(\dfrac{1}{n_{i\cdot}} + \dfrac{1}{n_{\cdot j}}\right)$. All other observations in row i are assigned $n_{ij} - \dfrac{Nn_{ij}}{n_{i\cdot}}$ and all other observations in column j are assigned $n_{ij} - \dfrac{Nn_{ij}}{n_{\cdot j}}$. The remaining observations are assigned n_{ij}. Returning to our example, and constructing vector $A_1B_1^*$ (for case I), each observation in cell A_1B_1 is assigned $N + n_{ij} - Nn_{ij}\left(\dfrac{1}{n_{i\cdot}} + \dfrac{1}{n_{\cdot j}}\right) = 42 + 8 - (42)(8)\left(\dfrac{1}{24} + \dfrac{1}{14}\right) = 12$. All other observations from level A_1 (i.e., A_1B_2, A_1B_3) receive a score of $n_{ij} - \dfrac{Nn_{ij}}{n_{i\cdot}} = 8 - \dfrac{(42)(8)}{24} = -6$. All other observations from level B_1 (i.e., A_2B_1) are assigned $n_{ij} - \dfrac{Nn_{ij}}{n_{\cdot j}} = 8 - \dfrac{(42)(8)}{14} = -16$. All remaining cells are assigned $n_{ij} = 8$.

The design matrices of the proposed coding method for both case I and case II of our example (see Table 4.4) are presented in Table 4.7, and the corresponding correlation matrices are presented in Table 4.8. Note that the vectors of the

TABLE 4.7
Design Matrix for Case I and II Using the Proposed System

	n	$A_1{}^*$	$B_1{}^*$	$B_2{}^*$	$AB_{11}{}^*$	$AB_{12}{}^*$	Y†
				Case I			
(A_1B_1)	8	18	28	−14	12	−6	–
(A_2B_1)	6	−24	28	−14	−16	8	–
(A_1B_2)	8	18	−14	28	−6	12	–
(A_2B_2)	6	−24	−14	28	8	−16	–
(A_1B_3)	8	18	−14	−14	−6	−6	–
(A_2B_3)	6	−24	−14	−14	8	8	–

	n	$A_1{}^*$	$B_1{}^*$	$B_2{}^*$	$AB_{11}{}^*$	$AB_{12}{}^*$	Y†
				Case II			
(A_1B_1)	8	21	26	−14	13	−7	–
(A_2B_1)	8	−21	26	−14	−13	7	–
(A_1B_2)	7	21	−16	28	−8	14	–
(A_2B_2)	7	−21	−16	28	8	−14	–
(A_1B_3)	6	21	−16	−14	−8	−7	–
(A_2B_3)	6	−21	−16	−14	8	7	–

†A score is given for each individual. The number of scores for each cell is indicated by the first column (n).

TABLE 4.8
Correlation Matrices for Unequal but Proportional Cell Frequencies
Using the New Coding System

			Case I		
1.000					
0	1.000				
0	−.500	1.000			
0	0	0	1.000		
0	0	0	−.500	1.000	
.039	.511	.072	−.197	.049	1.000

			Case II		
1.000					
0	1.000				
0	−.555	1.000			
0	0	0	1.000		
0	0	0	−.555	1.000	
−.052	.576	−.107	−.197	−.095	1.000

different effects in Table 4.7 are uncorrelated. For example, to check if vectors A_1^* and AB_{11}^* are correlated we calculate the product of these two vectors weighted by the appropriate cell frequencies. Thus $8(18)(12) + 6(-24)(-16) + 8(18)(-6) + 6(-24)(8) + 8(18)(-6) + 6(-24)(8) = 0$.

The reader can verify by himself that by using the method any pair of vectors (not from the same effect) is uncorrelated. Consequently, the different factors are uncorrelated, as indicated in Table 4.8.

As a last step, the multiple correlations of the different variables based on the new coding system are calculated:

	Case I	Case II
$R^2(\alpha_i, \beta_j, \alpha\beta_{ij})$	.34947	.43917
$R^2(\alpha_i, \alpha\beta_{ij})$	.04367	.04180
$R^2(\beta_j, \alpha\beta_{ij})$	.34795	.43650
$R^2(\alpha_i, \beta_j)$	.30732	.39999
$R^2(\alpha\beta_{ij})$	.04216	.03918
$R^2(\alpha_i)$	.00152	.00272
$R^2(\beta_j)$	.30580	.39728

It can be readily verified that these multiple correlations satisfy the requirements of Equation 3.

In the present section we have shown that by using a certain coding system the unequal but proportional cell frequencies case can be reduced to an orthogonal design. It should be emphasized, again, that the coding system that we have introduced is only one of many that may be appropriate. Gocka (1973) has presented a somewhat different coding system that also yields an orthogonal design for the proportional case, and yet another alternative method (Keren & Lewis, 1976) is presented in a later section. The common denominator to all of these coding methods is that they make explicit use of the proportionality of sample sizes which is a necessary requirement to achieve orthogonality. The question of how to interpret the results given a particular coding method is discussed in the next section.

Unequal Disproportionate Cell Frequencies

We are now ready to discuss the more general (and probably more frequent) case of unequal n's when cell frequencies are not necessarily proportional. The reader is probably convinced by now that the three different methods (Overall & Spiegel, 1969) are not going to yield the same results in the case of unequal and nonproportional cell frequencies. As was shown in the previous section, even for proportional n's the 1, 0, -1 coding method does not necessarily yield an orthogonal design, a conclusion which will still be valid if we eliminate the proportionality assumption. The alternative coding system proposed earlier was designed particularly for the case of proportional n's. However, when cell frequencies are unequal and disproportionate, there is no single coding method that will lead to an orthogonal design matrix. In other words, any unbalanced design will inherently be nonorthogonal.

Two different approaches to the problem have emerged in the recent literature. One (following Overall & Spiegel, 1969; Overall, Spiegel, & Cohen, 1975) was mainly concerned with the problem of orthogonality. Implicitly, these authors have correctly realized that for nonorthogonal designs there is no single "correct" and unambiguous partitioning of the Y variance. Consequently, they suggested that the three methods that were previously discussed should be interpreted differently and be applied in different situations. The question of which method is preferable and under what conditions has been debated in the recent literature (Bogartz, 1975; Howell & McConaughy, 1982; Joe, 1971; Rawlings, 1972, 1973; Wolf & Cartwright, 1974; and others) and has often caused confusion. It will be shown briefly that these three methods are simply testing different hypotheses. In addition, it will be argued that the three methods are not necessarily exhaustive, and other meaningful hypotheses can be stated that should be treated differently.

An alternative approach has been suggested by Appelbaum and Cramer (1974), which treats the analysis of variance (both orthogonal and nonorthogonal) as a series of model comparisons. This procedure tries to find the best fitting model to the data at hand, and the question of whether the design is balanced or not becomes a secondary issue. For a closer look at the model comparison approach, consider a two-way fixed-effects design. There are several competing models that may describe the population cell means μ_{ij}:

1. $\mu_{ij} = \mu$
2. $\mu_{ij} = \mu + \alpha_i$
3. $\mu_{ij} = \mu + \beta_j$
4. $\mu_{ij} = \mu + \alpha_i + \beta_j$
5. $\mu_{ij} = \mu + \alpha\beta_{ij}$
6. $\mu_{ij} = \mu + \alpha_i + \alpha\beta_{ij}$
7. $\mu_{ij} = \mu + \beta_j + \alpha\beta_{ij}$
8. $\mu_{ij} = \mu + \alpha_i + \beta_j + \alpha\beta_{ij}$

Model 8, which is the most complete model, contains the main effect $A(\alpha_i)$, the main effect $B(\beta_j)$ and the interaction $AB_{ij}(\alpha\beta_{ij})$. The other models are derived from model 8 by dropping either main effect or the interaction or any combination of them. The model comparison procedure involves comparing the fit of one model relative to a second model, where one or more effects have been omitted from the latter.

For model comparisons, we may utilize the general linear model theory (Scheffé, 1959). For comparing any two models Ω and ω, we use

$$F = \left[\frac{df(\Omega)}{df(\omega - \Omega)} \right] \left[\frac{SS_e(\omega) - SS_e(\Omega)}{SS_e(\Omega)} \right] \tag{6}$$

where ω is always the more restricted model (i.e., with less parameters than Ω), $SS_e(\omega)$ and $SS_e(\Omega)$ are the residual sum of squares for ω and Ω, respectively, and $df(\omega - \Omega)$ and $df(\Omega)$ are the appropriate degrees of freedom for the numerator and denominator, respectively. Note that Equation 6 can be easily translated into the terminology of Overall and Spiegel (1969) which was described earlier. Because

$$SS_e(\omega) = SS_T[1 - R^2(\omega)] \tag{7}$$

and

$$SS_e(\Omega) = SS_T[1 - R^2(\Omega)] \tag{8}$$

where $R^2(\Omega)$ and $R^2(\omega)$ are the multiple R^2s for regression of the dependent variable on the two models respectively, and SS_T is the total sum of squares, we can substitute the expressions of $SS_e(\omega)$ and $SS_e(\Omega)$ in Equation 6 and by rearranging, we obtain

$$F = \frac{df(\Omega)}{df(\omega - \Omega)} \frac{R^2(\Omega) - R^2(\omega)}{1 - R^2(\Omega)} \tag{9}$$

As will be pointed out shortly, the three methods proposed by Overall and Spiegel can readily be expressed in terms of model comparisons (see Herr & Gaebelein, 1978; Lewis & Keren, 1977).

To further illustrate model comparisons, consider the following hypothetical

TABLE 4.9
Cell Means and Weights
for a Hypothetical 2 × 3 Design

	Cell Means μ_{ij}		
	B_1	B_2	B_3
A_1	60	120	180
A_2	240	240	240

	Weights ω_{ij}			
	B_1	B_2	B_3	$\omega_{i\cdot}$
A_1	.1	.1	.3	.5
A_2	.3	.1	.1	.5
$\omega_{\cdot j}$	.4	.2	.4	

example of a 2 × 3 design. Cell means (μ_{ij}) and cell weights (ω_{ij}) are provided in Table 4.9. We now proceed with a detailed analysis of the different tests one may consider. Starting with the case of testing a null hypothesis for the main effect A

$$H: \alpha_i = 0 \text{ (under the restriction } \Sigma\alpha_i = 0)$$

Several model comparisons can be made, each implying different assumptions and consequently testing somewhat different hypotheses (Herr & Gaebelein 1978). Specifically, to test the above hypothesis, one may compare models 1–2 3–4, and 7–8.

The comparison of models 7–8 actually assumes that model 8 holds and is thus a test of model 7 (i.e., a test of the hypothesis that model 7 fits the population). This corresponds exactly to method I of Overall and Spiegel (1969) and the appropriate F ratio is

$$F = \frac{N - ab}{a - 1} \times \frac{R^2(\alpha_i, \beta_j, \alpha\beta_{ij}) - R^2(\beta_j, \alpha\beta_{ij})}{1 - R^2(\alpha_i, \beta_j, \alpha\beta_{ij})} \quad (10)$$

Note that both models 7 and 8 contain the main effect B and an interaction term. Following the terminology of Appelbaum and Cramer, this kind of test will be termed "*A eliminating B and AB.*" By eliminating it is meant that out test takes into account and eliminates the confounding effects of other factors when they are present.

The comparison of models 7 and 8 implies that we are testing the hypothesis of equality of unweighted means:

$$H: \mu_1. = \mu_2.$$

where $\mu_1.$ stands for the *unweighted* means of each row (i.e., cell means are treated equally regardless of cell sizes). In our example

$$\mu_1. = \frac{60 + 120 + 180}{3} = 120$$

$$\mu_{2\cdot} = \frac{240 + 240 + 240}{3} = 240$$

The second possible comparison is that between models 3 and 4. Because both models do not contain an interaction term (but do contain a B effect), we will refer to it as "*A eliminating B and ignoring AB.*" Ignoring is meant here literally: An ignored factor is assumed to be nonexistent.[6] An important point to note is that following Scheffé (1959), the comparison here amounts to assuming that model 4 holds and is thus a test of model 3. The assumption that model 4 holds implies that we assume all $\alpha\beta_{ij} = 0$. Consequently, the error term for the F test should result from pooling the within cell and interaction terms (Lewis & Keren, 1977), a point that has been neglected by several researchers. The appropriate F ratio is

$$F = \frac{N - a - b + 1}{a - 1} \; \frac{R^2(\alpha_i, \beta_j) - R^2(\beta_j)}{1 - R^2(\alpha\beta_{ij}, \beta_j)} \tag{11}$$

This test is what Overall and Spiegel termed method II except that they did not pool the error term on grounds of conservatism (Overall & Spiegel, 1973). As pointed out previously, the question is not whether one is conservative or not, but rather what assumptions are implied by a certain test. Comparing models 3 and 4 implies the assumption of all $\alpha\beta_{ij} = 0$, which in turn implies that one should pool the error term. For a more elaborate discussion on the pooling problem, the reader is referred to Lewis and Keren (1977).

The hypothesis for this comparison is more complex and difficult to describe. It is actually testing whether or not a row effect explains a significant amount of variability in the presence of, or adjusting for, column effects and ignoring interactions (Herr & Gaebelein, 1978). Carlson and Timm (1974) show that this hypothesis is equivalent to testing:

$$H: \left(n_{11} - \frac{n^2_{11}}{n_{\cdot 1}}\right) \mu_{11} + \left(n_{12} - \frac{n^2_{12}}{n_{\cdot 2}}\right) \mu_{12} + \left(n_{13} - \frac{n^2_{13}}{n_{\cdot 3}}\right) \mu_{13}$$

$$- \frac{n_{11}n_{21}}{n_{\cdot 1}} \mu_{21} - \frac{n_{12}n_{22}}{n_{\cdot 2}} \mu_{22} - \frac{n_{13}n_{23}}{n_{\cdot 3}} \mu_{23} = 0$$

They also argue that this is a peculiar hypothesis that a researcher rarely would be interested in testing. Indeed, the hypothesis as stated by Carlson and Timm is a complex one and does not provide a readily intuitive interpretation, a claim that has been further echoed by Howell et al. (1982). However, in terms of model comparisons it is clearly a sensible test which may often be of interest. Herr and

---

[6] "*A ignoring B*" indicates the nonexistence of factor *B* and normally the nonexistence of interaction as well. Consequently, one may "ignore interaction and eliminate *B*" but usually not ignore *B* and eliminate interaction." When cell frequencies are proportional $\left(\text{i.e., } n_{ij} = \frac{n_{i\cdot}n_{\cdot j}}{N}\right)$ independence between rows and columns is guaranteed and consequently in this case there is no difference between eliminating and ignoring.

Gaebelein (1978) have stated: "The model-comparison approach is a regression-oriented view of the problem, whereas the parametric hypothesis approach is an effect-oriented view of the problem" (p. 209). It is important to emphasize, however, that these two views are not independent. At any rate, the regression point of view seems to be preferable if just for the fact that model comparisons are more meaningful compared to a parametric-hypothesis approach that may yield certain tests which, on the surface, may look peculiar though they are not necessarily so. Also, as pointed out by Howell et al. (1982), if there is sufficient reason to believe that there are no interactions, the hypothesis becomes meaningful.

Using again the data of Table 4.9 (and assuming that weights reflect cell frequencies with a total of 100), this hypothesis is testing whether the row of the weighted column averages, equals to the simple weighted average of the first row. The simple weighted average of row 1 is

$$\mu_1^* = \frac{10}{50}\,60 + \frac{10}{50}\,120 + \frac{30}{50}\,180 = 144$$

To calculate the other mean, one has first to establish the weighted mean of each column:

$$\mu_{\cdot 1} = \frac{10}{40}\,60 + \frac{30}{40}\,240 = 195$$

$$\mu_{\cdot 2} = \frac{10}{20}\,120 + \frac{10}{20}\,240 = 180$$

$$\mu_{\cdot 3} = \frac{30}{40}\,180 + \frac{10}{40}\,240 = 195$$

and then get the mean of the column weighted means, weighted by the corresponding weights from the first row (the same ones used to obtain μ_1^*.). Because weighted column means are used we designate this mean as $\mu_{1\cdot(q)}^*$

$$\mu_{1\cdot(q)}^* = \frac{10}{50}\,195 + \frac{10}{50}\,180 + \frac{30}{50}\,195 = 192$$

Finally, one may want to compare models 1 and 2, which is the case of "*ignoring both B and AB.*" Again, following Scheffé (1959), the assumption here is that model 2 holds and model 1 is being tested. Since model 2 assumes that both all $\beta_j = 0$ and all $\alpha\beta_{ij} = 0$, the error term in this case should be a pooling of three terms—namely, the within cell, the interaction effect, and the main effect of B eliminating A. Consequently, the F ratio for this test will be

$$F = \frac{N - a}{a - 1}\,\frac{R^2(\alpha_i) - 0}{1 - R^2(\alpha_i)} \tag{12}$$

which is method III of Overall and Spiegel except for the change in the error term that has been discussed previously.

The test corresponding to the comparison of models 1 and 2 is

$$H: \mu_1^* = \mu_2^*.$$

where μ_i^* stands for the weighted means of each row (weighted by the corresponding cell frequencies of each row). In our example, suppose again that weights in Table 4.9 reflect cell frequencies with a total of 100. Then

$$\mu_1^* = \left(\frac{10}{50}\right) 60 + \left(\frac{10}{50}\right) 120 + \left(\frac{30}{50}\right) 180 = 144$$

$$\mu_2^* = \left(\frac{30}{50}\right) 240 + \left(\frac{10}{50}\right) 240 + \left(\frac{10}{50}\right) 240 = 240$$

It is important to emphasize that the choice of models to be compared and the nature of the means (i.e., weighted, unweighted, etc.) that are tested for equality are not independent questions. In fact, the choice of models to be compared determines the nature of the weighting of the means as reflected in the estimate (Blair & Higgins, 1978). The notion that these two aspects can be determined independently as suggested, for example, by Herr and Gaebelien (1978) is unjustified. Thus parameters are estimated by equations that include the sample size, and these estimates depend on the choice of model.

To test the effect of factor B one may compare models 1–3, 2–4, or 6–8. The analysis and interpretations of these three different comparisons are similar to the corresponding comparisons for factor A which were discussed previously. Whichever test is used for A does not necessarily imply that the same test has to be applied for B. For example, one might test "A eliminating B and ignoring AB" (i.e., test $\mu_1^* = \mu_2^*$). That is to say, the nature of the hypothesis regarding factor A and B is not necessarily dependent, and one might have sufficient reasons to test somewhat different hypotheses for A and B.

To test for interaction, the possible comparisons are between models 1–5, 2–6, 3–7 and 4–8. The comparisons of models 1–5 ignore both main effects, whereas comparisons of 2–6 and 3–7 ignore one main effect and eliminate the other. These comparisons would seldom be used because under normal circumstances one would not wish to ignore main effects when testing for interaction.

The most likely comparison for testing the interaction null hypothesis

$$H: \alpha\beta_{ij} = 0 \quad \text{(with the restriction } \sum_i \alpha\beta_{ij} = \sum_j \alpha\beta_{ij} = 0\text{)}$$

is that between models 4 and 8. There is no disagreement among different researchers concerning the test of interaction. Indeed, Overall and Spiegel (1969) have proposed this test for all their three methods, and the same test is also given by Appelbaum and Cramer (1974). The F ratio for this test is

$$F = \frac{N - ab}{(a - 1)(b - 1)} \cdot \frac{R^2(\alpha_i,\beta_j,\alpha\beta_{ij}) - R^2(\alpha_i,\beta_j)}{1 - R^2(\alpha_i,\beta_j,\alpha\beta_{ij})} \qquad (13)$$

Clearly, there is no pooling in this case and the error term is simply the mean square within cells. As mentioned by Appelbaum and Cramer (1974), Herr and Gaebelein (1978), Keren and Lewis (1976), and others, one should always begin the analysis by test of interaction (i.e., comparing models 4 and 8). There are several reasons for this preference: The test of interaction is the least ambiguous one and implies the weakest assumptions. It also provides important information as to which tests we should proceed with and what assumptions one could make.[7]

It is important to emphasize that the foregoing discussion assumes the use of a *full-rank* model, which is achieved by adding the following restrictions on the models (Scheffé, 1959):

$$\sum_i \alpha_i = 0$$

$$\sum_j \beta_j = 0$$

$$\sum_i \alpha\beta_{ij} = \sum_j \alpha\beta_{ij} = 0 \qquad (14)$$

The question of whether to use a *full-rank* model or not (i.e., whether to place additional restrictions on the models) is an important one. If one prefers the *non-full-rank* model, by avoiding the use of the above restrictions, then models, 5, 6 7, and 8 are actually identical. Scheffé (1959) provides convincing arguments for the use of a *full-rank* model, the most important one being that in a *non-full-rank* model the parameter values are not identifiable. Carlson and Timm (1974) have argued in the same line, and have concluded that: "The analysis of a two-way design with unequal cell numbers and data in every cell is complex; however, the complexities are very easy to understand with the full rank model formulation" (p. 70).

Additional Considerations: Sample vs Population, Weighting and Coding

It has been argued in a previous section that cell frequencies have to be taken into account whenever there is a departure from a perfectly balanced design. It was shown, for example, that for unequal but proportional cell frequencies

---

[7]In particular this is important with regard to decisions as to which terms to pool into the error term as was discussed earlier. Note that one has to have sufficient evidence to assume that the effect to be pooled are indeed zero, and relying only on a significance test in this respect might not be sufficient. A situation in which the researcher also has previous knowledge to support his assumptions of zero effects is preferable.

rthogonality can be achieved if an appropriate coding method is used—one that
ιkes into account the cell frequencies.

An important related issue concerns the specifications of the population to
hich inferences are being made, and the sampling procedures used. With regard
» the population of interest, one might distinguish between nonexperimental and
xperimental situations (Keren and Lewis, 1977). In the former there is a natural
opulation (e.g., population of graduate students in the U.S. classified according
ɔ sex and socio-economic variables) and thus natural weights. Independent of
⁻hether such a situation is characterized by conditional or unconditional sam-
ling, the coding system should reflect the natural population cell weights, even
⁻ the sample sizes do not (see Humphreys and Dachler, 1969; Humphreys and
ʃeishman, 1974). In the case of an experimental situation where variables are
ɔntrolled by the experimenter and there is no natural population being sampled,
ιe researcher has more freedom. A natural choice would be equal weights,
⁻hich is implicitly adopted by most psychologists. However, the experimenter
ιay want to reflect certain relationships that exist in the real world. In that case
ιe should probably avoid equal weights under certain circumstances. Such an
ɔpproach would be congruent with Brunswik's "representative design"
Brunswik, 1956), which he has strongly advocated. Finally, one may encounter
ɔartially experimental" conditions, a situation that lies between the above two
xtremes, in which case cell weights should reflect the population associated
ⁱith the nonexperimental individual variables. The list of sources for unequal
ell frequencies that was presented earlier (but is not necessarily exhaustive),
hould provide additional clues for the final decision. Keren and Lewis (1976)
rovide a framework in which that consideration can be incorporated. A brief
ummary of this approach is provided in the following, and the interested reader
; referred to the original source for additional elaborations.

Consider again the eight competing models presented earlier. The approach
ιken here is to define the parameters of a given model to be those that minimize
ιe mean square discrepancy between the model and the actual population means
henceforth referred to as the *residual variance*). For example, in model 2 μ and
ᵢ must minimize $\Sigma_i\Sigma_j\omega_{ij} (\mu_{ij} - \mu - \alpha_i)^2$. Each cell of the design is associated
ⁱith a positive weight ω_{ij} with the property that $\Sigma_i\Sigma_j \omega_{ij} = 1$, and the grand
ιean, which is the same for all models, $\mu = \Sigma_i\Sigma_j\omega_{ij}\mu_{ij}$. The weights are in-
ʃuded primarily to give the greatest possible generality to this approach. Each
ⱽeight has a natural interpretation as the probability for the corresponding cell of
he population under study, which might be a naturally occurring one, a com-
ʃletely hypothetical population, or a combination of the two.

The restrictions we have added to the eight models (Equation 14) in order to
chieve uniqueness are also weighted in the present approach and are

$$\sum_i \sum_j \omega_{ij}\alpha_i = 0$$

$$\sum_i \sum_j \omega_{ij}\beta_j = 0$$

$$\sum_i \omega_{ij}\alpha\beta_{ij} = \sum_j \omega_{ij}\alpha\beta_{ij} = 0 \qquad (15)$$

for all i and j. Interpreting ω_{ij} as a probability, these restrictions imply that in ou population the means of the row and column effects are both zero, as are a conditional row and column means of the interaction effects.

Although the same symbols are used in different models, the best fitting value need not remain the same from model to model for the same population. Th introduction of additional parameters may change the optimal choice of the orig inal parameter values. Also note that models 5 through 8 contain interaction term $\alpha\beta_{ij}$. Fitting model 5 with the restrictions in equation 15 leads to the equation

$$\alpha\beta_{ij} = \mu_{ij} - \mu - \alpha_i - \beta_j \qquad (16)$$

where μ, α_i, and β_j are the values taken from model 4. Thus, at least for the pur interaction model, $\alpha\beta_{ij}$ are just the residual values from the best-fitting additiv model. In fact, based on the restrictions in Equation 15, the choice of $\alpha\beta_{ij}$ i Equation 16 minimizes the residual variance for each of the models in which $\alpha\beta$ appears.

Table 4.10 describes the results of fitting all eight models to a set of popula tion means, minimizing the residual variance and using the restrictions in Equa tion 15. The asterisk in this context indicates *ignoring;* hence α_i^* is referred to a row effects ignoring columns, β_j^* as effects of columns ignoring rows, and α_i an β_j as the corresponding effects eliminating columns and rows respectively. Not that the interaction effects in Table 4.10 can be referred to unambiguously because their values are not changed when terms for rows and/or columns ar introduced. In addition, the presence or absence of interaction terms do no change the values of row and column effects. Thus we only need the eliminating

TABLE 4.10
Parameter Values and Residual Variances
for Models in a Two-Way Design

Model	Parameter Values	Residual Variance
1	μ	$\Sigma\Sigma\omega_{ij}(\mu_{ij} - \mu)^2$
2	μ, α_i^*	$\Sigma\Sigma\omega_{ij}(\mu_{ij} - \mu - \alpha_i^*)^2$
3	μ, β_j^*	$\Sigma\Sigma\omega_{ij}(\mu_{ij} - \mu - \beta_j^*)^2$
4	$\mu, \alpha_{ij}, \beta_j$	$\Sigma\Sigma\omega_{ij}\gamma_{ij}^2$
5	μ, γ_{ij}	$\Sigma\Sigma\omega_{ij}(\alpha_i + \beta_j)^2$
6	$\mu, \alpha_i^* \gamma_{ij}$	$\Sigma\Sigma\omega_{ij}(\alpha_i + \beta_j)^2$
7	$\mu, \beta_j^*, \gamma_{ij}$	$\Sigma\Sigma\omega_{ij}(\alpha_i + \beta_j - \beta_j^*)^2$
8	$\mu, \alpha_i, \beta_j, \gamma_{ij}$	0

gnoring terminology for rows and columns to refer unambiguously to their ffects.

Consider again the hypothetical example in Table 4.9. The overall level (μ) 'hich is a weighted average of the μ_{ij} is 192. For fitting model 2 the row effects re defined as:

$$\alpha_i^* = \frac{\displaystyle\sum_j \omega_{ij}\,\mu_{ij}}{\displaystyle\sum_j \omega_{ij}} - \mu \tag{17}$$

nd for our particular example these are equal to:

$$\alpha_1^* = \frac{(.1)60 + (.1)120 + (.3)180}{.5} - 192 = -48$$

$$\alpha_2^* = \frac{(.3)240 + (.1)240 + (.1)240}{.5} - 192 = 48$$

ote that these values are also correct for model 6, so that including interaction 1 the model has no influence on the other parameter values.

For fitting model 3, the column effects are defined as

$$\beta_j^* = \frac{\displaystyle\sum_i \omega_{ij}\,\mu_{ij}}{\displaystyle\sum_i \omega_{ij}} - \mu$$

'hich for our example yields:

$$\beta_1^* = \frac{(.1)60 + (.3)240}{.4} - 192 = 3$$

$$\beta_2^* = \frac{(.1)120 + (.1)240}{.2} - 192 = -12$$

$$\beta_3^* = \frac{(.3)180 + (.1)240}{.4} - 192 = 3$$

hese values also apply to model 7, in which interaction has been included. For pplying model 4 we have to solve simultaneously the equations

$$\alpha_i = \left[\frac{\displaystyle\sum_j \omega_{ij}\mu_{ij}}{\displaystyle\sum_j \omega_{ij}} - \mu\right] - \frac{\displaystyle\sum_j \omega_{ij}\beta_j}{\displaystyle\sum_j \omega_{ij}}$$

$$\beta_j = \left[\frac{\sum_i \omega_{ij} \mu_{ij}}{\sum_i \omega_{ij}} - \mu \right] - \frac{\sum_i \omega_{ij} \alpha_i}{\sum_i \omega_{ij}}$$

which yield new values for row and column effects (eliminating column and row effects, respectively). In our example, these are

$$\alpha_1 = -60 \qquad \alpha_2 = 60$$

$$\beta_1 = 27 \qquad \beta_2 = -12 \qquad \beta_3 = 33$$

The values of $\alpha\beta_{ij}$ are given by applying equation 16 and yield

$$\alpha\beta_{11} = -45 \qquad \alpha\beta_{12} = 0 \qquad \alpha\beta_{13} = 15$$

$$\alpha\beta_{21} = 15 \qquad \alpha\beta_{22} = 0 \qquad \alpha\beta_{23} = -45$$

These values apply to models 5 through 8, which is to say that interaction is unaffected by the presence of other terms in the model.

To see the importance of choice of weight, we might briefly consider the effect of setting $\omega_{ij} = \frac{1}{6}$. Now the various parameter values for our example are

$$\mu = 180$$

$$\alpha_1 = \alpha_1^* = -60 \qquad \alpha_2 = \alpha_2^* = 60$$

$$\beta_1 = \beta_1^* = -30 \qquad \beta_2 = \beta_2^* = 0 \qquad \beta_3 = \beta_3^* = 30$$

$$\alpha\beta_{11} = -30 \qquad \alpha\beta_{12} = 0 \qquad \alpha\beta_{13} = 30$$

$$\alpha\beta_{21} = 30 \qquad \alpha\beta_{22} = 0 \qquad \alpha\beta_{23} = -30$$

In this case the requirements of proportionality are satisfied; hence there is no difference between ignoring and eliminating effects.

Note that parameter values have changed as a consequence of changing weights. Thus the choice of weights is of practical importance for the definition of parameters. The only exception to this conclusion is that if there is no interaction for one set of weights, there is no interaction for any other set. Thus if an additive model fits the cell means exactly, this fit is independent of the weights.

A most valuable aspect of the approach just presented is that it allows for the definition of variance components accounted for by an effect. This can be done in terms of model comparisons by defining variance components as the difference between residual variances. We will not elaborate on this issue further, and the interested reader is referred to Keren and Lewis (1976).

Finally, we want to present the multiple regression approach using dummy variables based on our weighting system. In the present context we will limit ourselves to the case of unequal but proportional cell frequencies. A more elaborate presentation can be found in Keren and Lewis (1976).

To illustrate, consider again the data in Table 4.4, both cases I and II. The weights chosen are based on the cell frequencies (i.e., $\omega_{ij} = n_{ij}/N$). To construct the design matrix, we start with levels of factor A. Assuming a levels, we construct $a - 1$ vectors (variables as follows: Each observation at level i is assigned a score of 1 on the ith variable and zero on all the others, except those at level a (the last level of variable A). If n_i represents the number of observations at level i of factor A, and n_a the number of observations on the last level of variable A, each observation at level a is assigned a score of $-\dfrac{n_i}{n_a}$, on the ith variable. For example, in case I of Table 4.4, the vector A_1 consists of 1's for each observation at level A_1 and $\dfrac{n_1.}{n_\alpha.} = -\dfrac{24}{18} = -\dfrac{4}{3}$ for each observation at level A_2.

We proceed the same way for factor B, constructing $b - 1$ new variables and assigning scores of $-\dfrac{n_{.j}}{n_b.}$ to each observation at level b of factor B on the jth variable. For example, in case II of Table 4.4, vector B_1 consists of 1's for each observation at level B_1, 0's for each observation at level B_2 and $\dfrac{n_{.2}}{n_{.b}} = -\dfrac{16}{12}$ $= -\dfrac{4}{3}$ for each observation at level B_3. For vector B_2 we assign 0's for each observation at level B_1, 1's for each observation at level B_2, and $\dfrac{n_{.j}}{n_{.b}} = -\dfrac{14}{12}$ $= \dfrac{7}{3}$ for each observation at level B_3.[8]

Finally, $(a - 1)(b - 1)$ new variables are constructed for the interaction. For each combination of variable i from factor A and variable j from factor B, take the products of their scores to construct scores on a new interaction variable. The design matrices for cases I and II using the aforementioned coding system are presented in Table 4.11. The reader can easily verify that vectors from different effects are indeed orthogonal. Note, however, that when checking for orthogonality one has to take into account also the cell frequencies that are added in the first column of Table 4.11. For instance, to check whether vectors A_1 and B_1 are orthogonal, for case I we calculate

$$(1)(1) + 6\left(-\frac{4}{3}\right)(1) + 8(1)(0) + 6\left(-\frac{4}{3}\right)(0) + 8(1)(-1) + 6\left(-\frac{4}{3}\right)(-1) = 0$$

and for case II

$$(1)(1) + 8(-1)(1) + 7(1)(0) + 7(-1)(0) + 6(1)\left(-\frac{4}{3}\right) + 6(-1)\left(-\frac{4}{3}\right) = 0$$

---

[8]In this example weights were based on cell frequencies $\left(\text{i.e., } \omega_{ij} = \dfrac{n_{ij}}{N}\right)$ and because N is a constant the cell frequencies are actually serving as weights. In general one may, though not necessarily, use cell frequencies as weights. If cell frequencies are not used as weights, simply exchange ω for n and use the same procedure as described previously.

TABLE 4.11
Design Matrix for Proportional Cell Frequency
Based on the Weighting Method Proposed by Keren and Lewis (1976)

					Case I			
		(n_{ij})	A_i	B_1	B_2	A_1B_1	A_1B_2	Y[†]
(A_1B_1)	G1	(8)	1	1	0	1	0	—
(A_2B_1)	G2	(6)	−4/3	1	0	−4/3	0	—
(A_1B_2)	G3	(8)	1	0	1	0	1	—
(A_2B_2)	G4	(6)	−4/3	0	1	0	−4/3	—
(A_1B_3)	G5	(8)	1	−1	−1	−1	−1	—
(A_2B_3)	G6	(6)	−4/3	−1	−1	4/3	4/3	—

					Case II			
		(n_{ij})	A_i	B_1	B_2	A_1B_1	A_1B_2	Y[†]
(A_1B_1)	G1	(8)	1	1	0	1	0	—
(A_2B_1)	G2	(8)	−1	1	0	−1	0	—
(A_1B_2)	G3	(7)	1	0	1	0	1	—
(A_2B_2)	G4	(7)	−1	0	1	0	−1	—
(A_1B_3)	G5	(6)	1	−4/3	−14/12	−4/3	−14/12	—
(A_2B_3)	G6	(6)	−1	−4/3	−14/12	4/3	14/12	—

†A score is given for each individual. The number of scores for each cell is indicated by the first column (n).

For the more general case of unequal and nonproportional cell frequencies, the multiple regression procedure of this approach is presented in detail in Keren and Lewis (1976).

An important point entailed by the approach taken here, is that coding depends on cell weights, which in turn describe the population to which we wish to generalize. The question of which is the appropriate coding system has become a controversial issue in the recent literature. In the present text chapter I tried to emphasize (implicitly and explicitly) that there is no one "correct" coding system (Keren and Lewis, 1977). Different coding methods define different main effects and interactions (Scheffé, 1959), and consequently lead to the testing of different hypotheses. We tried to illuminate in this chapter some of the considerations a researcher should take into account when deciding on what is the appropriate coding system to be used for a particular situation. Those considerations include the way the data were obtained (sampling considerations), the nature of the phenomena under investigation, and the hypotheses the researcher is interested in testing.

FINAL COMMENTS AND A BRIEF SUMMARY

A major guiding principle followed by most articles on nonorthogonal designs has been "that the method for the analysis of variance of data from nonorthogonal

esigns should estimate the same parameters and test the same hypotheses as can
therwise be estimated and tested in a balanced analysis of variance experimental
esign involving the same factors" (Overall et al., 1975, p. 184). This tenet has
een further endorsed by Appelbaum and Cramer (1974), and Cramer and Ap-
elbaum (1980) who proposed that "having decided to employ the method of
ast squares . . . one is left only with the selection of possible models and
iodel comparisons. The models selected are logically independent of the ob-
erved numbers of observations per cell" (Appelbaum & Cramer, 1974, p 336).

Whether these guidelines should invariably be followed, is in my opinion
uestionable. In particular, although models and observed numbers are logically
idependent, the choice of which models one wants to test should not always be
idependent of data. As mentioned by Keren and Lewis (1977), there are differ-
it sources that may account for an unbalanced design, some of which would
:come apparent by a simple examination of the observed data. For instance,
insider an experiment in which subjects have to show up twice. Furthermore,
ippose that in one of the conditions many subjects fail to show for the second
:ssion, based on their experience on the first session. Should researchers neglect
e possible effects that the treatment had on the number of subjects in each cell,
id attempt to estimate the same parameters and test the same hypotheses as they
ould have done in the case of a balanced design? And what about the case in
hich the unequal cell frequencies reflect true differences in the original popula-
on?

Howell and McConaughy (1982) suggested that the appropriate method for
ilculating least squares analysis of variance with unequal frequencies, should
:pend on the particular questions the experimenter want to answer. Indeed, as
as shown in this chapter different methods address different questions, and as
oposed by Howell and McConaughy, the question should be put before the
iswer. Moreover, the exact nature of the question should be determined (among
her things) by the apparent or hypothesized source for the unequal cell frequen-
es, as reflected in the sample data. All said, how should the experimenter
oceed when facing an unbalanced design? We suggest that several aspects
iould be considered before a decision is made. In particular, the researcher is
icouraged to consider the following:

1. The nature of the population under investigation based on previous knowledge the researcher might have.

2. The nature of the sampling procedure employed.

3. The nature of the treatments (independent variables) involved and the
   extent to which they might effect cell frequencies.

4. Is there any previous knowledge suggesting the existence (or nonexistence) of main effects and/or interactions?

5. What are the main questions (hypotheses) the researcher would like to
   test?

The decision as to which analysis to employ should depend on these conside
ations that will probably lead to the most appropriate analysis, and will als
enable the researcher to interpret correctly the results of the analysis. Unlik
many previous researchers who strongly recommended one single (or very few
method(s), the point of view advocated in this chapter is that there is a very larg
number of potential methods, and that several considerations (some of which a
to a certain extent "subjective") have to be taken into account for the final choic

In the introduction to this chapter we stated a nonexistence theorem, namel
that there is no way to partition the response variance uanmbiguously whe
unequal and disproportionate cell frequencies are involved. The fact that sever
methods can be employed for the same set of data and yet yield different solu
tions is a manifestation of this statement. In fact, two researchers may analy
the same set of data by using two different methods and consequently obtai
different results. Such a state of affairs is likely to occur if the two experimente
differ in their evaluations on some of the considerations listed earlier, and th
question who employed the "correct" method is in many instances unanswerabl
Thus the purpose of the present chapter was not to suggest the "correct" metho
for dealing with unbalanced designs, but rather to present the reader with a set
possible methods and the relevant considerations to be taken into account
order to reduce the ambiguity that has developed around this topic.

It might be argued that the discrepancies between the different solutions,
dictated by different methods, are rather small and insignificant, and that for a
practical purposes any method will do. For example, Chilag (1975) conducted
simulation study in which she compared the three different methods of Overa
and Speigel (1960) and the unweighted means method (Winer, 1971). Chila
(1975) found that: "For the populations and design studied, all four methods w
have the same power and the same significance level even though the sums
squares for the effets are different" (p. 1). Whether this conclusion can be gene
alized to other populations and designs beyond those that were studied is que
tionable. In a more recent study, Milligan, Wong, and Thompson (1987) reporte
the results of a Monte Carlo simulation study from which they concluded th
standard computational routines for unequal cell sizes are non-robust. The
proposed that the lack of robustness can, at least partly, be accounted for by th
unequal cell frequencies and thus warned that such studies should be interprete
with care. Given that unbalanced designs may frequently occur and often cann
be avoided, robustness properties should indeed be further studied.

APPENDIX A: CONSTRUCTION AND PROOFS
OF A CODING SYSTEM FOR THE CASE OF
PROPORTIONAL N'S WHICH WILL ALWAYS
MAINTAIN ORTHOGONALITY

To construct a coding system which will maintain the requirement
orthogonality for proportional n's, we start by defining dummy variables for

two-way analysis, with I levels of factor A and J levels of factor B. G is defined as a variable that assigns a score of 1 to all subjects. A_i, $i = 1 \ldots I$, is a variable which assigns a score of 1 to each subject observed at level i of factor A and 0 to all others. B_j, $j = 1 \ldots J$, is defined similarly for each level of factor B. Likewise, AB_{ij}, $i = 1 \ldots I, j = 1 \ldots J$, assigns a score of 1 to each observation in the ijth cell of the design and a score of 0 to all others.

The goal now is to construct A_i^* and B_j^* from A_i and B_j, which are orthogonal to G (i.e., the vector products $G'A_i^*$ and $G'B_j^*$ are all zero), and describe the effects of A and B respectively. It will be shown briefly that the products $(A_i^*)'B_j^*$ are all zero in the case of proportional n's. Next, AB_{ij}^* are constructed from AB_{ij}, which are orthogonal to A_i^*, B_j^*, and G. Any particular AB_{ij}^* is orthogonal to all A_i^* and B_j^* in the case of proportional n's. Thus in the case of proportional cell sizes, the constructed variables define four mutually orthogonal subspaces, which are denoted by $\{G\}$, $\{A^*\}$, $\{B^*\}$, and $\{AB^*\}$. Moreover, in these cases the sum of squares of the dependent variable in the experiment accounted for by the last three of these (when they are used as predictors in multiple regression) is equal to SS_A, SS_B, and SS_{AB}, respectively, as obtained from the conventional ANOVA formulas.

To construct A_i^*, we make use of the following result: Given vectors x and y,

$$y^* = y - x(x'y)/x'x \tag{1}$$

is orthogonal to x. To see this, we need only to evaluate the product $x'y^*$

$$x'y^* = x'y - (x'x)(x'y)/(x'x) = 0$$

For $x = G$, and $y = A_i$, we therefore obtain by substituting in (1)

$$A_i^* = A_i - G(G'A_i)/(G'G) \tag{1a}$$

This can be simplified once we evaluate the products $G'G$ and $G'A_i$. In particular, because all observations have a score of 1 on G, $G'G = N$, the total number of observations in the experiment. Because only the $n_i.$ observations at level i of factor A have a score of 1 on A_i (and all the others have a score of 0), the products $G'A_i = n_i.$. Substituting these two results in (1a) we obtain

$$A_i^* = A_i - G(n_i./N) \tag{2}$$

so that the score on A_i^* of a subject observed at level i of factor A is $(N - n_i.)/N$, whereas all others have a score of $-n_i./N$.

We may construct B_j^* in a similar fashion and obtain the equation

$$B_j^* = B_j - G(G'B_j)/(G'G) = B_j - G(n_{.j}/N) \tag{3}$$

Thus the score of an observation on B_j^* will be $(N - n_{.j})/N$ or $-n_{.j}/N$, depending on whether it was observed at level j of factor B or not.

Now we wish to show that A_i^* and B_j^* are indeed orthogonal in the case of proportional n's. To do this we simply expand the product

$$(A_i^*)'B_j^* = [A_i - G(n_i./N)]'[B_j - G(n._j/N)]$$
$$= A_i'B_j - G'B_j(n_i./N) - A_i'G(n._j/N)$$
$$+ G'G(n_i.n._j/N^2)$$

The only one of these products that was not previously discussed is $A_i'B_j$. The terms in this product will be 1 only for the individuals in the jth cell of the design, so that $A_i'B_j = n_{ij}$.

Thus

$$(A_i^*)'B_j^* = n_{ij} - (n_i.n._j)/N - (n_i.n._j)/N + (n_i.n._j)/N$$
$$= n_{ij} - (n_i.n._j)/N \tag{4}$$

Cell sizes are said to be proportional whenever

$$n_{ij} = (n_i.n._j)/N$$

and, of course, equal cell sizes are a special case. Thus A_i^* and B_j^* are orthogonally exactly in these cases.

Next, we want to construct AB_{ij}^* (from AB_{ij}), which will be orthogonal to A_i^*, B_j^*, and G. Using an extension of Equation (1) we have

$$AB_{ij}^* = AB_{ij} - A_i^*(AB_{ij}'A_i^*)/[(A_i^*)'A_i^*] - B_j^*(AB_{ij}'B_j^*)/[(B_j^*)'A_i^*]$$
$$- G(AB_{ij}'G)/(G'G) \tag{5}$$

To deal further with this expression, we have to evaluate the vector products. By using Equation 2 the vector products can be written as

$$(A_i^*)'A_i^* = [A_i - G(n_i./N)]'[A_i - G(n_i./N)]$$
$$= A_i'A_i - G'A_i(n_i./N) - A_i'G(n_i./N)$$
$$+ G'G(n_i./N)^2$$
$$= n_i. - 2n_i^2./N + n_i^2./N = n_i.(1 - n_i./N) \tag{6}$$

Similarly, from Equation 3 we obtain

$$(B_j^*)'B_j^* = n._j(1 - n._j/N) \tag{7}$$

Finally we evaluate

$$(AB_{ij})'A_i^* = (AB_{ij})'[A_i - G(n_i./N)] = (AB_{ij})'A_i - (AB_{ij})'G(n_i./N)$$
$$= n_{ij}(1 - n_i./N) \tag{8}$$

and in a similar way we obtain

$$(AB_{ij})'B_j^* = n_{ij}(1 - n._j/N) \tag{9}$$

Substituting Equations 6, 7, and 9 into 5 we obtain

$$AB_{ij}^* = AB_{ij} - A_i^*(n_{ij}/n_i.) - B_j^*(n_{ij}/n._j) - G(n_{ij}/N) \tag{10}$$

and using the values of A_i^* and B_j^* in (2) and (3), we can finally express AB_{ij}^* as follows:

$$AB_{ij}^* = AB_{ij} - [A_i - G(n_i./N)](n_{ij}/n_i.) - [B_j - G(n._j/N)](n_{ij}/n._j)$$
$$- G(n_{ij}/N) = AB_{ij} - A_i(n_{ij}/n_i.) - B_j(n_{ij}/n._j) + G(n_{ij}/N) \qquad (11)$$

In order to check for orthogonality of AB_{ij}^* to A_g^* and B_h^* where $g \neq i$, $h \neq j$, we employ Equation 10. Consider the product

$$(A_g^*)'AB_{ij}^* = (A_g^*)'[AB_{ij} - A_i^*(n_{ij}/n_i.) - B_j^*(n_{ij}/n._j) - G(n_{ij}/N)]$$
$$= (A_g^*)'AB_{ij} - (A_g^*)'A_i^*(n_{ij}/n_i.) - (A_g^*)'B_j^*(n_{ij}/n._j)$$
$$- (A_g^*)'G(n_{ij}/N) \qquad (12)$$

As was shown previously, for equal or proportional n's

$$(A_g^*)'B_j^* = 0$$

and in general

$$(A_g^*)'G = 0.$$

We only need to expand the first two terms of Equation 2:

$$(A_g^*)'AB_{ij}^* - (A_g^*)'A_i^*(n_{ij}/n_i.) = [A_g - G(n_g./N)]'AB_{ij}$$
$$- [A_g - G(n_g./N)]'[A_i - G(n_i./N)](n_{ij}/n_i.)$$

$$= A_g'AB_{ij} - G'AB_{ij}(n_g./N) - [A_g'A_i - G'A_i(n_g./N) - A_g'G(n_i./N)$$
$$+ G'G(n_g.n_i./N^2)](n_{ij}/n_i.)$$

$$= 0 - n_{ij}n_g./N - [0 - (n_i.)(n_g.)/N - (n_g.)(n_i.)/N + (n_g.)(n_i.)/N]n_{ij}/n_i.$$

$$= -(n_{ij})n_g./N + (n_{ij})(n_g.)/N = 0.$$

A similar proof establishes the result for $(B_h^*)'A_{ij}^*$.

Thus we have defined four sets of variables, G, A_i^*, B_j^*, and AB_{ij}^*, with the property, in the case of proportional n's, that any member of one set is orthogonal to any member of the other sets. The last three sets can be used as predictors of the dependent variable in a two-way experiment with proportional n's, knowing that they will account for nonoverlapping variance.

REFERENCES

Appelbaum, M. I., & Cramer, E. M. (1974). Some problems in the nonorthogonal analysis of variance. *Psychological Bulletin, 75,* 335–343.

Blair, R. C., & Higgins, J. J. (1978). Tests of hypotheses for unbalanced factorial designs under various regression/coding method combinations. *Educational and Psychological Measurement, 38,* 621–631.

Bogartz, W. (1975). Coding dummy variables is a waste of time: Reply to Wolf and Cartwright, among others. *Psychological Bulletin, 82,* 80.

Brunswik, E. (1956). Historical and thematic relations of psychology to other sciences. *Scientifi Monthly, 83,* 151–161.

Carlson, J. E., & Timm, N. H. (1974). Analysis of nonorthogonal fixed effects designs. *Psycholog ical Bulletin, 81,* 563–570.

Chilag, N. (1975). *A Monte Carlo study of unbalanced ANOVA designs.* Unpublished master thesis, University of Illinois at Urbana-Champaign.

Cohen, J. (1968). Multiple regression as a general data-analytic system. *Psychological Bulletin, 7(426–443.*

Cohen, J. (1982). "New-look" multiple regression/correlation analysis. In G. Keren (Ed.) *Statistic and methodological issues in psychology and social sciences research.* Hillsdaie, NJ: Lawrenc Erlbaum Associates.

Cohen, J., & Cohen, P. (1975). Applied multiple regression/correlation analysis for the behavior sciences. Hillsdale, NJ: Lawrence Erlbaum Associates.

Cramer, E. M., & Appelbaum, M. I. (1980). Nonorthogonal analysis of variance—once again *Psychological bulletin, 87,* 51–57.

Darlington, R. B. (1968). Multiple regression in psychological research and practice. *Psychologica Bulletin, 69,* 161–182.

Glass, G. V., & Stanley, J. C. (1970). *Statistical methods in education and psychology.* Englewoo Cliffs, NJ: Prentice-Hall.

Gocka, E. F. (1973). Regression analysis of proportional cell data. *Psychological Bulletin, 80,* 25 27.

Herr, D. G., & Gaebelein, J. (1978). Nonorthogonal two-way analysis of variance. *Psychologica Bulletin, 85,* 207–216.

Howell, D. C., & McConaughy, S. H. (1982). Nonorthogonal analysis of variance: Putting th question before the answer. *Educational and Psychological Measurement, 42,* 10–24.

Humphreys, L. G., & Dachler, H. P. (1969). Jenson's theory of intelligence. *Journal of Education al Psychology, 60,* 419–426.

Humphreys, L. G., & Fleishman, A. (1974). Pseudo-orthogonal and other analysis of varianc designs involving individual-differences variables. *Journal of Educational Psychology, 66,* 464 472.

Joe, G. W. (1971). Comment on Overall and Spiegel's "Least squares analysis of experiment data." *Psychological Bulletin, 75,* 364–366.

Keren, G., & Lewis, C. (1976). Nonorthogonal designs: Sample versus population. *Psychologica Bulletin, 83,* 817–826.

Keren, G., & Lewis, C. (1977). A comment on coding in nonorthogonal designs. *Psychologica Bulletin, 84,* 346–348.

Kerlinger, F. N., & Pedhazur, E. J. (1973). *Multiple regression in behavioral research.* New York Holt, Rinehart & Winston.

Lewis, C., & Keren, G. (1977). You can't have your cake and eat it too: Some considerations of th error term. *Psychological Bulletin, 84,* 1150–1154.

Milligan, G. W., Wong, D. S., & Thompson, P. A. (1987). Robustness properties of nonorthogona analysis of variance. *Psychological Bulletin, 101,* 464–470.

Myers, J. L. (1978). *Fundamentals of experimental design* (3rd ed.). Boston: Allyn & Bacon.

Overall, J. E., & Spiegel, D. K. (1969). Concerning least squares analysis of experimental data *Psychological Bulletin, 72,* 311–322.

Overall, J. E., & Spiegel, D. K. (1973). Comment on "regression analysis of proportional cel data." *Psychological Bulletin, 80,* 28–30.

Overall, J. E., Spiegel, D. K., & Cohen, J. (1975). Equivalence of orthogonal and nonorthogona analysis of variance. *Psychological Bulletin, 82,* 182–186.

Rawlings, R. R., Jr. (1972). Note on nonorthogonal analysis of variance. *Psychological Bulletin, 79,* 168–169.

cheffé, H. (1959). *The analysis of variance*. New York: Wiley.

peed, F. M., & Hocking, R. R. (1976). The use of the R( )-notation with unbalanced data. *The American Statistician, 30,* 30–34.

Vainer, H. (1982). Robust statistics: A survey and some prescriptions. In G. Keren (Ed.), *Statistical and methodological issues in psychology and social science research* (pp. 187–214). Hillsdale, NJ: Lawrence Erlbaum Associates.

Viner, B. J. (1971). *Statistical principles in experimental design* (2nd ed.). New York: McGraw-Hill.

Volf, G., & Cartwright, B. (1974). Rules for coding dummy variables in multiple regression. *Psychological Bulletin, 81,* 173–179.

5 MANOVA and MANCOVA: An Overview

Neil H. Timm
University of Pittsburgh

INTRODUCTION

Most students in psychology, education, and the social sciences are familiar with the application of the basic principles of univariate analysis of variance (ANOVA) and covariance (ANCOVA) analysis in the design of experiments; that is, reaching valid conclusions about population parameters through tests of hypotheses and the establishment of simultaneous confidence intervals. When introduced to the univariate principles of ANOVA and ANCOVA, students may have learned the concepts via "partitioning the observed total sum of squares" following Fisher (1925); the overparameterized less than full rank model following Scheffé (1959) and more recently Searle (1971, 1987) and Rao (1973); the full rank linear model popularized by Hocking and Speed (1975), Timm and Carlson (1975), and Hocking (1985); or the coordinate-free geometric approach discussed by Herr (1980). Although all of these approaches have natural generalizations to multivariate analysis of variance (MANOVA) and covariance (MANCOVA) analysis, the multivariate generalizations are complicated by the number of hypotheses that may be tested, the difficulty of choosing among numerous test statistics, and the fact that a computer software program must be available to the researcher to perform the mathematical calculations. Nonorthogonal designs, the analysis of repeated measurements, designs in which the errors form a stationary spacial process, multiresponse designs, and designs in which repetitions of a basic design leads to independent multivariate stationary time series add additional complications to MANOVA and MANCOVA methodologies.

This chapter reviews and integrates the various approaches to the analysis of variance: full rank models; reparameterized less than full rank models; the geometry of the analysis of covariance; restricted full rank models; a general discussion of multivariate estimation, hypothesis testing, and the multivariate general linear model; and some general MANOVA and MANCOVA principles.

FUNDAMENTALS: FULL RANK MODEL

Before formulating and developing abstract concepts of general linear models, estimation of population parametric, likelihood ratio tests, vector spaces, and projection operations, we illustrate these ideas through a very simple two-sample example. To provide inferences about the means of a random variable Y in two populations with means μ_1, and μ_2, a random sample of size N_i ($i = 1, 2$) is drawn from each population. Letting Y_{ij} denote the jth observation from the ith population, the expectation of Y_{ij} is $E(Y_{ij}) = \mu_i$, for $i = 1, 2$. The observed random variable Y_{ij} is not equal to $E(Y_{ij})$, the difference $\epsilon_{ij} = Y_{ij} - E(Y_{ij})$ is an unobserved random variable with mean equal to zero and variance σ^2. We further assume that the covariance between every pair of different ϵ_{ij} is zero, cov $(\epsilon_{ij}, \epsilon_{i'j'}) = 0$ for $i \neq i'$ and $j \neq j'$. With this, the model equation for the observed random variable Y_{ij} is given by

$$\Omega: Y_{ij} = \mu_i + \epsilon_{ij} \quad i = 1, 2; \quad j = 1, \ldots, N_i; \tag{1}$$

and

$$E(Y_{ij}) = \mu_i$$
$$V(Y_{ij}) = \sigma^2. \tag{2}$$

Equation 1 is called the *linear model* and Equation 2 is called the *Gauss–Markoff setup*. If we add the assumption of normality, it follows that the ϵ_{ij} are independently normally distributed, $\epsilon_{ij} \sim \text{IN}(0, \sigma^2)$ or

$$Y_{ij} \sim \text{IN}(\mu_i, \sigma^2) \quad i = 1, 2. \tag{3}$$

Letting N_1 and 2 and $N_2 = 3$,

$$Y_{ij} = \mu_i + \epsilon_{ij} \quad i = 1, 2; \quad j = 1, 2, 3. \tag{4}$$

To see how this fits into a more general linear model format, let y_{ij} be the observed value of the random variable Y_{ij} and define the vector $\mathbf{y}' = (y_{11}, y_{12}, y_{21}, y_{22}, y_{23})$.

With the indicator variable w_i, $i = 1, 2$ defined:

$$w_i = \begin{cases} 1 & \text{if the observation is from group } i \\ 0 & \text{otherwise} \end{cases} \tag{5}$$

so that:

$$W = \begin{bmatrix} 1 & 0 \\ 1 & 0 \\ 0 & 1 \\ 0 & 1 \\ 0 & 1 \end{bmatrix} \tag{6}$$

and with $\mu' = (\mu_1, \mu_2)$, Expression 4 is conveniently expressed in compact form as $y = W\mu + \epsilon$. The design or model matrix simply consists of 1's and 0's to indicate group membership. In general for p populations, the $N \times 1$ observation vector y has the form

$$\Omega: \quad \underset{N \times 1}{y} = \underset{N \times p}{W} \underset{p \times 1}{\mu} + \underset{N \times 1}{\epsilon} \tag{7}$$

where the design matrix W is of rank $p \le N$.

$$E(Y) = W\mu \qquad V(Y) = \sigma^2 I_N. \tag{8}$$

The parametric vector μ in Equation 7 is not constrained under Ω, so the model is termed the *unrestricted full rank model*. It is of full rank because the design matrix has full column rank, p, $R(W) = p$. For testing hypotheses about the elements of the parametric vector μ, we further assume that Y follows an N-variate multivariate normal distribution with mean and variance given in Equation 8. Letting the notation $N(\mu, \Sigma)$ represent the multivariate normal distribution with mean vector, μ, and covariance matrix, Σ, the general model is also written as

$$Y \sim N(W\mu, \sigma^2 I_N) \tag{9}$$

Assuming for the moment that $\mu_1 = \mu_2 = \mu$ where the population parametric μ has linear structure

$$E(Y_{ij}) = \alpha + \beta x_{ij} \tag{10}$$

Then the linear model becomes:

$$\begin{bmatrix} y_{11} \\ y_{12} \\ y_{21} \\ y_{22} \\ y_{32} \end{bmatrix} = \begin{bmatrix} 1 & x_{11} \\ 1 & x_{12} \\ 1 & x_{21} \\ 1 & x_{22} \\ 1 & x_{32} \end{bmatrix} \begin{bmatrix} \alpha \\ \beta \end{bmatrix} + \begin{bmatrix} \epsilon_{11} \\ \epsilon_{12} \\ \epsilon_{21} \\ \epsilon_{22} \\ \epsilon_{32} \end{bmatrix}$$

$$y = X\beta + \epsilon \tag{11}$$

More generally, we may have N observations, y_i, $i = 1, \ldots, N$ corresponding to independent inputs $x_{i1}, x_{i2}, \ldots, x_{ik}$ for $i = 1, \ldots, N$. Using matrix notation for the general linear relationship,

$$y_i = \beta_0 + x_{i1}\beta_1 + \ldots + x_{ik}\beta_k + \epsilon_i \tag{12}$$

let,

$$\mathbf{y} = \begin{bmatrix} y_1 \\ y_2 \\ \cdot \\ \cdot \\ \cdot \\ y_N \end{bmatrix} \quad \boldsymbol{\beta} = \begin{bmatrix} \beta_0 \\ \beta_1 \\ \cdot \\ \cdot \\ \beta_k \end{bmatrix} \quad \boldsymbol{\epsilon} = \begin{bmatrix} \epsilon_1 \\ \epsilon_2 \\ \cdot \\ \cdot \\ \cdot \\ \epsilon_N \end{bmatrix}$$

$$N \times 1 \qquad q \times 1 \qquad N \times 1$$

with the matrix of x_{ij}'s defined as

$$\mathbf{X} = \begin{bmatrix} 1 & x_{11} & x_{12} & \cdots & x_{1k} \\ 1 & x_{21} & x_{22} & \cdots & x_{2k} \\ \cdot & & \cdot & & \cdot \\ \cdot & & \cdot & & \cdot \\ \cdot & & \cdot & & \cdot \\ 1 & x_{N1} & x_{N2} & \cdots & x_{Nk} \end{bmatrix}$$

$$N \times q$$

Then, the matrix form of Equation 12 becomes

$$\Omega: \quad \underset{N \times 1}{\mathbf{y}} = \underset{N \times q}{\mathbf{X}} \underset{q \times 1}{\boldsymbol{\beta}} + \underset{N \times 1}{\boldsymbol{\epsilon}} \qquad (13)$$

assuming $E(\boldsymbol{\epsilon}) = 0$ and the $V(\boldsymbol{\epsilon}) = \boldsymbol{\Sigma}$, where $\boldsymbol{\epsilon}$ follows a multivariate normal distribution, $\mathbf{X}$ represents a matrix of q "independent" variables observed on each of the N individuals, $\boldsymbol{\beta}$ is an unknown vector of population parametrics, and $\mathbf{X}$ is a full rank matrix, an alternative form of Equation 13 is

$$E(\mathbf{y}) = \mathbf{X}\boldsymbol{\beta}$$

$$V(\mathbf{y}) = \sigma^2 \mathbf{I}$$

$$\mathbf{y} \sim N(\mathbf{X}\boldsymbol{\beta}, \sigma^2 \mathbf{I}). \qquad (14)$$

No restrictions are placed on the parametric vector $\boldsymbol{\beta}$, thus Equation 14 is also an unrestricted full rank model. The linear model literature refers to this equation as the general regression model. When the model matrix contains only 0's and 1's so that $\mathbf{X} \equiv \mathbf{W}$ and has full column rank, we are usually investigating means in the analysis of variance.

Instead of letting $\mu_1 = \mu_2 = \mu$ with linear structure, let's assume that

$$Y_{ij} = \mu_i + \gamma z_{ij} + \epsilon_{ij}, \qquad (15)$$

where as usual $\epsilon_{ij} = Y_{ij} - E(Y_{ij})$ and $\epsilon_{ij} \sim IN(0, \sigma^2)$ so that

$$E(Y_{ij}) = \mu_i + \gamma z_{ij}. \qquad (16)$$

For the observations in Equation 4, we have that

$$\begin{bmatrix} y_{11} \\ y_{12} \\ y_{21} \\ y_{22} \\ y_{23} \end{bmatrix} = \begin{bmatrix} 1 & 0 \\ 1 & 0 \\ 0 & 1 \\ 0 & 1 \\ 0 & 1 \end{bmatrix} \begin{bmatrix} \mu_1 \\ \mu_2 \end{bmatrix} + \begin{bmatrix} z_{11} \\ z_{21} \\ z_{21} \\ z_{22} \\ z_{23} \end{bmatrix}^{\gamma} + \begin{bmatrix} \epsilon_{11} \\ \epsilon_{11} \\ \epsilon_{21} \\ \epsilon_{22} \\ \epsilon_{23} \end{bmatrix}$$

$$\Omega: \quad \mathbf{y} \quad = \quad \mathbf{W}\boldsymbol{\mu} \quad + \quad \mathbf{Z}\boldsymbol{\gamma} \quad + \quad \boldsymbol{\epsilon}, \tag{17}$$

which incorporates both the analysis of variance matrix $\mathbf{W}$ and the regression matrix $\mathbf{Z}$. By writing Equation 17 as

$$E(\mathbf{y}) = [\mathbf{WZ}] \begin{pmatrix} \boldsymbol{\mu} \\ \boldsymbol{\gamma} \end{pmatrix} = \mathbf{X}^* \boldsymbol{\theta}^* \tag{18}$$

the model takes the form

$$E(\mathbf{y}) = \mathbf{X}^* \boldsymbol{\theta}^*, \tag{19}$$

which is similar to Equation 14 provided the columns of $\mathbf{Z}$ are linearly independent of those of $\mathbf{W}$ and the matrix $\mathbf{X}^*$ has full column rank. Traditionally, such models are termed analysis of covariance, a common application of the model is with pretest scores z_{ij} and posttest scores y_{ij}.

Our discussion so far has been limited to full rank linear model structure. Having defined the model, one next wants to estimate the population parametrics, test hypotheses about the parameters, and establish simultaneous confidence intervals. To estimate the elements of $\boldsymbol{\mu}$ in Equation 7 under assumption Equation 8, the method of least squares is employed so that the error sum of squares

$$Q_{\Omega} = \sum_{i=1}^{N} \epsilon_i^2 = \boldsymbol{\epsilon}' \boldsymbol{\epsilon} = (\mathbf{y} - \mathbf{W}\boldsymbol{\mu})'(\mathbf{y} - \mathbf{W}\boldsymbol{\mu}) \tag{20}$$

is minimized to obtain the least squares estimator of $\boldsymbol{\mu}$. Taking the partial derivative of Q_{Ω} with respect to $\boldsymbol{\mu}$ and equating the results to zero yield the normal equations

$$(\mathbf{W}'\mathbf{W})\boldsymbol{\mu} = \mathbf{W}'\mathbf{y} \tag{21}$$

because $\mathbf{W}$ is of full rank and the $R(\mathbf{W}) = R(\mathbf{W}'\mathbf{W}) = p$, the inverse of $\mathbf{W}'\mathbf{W}$ exists so that the unique solution to the normal equations is

$$\hat{\boldsymbol{\mu}}_{\Omega} = \bar{\mathbf{y}}, \tag{22}$$

a $p \times 1$ vector of cell means.

The estimate of $\boldsymbol{\mu}$, $\hat{\boldsymbol{\mu}}_{\Omega} = \bar{\mathbf{y}}$ is unique. Hence, all linear parametric functions, $\psi = \mathbf{c}'\boldsymbol{\mu}$, which are linear combinations of the means, are always estimable and estimated by $\hat{\psi} = \mathbf{c}'\hat{\boldsymbol{\mu}}_{\Omega}$ and an unbiased estimator of ψ because

$$E(\hat{\psi}) = E(\mathbf{c}'\hat{\boldsymbol{\mu}}_\Omega) = \mathbf{c}'(\mathbf{W}'\mathbf{W})^{-1}(\mathbf{W}'\mathbf{W})\boldsymbol{\mu} = \mathbf{c}'\boldsymbol{\mu} = \psi \qquad (23)$$

The variance of the estimator $\hat{\psi}$, which has minimum variance among a[ll] linear unbiased estimations, is given by

$$V(\hat{\psi}) = V(\mathbf{c}'\hat{\boldsymbol{\mu}}_\Omega) = \sigma^2\mathbf{c}'(\mathbf{W}'\mathbf{W})^{-1}\mathbf{c}. \qquad (24)$$

(see, e.g., Timm, 1975, p. 175).

Establishing an unbiased estimator for the common variance σ^2, the error sum of squares in Equation 20 is divided by $N - p$ and $\boldsymbol{\mu}$ is replaced by $\hat{\boldsymbol{\mu}}_\Omega$.

$$\begin{aligned}
\hat{\sigma}^2_\Omega &= (\mathbf{y} - \mathbf{W}\hat{\boldsymbol{\mu}}_\Omega)'(\mathbf{y} - \mathbf{W}\hat{\boldsymbol{\mu}}_\Omega)/(N - p) \\
&= (\mathbf{y}'\mathbf{y} - \mathbf{y}'\mathbf{W}\hat{\boldsymbol{\mu}}_\Omega)/(N - p) \\
&= (\mathbf{y}'(\mathbf{I} - \mathbf{W}(\mathbf{W}'\mathbf{W})^{-1}\mathbf{W}')\mathbf{y})/(N - p).
\end{aligned} \qquad (25)$$

To prove that $\hat{\sigma}^2_\Omega$ is an unbiased estimation for σ^2, recall that for a random vecto[r] $\mathbf{Y}$ and a symmetric matrix $\mathbf{A}$ that the expectation of a quadratic form $\mathbf{Y}'\mathbf{AY}$ i[s] given by

$$E(\mathbf{Y}'\mathbf{AY}) = \text{Tr}[\mathbf{A}(\sigma^2\mathbf{I})] + \boldsymbol{\mu}'\mathbf{A}\boldsymbol{\mu} \qquad (26)$$

(where Tr denotes the trace operator) if $E(\mathbf{Y}) = \boldsymbol{\mu}$ and $V(\mathbf{Y}) = \sigma^2\mathbf{I}$. That is,

$$\begin{aligned}
E(\hat{\sigma}^2_\Omega) &= \frac{1}{(N - p)} \text{Tr}\,(\mathbf{I} - \mathbf{W}(\mathbf{W}'\mathbf{W})^{-1}\mathbf{W}')\sigma^2 + \boldsymbol{\mu}'\mathbf{W}'(\mathbf{I} - \mathbf{W}(\mathbf{W}'\mathbf{W})^{-1}\mathbf{W}')\mathbf{W} \\
&= \text{Tr}\,[\sigma^2(\mathbf{I} - \mathbf{W}(\mathbf{W}'\mathbf{W})^{-1}\mathbf{W}')]/N - p) \\
&= (N - p)\sigma^2/(N - p) = \sigma^2
\end{aligned} \qquad (27)$$

because the matrix $(\mathbf{I} - \mathbf{W}(\mathbf{W}'\mathbf{W})^{-1}\mathbf{W}')$ is idempotent, the $\text{Tr}(\mathbf{I} - \mathbf{W}(\mathbf{W}'\mathbf{W})^{-1}\mathbf{W}')$ equals the rank of $\mathbf{I} - \mathbf{W}(\mathbf{W}'\mathbf{W})^{-1}\mathbf{W}' = N - p$.

Although no distributional assumptions are required to obtain the least square[s] estimator of $\boldsymbol{\mu}$, of parametric functions ψ under Ω or an unbiased estimator o[f] σ^2, to test linear hypotheses under Ω of the form

$$\omega: \qquad H: \mathbf{C}\boldsymbol{\mu} = \boldsymbol{\xi}, \qquad (28)$$

where $\boldsymbol{\xi}$ is a specified known vector of constants and $\mathbf{C}$ is a $q \times p$ matrix of ran[k] $q \leq p$ or to determine confidence intervals for parametric functions, one assume[s] that $\mathbf{y}$ has a multivariate normal distribution as represented in Equation 9. Wit[h] distributional assumptions under Ω, parameter estimation may be accomplishe[d] using the maximum likelihood estimation procedure. The likelihood functio[n] under normal theory is

$$L(\boldsymbol{\mu},\sigma^2) = (2\pi)^{-N/2}|\sigma^2\mathbf{I}_N|^{1/2}e^{-\boldsymbol{\epsilon}'\boldsymbol{\epsilon}/2\sigma^2}. \qquad (29)$$

Maximizing Equation 29 with respect to μ is equivalent to solving $\partial[\ln_e L(\mu, \sigma^2)]/\partial\mu = 0$. The solution is the maximum likelihood estimator of μ which is identical to the least squares estimator. Taking the $\partial[\ln_e L(\mu, \sigma^2)]/\partial\sigma^2$ and equating the result to zero yield the maximum likelihood estimator for σ^2

$$\hat{\sigma}^2_{ML} = (y - W\hat{\mu}_\Omega)'(y - W\hat{\mu}_\Omega)/N, \tag{30}$$

which is not an unbiased estimator of σ^2. Multiply Equation 30 by the ratio $N/(N - p)$ yields $\hat{\sigma}^2_\Omega$, which is an unbiased estimator.

To understand geometrically the estimator of the parameter vector under linear model theory, consider the vector y in an N-dimensional space V_N and let V_p denote the space spanned by the columns of the model matrix. Then $W\hat{\mu}_\Omega = \hat{\theta}_\Omega = \hat{y}$ may be interpreted as the vector that comes closest to y as possible; that is,

$$W\hat{\mu}_\Omega = W(W'W)^{-1}W'y = Py = \hat{y} \tag{31}$$

is the projection of y onto V_p where

$$P = W(W'W)^{-1}W' \tag{32}$$

in the projection operator. Furthermore, $y'P'(I - P)y = 0$ because P is symmetric and idempotent ($P^2 = P$), $\hat{y}$ is orthogonal to $y - W\hat{\mu}_\Omega$. From the orthogonality of vectors,

$$\|y\|^2 = \|W\hat{\mu}_\Omega\|^2 + \|y - W\hat{\mu}_\Omega\|^2. \tag{33}$$

The vector $y - W\hat{\mu}_\Omega$ measures the error in estimating y by $\hat{y}$, (Fig. 5.1).

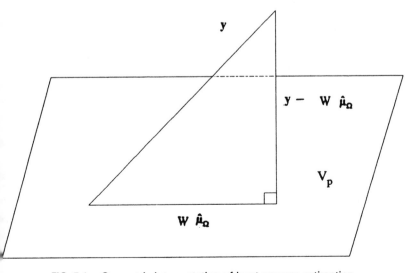

FIG. 5.1. Geometric interpretation of least squares estimation.

To test the null hypothesis specified in Equation 28 under normal theory, th likelihood ratio criterion

$$\lambda = \frac{L(\hat{\omega})}{L(\hat{\Omega})} \tag{34}$$

is employed to obtain a likelihood ratio test (LRT). $L(\hat{\Omega})$ is the maximum valu of $L(\mu, \sigma^2)$ under Ω and $L(\hat{\omega})$ is the maximum value of $L(\mu, \sigma^2)$ maximize under the hypothesis, under ω, which limits the range of the population para metrics. For a test of size α, the null hypothesis is rejected for small values of such that the $Pr(\lambda < \lambda_0) = \alpha$. Under Ω,

$$L(\hat{\Omega}) = (2\pi\hat{\sigma}^2_{ML})^{-N/2} e - (y - W \hat{\mu}_\Omega)'(y - W \hat{\mu}_\Omega)/2\hat{\sigma}^2_{ML}$$

$$= \left(\frac{1}{2\pi\hat{\sigma}^2_{ML}}\right)^{N/2} e^{-N/2}. \tag{35}$$

where

$$\hat{\sigma}^2_{ML} = \frac{(y - W\hat{\mu}_\Omega)'(y - W\hat{\mu}_\Omega)}{N}$$

Under ω, maximizing Equation 29 with respect to μ is equivalent to solving th likelihood equation $\partial[\ln_e L(\mu, \sigma^2)]/\partial\mu = 0$ under the null hypothesis. That is th least squares criterion under ω

$$Q_\omega = \min_{C\mu = \xi} (y - W\mu)'(y - W\mu) \tag{36}$$

is minimized subject to the constraint or restriction that $C\mu = \xi$. Introducing vector of language multipliers λ, the function

$$G = (y - W\mu)'(y - W\mu) + 2\lambda'(C\mu - \xi) \tag{37}$$

is minimized. Taking the partial derivatives of G with respect to μ and λ an equating them to zero yields the equations

$$(W'W)\mu_\omega + C'\lambda = W'y$$

$$C\mu_\omega = \xi. \tag{38}$$

From the first equation $\mu_\omega = \hat{\mu}_\Omega - (W'W)^{-1}C'$ and multiplying by C,

$$\lambda = [C(W'W)^{-1}C']^{-1}(C\hat{\mu}_\Omega - \xi) \tag{39}$$

so that the best estimator of μ under the hypothesis is

$$\hat{\mu}_\omega = \hat{\mu}_\Omega - (W'W)^{-1}C'[C(W'W)^{-1}C']^{-1}(C\hat{\mu}_\Omega - \xi). \tag{40}$$

Thus, the maximum likelihood estimator of μ under the hypothesis is the same a the least squares estimator. Taking the partial derivative of G with respect to σ^2

$$\frac{\partial G}{\partial \sigma^2} = \frac{-N}{2\sigma^2} + \frac{(y - W\hat{\mu}_\omega)'(y - W\hat{\mu}_\omega)}{2\sigma^4} \tag{41}$$

nd equating the result to zero, the maximum likelihood estimator of σ^2 under ω
s obtained:

$$\hat{\sigma}_\omega^2 = (\mathbf{y} - \mathbf{W}\hat{\boldsymbol{\mu}}_\omega)'(\mathbf{y} - \mathbf{W}\hat{\boldsymbol{\mu}}_\omega)/N. \tag{42}$$

Hence

$$L(\hat{\omega}) = (2\pi\hat{\sigma}_\omega^2)^{-N/2}e^{-(\mathbf{y}-\mathbf{W}\hat{\boldsymbol{\mu}}_\omega)'(\mathbf{y}-\mathbf{W}\hat{\boldsymbol{\mu}}_\omega)/2\hat{\sigma}_\omega^2}$$

$$= \left(\frac{1}{2\pi\hat{\sigma}_\omega^2}\right)^{N/2} e^{-N/2}$$

where

$$\hat{\sigma}_\omega^2 = \frac{(\mathbf{y} - \mathbf{W}\hat{\boldsymbol{\mu}}_\omega)'(\mathbf{y} - \mathbf{W}\hat{\boldsymbol{\mu}}_\omega)}{N}$$

o that the likelihood ratio criterion λ becomes

$$\lambda = \left[\frac{(\mathbf{y} - \mathbf{W}\hat{\boldsymbol{\mu}}_\Omega)'(\mathbf{y} - \mathbf{W}\hat{\boldsymbol{\mu}}_\Omega)}{(\mathbf{y} - \mathbf{W}\hat{\boldsymbol{\mu}}_\omega)'(\mathbf{y} - \mathbf{W}\hat{\boldsymbol{\mu}}_\omega)'}\right]. \tag{43}$$

Letting $\hat{Q}_\Omega = (\mathbf{y} - \mathbf{W}\hat{\boldsymbol{\mu}}_\Omega)'(\mathbf{y} - \mathbf{W}\hat{\boldsymbol{\mu}}_\Omega)$ and $\hat{Q}_\omega = (\mathbf{y} - \mathbf{W}\hat{\boldsymbol{\mu}}_\omega)'(\mathbf{y} - \mathbf{W}\hat{\boldsymbol{\mu}}_\omega)$ notice
that

$$\hat{Q}_\omega = \hat{Q}_\Omega + \boldsymbol{\lambda}'[\mathbf{C}(\mathbf{W}'\mathbf{W})^{-1}\mathbf{C}']^{-1}\boldsymbol{\lambda}$$

$$= \hat{Q}_\Omega + (\mathbf{C}\boldsymbol{\mu}_\Omega - \boldsymbol{\xi})'[\mathbf{C}(\mathbf{W}'\mathbf{W})^{-1}\mathbf{C}']^{-1}(\mathbf{C}\hat{\boldsymbol{\mu}}_\Omega - \boldsymbol{\xi}) \tag{44}$$

r

$$\hat{Q}_\omega - \hat{Q}_\Omega = (\mathbf{C}\hat{\boldsymbol{\mu}}_\Omega - \boldsymbol{\xi})'[\mathbf{C}(\mathbf{W}'\mathbf{W})^{-1}\mathbf{C}']^{-1}(\mathbf{C}\hat{\boldsymbol{\mu}}_\Omega - \boldsymbol{\xi}) \tag{45}$$

o that

$$\Lambda = \lambda^{2/N} = \frac{\hat{Q}_\Omega}{\hat{Q}_\omega} = \frac{\hat{Q}_\Omega}{\hat{Q}_\Omega + (\hat{Q}_\omega - \hat{Q}_\Omega)}$$

$$= \frac{1}{1 + (\hat{Q}_\omega - \hat{Q}_\Omega)/\hat{Q}_\Omega}. \tag{46}$$

However, $\hat{Q}_\Omega$ and $\hat{Q}_\omega - \hat{Q}_\Omega$ are statistically independent and under normality
ave noncentral chi-square distributions;

$$\hat{Q}_\Omega \sim \sigma^2\chi^2(N - p, \delta = 0)$$

$$(\hat{Q}_\omega - \hat{Q}_\Omega) \sim \sigma^2\chi^2(q,\delta) \tag{47}$$

where

$$\delta = (\mathbf{C}\boldsymbol{\mu} - \boldsymbol{\xi})'[\mathbf{C}(\mathbf{W}'\mathbf{W})^{-1}\mathbf{C}']^{-1}(\mathbf{C}\boldsymbol{\mu} - \boldsymbol{\xi})/\sigma^2 \tag{48}$$

the noncentrality parameter of the noncentral chi-square distribution (Timm,
975, p. 179). Forming the ratio

$$F = \frac{(\hat{Q}_\omega - \hat{Q}_\Omega)/q}{\hat{Q}_\Omega/(N - p)} \qquad (49)$$

and applying the definition of the noncentral F distribution, the statistic F has a noncentral F distribution with parametric q and $N - p$ and noncentrality parametric δ defined in Equation 48. Returning to Equation 46

$$\lambda = \left[\frac{1}{1 + q\, F/(N - p)} \right]^{N/2}$$

and if $F \to 0$, $\lambda \to 1$, and as $F \to +\infty$, $\lambda \to 0$. Thus, rejecting the null hypothesis specified in Equation 28 for small values of λ is equivalent to rejecting for large values of F. Testing Equation 28 at the level of significance α, H is rejected if

$$F > F^\alpha(q, N - p).$$

Where F^α is the upper α percentage point of the central F distribution, $\nu_h = q = R(C)$ is the hypothesis degrees of freedom and $N - p$ is the degrees of freedom for error, the rank of the projection matrix $(\mathbf{I} - \mathbf{P}) = (\mathbf{I} - \mathbf{W}(\mathbf{W}'\mathbf{W})^{-1}\mathbf{W}')$

The specification of the null hypothesis under ω allows researchers to specify which functions of the cell means are of interest to them in any experimental design under Ω without being concerned about which functions are estimable because all linear combinations of the parameters are estimable. Hence, more thought and consideration can be devoted to determining the full row rank hypothesis test matrix $\mathbf{C}$ with no confusion about what is being tested even though the matrix $\mathbf{C}$ is not unique for a specific hypothesis. To see that it is not unique, suppose the hypothesis under ω is multiplied by a nonsingular matrix $\mathbf{T}$. Then the hypothesis sum of squares in Equation 46 becomes

$$\begin{aligned}
(\mathbf{TC}\hat{\boldsymbol{\mu}}_\Omega - \mathbf{T}\boldsymbol{\xi})'[\mathbf{TC}(\mathbf{W}'\mathbf{W})^{-1}\mathbf{C}'\mathbf{T}']^{-1}(\mathbf{TC}\hat{\boldsymbol{\mu}}_\Omega - \mathbf{T}\boldsymbol{\xi}) \\
= (\mathbf{C}\hat{\boldsymbol{\mu}}_\Omega - \boldsymbol{\xi})'\mathbf{T}'[\mathbf{TC}(\mathbf{W}'\mathbf{W})^{-1}\mathbf{C}'\mathbf{T}']^{-1}\mathbf{T}(\mathbf{C}\hat{\boldsymbol{\mu}}_\Omega - \boldsymbol{\xi}) \\
= (\mathbf{C}\hat{\boldsymbol{\mu}}_\Omega - \boldsymbol{\xi})'[\mathbf{C}(\mathbf{W}'\mathbf{W})^{-1}\mathbf{C}']^{-1}(\mathbf{C}\hat{\boldsymbol{\mu}}_\Omega - \boldsymbol{\xi}) \\
= \hat{Q}_\omega - \hat{Q}_\Omega,
\end{aligned}$$

which shows that the hypothesis sum of squares is invariant under nonsingular transformations.

In analysis of variance designs, the vector $\boldsymbol{\xi}$ in the null hypothesis under ω, H: $\mathbf{C}\boldsymbol{\mu} = \boldsymbol{\xi}$ is usually equal to the zero vector. If a hypothesis of the form H: $\mathbf{C}\boldsymbol{\mu} =$ involving q linearly independent estimable functions $\psi = \mathbf{c}'\boldsymbol{\mu}$ is rejected, an experimenter usually wants to know with some confidence which of the q functions or linear combinations of the q functions led to the rejection of the hypothesis. Following Scheffé (1959, pp. 68–69), let L denote the set of all linear combinations: $\psi_1, \psi_2, \ldots, \psi_q$; then the S method of multiple comparisons states that under Ω the probability is $1 - \alpha$ that simultaneously for all $\psi \in L$

$$\hat{\psi} - S\hat{\sigma}_{\psi} \le \psi \le \hat{\psi} + S\hat{\sigma}_{\psi}, \tag{50}$$

where the estimater of ψ is $\hat{\psi} = \mathbf{c}'\hat{\mathbf{\mu}}_{\Omega}$, the constant S is defined by

$$S^2 = qF^{\alpha}(q, N - p) \tag{51}$$

and $\hat{\sigma}_{\psi}$ is the square root of the expression given in Equation 24 with σ^2 replaced by $\hat{\sigma}_{\Omega}^2$;

$$\hat{\sigma}_{\hat{\psi}} = [\hat{\sigma}_{\Omega}^2 \mathbf{c}'(\mathbf{W}'\mathbf{W})^{-1}\mathbf{c}]^{1/2}. \tag{52}$$

Furthermore, the hypothesis H: $\mathbf{C\mu} = \mathbf{0}$ is equivalent to the hypothesis H: All ψ_i's $= 0$ for $\psi_i \in L$, hence the F ratio defined in Equation 25 will lead to rejection of the null hypothesis if and only if at least one $\psi \in L$ is significantly different from zero. Equation 49 applies to all $\psi \in L$, so for any $\psi \in L$ the probability is certainly greater than or equal to $1 - \alpha$. Combining the overall F test with the S method applied to full rank models, experimenters have a powerful statistical procedure to help them in the analysis of many experimental designs.

In our discussion so far we have limited our comments to model matrices of full rank. Because $\mathbf{W}$, $\mathbf{X}$, and $\mathbf{X}^*$ are all of full rank we can replace $\mathbf{W}$ with $\mathbf{X}$ or $\mathbf{X}^*$ in all our general expressions derived using the $\mathbf{W}$ matrix. Due to the special structure of $\mathbf{X}^*$, more will be said about the analysis of covariance model. In general then we have the following result.

Under the Gauss–Markoff setup, $\mathbf{y} = \mathbf{X\beta} + \mathbf{\epsilon}$, where $\mathbf{\theta} = \mathbf{X\beta} \in \Omega$ and Ω is an r-dimensional subspace $V_r \subset V_N$. Consider the problem of testing the hypothesis $\mathbf{\theta} \in \omega$, where ω is an $(r - g)$-dimensional subspace of V_r. Furthermore, assume that the random vector $\mathbf{Y}$ has a multivariate normal distribution with mean $\mathbf{\eta} = \mathbf{X\beta}$ and variance $\sigma^2\mathbf{I}$, $\mathbf{Y} \sim N(\mathbf{\eta}, \sigma^2\mathbf{I})$. Let $\mathbf{C}$ be a matrix of order $g \times q$ of rank $g < r$, where r is the full column rank of the model matrix $\mathbf{X}$ such that the linearly independently parametric functions $\mathbf{C\beta}$ are individually estimable and

$$\hat{Q}_{\omega} = \min(\mathbf{y} - \mathbf{X\beta})'(\mathbf{y} - \mathbf{X\beta}),$$

subject to the condition that $\mathbf{C\beta} = \mathbf{\xi}$ for a specified vector $\mathbf{\xi}$. Then if the hypothesis

$$H_0: \mathbf{C\beta} = \mathbf{\xi}$$

is true, the ratio

$$\frac{Q_h/\nu_h}{Q_e/\nu_e} \sim F(\nu_h, \nu_e, \delta = 0)$$

has a central F distribution with degrees of freedom

$$g = \nu_h = R(\mathbf{C})$$

and

$$\nu_e = N - R(\mathbf{X}) = N - r = \nu_e.$$

With

$$Q_h = \hat{Q}_\omega - \hat{Q}_\Omega$$
$$= (\mathbf{C}\hat{\boldsymbol{\beta}} - \boldsymbol{\xi})'[\mathbf{C}(\mathbf{X}'\mathbf{X})^{-1}\mathbf{C}']^{-1}(\mathbf{C}\hat{\boldsymbol{\beta}} - \boldsymbol{\xi})$$
$$Q_e = \hat{Q}_\Omega = \mathbf{y}'(\mathbf{I} - \mathbf{X}(\mathbf{X}'\mathbf{X})^{-1}\mathbf{X}')\mathbf{y}$$
$$\hat{\boldsymbol{\beta}} = (\mathbf{X}'\mathbf{X})^{-1}\mathbf{X}'\mathbf{y}.$$

For a geometric interpretation of the F test, let V_r denote the space spanned b the columns of $\mathbf{X}$, V_{r-g} the hypothesis subspace of V_r, and V_g the orthocompl ment of V_{r-g} relative to V_r. In minimizing Q_Ω, the estimate of $\mathbf{X}\boldsymbol{\beta}$ is $\mathbf{X}\hat{\boldsymbol{\beta}} = \hat{\boldsymbol{\theta}}_\Omega$ obtained under the general model Ω. In minimizing Q_ω, the estimate of $\mathbf{X}\boldsymbol{\beta}$ $\mathbf{X}\hat{\boldsymbol{\beta}}_\omega$, is acquired under the constraint imposed by the hypothesis, so let $\hat{\boldsymbol{\theta}}_\omega$ $\mathbf{X}\hat{\boldsymbol{\beta}}_\omega$. By using the geometry of least-squares estimation shown in Fig. 5.1, $\hat{\boldsymbol{\theta}}_\Omega$ the projection of $\mathbf{y}$ on V_r and $\hat{\boldsymbol{\theta}}_\omega$ is the projection of $\mathbf{y}$ on V_{r-g}, so that

$$Q_\omega = \|\mathbf{y} - \hat{\boldsymbol{\theta}}_\omega\|^2 \text{ and } Q_\Omega = \|\mathbf{y} - \hat{\boldsymbol{\theta}}_\Omega\|^2$$

and

$$Q_h = Q_\omega - Q_\Omega = \|\hat{\boldsymbol{\theta}}_\Omega - \hat{\boldsymbol{\theta}}_\omega\|^2$$

by the orthogonality of the projections. Pictorially, the relations among $\hat{Q}_\omega$, $\hat{Q}_\Omega$ and Q_h are shown in Fig. 5.2 where we see that

$$\hat{Q}_\omega = (\hat{Q}_\omega - \hat{Q}_\Omega) + \hat{Q}_\Omega$$
$$SS_T = \quad SS_H \quad + SS_e$$

or the total sum of squares = the hypothesis sum of square + the error sum squares. Furthermore, $\hat{Q}_\Omega \in V_r^\perp$ of dimension $(N - r)$, $\hat{Q}_\omega \in V_{N-r+g}$ dimension $N - r + g$ and $Q_h \in V_g$ of dimension g; the degrees of freedom of th F statistic correspond to the dimension of the subspaces. From Fig. 5.2, a visu interpretation of the F statistic is as $\hat{\boldsymbol{\theta}}_\Omega$ and $\hat{\boldsymbol{\theta}}_\omega$ differ, the best estimate of $\boldsymbol{\theta}$ und Ω and ω, Q_h increases so that the value of F becomes large yielding rejection the null hypothesis.

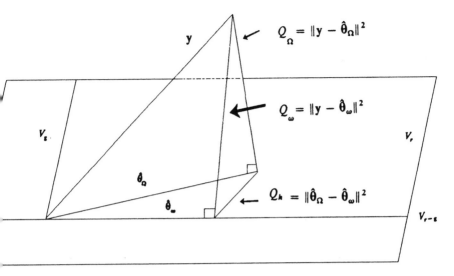

FIG. 5.2.   Geometric interpretation of the F statistic.

FUNDAMENTALS:
LESS THAN FULL RANK MODELS

Our discussion so far has been limited to full rank unrestricted linear models because the model matrix was always of full rank and the parameter vector was not constrained. We now discuss overparameterized less than full rank models. To begin our discussion, lets again review the two-sample example; however, instead of letting $E(Y_{ij}) = \mu_i$ for $i = 1, 2$ we let $\mu_i = \mu + \alpha_i$. That is, we let the cell mean equal an overall common constant μ and a unique effect α_i. With this parameterization, Equation 53 becomes

$$\Omega: Y_{ij} = \mu + \alpha_i + \epsilon_{ij} \; i = 1, 2; j = 1, 2, \ldots, N_i$$

$$E(Y_{ij}) = \mu + \alpha_i$$

$$V(Y_{ij}) = \sigma^2. \tag{53}$$

Letting $N_1 = 2$ and $N_2 = 3$, we see that the matrix representation of Equation 53 is:

$$\begin{bmatrix} y_{11} \\ y_{12} \\ y_{21} \\ y_{22} \\ y_{31} \end{bmatrix} = \begin{bmatrix} 1 & 1 & 0 \\ 1 & 1 & 0 \\ 1 & 0 & 1 \\ 1 & 0 & 1 \\ 1 & 0 & 1 \end{bmatrix} \begin{bmatrix} \mu \\ \alpha_1 \\ \alpha_2 \end{bmatrix} + \begin{bmatrix} \epsilon_{11} \\ \epsilon_{12} \\ \epsilon_{21} \\ \epsilon_{22} \\ \epsilon_{23} \end{bmatrix}$$

or that $\mathbf{y} = \mathbf{X}\boldsymbol{\beta} + \boldsymbol{\epsilon}$. However, because the first column of the model matrix is the sum of the last two, the model matrix no longer has full column rank; the model is overparameterized and less than full rank. There are three parameters but only two linearly independent estimates, the rank of the model matrix.

In general, under Ω in Equation 13 when the model matrix is less than full rank, $R(\mathbf{X}) = r < q$, the normal equations.

$$(\mathbf{X'X})\boldsymbol{\beta} = \mathbf{X'y}, \tag{54}$$

which result when minimizing the error sum of squares Q_Ω in Equation 20. However, these equations do not have a unique solution if the rank of $\mathbf{X}$ is less than the number of columns in the model matrix because the inverse $(\mathbf{X'X})^-$ does not exist. To overcome this problem, three commonly used approaches have been discussed by authors of experimental design texts: the generalized inverse, estimable function approach, model restrictions or side conditions, and reparametrization.

Generalized Inverse

Although Equation 54 does not have a unique solution, a general solution set for the normal equations is

$$\hat{\boldsymbol{\beta}} = (\mathbf{X'X})^- \mathbf{X'y} + (\mathbf{I} - \mathbf{H})\mathbf{z}, \tag{55}$$

where $\mathbf{H} = (\mathbf{X'X})^-(\mathbf{X'X})$, $\mathbf{z}$ is an arbitrary vector, and $(\mathbf{X'X})^-$ is a g-inverse of $(\mathbf{X'X})$, any matrix that satisfies the condition

$$(\mathbf{X'X})(\mathbf{X'X})^- (\mathbf{X'X}) = (\mathbf{X'X}). \tag{56}$$

With $\hat{\boldsymbol{\beta}}$ defined in Equation 55, certain linear combinations of the elements of $\boldsymbol{\beta}$, often called parametric functions, are uniquely estimable and independent of the solution.

A parametric function $\psi = \mathbf{c'}\boldsymbol{\beta}$ is said to be estimable if there exists a vector $\mathbf{a}$ such that $E(\mathbf{a'Y}) = \mathbf{c'}\boldsymbol{\beta}$. $\tag{57}$

That is, $\psi = \mathbf{c'}\boldsymbol{\beta}$ has a linear unbiased estimate given by $\mathbf{a'Y}$. This implies that ψ is estimable if and only if $\mathbf{c'} = \mathbf{a'X}$; that is, $\mathbf{c'}$ is a linear combination of the rows of $\mathbf{X}$ or if $\mathbf{c}$ is a vector in the space spanned by the columns of $\mathbf{X'}$, written as $\mathbf{c} \in V(\mathbf{X'})$, or equivalently, $\mathbf{c} \in V(\mathbf{X'X})$. If the $R(\mathbf{X}) = r$, there are only r linearly independent estimable functions. For known $\mathbf{c}$, obtaining a vector $\mathbf{a}$ such that $\mathbf{c} = \mathbf{a'X}$ is not necessarily easy when the $R(\mathbf{X})$ is large. Even if you found one, how do you know it is the "best" one? Geometrically, following Scheffé (1959, p. 15), suppose an unbiased estimate $\psi = \mathbf{c'}\boldsymbol{\beta}$ is found such that $E(\mathbf{a'Y}) = \mathbf{c'}\boldsymbol{\beta}$. To find the "best" one, we would substitute for the vector $\mathbf{a}$, the projection of $\mathbf{a}$ onto the space spanned by the columns of $\mathbf{X}$,

$$\mathbf{a^*} = \mathbf{P}_V\mathbf{a}$$

$$= \mathbf{X}(\mathbf{X'X})^-\mathbf{Xa} \tag{58}$$

o that

$$\hat{\psi} = \mathbf{a}^{*\prime}\mathbf{y} = \mathbf{a}'\mathbf{X}(\mathbf{X}'\mathbf{X})^-\mathbf{X}'\mathbf{y}$$
$$= \mathbf{c}'(\mathbf{X}'\mathbf{X})^-\mathbf{X}'\mathbf{y}$$
$$= \mathbf{c}'\hat{\boldsymbol{\beta}} \tag{59}$$

s the desired "best" estimate.

Alternatively, if $\mathbf{c}' = \mathbf{a}'\mathbf{X}$, then $\mathbf{c}'\mathbf{H} = \mathbf{a}'\mathbf{X}\mathbf{H} = \mathbf{a}'\mathbf{X}(\mathbf{X}'\mathbf{X})^-\mathbf{X}'\mathbf{X} = \mathbf{a}'\mathbf{X} = \mathbf{c}'$; f $\mathbf{c}'\mathbf{H} = \mathbf{c}'$, then $\mathbf{c}' = \mathbf{c}'(\mathbf{X}'\mathbf{X})^-\mathbf{X}'\mathbf{X} = \mathbf{a}'\mathbf{X}$ by setting $\mathbf{a}' = \mathbf{c}'(\mathbf{X}'\mathbf{X})^-\mathbf{X}'$. A necessary and sufficient condition that $\mathbf{c}'\boldsymbol{\beta}$ be uniquely estimable is that $\mathbf{c}' = \mathbf{c}'\mathbf{H}$ because, for any $\hat{\boldsymbol{\beta}}$, $\mathbf{c}'\hat{\boldsymbol{\beta}} = \mathbf{c}'\mathbf{H}\hat{\boldsymbol{\beta}} = \mathbf{c}'(\mathbf{X}'\mathbf{X})^-\mathbf{X}'\mathbf{y} = \mathbf{a}'\mathbf{X}(\mathbf{X}'\mathbf{X})^-\mathbf{X}'\mathbf{y} = \mathbf{a}^{*\prime}\mathbf{y}$ is unique when $\mathbf{c}'\boldsymbol{\beta}$ is estimable.

Furthermore, $\mathbf{c}'\boldsymbol{\beta}$ is unbiased for $\mathbf{c}'\boldsymbol{\beta}$ because

$$E(\mathbf{c}'\hat{\boldsymbol{\beta}}) = E(\mathbf{c}'(\mathbf{X}'\mathbf{X})^-\mathbf{X}'\mathbf{Y}) + \mathbf{c}'(\mathbf{I} - \mathbf{H})\mathbf{z}$$
$$= \mathbf{c}'(\mathbf{X}'\mathbf{X})^-\mathbf{X}'E(\mathbf{Y})$$
$$= \mathbf{c}'(\mathbf{X}'\mathbf{X})^-\mathbf{X}'\mathbf{X}$$
$$= \mathbf{c}'\mathbf{H}$$
$$= \mathbf{c}'\boldsymbol{\beta}$$

f and only if $\mathbf{c}' = \mathbf{c}'\mathbf{H}$. Because $\mathbf{c}' = \mathbf{c}'\mathbf{H}$ if and only if $\mathbf{c}' = \mathbf{t}'\mathbf{H}$ for arbitrary vectors $\mathbf{t}$ by the idempotency property of $\mathbf{H}$.

The parametric function $\psi = \mathbf{c}'\boldsymbol{\beta}$, where $\boldsymbol{\beta}$ is such that $(\mathbf{X}'\mathbf{X})\boldsymbol{\beta} = \mathbf{X}'\mathbf{y}$, has a unique linear unbiased estimator given by $\mathbf{c}'\hat{\boldsymbol{\beta}} = \mathbf{c}'(\mathbf{X}'\mathbf{X})^-\mathbf{X}'\mathbf{y}$ if and only if $\mathbf{c}'\mathbf{H} = \mathbf{c}'$, where in general, for arbitrary vectors $\mathbf{t}$ such that $\mathbf{c}' = \mathbf{t}'\mathbf{H}$, $\mathbf{c}'\boldsymbol{\beta} = \mathbf{t}'(\mathbf{X}'\mathbf{X})^-\mathbf{X}'\mathbf{X}(\mathbf{X}'\mathbf{X})^-\mathbf{X}'\mathbf{y} = \mathbf{t}'\mathbf{H}\hat{\boldsymbol{\beta}}. \tag{60}$

If $(\mathbf{X}'\mathbf{X})^-$ is constructed such that $(\mathbf{X}'\mathbf{X})^-\mathbf{X}'\mathbf{X}(\mathbf{X}'\mathbf{X})^- = (\mathbf{X}'\mathbf{X})^-$, then $\mathbf{c}'\hat{\boldsymbol{\beta}} = \mathbf{t}'(\mathbf{X}'\mathbf{X})^-\mathbf{X}'\mathbf{y}$.

The variance of the estimator $\mathbf{c}'\hat{\boldsymbol{\beta}}$ of $\mathbf{c}'\boldsymbol{\beta}$ is

$$V(\mathbf{c}'\hat{\boldsymbol{\beta}}) = \sigma^2\mathbf{c}'(\mathbf{X}'\mathbf{X})^-\mathbf{c}. \tag{61}$$

To prove Equation 61 we recall that $\mathbf{X} = \mathbf{X}(\mathbf{X}'\mathbf{X})^-\mathbf{X}'\mathbf{X}$ and, if $\mathbf{c}'\boldsymbol{\beta}$ is estimable, $\mathbf{c} = \mathbf{X}'\mathbf{a}$. Thus

$$V(\mathbf{c}'\hat{\boldsymbol{\beta}}) = \mathbf{c}'(\mathbf{X}'\mathbf{X})^-\mathbf{X}'(\sigma^2\mathbf{I})\mathbf{X}(\mathbf{X}'\mathbf{X})^-\mathbf{c}$$
$$= \sigma^2\mathbf{c}'(\mathbf{X}'\mathbf{X})^-\mathbf{X}'\mathbf{X}(\mathbf{X}'\mathbf{X})^-\mathbf{c}$$
$$= \sigma^2\mathbf{a}'\mathbf{X}(\mathbf{X}'\mathbf{X})^-\mathbf{X}'\mathbf{X}(\mathbf{X}'\mathbf{X})^-\mathbf{X}'\mathbf{a}$$
$$= \sigma^2\mathbf{a}'\mathbf{X}(\mathbf{X}'\mathbf{X})^-\mathbf{X}'\mathbf{a}$$
$$= \sigma^2\mathbf{c}'(\mathbf{X}'\mathbf{X})^-\mathbf{c}$$

To see how this general theory would work for the model specified in Equation 53, observe that

$$(\mathbf{X'X}) = \begin{pmatrix} N & N_1 & N_2 \\ N_1 & N_1 & O \\ N_2 & O & N_2 \end{pmatrix} , \tag{62}$$

where $N = N_1 + N_2$ and the inverse of $(\mathbf{X'X})$ does not exist. To construct a g-inverse for $(\mathbf{X'X})$, one can delete the dependent rows and corresponding columns, replace the entries with zeroes and find the inverse of the remaining matrix (Timm, 1975, p. 52). Then, a g-inverse of $\mathbf{X'X}$ is:

$$(\mathbf{X'X})^- = \begin{pmatrix} 0 & 0 \\ 0 & \mathbf{D}^{-1} \end{pmatrix} = \begin{pmatrix} 0 & 0 & 0 \\ 0 & \frac{1}{N_1} & 0 \\ 0 & 0 & \frac{1}{N_2} \end{pmatrix} \tag{63}$$

and

$$\mathbf{H} = (\mathbf{X'X})^-(\mathbf{X'X}) = \begin{pmatrix} 0 & 0 & 0 \\ 1 & 1 & 0 \\ 1 & 0 & 1 \end{pmatrix}$$

$$\hat{\boldsymbol{\beta}} = (\mathbf{X'X})^-\mathbf{X'y} + (\mathbf{I} - \mathbf{H})\mathbf{z} = \begin{pmatrix} 0 \\ \bar{y}_1 \\ \bar{y}_2 \end{pmatrix} + \begin{pmatrix} z_1 \\ -z_1 \\ -z_2 \end{pmatrix}$$

and setting $z_1 = \bar{y} = (N_1\bar{y}_1 + N_2\bar{y}_2)/(N_1 + N_2)$, a general solution may take the form

$$\hat{\boldsymbol{\beta}} = \begin{pmatrix} \bar{y} \\ \bar{y}_1 - \bar{y} \\ \bar{y}_2 - \bar{y} \end{pmatrix} .$$

However, because $\mathbf{c'H} \neq \mathbf{c'}$ for $\mathbf{c'} = (1, 0, 0)$, μ is not uniquely estimable. Using Equation 60 and $(\mathbf{X'X})^-$ defined in Equation 63, the general form of parametric functions with unique linear unbiased estimates for arbitrary vectors $\mathbf{t}$ take the form

$$\psi = \mathbf{t'\boldsymbol{\beta}} = \mathbf{t'H}$$

$$= (t_0, t_1, t_2)' \begin{pmatrix} 0 & 0 & 0 \\ 1 & 1 & 0 \\ 1 & 0 & 1 \end{pmatrix} \begin{pmatrix} \mu \\ \alpha_1 \\ \alpha_2 \end{pmatrix}$$

$$\psi = (t_1 + t_2)\mu + t_1\alpha_1 + t_2\alpha_2 \tag{64}$$

with unique solutions given by

$$\hat{\psi} = \mathbf{t'H(X'X)^-y}$$

$$= \mathbf{t'} \begin{pmatrix} 0 & 0 & 0 \\ 1 & 1 & 0 \\ 1 & 0 & 1 \end{pmatrix} \begin{pmatrix} 0 \\ \bar{y}_1 \\ \bar{y}_2 \end{pmatrix}$$

$$\hat{\psi} = t_1 \bar{y}_1 + t_2 \bar{y}_2. \tag{65}$$

Choosing $\mathbf{t'} = \mathbf{t'_1} = (0, 1, -1)$ and $\mathbf{t'} = \mathbf{t'_2} = (0, 1/N_1, 1/N_2)$, we observe that the parametric functions

$$\psi_1 = \mathbf{t'_1 \beta} = \alpha_1 - \alpha_2$$

$$\psi_2 = \mathbf{t'_2 \beta} = \mu + (N_1 \alpha_1 + N_2 \alpha_2)/(N_1 + N_2) \tag{66}$$

have unique estimates

$$\hat{\psi}_1 = \bar{y}_1 - \bar{y}_2$$

$$\hat{\psi}_2 = \bar{y} = (N_1 \bar{y}_1 + N_2 \bar{y}_2)/(N_1 + N_2). \tag{67}$$

Furthermore, no $\mathbf{t}$ exists to estimate μ; but, $\psi = \mu + \alpha_1$ or $\psi = \mu + \alpha_2$ are uniquely estimable and estimated by $\hat{\psi}_1 = \bar{y}_1$ and $\hat{\psi}_2 = \bar{y}_2$.

Provided the g linearly independent functions $\mathbf{C\beta}$ are individually estimable, hypothesis of the form H_0: $\mathbf{C\beta} = \boldsymbol{\xi}$ can be tested with the statistic defined in equation 49 by replacing $\mathbf{W}$ with $\mathbf{X}$ and the ordinary inverse with a g inverse and by $\mathbf{\beta}$ (Timm, 1975, pp. 171–183):

$$F = \frac{(\mathbf{C\hat{\beta}} - \boldsymbol{\xi})'(\mathbf{C(X'X)^-C'})^{-1}(\mathbf{C\hat{\beta}} - \boldsymbol{\xi})/g}{\mathbf{y'(I - X(X'X)^-X')y}/(N - r)} \tag{68}$$

where $r = R(\mathbf{X})$ and $g = R(\mathbf{C})$.

Model Restrictions or Side Conditions

Another approach to solving the normal equations defined in Equation 54 is to increase the model defined by Equation 53 to full rank by augmenting the model matrix $\mathbf{X}$ with a matrix $\mathbf{R}$ where $\mathbf{R\beta} = \mathbf{0}$ so that the rows of $\mathbf{R}$ are linearly independent of the rows of $\mathbf{X}$, the row space of $\mathbf{R}$ and the row space of $\mathbf{X}$ satisfy the condition that $\mathbf{X} \cap \mathbf{R} = \{\mathbf{0}\}$; that is, to add nonestimable restrictions or side conditions to the model parameters. Replacing $\mathbf{X}$ with $\begin{pmatrix} \mathbf{X} \\ \mathbf{R} \end{pmatrix}$ in Equation 54, we see that

$$(\mathbf{X'X + R'R)\beta} = (\mathbf{X'y + R\theta}) \tag{69}$$

are the new normal equations. Now, the model matrix has full rank and

$$\hat{\mathbf{\beta}} = (\mathbf{X'X + R'R})^{-1}(\mathbf{X'y + R\theta}) \tag{70}$$

is a unique solution to the model with the nonestimable restrictions added to the model.

To illustrate the notion of side conditions, we again use our simple two-group example. The first task is to create "natural" side conditions for the matrix $\mathbf{R}$. Letting $\mu_1 = \mu + \alpha_1$ and $\mu_2 = \mu + \alpha_2$, observe that

$$\frac{N_1\mu_1 + N_2\mu_2}{N_1 + N_2} = \mu + \frac{N_1\alpha_1 + N_2\alpha_2}{N_1 + N_2}. \tag{71}$$

To give meaning to the constant μ, one might select the side condition

$$\mathbf{R}\boldsymbol{\beta} = N_1\alpha_1 + N_2\alpha_2 = 0 \tag{72}$$

or $\mathbf{R} = (0, 2, 3)$ for our two sample example. By Equation 64, the parametric function $\mathbf{R}$ is not estimable. By adding $\mathbf{R}$ to the model matrix $\mathbf{X}$, we increase the model matrix to full rank three

$$R\left(\begin{matrix} \mathbf{X} \\ \mathbf{R} \end{matrix}\right) = \begin{bmatrix} 1 & 1 & 0 \\ 1 & 1 & 0 \\ 1 & 0 & 1 \\ 1 & 0 & 1 \\ 1 & 0 & 1 \\ 0 & 2 & 3 \end{bmatrix} = 3.$$

Performing the normal equation calculations, Equation 69 becomes

$$\left[\begin{pmatrix} 5 & 2 & 3 \\ 2 & 2 & 0 \\ 3 & 0 & 3 \end{pmatrix} + \begin{pmatrix} 0 & 0 & 0 \\ 0 & 4 & 6 \\ 0 & 6 & 9 \end{pmatrix}\right]\begin{pmatrix} \mu \\ \alpha_1 \\ \alpha_2 \end{pmatrix} = \begin{pmatrix} 5\bar{y} \\ 2\bar{y}_1 \\ 3\bar{y}_2 \end{pmatrix}, \tag{73}$$

which has the solution

$$\hat{\mu} = \frac{2\bar{y}_1 + 3\bar{y}_2}{(2 + 3)} = \frac{N_1\bar{y}_1 + N_2\bar{y}_2}{N_1 + N_2} = \bar{y}$$

$$\hat{\alpha}_1 = \bar{y}_1 - \bar{y}$$

$$\hat{\alpha}_2 = \bar{y}_2 - \bar{y}. \tag{74}$$

That is, the parametric functions μ, α_1, and α_2 become estimable when the side conditions are part of the model because we now have a full rank model. The parametric function $\psi = \alpha_1 - \alpha_2$ is again estimable and estimated by $\hat{\psi} = \hat{\alpha}_1 - \hat{\alpha}_2 = \bar{y}_1 - \bar{y}_2$.

An alternative model is to use the set of restrictions $\alpha_1 + \alpha_2 = 0$. This might be appropriate if we were interested in an unweighted average of parameters because then for $\mu_1 = \mu + \alpha_1$ and $\mu_2 = \mu + \alpha_2$,

$$\frac{\mu_1 + \mu_2}{2} = \mu + \frac{\alpha_1 + \alpha_2}{2}. \tag{75}$$

With this set of restrictions,

$$\hat{\mu} = \frac{\bar{y}_1 + \bar{y}_2}{2} = \bar{y}*$$

$$\hat{\alpha}_1 = \bar{y}_1 - \bar{y}*$$

$$\hat{\alpha}_2 = \bar{y}_2 - \bar{y}*. \tag{76}$$

Again, the parametric functions μ, α_1, and α_2 become estimable when the new side conditions become part of the model; however, the individual estimates in Equation 74 are not the same as those obtained in Equation 76. Observe, however, that the parametric function $\psi = \alpha_1 - \alpha_2$ is again estimable and estimated by $\hat{\psi} = \hat{\alpha}_1 - \hat{\alpha}_2 = \bar{y}_1 - \bar{y}_2$; it was invariant to the nonestimable restrictions.

Reparameterization

Another method of solving Equation 54 is to reparameterize the model or reduce the system to full rank r by solving for only r linear parametric functions. The technique is to introduce a new set of unknowns $\boldsymbol{\beta}* = \mathbf{C}\boldsymbol{\beta}$ where $\boldsymbol{\beta}*$ is an $r \times 1$ vector and the $R(\mathbf{C}) = r$ such that

$$(\mathbf{X}'\mathbf{X}) = \mathbf{BC}. \tag{77}$$

Then

$$(\mathbf{X}'\mathbf{X})\boldsymbol{\beta} = \mathbf{X}'\mathbf{y}$$

$$\mathbf{BC}\boldsymbol{\beta} = \mathbf{X}'\mathbf{y}$$

$$(\mathbf{B}'\mathbf{B})\mathbf{C}\boldsymbol{\beta} = \mathbf{B}'\mathbf{X}'\mathbf{y}$$

$$\hat{\boldsymbol{\beta}}* = (\mathbf{B}'\mathbf{B})^{-1}\mathbf{B}'\mathbf{X}'\mathbf{y} \tag{78}$$

and $\boldsymbol{\beta}*$ is a reparameterized vector of unknown parameters. To find the matrix $\mathbf{B}$ in Equation 77, $\mathbf{C}$ must be selected so that the rows of $\mathbf{C}$ are in the row space of $\mathbf{X}'\mathbf{X}$, because $(\mathbf{X}'\mathbf{X}) = \mathbf{BC}$ or so that the

$$R\begin{pmatrix} \mathbf{X}'\mathbf{X} \\ \mathbf{C} \end{pmatrix} = R(\mathbf{X}'\mathbf{X}) = R(\mathbf{C}) = r. \tag{79}$$

Given $\mathbf{C}$, $\mathbf{B}$ is determined by

$$\mathbf{B} = \mathbf{B}(\mathbf{CC}')(\mathbf{CC}')^{-1} = (\mathbf{X}'\mathbf{X})\mathbf{C}'(\mathbf{CC}')^{-1}. \tag{80}$$

In experimental designs, $\mathbf{C}$ is chosen such that the vector of new parameters $\mathbf{B}*$ have a meaningful interpretation. For example, if

$$\mathbf{C} = \begin{pmatrix} 1 & \frac{1}{2} & \frac{1}{2} \\ 0 & 1 & -1 \end{pmatrix} \tag{81}$$

or

$$C = \begin{pmatrix} 1 & \frac{2}{5} & \frac{3}{5} \\ 0 & 1 & -1 \end{pmatrix}$$

for our two-sample example, then

$$\boldsymbol{\beta}^* = \begin{bmatrix} \mu = \dfrac{\alpha_1 + \alpha_2}{2} \\ \\ \alpha_1 - \alpha_2 \end{bmatrix} \tag{82}$$

or

$$\boldsymbol{\beta}^* = \begin{bmatrix} \mu + \dfrac{2\alpha_1 + 3\alpha_2}{5} \\ \\ \alpha_1 - \alpha_2 \end{bmatrix}.$$

Meaningful interpretation under reparameterization really means that the parametric function $\psi = \mathbf{c}'\boldsymbol{\beta}$, an element of $\boldsymbol{\beta}^*$, is estimable. For models with side conditions, we also saw that the notion of estimable functions was important because the restriction matrix $\mathbf{R}$ should not contain estimable functions in $\mathbf{R}\boldsymbol{\beta}$. This condition ensures that the solution to the normal equations given by Equation 70 is just one solution of the general case given by Equation 55. This is not the case if $\mathbf{R}$ contains estimable functions, as becomes evident in the next section.

For models, with nonestimable side conditions, parameters not estimable in the less than full rank models become estimable (have meaning) in terms of the new full rank model and hypotheses not testable using the less than full rank model become testable in the restricted model. For our simple example, the correspondence is illustrated in Table 5.1. To avoid the confusion introduced by side conditions and reparameterization, we can either choose to discuss less than full rank models or simple full rank mean (μ_{ij}) models. The approach taken in

TABLE 5.1
Comparing Hypotheses Across Models

Less than Full Rank	Full Rank with Nonestimable Restrictions	Full Rank
$H_0: \mu + \dfrac{N_1\alpha_1 + N_2\alpha_2}{N_1 + N_2} = 0$	$H_0: \mu = 0$ where $N_1\alpha_1 + N_2\alpha_2 = 0$	$H_0: \dfrac{N_1\mu_1 + N_2\mu_2}{N_1 + N_2} = 0$
$H_0: \mu + \dfrac{\alpha_1 + \alpha_2}{2} = 0$	$H_0: \mu = 0$ where $\alpha_1 + \alpha_2 = 0$	$H_0: \dfrac{\mu_1 + \mu_2}{2} = 0$
$H_0: \mu + \alpha_2 = 0$	$H_0: \mu = 0$ where $\alpha_2 = 0$	$H_0: \mu_2 = 0$
$H_0: \alpha_1 = \alpha_2$	$H_0: \alpha_1 = \alpha_2 = 0$ where $\alpha_1 + \alpha_2 = 0$	$H_0: \mu_1 = \mu_2$

his chapter is to stress mean models in the multivariate case because Timm 1975) already reviewed the less than full rank multivariate model theory.

GEOMETRY: ANCOVA MODEL

n Fig. 5.2, we represented the familiar geometric interpretation of the F statistic nd we presented the general form of the analysis of covariance model in Equaion 17. This is where most authors stop their geometric discussion of ANOVA. he purpose of this section is to extend the geometry, following Scheffé (1959, hap. 6), to analysis of covariance models.

For the ANCOVA model, let

$$\Omega^*: Y = \underset{n \times p}{X} \quad \underset{p \times 1}{\beta} + \underset{n \times h}{Z} \quad \underset{h \times 1}{\gamma} + \underset{n \times p}{\epsilon} \quad (83)$$
$$\epsilon \sim N(0, \sigma^2 I),$$

here we may have $R\beta = 0$ estimable side conditions imposed to make the ements of β estimable so that the row space of X and R satisfy $R \cap X = \{0\}$. et V_0 denote the space spanned by the columns of X and V_1 the space spanned y the columns of Z. Then $E(Y) = \eta \in V = V_0 + V_1$. Further, assume $V_0 \cap V_1 = \{0\}$ so that

$$E(Y) = \eta = \eta_0 + \eta_1 = X\beta + Z\gamma \quad (84)$$

here $\eta_i \in V_i$ is unique and the $R(V_1) = h$ so that the γ_j's are unique. Now lets write $V = V_0 \oplus V_1 = V_0 \oplus V^*$ where V^* is the orthocomplement of V_0 in V $\subset V_N$. Then,

$$Y = X\beta_0 + Z^*\gamma + \epsilon \quad (85)$$

here the columns of Z^* span V^*. Furthermore, let P and $I - P = Q$ denote ojection operations onto V_0 and $V_0^\perp$ in V_N. Then,

$$Y = X\beta_0 + Z^*\gamma + \epsilon$$
$$Y = (X\beta + PZ\gamma) + QZ\gamma + \epsilon \quad (86)$$

here $(X\beta + PZ\gamma) \in V_0$ and $QZ\gamma \in V^*$. The decomposition of the mean ctor η is shown in Fig. 5.3.

$$E(Y) = \eta = X\beta + Z\gamma$$
$$= \eta_0 + \eta_1$$
$$= X\beta_0 + Z^*\gamma$$
$$= (X\beta + PZ\gamma) + Z^*\gamma. \quad (87)$$

To estimate β under Ω^*, recall from the ANOVA model Ω: $Y = X\beta + \epsilon$ with $\beta = 0$ that there exists a $\hat{\beta}$ such that

$$\hat{\mathbf{y}} = \hat{\boldsymbol{\theta}}_\Omega = \mathbf{PY} = \mathbf{X\beta} \quad \text{and} \quad \mathbf{R\beta} = 0$$

uniquely where $\mathbf{PY}$ is the projection of $\mathbf{Y}$ on V, the space spanned by the column of $\mathbf{X}$. Suppose the solution under Ω is $\hat{\boldsymbol{\beta}} = \mathbf{Ay}$ and let $\mathbf{Z}$ be spanned by $[\mathbf{z}_1, \mathbf{z}_2, \ldots, \mathbf{z}_h]$. Consider

$$\mathbf{PZ} = [\mathbf{Pz}_1, \ldots, \mathbf{Pz}_h] = [\mathbf{X\beta}^{(1)}, \ldots, \mathbf{X\beta}^{(y)}] \text{ where } \boldsymbol{\beta}^{(j)} = \mathbf{Az}_j.$$

Then,

$$\mathbf{PZ\gamma} = \sum_j \gamma_j \mathbf{X\beta}^{(j)} = \mathbf{X} \sum_j \gamma_j \boldsymbol{\beta}^{(j)}$$

so that

$$\mathbf{Y} = \mathbf{X\beta} + \mathbf{PZ\gamma} + \mathbf{QZ\gamma} + \boldsymbol{\epsilon}$$

$$= \mathbf{X}(\boldsymbol{\beta} + \gamma_1 \boldsymbol{\beta}^{(1)} + \ldots + \gamma_h \boldsymbol{\beta}^{(h)}) + \mathbf{QZ\gamma} + \boldsymbol{\epsilon}$$

$$\mathbf{Y} = \mathbf{X\beta}_0 + \mathbf{QZ\hat{\gamma}} + \boldsymbol{\epsilon}.$$

Hence, the projection of $\mathbf{Y}$ onto V becomes

$$\mathbf{P_V Y} = \mathbf{P_{V0} Y} + \mathbf{P_{V*} Y}$$

$$= \mathbf{X\hat{\beta}_0} + \mathbf{Z^* \gamma}.$$

That is, the estimate of $\boldsymbol{\beta}$ under Ω^* is

$$\hat{\boldsymbol{\beta}}_{\Omega*} = \hat{\boldsymbol{\beta}}_0 - \hat{\gamma}_1 \boldsymbol{\beta}^{(1)} - \ldots - \hat{\gamma}_h \boldsymbol{\beta}^{(h)} \tag{88}$$

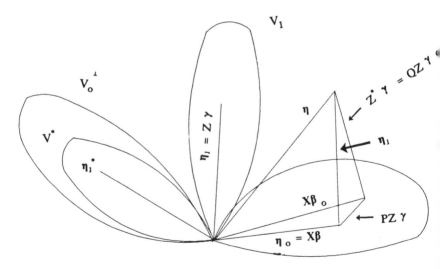

FIG. 5.3. Decomposition of $\boldsymbol{\eta} = \mathbf{X}\boldsymbol{\beta} + \mathbf{Z}\boldsymbol{\gamma}$.

or formula 6.2.10 derived by Scheffe (1959, p. 203). This shows that the esti-mate of $\boldsymbol{\beta}$ under Ω^* is the estimate under Ω ($\hat{\boldsymbol{\beta}}_0$), adjusted by the covariates. Using matrix algebra to find $\hat{\boldsymbol{\beta}}_{\Omega*}$, Equation 88 becomes

$$\hat{\boldsymbol{\beta}}_{\Omega*} = (\mathbf{X'X})^-\mathbf{X'y} - (\mathbf{X'X})^-\mathbf{X'Z}\hat{\boldsymbol{\gamma}} \tag{89}$$

$$\hat{\boldsymbol{\gamma}} = (\mathbf{Z'QZ})^{-1}\mathbf{Z'Qy}$$

$$\mathbf{Q} = \mathbf{I} - \mathbf{X(X'X)}^-\mathbf{X'} = (\mathbf{I} - \mathbf{P}) \tag{90}$$

as shown in Timm (1975, p. 472).

To test hypotheses about $\boldsymbol{\gamma}$ and $\boldsymbol{\beta}$ under Ω^*, we again want to obtain an orthogonal decomposition of the observation vector similar to Fig. 5.2. From Fig. 5.3, $V^* \subseteq V_0^\perp$ and

$$V = V_0 \oplus V^*$$

$$V \oplus V^\perp = V_N$$

$$V_0 \oplus V_0^\perp = V_N$$

so that

$$V_0 \oplus V_0^\perp = V_0 \oplus V^* \oplus V^\perp$$

and

$$V_0^\perp - V^* = V.$$

Considering $\mathbf{Y} \in V_N$ we have that

$$\mathbf{Y} = \mathbf{P_V Y} + \mathbf{P_V^\perp Y}$$

$$\mathbf{Y} = (\mathbf{P_{V0} Y} + \mathbf{P_{V*} Y}) + (\mathbf{P_{V0}^\perp Y} - \mathbf{P_{V*} Y})$$

$$= \mathbf{X}\hat{\boldsymbol{\beta}}_0 + \mathbf{QZ}\hat{\boldsymbol{\gamma}} + \text{Residual}. \tag{91}$$

From Figs. 5.1 and 5.2,

$$Q_\Omega^* = \|\mathbf{y} - \hat{\boldsymbol{\theta}}_{\Omega*}\|^2 \tag{92}$$

is the error sum of squares under Ω^* where $\hat{\boldsymbol{\theta}}_{\Omega*} = \mathbf{P_V Y}$. But $\mathbf{y} - \mathbf{P_V Y} = \mathbf{P_V^\perp Y}$ so that

$$\hat{Q}_{\Omega*} = \|\mathbf{P_V^\perp Y}\|^2$$

$$= \|\mathbf{P_{V0}^\perp Y}\|^2 - \|\mathbf{P_{V*} Y}\|^2$$

$$= \mathbf{y'Qy} - \hat{\boldsymbol{\gamma}}'(\mathbf{Z'QZ})\hat{\boldsymbol{\gamma}}$$

$$\hat{Q}_{\Omega*} = \hat{Q}_\Omega - \hat{\boldsymbol{\gamma}}'(\mathbf{Z'QZ})\hat{\boldsymbol{\gamma}} \tag{93}$$

is the ANCOVA residual sum of squared with degrees of freedom $\nu_e = N - r -$ the rank of $V^\perp$.

To test hypotheses under Ω^* is more complicated than under Ω because now the parameter vector has two components $\boldsymbol{\beta}$ and $\boldsymbol{\gamma}$, whereas, under Ω we only had $\boldsymbol{\beta}$. In addition, under Ω,

$$\mathbf{V}_N = \mathbf{V}_r \oplus \mathbf{V}_{N-r}^{\perp}$$
$$= \mathbf{V}_g \oplus \mathbf{V}_{r-g} \oplus \mathbf{V}_{N-r}^{\perp},$$

where $\mathbf{V}_{r-g}$ was the hypothesis test space. Now, the diagram is complicated by $\mathbf{V}^*$:

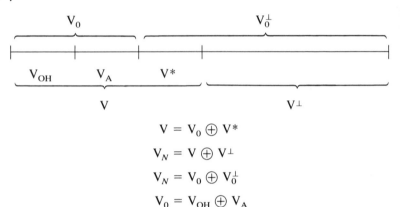

$$V = V_0 \oplus V^*$$
$$V_N = V \oplus V^{\perp}$$
$$V_N = V_0 \oplus V_0^{\perp}$$
$$V_0 = V_{OH} \oplus V_A$$

To test H_γ the hypothesis that $\boldsymbol{\gamma} = \mathbf{0}$, the Ω^* model reduces to the ANOVA Ω model under H_γ so that the hypothesis sum of squares becomes

$$Q_h = \hat{Q}_\omega - \hat{Q}_{\Omega^*}$$
$$= \hat{Q}_\Omega - \hat{Q}_{\Omega^*}$$
$$= \hat{\boldsymbol{\gamma}}'(\mathbf{Z}'\mathbf{QZ})\hat{\boldsymbol{\gamma}}$$
$$= \|\mathbf{P}_{V^*}\mathbf{Y}\|^2$$
$$= SS_{H_\gamma} \qquad\qquad (94)$$

from Equation 93 where the degrees of freedom is the rank of $\mathbf{Z} = h$. To test ω^* $H: \mathbf{C}\boldsymbol{\beta} = \mathbf{0}$ under Ω^* we begin with the test of H_β under Ω. Under Ω, $\mathbf{V}^* = \{\mathbf{0}\}$ and

$$SS_H = \|\mathbf{P}_{VA}\mathbf{Y}\|^2 = \|\mathbf{P}_{VOH}^{\perp}\mathbf{Y}\|^2 - \|\mathbf{P}_{V0}^{\perp}\mathbf{Y}\|^2.$$

However,

$$\hat{Q}_{\Omega^*} = \|\mathbf{P}_{V0}^{\perp}\|^2 - \|\mathbf{P}_{V^*}\mathbf{Y}\|^2.$$

Letting

$$\hat{\boldsymbol{\gamma}}_{H'}(\mathbf{Z}'\mathbf{Q}_H\mathbf{Z})\hat{\boldsymbol{\gamma}}_H = \|\mathbf{P}_{V^{**}}\mathbf{Y}\|^2$$

e error sum of squares under ω^* is

$$\hat{Q}_{\omega*} = \|P_{VA}Y\|^2 - \|P_{V**}Y\|^2$$

$$= \hat{Q}_\omega - \|P_{V**}Y\|^2$$

nd the hypothesis sum of squares is $SS_{H_\beta} = \hat{Q}_{\omega*} - \hat{Q}_{\Omega*}$ with degrees of freedom
$- (r + h - g) - (N - r - h) = g.$
The geometric interpretation of the ANCOVA model is represented in Fig.
.4. Figure 5.4 shows clearly the relationship between the hypothesis sum of
quares for ANOVA and ANCOVA models. Under Ω: $Y = X\beta + \epsilon$ the hypoth-
sis sum of squares to test ω: $C\beta = 0$ is

$$SS_H = \hat{Q}_\omega - \hat{Q}_\Omega.$$

nder Ω^*: $Y + X\beta + Z\gamma + \epsilon$, to test H_γ: $\gamma = 0$

$$SS_{H_\gamma} = \hat{Q}_\Omega - \hat{Q}_{\Omega*}$$

nd to test ω^*: $C\beta = 0$ we have

$$SS_{H_\beta} = \hat{Q}_{\omega*} - \hat{Q}_{\Omega*}.$$

urthermore,

$$\hat{Q}_\omega - \hat{Q}_{\omega*} = \|P_{V**}Y\|^2$$

$$\hat{Q}_\Omega - \hat{Q}_{\Omega*} = \|P_{*V*}Y\|^2$$

rm right triangles.

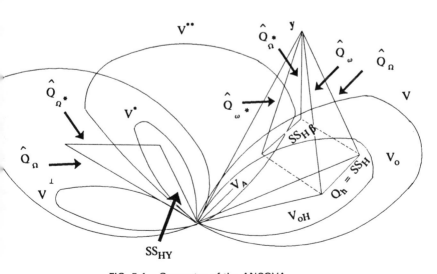

FIG. 5.4. Geometry of the ANCOVA.

FUNDAMENTALS:
RESTRICTED FULL RANK MODEL

When considering full rank models as defined in Equation 7 or 13 one may wan
to introduce restrictions on the population parameters. For example, in the sim
ple linear regression model, $y_i = \alpha + \beta x_i + \epsilon_i$ one may want to conside
regression through the origin by adding the estimable restriction $\alpha = 0$ to th
model. For the two-way full rank ANOVA model $y_{ij} = \mu_{ij} + \epsilon_{ij}$, one may want t
add to the model the estimable no interaction restriction

$$\mu_{ij} - \mu_{i'j} - \mu_{ij'} + \mu_{i'j'} + 0$$

to the model. In general, the restricted full rank model takes the followin
general form:

$$\tilde{\Omega}: \quad \underset{N \times 1}{y} \;=\; \underset{N \times p}{W} \quad \underset{p \times 1}{\mu} \;+\; \underset{N \times 1}{\epsilon} \tag{95}$$

$$\underset{s \times p}{R} \quad \underset{p \times 1}{\mu} \;=\; \underset{s \times 1}{\theta}$$

$$E(y) = W\mu$$

$$V(y) = \sigma^2 I,$$

where the $R(W) = p$ and the $R(R) = s \leq p$ and

$$Y \sim N(W\mu, \sigma^2 I). \tag{96}$$

For experimental designs that do not require the parameter vector μ to be re
stricted, we see that Equation 95 reduces to Equation 7, the unrestricted mode
$\tilde{\Omega}$. Hence, the model specified under $\tilde{\Omega}$ may be considered the general full ran
representation.

Estimating the parameters under $\tilde{\Omega}$, the error sum of squares $Q_\Omega = (y -$
$W\mu)'(y - W\mu)$ is minimized subject to the restrictions $R\mu = \theta$. That is, unde

$$Q_\Omega = \min (y - W\mu)'(y - W\mu)$$

$$R\mu = \theta \tag{97}$$

is minimized. From Equation 40 in the unrestricted model, we see that th
restricted estimate of μ is

$$\mu_{\tilde{\Omega}} = \hat{\mu}_\Omega - (W'W)^{-1}R'(R(W'W)^{-1}R')^{-1}(R\hat{\mu}_\Omega - \theta) \tag{98}$$

by associating $R\mu = \theta$ with $C\mu = \xi$. In Equation 98, $\hat{\mu}_\Omega$ is the unrestricte
estimator of μ and $\hat{\mu}_{\tilde{\Omega}}$ is the restricted estimator. Replacing W with X and
with β, a general solution to Equation 97 becomes for the less than full ran
restricted model

$$\hat{\beta}_{\tilde{\Omega}} = \hat{\beta} - (X'X)^{-}R'(R(X'X)^{-}R')^{-1}(R\hat{\beta} - \theta). \tag{99}$$

Now, however, $\hat{\boldsymbol{\beta}}_{\tilde{\Omega}}$ is not a solution to the normal equations $(\mathbf{X}'\mathbf{X})\,\boldsymbol{\beta} = \mathbf{X}'\mathbf{y}$, which was the case when the restrictions were nonestimable parametric functions. Replacing $\mathbf{C}$ by $\mathbf{R}$ and $\boldsymbol{\xi}$ by $\boldsymbol{\theta}$ in Equation 44, the error sum of square under $\tilde{\Omega}$ becomes

$$\hat{Q}_{\tilde{\Omega}} = \hat{Q}_{\Omega} + (\mathbf{R}\hat{\boldsymbol{\mu}}_{\Omega} - \boldsymbol{\theta})'(\mathbf{R}(\mathbf{W}'\mathbf{W})^{-1}\mathbf{R}')^{-1}(\mathbf{R}\hat{\boldsymbol{\mu}}_{\Omega} - \boldsymbol{\theta}) \qquad (100)$$

with expected value in general given by

$$E(\hat{Q}_{\tilde{\Omega}}) = (N - r + s)\sigma_{\tilde{\Omega}}^2, \qquad (101)$$

where $r = R(\mathbf{X}) \le p = R(\mathbf{W})$ and $s = R(\mathbf{R})$. If $s = 0$, the estimator of $\sigma_{\tilde{\Omega}}^2$ reduces to the estimator for σ_{Ω}^2 in the unrestricted model.

To test the hypothesis under $\tilde{\Omega}$ of the form

$$\tilde{\omega}: H: \mathbf{C}\boldsymbol{\mu} = \boldsymbol{\xi}, \qquad (102)$$

where $\mathbf{C}$ is a $q \times p$ matrix of rank q and $\boldsymbol{\xi}$ is a specified vector of constants and $\mathbf{Y}$ is distributed as in Equation 96, we again use the LRT criterion.

To maximize the likelihood function under $\tilde{\omega}$, let

$$\mathbf{Q} = \begin{pmatrix} \mathbf{R} \\ \mathbf{C} \end{pmatrix} \quad \text{and} \quad \boldsymbol{\eta} = \begin{pmatrix} \boldsymbol{\theta} \\ \boldsymbol{\xi} \end{pmatrix}. \qquad (103)$$

In forming the matrix $\mathbf{Q}$, the hypothesis under $\tilde{\omega}$ can be tested only if it is consistent with the restrictions $\mathbf{R}\boldsymbol{\mu} = \boldsymbol{\theta}$. That is, no row of $\mathbf{C}$ can be identical to a row of $\mathbf{R}$, inconsistent with the restrictions or dependent on the rows of $\mathbf{R}$ and/or the rows of $\mathbf{C}$. That is, the rows of $\mathbf{Q}$ must be linearly independent so that the $R(\mathbf{Q}) = s + q > s$. A hypothesis test matrix $\mathbf{C}$ that specifies a hypothesis of interest may itself be of full row rank but when the augmented matrix $\mathbf{Q}$ is formed some rows of $\mathbf{C}$ might have to be detected for the matrix $\mathbf{Q}$ to have full rank. When $\mathbf{C}$ is totally dependent on the rows of the matrix $\mathbf{R}$, the hypothesis is not testable because the rank of $\mathbf{Q}$ would be s. Following the derivation of the LRT for the full rank unrestricted model, the least square criterion under $\tilde{\omega}$ is minimized:

$$\mathbf{Q}_{\tilde{\omega}} = \min(\mathbf{y} - \mathbf{W}\boldsymbol{\mu})'(\mathbf{y} - \mathbf{W}\boldsymbol{\mu})$$

$$\mathbf{Q}\boldsymbol{\mu} = \boldsymbol{\eta} \qquad (104)$$

Using Equation 40,

$$\hat{\boldsymbol{\mu}}_{\tilde{\Omega}} = \hat{\boldsymbol{\mu}}_{\Omega} - (\mathbf{W}'\mathbf{W})^{-1}\mathbf{Q}'[\mathbf{Q}(\mathbf{W}'\mathbf{W})^{-1}\mathbf{Q}']^{-1}(\mathbf{Q}\hat{\boldsymbol{\mu}}_{\Omega} - \boldsymbol{\xi}), \qquad (105)$$

which is also the maximum likelihood estimate for $\boldsymbol{\mu}$ under $\tilde{\omega}$. Forming the likelihood ratio λ, it can be shown that

$$\lambda = \left[\frac{(\mathbf{y} - \mathbf{W}\hat{\boldsymbol{\mu}}_{\tilde{\Omega}})'(\mathbf{y} - \mathbf{W}\hat{\boldsymbol{\mu}}_{\tilde{\Omega}})}{(\mathbf{y} - \mathbf{W}\hat{\boldsymbol{\mu}}_{\tilde{\omega}})'(\mathbf{y} - \mathbf{W}\hat{\boldsymbol{\mu}}_{\tilde{\omega}})} \right]^{N/2} \qquad (106)$$

by following the proof given in the unrestricted case. From Equation 100,

$$\hat{Q}_{\bar{\Omega}} = \hat{Q}_{\Omega} + (\mathbf{R}\hat{\boldsymbol{\mu}}_{\Omega} - \boldsymbol{\theta})'(\mathbf{R}(\mathbf{W}'\mathbf{W})^{-1}\mathbf{R}'(\mathbf{R}\hat{\boldsymbol{\mu}}_{\Omega} - \boldsymbol{\theta}) \qquad (107)$$

and following Equation 44

$$\hat{Q}_{\bar{\omega}} = \hat{Q}_{\Omega} + (\mathbf{Q}\hat{\boldsymbol{\mu}}_{\Omega} - \boldsymbol{\eta})'(\mathbf{Q}(\mathbf{W}'\mathbf{W})^{-1}\mathbf{Q}'(\mathbf{Q}\hat{\boldsymbol{\mu}}_{\Omega} - \boldsymbol{\eta}) \qquad (108)$$

or replacing $\mathbf{Q}$ and $\boldsymbol{\eta}$ by the partitioned matrices in Equation 91 and using the formula for finding the inverse of the partitioned matrix $(\mathbf{Q}(\mathbf{W}'\mathbf{W})^{-1}\mathbf{Q}')^{-1}$,

$$\hat{Q}_{\bar{\omega}} - \hat{Q}_{\Omega} = (\mathbf{C}\hat{\boldsymbol{\mu}}_{\bar{\Omega}} - \boldsymbol{\xi})'[\mathbf{C}\mathbf{A}(\mathbf{W}'\mathbf{W})^{-1}\mathbf{C}']^{-1}(\mathbf{C}\hat{\boldsymbol{\mu}}_{\bar{\Omega}} - \boldsymbol{\xi}), \qquad (109)$$

where

$$\mathbf{A} = \mathbf{I} - (\mathbf{W}'\mathbf{W})^{-1}\mathbf{R}'(\mathbf{R}(\mathbf{W}'\mathbf{W})^{-1}\mathbf{R}')^{-1}\mathbf{R}$$

and

$$\mathbf{A}^2 = \mathbf{A}.$$

Following Equation 46, and substituting $\hat{\boldsymbol{\mu}}_{\bar{\Omega}}$ and $\hat{\boldsymbol{\mu}}_{\bar{\omega}}$ for $\hat{\boldsymbol{\mu}}_{\Omega}$ and $\hat{\boldsymbol{\mu}}_{\omega}$ in Equation 43,

$$\Lambda = \lambda^{2/N} = \frac{\hat{Q}_{\bar{\Omega}}}{\hat{Q}_{\bar{\omega}}} = \frac{\hat{Q}_{\bar{\Omega}}}{\hat{Q}_{\bar{\Omega}} + (\hat{Q}_{\bar{\omega}} - \hat{Q}_{\bar{\Omega}})}$$

$$= \frac{1}{1 + (\hat{Q}_{\bar{\omega}} - \hat{Q}_{\bar{\Omega}})/\hat{Q}_{\bar{\Omega}}} \qquad (110)$$

to test H: $\mathbf{C}\boldsymbol{\mu} = \boldsymbol{\xi}$, we reject H if

$$F = \frac{(\hat{Q}_{\bar{\omega}} - \hat{Q}_{\bar{\Omega}})/q}{Q/(N - p + s)} > F^{\alpha}(q, N - p + s) \qquad (111)$$

at the significance level α. Again, replacing $\mathbf{W}$ by $\mathbf{X}$ where the $R(\mathbf{X}) = r \leq R(\mathbf{W}) = p$, $\boldsymbol{\mu}$ by $\boldsymbol{\beta}$ and $(\mathbf{W}'\mathbf{W})^{-1}$ with $(\mathbf{X}'\mathbf{X})^{-}$ the general less than full rank results follow immediately. For example,

$$\hat{Q}_{\bar{\Omega}} = \hat{Q}_{\Omega} + (\mathbf{R}\boldsymbol{\beta} - \boldsymbol{\theta})'(\mathbf{R}(\mathbf{X}'\mathbf{X})^{-}\mathbf{R}')^{-1}(\mathbf{R}\hat{\boldsymbol{\beta}} - \boldsymbol{\theta}) \qquad (112)$$

and

$$\hat{Q}_{\bar{\omega}} - \hat{Q}_{\bar{\Omega}} = (\mathbf{C}\hat{\boldsymbol{\beta}}_{\bar{\Omega}} - \boldsymbol{\xi})'[\mathbf{C}\mathbf{A}(\mathbf{X}'\mathbf{X})^{-}\mathbf{C}']^{-1}(\mathbf{C}\hat{\boldsymbol{\beta}}_{\bar{\Omega}} - \boldsymbol{\xi}), \qquad (113)$$

where

$$\mathbf{A} = \mathbf{I} - (\mathbf{X}'\mathbf{X})^{-}\mathbf{R}'(\mathbf{R}(\mathbf{X}'\mathbf{X})^{-}\mathbf{R}')^{-1}\mathbf{R}.$$

To obtain simultaneous confidence intervals, we again use the general form specified in Equation 50 with

$$S^2 = q\, F^{\alpha}(q, N - p + s)$$

$$\hat{\sigma}_{\hat{\psi}} = \hat{\sigma}_{\bar{\Omega}}(\mathbf{c}'\mathbf{A}(\mathbf{W}'\mathbf{W})^{-1}\mathbf{c})^{1/2}$$

$$\hat{\psi} = \mathbf{c}'\hat{\boldsymbol{\mu}}_{\bar{\Omega}}. \qquad (114)$$

THE MULTIVARIATE LINEAR MODEL: ESTIMATION

To extend the concepts of ANOVA and ANCOVA to the multivariate case, one merely has to replace the random $N \times 1$ vector $\mathbf{Y}$ by a random $N \times p$ matrix $\mathbf{Y}$ where each column of $\mathbf{Y}$ represents one of p variables. For the moment, we assume that the model matrix $\mathbf{W}$ of order $N \times q$ is the same for each variable, a reasonable assumption for the analysis of variance. Because we have p variables, the parameter vector becomes a matrix of variables, one column for each variate. The restrictions on the model parameters is again represented by a matrix $\mathbf{R}$, however, because the model parameters are elements of a matrix, we may post multiply the parameter matrix by a matrix $\mathbf{A}$ to add additional restrictions to the parameters across variables. With this, the restricted full rank multivariate linear model takes the following general form.

$$\tilde{\Omega}: \quad \underset{N \times p}{\mathbf{Y}} = \underset{N \times q}{\mathbf{W}} \quad \underset{q \times p}{\mathbf{U}} + \underset{N \times p}{\mathbf{E}_0}$$

$$\underset{r \times q}{\mathbf{R}} \underset{q \times p}{\mathbf{U}} \underset{p \times n}{\mathbf{A}} = \underset{r \times p}{\text{\textcircled{H}}}$$

$$E(\mathbf{Y}) = \mathbf{WU}$$

$$V(\mathbf{Y}) = \mathbf{I},$$

where

\textcircled{X} is a Kronecker product and

$\mathbf{Y}$ $(N \times p)$ is a matrix of observations

$\mathbf{U}$ $(q \times p)$ is a nonrandom matrix of parameters, usually population means

$\mathbf{W}$ $(N \times q)$ is the full rank model matrix of rank $q < N$

$\mathbf{R}$ $(r \times q)$ is a known real matrix of rank $r < q$

\textcircled{H} $(r \times p)$ is a specified matrix of known constants

$\mathbf{A}$ $(p \times t)$ is a known matrix of rank $t \leq p$

and each row $\mathbf{Y}'_i$ of $\mathbf{Y}$ is independent and has a p variate normal distribution. Removing the restrictions $\mathbf{RUA} = \text{\textcircled{H}}$ from the model, we have the unrestricted full rank model as in the univariate case.

To estimate $\mathbf{U}$ and $\mathbf{\Sigma}$ under $\tilde{\Omega}$, the least squares criterion

$$\text{Tr}(\mathbf{E}_0'\mathbf{E}_0) = \text{Tr}[(\mathbf{Y} - \mathbf{WU})'(\mathbf{Y} - \mathbf{WU})]$$

is used, where Tr denotes the trace operation. Letting

$$F = \text{Tr}[(\mathbf{Y} - \mathbf{WU})'(\mathbf{Y} - \mathbf{WU})] + 2\,\text{Tr}\,[\mathbf{\Delta}'(\mathbf{RUA} - \mathbf{H})],$$

157

where Δ' is a matrix of Lagrange multipliers, and differentiating F with respect to U and Δ', the restricted multivariate linear model normal equations are directly obtained.

$$(W'W)\hat{U}_{\hat{\Omega}} + R'\Delta A' = W'Y$$

$$R \hat{U}_{\hat{\Omega}} A = H. \qquad (116)$$

Letting $\hat{U}_{\Omega} = (W'W)^{-1}W'Y$ represent the unrestricted estimator of U, the first equation 116 yields

$$\hat{U}_{\hat{\Omega}} = \hat{U}_{\Omega} - (W'W)^{-1}R'\Delta A'.$$

Premultiplying $\hat{U}_{\hat{\Omega}}$ by R and postmultiplying by A, we have that

$$\textcircled{H} = R\hat{U}_{\Omega}A - R(W'W)^{-1}R'\Delta A'A$$

or

$$R(W'W)^{-1}R'\Delta(A'A) = R\hat{U}_{\Omega}A - \textcircled{H}$$

so that

$$\Delta = (R(W'W)^{-1}R')^{-1}(R\hat{U}_{\Omega}A - \textcircled{H})(A'A)^{-1}.$$

Hence, from Equation 116 the restricted least squares estimator of U under $\tilde{\Omega}$ is

$$\hat{U}_{\hat{\Omega}} = \hat{U}_{\Omega} - (W'W)^{-1}R'(R(W'W)^{-1}R')^{-1}(R\hat{U}_{\Omega}A - \textcircled{H})(A'A)^{-1}A', \quad (117)$$

which is very similar to the estimator obtained in the univariate case, Equation 98.

To obtain an unbiased estimator of Σ under $\tilde{\Omega}$, the estimated restricted error sum of squares and product (SSP) matrix under $\tilde{\Omega}$ is divided by $N - q - r$

$$S_{\hat{\Omega}} = \hat{Q}_{\hat{\Omega}}/(N - q - r), \qquad (118$$

where

$$\hat{Q}_{\hat{\Omega}} = (Y - W\hat{U}_{\hat{\Omega}})'(Y - W\hat{U}_{\hat{\Omega}})$$

the estimated restricted SSP matrix.

Under Equation 115, the best linear unbiased estimator (BLUE) of U is given by Equation 117. If $\psi = c'Ua$ is estimated by $\hat{\psi} = c'U_{\hat{\Omega}}a$ under $\tilde{\Omega}$, $\hat{\psi}$ is the unique linear unbiased estimate of ψ and has minimum variance among all linear unbiased estimates (see, e.g., Timm, 1975, p. 188).

THE MULTIVARIATE LINEAR MODEL: HYPOTHESIS TESTING

To test the hypothesis

$$\bar{\omega}: H: CUA = \Gamma \qquad (119$$

nder $\tilde{\Omega}$ where $C(\nu_h xq)$ is a known matrix of real numbers of rank $\nu_h < q$, $A(p \times t)$ is a known real matrix of rank $t < p$, and $\Gamma(\nu_h xt)$ is a matrix of known constants, the partitioned matrices

$$Q = \begin{pmatrix} R \\ C \end{pmatrix} \qquad \Psi = \begin{pmatrix} \textcircled{H} \\ \Gamma \end{pmatrix} \tag{120}$$

re formed and the expression $\mathrm{Tr}[(Y - WU)'(Y - WU)]$ is minimized subject to the restriction $QUA = \Psi$ under $\tilde{\omega}$.

Provided no row of C is equal to any row of R or dependent on the rows of R and/or other rows of C and that the rank of the matrix A is t, that the expression for the hypothesis is not inconsistent with the restrictions on the model, the independently distributed hypothesis and error sum of squares and products matrices for testing Equation 119 are given by

$$S_h = (C\hat{U}_{\tilde{\Omega}}A - \Gamma)'(CF(W'W)^{-1}C')^{-1}(C\hat{U}_{\Omega}A - \Gamma)$$

$$S_e = A'\hat{Q}_{\tilde{\Omega}}A$$

$$F = I - (W'W)^{-1}R'(R(W'W)^{-1}R')^{-1}R. \tag{121}$$

When the null hypothesis is true, S_h and S_e are distributed as central Wishart matrices

$$S_h \sim W_t(\nu_h, A'\Sigma A)$$

$$S_e \sim W_t(N - q - r, A'\Sigma A). \tag{122}$$

Letting $\lambda_1, \lambda_2, \ldots, \lambda_s$ with $s = \min(t, \nu_h)$ denotes the roots of the determinatal equation

$$|S_h - \lambda S_e| = 0 \tag{123}$$

hypothesis of the form H_0: $CUA = \Gamma$ may be tested using several multivariate test criteria.

Using the likelihood ratio criterion to test Equation 119, following the univariate case,

$$\lambda = \left\{ \frac{|(Y - W\hat{U}_{\tilde{\Omega}})'(Y - W\hat{U}_{\tilde{\Omega}})|}{|(Y - W\hat{U}_{\tilde{\omega}})'(Y - W\hat{U}_{\tilde{\omega}})|} \right\}^{N/2}$$

or

$$\Lambda = \lambda^{2/N} = \frac{|S_e|}{|S_e + S_h|} = \prod_i \nu_i,$$

where the ν_i are the roots of the determinantal equation $|S_e + \nu(S_e + S_h)| = 0$. The null hypothesis is rejected at the significant level if

$$\Lambda = \prod_{i=1}^{s} \nu_i = \prod_{i=1}^{s} (1 + \lambda_i)^{-1} < U^\alpha(t, \nu_h, \nu_e), \tag{124}$$

where Λ is distributed as a product of independent beta variables, $t = R(A)$, $v_h = R(C)$, and $v_e = N - q - r$, or equivalently with v_i the eigenvalues of the characteristic equation $|S_h - \lambda S_e| = 0$,

$$\Lambda = \frac{|S_e|}{|S_e + S_h|} = \prod_{i=1}^{s} (1 + \lambda_i)^{-1}$$

and $s = \min(t, v_h)$.

An alternative to the LRT is the union intersection test criterion. The multivariate hypothesis in Equation 119 $CBA = \Gamma$ is true if and only if $b'CBAa = b'a$ for all a and b. the multivariate hypothesis is true if and only if every univariate hypothesis is true and is rejected if at least one univariate hypothesis is rejected. Clearly, each $H_0: b' a = 0$ region of acceptance is the intersection of the acceptance regimes of all univariate regions over b is

$$\bigcap_a \frac{a'S_h a}{a'S_e a} \le \frac{v_h}{v_e} F^{\alpha*}(v_h, v_e)$$

for fixed a. Maximizing the ratio over a shows that the

$$\max_a \frac{a'S_h a}{a'S_e a} = \lambda_1$$

the largest eigenvalue of $|S_h - \lambda S_e| = 0$. Letting $\theta_s = \lambda_1/1 + \lambda_1$ denote the largest root of $|S_h - \theta(S_h + S_e)| = 0$. The hypothesis in Equation 119 is rejected for large values of θs. That is, the null hypothesis is rejected if the

$$P\{\theta_s > \theta^\alpha (s, m, n)|H_0\} = \alpha,$$

where

$$s = \min(t, v_h)$$

$$m = \tfrac{1}{2}(|v_h - t| - 1)$$

$$n = \tfrac{1}{2}(v_e - t - 1)$$

(see, e.g., Timm, 1975, p. 584).

Whenever the $R(C) = 1$ or the $R(A) = 1$ or $s = \min(t, v_h) = 1$, the likelihood ratio test and the union intersection criterion are equivalent. When this is not the case, the two procedures may lead to different results for testing the same null hypothesis.

The likelihood ratio test (LRT) and the union intersection test (UIT) criterion are only two of many other procedures developed to test Equation 119. All of the criterion involve the roots of the determinantal equation $|S_h - \lambda S_e| = 0$. However, no procedure is uniformly most powerful. The advantage of the UIT over all others proposed is that it leads to the construction of exact simultaneous confidence intervals. For the LRT only approximate intervals may be formed. In addition, the LRT depends on the assumption of specific joint distribution form; this is not the case for UITs. Wilks (1932) applied the principle of the likelihood ratio in the development of the Λ criterion in some special cases of multivariate analysis and Roy (1953) was the first to apply the union intersection method in the analysis of variance.

To construct simultaneous confidence intervals following the test of the multivariate hypothesis, let parametric functions $\psi = \mathbf{c}'\mathbf{U}\mathbf{a}$ and

$$\hat{\psi} = \mathbf{c}'\hat{\mathbf{U}}_{\hat{\Omega}}\mathbf{a}$$
$$\hat{\sigma}_{\hat{\psi}}^2 = \text{Var}(\hat{\psi})$$
$$\mathbf{C}_o^2 = \nu_e(\theta^\alpha/(1 - \theta^\alpha))$$

Then $100(1 - \alpha)\%$ simultaneous confidence intervals take the form

$$\hat{\psi} - \mathbf{C}_0\hat{\sigma}_{\hat{\psi}} \leq \psi \leq \hat{\psi} + \mathbf{C}_0\hat{\sigma}_{\hat{\psi}} \tag{125}$$

when testing H_0: $\mathbf{CBA} = \Gamma$ using the UIT criterion.

MANOVA AND MANCOVA: SOME GENERAL PRINCIPLES

To illustrate the general multivariate theory for a restricted full rank multivariate design consider the situation where a vector of dependent variates are obtained repeatedly over p conditions or are repeated measurements and for each repeated observation there is associated a unique covariate. A design of this type for two groups may take the form shown in Table 5.2 when $\mathbf{Y}$ is the criterion measure and $\mathbf{Z}$ is the covariate. For the data in Table 5.2, the parameter matrix

$$\mathbf{U} = \begin{bmatrix} \mu_{11} & \mu_{12} & \mu_{13} \\ \mu_{21} & \mu_{22} & \mu_{23} \\ \beta_{11} & \beta_{12} & \beta_{13} \\ \beta_{21} & \beta_{22} & \beta_{23} \end{bmatrix}$$

and design matrix $\mathbf{X} = [\mathbf{XZ}$ is defined by

$$\begin{pmatrix} \mathbf{1}_{N1} & \mathbf{0}_{N1} & \mathbf{Z}_1 0 \\ \mathbf{0}_{N2} & \mathbf{1}_{N2} & 0\mathbf{Z}_2 \end{pmatrix}.$$

Letting

$$\mathbf{R} = (0\ 0\ 1\ -\ 1)$$

$$\mathbf{A} = \begin{pmatrix} 1 & 0 \\ -1 & 1 \\ 0 & -1 \end{pmatrix}$$

TABLE 5.2
MANCOVA with Repeated Measures

		C_1		C_2		C_3	
				Conditions			
G_1	s_1	y_{111}	z_{111}	y_{12}	z_{112}	y_{113}	z_{113}
	s_2	y_{121}	z_{121}	y_{122}	z_{122}	y_{123}	z_{123}
	$\vdots$	$\vdots$	$\vdots$	$\vdots$	$\vdots$	$\vdots$	$\vdots$
	s_{N1}	y_{1N11}	z_{1N11}	y_{1N12}	z_{1N12}	y_{1N13}	z_{1N13}
G_2	s_1'	y_{211}	z_{211}	y_{212}	z_{212}	y_{213}	z_{213}
	s_2	y_{221}	z_{221}	y_{222}	z_{222}	y_{223}	z_{223}
	$\vdots$	$\vdots$	$\vdots$	$\vdots$	$\vdots$	$\vdots$	$\vdots$
	s_{N2}	y_{2N21}	z_{2N21}	y_{2N22}	z_{2N22}	y_{2N23}	z_{2N23}

the restriction

$$\mathbf{RUA} = \mathbf{0}$$

implies there is no interaction in the regression lines; that is,

$$\beta_{11} - \beta_{13} - \beta_{12} + \beta_{23} = 0 \qquad \beta_{12} - \beta_{13} - \beta_{22} + \beta_{23} = 0$$

$$\beta_{12} - \beta_{23} - \beta_{13} + \beta_{33} = 0 \qquad \beta_{22} - \beta_{23} - \beta_{32} + \beta_{33} = 0$$

or the lines are parallel. To test now that there is no difference in intercepts across conditions

$$\tilde{\omega}: H: \begin{pmatrix} \mu_{11} \\ \mu_{21} \end{pmatrix} = \begin{pmatrix} \mu_{12} \\ \mu_{22} \end{pmatrix} = \begin{pmatrix} \mu_{13} \\ \mu_{23} \end{pmatrix}$$

the matrix

$$\mathbf{C} = \mathbf{I}_2 \quad \text{and} \quad \mathbf{A} = \begin{pmatrix} 1 & 0 \\ -1 & 1 \\ 0 & -1 \end{pmatrix}$$

employing the restricted full rank multivariate model. In this example, the restriction transformed the intra-class model, one with multiple slopes, to the single-slope analysis of covariance model.

The general restricted full rank multivariate linear model as specified in Equation 115 may be used to represent many MANOVA and MANCOVA models and to test hypothesis represented by Equation 119. This includes orthogonal and nonorthogonal designs, numerous multivariate repeated measures data sets, multivariate mixed models, and other designs that meet the general condition that the design or model matrix is the same for each dependent variate in the observation matrix $\mathbf{Y}$ (Timm, 1980). In addition, the multivariate tests assume multinormality. If one cannot transform the data to normality, multivariates nonparametric methods may be employed (Puri & Sen, 1971). Depending on the multivariate test criterion, different criteria may lead to different results and no criterion is uniformly most powerful (Lehmann, 1959). Moreover, there are numerous step-down procedures that may be used to test MANOVA and MAN-COVA hypothesis (Mudholkar & Subbaiah, 1980). MANOVA and MANCOVA designs are a subset of a more general class of designs referred to as multiple-design multivariate (MDM) models where the design or model matrix may vary across dependent variates (McDonald, 1975). A further generalization of the MDM model is a model developed by Kleinbaum (1973), called the Generalized Growth Curve Multivariate (GGCM) Model. His most general design incorporates the notion of a multiple-design to solve the problem of incomplete or missing data within multivariate observation vectors.

REFERENCES

Fisher, R. A. (1925). *Statistical methods for research workers.* Edinburgh: Oliver & Boyd.

Herr, O. G. (1980). On the history of the use of geometry in the general linear model. *The American Statistician, 34,* 43–47.

Hocking, R. R. (1985). *The analysis of linear models.* Monterey, CA: Brooks/Cole.

Hocking, R. R., & Speed, F. M. (1975). A full rank analysis of some linear model problems. *Journal of the American Statistical Association, 70,* 706–712.

Kleinbaum, D. G. (1973). A generalization of the growth curve model which allows missing data. *Journal of Multivariate Analysis, 3,* 117–124.

Lehmann, E. L. (1959). *Testing statistical hypothesis.* New York: Wiley.

McDonald, L. L. (1975). Tests for the general linear hypothesis under the multiple design multivariate linear model. *Annals of Mathematical Statistics, 3,* 461–466.

Mudholkar, G. S., & Subbaiah, P. (1980). A review of step-down procedures for multivariate analysis of variance. In R. P. Gupta (Ed.), *Multivariate statistical analysis* (pp. 161–178). New York: North-Holland.

Puri, M. L., & Sen, P. K. (1971). *Non-parametric methods in multivariate analysis.* New York: Wiley.

Rao, C. R. (1973). *Linear statistical inference and its applications* (2nd ed.). New York: Wiley.

Roy, S. N. (1953). On a heuristic method of test construction and its use in multivariate analysis. *Annals of Mathematical Statistics, 24,* 220–238.

Scheffé, H. (1959). *The analysis of variance.* New York: Wiley.

Searle, S. R. (1971). *Linear models.* New York: Wiley.

Searle, S. R. (1987). *Linear models for unbalanced data.* New York: Wiley.

Timm, N. H. (1975). *Multivariate analysis with applications in education and psychology.* Monterey, CA: Brooks/Cole.

Timm, N. H., & Carlson, J. E. (1975). Analysis of variance through full rank models. *Multivariate Behavioral Research Monograph, 75*(1), 120.

Timm, N. H. (1980). Multivariate analysis of variance of repeated measures. In P. R. Krishnaiah (Ed.), *Handbook of statistics* (Vol. 1, pp. 41–87). New York: North-Holland.

Wilks, S. S. (1932). Certain generalizations in the analysis of variance. *Biometrika, 39,* 17–31.

6 Set Correlation

Jacob Cohen
New York University

By now, it is widely appreciated that multiple regression/correlation analysis (MRC) can be used as a general data-analytic system (J. Cohen, 1968, 1982a; J. Cohen & P. Cohen, 1983; Pedhazur, 1982). As a realization of the univariate general linear model, it incorporates the analysis of variance (ANOVA) and the analysis of covariance (ANCOVA) as special cases, and is not constrained to the neat balanced layouts or categorical independent variables ("treatments," "diagnosis") that characterizes their textbook presentation. With MRC, one can use graduated ("continuous") independent variables, study interactions and other nonlinear relationships involving such variables, and represent missing data as positive information. Moreover, one can readily generalize the notion of "adjusting" for covariates," used in ANCOVA for categorical independent variables, to graduated variables in "the analysis of partial variance" (APV). MRC also offers the obvious benefit of a common framework for apparently diverse techniques, with a common effect size measure (proportion of variance accounted for), and is replete with least squares parameter estimation, hypothesis testing, and power analysis.

The versatility of MRC as a general data-analytic method is largely due to the use of sets of independent variables representing research factors as the units of analysis, and the varied use of partialling.

SETS AS RESEARCH FACTORS

Virtually any information can be represented by a suitably chosen set of quantitative variables: nominal (qualitative, categorical) scales, curvilinearly related

165

quantitative (ratio, interval, ordinal) scales, variables with missing data, and interactions (conditional relationships) of any order among research factors of any kind. Research factors are the functional entities in an analysis— experimental condition, age, socioeconomic status, trial block, diagnosis, and so forth. A research factor is represented as a set of one or more variables, and the set is the basic unit of analysis.

PARTIALLING

By partialling a set of X_P from a set X, a new set $X \cdot X_P$ is produced whose variables have zero correlations with those in set X_P. These X_P-partialled X variables are what would result if from each variable in set X one would subtract the value "predicted" for it by a multiple linear regression equation in which it is the dependent variable and the variables in set X_P are the independent variables. Each variable in set $X \cdot X_P$ thus contains what remains (is "residual") in it after that part of it that is linearly related to set X_P is removed. This powerful device has several uses in data analysis, including the statistical control of irrelevant or spurious sources of variance, the representation of curvilinear components and of interactions (J. Cohen, 1978), and the analysis of contrast functions among means.

Now, all this refers to the independent variables, the right-hand side of the equation, which is where the multiplicity of MRC resides. The left-hand side contains the single variable y. MRC is sometimes called a multivariate method, but it is, strictly speaking, univariate. Only when the singular y is replaced by a plural set of variables Y whose interrelationships are taken into account in the analysis does the method properly become multivariate.

Now, consider the benefits that would accrue from a generalization of MRC such that a set Y could be related to a set X, either of them partialled, if and as necessary. The possibility of representing "virtually any information" and the use of partialling for control and specification would now extend to the left-hand side, the dependent variables, as well. The resulting method, set correlation (SC), is a realization of the general *multivariate* linear model, and has the following properties:

1. It is a generalization of MRC, a truly multivariate MRC, and can employ the structural features of MRC (e.g., hierarchical analysis) with dependent research factors of any kind.

2. SC bears the same relationship to the standard multivariate methods that MRC does to the standard univariate methods. Thus, multivariate analysis of variance (MANOVA) and covariance (MANCOVA) are special cases of SC.

3. Its generality frees it from the latter's requirement of nominal scale research factors, making possible multivariate analysis of partial variance and other novel analytic methods.

4. SC provides a single framework of measures of association, parameter estimation, hypothesis testing, and statistical power analysis that encompasses most of the standard data-analytic methods.

CANONICAL ANALYSIS

The traditional multivariate correlation method is Hotelling's (1936) canonical analysis (CA). Also, the application of CA to variously partialled correlation matrices has been described by Roy (1957), Hooper (1962), Rao (1975), Timm and Carlson (1976), and others. Yet it is not an entirely satisfactory general tool for multivariate analysis.

In CA, the strength of the overall relationship between two sets of variables X and Y is measured by a series of canonical correlations (C), each a product-moment correlation between weighted linear combinations of the x_i variables of X and the y_j variables of Y. These are called x- and y-canonical factors (cf's), or canonical variates. The weights are such as to maximize the Cs between paired cf's subject to the further condition that each cf correlate zero with all but its paired cf. The number of such cf pairs (and hence of C's) is the lesser of the number of variables in the two sets, min(k_Y,k_X), here designated as q. Thus, the X,Y relationship is efficiently summarized by q correlations between as many pairs of weighted combinations of X and Y, each in turn extracting as much (new) between set covariance as possible.

In a seminal article, Rozeboom (1965) showed that the strength of relationship between two sets can be quantified by the degree of overlap of the spaces they span, and the cf's are covariance-maximizing principal components of the between set correlations. These are exactly analogous to the familiar variance-maximizing principal components extracted from the correlations among the members of a set in factor analysis.

Two problems arise with the use of CA. First, it provides q C's where a single measure of the strength of the overall relationship, some generalization of multiple R^2, is desired. The second is the limited utility of the cf's in the understanding of the nature of the X,Y relationship. Efforts to interpret these through the weights of factor loadings of the variables frequently read like laundry lists and are seldom convincing. In light of Rozeboom's demonstration that they are principal components of the between-set covariances, this is hardly surprising, because we have known in factor analysis for over half a century that principal components are not interpretable as functional unities. Thurstone invented rotation to simple structure in order to achieve substantive meaningfulness. Accordingly, the rotation of cf's to simple structure has been advocated (Cliff & Krus 1976). This may occasionally help, but simple structure in factor analysis i predicated on the employment of many variables so as to provide broad coverag of some behavioral domain; simple structure merely implements the expectatio that most of the correlations between many variables and several factors repre senting the functional unities in a domain will be zero or negligible. However variables analyzed in CA are in general not so selected, and the simple structur rationale does not obtain. Thus, the q pairs of cf's, original or rotated, canno serve as our primary analytic device. Instead, in SC, we work directly with th original variables, and by means of partialling, we carve out of the overal association the relationships between substantively meaningful components.

ELEMENTS OF SET CORRELATION

The technical literature contains the derivations and proofs of the elements of SC The most important sources are Wilks (1932) and Rozeboom (1965), who firs gave the derivation and rationale for whole and partial multivariate $R^2_{Y.X}$. Hooper described trace correlation for whole (1959) and partialled (1962) sets. Roy (1957) and Rao (1973) described the CA of partial correlations, and Timm and Carlson (1976) that of semipartial and bipartial correlations. Van den Burg and Lewis (1988) recently published a comprehensive description and proofs of the properties of multivariate $R^2_{Y.X}$ and trace correlation for whole and partialled sets

In what follows, the symbols Y_B and X_B represent *basic* sets: Set Y_B may be a set of dependent variables Y, or a set of dependent variables Y from which another set Y_P has been partialled, represented as $Y \cdot Y_P$. Similarly, set X_B may be a set of independent variables X, or a set of independent variables X from which another set X_P has been partialled, $X \cdot X_P$. All references to sets Y and X in subscripts and in the formula that follow are to be understood to mean Y_B and X_B, the "left-hand" and "right-hand" sets, whether or not either is a partialled set.

Measures of Multivariate Association

It is desirable that a measure of association between sets be a natural generaliza- tion of multiple R^2, bounded by 0 and 1, invariant over full rank (nonsingular) linear transformation (e.g., rotation) of either or both sets, symmetric (i.e., $R^2_{Y.X} = R^2_{X.Y}$), and not decrease in value when a variable is added to either side. Of the measures of multivariate association that have been proposed (Cramer & Nicewander, 1979), three have been found to be particularly useful for SC, multivariate R^2, and the symmetric (T^2) and asymmetric (P^2) squared trace correlations.

$R^2_{Y,X}$, Proportion of Generalized Variance

Using determinants of correlation matrices,

$$R^2_{Y,X} = 1 - |\mathbf{R}_{YX}| \, / \, (|\mathbf{R}_Y| \, |\mathbf{R}_X|),$$

where $\mathbf{R}_{YX}$ is the full correlation matrix of the Y_B and X_B variables,
$\mathbf{R}_Y$ is the matrix of correlations among the variables of set Y_B, and
$\mathbf{R}_X$ is the matrix of correlations among the variables of set X_B.

This equation also holds when variance-covariance or sums of squares-products matrices replace the correlation matrices.

$R^2_{Y,X}$ may also be written as a function of the q squared canonical correlations (C^2) where $q = \min(k_Y, k_X)$, the number of variables in the smaller of the two basic sets:

$$R^2_{Y,X} = 1 - (1 - C^2_1)(1 - C^2_2) \ldots (1 - C^2_q).$$

$R^2_{Y,X}$ is a generalization of the simple bivariate r^2 and of multiple R^2, and is properly interpreted as the proportion of the generalized variance of set Y_B accounted for by set X_B (or vice versa, because it is symmetric). Generalized variance (Wilks, 1932) is the generalization of the univariate concept of variance to a set of variables and is defined as the determinant of the variance–covariance matrix of the variables in the set. One may interpret proportions of generalized variance much as one does proportions of variance of a single variable. $R^2_{Y,X}$ may also be interpreted geometrically as the degree of overlap of the spaces defined by the two sets, and is therefore invariant over nonsingular transformations of the two sets, so that, for example, $R^2_{Y,X}$ does not change with changes in the coding (dummy, effects, or contrast) of nominal scales.

$R^2_{Y,X}$ makes possible a multiplicative decomposition in terms of squared (multivariate) *partial* (but not semipartial) correlations. For example, with set X made up of the subsets A, B, and C, the following relationship holds:

$$1 - R^2_{Y,X} = (1 - R^2_{Y,A})(1 - R^2_{Y \cdot A, B \cdot A})(1 - R^2_{Y \cdot AB, C \cdot AB})$$

The R^2's on the right (except the first) are squared multivariate *partial* correlations. It is also the case that the multivariate partial R^2 can be written as a function of whole multivariate R^2's:

$$R^2_{Y \cdot Z, X \cdot Z} = (R^2_{Y,XZ} - R^2_{Y,Z})/(1 - R^2_{Y,Z}).$$

where $R^2_{Y,XZ}$ is the multivariate R^2 between set Y and the combined sets X and Z (J. Cohen & P. Cohen, 1983, p. 143).

Both these properties of $R^2_{Y,X}$ are proper generalizations from multiple R^2, that is, they hold when set y is a single variable, y. However, the following relationship for the *semipartial* R^2 from multiple R^2,

$$R^2_{y,(x \cdot 2)} = R^2_{y,xz} - R^2_{y,z},$$

(J. Cohen & P. Cohen, 1983, p. 142) does not generalize to multivariate R^2. Thus, multivariate R^2 affords a multiplicative, but not an additive decomposition.

$T^2_{Y,X}$ and $P^2_{Y,X}$, Proportions of Additive Variance

Two other useful measures of multivariate association are based on the trace of the between set variance–covariance matrix of the basic Y and X matrices,

$$\mathbf{M}_{Y,X} = \mathbf{C}_{YY}^{-1}\mathbf{C}_{YX}\mathbf{C}_{XX}^{-1}\mathbf{C}_{XY}.$$

The eigenstructure of this matrix is basic to CA, and its trace, $V_{Y,X}$, is used in testing multivariate association (see, e.g., Anderson, 1984, p. 326; Pillai, 1960).

Now, $V_{Y,X}$ is symmetrical ($V_{Y,X} = V_{X,Y}$), invariant over nonsingular linear transformation of either or both sets, and cannot decrease with the addition of variables to either set. But it cannot serve as a measure of association because it increases indefinitely as the number of variables increase. It can be shown that it equals $\Sigma_q C^2$, the sum of the q squared canonical correlations. Its maximum, therefore, is q. One way to render a measure of association from $V_{Y,X}$ is to divide it by q. The result,

$$T^2_{Y,X} = V_{Y,X}/q = \Sigma_q C^2/q,$$

the mean of the q squared canonical correlations, is defined as the symmetric squared trace correlation, because $T^2_{Y,X} = T^2_{X,Y}$. Each canonical factor has unit variance, so the maximum total canonical variance is q, and $T^2_{Y,X}$ is a proportion of variance measure, that is, the proportion of the total canonical variance that the sets account for in each other. Equivalently, and more simply, it is the proportion of the total variance of the smaller set accounted for by the larger. However, unlike $R^2_{Y,X}$, increasing the smaller of the two sets increases q and may result in a drop in $T^2_{Y,X}$.

$T^2_{Y,X}$ offers an interesting identity. Nominal scales (categorical variables) can be coded as sets of variables that can then be employed in correlational analysis (see J. Cohen & P. Cohen, 1983), thus it is possible to analyze contingency tables by means of SC. A two-way frequency table that is routinely subjected to a chi-square test can instead be represented as two sets of variables and analyzed by SC (with certain advantages (see J. Cohen, 1988a). The $T^2_{Y,X}$ from the resulting analysis is demonstrably equal to the Cramér ϕ^2 statistic employed as a measure of association for contingency tables (Srikantan, 1970). In a $2 \times k$ table, therefore, the Cramér ϕ^2 also equals the multiple R^2 of the dichotomy with the K-level categorical variable and thus has a proportion of variance interpretation.

Another way to derive a measure of association from $V_{Y,X}$ is to divide it by k_Y, the number of dependent variables, which produces

$$P^2_{Y,X} = V_{Y,X}/k_Y,$$

defined as the *asymmetric* squared trace correlation, asymmetric because $P_{X,Y}^2 \neq P_{Y,X}^2$, but rather, when set X is dependent,

$$P_{X,Y}^2 = V_{Y,X}/k_X$$

In contrast to the multiplicative decomposition in terms of squared multivariate partial correlations made possible by $R_{Y,X}^2$, additive decomposition in terms of squared *semi*partials can be effected with $P_{Y,X}^2$. It can be shown, for example, that with set X made up of the subsets A, B, and C,

$$P_{Y,X}^2 = P_{Y,A}^2 + P_{Y,B\cdot A}^2 + P_{Y,C\cdot AB}^2,$$

the P^2's on the right (except the first) being P^2's for X semipartial association (discussed later).

A space may be defined by a set of variables and any nonsingular linear transformation (e.g., rotation) of these variables defines the same space. Consider a nonsingular linear transformation (e.g., a factor-analytic) rotation of the y variables to any orthogonal position. Find the multiple R^2's of each of the orthogonalized y variables with the variables in set X. Their sum equals $V_{Y,X}$, so the mean of these multiple R^2's is $P_{Y,X}^2$. $P_{Y,X}^2$ also permits a proportion of variance interpretation, but unlike $R_{Y,X}^2$, the definition of variance is additive, the sum of the unit variances of the (standardized) y variables.

When the number of dependent variables does not exceed the number of independent variables, $P_{Y,X}^2 = T_{Y,X}^2$, but when $K_Y > k_X$, its maximum is not unity but k_X/k_Y. This is reasonable—you cannot expect to be able to account for all the variance in five (nonredundant) y variables by two x variables, but, at most, $\frac{2}{5}$ of it. Thus, implicitly, $P_{Y,X}^2$ defines multivariate association in such a way as to preclude perfect association in these circumstances. In their analysis of the properties of these measures, van den Burg and Lewis (1988) argued that together with $R_{Y,X}^2$, $P_{Y,X}^2$ rather than $T_{Y,X}^2$ is a direct generalization of multiple R^2.

They are averages of C^2's or multiple R^2's, so there are circumstances where neither $T_{Y,X}^2$ nor $P_{Y,X}^2$ seems appropriate. When SC deals with research factor sets that define unitary entities, for example, religion as a four-category nominal scale or response magnitude (rm) represented polynomially as rm, rm^2, and rm^3. Averaging proportions of variance over such elements distorts the magnitude of their collective association with other sets. Only $R_{Y,X}^2$, which cumulates association over the elements of the set, seems appropriate in such circumstances.

In the final analysis, however, analysts must be guided by their substantive and methodological conceptions of the problem at hand in their choice of a measure of association.

Partialling

The varied uses of partialling (residualization), made familiar by MRC, make possible in SC a functional analysis directly in terms of research factors and their elements. Staying for the moment with MRC, let the basic X set (X_B) be $X \cdot X_P$, set X from which another set X_P has been partialled. Then $X \cdot X_P$ may be used in any of the following ways:

1. The statistical control of the research factor(s) in set X_P when relating X to y. If the causal model posits a direct effect of X on y, then $X \cdot X_P$ "holds X_P constant"; were X_P not partialled from X, the effect found for X may be a spurious consequence of the operation of X_P. Partialling X_P also has the effect of reducing the error variance, thus increasing the statistical power of the test of X. The analysis of covariance (set X defining group membership) is a special case of this type of use and the "analysis of partial variance" (set X unconstrained) the more general case (J. Cohen & P. Cohen, 1983, chap. 10).

2. The representation of interaction of any order between research factors of any kind. For example, the $U \times V$ interaction set is constructed as a set $X \cdot X_P$ where $X = U*V$, the set of $k_U k_V$ product variables that result from multiplying each of the variables in research factor U by each of the variables in research factor V, and set $X_P = UV$, which represents the $k_Y + k_X$ variables of the combined U and V research factors (J. Cohen & P. Cohen, 1983, chap. 8).

3. The representation of curve components in polynomial (curvilinear) regression. For example, for the cubic component of a variable v, $X = v^3$ and set X_P is made up of v and v^2 (J. Cohen, 1978; J. Cohen & P. Cohen, 1983, chap. 6).

4. The representation of a specified contrast within a set of y means of the categories of a nominal scale. Here, set X is made up of a single, suitably coded variable and set X_P contains the remaining variables containing other contrasts (J. Cohen & P. Cohen, 1983, chap. 5). For example, for dummy coding for three experimental groups and one control group, one creates three variables, each of which codes one of the experimental groups 1 and the other three groups 0. When one of these variables makes up set X and the other two set X_P, the resulting set $X \cdot X_P$ effects a contrast (here a simple difference) between the y mean of one of the experimental groups and the mean of the control group.

5. The "purification" of a variable to its "uniqueness," as when X is one subtest of a battery of correlated measures, and X_P contains the remaining subtests. Examples of X are the digit symbol subtest score of the Wechsler Adult Intelligence Scale or the schizophrenia scale of the Minnesota Multiphasic Personality Inventory, with set X_P in each case the remaining subtest or scale scores of the battery. Similarly, one may assign a subset of scores to X and another subset to X_P.

6. The incorporation of missing data as positive information. Here, X is a research factor whose missing data have been "plugged" with an arbitrary constant and X_P is a dichotomy distinguishing subjects with missing data (scored 1) from those with data present (scored 0) (J. Cohen & P. Cohen, 1983, chap. 7). This procedure not only avoids the loss of cases, but, of particular importance

hen missingness is not random, carries it as a variable whose correlates can be
udied.

In SC, the partialling devices described earlier for X_B may equally be em-
loyed for Y_B as $Y \cdot Y_P$. Thus, for example, one may control a dependent variable
r age, sex, and socioeconomic status, or represent curve components, interac-
ons, missingness, or uniqueness of a dependent variable or set of dependent
ariables.

he Five Types of Association

iven the option of partialling, there are five types (see Table 6.1) of association
ossible in SC:

Formulas for the necessary matrices to compute the measures of association
r these five types are given in J. Cohen (1982b, Table 1). The use of these types
f association are described in the examples.

upplementary Analysis

ollowing an SC analysis, further analytic detail is provided by correlational and
gression output for the individual basic x and y variables, each a single variable
 their respective sets. Thus, it is for these variables, partialled or whole depend-
g on the type of association that the following are given:

1. The within set correlations for each set. If the set has been partialled, these
   are partial correlations.
2. The rectangular matrix of between set correlations. Depending on the type
   of association, these are either "whole" (simple, unpartialled) correlations, partial correlations (when $Y_P = X_P$), Y semipartial, X semipartial, or
   bipartial correlations (when both sets are partialled and $Y_P \neq X_P$).

TABLE 6.1
Types of Association

	Dependent Set Y_B		Independent Set X_B
Whole	set Y	with	set X
Partial	set $Y \cdot Y_P$	with	set $X \cdot X_P$ (where $X_P = Y_P$)
Y semipartial	set $Y \cdot Y_P$	with	set X
X semipartial	set Y	with	set $X \cdot X_P$
Bipartial	set $Y \cdot Y_P$	with	set $X \cdot X_P$ (where $X_P \neq Y_P$)

3. A multiple regression analysis for each variable in Y_B on the variables in set X_B: standardized regression coefficients (βs) and their t test values, and the multiple R^2 and its F test value. Correlations among the regression predicted y_B's are also given.

The information provided by the analysis of these individual basic variables serves to facilitate the interpretation of the SC results of the X_B and Y_B sets that they constitute.

HYPOTHESIS TESTING, ESTIMATION, AND STATISTICAL POWER TESTING THE NULL HYPOTHESIS

For purposes of testing the hypothesis of no association between sets X_B and Y_B we treat Y_B as the dependent variable set, X_B as independent, and employ the fixed model. Wilks's likelihood ratio Λ is the ratio of the determinant of the error covariance matrix $\mathbf{E}$ to the determinant of the sum of the error and hypothesis covariance matrices,

$$\Lambda = |\mathbf{E}| \, / \, |\mathbf{E} + \mathbf{H}|,$$

where $\mathbf{H}$ is the variance-covariance accounted for in the variables in Y_B by X_B

$$\mathbf{H} = \mathbf{C}_{Y_B X_B} \mathbf{C}_{X_B X_B}{}^{-1} \mathbf{C}_{X_B Y_B}.$$

The definition of $\mathbf{E}$ depends on whether the test is to employ Model 1 or Model 2 error. Model 1 error is defined as

$$\mathbf{E}_1 = \mathbf{C}_{Y_B Y_B} - \mathbf{C}_{Y_B, XX_P} \mathbf{C}_{XX_P}{}^{-1} \mathbf{C}_{XX_P, Y_B},$$

that is, the residual Y_B variance–covariance matrix when covariance associated with sets X and X_P has been removed.

Model 2 error is employed when there exists a set G, made up of variables in neither X nor X_P, that can be used to account for additional variance in $\mathbf{C}_{Y_B Y_B}$ and thus reduce $\mathbf{E}$ below $\mathbf{E}_1$ in the interest of unbiasedness and increased statistical power. This occurs when, with multiple research factors, the analyst wishes to use "pure" error, for example, the within cell variance in a factorial design. In this case, the error-reducing set G is made up of the variables comprising the research factors ("main effects") and interactions other than the factor or interaction under test, as is done traditionally in both univariate and multivariate factorial designs.

$$\mathbf{E}_2 = \mathbf{C}_{Y_B Y_B} - \mathbf{C}_{Y_B, XX_P G} \mathbf{C}_{XX_P G}{}^{-1} \mathbf{C}_{XX_P G, Y_B}.$$

In whole and Y semipartial association, where X_P does not exist, it is dropped from E_1 and E_2. Formulas for the H and E matrices for the five types of association are given in J. Cohen (1982b, Table 2).[1]

The diagonal values of the error matrix employed in a given analysis are used for the significance tests of the β's and multiple R^2's of the supplementary analyses of the individual basic variables.

When Model 1 error (no set G) is used, for the whole and partial types of association, it can be shown that

$$\Lambda = 1 - R^2_{Y,X}.$$

Once Λ is determined for a sample, Rao's F test (1973) may be applied to test the null hypothesis. As adapted for SC, the test is quite general, covering all five types of association and both error models. When k_Y or $k_X = 1$, where multivariate $R^2_{Y,X}$ specializes to multiple R^2, the Rao F test specializes to the standard null hypothesis F test for MRC. For this case, and for the case where the smaller set is made up of no more than two variables, the Rao F test is exact; otherwise, it provides a good approximation (J. Cohen & Nee, 1987).

$$F = (\Lambda^{-1/s} - 1)(v/u),$$

where

$u = $ numerator $df = k_Y k_X$,

$v = $ denominator $df = ms + 1 - u/2$, where

$m = n - \max(k_{Y_P}, k_{X_P} + k_G) - (k_Y + k_X + 3)/2$, and

$s = \sqrt{(k_Y^2 k_X^2 - 4)/(k_Y^2 + k_X^2 - 5)}$,

except that when $k_Y^2 k_X^2 \, 4$, $s \leq 1$. For partial $R^2_{Y,X}$, set $X_P = $ set Y_P, so $k_{X_P} = k_{Y_P}$ is the number of variables in the set that is being partialled. k_{Y_P}, k_{X_P}, and k_G are zero when the set does not exist for the type of association or error model in question. The standard F tables are used (but note that v need not be an integer and that when $q > 1$, v will be greater than the sample size, n).

The test assumes that the variables in X are fixed and those in Y are multivariate normal, but the test is quite robust against assumption failure (J. Cohen & Nee, 1989; Olson, 1974).

As an illustration of the use of the Rao F test, consider the SC analysis of the

---

[1]Table 2 in J. Cohen (1982b) contains errors in two of the matrix expressions for the Y semipartial. The expression for H should read (in the notation of that article)

$$C_{D \cdot C, B \cdot C} C_{B \cdot C}^{-1} C'_{D \cdot C, B \cdot C}$$

and in E_2, B should be replaced by B·C. E_1 is correct as is. I am indebted to Charles Lewis for this correction. See also Lewis & Keren (1977) and van den Burg & Lewis (1990).

following MANOVA design of a research in clinical diagnosis. For $n = 97$ cases distributed over four $(= g)$ psychiatric diagnostic groups (set X), scores on five cognitive measures were obtained. To control for possibly contaminating effects of demographic variables, a covariate set $(X_P = Y_P)$ made up of the variables sex, years of education, age, and age^2 was used. The analysis relates the nominal scale of diagnosis $(k_X = g - 1 = 3)$ to the cognitive measures $(k_Y = 5)$, with the covariate set partialled from both $(k_{X_P} = k_{Y_P} = 4)$.

The measures of partial association are found to be $R^2_{Y,X} = .3016$, $T^2_{Y,X} = .1100$, and $P^2_{Y,X} = .0660$. The Rao F test's ingredients are found as $\Lambda = .6984$, $s = 2.76$, with df of $u = 15$, $v = 235.05$. Substituting gives Rao $F = 2.176$, $p < .05$.

Estimators of the Population $R^2_{Y,X}$, $T^2_{Y,X}$, and $P^2_{Y,X}$

The positive bias (overestimation) of the population multiple R^2 by its sample value is well known to data analysts, as is Wherry's (1931) formula for "shrinking" it to a nearly unbiased estimate. Bias in R^2 decreases as n increases, and increases with k_X, the numerator df of the F test. In SC, $R^2_{Y,X}$ and the other measures of association are even more strongly positively biased. "Shrunken" values for the three measures of association in SC are given by

$$\hat{R}^2_{Y,X} = 1 - (1 - R^2_{Y,X})[(v + u)/v]^s,$$

$$\hat{T}^2_{Y,X} = 1 - (1 - T^2_{Y,X})[(w + u)/u],$$

where w is the denominator df of the Pillai (1960) F test for $T^2_{Y,X}$,

$$w = q[n - k_Y - k_X - \max(k_{Y_P}, k_{X_P}) - 1]$$

(Cohen & Nee, 1984), and

$$\hat{P}^2_{Y,X} = \hat{T}^2_{Y,X}(k_X/k_Y).$$

When $q = 1$, both $\hat{R}^2_{Y,X}$ and $\hat{T}^2_{Y,X}$ specialize to Wherry's (1931) formula for the shrunken multiple R^2, as does $\hat{P}^2_{Y,X}$ when $k_Y = 1$.

The degree of positive bias in these measures also decreases as n increases and increases with the numerator df of the Rao F test, the *product* of the numbers of variables in the two sets $(u = k_Y k_X)$.

In the previous example, (where $u = 15$, $v = 235.1$, and $s = 2.76$), the $R^2_{Y,X}$ of .3016 shrinks to .1715, the $T^2_{Y,X}$ of .1100 (for $u = 15$ and $w = 252$) shrinks to .0570, and the $P^2_{Y,X}$ of .0660 shrinks to .0342, which are, respectively, 43%, 48%, and 48% shrinkage. Had there been six diagnostic groups instead of four, u would be 25, v 309.84, s 3.72 and w 410, and the shrunken values are $\hat{R}^2_{Y,X} = .0683$, $\hat{T}^2_{Y,X} = .0557$, and $\hat{P}^2_{Y,X} = .0334$, shrinkages respectively of 77%, 49%, and 49%.

It is instructive to compare this shrinkage with that of MRC. First note that because MRC is the special case of SC where there is only one dependent

ariable, $R_{Y,X}^2 = T_{Y,X}^2 = P_{Y,X}^2 =$ multiple R^2, and the previous formulas special-
e to the standard Wherry (1931) shrinkage formula. Now for $n = 97$, with one
dependent variable, five independent variables and four variables in a covariate
t, a multiple R^2 of .3016 shrinks to .2204, with shrinkage of 27%, far less than
efore.

The very large degree of shrinkage in SC with what would be considered a
airly large n and not very many variables in the two sets is to be expected unless
e observed association is quite strong.

ower Analysis

he power of a statistical test is the probability of rejecting the null hypothesis,
iven the significance criterion (α), n, the degrees of freedom of the test, and the
ffect size, that is, the degree of departure from the null condition in the popula-
on.

For SC, and therefore for multivariate methods in general, power analysis is
omplicated by the fact that the effect size is not a simple function of a measure
f association, for example, $R_{Y,X}^2$, but rather is inversely related to the sth root of
e complement of $R_{Y,X}^2$, where s is itself a complex function of k_Y and k_X, and
epends also on the type of association and error model. Thus, power increases
s the strength of association increases, but decreases (as shrinkage increases)
ith $k_Y k_X$ ($= u$, the numerator df of the Rao F test of $R_{Y,X}^2$). As always, power
ncreases with n and α. A comprehensive treatment of power analysis in SC is
herefore well beyond the scope of this chapter. To actually perform a power
nalysis, the reader is referred to J. Cohen (1988b, chap. 10), which is replete
ith formulas, tables, and many worked examples.

Table 6.2 was prepared to give the reader a feel for the relationship to power
f the parameters that determine it: the significance criterion, sample size, num-
ers of variables in the two sets, and $R_{Y,X}^2$. The power values in the table hold
rictly for whole and partial association.

In keeping with its modest purpose, Table 6.2 gives power for only a few
elected values of the relevant parameters. The reader is warned not to take the
aree levels of $R_{Y,X}^2$ as operationally defining small, medium, and large effect
zes (because $R_{Y,X}^2$ is not an effect size parameter), or to interpolate between
ose or between the values of the other parameters. Another warning must be
ssued: The $R_{Y,X}^2$ values are *population* values; the $R_{Y,X}^2$ values found in samples,
s we have seen, are positively biased, so the investigator should think in terms
f shrunken $\hat{R}_{Y,X}^2$ in setting estimates for power analysis.

That said, certain implications may be drawn from the table:

1. At the frequently preferred $\alpha = .01$ level, a small degree of association is
   very unlikely to be detected except for very large n and few variables.
   Even at $\alpha = .05$, the situation is not much improved.

TABLE 6.2
Power as a Function of $R^2_{Y,X}$, n, k_y, k_x, and α

$R^2_{Y,X}$	n	k_y, k_x									
		2,2	2,4	2,8	2,16	4,4	4,8	4,16	8,8	8,16	16,1
					$\alpha = .01$						
.05	50	06	04	03	02	03	02	02	02	01	01
	100	19	12	07	04	07	04	03	03	02	02
	200	50	35	22	12	22	13	07	07	04	03
	500	96	91	79	59	79	60	38	38	21	11
.20	50	53	36	21	09	22	11	05	06	03	02
	100	93	84	67	43	67	45	24	25	12	06
	200	*	*	99	93	99	93	77	78	52	28
	500	*	*	*	*	*	*	*	*	*	96
.40	50	97	90	73	42	74	49	22	26	11	05
	100	*	*	*	97	*	97	83	84	56	29
	200	*	*	*	*	*	*	*	*	99	90
	500	*	*	*	*	*	*	*	*	*	*
					$\alpha = .05$						
.05	50	20	15	11	08	11	09	07	07	06	06
	100	41	30	21	14	21	15	11	11	09	07
	200	73	60	45	31	45	32	21	22	15	11
	500	99	97	92	80	92	80	63	63	44	29
.20	50	76	62	44	27	45	30	18	19	12	09
	100	98	95	86	68	86	70	48	50	32	20
	200	*	*	*	98	*	98	92	92	75	53
	500	*	*	*	*	*	*	*	*	*	99
.40	50	99	97	90	69	90	73	47	51	29	17
	100	*	*	*	99	*	99	95	95	79	54
	200	*	*	*	*	*	*	*	*	*	97
	500	*	*	*	*	*	*	*	*	*	*

2. At $R^2_{Y,X} = .20$, a sample of 100 gives satisfactory power at $\alpha = .01$ only for problems with small set sizes; at $\alpha = .05$, somewhat larger sets (say up to $u = 20$) will yield adequate power.

3. For $R^2_{Y,X} = .40$, at $\alpha = .01$, $n = 50$ will provide adequate power only for small set sizes; at $\alpha = .05$, somewhat larger sets (say, up to $u = 25$) will yield adequate power.

4. The table makes clear the dependence of power on u: Note the close similarity in power values in each row between the entries for 2,8 and 4,4 ($u = 16$), and for 2,16 and 4,8 ($u = 32$).

To quote from the detailed treatment of power in SC, "Multivariate or otherwise, the same old principle applies—the fewer variables the better—less is more" (J. Cohen, 1988b, p. 477).

uarding Against Type I Error Inflation

multivariate significance test treats the variables in a set simultaneously, that
, it takes into account the correlations among the variables. Thus, it provides
aformation different from what is obtained from a series of univariate tests on
ae individual variables. However, the multivariate test has the virtue of provid-
ag a valid test of the null hypothesis that all the population multiple R^2's of the
adividual y variables with set X are zero, or, equivalently that all the r's between
ets are zero. To provide some protection against the inflation of experimentwise
ype I errors ("probability pyramiding"), it is prudent practice to require that the
multivariate test be significant as a precondition for performing tests on individu-
l variables.

In SC, in the interest of full exploitation of a data set, one may find oneself
performing many significance tests, both univariate and multivariate (on subsets
f variables), with the attendant risk of Type I errors. Considering only univariate
ests, with k_Y dependent and k_X independent variables, there are $k_Y k_X$ correlation
oefficients and the same number of regression coefficients. Even for such mod-
st set sizes as 3 and 5, that comes to 30 tests, a considerable number.

This problem does not lend itself to any easy mechanical solution, but some
general suggestions may, when combined with the scientific judgment of a com-
petent investigator, serve to keep the rate of invalid null hypothesis rejections to a
olerable minimum. These are essentially those proposed by J. Cohen and P.
Cohen (1983, pp. 166–176) and P. Cohen (1982), generalized to the larger arena
of SC:

1. Avoid the use of more variables or more sets of variables than are needed
   to frame the issues—"less is more."
2. Distinguish confirmatory (conclusion-seeking) from exploratory research
   or aspects of a single research. Exploratory research, by definition, yields
   hypotheses to be tested in future research, so error inflation is subject to
   later correction. It is when conclusions are to be drawn that the problem
   needs to be seriously addressed. When a single investigation incorporates
   both aspects, a hierarchical approach with the exploratory issues entering
   last is optimal if consistent with theory.
3. Some technical tools are helpful:
   (a) When possible, combine research factors into (larger) sets and require
       that the latter be statistically significant as a condition for testing the
       former. This employs the same logic as the Fisher "protected" (LSD)
       test on pairs of means. For example, for a set Y one may be interested
       in testing the association of set X with the individual y variables, or the
       unique aspects of these variables (y_j from which all the remaining y
       variables are partialled), or the unique aspects of subsets of set Y. It
       would be advisable to establish that the association of sets Y and X was

statistically significant as a condition for testing elements of Y. Th
same would hold for X and its elements. (Note, however, the caveat i
the first illustrative example.)

(b) Use a Bonferroni approach: To maintain an experimentwise Type
error rate no greater than α_F, divide α_E by the total number of signifi
cance tests to be performed, and use the latter criterion for each test
Or, if it is desired that some tests have greater power than others
divide α_E unequally, assigning larger portions of it to these tests.

(c) Or, more simply, use more stringent criteria for each test than th
conventional .05 or .01 levels: use .005 or even .001. This goes in th
same direction as the Bonferroni test without its (possibly unneces
sary) precision.

COMPUTATION

The original article on SC (J. Cohen, 1982b) contains all the formulas necessary
for SC and the supplementary analyses. More to the point, there exist SC compu
ter programs for mainframe (J. Cohen & Nee, 1983) and personal computers (J.
Cohen, 1989; Eber & J. Cohen, 1987). The most recent and complete of these i
SETCOR (J. Cohen, 1989), which is a supplementary module for SYSTAT
(Wilkinson, 1988), is user-friendly and integrated with all of SYSTAT's dat
analysis and handling capabilities.

APPLICATIONS OF SET CORRELATIONS

Conventional Multivariate Methods

SC is on the one hand a generalization of the MRC system (itself a generalization
of the standard univariate methods) and on the other a generalization of the
standard multivariate methods. The latter generalization may be accomplished in
the same way that MRC generalizes the standard univariate methods, that is,
with a single y replaced by a set Y_B, with multiple (semipartial or partial) R^2
replaced by multivariate (semipartial, partial, or bipartial) $R^2_{Y,X}$ (or $T^2_{Y,X}$ or $P^2_{Y,X}$)
and tested by Rao's F or one of the other tests (Olson, 1976).

For example, a multivariate analysis of variance (MANOVA) with a single
factor ("one-way") calls for the whole association between a set of dependent
variables Y ("scores"), and a set X ("groups" or "conditions"), an appropriately
coded nominal scale. All the advantages of the MRC system are inherent in this
generalization, including measures of strength of association and the availability
of different coding methods (dummy, effects, contrast) for X to represent the
comparisons of interest. The supplementary multiple regressions of the y vari-

bles on X, which is part of the standard SC output for the overall association, ields the β's with their t tests for the individual contrast functions of the group neans of the y variables. If one wishes the contrasts' effect sizes expressed as roportions of y variance accounted for, one can do a series of X semipartial nalyses where X_B is $x_i \cdot X_{i'}$, where $X_{i'}$ signifies the non-i subset of X (J. Cohen & . Cohen, 1983, chap. 5).

For multiple research factors, that is, factorial design MANOVA, the type of C association is X semipartial, Y versus $X \cdot X_P$. Any research factor ("main ffect") is carried by an appropriately coded set X, and (assuming non-rthogonality) the make-up of X_P depends on the causal model. It may contain ne or more or all of the other research factors, or it may be empty and thus :duce to whole association (e.g., U ignoring V and W). For conditional relation-hips (interactions among factors), X contains the product set for the factors nvolved and X_P the factors and lower-order products (if any), exactly as in 1RC. It is conventional to use Model 2 ("within cell") error in ANOVA and NCOVA, so the analysis for each research factor and interaction would include s the error-reducing set G all the other research factors and interactions up to the ighest order. Research factors and interactions yielding significant results may e followed up by single df contrasts in the form $X \cdot X_P$ as described earlier. For xample, in following up a significant $U \cdot V$ in a two factor ($U \times V$) design, a ingle df contrast u_i will have partialled from it not only the research factor V, but lso the other variables in the U research factor ($U_{i'}$). Similarly, a single interac-ion contrast uv_{ij} will have partialled from it both the other product variables in ne $U*V$ set and also factors U and V. Again, these procedures are exactly those mployed for single contrasts in MRC.

MANCOVA versions of any of the aforementioned designs (or any other NOVA design) involve only the addition of a set of covariates partialled from oth Y and X. For a one-factor design, the type of association is the partial, $Y \cdot Y_P$ vith $X \cdot X_P$, where $X_P = Y_P$ is the covariate set. For multifactor covariance lesigns, where other factors may need to be partialled in defining X_B, the ssociation type is generally bipartial, with the Y_P the covariate set and X_P the ovariate set plus whatever other research factors are needed. For example, in esting $U \cdot V$ in a two-factor design with a covariate set C, Y_B is $Y \cdot C$ and X_B is $I \cdot VC$, with VC being the combined V and C sets serving as X_P. We define this as ipartial because X_P does not equal Y_P. Single df contrasts expressed as β's and heir t test values may be obtained from the supplementary regression analyses, r, if a proportion of variance metric is desired, by running new SC analyses with he covariate set included in the partialling of the single variable, that is, $X_B = i \cdot U_{i'} VC$.

Discriminant function analysis (DFA) is a multivariate procedure that relates nembership in g groups to a set of scores. It solves for sets of weights that yield inearly weighted composites of the scores that maximally discriminate (in terms f the F ratio or eta-square) among the groups and are mutually orthogonal. DFA is a special case of CA, and can be accomplished by applying the latter to the scores as one set of variables and any form of nominal coding of group membership as the other. The resulting canonical weights are proportional to (and therefore functionally equivalent with) the discriminant weights. When there are only two groups, DFA reduces to MRC (because there is only one variable in one of the sets, the group dichotomy), as does CA.

DFA is employed for "predicting" group membership much as MRC may be employed in "predicting" a single y. But it is also frequently used as an aid to understanding group membership, and here it suffers the inadequacies of its parent, CA, as described earlier. SC provides a superior alternative, as was suggested in the discussion of MANOVA. Depending on the investigator's interest or specific hypotheses, a coding method for groups as set X_B may be chosen so as to compare each group with all groups (effects coding), or with a control or reference group (dummy coding), or to effect other contrasts among group means (contrast coding, orthogonal polynomials), as is done in MRC (J. Cohen & P. Cohen, 1983; Pedhazur, 1982). Single df contrasts can be evaluated as described in the SC approach to MANOVA. Further analytic elaboration of the contrasts may be obtained by assessing unique contributions of subsets of y variables or single y variables by analyzing partialled $Y \cdot Y_P$ sets with contrasts represented by $x_i \cdot X_{i'}$ in bipartial analyses (see the illustrative example, *A Hierarchical Analysis of a Nominal Scale and its Contrasts*).

New Analytic Possibilities

The SC approach to standard multivariate designs enhances their scope and yields additional analytic detail, yet its greatest interest lies in the possibilities it affords for analytic innovations. Prominent among these are analyses that employ Y_B as a partialled set.

One such possibility is the analysis of unique variance components of a single variable or subset of variables in a battery of tests. Many studies employ a group of measures or formal battery of tests as a set of dependent variables that together are designed to cover some domain such as intelligence, personality, values, or psychiatric status. The variables in the battery typically are correlated (sometimes substantially so) with one or more common factors underlying them. The investigator's interest often extends beyond the global construct defined by the battery to the unique variance of single variables or to common variance of subsets of the battery. Thus, an investigator of the correlates of educational intervention and demographic correlates of performance on the subtests of the Wechsler Intelligence Scale for Children may well be interested not only in the subtest aggregate but also in components specific to a single subtest or group of subtests that take the $Y \cdot Y_P$ form. An example of the former is the Mazes subtest partialling all other subtests and of the latter the perceptual organization subtests (picture arrangement, picture completion, block design, and object assembly gain partialling all the others. Because many such components can be created, he reader is reminded of the discussion of Type I error inflation.)

Other novel analytic forms are illustrated in the following examples.

ILLUSTRATIVE EXAMPLES

The following examples are drawn from previous publications (chiefly J. Cohen 982b, but also from J. Cohen, 1988b, and 1989). In the interest of saving space o emphasize the conceptual issues, only selected results are presented here; the original sources usually provide greater detail (e.g., shrunken $R_{Y,X}^2$'s, trace correlations, F ratios, exact p values).

A Simple Whole Association

An investigation generates data for 48 college sophomores on three physiological measures (set $X_B = P_1, P_2, P_3$) and two behavioral rating scales (set $Y_B = S_1, S_2$). The SC analysis yields $R_{Y,X}^2 = .367$, $T_{Y,X}^2 = P_{X,X}^2 = .202$. The shrunken values are given respectively as .275, .147, and .147. The Rao $F = 3.675$ for $u = 6$ and $= 86$ df ($p < .01$).

With the overall association being significant, we can go on to assess the results of the supplementary analysis. The multiple R^2 for S_1 and S_2 with the X set are .193 and .175, respectively, both significant (at $\alpha = .05$). For S_1, P_1's β is 391, and for S_2, P_3's beta is .517, with both ts significant at $\alpha = .05$. Note the isk of experimentwise Type I error in using the .05 criterion for the ts: although somewhat protected by the .01 significance level of the overall test, the risk of dentifying a true null or trivial effect among the six βs is rather greater than .05. For example, if five of the six population βs were 0, the probability of one or more of these reaching significance at the .05 level would fall between $1 - .95)^5 = .23$ and $5(.05) = .25$ (the Bonferroni value).

J. Cohen (1989) provided complete SETCOR output for this problem including the within- and between-set correlations and a complete canonical analysis.

A Multivariate Analysis of Partial Variance

Conventional ANCOVA and MANOVA "adjust for" (partial out) a covariate set n comparing groups on scores. In MRC terms, ANCOVA relates a score (y) to a nominally coded group membership set X. J. Cohen and P. Cohen (1983, pp. 402–406) generalize this to the case where X is not constrained to be group membership, but can be any kind of research factor(s), including one or more quantitative scales, and call this generalization the analysis of partial variance APV). This idea readily generalizes further to the multivariate analysis of partial variance (MAPV), where the single y is generalized to the set Y_B.

In a large-scale longitudinal study of childhood and adolescent mental healt▌ (P. Cohen & Brook, 1987), data were obtained on personal qualities the subject▌ admired and what they thought other children admired. The admired qualitie▌ were organized into scales for antisocial, materialistic, and conventional value▌ for the self and also as ascribed to others. In one phase of the investigation, th▌ researchers addressed the relationship between the self and other values. It ha▌ been found that several of these scales exhibited sex differences, were non linearly (specifically quadratically) related to age, and/or were differently relate▌ to age for the two sexes. For the self–other association to be assessed free of th▌ confounding influence of age, sex, and their interactions, it was necessary t▌ partial these effects from the association. Accordingly, a covariate set was con- stituted of the variables age, age^2, sex, sex times age, and sex times age^2, wit▌ sex coded 0–1 (dummy coding). The type of association is partial, with set X th▌ self scales (Antiso_s, Mater_s, Conven_s), set Y the other scales, and the covariat▌ set being partialled from both ($X_P = Y_P$). The main results are given in Table 6.3

The degree of association is substantial, the self scales accounting for 43% o▌ the generalized variance of the other scales with the curvilinear (quadratic▌ effects of age, sex, and their interaction removed. With both these sets partialle▌ by the covariates, all the between- and within-set correlations are partial correla- tion coefficients, and it is on these partialled variables that the multiple regres-

TABLE 6.3
Self versus Other Values in Childhood and Adolescence,
Partialled for Quadratic Age, Sex, and their Interactions
($n = 755$)

$$R^2_{Y,X} = .429 \qquad \hat{R}^2_{Y,X} = .422$$
$$\text{Rao } F = 52.169^* \ (df: u = 6, v = 1810.9)$$

Correlations among basic variables (partial correlations):

	Set Y_B			Set X_B		
	Antiso_o	Mater_o	Conven_o	Antiso_s	Mater_s	Conven_s
Antiso_o	1.000					
Mater_o	.200	1.000				
Conven_o	−.417	.105	1.000			
Antiso_s	.393	.077	−.066	1.000		
Mater_s	.133	.456	.046	.206	1.000	
Conven_s	−.111	.120	.351	−.258	.063	1.000

Betas and Multiple R^2's of Y_B variables on set X_B:

	Antiso_o	Mater_o	Conven_o
Antiso_s	.377*	.009	.022
Mater_s	.056	.448*	.018
Conven_s	−.017	.094*	.356*
Multiple R^2	.157*	.216*	.124*

$^*P < .01$

ions are performed. For example, the significant β = .377 for Antiso_s in stimating Antiso_o is not only partialled by the covariate set, but Antiso_s is urther partialled by Mater_s and Conven_s in the regression equations. Each _s self) scale has a significant β with its paired _o (other) scale and, in addition, the Conven_s's beta for estimating Mater_o is significant. Each of the _o scales has a ignificant multiple R^2 with the _s scales, that for Mater_o being the largest.

Note that if the X set had been a categorical variable (mother's marital status, eligious affiliation), the SC analysis would have exactly the same structure and he design identifiable as a conventional MANOVA. The covariate set employed, owever, is hardly of the kind encountered in textbook examples, and illustrates he flexibility of the method. Not only can one "adjust" for nonlinearly related ariables and interactions, but for missing data and categorical variables. These lternatives are described for MRC in J. Cohen and P. Cohen (1983, pp. 38–02), and are readily applied in SC.

A HIERARCHICAL ANALYSIS
OF A QUANTITATIVE SET
AND ITS UNIQUE
COMPONENTS

n a survey of the subjective sense of "General Well-Being" in the adult U.S. opulation by the National Center for Health Statistics[2] of 3,777 respondents, a ortion of the data was organized into five- or six-item clusters whose sums were alled Physical Well-Being (Pw), Depression scored negatively (Dp), and Life iatisfaction (Ls). Although discriminable, the three scales had intercorrelations f .63, .61, and .71. When treated as a set representing General Well-Being, they argely reflect their substantial common factor. When, however, from each of the hree the other two are partialled, the resulting variable is a measure of that which s unique to the scale (including a likely large amount of measurement error). An iC analysis addressed the association of the set as a whole and of its unique omponents with a hierarchical, cumulatively partialled series of four demo-graphic research factors: age, sex, race (Black vs. other), and education, repre-iented by years of education and its square. (Prior analyses had found that neither ige[2] nor interactions among these variables made significant contributions.)

Table 6.4 presents the $R^2_{Y,X}$ values for the three-variable set Y (= Pw, Dp, Ls) n the first column, and for each unique component in the remaining three columns. The first four rows constitute a hierarchical series of research factors with each being partialled by those preceding it in the hierarchy. The fifth is for ill the demographic research factors combined into a single set. Except for :ducation, the research factors are each one-variable sets, as are also the unique

[2]I thank Harold Dupuy of that agency for providing background information and permission to use these data, which are taken from their health and nutrition examination survey.

TABLE 6.4
$R^2_{Y,X}$'s for the Association of General Well-Being
and its Unique Components with Hierarchically Organized
Demographic Research Factors ($n = 3,777$)[a]

	Y_B			
	General Well-Being:	Unique Components		
X_B	Pw,Dp,Ls	Pw · Dp,Ls	Dp · Pw,Ls	Ls · Pw,D
Age	.020	.011	.014	(.000)
Sex · Age	.027	(.000)	.005	(.003)
Race · Age,Sex	.030	.014	.004	.004
Educ · Age,Sex,Race	.035	.018	(.003)	(.002)
Age,Sex,Race,Educ	.109	.043	.026	.009

[a] Except for the values in parentheses, all $R^2_{Y,X}$ in the table yield F ratios significan at $P < .001$.

components of the dependent variables, so that the $R^2_{Y,X}$'s given in the last thre columns specialize to r^2's between single variables; of the latter, the values in th first row are y semipartials and in the next two rows bipartials. The $R^2_{Y,X}$'s of th fourth and fifth rows in the columns for unique components and those in the fir three rows of the first column specialize to multiple R^2's, because in all thes cases one variable (either y or x) is being related to two or more. Only two $R^2_{Y,X}$ in the table are between sets of two or more variables, the last two in the fir column.

Thus, the column for each of the unique components contains the results of hierarchical *multiple* R^2, and the entries for the successively partialled researc factors are additive; each sum equals the multiple R^2 for that component with a four research factors. Such is, however, not the case for the three-variable set the first column, nor in the general case for multivariate increments to $R^2_{Y,X}$ (semipartials or bipartials), as noted in the earlier discussion of $R^2_{Y,X}$'s propertie .109 is not the sum of the values above it—they are not cumulative increments a total $R^2_{Y,X}$.

We note that the values in Table 6.4 are generally small, even though, with th exceptions noted, "highly" significant. Given the very large sample, it is n surprising that the Rao F ratios are large, even for small $R^2_{Y,X}$. For example, f the trivially small $R^2_{Y,X} = .004$ for Race·Age,Sex with the Depression uniqu ness, $F(1,3771) = 16.64$, $p = .00019$ using Model 2 error. Substantively, note that the set of four demographic factors account for .109 of the generalize variance of the General Well-Being set. Education (as partialled) accounts f more of this variance and age less than might have been anticipated. Howeve for unique Depression, their relative magnitudes are reversed. Other findings interest are the marked difference in variance accounted for in unique Physic

Well-Being (.043) and unique Life Satisfaction (.009) and the fact that only race (as partialled) makes a significant contribution to the latter, indeed to all three unique components.

A Hierarchical Analysis of a Nominal Scale and its Contrasts

In data sets where Y_B is a nominal scale, that is, a set of mutually exclusive categories, or groups, the investigator's interest is likely to extend beyond the category-set taken as a whole to one-df contrasts among the groups with regard to the research factors in set X_B. In simple applications, X_B is a string of independent variables that are not further differentiated, and the contrasts are between centroids (vectors of k_X means) of the groups. This analytic form was discussed earlier, but there the perspective was that "groups" was the independent variable set and "scores" dependent, the usual circumstance in experiments. This makes little difference in the analysis because of the symmetry of SC.

The example that follows extends this design by assessing not only the linear aspects of the research factors, but also their interactions and quadratic aspects, related in hierarchical form both to the overall nominal scale and to specific contrasts. The most important difference between this and the preceding example lies in the use of partialling to make specific one-df contrasts between groups, rather than unique components of correlated scores. Although these are substantively quite different, they are structurally the same.

The data analyzed in Table 6.5 are a portion of those gathered in a study of the level of care required by the adult inpatients of the New York State psychiatric hospital system.[3] For virtually all such patients in residence on a given date ($n = 21,892$), the following variables were determined: age, length of stay (in months), and diagnosis, coded 1 = schizophrenic (74%), 0 = all other, mostly organic brain syndrome. The dependent variable set, Outcome, was a nominal scale defined as the next change of status occurring in the ensuing 2 years. The groups thus defined were: Died (Di, 2.1%), Discharged (Ds, 6.7%), AWOL (Aw, 3.1%). Family Care (Fc, 4.9%), and the balance, Stayed (83.2%). Outcome was represented by four dichotomous variables using dummy coding, with Stayed serving as the reference group. In this coding method, when from each of the four dummy variables the other three are partialled, the resulting variable effects a contrast between that group and the reference group (J. Cohen & P. Cohen, 1983, pp. 183–198). Thus, for example, the third variable in the Outcome set, AWOL, is scored 1 for patients going AWOL and 0 for all the others. When the other three variables are partialled from it to create AWOL·Died, Discharged, Family Care, the latter effects a contrast between the AWOL group and the

[3] I gratefully acknowledge the efforts of Patricia Cohen of the New York State Psychiatric Institute and the Columbia School of Public Health for her provision and preparation of these data.

TABLE 6.5
Status Change in a Psychiatric Hospital Population
as a Quadratic Function of Age and Length of Stay, and Diagnosis

a. Setwise Hierarchical Analyses with Dummy-Coded Outcome: $R^2_{Y,X}$

		Y_B			
	Outcome Set[a]		Contrast with Stayed[b]		
$X_B{}^c$	Di,Ds,Aw,Fc	Di	Ds	Aw	Fc
A,L,D	.236	.020	.140	.087	.007
TWI · A,L,D	.075	.003	.038	.034	.002
A^2,L^2 · A,L,D	.045	.002	.037	.004	.003
A,L,D,TWI,A^2,L^2	.346	.025	.215	.125	.012

b. β's by X_B Sets on Constrast with Stayed

		Contrast with Stayed[b]			
		Di	Ds	Aw	Fc
A,L,D	Age	.11	−.13	−.19	−.04
	Length of Stay	−.09	−.30	−.15	−.04
	Diagnosis	−.05	.12	.08	.06
TWI · A,L,D	A × L	.01	.19	.17	−.03
	A × D	−.05	−.03	−.08	.04
	L × D	.04	−.02	.00	−.02
A^2,L^2 · A,L,D	A^2	.04	−.02	.03	−.06
	L^2	.03	.19	.06	−.01

Note: With $n = 21,892$, all $R^2_{Y,X}$ values are significant at $P < 10^{-9}$, and all β's of .03 or more at $P < .001$.

[a]Di,Ds,Aw,Fc = Died, Discharged, AWOL, Family Care

[b]Each of these is a dummy variable from which the other three dummy variables coding Outcome are partialled, e.g., Ds = Ds · Di,Aw,Fc.

[c]A,L,D = Age, Length of stay, Diagnosis
    TWI = Two-way interaction: A × L, A × D, L × D
    A^2,L^2 = The squares of age and length of stay

Stayed group. The Y_B sets, then, are the four-variable Outcome set and each of these four from which the other three are partialled.

The structure of the analysis on the X_B side is setwise hierarchical, with the first three rows of Panel a of Table 6.5 giving the results for the following sets:

1. The main effects age, length of stay, diagnosis (A,L,D).
2. The two-way interactions A × L, A × D, L × D (TWI·A,L,D).
3. The quadratic aspects of age and length of stay (A^2,L^2·A,L,D,TWI).

The fourth row collects all the independent variables into a single (whole) set.

The entries in Panel *a* are $R^2_{Y.X}$'s, but, as was the case in the preceding example, for the single partialled y_B variables (here contrasts, their uniqueness), they specialize to multiple R^2's, albeit on partialled variables. For example, .037 is the multiple R^2 of the single dependent variable Ds·Di,Aw,Fc with the two independent variables A^2·A,L,D,TWI and L^2·A,L,D,TWI. Thus, the Discharged group is distinguished from the Stayed group, .037 of the variance of that distinction being accounted for by the combined quadratic (simple curvilinear) aspects of age and length of stay. Also, as in the preceding example, because of the hierarchical organization of the X_B sets, these multiple R^2's are additive to the total multiple R^2 in the fourth row, where the three sets (eight variables) are related to each contrast with Stayed; for example, for Discharged versus Stayed, .140 + .038 + .037 = .215.

The enormous *n* results in even the smallest $R^2_{Y.X}$ in Panel *a* (.002) being "highly" significant ($p < 10^{-9}$!). One salutary effect of working with such large samples is that it brings forcibly to home the point frequently made by critics of the shibboleth of hypothesis testing to the effect that the null hypothesis, taken literally, is always false. Thus, its use as a conventional arbiter of what to interpret from an analysis breaks down here. We are then forced to do what we always should—make our interpretations in the light of the *magnitudes* of the effect sizes, both absolutely and relative to effect sizes in the substantive area under study. If $R^2_{Y.X}$ values less than .02 are discounted as trivial, some illustrative interpretations are: the variable's age, length of stay, and diagnosis, together with their interactive and quadratic aspects, account to a moderate degree (.346) for overall status change (Outcome). Although as is usually the case, most of the association is due to linear aspects of these variables (.215), the contributions of their interactions (.075) and the quadratic components (.045) are by no means trivial. Furthermore, the status categories that are distinct from Stayed are Discharged (.215) and AWOL (.125), but for the latter, the quadratics make only a trivial contribution. With no null hypothesis to affirm invalidly, we can nevertheless say that in regard to the research factors studied, Family Care status is virtually indistinguishable (.012) from Stayed and Died only barely so (.025), and whatever predictability obtains for all but Discharged status resides entirely in the linear aspects of the research factors.

The X_B sets each contain multiple (two or three) variables, so the $R^2_{Y.X}$ values in Panel *a* do not reveal the microstructure of the effects, that is, the unique effects of A in the first set, A × L in the second, L^2 in the third, and so forth. In Table 6.4 for the preceding example, this kind of information was conveyed by $R^2_{Y.X}$'s of various kinds, each from a separate SC analysis. However, when Y_B is a single variable (partialled or not) so that $R^2_{Y.X}$ specializes to multiple R^2, an alternative means is available from the supplementary analysis via the standardized partial regression coefficients (β's) of the variables in each X_B set. Panel *b* of Table 6.5 gives these β's for each contrast variable (e.g., Di·Ds,Aw, Fc) on each of the X_B sets (e.g., TWI·A,L,D).

The largest β (−.30) occurs for the most predictable contrast, Discharged versus Stayed, and indicates a sharply declining relative probability of discharge with increasing length of stay. The relationship is, however, curvilinear, the regression curve flattening with longer residence, as evidenced by a substantial positive (concave upward) β of .19, for the partialled L². Moreover, because the β for A × L is also large and positive (.19), the declining probability of discharge with increasing length of stay is sharper with younger patients. The same pattern, although attenuated, holds also for the AWOL versus Stayed contrast although here age takes on greater importance (−.19), even more so than for Died versus Stayed (.11), where it is quite understandably the most important predictor. Finally, it is of some interest that except for the regression of Discharged versus Stayed on diagnosis (.12), the latter and its interactions make virtually no net contribution to the prediction of status change.

Given the presence in this study of a logical reference group (Stayed), the use of partialled dummy variables provided the comparisons of interest. For studies of different logical structure or substantive concerns, different comparisons could be obtained by employing other nominal scale coding methods (J. Cohen & P. Cohen, 1983, chap. 5). For example, partialled effects-coded variables would yield the comparison of each group with the unweighted centroid of the centroids of all the groups, thus comparing each group with all the other groups rather than with a single reference group. Finally, yet other kinds of comparisons can be represented by the method of contrast coding. Indeed, with appropriate coding, any comparison can be made.

Bipartial Association Among Three Sets

The data for the next example were taken from an experiment on the effects of maternal nutrition during pregnancy on somatic and behavioral characteristics of newborn infants.[4] The subjects were 650 pregnant women coming to a prenatal clinic who were randomly assigned to three groups (High Protein Supplement, Balanced Protein/Calorie Supplement, Routine Care Control), treated, and followed to term. Their newborns were weighed and measured at birth and, within 48–99 hours after birth, were subjected to a 19-item behavioral examination assessing degree of neurological development via muscle tone and reflexes. A factor analysis of these items suggested four factors, scores for which were generated by adding the highly loaded items for each factor.

The major issues addressed were (a) the effects of the two forms of dietary supplement on the somatic characteristics of the newborns and (b) on their behavior as represented by the four factor scores, and also (c) the relationship

---

[4] I am indebted to David Rush, Mervyn W. Susser, and Zena Stein of the School of Public Health of Columbia University for permission to use these data.

etween somatic characteristics and behavior. Various maternal attributes with
potential effects on their babies served as a covariate (control) set. Concretely,
the major analysis used the following research factors:

1. Treatment (TRT): two dummy variables with the control group as reference.
2. Maternal attribute controls (COV): prepregnant weight, gestation, and
   weight at time of clinic registration, parity, and number of previous low-
   birthweight babies (five variables).
3. Newborn somatic characteristics (SOM): birthweight, length, and head
   circumference.
4. Newborn behavior (BEH): the four factor-analytically derived scores.
5. Age at examination (in hours) and sex.

Before turning to the main analysis, I seize the opportunity to offer evidence
on an important issue in research on the newborn and simultaneously illustrate a
methodological point. The physical maturity of the infant at birth, a matter of
considerable medical importance, was assessed by measuring its "age" from
conception, using as a reference the date of the onset of the mother's last men-
strual period as reported by her at the time of clinic registration (during, on
average, the sixteenth week of pregnancy). The accuracy of this datum (Gestation) is suspect, and besides, the theoretical question arises as to whether the
"postconceptual age" at birth provides any relevant information beyond that of
the observable somatic characteristics, or (more simply) given its size, does it
matter how "old" the newborn is? This issue was directly addressed by partialling
SOM and sex from Gestation and relating it to the suitably partialled BEH set. Its
$R^2_{Y.X}$ (a multiple R^2) was .014, which is not significant even at $\alpha = .05$. When
each of the other variables was similarly treated, with Gestation included among
the variables that were partialled, the $R^2_{Y.X}$'s for these unique BEH scores were
larger and significant at $\alpha = .01$. These results suggest that the postconceptual
age at birth as determined from the mother's reported date of last menstruation
yields no information relevant to the newborn's behavior beyond what is available from measuring its weight, length, and head circumference.

In the main analysis, the three research factors to be related were treatment,
newborn somatic characteristics, and newborn behavior. The maternal attributes
were to be statistically controlled as a covariate set, thus they were partialled
from each research factor. Furthermore, to control for sex differences, it was
partialled from both the somatic and behavior research factors. Finally, because
the behavioral examination took place at varying intervals after birth, age at
examination was also partialled from the behavior scores. Thus, the following
three factors, as partialled, were related to each other in the SC analysis: (a)
TRT·COV, (b), SOM·COV,sex, and (c) BEH·COV,sex,age.

TABLE 6.6
Nutritional Supplementation during Pregnancy and the Somatic
and Behavioral Characteristics of Newborn ($n = 650$)

a. Association between Research Factors: Bipartial $R^2_{Y,X}$

	TRT · COV	SOM · COV,sex
SOM · COV,sex	.010	
BEH · COV,sex,age	.018	.300*

b. β's and Multiple R^2 of BEH · COV,sex,age on SOM · COV,sex

	Partialled BEH Scores			
	I	II	III	IV
	βs			
Partialled SOM Scores				
Birthweight	.08	.29*	.20*	.15
Length	.37*	−.16*	.13	−.02
Head Circumference	−.03	−.09	.09	.18*
Multiple R^2	.160*	.039*	.133*	.087*

Note: TRT = 2 dummy-coded nutritional supplementation variables; SOM = 3 somatic characteristics of newborn; BEH = 4 behavior factor characteristics of newborn; COV = 5 maternal attribute variables.
*$P < .001$

Panel a of Table 6.6 gives the $R^2_{Y,X}$'s for each pair. The partialling sets are not exactly the same for the three sets, so the type of association is defined as bipartial. Note that the two $R^2_{Y,X}$'s with TRT·COV summarize a MANOVA, but with additional variables partialled from SOM (sex) and BEH (sex and age at examination). Clearly, the results provide no evidence to suggest the existence of treatment effects on either the somatic or behavioral characteristics of the newborn, the $R^2_{Y,X}$ values being both trivial and despite the large sample size ($n = 650$), nonsignificant by any conventional standard ($p > .15$).

The association of BEH and SOM, as partialled, constitutes another example of the multivariate analysis of partial variance (MAPV). X_B here is a set of three quantitative variables (SOM), but the association is controlled by covariates (COV and sex), with age additionally partialled from BEH. The association is quite substantial ($R^2_{Y,X} = .300$), and highly significant. (The $P^2_{Y,X} = T^2_{Y,X} = .108$, which average the three canonical R^2's, is also relatively large). Thus, although the nutritional intervention had no demonstrable effects on either the newborns' physical or behavioral characteristics, there is a material relationship between these two research factors.

The supplementary analyses provide the multiple R^2's and β's relating the three partialled SOM scores to each of the dependent partialled BEH scores

(Table 6.6, Panel *b*). It is interesting to note that despite fairly high (partial) correlations among the SOM measures of .60, .70, and .46 (available from the SC printout), they give rise to distinctively different patterns of β's and levels of $R_{Y,X}^2$'s in estimating the four partialled BEH scores.

Contingency Tables

I have argued that any information can be represented as a basic set of variables and therefore SC can be applied to study relationships between research factors unconstrained by the level of their scaling when suitable coding is used. We have already seen that purely nominal data can be coded by various means and employed in SC (psychiatric status, treatment group). Contingency tables portray the joint occurrence of levels or categories of two or more nominal scales and are therefore subject to analysis by SC, a novel alternative to the traditional contingency table chi-square analysis and the more recently developed approach via log-linear models. J. Cohen (1988a) gave a detailed SC reanalysis of a contingency example analyzed by Zwick and Cramer (1986) using several different multivariate techniques. The SC analysis gives the same results for the overall association as the other methods, but provides greater interpretive yield by assessing specific hypotheses about the details of the association.

An artificial example (from J. Cohen, 1982b) relates psychiatric diagnosis to work history for 100 patients. Panel *a* of Table 6.7 provides the 3 × 4 contingency table of joint frequencies, together with the conventional results: Chi-square (6) = 14.333, p = .026, and Cramér ϕ^2 = .0717. To apply SC, the 100 cases were first effects-coded for the three diagnostic groups as shown in Panel *b*: d_1 = 1,0,−1 and d_2 = 0,1,−1. Then the four categories of work history were contrast-coded to yield the contrasts: w_1 steady or many jobs versus little or no work (1,1, −1,−1), w_2 = steady versus many jobs (1,−1,0,0), and w_3 = little versus no work (0,0,1,−1). The five resulting variables were intercorrelated for the 100 subjects to produce the correlation matrix in Panel *b* of Table 6.7. When Diagnosis (d_1, d_2) is related to Work History (w_1, w_2, w_3) by SC (Panel *c*),$R_{Y,X}^2$ = .139, $F(6,190)$ = 2.463, p < .026. Note that this p value agrees to three places (two significant digits) with the p value of the contingency table chi-square (6) = 14.333. Furthermore, the Bartlett test of the multivariate null hypothesis yields an almost identical chi-square (6) = 14.380, with p = .026, again agreeing.

A problem posed by the standard multivariate significance tests is their assumption of multivariate normality for at least one of the sets, an assumption that is patently not met by contingency tables. However, Monte Carlo simulations with 31 contingency tables of varying size (2 × 3, 3 × 4, 4 × 6) and skewness of marginals for random samples of 1,000 analyses with sample sizes of 30, 60, 120, and 240 showed that the Rao F test was quite robust; there was good agreement between nominal and actual p values for the Rao F test for both Type I errors and power (J. Cohen & Nee, 1989). For example, for n of 60 or more, the

TABLE 6.7
Psychiatric Diagnosis and Work History ($n = 100$)

a. Basic Data: Contingency Table

Work History

Diagnosis	Steady Job (s)	Many Jobs (m)	Little Work (1)	No Work (o)	Total
Schizophrenia-sc	9	3	12	6	30
Neurosis-n	20	6	12	2	40
Pers Disord-pd	11	11	6	2	30
Total	40	20	30	10	

Chi-Square (6) = 14.333, p = .026, Cramer ϕ^2 = .0717

b. Correlation Matrix of Effects-Coded Diagnosis and Contrast-Coded Work History

	Diagnosis		Work History		
	d_1	d_2	w_1	w_2	w_3
d_1: sc = 1, ne = 0, pd = −1	1.00				
d_2: sc = 0, ne = 1, pd = −1	.47	1.00			
w_1: (s + m) − (1 + o)	−.26	−.05	1.00		
w_2: s − m	.10	.19	.22	1.00	
w_3; 1 − o	.04	.08	−.41	−.09	1.00

c. Effects of Diagnosis on Work History Contrasts: $R^2_{Y,X}$

X_B	Y_B	$R^2_{Y,X}$	F	u,v	p
1. Diagnosis (d_1,d_2)	Work (w_1,w_2,w_3)	.139	2.463	6,190	.026
2. "	$w_1 \cdot w_2,w_3$	.096	5.056	2,95	.008
3. "	$w_2 \cdot w_1,w_3$	.049	2.470	2,95	.090
4. "	$w_3 \cdot w_1,w_2$	.018	.847	2,95	.432
5. Schizophrenia Effect ($d_1 \cdot d_2$)	$w_1 \cdot w_2,w_3$	.093	9.485	1,96	.002
6. Neurosis Effect ($d_2 \cdot d_1$)	"	.008	.851	1,96	.359

actual rates overall for the .01 and .05 levels were .012 and .050. (For $n = 30$, the results were poorer, but not intolerable, .023 and .056.) The close agreement in the example between the ps for the Rao and Bartlett tests with that of the contingency table chi-square, which is distribution-free, is therefore to be expected.

Although for the overall association $R^2_{Y,X} = .139$, the $T^2_{Y,X} = .0717$, exactly equal to the Cramér statistic found for the table, as already noted. However, for all the remaining tests in Panel c, because $k_Y = 1$, $R^2_{Y,X} = T^2_{Y,X} = P^2_{Y,X}$ = multiple R^2 or bivariate r^2, depending on whether $k_X = 2$ or 1.

As a strategy to minimize Type I error inflation, the analysis proceeds by requiring the protection that more inclusive sets yield significant association ($\alpha = .05$) as a condition for investigating their constituent subsets (discussed earlier). The overall association was found to be significant, so Diagnosis was then related to each of the three contrasts of Work History (panel c, lines 2–4). Of these, only $w_1 \cdot w_2, w_3$, which compares the unweighted mean of the means (here proportions) for steady and many jobs with that for little or no work, yields moderate and significant association ($R^2_{Y,X} = .096$, $p < .01$). Thus the three diagnostic groups are not equal in employment history when it is dichotomized in that way. When the elements of Diagnosis are then pursued by scrutinizing its unique Schizophrenia ($d_1 \cdot d_2$) and Neurosis ($d_2 \cdot d_1$) effects in relationship to this dichotomy ($w_1 \cdot w_2, w_3$), it is found that it is the former that essentially accounts (negatively) for the overall Diagnosis effect ($R^2_{Y,X} = .093$, $r = -.304$, $p < .01$).[5] Thus, the nub of the association between Diagnosis and Work History is the specific association of schizophrenia with little or no past employment.

It is useful to note that had different coding methods or different contrasts been used, the same overall $R^2_{Y,X} = .139$ with the same F ratio would have been found, because alternative coding for a nominal scale is simply a nonsingular linear transformation (rotation of axes) of the space defined by that set, and $R^2_{Y,X}$, $T^2_{Y,X}$, and $P^2_{Y,X}$ remain invariant over such transformation, that is, the size of the pie does not change. However, constituent parts of the overall association would have different meanings and therefore different proportions of variance, that is, we would have cut the same pie into different pieces. For example, an alternate coding, after yielding a different correlation matrix but the same overall $R^2_{Y,X}$, $T^2_{Y,X}$, and $P^2_{Y,X}$ might lead to the specific finding that schizophrenics differ from neurotics in the incidence of Steady Job as opposed to the other work histories.

Once it is appreciated that nominally scaled research factors are simply sets of variables, some possibilities of expansion to novel analytic forms come readily to mind. "Multiway" tables of joint frequencies simply imply that more than two research factors are in play, and the specific analytic procedure depends on the purpose or causal model underlying the analysis. Additional research factors may be partialled from the independent or dependent research factors to effect an ANCOVA-like analysis, or one for which semipartial or bipartial analysis is appropriate. Also, additional research factors and interactions might be added to the right-hand side to effect a factorial designlike analysis. Or, of course, additional research factors might be added both for control via partialling and to serve as main effects and interactions.

Other possibilities may occur to the reader. Among these, the use of quantitative research factors together with two-way or multi-way tables deserves atten-

---

[5] The Personality Disorder effect is not explicitly available from this analysis. It may be found by some tedious algebra or, more readily, by recoding Diagnosis so that it is explicitly represented and finding its bipartial r^2 with $w_1 \cdot w_2, w_3$. It is not significant.

tion. In the example, controlling the Diagnosis-Work History association for age, length of hospitalization, and sex, by combining these into a covariate set (possibly including quadratic and interactions as in the psychiatric status example of Table 6.5), recommends itself.

These considerations serve to underscore the flexibility and generality of the SC system. Information in any form may be represented as sets of variables, sets may be partialled from other sets for control or for the specification of research issues, and the strength and nature of the association between research factors determined. Subsets or single variables, partialled as necessary, represent the functional components whose relationships provide the analytic detail necessary for understanding associations. Issues of statistical power may be addressed in research planning. Attention to logical or causal structures and assessments of the magnitude and statistical significance of hypothesized relationships can thus come to the fore.

ACKNOWLEDGMENTS

This chapter is a reworking and updating of the basic reference on set correlation (J. Cohen, 1982b, reprinted as Appendix 4 in J. Cohen & P. Cohen, 1983). The new material includes estimators of the measures of association ("shrinkage" formulas) (Cohen & Nee, 1984), power analysis (J. Cohen, 1988b, chap. 10), robustness (Cohen & Nee, 1989), examples from the SETCOR manual (J. Cohen, 1989), and properties of the measures of association (van den Burg & Lewis, 1988). Conceptual and practical issues are emphasized and much of the technical detail is omitted.

I gratefully acknowledge my indebtedness to my wife, Patricia Cohen, for critical discussion and stimulating interaction.

REFERENCES

Anderson, T. W. (1984). *An introduction to multivariate statistical analysis* (2nd ed.). New York: Wiley.

Cliff, N. & Krus, D. J. (1976). Interpretation of canonical analysis: Rotated versus unrotated solutions. *Psychometrika, 41*, 35–42.

Cohen, J. (1968). Multiple regression as a general data-analytic system. *Psychological Bulletin, 70*, 426–423.

Cohen, J. (1978). Partialed products *are* interactions; partialed powers *are* curve components. *Psychological Bulletin, 85*, 858–866.

Cohen, J. (1982a). "New-look" multiple regression/correlation analysis and the analysis of variance/covariance. In G. Keren (Ed.), *Statistical and methodological issues in psychology and social science research* (pp. 41–69). Hillsdale, NJ: Lawrence Erlbaum Associates.

Cohen, J. (1982b). Set correlation as a general multivariate data-analytic method. *Multivariate Behavioral Research, 17*, 301–341.

Cohen, J. (1988a). Set correlation and contingency tables. *Applied Psychological Measurement, 12,* 425–434.

Cohen, J. (1988b). *Statistical power analysis for the behavioral sciences* (2nd ed.). Hillsdale, NJ: Lawrence Erlbaum Associates.

Cohen, J. (1989). SETCOR: *A supplementary module for SYSTAT and SYGRAPH.* Evanston, IL: SYSTAT, Inc.

Cohen, J., & Cohen, P. (1983). *Applied multiple regression/correlation analysis for the behavioral sciences* (2nd ed.). Hillsdale, NJ: Lawrence Erlbaum Associates.

Cohen, J., & Nee, J. C. M. (1983). CORSET, A Fortran IV program for set correlation. *Educational and Psychological Measurement, 43,* 817–820.

Cohen, J., & Nee, J. C. M. (1984). Estimators for two measures of association for set correlation. *Educational and Psychological Measurement, 44,* 907–917.

Cohen, J., & Nee, J. C. M. (1987). A comparison of two noncentral F approximations, with applications to power analysis in set correlation. *Multivariate Behavioral Research, 22,* 483–490.

Cohen, J., & Nee, J. C. M. (1989). Robustness of Type I error and power in set correlation analysis of contingency tables. *Multivariate Behavioral Research, 23.*

Cohen, P. (1982). To be or not to be: The control and balancing of Type 1 and Type 2 errors in research. *Journal of Evaluation and Program Planning, 5,* 247–253.

Cohen, P., & Brook, J. (1987). Family factors related to the persistence of psychopathology in childhood and adolescence. *Psychiatry, 50,* 332–345.

Cramer, E. M., & Nicewander, W. A. (1979). Some symmetric, invariant measures of set association. *Psychometrika, 44,* 43–54.

Eber, H. W., & Cohen, J. (1987). *SETCORAN, A PC program to implement set correlation as a general multivariate data-analytic method* [Computer program]. Atlanta, GA: Psychological Resources.

Hooper, J. W. (1959). Simultaneous equations and canonical correlation theory. *Econometrica, 27,* 245–256.

Hooper, J. W. (1962). Partial trace correlations. *Econometrica, 30,* 324–331.

Hotelling, H. (1936). Relations between two sets of variables. *Biometrika, 28,* 321–377.

Lewis, C., & Keren, G. (1977). You can't have your cake and eat it too: Some considerations of the error term. *Psychological Bulletin, 84,* 1150–1154.

Olson, C. L. (1974). Comparative robustness of six tests in multivariate analysis of variance. *Journal of the American Statistical Association, 69,* 894–908.

Olson, C. L. (1976). On choosing a test statistic in multivariate analysis of variance. *Psychological Bulletin, 83,* 579–586.

Pedhazur, E. J. (1982). *Multiple regression in behavioral research* (2nd ed.). New York: Holt, Rinehart & Winston.

Pillai, K. C. S. (1960). *Statistical tables for tests of multivariate hypotheses.* Manila: The Statistical Institute, University of the Philippines.

Rao, C. R. (1975). *Linear statistical inference and its applications* (2nd ed.). New York: Wiley.

Roy, S. N. (1957). *Some aspects of multivariate analysis.* New York: Wiley.

Rozeboom, W. W. (1965). Linear correlations between sets of variables. *Psychometrika, 30,* 57–71.

Srikantan, K. S. (1970). Canonical association between nominal measurements. *Journal of the American Statistical Association, 65,* 284–292.

Timm, N. H., & Carlson, J. E. (1976). Part an bipartial canonical correlation correlation analysis. *Psychometrika, 41,* 159–176.

van den Burg, W., & Lewis, C. (1988). Some properties of two measures of multivariate association. *Psychometrika, 53,* 109–122.

van den Burg, W., & Lewis, C. (1990). Testing multivariate partial, semipartial and bipartial correlation coefficients. *Multivariate Behavioral Research, 25,* 335–340.

Wherry, R. J. (1931). The mean and second moment coefficient of the multiple correlation coefficient in samples from a normal population. *Biometrika, 22,* 353–361.

Wilkinson, L. (1988). *SYSTAT: The system for statistics.* Evanston IL: Systat, Inc.

Wilks, S. S. (1932). Certain generalizations in the analysis of variance. *Biometrika, 24,* 471–494.

Zwick, R., & Cramer, E. M. (1986). A multivariate perspective on the analysis of categorical data. *Applied Psychological Measurement, 10,* 141–145.

II BAYESIAN STATISTICS

The chapters in this section describe an approach to inferential statistics that differs in several fundamental ways from what is usually taught in introductory courses. The standard approach is often referred to as sampling theory inference because of its emphasis on the behavior of repeated (hypothetical) samples similar to the one actually obtained. It forms the basis for most of the statistically oriented chapters in this book.

Bayesian inference, on the other hand, makes no reference to repeated sampling. Instead, it provides a framework for making direct probability statements about unknown parameters, such as population means, based on the data at hand as well as any previously available information. The origin of this approach is associated with the eighteenth century mathematician Thomas Bayes, whose theorem regarding conditional probabilities forms the basis of its primary inferential mechanism. Nevertheless, most of the important developments in Bayesian statistics have been relatively recent.

Chapter 7, by Winkler, introduces several forms of Bayes' Theorem, working with probabilities for single events, as well as discrete and continuous random variables. The author then discusses issues associated with expressing prior knowledge and information contained in the sample data in a form that facilitates the application of Bayes' Theorem. Bayesian approaches to problems in estimation, hypothesis testing, prediction and decision making are explained and compared with their sampling theory alternatives.

In chapter 8, Lewis considers the application of Bayesian ideas to the analysis of variance. The role of prior information is not discussed in this introduction. Instead, the emphasis is on the comparison between Bayesian and sampling theory interpretations, contrasting the simplicity of the former with the convoluted logic of the latter. A variety of designs are illustrated with examples including one-way and factorial designs involving between-groups and/or repeated measures factors. As an alternative to hypothesis testing, interval estimation of planned contrasts is discussed, with attention given to the problem of simultaneous inference. Lewis contends that researchers familiar with the sampling theory approach to interval estimation in the analysis of variance need not learn any new computational techniques to apply Bayesian inference to their data. They should simply re-interpret their results in Bayesian terms.

7 Bayesian Statistics: An Overview

Robert L. Winkler
Duke University
INSEAD, Fontainebleau, France

INTRODUCTION

In the Bayesian approach to statistics, an attempt is made to utilize all available information in order to reduce the amount of uncertainty present in an inferential or decision-making problem. As new information is obtained, it is combined with any previous information to form the basis for making inferences or decisions. The formal mechanism used to combine the new information with the previously available information is known as *Bayes' theorem:* This explains why this general approach to statistics is known as Bayesian statistics. Bayes' theorem involves the use of probabilities, which is only natural, since probability can be thought of as the mathematical language of uncertainty. At any given point in time, the statistician's state of information about some uncertain quantity can be represented by a set of probabilities. When new information is obtained these probabilities are revised in order that they may represent all of the available information.

An important feature of the Bayesian approach is the notion that any variable about which the statistician is uncertain can be treated as a random variable. This means, for example, that parameters of statistical models (e.g., a Bernoulli proportion, a normal mean, a regression coefficient) can be viewed as random variables instead of as fixed, unknown quantities. As a result, probability distributions for such parameters can be considered and can be updated as new information is obtained. Indeed, the primary inferential statement about a parameter is a probability distribution for the parameter, and other types of inferences, such as point estimates, interval estimates, and tests of hypotheses, if desired, are viewed as secondary and are based on this probability distribution. Therefore, the main concern in Bayesian statistics is the determination of probability distributions for variables of interest and the revision of such distributions to reflect new information.

Bayes' theorem dates back over two centuries (Bayes, 1763), but its use as the basis for the Bayesian approach to statistics is relatively recent. Prior to the last three decades, virtually all statistical methodology was non-Bayesian in nature, based on what is often called the classical approach to statistics. Important foundational work by deFinetti (1937) and Savage (1954) helped to generate some interest in Bayesian statistics, and early books in the area (e.g., Raiffa & Schlaifer, 1961; Schlaifer, 1959) provided further motivation for Bayesian work. During the late 1950s and 1960s, the Bayesian approach to statistics was viewed by many statisticians as quite controversial, and the classical and Bayesian schools were often at odds. Now the controversy has died down for the most part, and Bayesian methods are accepted by the statistical community. The amount of work in Bayesian statistics has increased steadily over the past three decades; as of this writing there is considerable Bayesian activity at major statistics departments in many countries and at least one group (the Institute of Statistics and Decision Sciences at Duke University) almost entirely Bayesian in orientation.

Because this book is intended for a psychology/social sciences audience, it should be noted that psychologists have been exposed over the years to more material concerning Bayesian methods than have researchers in other areas where experimental data are frequently collected and analyzed. Beginning with Edwards, Lindman, and Savage (1963), numerous articles concerning Bayesian procedures vis-à-vis classical procedures have appeared in psychological journals (e.g., Bakan, 1966; Edwards, 1965; Pitz, 1978; Wilson, Miller, & Lower, 1967), and some psychologists have been deeply concerned about the philosophical implications of various statistical procedures (e.g., Meehl, 1967). A text on Bayesian statistics has been authored by a psychologist (Phillips, 1973). Moreover, many psychologists are actively involved in research in the area of human behavior in inferential and decision-making situations, and Bayes' theorem is frequently used as a normative standard of comparison (e.g., see Kahneman, Slovic, & Tversky, 1982; Slovic & Lichtenstein, 1971). Finally, Bayesian methods play an important role in prescriptive decision analysis, an area of interest in its own right to some psychologists (see von Winterfeldt & Edwards, 1986) in addition to its interactions with descriptive behavioral decision theory.

The purpose of this chapter is to provide an overview of the Bayesian approach to statistics. In the following section, Bayes' theorem is presented and illustrated with examples involving a single event, a Bernoulli process, a Poisson process, and a normal process. The two inputs needed for the application of Bayes' theorem are a prior distribution and a likelihood function, and modeling issues concerning the assessment of these inputs are covered in the third section. As noted earlier, the primary Bayesian inferential statement about a variable of interest is a probability distribution for the variable, and the output of Bayes' theorem is a posterior distribution. The use of posterior distributions in problems of estimation and hypothesis testing, prediction, and decision making under uncertainty is discussed in subsequent sections, with some comparisons of Bayesian and classical approaches where appropriate. A brief summary is given in the final section.

BAYES' THEOREM

Bayes' theorem is nothing more than a procedure for finding conditional probabilities, and it can be derived easily from the usual definition of conditional probability. The simplest form of Bayes' theorem involves a conditional probability for a single event E:

$$P(E|y) = \frac{P(E)P(y|E)}{P(E)P(y|E) + P(\bar{E})P(y|\bar{E})}, \tag{1}$$

where $\bar{E}$ represents the complement of E. Here y represents new information, $P(E)$ and $P(\bar{E})$ are called prior probabilities because they are the probabilities of E and $\bar{E}$ before y is observed, and $P(y|E)$ and $P(y|\bar{E})$ are likelihoods. Bayes' theorem provides the posterior probability $P(E|y)$, the probability of E after y is observed. Of course, once $P(E|y)$ is known, $P(\bar{E}|y) = 1 - P(E|y)$ can also be determined.

A simple, yet realistic, example serves to illustrate Bayes' theorem. An important topic of interest in medicine is the diagnosis of coronary artery disease. A number of tests are available to the physician who is attempting to diagnose the presence or absence of coronary artery disease in a patient. One test that is commonly used is an electrocardiogram (EKG) taken while the patient exercises on a treadmill or a stationary bicycle. This exercise test is by no means a perfect predictor of the presence or absence of coronary artery disease, but it does provide some useful information. Using a 1.0 mm ST depression in the EKG as a cutoff point between a positive and a negative exercise test, various studies have indicated that approximately 70% of patients with coronary artery disease have a positive reading on the test whereas only about 10% of those without the disease have a positive reading (Lipscomb, 1977). This differential between the "correct positive rate" and the "false positive rate" indicates that the exercise test can be useful as a diagnostic tool.

Prior to conducting an exercise test, suppose that a physician considers all of the available information concerning the patient (e.g., age, sex, past medical history, current symptoms, resting EKG) and feels that there is a .10 chance that the patient has coronary artery disease. The patient then undergoes an exercise test, and the outcome of the test is positive. What is the revised probability that the patient has coronary artery disease?

The prior probability of coronary artery disease, as provided by the physician is .10. Furthermore, the past data concerning the exercise test provide the likelihoods, $P(y|E) = .7$ and $P(y|\bar{E}) = .1$, where y represents the positive reading of the exercise test and E represents the presence of coronary artery disease. Thus from Bayes' theorem, the posterior probability of E is

$$P(E|y) = \frac{.1(.7)}{.1(.7) + .9(.1)} = .44.$$

The positive exercise test increases the probability of coronary artery disease from .10 to .44. Although this is certainly not a definitive diagnosis, it represents a sizable shift in the probability of E and it does suggest that further tests should be run to obtain more information.

What if the exercise test had yielded a negative result? The likelihoods would then be .3 and .9 instead of .7 and .1; 30% of diseased patients and 90% of nondiseased patients are expected to have a negative reading. With a prior probability of .10, as given previously, a negative reading would yield a posterior probability of coronary artery disease of .04. Just as the positive test increases the probability that the disease is present, the negative test decreases this probability. The physician and the patient would still have to decide whether additional tests would be worthwhile, but the negative exercise test would be viewed as good news.

Bayes' theorem can be applied repeatedly as new information is obtained. If the patient has a positive reading on the exercise test and another test, such as the measurement of total serum cholesterol, is run, the posterior probability of coronary artery disease following the exercise test is the prior probability relative to the cholesterol test. From Lipscomb (1977), it appears that with a cutoff cholesterol value of 280, the probability of a positive result on the cholesterol test is .5 for an individual with coronary artery disease and .3 for an individual without the disease. If y_1 denotes the result of the exercise test and y_2 denotes the value of the cholesterol test, the probability revision after seeing the cholesterol test can be done via Bayes' theorem, with all of the probabilities conditional on the result of the exercise test:

$$P(E|y_1, y_2) = \frac{P(E|y_1)P(y_2|E, y_1)}{P(E|y_1)P(y_2|E, y_1) + P(\bar{E}|y_1)P(y_2|\bar{E}, y_1)}. \tag{2}$$

Here it would be expected that if the physician knew whether the patient was diseased or not, the result of the cholesterol test would be independent of the result of the exercise test. This is called *conditional independence* because it is conditional upon E or $\bar{E}$, and it implies that the likelihoods in Equation (2) can be simplified as follows:

$$P(y_2|E, y_1) = P(y_2|E)$$

ınd

$$P(y_2|\bar{E},y_1) = P(y_2|\bar{E}).$$

Therefore, a positive cholesterol test yields likelihoods of .5 and .3 for E and $\bar{E}$, respectively, and the posterior probability of E following a positive exercise test and a positive cholesterol test is

$$P(E|y_1,y_2) = \frac{.44(.5)}{.44(.5) + .56(.3)} = .57.$$

The initial probability of coronary artery disease, .10, thus increases to .44 after a positive exercise test and then increases further to .57 after a positive cholesterol test. If the cholesterol test were negative, on the other hand, the second application of Bayes' theorem would yield

$$P(E|y_1,y_2) = \frac{.44(.5)}{.44(.5) + .56(.7)} = .36.$$

A negative cholesterol test reduces the probability of coronary artery disease, but the probability is still much higher than the initial value of .10. It might be said that the positive exercise test provides more positive evidence for the presence of the disease than the negative cholesterol test provides negative evidence. The two tests do not "cancel each other out." The same result would occur if the results of the tests were reversed; a negative exercise test and a positive cholesterol test yield a posterior probability of .065, which is less than the original probability of .10. Once again the evidence provided by the exercise test appears stronger than the evidence provided by the cholesterol test.

The medical example involves the revision of a probability for a single event, the presence of coronary artery disease. In statistics, parametric models are widely used, and interest centers upon certain parameters. Just as Bayes' theorem can be used to revise probabilities for a single event, it can be used to revise probability distributions for a parameter of a statistical model. If the prior distribution of a parameter θ is discrete and the new information y comes from a discrete model, then Bayes' theorem can be expressed in the form

$$P(\theta_i|y) = \frac{P(\theta_i)P(y|\theta_i)}{\sum\limits_{j=1}^{J} P(\theta_j)P(y|\theta_j)}, \tag{3}$$

where $\theta_1, \ldots, \theta_j$ represent the possible values of θ. The $P(\theta_i)$ are the prior probabilities, the $P(\theta_i|y)$ are the posterior probabilities, and the likelihoods $p(y|\theta_i)$ come from the statistical model that is being used to represent the data-generating process.

For example, suppose that a psychologist is interested in the ability of people to discriminate correctly between two stimuli. The psychologist plans to conduct an experiment in which individuals will be presented with the two stimuli and asked which one has greater magnitude. A choice between the two stimuli must be made in each case; stating that they are equal in magnitude is not an acceptable response. For this question, the result for each subject will either be a correct answer or an incorrect answer. For this dichotomous process, the psychologist feels that the possible sequences of outcomes are exchangeable. That is, for any number of subjects and any observed sequence of responses, all sequences with the same number of correct answers and the same number of incorrect answers are viewed as equally likely. For a dichotomous process, exchangeability implies that the Bernoulli model is an appropriate model. The parameter of interest is thus a Bernoulli parameter, the probability that a randomly-selected individual from the population of concern will correctly discriminate between the two stimuli.

The psychologist decides to consider three possible values of the Bernoulli parameter θ: .5, which implies that people simply cannot discriminate between the two stimuli; .7, which implies a moderate ability to discriminate correctly; and .9, which implies a high degree of correct discrimination. Prior to the experiment, very little information is available regarding θ, and the prior probabilities are taken to be $P(\theta = .5) = P(\theta = .7) = P(\theta = .9) = \frac{1}{3}$. The experiment is then conducted, and in a sample of 50 subjects, 36 correct answers and 14 incorrect answers are observed. The likelihoods, which are the probabilities for this new information conditional upon the different values of θ, can be found from the binomial distribution, where r represents the number of correct discriminations, n represents the sample size, and $\binom{n}{r}$ is a combinatorial term frequently called a binomial coefficient:

$$P(r = 36|n = 50, \theta = .5) = \binom{50}{36}(.5)^{36}(.5)^{14} = .0008,$$

$$P(r = 36|n = 50, \theta = .7) = \binom{50}{36}(.7)^{36}(.3)^{14} = .1189,$$

and

$$P(r) = 36|n = 50, \theta = .9) = \binom{50}{36}(.9)^{36}(.1)^{14} = .0002.$$

From Bayes' theorem, the posterior distribution of θ can be found, as follows:

$$P(\theta = .5|r) = \frac{(\frac{1}{3})(.0008)}{(\frac{1}{3})(.0008) + (\frac{1}{3})(.1189) + (\frac{1}{3})(.0002)} = .0067,$$

$$P(\theta = .7|r) = \frac{(\frac{1}{3})(.1189)}{(\frac{1}{3})(.0008) + (\frac{1}{3})(.1189) + (\frac{1}{3})(.0002)} = .9916,$$

and

$$P(\theta = .9|r) = \frac{(\frac{1}{3})(.0002)}{(\frac{1}{3})(.0008) + (\frac{1}{3})(.1189) + (\frac{1}{3})(.0002)} = .0017.$$

The evidence is overwhelmingly in favor of $\theta = .7$, a moderate ability to discriminate correctly between the stimuli.

For an example with a different statistical model of a data-generating process, consider an industrial psychologist who is interested in the rate at which a certain worker can complete a particular repetitive task. It is assumed that the data-generating process can be represented as a Poisson process. Given any sequence of observed completion times (times elapsed between successive completions), changes in the order in which these times occur do not change the probability of the sequence. The Poisson parameter λ is the intensity of the process, or the average rate at which the task is completed. This rate will be expressed in terms of completions per hour.

The industrial psychologist has observed other workers performing the same task in the past, and, on the basis of this past information, decides to consider the values 1.0, 1.2, 1.4, and 1.6 for λ, with prior probabilities $P(\lambda = 1.0) = .1$, $P(\lambda = 1.2) = .2$, $P(\lambda = 1.4) = .5$, and $P(\lambda = 1.6) = .2$. The worker is then observed for a period of 10 hours, and during this period the task is completed exactly 11 times, with the eleventh completion occurring just at the end of the tenth hour. For a Poisson process with intensity λ per hour, the expected number of completions in 10 hours is simply 10λ, and the likelihoods in this example can be found from the Poisson distribution:

$$P(r = 11|\lambda = 1.0) = e^{-10(1.0)} [10(1.0)]^{11}/11! = .1137,$$

$$P(r = 11|\lambda = 1.2) = e^{-0(1.2)} [10(1.2)]^{11}/11! = .1144,$$

$$P(r = 11|\lambda = 1.4) = e^{-10(1.4)} [10(1.4)]^{11}/11! = .0844,$$

and

$$P(r = 11|\lambda = 1.7) = e^{-10(1.6)} [10(1.6)]^{11}/11! = .0496.$$

From Bayes' theorem, the posterior probabilities for the four possible values of λ are

$$P(\lambda = 1.0|r) = \frac{(.1)(.1137)}{(.1)(.1137) + (.2)(.1144) + (.5)(.0844) + (.2)(.0496)} = .1316,$$

$$P(\lambda = 1.2|r) = \frac{(.2)(.1144)}{(.1)(.1137) + (.2)(.1144) + (.5)(.0844) + (.2)(.0496)} = .2649,$$

$$P(\lambda = 1.4|r) = \frac{(.5)(.0844)}{(.1)(.1137) + (.2)(.1144) + (.5)(.0844) + (.2)(.0496)} = .4886,$$

and

$$P(\lambda = 1.6|r) = \frac{(.2)(.0496)}{(.1)(.1137) + (.2)(.1144) + (.5)(.0844) + (.2)(.0496)} = .1149.$$

The evidence from the sample of 10 hours does not cause large changes in the probabilities, although the probability of the highest possible value of λ, 1.6, decreases from .2 to .1149. The probability that $\lambda = 1.4$ decreases slightly, whereas the probabilities for the lower values of λ increase by about 30% from .1 and .2 to .1316 and .2649. If more information is desired, the worker could be observed for a greater length of time, of course.

In the Bernoulli and Poisson examples, the sample information y is discrete in nature. If the prior distribution of a parameter θ is discrete but the new information y comes from a continuous model, then Bayes' theorem can be expressed in the form

$$P(\theta_i|y) = \frac{P(\theta_i)f(y|\theta_i)}{\sum\limits_{j=1}^{J} P(\theta_j)f(y|\theta_j)}. \tag{4}$$

The difference between Equations 3 and 4 is that the likelihoods are probabilities in 3 and densities in 4, because the model used to represent the process generating y is discrete in 3 and continuous in 4. It should be noted that as in non-Bayesian procedures involving likelihood functions, the likelihoods in 3 or 4 could all be multiplied by the same positive constant without affecting the results. Thus, terms in $P(y|\theta)$ or $f(y|\theta)$ not involving θ can be factored out to simplify computations if desired.

The continuous model that is used most frequently in statistics to represent a data-generating process is the normal, or Gaussian, model. Suppose that an educator who has developed a new standardized test feels that scores of sophomores at a large state university will be approximately normally distributed with a standard deviation of 30 points. The educator is somewhat uncertain about the mean of the process, denoted by μ, but assesses prior probabilities $P(\mu = 115) = .2$, $P(\mu = 120) = .6$, and $P(\mu = 125) = .2$. The test is then administered to a random sample of 100 sophomores, and the average score turns out to be $\bar{x} = 126$. The likelihoods in this example can be found from the standard normal density function, since the average score has a normal distribution with mean μ and standard deviation $30/\sqrt{100} = 3$:

$$f(\bar{x} = 126|\mu = 115) = \phi\left(\frac{126 - 115}{3}\right)\bigg/ 3 = f_{N*}(3.67)/3 = .0002,$$

$$f(\bar{x} = 126|\mu = 120) = \phi\left(\frac{126 - 120}{3}\right)\bigg/ 3 = f_{N*}(2.00)/3 = .0180,$$

and

$$f(\bar{x} = 126|\mu = 125) = \phi \left(\frac{126 - 125}{3} \right) \Big/ 3 = f_{N*}(-0.33)/3 = .1259.$$

where ϕ represents the standard normal density function. Given these likelihoods, Bayes' theorem can be used to revise the distribution of μ:

$$P(\mu = 115|\bar{x} = 126) = \frac{(.2)(.0002)}{(.2)(.0002) + (.6)(.0180) + (.2)(.1259)} = .001,$$

$$P(\mu = 120|\bar{x} = 126) = \frac{(.6)(.0180)}{(.2)(.0002) + (.6)(.0180) + (.2)(.1259)} = .300,$$

and

$$P(\mu = 125|\bar{x} = 126) = \frac{(.2)(.1259)}{(.2)(.0002) + (.6)(.0180) + (.2)(.1259)} = .699,$$

The sample mean of 126 is high enough to virtually eliminate $\mu = 115$ from contention, and 125 is now the most likely value of μ although $\mu = 120$ has a posterior probability of .300.

The Bernoulli, Poisson, and normal examples that have been given in this chapter are quite artificial in one important sense. It is highly unrealistic to assume in these instances that there are only a few possible values of θ, the parameter of interest. If θ is the probability of correct discrimination between two stimuli, the assumption that θ must be either .5, .7, or .9 seems to be at best a rough approximation. The first value, .5, has an intuitively reasonable interpretation in that it implies that people simply cannot discriminate between the two stimuli. The interpretation of $\theta = .7$ and $\theta = .9$ as representing moderate and high abilities to discriminate, respectively, is not unreasonable, but why are values such as .65, .736, and so on, excluded from consideration? Unless there is strong reason to believe that only .5, .7, and .9 are possible, the discrete example must be viewed as an approximation in which, for example, $\theta = .7$ might really represent something like .6 < θ < .8. Similar arguments can be made in the Poisson and normal examples.

The approximation provided by a discrete probability distribution for θ can be improved by increasing the number of values considered for θ. Ideally, however, the possibility of treating θ as a continuous random variable should be allowed. If the prior distribution of θ is represented by a density function $f(\theta)$, then the posterior distribution is also represented by a density function $f(\theta|y)$. The continuous analogues of Equations 3 and 4 are

$$f(\theta|y) = \frac{f(\theta)P(y|\theta)}{\int_{-\infty}^{\infty} f(\theta)p(y|\theta)d\theta} \tag{5}$$

and

$$f(\theta|y) = \frac{f(\theta)f(y|\theta)}{\displaystyle\int_{-\infty}^{\infty} f(\theta)f(y|\theta)d\theta} .$$

(6

Bayes' theorem with continuous prior and posterior distributions, then, is repre
sented by Equations 5 and 6.

Conceptually, Equations 5 and 6 provide a convenient way to revise densit,
functions in the light of sample information. In practice, however, it may prov
quite difficult to apply these formulas analytically. If the product of the prio
density function and the likelihood function is not a fairly simple mathematica
function, it may be a formidable task indeed to carry out the integration in th
denominator of Bayes' theorem. For instance, in the Poisson example, suppos
that the prior distribution of λ, the rate at which the task is completed, is a norma
distribution with mean 1.35 and standard deviation .20. The numerator of equa
tion 8.5 is the product of this normal distribution and the Poisson probability tha
the number of completions is 11 given that the Poisson mean is 10λ, and th
normalizing factor is provided by the denominator of Equation 5, which is th
integral of this product over the parameter space. The integral in the denominato
actually is tractable in this case, but the posterior distribution is not of a well
known form and is not particularly easy to work with. Other examples can b
found in which the integration in the denominator simply cannot be carried ou
analytically.

One way to avoid the problems that can be encountered because of the integra
tion in the denominator of Bayes' theorem is to carry out the integration numer
ically. With today's computers, calculating and displaying posterior distribution
is much easier than it might have been just a relatively short time (say, tw
decades) ago. Faster computers and improved techniques for evaluating integral
numerically make it feasible to work with complicated models with many param
eters. For a discussion of "Bayesian calculation," see Berger (1985, sect. 4.9)

Another alternative, one permitting analytical results, is to restrict the prio
distribution in such a way that the product of the prior density function and th
likelihood function is relatively easy to work with. The restriction used mos
often is to require the prior distribution to be a member of the family of distribu
tions that is conjugate to the likelihood function. A brief definition of a conjugate
family of prior distributions is that a prior distribution is conjugate to the likeli
hood function when the prior density function is of the same mathematical form
as the likelihood function insofar as factors involving the parameter θ are in
volved. The multiplication of the prior density and the likelihood function is the
analogous to the multiplication of two likelihood functions from independen
samples, and the combination of prior information and sample information vi
Bayes' theorem can be likened to the pooling of information from independen
samples. When the prior distribution is a conjugate distribution, the posterio

distribution is also a conjugate distribution, which means that any future revision of the posterior distribution will also be relatively easy to handle. For detailed developments of the notion of conjugate distributions in Bayesian analysis, see Raiffa and Schlaifer (1961), DeGroot (1970), and LaValle (1970).

In the Bernoulli example involving the probability that an individual can correctly discriminate between two stimuli, the likelihood function is

$$P(r = 36|n = 50,\theta) = \binom{50}{36} \theta^{36}(1 - \theta)^{14}.$$

As noted earlier, a likelihood function can always be multiplied by a positive constant without affecting the inferences that are drawn from the likelihood function. Thus, the likelihood function in this example can be multiplied by the reciprocal of the combinatorial term $\binom{50}{36}$, leaving a likelihood function of the form $\theta^{36}(1 - \theta)^{14}$. In fact, if the likelihoods were originally generated from the actual sequence of observations without bringing in the binomial distribution, the result would be $\theta^{36}(1 - \theta)^{14}$. In general, the likelihood function can be expressed as $\theta^r(1 - \theta)^{n-r}$, where n represents the sample size and r represents the number of correct discriminations. Note that once the assumption of a Bernoulli process is invoked, the form of the likelihood function is determined, and only r and n are needed from the sample in order to state the likelihood function. Other details, such as the exact sequence of correct and incorrect discriminations, are not needed, although such details may be of interest in checking to see whether the original assumption that the process behaves like a Bernoulli process seems reasonable. As a result, r and n are called sufficient statistics in this example, and since n is predetermined by the psychologist who is conducting the experiment, r is the only statistic that must be computed from the experimental results.

When the data-generating process is assumed to be a Bernoulli process, then, a conjugate prior distribution must have a density function of the same form as the likelihood function $\theta^r(1 - \theta)^{n-r}$ and it must also be a proper density function. The family of distributions satisfying these requirements is the family of beta distributions. If the prior distribution of θ is a beta distribution with density function

$$f(\theta) = \frac{(a + b + 1)!}{a!b!} \theta^a (1 - \theta)^b \text{ for } 0 \le \theta \le 1,$$

where $a > -1$ and $b > -1$, then the posterior distribution of θ is a beta distribution with density function

$$f(\theta|y) = \frac{(a + b + n + 1)!}{(a + r)! (b + n - r)!} \theta^{a+r}(1 - \theta)^{b+n-r} \text{ for } 0 \le \theta \le 1.$$

That is, if the prior distribution is a beta distribution with parameters a and b, the posterior distribution is a beta distribution with parameters $a^* = a + r$ and $b^* = b + n - r$. A beta distribution with parameters a and b has mean $(a + 1)/(a + b$

+ 2) and variance $(a + 1)(b + 1)/(a + b + 2)^2(a + b + 3)$, and some tables of beta probabilities are available (e.g., Schlaifer, 1969).

Suppose that the psychologist interested in the discrimination between two stimuli assesses a prior distribution that is a beta distribution with $a = 6$ and $b = 2$. From beta tables, the quartiles of this distribution are .61, .71, and .80. The mean and standard deviation are .70 and .14. After the sample of $n = 50$ observations with $r = 36$ correct discriminations, the posterior distribution of θ is a beta distribution with $a + r = 42$ and $b + n - r = 16$. The quartiles of this distribution are .69, .73, and .77, the mean is .717, and the standard deviation is .06. The new information has shifted the mean and the median of the distribution up slightly and has reduced the dispersion of the distribution considerably.

In the Poisson example involving the rate at which a task is completed, the likelihood function is

$$P(r = 11|\lambda = e^{-10\lambda}(10\lambda)^{11}/11!,$$

which can be simplified to $\lambda^{11}e^{-10\lambda}$ by factoring out terms not involving λ. In general, the likelihood function for a sample from a Poisson process can be expressed as $\lambda^r e^{-t\lambda}$, where t represents the length of time (the number of hours in this example) for which the process is observed and r represents the number of occurrences (completed tasks in this example) during that time period. Thus, r and t are sufficient statistics, with t being predetermined by the industrial psychologist in the example and r being observed when the sample is taken.

Because the likelihood function for a sample from a Poisson process is of the form $\lambda^r e^{-t\lambda}$, a conjugate prior distribution in the Poisson case must have a density proportional to this same form. The appropriate family is the family of gamma distributions. If the prior distribution of λ is a gamma distribution with density function

$$f(\lambda) = e^{-a\lambda}a^{b+1}\lambda^b/\Gamma(b + 1) \text{ for } \lambda \geq 0,$$

where $a > 0$, $b > -1$, and Γ represents the gamma function, then the posterior distribution of λ is a gamma distribution with density function

$$f(\lambda|r) = e^{-(a+t)\lambda}(a + t)^{b+r+1}\lambda^{b+r}/\Gamma(b + r + 1) \text{ for } \lambda \geq 0.$$

As in the Bernoulli case with a conjugate beta prior distribution, the Bayesian revision in the Poisson case with a conjugate gamma distribution can be expressed in terms of the simple addition of prior parameters and sample statistics. The only difference between the prior and posterior gamma distributions is that the prior parameters a and b are replaced by $a^* = a + t$ and $b^* = b + r$, respectively. The mean and variance of a gamma distribution with parameters a and b are $(b + 1)/a$ and $(b + 1)/a^2$. Gamma probabilities can be found from tables of chi-square probabilities (see, for example, Novick & Jackson, 1974).

On the basis of past information concerning the performance of other workers and limited knowledge about the worker now being considered, the industrial

sychologist assesses a gamma prior distribution for λ with parameters $a = 6$ and
$= 7$. This distribution has mean 1.33 and standard deviation .471, and its
uartiles (from chi-square tables) are 1.17, 1.28, and 1.61. After the sample of t
$= 10$ hours with $r = 11$ completed tasks, the posterior distribution of λ is a
amma distribution with $a + t = 16$ and $b + r = 18$. The average rate of
ompletions per hour during the sample is $r/t = 1.1$, which is less than the prior
nean of λ, 1.33. As a result, the posterior mean, 1.19, is less than the prior mean
out greater than the sample average). This shift is also evident in the quartiles
f the posterior distribution, which are .99, 1.17, and 1.36. The first quartile,
nedian, and third quartile are .18, .11, and .25 less, respectively, than their
rior counterparts. The information provided by the sample reduces the standard
eviation of λ from its prior value, .471, to a posterior standard deviation of
272.

In the normal example involving scores on a new test, the likelihood function

$$f(\bar{x} = 126|\mu) = \frac{1}{3\sqrt{2\pi}} e^{-(126-\mu)^2/2(9)}.$$

s in the Bernoulli and Poisson examples, the terms not involving the parameter
f interest can be factored out, leaving $e^{-(126-\mu)^2/18}$ as a likelihood function. If $\bar{x}$
epresents the sample mean and n represents the sample size, the likelihood
unction can be written in the form $e^{-n(\bar{x}-u)^2/1800}$, where 1800 is twice the
ariance of the distribution of test scores. Here $\bar{x}$ and n are sufficient statistics,
ith n being predetermined and $\bar{x}$ being calculated from the n sample values.
ote that the sample variance is not needed because it is assumed that the
ariance of test scores is known to be 900.

A conjugate prior distribution for μ must be a proper distribution with a
ensity proportional to $e^{-b(a-\mu)^2/1800}$. Multiplying this expression by
$/1800\pi)^{1/2}$ yields a normal density function for μ with mean a and variance
)0/b. When the prior density is of this form,

$$f(\mu) = \frac{\sqrt{b}}{30\sqrt{2\pi}} e^{-b(\mu-\alpha)^2/1800},$$

here $b > 0$, the posterior density of μ is a normal density with mean $(ba +$
$\bar{x})/(b + n)$ and variance $900/(b + n)$:

$$f(\mu|\bar{x}) = \frac{\sqrt{b + n}}{30\sqrt{2\pi}} e^{-(b+n)[\mu-(b\alpha+n\bar{x})/(b+n)]^2/1800}.$$

he posterior mean is a weighted average of the prior mean a and the sample
nean $\bar{x}$, and the posterior variance is smaller than the prior variance by a factor of
$/(b + n)$. Of course, probabilities involving μ can be found from prior and
osterior distributions through the use of tables of standard normal probabilities.

Suppose that prior to observing the sample of test scores from $n = 10$ sophomores, the distribution of the population mean μ is a normal distribution with mean 120 and variance 6. Then $a = 120$ and $b = 900/6 = 150$. After the average score in the sample is computed and found to be 126, the posterior distribution of μ is a normal distribution with mean $(ba + n\bar{x})/(b + n) = 122.$ and variance $900/(b + n) = 3.6$.

In most applications involving normally-distributed populations, it is probably unrealistic to assume that the population variance is known for certain. If the population variance is denoted by σ^2, then a realistic approach in most situations would be to assume that both parameters μ and σ^2 are unknown. Relaxing the known-variance assumption leads to a likelihood function of the form

$$\prod_{j=1}^{n} \frac{1}{\sigma\sqrt{2\pi}} e^{-(x_j - \mu)^2/2\sigma^2},$$

which can be simplified to

$$\sigma^{-n} e^{-n(\bar{x} - \mu)^2/2\sigma^2} e^{-(n-1)s^2/2\sigma^2},$$

where $s^2 = \sum_{j=1}^{n} (x_j - \bar{x})^2/(n - 1)$ represents the sample variance. Now that the population variance is no longer assumed known, the sample variance s^2 joins the sample size n and the sample mean $\bar{x}$ as sufficient statistics.

The conjugate family of distributions in the normal case with both mean and variance unknown is the family of normal-inverted-gamma distributions. A normal-inverted-gamma distribution consists of a conditional normal distribution for μ given σ^2 and a marginal inverted-gamma distribution for σ^2 (which implies a marginal gamma distribution for $1/\sigma^2$). For inferences about μ, the marginal distribution of μ is of interest, and when μ and σ^2 have a normal-inverted-gamma distribution, the marginal distribution of μ is a Student t distribution.

If the prior normal-inverted-gamma distribution of μ and σ^2 has density

$$f(\mu,\sigma^2) = f(\mu|\sigma^2)f(\sigma^2) = \frac{\sqrt{b}}{\sigma\sqrt{2\pi}} e^{-b(\mu-a)^2/2\sigma^2} \frac{(dc/2)^{d/2}}{\Gamma(d/2)c^{d+2}} e^{-dc/2\sigma^2},$$

where $b > 0$, $c > 0$, and $d > 0$, then the conditional prior distribution of μ given σ^2 is a normal distribution with mean a and variance σ^2/b. The marginal prior distribution of μ is a Student t distribution with d degrees of freedom, mean a and variance $[d/(d - 2)]c/b$, with $d > 1$ required for the existence of the mean and $d > 2$ required for the existence of the variance. The uncertainty about σ means that σ^2 in the variance of μ is replaced by the expected value of σ^2 from the marginal prior distribution of σ^2. This marginal prior distribution of σ^2 is an inverted-gamma distribution with mean $[d/(d - 2)]c$ and variance $2d^2c^2/(d - 2)^2(d - 4)$. Probabilities involving σ can be found from tables of the Student t distribution, and probabilities involving σ^2 can be related to inverse chi-square probabilities, for which some tables are available (Isaacs, Christ, Novick, & Jackson, 1974; Novick & Jackson, 1974).

Given the normal-inverted-gamma density just described, and given a sample of size n with sample mean $\bar{x}$ and sample variance s^2, the posterior normal-inverted-gamma density for μ and σ^2 is of the same form as the prior density with the prior parameters a, b, c, and d replaced by

$$a^* = (ba + n\bar{x})/(b + n),$$

$$b^* = b + n,$$

$$c^* = \{dc + ba^2 + (n - 1)s^2 + n\bar{x}^2 - [(ba + n\bar{x})^2/(b + n)]\}/(d + n),$$

and $d^* = d + n,$

respectively. As in the known-variance case, the posterior mean of μ is a weighted average of the prior mean and the sample mean, and the sample size n is simply added to b, which might be thought of in terms of the "amount of prior information" concerning μ, and to d, which might be thought of in terms of the "amount of prior information" concerning σ^2. The revision of c is a bit more complicated, because new information about the variance σ^2 is provided not just by the sample variance s^2, but also by any differences between the prior mean of μ, a, and the sample mean $\bar{x}$. When a and $\bar{x}$ are equal, the revision of c simplifies to $[dc + (n - 1)s^2]/(d + n)$, which can be rewritten as a weighted average $(dc + nv)/(d + n)$ if $v = \Sigma_{j=1}^{n} (x_j - \bar{x})^2/n = (n - 1)s^2/n$ is used instead of s^2.

Returning to the educator and the standardized test, suppose that the prior distribution for μ and σ^2 is normal-inverted-gamma with $a = 120$, $b = 150$, $c = 900$, and $d = 50$. The choices of a and b agree with the values used in the previous illustration of the known-variance case. The prior mean of μ, 120, is the same in the two cases, but the prior variance of μ is slightly larger in the unknown-variance case (6.25, as opposed to 6.00) because of the uncertainty about σ^2 and the resulting need to multiply by $d/(d - 2)$. Moreover, $c = 900$ appears to be consistent with the assumption of a variance of 900. If d were allowed to increase without bound, the results from the unknown-variance case would approach the results from the known-variance case. With $d = 50$, the prior mean of the variance σ^2 is 937.5, which is larger than 900 because of the factor $d/(d - 2)$, and the standard deviation of σ^2 is 195.5. Note that $d < b$, indicating that there is less prior information available about σ^2 than about μ.

The educator observes the sample of 100 scores and, as before, calculates the sample mean, $\bar{x} = 126$. With σ^2 unknown, it is also necessary to calculate the sample variance, and the result is $s^2 = 625$. Combining the prior information and the sample information yields a posterior normal-inverted-gamma distribution with parameters $a^* = 122.4$, $b^* = 250$, $c^* = 726.9$, and $d^* = 150$. The population mean μ now has an expected value of 122.4 and a variance of 2.95. As for σ^2, its posterior mean and standard deviation are 736.7 (a considerable reduction from 937.5 due to the sample variance of 625) and 86.23, respectively.

This section has involved the revision of prior probabilities via Bayes' theorem for a single event, a Bernoulli process, a Poisson process, and a normal process. For the parametric models (Bernoulli, Poisson, and normal), probability revision has been done with discrete prior distributions and with conjugate prior distributions. The notion of conjugate prior distributions has been developed briefly and illustrated. The presentation of this sort of material is somewhat mechanical in nature, with formulas presented and illustrated for the various cases considered. Revision formula for other parameters such as differences in means, differences in variances, regression coefficients, and parameters of more complex models are available. Mechanical steps can be relegated to the computer, of course, and some computer packages for Bayesian revision have been developed (see Press, 1989). It is important to look beyond the mechanics of probability revision to the underlying modeling issues. Thus, the generation of the necessary inputs to the revision process, the prior distribution and the likelihood function, is discussed briefly in the next section.

ASSESSMENT OF LIKELIHOOD FUNCTIONS AND PRIOR DISTRIBUTIONS

Once the likelihood function and the prior distribution have been determined, the generation of a posterior distribution is a conceptually straightforward step. If the prior distribution is a member of the appropriate conjugate family, then the posterior distribution can be determined analytically. If not, the posterior distribution can be found numerically. Either way, once the inputs are determined, the die is cast. The statistician's opportunity to capture the important aspects of the real-world situation at hand comes when the inputs are determined. If the likelihood function is a poor representation of the actual data-generating process or if the prior distribution is a poor reflection of the prior information available to the statistician, then even though the application of Bayes' theorem is "correct," the results may not be very meaningful. Bayesian statistics certainly does not have a monopoly on this type of problem. Modeling is just as crucial in classical statistics as it is in Bayesian statistics. Indeed, in any modeling, quantitative or otherwise, the output of the model is only as good as the inputs. A statistician, classical or Bayesian, can use a Bernoulli model and perform all sorts of calculations correctly with that model, but the effort will all be for naught (or worse than that, if the results mislead naive or even sophisticated readers) if the assumptions underlying the Bernoulli model are violated grossly. This is not to say that the assumptions of a model need to be met exactly; it would be surprising if they could be met exactly except in the simplest of real-world situations. What is needed is an understanding of the assumptions and some care in attempting to determine whether the assumptions provide a reasonable approximation and to investigate the effects on inferences of possible violations of the assumptions.

In the Bayesian approach to statistics, new information is incorporated into the analysis via the likelihood function. Likelihoods can be assessed directly without the use of any model, but the assessment and computational aspects of the analysis are generally simplified if a parametric model is used to represent the data-generating process. The step of choosing a parametric model is no different in a Bayesian analysis than it is in a classical analysis. Furthermore, although it may be possible to examine some data from the process to investigate the suitability of alternative models, the ultimate choice of a model is subjective in nature.

Consider once again the example involving the psychologist who is interested in the ability of people to discriminate correctly between two stimuli. Suppose that each subject in the experiment is presented with the discrimination task several times, with other discrimination tasks inserted to provide some "noise." Ignoring the extraneous tasks, the psychologist has for each subject a series of results for the discrimination task of interest. The simplest and most appealing model for this situation is that of a Bernoulli process, but the applicability of this process must be examined carefully. It might be, for instance, that some learning occurs during the experiment, so that the probability of a correct discrimination changes. Even though no feedback is provided, the subject may somehow become attuned to the type of task that is being used. Another possibility is that despite the noise introduced by the extra trials with other tasks, the subject might recognize the repetitions of the task of interest, in which case the responses might not be independent. Might a model allowing for some change in the probability of a correct discrimination (perhaps some sort of a learning model), or a model allowing for some dependence (perhaps a Markovian model), be more appropriate than a Bernoulli model? The psychologist may feel that a Bernoulli model is appropriate but might want to look at the actual sequences of responses to make sure that the data and the model are not seriously at odds. If, for instance, the sequences tend to begin with a mixture of correct and incorrect discriminations and end with a series of correct discriminations, the psychologist might conclude that some learning is occurring and the Bernoulli model is therefore not appropriate. The investigation of the data could include informal "eyeballing" of the data as well as more formal measures and tests of independence and stationarity.

In general, the statistician would like to use the simplest model that provides a reasonable representation of the situation at hand. Thus, simplifying properties such as exchangeability are very important properties to consider. An informal definition of exchangeability is that a process is exchangeable if for any number of observations and sequence of outcomes, all sequences with the same outcomes are viewed as equally likely. If a process is exchangeable, then the observations may be treated as independent and identically distributed with some common distribution. When the observations are dichotomous, the Bernoulli model is the simplest model available. When the observations are continuous, then they have some common density function $f(x|\theta)$, and various models might be considered to represent f. A common choice for f is the normal density function, and various formal and informal procedures are available to test for normality.

The examples in this chapter have involved very simple models of data-generating processes, and the availability of "fancier" models should be emphasized. For example, second-order models, which are often called hierarchical models, might be suitable in certain situations. Suppose that each individual is assumed to have some innate level of intelligence, and these levels, of course, differ from person to person. A score on an IQ test is not a perfect measure of an individual's level of intelligence, but it does provide some information about that level. Here the observed datum for an individual is the score on the IQ test, and presumably the distribution of that score depends on the individual's level of intelligence. For instance, the score might be normally distributed with mean equal to the level of intelligence and with some error variance. This is the first-order model. Since levels of intelligence differ from person to person, there is also a distribution of intelligence levels across the population. Perhaps this distribution, which is a second-order distribution, could also be assumed to be normal. To make inferences about the mean and variance of the level of intelligence in the population, a second-order model is necessary because the mean and variance are two steps removed from the actual data. The intermediate step involves the individual's level of intelligence, which is unobservable (or observable only with some error). Second-order models are among the models discussed in Lindley (1972) and Berger (1985). Other models, including models frequently used by classical statisticians, are discussed from the Bayesian viewpoint in Box and Tiao (1973) and Press (1989).

Excellent examples of more complex models of data-generating processes can be found in the econometric literature, and the study of some of these models from the Bayesian viewpoint is presented in Zellner (1971). Such models range from linear regression models with identically distributed normal error terms to models involving autocorrelated errors, heteroscedastic errors, errors in the variables, nonlinear regression, autoregression, distributed lags, and simultaneous equations. Models for dealing with time-series data and forecasting are developed in West and Harrison (1989). As the model becomes more complicated, the likelihood function tends to become more complicated and the number of parameters generally increases. Thus, statisticians are pleased when it appears that a simple linear regression with identically distributed normal error terms is a suitable model. On the other hand, many of them are well aware of the need to carefully check the assumptions underlying this model and are willing to work with more complex models if assumptions such as linearity, normality, independence, or homoscedasticity are violated. Moreover, the Bayesian approach often enables a statistician to avoid some problems that create stumbling blocks in a classical analysis. For example, prior information can overcome identification problems that may arise in classical analyses of multiparameter problems (e.g., see Winkler & Gaba, 1990).

When a parametric model is chosen to represent a data-generating process, the statistician's interest generally focuses on the parameters of that model. Data from a sample or experiment provide information about the parameters, and this is brought into the formal analysis via the likelihood function. In the classical approach to statistics, inferences are often based directly on the likelihood function. Examples are maximum likelihood estimators and likelihood ratio tests. In the Bayesian approach to statistics, the likelihood function represents one input to the analysis, and the prior distribution represents another input. When a parametric model is used to represent the data-generating process, the choice of a model dictates the parameters for which a prior distribution is needed.

The prior distribution of a parameter is supposed to represent the information available about the parameter before the new information (i.e., the new sample or the new experiment) is observed. If the past information consists exclusively of past data from a previous sample, then the prior distribution is said to be data-based, and the combination of prior and sample information is directly analogous to the pooling of information from different samples. Often, however, much of the prior information will be of a more subjective nature, and the assessment of a prior distribution then involves the elicitation of subjective probabilities. The intent is to include all available information concerning the parameter of interest, and the formal justification for the consideration of subjective probabilities is provided by the axiomatic development of the theory of subjective probability (e.g., see de Finetti, 1970, 1972; Savage, 1954).

Various methods have been proposed and used for the assessment of subjective probability distributions. In the discrete case, the assessor could simply assess probabilities for the possible values of the parameter, perhaps using concepts such as lotteries or betting odds as mental aids in the assessment process. In the continuous case, the assessor might assess cumulative probabilities at a number of specific values of the parameter or assess some fractiles of the distribution. These assessments can be graphed and used as the basis for a cumulative distribution function. For discussions of assessment techniques, see Winkler (1967) and Spetzler and Staël von Holstein (1975). Of course, the assessment of subjective probabilities raises psychological questions concerning judgmental processes, and a review of the subjective probability literature from this viewpoint is provided in Hogarth (1975).

The assessment of prior distributions for use in Bayesian analysis raises some modeling questions in addition to questions concerning the assessment process. Just as the statistician's goal in the choice of a parametric model to represent a data-generating process should be to capture the real-world situation as accurately as possible with as simple a model as possible, the goal in the choice of a prior distribution should be to represent the prior information as accurately as possible with a prior distribution that simplifies the analysis as much as possible. Simple discrete prior distributions such as those considered in earlier examples are relatively easy to work with, but they often offer only very crude approximations of the prior information. It is usually more realistic to assume that the parameter is continuous and to assess a continuous prior distribution. Among continuous prior distributions, conjugate distributions lead to relatively tractable analyses. If a prior distribution is assessed subjectively, then, the statistician might attempt to find a member of the conjugate family of distributions that provides a good approximation to the assessed distribution. The question of how "good" the approximation should be in order to justify use of the conjugate distribution is, of course, a modeling issue. An alternative approach is to use an assessment technique that leads directly to a conjugate prior distribution. Since the conjugate prior distribution is of the same functional form (in terms involving the parameter of interest) as the likelihood function, the parameters of the prior distribution can be compared to sample statistics. If the prior information can be viewed as equivalent to the information that would be provided by a sample with certain sample statistics, then those sample statistics can be taken as the prior parameters. It should be emphasized that although conjugate prior distributions are convenient for analytical purposes, with today's computers posterior distributions can be determined numerically. Thus, if no member of the conjugate family seems to "fit" the assessed prior probabilities, the best option is to forego a conjugate analysis and proceed numerically.

Ultimately, inferences about a parameter are based on its posterior distribution. Therefore, questions concerning the goodness of certain approximations in terms of the prior distribution should be viewed in terms of the impact of the approximation on the posterior distribution. Sometimes fairly substantial changes in the prior distribution lead to relatively minor changes in the posterior distribution, in which case it is said that the posterior distribution is relatively insensitive to changes in the prior distribution. One situation of particular interest is that in which the sample information overwhelms the prior information (see Edwards, Lindman, & Savage, 1963). This might occur, for example, when a large sample is taken and the prior information is quite limited. The prior distribution then has very little impact on the posterior distribution, and the prior information is said to be diffuse relative to the sample information. Since the prior information contributes very little to the analysis, it is not worthwhile to spend much time on its assessment. Although there is some disagreement as to the criteria that should be used to arrive at the exact form of a diffuse distribution, certain diffuse prior distributions are encountered frequently. For the normal process with known variance, the conjugate family is the normal family, and a commonly-used representation of diffuseness is an improper normal prior distribution with infinite variance. In the notation presented earlier, this is a normal prior distribution for μ with $b = 0$. The posterior mean and variance of μ are then simply $\bar{x}$ and σ^2/n. Even in cases where the prior distribution is not diffuse, a supplementary analysis with a diffuse prior distribution is often conducted to see what the results look like when based on the sample information alone.

The discussion in this section of modeling issues that arise in Bayesian statistics has merely scratched the surface. As the situation being modeled becomes more complex, the modeling process generally becomes more difficult. For example, when observations are multivariate, possible dependence among variables might be very important. Assumptions underlying potential models of the data-generating process can be hard to check, and these models usually have many parameters. In turn, as the number of parameters increases, relationships among these parameters must be considered, and the assessment of a prior distribution becomes more difficult. In multiple regression, for instance, assessing a prior distribution for the regression coefficients and the error variance is by no means an easy task; see Kadane et al. (1980) for an approach to this assessment problem.

As the model becomes more complex, it may also be harder to investigate the sensitivity of inferences to deviations from the model. Nevertheless, the general approach to modeling is the same in complex situations as it is in relatively simple situations. Insofar as possible, the statistician should investigate the degree to which the model captures the real-world situation and the sensitivity of inferences or decisions to violations of the assumptions underlying the model. The issues of how best to conduct sensitivity analysis and how sensitive Bayesian inferences tend to be have received increasing attention recently under the label of "Bayesian robustness" (e.g., see Berger, 1984; Kadane, 1984).

ESTIMATION AND HYPOTHESIS TESTING

In Bayesian statistics, the primary concern involves the application of Bayes' theorem to combine prior and sample information and form a posterior distribution. The posterior distribution itself is the primary inferential statement in the Bayesian approach. Sometimes it is convenient for reporting purposes to summarize this distribution in some manner. Moreover, the emphasis in classical statistics on estimation and hypothesis testing has led to the development of Bayesian counterparts to classical estimates and tests. In this section the use of posterior distributions in problems of estimation and hypothesis testing is briefly discussed, with some comparison of Bayesian and classical approaches where appropriate. For a more detailed comparison of different approaches to statistics, see Barnett (1973).

One type of inferential procedure is that of point estimation, in which a single point, or single value, is used to estimate an unknown parameter. The classical statistician, of course, bases point estimates entirely on the sample information. Thus, a sample statistic is used to estimate an unknown parameter; for instance, the sample mean $\bar{x}$ might be used to estimate the mean μ of a particular process, and the sample proportion r/n might be used to estimate the parameter θ of a

Bernoulli process. A number of properties (e.g., sufficiency, unbiasedness, efficiency, consistency) have been put forth as good properties for estimators to possess.

In the Bayesian approach, any point estimate should be based on the posterior distribution, and the determination of such a point estimate amounts to choosing a measure of location for the distribution. Possible choices include, but are not limited to, the mean, median, and mode of the posterior distribution. If a loss function is available for the point estimation problem, the choice of an estimate becomes a decision-making problem with the objective of minimizing the expected loss. A symmetric squared-error loss function, for example, would result in the posterior mean being the optimal estimate. Certain comparisons with classical procedures are sometimes possible. If the prior distribution is uniform (one possible choice for a diffuse distribution), then the posterior mode is equal to the maximum likelihood estimate.

Another common form of estimation is interval estimation, in which the estimate is an interval of values rather than a single value. From the posterior distribution, the probability of any interval of values of the parameter can be determined. To find an interval containing 90% of the probability, the statistician could consider the interval from the .05 fractile to the .95 fractile, the interval from the .01 fractile to the .91 fractile, and so on. Two typical choices are (a) an interval that leaves the same amount of probability in each tail of the distribution and (b) a region (that need not be but usually is a single interval) for which the height of the density function for points outside the region is less than or equal to the height of the density function for points included in the region. The latter approach produces what is called a highest density region.

To illustrate Bayesian interval estimation, consider once again the known-variance case of the normal example from the section on Bayes' theorem. Here the parameter of interest is μ, the mean score on the test, and the posterior distribution for μ is a normal distribution with mean 122.4 and variance 3.6. An approximate 95% interval estimate for μ based on this posterior distribution has limits $122.4 \pm 1.96\sqrt{3.6}$, or 118.7 and 126.1. By comparison, a classical 95% confidence interval in this example has limits $126 \pm 1.96(30)/10$, or 120.1 and 131.9. In the unknown-variance case, both Bayesian and classical interval estimates involve the use of tables of the Student t distribution.

In the normal example, the limits of the Bayesian 95% interval estimate differ from the limits of the classical 95% interval estimate. This difference is due to the inclusion of prior information in the Bayesian analysis. An even more important difference between the two intervals involves their interpretation. The Bayesian interval is based on the posterior distribution of μ and can be interpreted as a probability statement about μ: The probability is approximately .95 that μ lies in the interval from 118.7 to 126.1. In the classical approach, the parameter μ is viewed as unknown but fixed. It is not a random variable, and the classical interval estimate is not a probability statement about μ. The randomness is associated with the way the sample is drawn, and the interpretation of the classical interval estimate is that if repeated independent samples of the same size ($n = 100$) were drawn, and a 95% confidence interval were found for each of the samples, then approximately 95% of these intervals would contain the true value of μ. The classical interpretation of confidence intervals is not as intuitively appealing as the Bayesian interpretation of interval estimates based on the posterior distribution, and many students and users of classical confidence intervals persist in interpreting these intervals as probability statements about μ rather than as probability statements about intervals generated by repeated sampling. The natural way to think about an interval estimate is in terms of a probability statement about μ, and the Bayesian approach addresses the question of interest directly.

Instead of estimating a parameter, a statistician may want to test a particular hypothesis concerning that parameter against some alternative hypothesis. In the Bayesian approach, the two hypotheses can be compared in terms of a posterior odds ratio, which is the ratio of the posterior probabilities of the hypotheses. If the two hypotheses of interest are labeled H_1 and H_2, the posterior odds ratios of H_1 to H_2 is $P(H_1|y)/P(H_2|y)$. A high odds ratio favors H_1, whereas a low odds ratio favors H_2. If one of the two hypotheses must be chosen, then it is necessary to determine a critical value of the odds ratio. Odds ratios above the critical value lead to the choice of H_1, whereas odds ratios below the critical value lead to the choice of H_2. As in any choice between two actions, two mistakes are possible: The statistician could choose H_1 when H_2 is, in fact, true, or H_2 could be chosen when H_1 is true. If these two mistakes are judged to be about equally serious, then the logical choice of a critical value for the odds ratio is one. When the posterior odds ratio is one, the two hypotheses are equally likely, so that a critical value of one amounts to a decision to choose the hypothesis that has the higher posterior probability. Of course, if one mistake is thought to be more serious than the other mistake, the critical value of the odds ratio should be adjusted accordingly.

Some comparisons can be made between Bayesian and classical hypothesis testing. Although classical tests are usually expressed in terms of critical regions for certain statistics (e.g., reject H_1 if $t \geq 1.7$), many tests used in practice are likelihood ratio tests. That is, the rejection region can be expressed in the form $LR \leq k$, where k is a critical value of the likelihood ratio LR. The likelihood ratio is, as the name implies, simply a ratio of the likelihoods associated with the two hypotheses: $LR = P(y|H_1)/P(y|H_2)$ for discrete data-generating processes, and $LR = f(y|H_1)/f(y|H_2)$ for continuous data-generating processes. But the likelihood ratio and posterior odds ratio are related, since Bayes' theorem can be expressed in terms of odds. The posterior odds ratio is equal to the product of the prior odds ratio (the ratio of the prior probabilities of H_1 and H_2) and the likelihood ratio. Thus, if the two hypotheses are equally likely a priori, the posterior odds ratio equals the likelihood ratio, and a Bayesian test is in fact a likelihood ratio test. When the prior odds ratio is not equal to one, of course, the posterior odds and the likelihood ratio are not equal, but the former might be thought of as an adjusted version of the latter.

As in interval estimation, the results of Bayesian and classical tests have different interpretations even when the numerical results happen to be similar. In classical hypothesis testing, the error probabilities are selected in advance (e.g., a significance level of .05 might be chosen by a statistician), and they are interpreted as the probabilities of errors in repeated samples (e.g., if the procedure were carried out repeatedly and H_1 were true, H_1 would be rejected about 5% of the time). In Bayesian hypothesis testing, the error probabilities are posterior probabilities calculated after the sample is observed, and they are interpreted as probabilities about H_1 and H_2 given that particular sample. In the known-variance case of the normal example from the second section, suppose that the hypotheses H_1: $\mu \geq 120$ and H_2: $\mu < 120$ are of interest. From the posterior distribution, $P(H_1|y) = P(\mu \geq 120|\bar{x} = 126) = 1 - \phi[(120 - 122.4)/1.9] = .896$ and $P(H_2|y) = P(\mu < 120|\bar{x} = 126) = .104$, where ϕ represents the standard normal cumulative distribution function. Here H_1 appears to be much more likely than H_2, with the posterior odds ratio equalling .896/.104 = 8.62.

Certain types of tests encountered frequently in classical analyses create some difficulties when studied from the Bayesian viewpoint. For example, consider the hypotheses H_1: $\mu = 120$ and H_2: $\mu \neq 120$. If the posterior distribution of μ is continuous, as it is when a normal prior distribution is assessed for μ, any single value such as 120 has a posterior probability of zero. As a result, it makes no sense to even contemplate the hypothesis that $\mu = 120$. What is generally meant by this sort of hypothesis is that μ is close to 120, but the notion of "close" is left quite vague. The Bayesian approach forces the statistician to explicitly state the hypothesis of interest. If it is $119 \leq \mu \leq 121$, then the posterior probability of the hypothesis can be computed.

A Bayesian approach to testing point null hypotheses such as H_1: $\mu = 120$ can be developed if the specific value in the point null hypothesis is assigned a nonzero prior probability. The prior distribution then typically consists of a mass of probability at the point null value (e.g., $\mu = 120$) with a continuous density function for the remaining probability. For example, a mass of one-half at $\mu = 120$ would imply a prior odds ratio of $P(\mu = 120)/P(\mu \neq 120) = .5/.5 = 1$. However, Bayesian inference for this situation, as reflected by posterior odds ratios, often leads to results that differ greatly from those obtained from classical methods, as reflected by observed classical significance levels (*P*-values). In particular, even when the data lead to a very low significance level, the *lower bound* on the posterior probability of the null hypothesis over a wide class of prior distributions can be quite large. Thus, a Bayesian might view the data as supportive of the null hypothesis when a classical statistician with the same data would be inclined to reject the null hypothesis. The difficulty relates to the fact that "classical error probabilities or *P*-values are completely misleading descriptions of the evidence against (the null hypothesis)" (Berger, 1985, p. 153). For more details, see Berger and Sellke (1987); Edwards, Lindman, and Savage (1963) is also very relevant.

Thus, although the primary inferential statement in Bayesian statistics is a posterior distribution, that distribution can be used as the basis for inferential statements of the type frequently used by classical statisticians, such as point estimates, interval estimates, and tests of hypotheses. The Bayesian approach provides an intuitively reasonable treatment of these topics, perhaps because the assignment of probability distributions to parameters permits estimates and tests to be interpreted in terms of probabilities concerning parameters instead of in terms of seemingly more awkward probabilities that concern the sample observations and are only conditional upon the parameters about which inferences are being made. Another way of saying this is simply that the Bayesian approach answers the real questions of interest directly rather than indirectly.

PREDICTION

The bulk of traditional statistical practice involves estimation and hypothesis testing, and the use of posterior distributions in problems of estimation and hypothesis testing has been discussed briefly. Another type of problem is that of predicting a future observation. In the Bayesian approach, a predictive distribution can be found for a future observation, and probability statements are based on this distribution. In the case of a discrete data-generating process and a discrete posterior distribution, for example, the predictive distribution for a future observation *x* after the data *y* have been observed is

$$P(x) = \sum_{j=1}^{J} P(\theta_j | y) P(x | \theta_j). \tag{7}$$

The probabilities $P(x|\theta_j)$ are obtained from the model chosen to represent the data-generating process. If we knew the actual value of θ, then this conditional probability distribution of *x* given θ could be used to make predictions about *x*. Since we do not know θ, conditional distributions of *x* given different values of θ are weighted by the posterior probabilities of the different values of θ in order to determine the predictive distribution.

In the example in the second section with a discrete prior distribution for the Poisson parameter λ, the average rate at which a worker completes a task, the posterior probabilities are $P(\lambda = 1.0|r) = .1316$, $P(\lambda = 1.2|r) = .2649$, $P(\lambda = 1.4|r) = .4886$, and $P(\lambda = 1.6|r) = .1149$. The conditional probabilities for *x*, the number of times the worker will complete the task in the next two hours, are

Poisson probabilities, and marginal, or predictive, probabilities for x are weighted averages of these Poisson probabilities. For example,

$$P(x = 0|\lambda = 1.0) = .3679,$$

$$P(x = 0|\lambda = 1.2) = .3012,$$

$$P(x = 0|\lambda = 1.4) = .2466,$$

and

$$P(x = 0|\lambda = 1.6) = .2019,$$

so that

$$P(x = 0) = .1316(.3679) + .2649(.3012) + .4886(.2466)$$
$$+ .1149(.2019) = .2719.$$

In a similar manner, predictive probabilities for the other values of x can be computed, and they are $P(x = 1) = .3499$, $P(x = 2) = .2294$, $P(x = 3) = .1020$, $P(x = 4) = .0345$, $P(x = 5) = .0095$, $P(x = 6) = .0022$, $P(x = 7) = .0004$, and $P(x = 8) = .0001$.

If the data-generating process is discrete and the prior distribution is continuous, the posterior distribution after y is observed is also continuous. Conditional probabilities $P(x|\theta)$ for different values of θ are then weighted by a density function $f(\theta|y)$ and the summation in Equation 7 is replaced by integration over θ:

$$P(x) = \int_{-\infty}^{\infty} f(\theta|y)P(x|\theta)d\theta. \tag{8}$$

Once again, the result is a marginal distribution for x that can be used for predictive purposes.

For example, if the data-generating process is Poisson and the prior distribution of λ is a gamma distribution with parameters a and b, then the posterior distribution for λ is also a gamma distribution, but with parameters $a^* = a + t$ and $b^* = b + r$, as discussed earlier. In the Poisson example involving the rate at which a task is completed, the gamma prior distribution with $a = 6$ and $b = 7$ given earlier leads to a posterior distribution with $a^* = 16$ and $b^* = 18$. Applying Equation 8 to find the predictive distribution for x, the number of times the worker will complete the task in the next 2 hours, yields a negative binomial distribution for x:

$$P(x) = \frac{(x + 18)!}{x! \ 18!} \left(\frac{2}{2 + 16}\right)^x \left(\frac{16}{2 + 16}\right)^{19}$$

for $x = 0, 1, 2, \ldots$. The predictive probabilities found by plugging different values of x into this formula are $P(x = 0) = .1067$, $P(x = 1) = .2252$, $P(x = 2) = .2502$, $P(x = 3) = .1946$, $P(x = 4) = .1189$, $P(x = 5) = .0608$, $P(x = 6) =$

.0270, $P(x = 7) = .0107$, $P(x = 8) = .0039$, $P(x = 9) = .0013$, $P(x = 10) = .0004$, and $P(x = 11) = .0001$. In some cases, of course, predictive probabilities may be desired before y is observed. In that case the conditional probabilities $P(x|\theta)$ are weighted by prior probabilities or densities instead of posterior probabilities or densities. Equations 7 and 8 are replaced by

$$P(x) = \sum_{j=1}^{J} P(\theta_j)P(x|\theta_j) \tag{9}$$

and

$$P(x) = \int_{-\infty}^{\infty} f(\theta)P(x|\theta)d\theta, \tag{10}$$

respectively. For the Poisson example with the discrete prior distribution, for instance, the Poisson probabilities .3679, .3012, .2466, and .2019 for $x = 0$ are weighted by the prior probabilities .1, .2, .5, and .2, giving

$$P(x = 0) = .1(.3679) + .2(.3012) + .5(.2466) + .2(.2019) = .2607.$$

Similar calculations for other values of x provide predictive probabilities for the worker completing the task once, twice, and so forth, in the next two hours: $P(x = 1) = .3463$, $P(x = 2) = .2343$, $P(x = 3) = .1074$, $P(x = 4) = .0375$, $P(x = 5) = .0106$, $P(x = 6) = .0025$, $P(x = 7) = .0005$, and $P(x = 8) = .0001$. If the prior distribution of λ is gamma with $a = 6$ and $b = 7$ instead of discrete, predictive probabilities for x based on the prior distribution can be found from the negative binomial formula

$$P(x) = \frac{(x + 7)!}{x! \, 7!} \left(\frac{2}{2 + 6}\right)^x \left(\frac{6}{2 + 6}\right)^8$$

for $x = 0, 1, 2, \ldots$.

Predictive distributions are found in a similar manner for continuous data-generating processes. If the prior distribution is continuous, then the predictive distribution for a future observation x has density

$$f(x) = \int_{-\infty}^{\infty} f(\theta)f(x|\theta)d\theta. \tag{11}$$

After the new information y has been observed, $f(\theta)$ is revised to $f(\theta|y)$, and the predictive density for a future x becomes

$$f(x) = \int_{-\infty}^{\infty} f(\theta|y)f(x|\theta)d\theta. \tag{12}$$

Certain combinations of likelihood functions and prior distributions (e.g., combinations in which the prior distribution is a member of the conjugate family) yield especially tractable results. For example, with a normal data-generating process with known variance, if the prior distribution of the mean μ is a normal distribution with mean a and variance σ^2/b, then the predictive distribution for a future observation from the process is normal with mean a and variance $(b + 1)\sigma^2/b$. The uncertainty about the future observation can be broken down into two sources of uncertainty: uncertainty about x due simply to the variability of the process, and uncertainty about the mean of the process. The former uncertainty contributes σ^2 to the variance of x, while the latter uncertainty contributes σ^2/b to the variance of x. Hence the total variance is $\sigma^2 + (\sigma^2/b)$, or $(b + 1)\sigma^2/b$. This can be generalized to the predictive distribution of a future sample mean $\bar{x}$ from a sample of size n; the distribution is normal with mean a and variance $(b + n)\sigma^2/bn$. Here the variance can be separated into the sum of σ^2/n (the uncertainty about $\bar{x}$ due to sampling variability, for fixed μ) and σ^2/b (the uncertainty about the mean μ of the process).

Probabilities for model parameters are not admitted in the classical approach to statistics, and without such probabilities, marginal probabilities for future observations cannot be determined. In the Poisson example, for instance, a classical statistician can use the Poisson distribution to make probability statements about a future observation x, but these probabilities are conditional upon λ, the Poisson parameter. Not having a distribution for λ, the classical statistician cannot make unconditional probability statements about x. Yet in many real-world problems, the inferences or decisions of interest concern such future observations. Inferences about the average rate at which a worker completes tasks may be of interest, but when a deadline is approaching and a contract includes monetary penalties for failure to meet the deadline, the variable of interest is the number of tasks completed by the deadline.

DECISION MAKING UNDER UNCERTAINTY

The primary focus in this chapter is on the inferential aspects of Bayesian statistics. The use of Bayes' theorem to revise probabilities provides posterior probabilities, the main inferential statements of interest in the Bayesian approach. But these probabilities can also be very important inputs in problems of decision making under uncertainty. Indeed, the motivation for much of the recent interest in Bayesian methods has been decision-theoretic in nature. The outcomes of decision-making problems often depend on particular events or variables, and the decision maker is frequently quite uncertain about the outcomes of the events or values of the variables. Probability theory provides a framework for the quantification of uncertainty and enables the decision maker to calculate expected payoffs, expected losses, and other measures of interest. In a full-fledged decision analysis, preferences are quantified in terms of utilities, which can deal with a single attribute such as monetary payoff or with multiple attributes (e.g., cost, length of life, and quality of life in a medical decision). Probabilities, representing uncertainties, and utilities, representing preferences, are combined via the calculation of expected utilities.

Bayesian analysis is particularly suitable for decision modeling because it provides probabilities both for unobservable parameters (prior and posterior distributions) and for observable events or variables (predictive distributions). This permits the determination of any sorts of expected values of interest and enables the decision maker to understand the upside potential and downside risk associated with a course of action. Moreover, the key aspect of Bayesian statistics, probability revision, becomes especially important in dynamic decision-making problems where sequences of decisions must be made over time and new information becomes available over time. Finally, by anticipating the possible reactions to new sample information before it is actually obtained, the decision maker can determine the expected value of the sample information and can thus decide whether or not to seek such information.

A lengthy discussion of the modeling of decision-making problems under uncertainty would be inappropriate here. Many books are available for those who would like to pursue this topic further; examples include Raiffa (1968), Keeney and Raiffa (1976), Lindley (1985), Bell, Raiffa, and Tversky (1988), Smith (1988), and Clemen (1991). The point of interest for the purposes of this chapter is that Bayesian procedures are of great value in the modeling of decision-making problems under uncertainty.

CONCLUSIONS

Bayesian statistics provides a unified framework within which to approach problems of inference and decision making under uncertainty. It uses probability, the mathematical language of uncertainty, to represent uncertainty quantitatively. Moreover, it operates in an intuitively appealing manner, similar in nature to the way individuals react qualitatively to uncertainty. At any given point, the statistician's uncertainty is represented by probabilities for uncertain quantities. As new information is then obtained, these probabilities are revised just as an individual revises judgments upon seeing new evidence.

The revision of probabilities is accomplished formally via Bayes' theorem, which requires two sets of inputs: the initial probabilities and the likelihoods of the new information given the possible values for the uncertain parameters or variables. The assessment of likelihoods can be done subjectively, but it is typically accomplished by modeling the data-generating process (the process generating the new information). For instance, some models commonly used for dichotomous processes are Bernoulli and Markov models; for a process generating a continuous variable, various distributions such as normal, lognormal, and gamma distributions might be considered as potential models. It is helpful to consider any available information (e.g., underlying theoretical models, empirical data) in the modeling process. Once the model is chosen, prior probabilities are assessed for any unknown parameters of the model. Bayes' theorem can then be used to revise these initial probabilities by multiplying them by the appropriate likelihoods and normalizing to arrive at posterior probabilities. Certain combinations of prior probabilities and likelihoods are easier to deal with analytically than others, but with today's computers, the posterior probabilities of interest can generally be found numerically if the problem proves intractable analytically.

The primary inferential statement in Bayesian statistics is a posterior distribution. If point estimates or other summary measures (interval estimates, tests of hypotheses) are desired they can be found from the posterior distribution. The resulting measures are sometimes similar to the results of an analysis using classical statistics, but this need not be the case. Indeed, the Bayesian approach is very different in spirit from the classical approach. For instance, in hypothesis testing the Bayesian approach provides probabilities for the various hypotheses; such probabilities are not permitted in the classical approach, which must deal with error probabilities that are probabilities of various possible sample outcomes (including some that were not observed as well as the outcome that was actually observed) conditional upon values of the parameters. Bayesian statistics answers more directly the questions of real interest; instead of asking how likely the sample outcome would be if the population proportion were one-half, for example, it asks how likely it is, given the evidence, that the population proportion is one-half.

The Bayesian approach also enables the statistician to find unconditional probabilities for future observables. These probabilities, which are labeled predictive probabilities, are of particular interest in forecasting what might occur in the future and in making decisions where the consequences (e.g., payoffs) depend on future events or variables. Although the primary focus in this chapter is on the inferential aspects of Bayesian statistics, the Bayesian approach plays a very important role in the modeling of decision-making problems under uncertainty.

As noted in the introduction, the consideration of the Bayesian approach as the primary paradigm for dealing with problems of statistical inference and decision making is relatively recent, with most of the work in this vein occurring in the past three decades. The interest in Bayesian statistics has steadily increased over this period, and there is a considerable amount of activity at this point. A sampling of recent Bayesian work is reported in Bernardo, DeGroot, Lindley, and Smith (1988), and a discussion of the present position in Bayesian statistics is presented in Lindley (1990). Other references given in this chapter provide additional details on both theoretical and applied aspects of Bayesian statistics for the interested reader.

REFERENCES

Bakan, D. (1966). The test of significance in psychological research. *Psychological Bulletin, 66,* 423–437.

Barnett, V. (1973). *Comparative statistical inference.* London: Wiley.

Bayes, T. (1763). An essay toward solving a problem in the doctrine of chance. *Philosophical Transactions of the Royal Society, 53,* 370–418. Reproduced with biography of Bayes in Barnard, G. A. (1958). Studies in the history of probability and statistics: IX. *Biometrika, 45,* 293–315.

Bell, D. E., Raiffa, H., & Tversky, A. (Eds.). (1988). *Decision making: Descriptive, normative, and prescriptive interactions.* Cambridge: Cambridge University Press.

Berger, J. O. (1984). The robust Bayesian viewpoint. In J. B. Kadane (Ed.), *Robustness of Bayesian analyses.* Amsterdam: North-Holland.

Berger, J. O. (1985). *Statistical decision theory and Bayesian analysis* (2nd ed.). New York: Springer-Verlag.

Berger, J. O., & Sellke, T. (1987). Testing a point null hypothesis: The irreconcilability of P-values and evidence. *Journal of the American Statistical Association, 82,* 112–139.

Bernardo, J. M., DeGroot, M. H., Lindley, D. V., & Smith, A. F. M. (Eds.). (1988). *Bayesian statistics 3.* Oxford: Clarendon Press.

Box, G. E. P., & Tiao, G. C. (1973). *Bayesian inference in statistical analysis.* Reading, MA: Addison-Wesley.

Clemen, R. T. (1991). *Making hard decisions: An introduction to decision analysis.* Boston: PWS-Kent.

de Finetti, B. (1937). La prévision: Ses lois logiques, Ses sources subjectives, *Annales de L'Institut Henri Poincaré, 7,* 1–68. Translated by H. E. Kyburg [Foresight: Its logical laws, its subjective sources] in H. E. Kyburg & H. E. Smokler (Eds.), *Studies in subjective probability.* New York: Wiley, 1964.

de Finetti, B. (1970). *Teoria delle probabilita.* Torino: Guilo Einaudi. Translated by A. Machi & A. Smith, *Theory of probability,* Vols. 1 and 2. London: Wiley, 1974 & 1975.

de Finetti, B. (1972). *Probability, induction, and statistics: The art of guessing.* London: Wiley.

DeGroot, M. H. (1970). *Optimal statistical decisions.* New York: McGraw-Hill.

Edwards, W. (1965). Tactical note on the relation between scientific and statistical hypotheses. *Psychological Bulletin, 63,* 400–402.

Edwards, W., Lindman, H., & Savage, L. J. (1963). Bayesian statistical inference for psychological research. *Psychological Bulletin, 70,* 193–242.

Hogarth, R. (1975). Cognitive processes and the assessment of subjective probability distributions. *Journal of the American Statistical Association, 70,* 271–289.

Isaacs, G. L., Christ, D. E., Novick, M. R., & Jackson, P. H. (1974). *Tables for Bayesian statisticians.* Iowa City: University of Iowa.

Kadane, J. B. (Ed.). (1984). *Robustness of Bayesian analyses.* Amsterdam: North-Holland.

Kadane, J. B., Dickey, J. M., Winkler, R. L., Smith, W. S., & Peters, S. C. (1980). Interactive elicitation of opinion for a normal linear model. *Journal of the American Statistical Association, 75,* 845–854.

Kahneman, D., Slovic, P., & Tversky, A. (Eds.). (1982). *Judgment under uncertainty: Heuristics and biases.* Cambridge: Cambridge University Press.

Keeney, R. L., & Raiffa, H. (1976). *Decisions with multiple objectives: Preferences and value trade-offs.* New York: Wiley.

La Valle, I. H. (1970). *An introduction to probability, decision, and inference.* New York: Holt, Rinehart & Winston.

Lindley, D. V. (1972). *Bayesian statistics: A review.* Philadelphia: Society for Industrial and Applied Mathematics.

Lindley, D. V. (1985). *Making decisions* (2nd ed.). London: Wiley.

Lindley, D. V. (1990). The 1988 Wald memorial lectures: The present position in Bayesian statistics. *Statistical Science, 5,* 44–89.

Lipscomb, K. (1977). *Cardiac diagnosis.* Dallas: University of Texas.

Meehl, P. E. (1967). Theory-testing in psychology and physics: A methodological approach. *Philosophy of Science, 34,* 103–115.

Novick, M. R., & Jackson, P. H. (1974). *Statistical methods for educational and psychological research.* New York: McGraw-Hill.

Phillips, L. D. (1973). *Bayesian statistics for social scientists.* London: Thomas Nelson.

Pitz, G. F. (1978). Hypothesis testing and the comparison of imprecise hypotheses. *Psychological Bulletin, 85,* 794–809.

Press, S. J. (1989). *Bayesian statistics: Principles, models, and applications.* New York: Wiley.

Raiffa, H. (1968). *Decision analysis.* Reading, MA: Addison-Wesley.

Raiffa, H., & Schlaifer, R. (1961). *Applied statistical decision theory.* Boston: Graduate School of Business Administration, Harvard University.

Savage, L. J. (1954). *The foundations of statistics.* New York: Wiley.

Schlaifer, R. (1959). *Probability and statistics for business decisions.* New York: McGraw-Hill.

Schlaifer, R. (1969). *Analysis of decisions under uncertainty.* New York: McGraw-Hill.

Slovic, P., & Lichtenstein, S. (1971). Comparison of Bayesian and regression approaches to the study of information processing in judgment. *Organizational Behavior and Human Performance, 6,* 651–730.

Smith, J. Q. (1988). *Decision analysis: A Bayesian approach.* London: Chapman & Hall.

Spetzler, C. A., & Staël von Holstein, C.-A. S. (1975). Probability encoding in decision analysis. *Management Science, 22,* 340–358.

von Winterfeldt, D., & Edwards, W. (1986). *Decision analysis and behavioral research.* Cambridge: Cambridge University Press.

West, M., & Harrison, P. J. (1989). *Bayesian forecasting and dynamic models.* New York: Springer-Verlag.

Wilson, W., Miller, H. L., & Lower, J. S. (1967). Much ado about the null hypothesis. *Psychological Bulletin, 67,* 188–196.

Winkler, R. L. (1967). The assessment of prior distributions in Bayesian analysis. *Journal of the American Statistical Association, 67,* 766–800.

Winkler, R. L., & Gaba, A. (1990). Inference with imperfect sampling from a Bernoulli process. In S. Geisser, J. S. Hodges, S. J. Press, & A. Zellner (Eds.), *Bayesian and likelihood methods in statistics and econometrics: Essays in honor of George A. Barnard* (pp. 303–317). Amsterdam: North-Holland.

Zellner, A. (1971). *An introduction to Bayesian inference in econometrics.* New York: Wiley.

8 Bayesian Methods for the Analysis of Variance

Charles Lewis
Educational Testing Service

INTRODUCTION

In this chapter, it is assumed that the reader has some familiarity with the basic concepts of Bayesian inference and of conventional analysis of variance. This allows attention to be focused on what happens when the two are brought together. For this purpose, extensive use is made of results presented by Box and Tiao (1973). This source provides, by far, the most extensive treatment of analysis of variance from a Bayesian point of view, and the interested reader will find in it proofs and generalizations of most of the material appearing here. This having been said, the author feels relieved of the obligation to make further reference to Box and Tiao. Although occasional reference to other relevant Bayesian (and non-Bayesian) work will be made, there has been no attempt to be systematic or exhaustive in this respect. Instead, the emphasis is on laying out, as clearly as possible, a Bayesian approach to analysis of variance. Readers wishing to see a similar approach for multivariate analysis of variance and covariance are referred to Woodworth (1979).

Prior Beliefs

Logically, the place for Bayesian inference to begin is with the specification of prior beliefs. This very important issue is almost completely sidestepped here. It is assumed that, in many cases at least, appropriate scientific reporting of experimental results should *not* include a description of the experimenter's personal posterior beliefs. Rather, the beliefs described should be those of someone whose prior knowledge was minimal compared with the information provided by the data themselves—a neutral observer, or reference person. For this purpose, so-called "improper" ("impossible" would be better) priors are routinely used. For instance, prior beliefs about a mean may be assumed to be uniformly distributed over the entire real line. There is, of course, no such probability distribution: it is merely a convenient fiction.

Edwards, Lindman, and Savage (1963) have provided a formal account of the degree of error resulting from the substitution of one prior for another in simple situations. To the author's knowledge, no such work has been done for the complex models that are commonly used in analysis of variance. Thus it is not really known how much is lost when more convenient but less realistic priors are used. What *is* known is that these priors typically give results that have close analogies to those obtained with conventional sampling theory analysis of variance. Thus they may be viewed as providing a first step for someone interested in making a relatively "painless" shift from non-Bayesian to Bayesian methods of inference. It is to just such a person that this chapter is primarily addressed. Once a person feels relatively comfortable with this level of Bayesian thinking, he or she is encouraged to consider the use of more precisely specified "proper" priors as discussed in detail by, for instance, Novick and Jackson (1974).

Models

Throughout this chapter, the models commonly used in analysis of variance are uncritically adopted. This is done primarily to facilitate comparisons between Bayesian and conventional results.

Normality and homogeneity of variance assumptions are almost certainly false—sometimes seriously so—in any experimental situation. When methods have been developed that give us the full flexibility of the conventional methods without requiring such strong assumptions, we should certainly use them. In the meantime, it may be best to regard the results of our analyses as based on a second (the improper priors were the first) convenient fiction. Thus we might say something like: "If our data *had* been independently sampled from normal distributions with equal variances, then the appropriate inferences would be . . . ' As with the choice of priors, the results of such an analysis will not differ much from those based on a variety of alternative models. There are, however, still other models, particularly those that allow for extreme observations (outliers) for which this generalization does not hold. Thus we should realize the potential weakness of the standard set of assumptions when reporting the results of our analyses.

FIXED EFFECT, BETWEEN SUBJECT DESIGNS

Assumptions

For this class of models, it is common to assume that the observations are mutually independent, given the parameters, and sampled from normal distributions with constant variance but possibly differing means. The parameters of interest are what will be called the *within-cell variance* and the *cell means,* reflecting the fact that the observations are typically classified into groups or cells, with observations in the same cell being treated simply as replications. Whether this classification occurs as a result of random assignment of subjects to conditions or is simply a statement of pre-existing circumstances makes no difference in the Bayesian statements that can be made about means and variances. It may, however, influence what linear combinations of the means we choose to consider for further analysis.

Prior beliefs about the means and variance are taken to be mutually independent. Beliefs about each mean separately, and about the *logarithm* of the variance, are assumed to be uniformly distributed from $-\infty$ to $+\infty$. This choice of improper reference priors leads to results which parallel those of conventional analysis of variance.

Results for One Cell Out of *k*

Most directly, based on the above assumptions, we have the fact that

$$t(\mu_i) = \frac{\mu_i - y_{i.}}{\sqrt{MS_w/n_i}} \tag{1}$$

follows a Student's *t*-distribution with $N - k$ degrees of freedom. Here μ_i denotes the true mean for cell i, $y_{i.}$ the corresponding sample mean based on n_i observations, MS_w the mean square within cells, N the total number of observations, and k the number of cells in the design.

Although Equation 1 looks like a result from conventional (i.e., sampling theory) analysis of variance, there are important differences. These can best be pointed out via an illustration. Suppose the dependent variable (y) consists of responses to an attitude question on a 7-point scale, where a response of 4 represents a neutral attitude. Further, suppose that in cell i, the sample mean response is 5.5 and that the standard error $\sqrt{MS_w/n_i} = .82$, with 24 degrees of freedom. If it is of interest to see whether the true mean for cell i exceeds the neutral value of 4, we begin by evaluating Equation 1 for $\mu_i = 4$:

$$t(4) = \frac{4 - 5.5}{.82} = \frac{-1.5}{.82} = -1.83.$$

Now the posterior probability that μ_i is greater than 4 is simply the area under a Student's *t*- distribution with 24 degrees of freedom above the value $t(4)$. In the present case, this probability is .96. Thus our neutral observer, based on the evidence of the sample data, should feel 96% certain that the true mean response here lies above the neutral point (4).

It may be worthwhile to explicitly contrast this with the corresponding statement in sampling theory inference. There, it would be said that, if the true mean response were indeed 4, 96% of the t-statistics computed as shown would have . value greater than -1.83. The different possible t-statistics arise from differen possible samples, all from a (normal) population of responses with mean 4. Thi statement is indirect in two ways. First, it only considers what would happen i an unknown parameter (the population mean) had a particular value. Second, i only refers to what would happen over repeated sampling. The Bayesian state ment, on the other hand, makes no assumption about the value of the populatio mean and is based on the present sample. Presumably, from the sampling theor statement, the researcher is supposed to acquire the feeling that the populatio mean is greater than 4. Better yet she/he should make the "decision" that th population mean is greater than 4. The Bayesian statement, in contrast, is a direc quantification of the degree of certainty one should have (based on the presen sample) that the population mean is greater than 4—albeit only an approxima tion, given the fact that the prior and model were chosen primarily for thei mathematical properties rather than their realism.

Additional use can be made of Equation 1 to make statements about inter vals.[1] First, based on the hypothetical sample statistics given previously, we ma construct a conventional 95% interval for μ_i (using $t_{24, .975} = 2.064$, the 97.5% point of the t-distribution with 24 degrees of freedom)

$$5.5 \pm (2.064)(.82) = 5.5 \pm 1.69.$$

Thus the interval is $(3.81, 7.19)$. The posterior probability for a neutral observe that μ_i is in this interval is .95. Thus such an observer is "95% confident" that th true mean response for cell i lies in this interval. It is important to stress that w are talking about the actual interval calculated here, and not about the samplinç behavior of future intervals. As always in Bayesian inference, we are dealing with simple, direct probability statements about unknown quantities (in this case μ_i), given known quantities (in this case y_i. and MS_w).

Before leaving the current example, we should consider yet another sort of probability statement, this one not about a parameter but about a new observa tion. Given the results of an experiment as before,

$$t(y_{i,n_i+1}) = \frac{y_{i,n_i+1} - y_i.}{\sqrt{MS_w \left(1 + \dfrac{1}{n_i}\right)}} \qquad (2$$

follows a Student's t-distribution, as before, with $N - k$ degrees of freedom. In Equation 2, $y_{i,n_i + 1}$ represents an observation not yet made or, in any event, no yet known to our neutral observer.

---

[1]These intervals have received a variety of names in the Bayesian literature: credible intervals credibility intervals, Highest Density Regions (HDRs), and Highest Posterior Density (HPD) inter vals. We shall simply refer to them as "intervals."

In this example, suppose $\sqrt{MS_w} = 1.64$ and $n_i = 4$. Then the standard error or the new observation is

$$(1.64)\sqrt{1 + .25} = 1.83.$$

To obtain the probability that $y_{i,n_i + 1}$ will be greater than 4, calculate $t(4)$

$$t(4) = \frac{4 - 5.5}{1.83} = -.82.$$

he area above $t(4)$, namely .79, is the desired probability. Thus our neutral bserver should not find the evidence very convincing that a new response in cell would be above the neutral point.
In the same spirit

$$5.5 \pm (1.83)(2.064) = 5.5 \pm 3.78:$$
$$(1.72, 9.28)$$

ives a 95% interval for the new observation. Its width reflects considerable ncertainty regarding a new response. (As a practical matter, the fact that it xtends beyond the highest possible response, namely 7, ought to remind us that he assumptions used to derive Equation 2 are, as always, false.)

Although this development parallels a sampling theory result,[2] the latter is ot widely used in conventional inference. Several Bayesian statisticians have rgued that such statements about new observations ought to be primary goals f inference. It is, after all, the responses themselves that researchers seek o understand, and not only parameters describing the population of re- ponses.

Results for Contrasts Among Cells

f we define a population contrast ψ (readers not familiar with this concept may vish to consult, for instance, Kirk, 1982, pp. 90–133) as

$$\psi = \sum_{i=1}^{k} c_i \mu_i \tag{3}$$

nd the corresponding sample contrast as

$$\hat{\psi} = \sum_{i=1}^{k} c_i y_i. \tag{4}$$

---

[2]Briefly, the sampling theory result is that over repeated replications of the experiment and amplings of an additional observation, the variable given in Equation 2 will be distributed according o Student's t with $N - k$ degrees of freedom.

then we have the Bayesian result that

$$t(\psi) = \frac{\psi - \hat{\psi}}{\sqrt{MS_w \sum\limits_i \frac{c_i^2}{n_i}}} \tag{5}$$

has a t-distribution whose degrees of freedom are those of the MS_w (namely $N - k$). Indeed, Equation 1 can be seen as a special case of this result, obtained by setting one c_i equal to unity and the rest equal to zero. (There is no need to make c_i sum to zero, although this may at times be a convenient restriction.) The distributional statement regarding Equation 5 is Bayesian because it describes uncertainty regarding the true value of ψ, given the sample information summarized in $\hat{\psi}$ and MS_w.

Undoubtedly the most common type of contrast is of the form $\mu_i - \mu_j$. As detailed earlier, we can make one-tailed probability statements using Equation 5. Here the most common regards the probability that

$$\mu_i - \mu_j > 0.$$

This is evaluated by finding the area above $t(0)$ for the t-distribution with appropriate degrees of freedom. Also as shown earlier, intervals for any ψ can be constructed and given a Bayesian interpretation.

To briefly illustrate suppose we wish to compare our cell i (having $y_{i.} = 5.5$ and $n_i = 4$) with cell j having $y_{j.} = 3.75$ and $n_j = 8$. Taking $c_i = 1$, $c_j = -1$, and all other weights zero, we have

$$\hat{\psi} = 5.5 - 3.75 = 1.75$$

with a standard error (using $\sqrt{MS_w} = 1.64$) of

$$\sqrt{MS_w \left(\frac{1}{n_i} + \frac{1}{n_j} \right)} = 1.64 \sqrt{\frac{1}{4} + \frac{1}{8}} = 1.00,$$

which would allow our neutral observer to make the following posterior probability statement:

$$\text{Prob}(\mu_i > \mu_j) = .95.$$

Similarly, he or she would be 95% certain that the true difference $\mu_i - \mu_j$ falls in the interval

$$1.75 \pm (2.064)(1.00):$$
$$(-.31, 3.81).$$

It is also possible to consider a contrast involving future observations and taking the form

$$\sum\limits_{i=1}^{k} c_i y_{i,n_i+1} . \tag{6}$$

This contrast has a mean of $\Sigma c_i y_i$, and a standard error given by

$$\sqrt{\sum_{i=1}^{k} c_i^2 \left(1 + \frac{1}{n_i} \right) MS_w} \tag{7}$$

with, as usual, reference to a t-distribution with $N - k$ degrees of freedom. To talk about the difference between a future observation from cell i and one from cell j, for instance, the appropriate 95% interval is given by

$$y_i - y_j \pm (2.064) \sqrt{\left(2 + \frac{1}{n_i} + \frac{1}{n_j} \right) MS_w}$$

or

$$1.75 \pm (2.064)(2.53):$$
$$(-3.47, 6.97).$$

Comparison of this interval with the one just obtained for $\mu_i - \mu_j$ illustrates how much less we would know about the responses themselves than about their means.

Possibilities for Simultaneous Inference

The main goal of analysis of variance as it is typically used to analyze experimental results is to make a statement, or statements, which refer to all the cells of the design. The types of statements discussed earlier may be used in combination to achieve this goal, provided that certain modifications are made. Indeed, this will be the approach developed in detail in this section.

The most commonly used tool for simultaneous inference in conventional analysis of variance is the F-test. This test has a Bayesian interpretation that should be mentioned, although it is not advocated for general use or discussed further in this chapter.

Just as intervals may be constructed for individual contrasts, it is possible to consider multidimensional regions for a set of contrasts or even for all possible contrasts.

Restricting our attention to contrasts whose weights sum to zero, such a region is given by referring

$$\sum_{i=1}^{k} n_i [(y_i - y_{..}) - (\mu_i - \mu_.)]^2 / [(k - 1)MS_w] \tag{8}$$

to a critical value from an F-distribution with $k - 1$ and $N - k$ degrees of freedom. Here $y_{..}$ is the sample grand mean and $\mu_.$ is defined by

$$\mu_. = \sum_{i=1}^{k} n_i \mu_i / N.$$

In its most common use, all contrasts of the form $\mu_i - \mu_j (i \neq j)$ are considered. These contrasts are simultaneously zero if and only if the differences $\mu_i - \mu$. are zero for $i = 1, \ldots, k$. Replacing these quantities by zeros in Equation 8 gives the usual F-statistic:

$$\sum_{i=1}^{k} n_i(y_i - y_.)^2 / [(k - 1)MS_w] = MS_B / MS_w. \qquad (9)$$

This statistic should be compared with, for instance, the 95th percentile of the appropriate F-distribution.

In these terms, the usual F-test (at the .05 level) is a check to see whether the values $\mu_i - \mu_j = 0$ (for all $i \neq j$) simultaneously lie within a 95% region for all contrasts. Unfortunately, a "significant" F-statistic provides no specific information about the separate contrasts. From this point of view, the F-test is not a particularly useful statistical tool (for Bayesians or sampling theorists).

In addition to the F-test, a variety of procedures exist for dealing directly with multiple contrasts in sampling theory analysis of variance. Scheffé's approach based on the F-distribution, Tukey's approach based on the Studentized range, and Dunn's approach based on the Bonferroni inequality all have direct Bayesian interpretations. (For a sampling theory discussion, see the chapter by Zwick in this volume.) In this chapter, only applications of the Bonferroni inequality will be further discussed. This is because the emphasis here will be on considering a limited number of planned contrasts—a purpose for which Bonferroni techniques are well suited.

Suppose the interest of the experimenter is in comparing each of a set of planned contrasts, $\psi_1, \ldots, \psi_h$, with zero. Moreover, suppose the signs of the weights for the ψ_i have been chosen so that the experimenter expects all the resulting contrasts will be positive. Then Equation 5 should be used with each ψ_i to obtain the h t-statistics $t_i(0)$, and the corresponding areas below the values under the t-density with $N - k$ degrees of freedom, say α_i. By the Bonferroni inequality, the posterior probability that all ψ_i are simultaneously greater than zero is at least

$$1 - \sum_{i=1}^{k} \alpha_i. \qquad (10)$$

To elaborate this result a bit, notice that α_i is the posterior probability that the statement "$\psi_i > 0$" is false. Thus it is the probability of making an "error" by pretending that $\psi_i > 0$ is true. Extending this across all contrasts

$$\sum_{i=1}^{h} \alpha_i \qquad (11)$$

s the expected (averaged over the posterior distribution of the ψ_i) number of errors made by pretending all ψ_i are positive. Now this expected number of errors must be greater than or equal to the probability of making at least one such error. Consequently Equation 10 gives a lower bound for the probability of making no errors when stating that all ψ_i are positive. This is the Bonferroni result. It may, of course, be of interest to report Equation 11, interpreting it directly as an expected number of errors associated with asserting that $\psi_i > 0$ for $i = 1, \ldots, h$.

Four points regarding the use of the Bonferroni inequality should be stressed. First, the probabilities or expected numbers of errors discussed here are statements of uncertainty about the true values of the contrasts. They do *not* refer to what might happen over repeated replications of the experiment. Second, there is no restriction on the choice of weights for ψ_i. They do *not* need to be orthogonal or even sum to zero. Third, there is no restriction on the type of statements that may be made about the ψ_i. For instance, if there were some difference between means that was expected to be small, the probability that the difference lies in an interval, such as $(-1, 1)$ for the rating scale example, might be included in a Bonferroni computation. Fourth, each additional contrast contributes to the overall uncertainty (or expected number of errors). Thus the total number of contrasts should be kept as small as possible in order to keep these quantities small. The most efficient way to do this is to consider only contrasts about which you have relatively strong expectations. Indeed, this is a natural place for the experimenter's prior beliefs to play a role: in the choice of planned contrasts.

It is also possible to use the Bonferroni approach to obtain simultaneous intervals for specified contrasts. Critical values of the t-distribution tabled by Dunn (1961) and reproduced, for instance, by Kirk (1982, p. 842) are helpful for this purpose.

If an interval with probability level $1 - \alpha_i$ is constructed for contrast ψ_i, then the simultaneous probability that all intervals under consideration contain their respective true contrast values is at least

$$1 - \Sigma \alpha_i.$$

These results, of course, strictly parallel the previous application of the Bonferroni inequality. The only difference is that here the α_i values are chosen in advance and the regions (intervals) are only known once the data have been analyzed. In the previous application, on the other hand, it was the regions that were chosen in advance ($\psi_i > 0$) and the α_i that only became known after analysis. The difference in emphasis is simply that between estimation and testing. With intervals, we want to simultaneously estimate a set of contrasts to a specified degree of precision. With prespecified regions, we want to state the degree of certainty associated with the hypothesis that all contrasts lie within their respective regions.

Factorial Designs

No attempt will be made here to discuss the many possible experimental designs that arise when combinations of two or more fixed factors are used to define cells. Instead, a few simple examples will be considered to illustrate a general approach.

Perhaps the simplest, and possibly the most frequently occurring factorial design consists of two factors, each with two levels, which are completely crossed. This may be illustrated as in Fig. 8.1(a).

For purposes of further analysis, it is convenient to rewrite the design in a one-way format, as in Fig. 8.1(b).

In this format, the usual questions about main effects and interaction may be translated into selection of contrast weights for the four cells. For instance, to compare the simple average levels of response to levels 1 and 2 of factor A, use the first line of contrast weights appearing in Table 8.1. The second line gives the corresponding contrast for factor B. The third line expresses the interaction between A and B in terms of the difference between cell differences.

Although it is *possible* to rephrase questions about main effects and interactions in terms of contrasts, one of the main reasons for re-expressing factorial designs in one-way terms is to avoid undue emphasis on these contrasts to the exclusion of others. Thus in the 2×2 design discussed previously, it might be useful to study the simple main effect of A at each level of B separately. This would involve using the contrast weights given in the first two lines of Table 8.2. Alternatively, the study might be such that the primary effect is expected when level 2 of factor A is combined with level 2 of factor B. In this case, we might be interested in comparing the mean for this cell with the average of the other three. The relevant contrast weights appear in the third line of Table 8.2.

Note that the contrasts discussed in Table 8.2 may be considered as alternatives, not merely supplementary to main effect-interaction contrasts. It is fairly

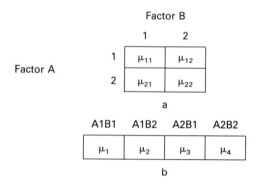

FIG. 8.1.   (a) A 2 × 2 design.   (b) A 2 × 2 design rewritten.

TABLE 8.1
Weights for Main Effects and Interaction

Source	A1B1	A1B2	A2B1	A2B2
A main effect	$1/2$	$1/2$	$-1/2$	$-1/2$
B main effect	$1/2$	$-1/2$	$1/2$	$-1/2$
A × B interaction	1	-1	-1	1

unusual in the author's experience that these latter arise naturally from the investigator's expectations. Instead, it often appears that, having chosen a factorial design, the investigator feels an obligation to test main effects and interactions when, in fact, a limited set of special planned contrasts would better suit her/his purposes. As mentioned earlier, these special contrasts should be chosen to reflect the investigator's prior expectations.

A second reason for choosing to rewrite factorial designs in one-way form is to emphasize the unity of the design and, hence, the need for overall probability statements in summarizing the results. The fact that a design containing more than one factor is being used in no way frees us from this need. On the contrary, the additional cells typically introduced by considering the effects of several factors make the concerns of simultaneous inference especially relevant. Once again, on grounds of simplicity, generality, and suitability for planned contrasts, the use of the Bonferroni inequality is suggested to control overall probabilities.

Analysis of a Factorial Example

To illustrate the aforementioned approach, an example will be taken from Keppel (1973, pp. 200–205), who describes a hypothetical investigation of the influence of reward (factor A) and drive (factor B) on learning. Monkeys serve as subjects and the six cells of this 3×2 design are defined by the number of grapes (1, 3, or 5) received after a correct response and the number of hours (1 or 24) of food deprivation. The dependent variable is the number of correct responses in 20 trials. There are four subjects per cell and the sample means for these subjects are given in Table 8.3. The mean square within cells (MS_w) is 18.33 with eighteen degrees of freedom.

TABLE 8.2
Weights for Other Contrasts of Interest

Source	A1B1	A1B2	A2B1	A2B2
A effect at B1	1	0	-1	0
A effect at B2	0	1	0	-1
A2B2 vs. "rest"	$-1/3$	$-1/3$	$-1/3$	1

TABLE 8.3
Sample Means

		Number of grapes (A)		
		1	3	5
Hours of depri-	1	3	10	14
vation (B)	24	11	12	10

Suppose that the primary research question concerns the effect of deprivation at each level of reward. Then the relevant contrasts are the simple main effects whose weights are given in Table 8.4.

Moreover, suppose that the primary interest is in estimation rather than testing. Thus we would like simultaneous intervals for these three contrasts. To obtain a simultaneous 95% probability level, we may use the Bonferroni inequality and take a level of

$$1 - .05/3 = .9833$$

for each interval separately. For actual computations, the interactive CADA (Novick, et al., 1980) statistical computer package was used.[3] It should be noted that CADA is useful for a wide variety of Bayesian analyses, including those for which specific prior information is relevant. In this case, the program for one-way analysis of variance was run and individual, user-specified contrasts were analyzed. It was possible to obtain intervals (called highest density regions, or HDRs in CADA) for any specified probability level. Although not strictly necessary, use of this program made the analysis much easier and is certainly recommended to the researcher. The actual intervals are given in Table 8.5.

Statistical interpretation of these results is as follows: based on the data of Table 8.3, a neutral observer should be at least 95% certain that the three mean differences specified by the weights in Table 8.4 all lie between their respective upper and lower limits as listed in Table 8.5.

Note that, although we would hardly expect a negative effect of 24 hours food deprivation on learning of a task for a food reward, such an effect cannot be ruled out for two of the three levels of reinforcement used in this study. Indeed, for the highest level, we have an upper limit of four additional correct responses for the mean effect of deprivations. Study of the cell means in Table 8.3 suggests the possibility that a ceiling effect may be operating here. (Monkeys with only 1 hour's deprivation had a mean level of 14 out of 20 correct responses.)

Most importantly, the extreme width of the intervals in Table 8.5—namely 16

---

[3]Information regarding CADA may be obtained by writing to the CADA Group, 306 Mullin Ave., Iowa City, IA 52246.

TABLE 8.4
Contrast Weights

Effect of deprivation with	(grapes, hours)					
	(1,1)	(3,1)	(5,1)	(1,24)	(3,24)	(5,24)
grape	−1	0	0	1	0	0
grapes	0	−1	0	0	1	0
grapes	0	0	−1	0	0	1

nits out of a total possible range of 40 for the differences—should tell us that we ave in fact learned very little about our contrasts from this study. This is not urprising when we consider that only four subjects per cell were used and that eppel undoubtedly introduced such a small example primarily to illustrate the omputational aspects of analysis of variance on an easily manageable scale. That *is* surprising is that an observation about the low power of the study does ot appear in Keppel's discussion of the results. Instead, he finds no significant ain effects, but does obtain a significant interaction ($F_{2,18} = 3.93, p < .05$). ccording to Keppel (1973), this is then interpreted by looking at the cell means, ore or less as though they were the true values: "Drive is relatively ineffective hen the animals are given 3 or 5 grapes, but hungry animals show learning uperior to that of less hungry animals when the reward is small [p. 204]."

Based on Table 8.5, we might rephrase this conclusion: Drive may or may not relatively ineffective when the animals are given three or five grapes, but ungry animals show learning that may be anywhere from marginally to dramatally superior to that of less hungry animals when the reward is small. These are atements in which we have at least 95% confidence in our role as neutral servers.

The difference between our analysis and that of Keppel is not merely Bayesian . sampling theory, but also estimation vs. testing. The more detailed picture ovided by taking an estimation approach, together with the direct belief statements resulting from a Bayesian analysis, account for the differences between ur conclusion and his.

TABLE 8.5
Simultaneous 95% Intervals for Contrasts

Effect of deprivation with	Lower limit	Upper limit
1 grape	0	16
2 grapes	−6	10
3 grapes	−12	4

DESIGNS HAVING REPEATED MEASURES

Assumptions and Notation

The most important observation to make about repeated measures designs is that they are essentially multivariate. (This point is discussed in detail by, for instance, Bock, 1975, pp. 447–505.) Thus when we obtain responses from a single subject under a number of conditions, it is appropriate to consider these as made up of a single response on each of several variables. In this framework, it is common to treat each subject's responses as a random sample from a multivariate normal distribution. The response vectors of separate subjects are assumed to be mutually independent, given the parameters. The normal distributions are assumed to have identical variance-covariance matrices and mean vectors that are identical for all subjects within a given cell (of the non-repeated measures part of the design), but which may differ from cell to cell, if there is more than one.

Prior beliefs about the variance-covariance matrix and the mean vectors are taken to be mutually independent. Beliefs about the means are taken to be uniformly distributed (independently for all elements of all vectors) and, if the variance-covariance matrix is denoted by Σ (pxp for a design having p repeated measures) its prior density is taken proportional to

$$|\Sigma|^{-1/2(p + 1)}. \tag{12}$$

This choice has the advantage of giving results that closely parallel parts of multivariate sampling theory analysis.

Finally, a word about notation. In general, a design will be thought of as having k distinct cells or groups of subjects with n_i subjects in the ith cell (N subjects in all). All subjects, regardless of which cell they are in, are supposedly measured on the same p repeated measures. The sample mean over n_i subjects in the ith cell on the jth repeated measure will be denoted by $y_{ij.}$ and the corresponding true mean by μ_{ij}. Instead of a mean square within cells, we must now consider a mean square and cross-products matrix S (pxp), for which the element in the jth row and j'th column is given by

$$s_{jj'} = \frac{\sum_{i=1}^{k} \sum_{l=1}^{n_i} (y_{ijl} - y_{ij.})(y_{ij'l} - y_{ij'.})}{N - k - p + 1}. \tag{13}$$

Notice that, when $p = 1$ (so there are actually no *repeated* measures), Equation 13 reduces to MS_w of the previous section.

Results for One Mean and for Contrasts Among Means

Paralleling an earlier result, we construct

246

$$t(\mu_{ij}) = \frac{\mu_{ij} - y_{ij\cdot}}{\sqrt{s_{jj}/n_i}},\tag{14}$$

which has a Student's t-distribution with $N - k - p + 1$ degrees of freedom. All of the results already given for one cell may be applied here, with MS_w replaced by s_{jj} and the degrees of freedom $N - k$ replaced by $N - k - p + 1$. In particular, the probability that μ_{ij} lies in a given region may be found and intervals for μ_{ij} may be constructed, following the same principles outlined there. Also, parallel statements may be made about $y_{ij,n_i + 1}$, the next observation on repeated measure j in cell i. Nothing changes except for the loss of degrees of freedom associated with measuring more than one variable for each subject. This loss of degrees of freedom does *not* occur in the sampling theory equivalent of Equation 4 and is a consequence for the Bayesian analysis that more than one variable has been measured.

When we turn to contrasts among means, we find that the extra structure demands new considerations. For the repeated measures situation, the contrasts to be considered have the form

$$\psi = \sum_{i=1}^{k} \sum_{j=1}^{p} c_i d_j \mu_{ij}.\tag{15}$$

Comparing this with the definition in Equation 3, we see that there is now not only a set of weights for the cells, $\{c_i\}$, but also a set $\{d_j\}$ for the repeated measures. Defining the corresponding sample contrast as

$$\hat{\psi} = \sum_i \sum_j c_i d_j y_{ij\cdot}.\tag{16}$$

it turns out that

$$t(\psi) = \frac{\psi - \hat{\psi}}{\sqrt{\sum_{i=1}^{k} (c_i^2/n_i) \sum_{j=1}^{p} \sum_{j'=1}^{p} (d_j d_{j'} s_{jj'})}}\tag{17}$$

as a t-distribution with $N - k - p + 1$ degrees of freedom.

For an illustration, suppose we consider a design with two groups (say male and female) and two repeated measures (say before and after treatment). To compare the effect of treatment for females with the effect for males, we might take

$$c_f = 1, c_m = -1$$

and

$$d_a = 1, d_b = -1.$$

Then the contrast Equation 15 takes the form

$$\psi = \mu_{f,a} - \mu_{f,b} - (\mu_{m,a} - \mu_{m,b})$$

and the denominator of Equation 17 becomes

$$\sqrt{\left(\frac{1}{n_f} + \frac{1}{n_m}\right)(s_{a,a} + s_{b,b} - 2s_{b,a})}.$$

To study the effect of treatment, averaged over males and females, we migh[t] keep d_a and d_b as above but use

$$c_f = \frac{n_f}{N} \text{ and } c_m = \frac{n_m}{N}$$

(at least if the numbers of males and females in the study reflect the proportion[s] of the sexes in the population of interest). This choice would give

$$\psi = \frac{n_f \mu_{f,a} + n_m \mu_{m,a}}{N} - \frac{n_f \mu_{f,b} + n_m \mu_{m,b}}{N}$$

and a denominator for Equation 17 of

$$\sqrt{\frac{1}{N}(s_{a,a} + s_{b,b} - 2s_{b,a})}.$$

Finally suppose we wished to compare the "base rate" for males and female[s]. Then we might take

$$c_f = 1, c_m = -1$$

and

$$d_a = 0, d_b = 1.$$

The contrast becomes

$$\psi = \mu_{f,b} - \mu_{m,b}$$

with a denominator for Equation 17 of

$$\sqrt{\left(\frac{1}{n_f} + \frac{1}{n_m}\right)s_{b,b}}.$$

Note that not all contrasts among means fit into the form of Equation 15. Fo[r] instance, there is no choice of c and d weights which allows a comparison o[f] females after treatment with males before treatment. This does not mean that n[o] such contrast may be considered within a Bayesian analysis, but merely that suc[h] contrasts no longer have t-distributions. Thus more complex methods, outsid[e] the scope of this elementary exposition, are required. (The interested reade[r] might consult, for instance, the discussion of the Behrens distribution in Novic[k]

nd Jackson [1974, pp. 251–255] and should know that such problems can be
andled within the CADA program package mentioned earlier.)

Returning to the form of Equation 15, a remark should be made about "pure"
:peated measures designs—those having only one group of subjects. For such
esigns $k = 1$

$$n_1 = N \qquad (18)$$

nd we may always take

$$c_1 = 1 \qquad (19)$$

I Equations 15, 16, and 17. Thus all contrasts are specified solely in terms of the
'eights (d_j) for the repeated measures.

imultaneous Inference and Factorial Designs

he likelihood ratio test commonly employed in sampling theory multivariate
nalysis (see, for instance, Bock, 1975, pp. 152–153) has a direct interpretation
I Bayesian terms. Specifically, for an α-level test it is a check to see whether the
ypothesized values for a set of contrasts lie within the joint $1 - \alpha$ highest
osterior density region for those contrasts. The simplest application of this is the
Iotelling's T^2 test, as it is applied for pure repeated measures designs. Just as
'ith the between-subjects F-test discussed in an earlier section, the check is to
:e whether all the contrasts $\mu_j - \mu_{j'}$ can simultaneously have the value zero
'ithin a region of size $1 - \alpha$.

As was noted in connection with the F-test, such summary checks are rela-
vely uninformative and do not provide direct probability statements about indi-
idual contrasts. The posterior probability that all such values are exactly correct
zero, no matter how much data have been collected. Consequently, we turn
gain to the Bonferroni inequality to develop simultaneous inference for designs
aving repeated measures. Because of its generality, this method may be applied
:re just as it was for between-subjects designs.

A set of planned contrasts having the form of Equation 15 is selected. The
:sired probability values for specified regions and/or the desired intervals are
btained for these contrasts via Equation 17. Finally, the lower bound for the
iint probability that the statements for all the contrasts are true is computed
sing Equation 10, where α_i is the probability that the statement for the ith
ntrast is false.

The extension of this procedure to designs having a factorial structure on the
:lls (groups of subjects) and/or the repeated measures is straightforward. Sim-
Iy rewrite each structure in a one-way form and select the contrasts of interest.
hese may correspond to main effects and interactions but *need* not. For illustra-
on, suppose we have a design with two between-subjects factors (A and B) and
vo repeated measures factors (C and D). Moreover, suppose $B1$ and $B2$ are

	Repeated measures					
Cells	C1D1	C1D2	C2D1	C2D2	C3D1	C3D2
A1B1	μ_{11}	μ_{12}	μ_{13}	μ_{14}	μ_{15}	μ_{16}
A1B2	μ_{21}	μ_{22}	μ_{23}	μ_{24}	μ_{25}	μ_{26}
A2B3	μ_{31}	μ_{32}	μ_{33}	μ_{34}	μ_{35}	μ_{36}
A2B4	μ_{41}	μ_{42}	μ_{43}	μ_{44}	μ_{45}	μ_{46}

FIG. 8.2.   A factorial design having repeated measures.

nested in $A1$, with $B3$ and $B4$ nested in $A2$ (thus two levels of A and four levels of B). Finally, suppose C (3 levels) and D (2 levels) are completely crossed, giving six repeated measures. The complete design may be represented as in Fig. 8.2.

To obtain conventional contrasts for this design, first construct contrast weights for the cells and repeated measures separately. These appear in Tables 8.6 and 8.7, respectively. (Note that only the values 1, -1, and 0 have been used in these tables. To interpret the magnitude of the final contrast, a rescaling of the weights may be necessary.)

An actual contrast is constructed using a set of cell weights and a set of repeated measures weights together, as indicated in Equation 15. The results of combining the weights in Tables 8.6 and 8.7 are interpreted in Table 8.8. Readers familiar with the MULTIVARIANCE program (Finn, 1978) will note similarities between the setup of that program for repeated measures designs and the development leading up to Table 8.8.

To close this section, it should be noted that the foregoing illustration was only employed to show the *possibility* of constructing contrasts corresponding to conventional main effects and interactions for a mildly complex design. It is almost inconceivable (at least to the author) that anyone would actually care about all these contrasts. In the following section, the value of choosing a few contrasts of interest for specific research questions will be stressed.

Analysis of a Repeated Measures Example

Data on the development of verbal ability in children, analyzed by Bock (1975, pp. 475–477) and by Finn and Mattsson (1978, chaps. 5–6), will be reanalyzed

TABLE 8.6
Weights for Cells

Source		A1B1	A1B2	A2B3	A2B4
Constant	(c_0)	1	1	1	1
A main effect	(c_1)	1	1	-1	-1
B within A	(c_2)	1	-1	0	0
B within A	(c_3)	0	0	1	-1

TABLE 8.7
Weights for Repeated Measures

ource		C1D1	C1D2	C2D1	C2D2	C3D1	C3D2
onstant	(d_0)	1	1	1	1	1	1
, main effect	(d_1)	1	1	−1	−1	0	0
? main effect	(d_2)	0	0	1	1	−1	−1
D main effect	(d_3)	1	−1	1	−1	1	−1
: × D interaction	(d_4)	1	−1	−1	1	0	0
, × D interaction	(d_5)	0	0	1	−1	−1	1

ere from a Bayesian point of view. Scaled scores on a vocabulary test are btained from 28 girls and 36 boys for four successive years, when the children re in grades 8, 9, 10, and 11. Thus there are two cells (girls and boys) and four epeated measures (vocabulary at grades 8 through 11). The primary research uestion, as stated by Bock, is whether girls complete their verbal development t an earlier age than boys. (The scaling as well as the validity of the test used to measure verbal development are critical to a check of the question. In what ollows, we make extensive use of an assumed interval character of the scale: It s assumed that intervals are comparable both over time and between sexes.) In nis context, it might be relevant to compare the mean score increase from grade 0 to grade 11 for girls and boys. Here we might expect to find the boys still mproving, whereas the girls had leveled off. Of course, if both were still improving, or both had leveled off, such a comparison would be inconclusive. Moreover, if the girls were consistently improving over all age levels measured, ut at a slower rate than the boys, then such a comparison would be misleading. f the choice of age levels is a good one, we might hope to find that the girls are ncreasing less between 10 and 11 than between 8 and 9, whereas the correspond-

TABLE 8.8
Contrasts for Conventional Effects

ell	Repeated measures weights					
eights	d_0	d_1	d_2	d_3	d_4	d_5
o	—	C main		D main	C × D interaction	
1	A main	A × C interaction		A × D interaction	A × C × D interaction	
2 3	B within A	C × B within A		D × B within A	C × D × B within A	

ing two increases for the boys are more nearly the same. The two relevant contrasts are

$$(\mu_{G,9} - \mu_{G,8}) - (\mu_{G,11} - \mu_{G,10}) \tag{20}$$

and

$$(\mu_{B,9} - \mu_{B,8}) - (\mu_{B,11} - \mu_{B,10}). \tag{21}$$

If both of these seem reasonable, we might include the difference between the two as a final check of the hypothesis:

$$[(\mu_{G,9} - \mu_{G,8}) - (\mu_{G,11} - \mu_{G,10})] - [(\mu_{B,9} - \mu_{B,8}) \\ - (\mu_{B,11} - \mu_{B,10})]. \tag{22}$$

The prediction is that Equation 20 will be positive, 21 not *too* positive, and 22 positive. Further consideration reveals that the prediction about Equation 21 is subsumed by those about Equations 20 and 22, namely that the girls are leveling off and that they are leveling off more than the boys. Thus to check Bock's prediction it will be enough to compute the simultaneous probability that Equations 20 and 22 are both positive.

We may note in passing that Equation 20 is an indication of the quadratic time trend for girls only, whereas 22 measures the sex by quadratic time trend interaction. Notice that overall sex differences are not checked—we have a much more specific prediction about the nature of these differences. Also, overall effects of time are not checked—they are undoubtedly present and not of particular interest here. Thus we have an example where conventional main effects and interactions may be safely ignored and our attention focused on the research question.

The observed means, y_{ij}, are given in Table 8.9 and the matrix **S** appears in Table 8.10. The posterior means of our contrasts are 1.37 and .79, respectively. Both are positive, a good sign. (Note that all values are quoted only to two decimal places. All computations, however, are carried out to seven significant digits. This may occasionally produce minor rounding discrepancies between results.)

To compute the "error terms" for these contrasts, we use the formula

$$\sqrt{\sum_i \frac{c_i^2}{n_i} \sum_j \sum_{j'} d_j d_{j'} s_{jj'}}. \tag{23}$$

TABLE 8.9
Observed Means

Sex	Grade			
	8	9	10	11
Girls	1.13	2.76	3.13	3.38
Boys	1.14	2.38	2.88	3.54

TABLE 8.10
S-matrix[a]

Grade	Grade			
	8	9	10	11
8	3.81			
9	3.41	4.60		
10	3.79	3.87	5.01	
11	3.05	3.26	3.63	3.95

[a]Within-sex sums of squares and cross products divided by $N - k - p + 1 = 59$. This is also the degrees of freedom for all t-values.

This requires that we explicitly identify the sets of values $\{c_i\}$ and $\{d_j\}$ for each contrast. In the case of the first contrast (20), because we are considering girls only, we may take

$$c_G = 1, \ c_B = 0. \tag{24}$$

The contrast among the grade levels implies

$$d_8 = -1, \ d_9 = 1, \ d_{10} = 1, \ d_{11} = -1. \tag{25}$$

For the second contrast (Equation 22), the values $\{d_j\}$ remain the same. Because we are now comparing girls with boys, however, the weights for the two sexes become

$$c_G = 1, \ c_B = -1. \tag{26}$$

As the first computing step in obtaining Equation 23 we need the value of

$$\sum_j \sum_{j'} d_j d_{j'} s_{jj'} = s_{8,8} + s_{9,9} + s_{10,10} + s_{11,11}$$

$$- 2s_{8,9} - 2s_{8,10} + 2s_{8,11}$$

$$+ 2s_{9,10} - 2s_{9,11} - 2s_{10,11} = 2.81.$$

For the first contrast, Equation 23 becomes

$$\sqrt{\frac{1}{28} (2.81)} = .32.$$

For the second, we have

$$\sqrt{\left(\frac{1}{28} + \frac{1}{36}\right)(2.81)} = .42.$$

The posterior probability that the first contrast is positive (i.e., that the mean increase in vocabulary score for girls is greater between grades 8 and 9 than between grades 10 and 11), is given by the area under the t-distribution with 5 degrees of freedom above the value

$$\frac{-1.37}{.32} = -4.32.$$

This probability is greater than .999. The posterior probability that the second contrast is positive (i.e., that the mean vocabulary scores for girls are leveling of more than those for boys when grades 10 and 11 are compared with grades 8 and 9), is equal to the area under the same t-distribution above

$$\frac{-.79}{.42} = -1.88.$$

The probability here is .967. Thus, using the Bonferroni inequality, the posterior probability that girls are leveling off *and* that they are leveling off faster than boys is at least

$$1 - (1 - .999) - (1 - .967) = .966.$$

For most purposes, this value should be sufficient to convince our neutral observer of the validity of Bock's prediction, at least for the vocabulary test used and the population of children sampled from.

CLOSING REMARKS

The above is an attempt to provide a simple introduction to Bayesian inference for analysis of variance. As such, it has done injustice to both aspects of the topic. Ignoring subjective beliefs, for instance, is a serious shortcoming from a Bayesian point of view, and adopting improper priors is hardly an adequate way to deal with the different opinions that are bound to exist among researchers. Such a step was taken here primarily to allow the simplest comparison with sampling theory results. It is safe to say, after all, that most readers of this chapter are not (yet) confirmed Bayesians. For such readers, the main advantage the above analyses have to offer is the simplicity of interpretation of result already obtainable from a sampling theory point of view. The idea that it's "all right" to talk about the probability that $2 < \mu < 3$ or that the hypothesis $\mu < 0$ is true is a major breakthrough of the Bayesian approach.

On the analysis of variance side, all models involving random effects have been avoided. This is not because Bayesian analyses for these models are not available. On the contrary, Box and Tiao (1973), for instance, devote several chapters to the subject. They have been avoided here because they require more advanced computation than is typically accessible to the researcher. (Some exceptions are found in the CADA programs.)

In discussing the analysis of variance, an approach that stresses the study of rechosen contrasts (rather than conventional main effects and interactions) has een advocated. One does not, of course, have to be a Bayesian to be sympathet- with this strategy. On the other hand, as mentioned earlier, concentrating on articular questions of interest is an idea that arises naturally once one is sensitive the existence of prior information and the desirability of using it in statistical ference.

This stress should not be interpreted as a statement denying the role of pri- arily exploratory research in science. On the contrary, science would certainly agnate if all research followed the lines developed in this chapter. For explora- ry work, the role of statistical inference (Bayesian or otherwise) seems very mited. Primary emphasis should instead be placed on insightful descriptions of e sample at hand, as developed, for instance, in the texts by Tukey (1977) and y Mosteller and Tukey (1977).

Within the context of the shortcomings noted above, it is hoped that the reader ill be left with the feeling that a Bayesian approach to the analysis of variance is oth feasible and desirable. The *feasibility* arises from the fact that no new omputations are required, beyond those employed in a sampling theory ap- roach, and that the familiar *t*-distribution suffices to provide all needed informa- on about probabilities. Thus Bayesian inference is seen to be closely related to s sampling theory alternative, and techniques learned in the context of the latter re easily transferred to the service of the former.

To appreciate the *desirability* of adopting a Bayesian approach, its *differences* ith sampling theory must be stressed. After all, if the two approaches are really similar, why should anyone bother to switch? Given that the primary goal of tatistical inference is to make statements about parameters (or future observa- ons) the big difference between Bayesian and sampling theory statements is eir degree of directness. The Bayesian statements are simple and direct, hereas those of sampling theory are complex and indirect. Take the interpreta- on of a 95% interval for a contrast ψ as an example. Note that exactly the same terval would be constructed by a sampling theorist and by a Bayesian with a ference prior. For the sampling theorist,

fixing the value of ψ, making an infinite number of replications of the experiment, and computing a 95% interval from the data of each replication, we would expect 95% of all such intervals to contain ψ. This is *not* a statement about the particular interval obtained for the present data, but refers only to the *procedure* employed for sampling data and constructing intervals.

or the Bayesian,

given the present data, and initial "ignorance" (represented by the reference prior), we should be 95% certain that the constructed interval contains ψ.

The Bayesian statement is a conditional one: Given something which i known, namely the data from our experiment, a degree of certainty is expressed about something which is unknown, namely the value of ψ. The sampling theory statement is also, according to a Bayesian at least, conditional, but the *wrong* conditioning is taking place. It is the unknown parameter value that is taken a given, rather than the known data. Indeed, as noted, the connection of the sampling theory statements to the data at hand is, at best, a tenuous one. It is no at all clear what one is supposed to think about a given computed interval from a sampling point of view. For the Bayesian, on the other hand, all attention is focused on the given interval, which refers directly to a posterior belief distribution. Results of future sampling or references to sampling distributions are irrelevant from this point of view.

To conclude, the difference between Bayesian and sampling theory statement may be stated even more sharply than before: Bayesian statements are directly relevant to the questions researchers ask. Sampling theory statements are no only indirect but of questionable relevance. Given this difference, the question posed earlier in this section may be rephrased. Why should anyone *not* switch from making sampling theory statements to making Bayesian ones?

REFERENCES

Bock, R. D. (1975). *Multivariate statistical methods in behavioral research.* New York: McGraw Hill.

Box, G. E. P., & Tiao, G. C. (1973). *Bayesian inference in statistical analysis.* Reading, MA Addison-Wesley.

Dunn, O. J. (1961). Multiple comparisons among means. *Journal of the American Statistical Association, 56,* 52–64.

Edwards, W., Lindman, H., & Savage, L. J. (1963). Bayesian statistical inference for psychological research. *Psychological Review, 70,* 193–242.

Finn, J. D. (1978). *User's guide. MULTIVARIANCE: Univariate and multivariate analysis of variance, covariance, regression and repeated measures.* Chicago: National Educational Resources

Finn, J. D., & Mattsson, I. (1978). *Multivariate analysis in educational research. Applications of the MULTIVARIANCE program.* Chicago: National Educational Resources.

Keppel, G. (1973). *Design and analysis: A researcher's handbook.* Englewood Cliffs, NJ: Prentice Hall.

Kirk, R. E. (1982). *Experimental design: Procedures for the behavioral sciences* (2nd ed.). Belmont, CA: Brooks/Cole.

Mosteller, F., & Tukey, J. W. (1977). *Data analysis and regression: A second course in statistics* Reading, MA: Addison-Wesley.

Novick, M. R., Hamer, R. M., Libby, D. L., Chen, J. J., & Woodworth, G. C. (1980). *Manual for the computer-assisted data analysis (CADA) monitor—1980.* Iowa City, IA: University of Iowa

Novick, M. R., & Jackson, P. H. (1974). *Statistical methods for educational and psychological research.* New York: McGraw-Hill.

Tukey, J. W. (1977). *Exploratory data analysis.* Reading, MA: Addison-Wesley.

Woodworth, G. C. (1979). Bayesian full rank MANOVA/MANCOVA: An intermediate exposition with interactive computer examples. *Journal of Educational Statistics, 4,* 357–404.

III CATEGORICAL DATA AND THE ANALYSIS OF FREQUENCIES

In their review of the current status of graduate training in statistics, methodology, and measurement in psychology, Aiken et al. (1990) have assessed the proficiency of graduate students to apply different techniques of statistics in their own research. According to their survey, more than fifty percent of graduate students lacked the competence required to apply basic nonparametric procedures. This section attempts to remedy that state of affairs.

Chapter 11, by Everitt, provides an introduction to the analysis of data collected in the form of count or frequencies. The chapter describes a number of useful methods accompanied by detailed examples that should facilitate comprehension. Readers who need further elaborated expositions of a particular method will find appropriate guidelines in the reference list at the end of the chapter.

One of the most frequently used (and misused) nonparametric procedures in psychology, and the social sciences in general, is the chi-square analysis of contingency tables. The application of that tool is deceptively simple. As early as 1949, D. Lewis and C. J. Burke cited no less than nine common errors made by practicing researchers who employed the chi-square test. Chapter 10, by Delucci, offers an updated review of potential pitfalls when applying the chi-square test and examines supplementary and alternative approaches.

Developments in the analysis of categorical data during the past two decades make an increasing use of *log-linear models*.

Chapter 9, by Brier, contains a simple and lucid formulation and interpretation of log-linear models and their underlying rationale. It outlines the ways in which these models can be used to describe relationships between underlying cell probabilities in contingency tables and shows how statistical inferences about the underlying probability structure should be performed.

9 Analysis of Categorical Data

Stephen S. Brier

INTRODUCTION

In this chapter we consider the analysis of data that are discrete or categorical in nature as opposed to measurements made on a continuous scale. Examples are numerous in the biological and social sciences: Americans may be classified according to ethnic background (e.g., English, Italian, Russian, etc.); in an opinion poll peoples' attitudes towards an issue may be recorded as "favor," "oppose," or "indifferent"; in a medical experiment patients may be classified in two ways as treated or not treated and as recovered and not recovered. Discrete data might also arise as a result of partitioning the range of a continuous variable (e.g., a family's income might be described as low, middle, or high).

In most statistical problems we are interested in relationships between two or more variables. When all variables are categorical the data are presented in the form of a contingency table. Table 9.1 presents the results of a survey of hospital patients analyzed by Cohen (1976). The contingency table in this case is called a 2 × 2 table because there are two variables each having two categories. Because a contingency table is a table of counts, discrete data are often referred to as counted data. Although we primarily consider contingency tables, the paper by Nerlove and Press (1976) deals with problems in which the response (dependent) variables are discrete while the explanatory (independent) variables are continuous. This would be the case if we were interested, for example, in how the concentration of poison affected the probability of death of an insect pest.

TABLE 9.1
Classification of Hospital Patients by Sex and Diagnosis

Sex	Schizophrenic	Not Schizophrenic
Male	43	15
Female	32	52

GENERATION OF CONTINGENCY TABLES

Before discussing the analysis of contingency tables we look at a number of different ways in which a table of counts might arise. To motivate the discussion we consider a hypothetical example involving the relationship of smoking habits and the incidence of lung cancer. We classify people as smokers or nonsmokers as well as being diseased or healthy. If a sample of people were cross-classified according to these two dichotomies we would present, in general, the following contingency table. In the labeling, "health" is the first variable (corresponding to rows) and "smoking habits" is the second variable (corresponding to columns). Thus X_{11} is the number of people in the first category of the first variable ("Health") and also in the first category of the second variable ("Smoking Habits"), that is, the number of diseased smokers. The categories of a contingency table are often referred to as cells (e.g., X_{11} is the count in the (1, 1) cell). Table 9.2 also gives the marginal totals: X_{1+} is the total number of diseased people whereas X_{+1} is the total number of smokers. A "+" indicates that we have summed over the categories of that variable. Finally the grand total, which is the sum over all levels of both variables, is denoted by X_{++}.

Perhaps the most traditional way of generating Table 9.2 would be via a multinomial sampling scheme. This scheme would be appropriate if we took a random sample of size N, where $N = X_{++}$, from the population of interest. If the N people were independently selected then the distribution of the observed table is given by the probability function

$$f(\mathbf{x}) = \binom{N}{x_{11}, x_{12}, x_{21}, x_{22}} p_{11}^{x_{11}} p_{12}^{x_{12}} p_{21}^{x_{21}} p_{22}^{x_{22}} \tag{1}$$

where p_{ij} is the probability of a randomly selected person falling in the (i, j)th cell. In general if $\mathbf{X} = (X_1, \ldots, X_r)$ represents a classification into r categories and $\mathbf{p} = (p_1, \ldots, p_r)$ is the corresponding probability vector then the probability function

$$g(\mathbf{x}) = \binom{N}{x_1, \ldots, x_r} \prod_{i=1}^{r} p_i^{x_i} \tag{2}$$

TABLE 9.2
Notation for a 2 × 2 Table

Health	Smoking Habits		Totals
	Smoker	Non-Smoker	
Diseased	X_{11}	X_{12}	X_{1+}
Healthy	X_{21}	X_{22}	X_{2+}
Totals	X_{+1}	X_{+2}	X_{++}

denoted as $M_r(N, \mathbf{p})$. Thus in this example $\mathbf{X} \sim M_4(N, \mathbf{p})$. It is well known that the expected value of a multinomial random variable is given by

$$E(\mathbf{X}) = Np \qquad (3)$$

so in our table the expected cells counts are

$$m_{ij} = E(X_{ij}) = Np_{ij}, \ i = 1, 2, j = 1, 2. \qquad (4)$$

It is important to note that under this sampling scheme the only number that is fixed beforehand is the grand total, $X_{++} = N$.

Another method of examining the relationship between cancer and smoking would be to take a sample of N_1 smokers and another independent sample of N_2 nonsmokers and within each sample classify people as diseased or healthy. Note that under this sampling plan the column margins are fixed because $X_{+1} = N_1$, $X_{+2} = N_2$. If the N_1 smokers are a simple random sample from the population of nonsmokers then the distribution of counts is

$$f(\mathbf{x}) = \binom{N_1}{x_{11}} (p_d^{(1)})^{x_{11}} (1 - p_d^{(1)})^{x_{21}} \binom{N_2}{x_{12}} (p_d^{(2)})^{x_{12}} (1 - p_d^{(2)})^{x_{22}} \qquad (5)$$

where $p_d^{(1)}$ is the probability of a smoker being diseased and $p_d^{(2)}$ is the probability of a nonsmoker being diseased. This type of sampling scheme is usually referred to as a *product multinomial scheme* because the distribution is a product of multinomials. The expected cell counts are

$$m_{11} = N_1 p_d^{(1)}, \ m_{21} = N_1(1 - p_d^{(1)})$$
$$m_{12} = N_2 p_d^{(2)}, \ m_{22} = N_2(1 - p_d^{(2)}). \qquad (6)$$

Instead of fixing the number of smokers and nonsmokers one could fix the numbers of diseased and healthy people in the sample. This would be the case if people were sampled from lists of hospital patients and were then questioned about their smoking habits. Sampling in this way would again yield a product multinomial distribution but now the row margins, X_{1+} and X_{2+}, would be fixed.

A third method of sampling fixes neither the grand total nor any of the marginal totals. We can observe people over a fixed time period and categorize them. Thus we might examine and question all persons applying for a job at large firm during a one-year period. In many instances it is reasonable to assum that the four counts generated in this way have independent Poisson distribu tions. If we use the general notation defined previously for the r-category classi fication, the Poisson probability function is

$$f(x) = e^{-\sum_i m_i} \left(\pi_i \frac{m_i^{x_i}}{x_i!} \right), \tag{7}$$

where the parameters, $\{m_i\}$, are the expected counts in each of the categorie:

We have briefly described the three primary classes of probability distribu tions useful for modelling contingency tables. For a detailed study of these an other discrete distributions the reader is referred to Johnson and Kotz (1969 There are other ways of generating the counts in Table 9.2: sample until predetermined number of smokers is found; sample until a predetermined num ber of diseased persons is found; sample until a predetermined number of dis eased smokers is found. The appropriate distribution in each of these cases is form of negative multinomial distribution. For details see Bishop, Fienberg, an Holland (1975). We do not consider the negative multinomial distribution in thi chapter because it is not a common sampling scheme and is not compatible wit the methodology developed for the other sampling schemes described here. W see in two later sections that the same methods of inference may be used fc multinomial, product multinomial, or Poisson sampling schemes.

FORMULATION AND INTERPRETATION
OF LOG-LINEAR MODELS

The counts in a contingency table are almost always a sample from a populatio of interest. We describe the population by describing the probability vector, $\mathbf{p}$, c cell probabilities. In this section we formulate a class of models for p that ar useful for representing relationships among categorical variables.

We begin with a 2×2 table and use the example given in Table 9.1 Corresponding to the table of counts there is a table of underlying cell proba bilities, $\mathbf{p}$ (see Table 9.3).

We say that sex and mental condition are independent if the conditional proba bility of being schizophrenic is the same for males and females, that is,

$$\frac{p_{11}}{p_{1+}} = \frac{p_{21}}{p_{2+}}. \tag{8}$$

Equivalently we could say that the conditional probability of being male is th same for schizophrenics and nonschizophrenics, that is,

$$\frac{p_{11}}{p_{+1}} = \frac{p_{12}}{p_{+2}} \tag{8a}$$

r, alternately, if the conditional odds of being schizophrenic is the same for males and females. Equations 8 and 8a are equivalent to a third representation of independence

$$p_{ij} = p_{i+}p_{+j}. \tag{8b}$$

Defining independence is clear-cut but measuring the amount of dependence is not. One possibility is the ratio of the odds of being schizophrenic for males and females

$$\left(\frac{p_{11}}{p_{12}}\right) \Big/ \left(\frac{p_{21}}{p_{22}}\right). \tag{9}$$

This ratio, called the *odds ratio or cross-product ratio,* will be denoted by α and can be rewritten as

$$\alpha = \frac{p_{11}p_{22}}{p_{21}p_{12}}. \tag{10}$$

We obtain two other measures of dependence by either taking the difference of the odds

$$\beta = \frac{p_{11}}{p_{12}} - \frac{p_{21}}{p_{22}} \tag{11}$$

or the difference in the conditional probability of being schizophrenic between males and females

$$\gamma = \frac{p_{11}}{p_{1+}} - \frac{p_{21}}{p_{2+}}. \tag{12}$$

Note that α may have any value between 0 and ∞ with 1 corresponding to independence. β lies between $-\infty$ and $+\infty$ while γ is between -1 and $+1$. For both β and γ, 0 corresponds to independence. The models we use are based on α because it has a number of desirable properties that the other measures do not:

1. α remains the same if rows and columns are interchanged.

2. If the levels of a variable are interchanged (e.g., listing females as the first sex) α is transformed to $1/\alpha$.

3. Multiplying either row by a constant number or either column by a constant number leaves α unchanged. If we take logarithms then

$$-\infty < \log \alpha < \infty \tag{13}$$

and $\log \alpha = 0$ corresponds to independence.

Using $\log \alpha$ as a measure of dependence between rows and columns, it is natural to postulate a model for the probabilities in Table 9.3 that is linear in the logarithms of the cell probabilities. The most general log-linear model for the 2 × 2 table is

$$\log p_{ij} = u + u_{1(i)} + u_{2(j)} + u_{12(ij)}, \quad i = 1, 2, j = 1, 2 \tag{14}$$

where the parameters are subject to the constraints

$$\sum_{i=1}^{2} u_{1(i)} = \sum_{j=1}^{2} u_{2(j)} = \sum_{i=1}^{2} u_{12(ij)} = \sum_{j=1}^{2} u_{12(ij)} = 0. \tag{15}$$

The parameters $\{u_{1(i)}\}$ are the main effects of variable 1 (sex), $\{u_{2(j)}\}$ are the main effects of variable 2 (mental condition), and $\{u_{12(ij)}\}$ represent the interaction between the two variables. The parameter u is not a free parameter because the constraint, $\Sigma_{i,j} p_{ij} = 1$, determines u after the other parameters are known. Due to the constraints in Equation 15 there is one independent u_1 parameter, one independent u_2 parameter, and one independent u_{12} parameter. Since the model in Equation 14 has as many parameters as there are independent cell probabilities, it is referred to as a saturated model.

A desirable feature of the log-linear model is that

$$u_{12(11)} = \tfrac{1}{4} \log \alpha \tag{16}$$

so that by setting $u_{12(11)} = 0$, from which it follows that $u_{12(ij)} = 0$ for all i, j, we obtain a model in which the two variables are independent. This feature is not present in models that are linear in the cell proabilities themselves, for example, if

$$p_{ij} = \mu + a_i + b_j + (ab)_{ij}, \quad i = 1, 2, j = 1, 2 \tag{17}$$

setting $(ab)_{ij} = 0$ does not produce a model in which Equation 8 is satisfied. See Bishop, Fienberg, and Holland (1975) for a discussion of this point. Another property of log-linear models is that we can use them to describe either cell probabilities or expected cell counts. All subscripted u-terms remain the same, only the parameter u is different in the two cases, differing by $\log N$. Perhaps the most important feature of models that are linear in the logarithmic scale is that setting certain parameters equal to zero produces models that describe interesting relationships among variables.

TABLE 9.3
Probabilities in a 2 × 2 Cross-Classification

	Schizophrenic	Not Schizophrenic	
Male	p_{11}	p_{12}	p_{1+}
Female	p_{21}	p_{22}	p_{2+}
	p_{+1}	p_{+2}	1

Because the saturated model is a linear model in the logarithms of the cell probabilities we can interpret the model parameters as contrasts in the log-probabilities

$$u_{12(11)} = \tfrac{1}{4} (\log p_{11} + \log p_{22} - \log p_{12} - \log p_{21}) \tag{18}$$

$$u_{1(1)} = \tfrac{1}{4} (\log p_{11} + \log p_{12} - \log p_{21} - \log p_{22}) \tag{19}$$

$$u_{2(1)} = \tfrac{1}{4} (\log p_{11} + \log p_{21} - \log p_{12} - \log p_{22}). \tag{20}$$

In general the subscripted "u-terms" in log-linear models can always be written as appropriate contrasts in the log probabilities in a manner similar to the way main effects and interactions are expressed as contrasts in treatment averages in analysis of variance models.

We have only considered 2×2 tables. In the general two-dimensional contingency table the row variable has I categories and the common variable has J categories. The saturated log-linear model is

$$\log p_{ij} = u + u_{1(i)} + u_{2(j)} + u_{12(ij)}, \quad i = 1, \ldots, I; j = 1, \ldots, J \tag{21}$$

where the u-terms satisfy constraints analogous to those in Equation 15. There are $(I - 1)(J - 1)$ independent interaction parameters, $u_{12(ij)}$, and they are defined by the cross product ratios in the 2×2 tables that may be extracted from the original table. If we set all u_{12} parameters equal to 0 we have independence of the row and column variables, as defined in Equation 8a.

Tables of higher dimension can be thought of as sets of two-dimensional tables. To illustrate the types of models that we will consider, we focus on a $2 \times 2 \times 2$ table. Generalizations of these models to larger tables will be apparent. Dyke and Patterson (1952) present a cross-classification of people into five dichotomous categories. We construct a cross-classification of people based on three of these: whether they read newspapers (variable 1), whether they listen to the radio (variable 2), and whether they have a good knowledge of cancer (variable 3). In the four models we present for this table we assume that the cell probabilities are known; we do not consider statistical inference about probabilities until later. Table 9.4 presents the table of observed counts, a table defining the notation for cell probabilities, and four tables illustrating possible log-linear models of interest.

In Table 9.4c the three variables are completely independent. This means that the conditional probability of being in either level of one variable is the same for all possible levels of the other variables. The cell probabilities satisfy the relationship

$$p_{ijk} = p_{i++}p_{+j+}p_{++k} \tag{22}$$

and the corresponding log-linear model is

$$\log p_{ijk} = u + u_{1(i)} + u_{2(j)} + u_{3(k)}. \tag{23}$$

TABLE 9.4
Possible Structures for a 2 × 2 × 2 Table

		C^+			C^-		
		R+	R−		R+	R−	
	N+	168	310	N+	138	357	C^+: Knowledgeable concerning cancer
(a)							R+: Radio listener
	N−	34	156		72	494	N+: Newspaper reader
		R+	R−	N−	R+	R−	
	N+	p_{111}	p_{121}	N+	p_{112}	p_{122}	
(b)							
	N−	p_{211}	p_{221}	N−	p_{212}	p_{222}	
		R+	R−		R+	R−	
	N+	.192	.288	N+	.128	.192	COMPLETE INDEPENDENCE OF VARIABLES
(c)							1, 2, and 3.
	N−	.048	.072	N−	.032	.048	
		R+	R−		R+	R−	
	N+	.18	.30	N+	.12	.20	INDEPENDENCE OF "MEDIA" and CANCER
(d)							KNOWLEDGE
	N−	.06	.06	N−	.04	.04	
		R+	R−		R+	R−	
	N+	.144	.096	N+	.0125	.0375	CONDITIONAL INDEPENDENCE OF VARIABLES 1
(e)							and 2 GIVEN 3.
	N−	.336	.224	N−	.0375	.1125	
		R+	R−		R+	R−	
	N+	.30	.15	N+	.035	.035	NO SECOND ORDER INTERACTION
(f)							
	N−	.30	.075	N−	.07	.035	

There are no interactions between the variables so the model only includes main effects.

Table 9.4d reflects the fact that if newspaper habits and radio habits were combined into one four-category "media" variable, cancer knowledge would be independent of this variable. Looking at the two tables corresponding to C^+ and C^- we see that the ratios of all four pairs of probabilities are equal. In terms of marginal probabilities the relationship among the cell probabilities is

$$p_{ijk} = p_{ij+}p_{++k}, \tag{24}$$

which leads to the log-linear model

$$\log p_{ijk} = u + u_{1(i)} + u_{2(j)} + u_{3(k)} + u_{12(ij)}. \tag{25}$$

Because there are no u_{13} parameters, each of the 2 × 2 tables cross-classifying variables 1 and 3 for the different levels of variable 2 has a cross-product ratio of 1. The analogous statement regarding variables 2 and 3 is also true.

In Table 9.4e both tables, corresponding to the different levels of cancer knowledge, exhibit independence of newspaper habits and radio habits. No other arrangement of the table produces cross-product ratios equal to 1. Hence we say that given the level of variable 3, variables 1 and 2 are independent. The cell probabilities satisfy

$$p_{ijk} = \frac{p_{i+k}\, p_{+jk}}{p_{++k}} \tag{26}$$

and the corresponding log-linear model is

$$\log p_{ijk} = u + u_{1(i)} + u_{2(j)} + u_{3(k)} + u_{13(ik)} + u_{23(jk)}. \tag{27}$$

In Table 9.4f we define

$$\alpha_{12}^{(k)} = \frac{p_{11k}\, p_{22k}}{p_{12k}\, p_{21k}}, \ k = 1, 2. \tag{28}$$

The term "no second order interaction" refers to the fact that $\alpha_{12}^{(1)} = \alpha_{12}^{(2)}$. Radio and newspaper habits are not independent but the amount of dependence (as measured by the cross-product ratio) is the same at both levels of cancer knowledge. This concept of "equal dependence" is symmetric in all three variables and is defined by the model

$$\log p_{ijk} = u + u_{1(i)} + u_{2(j)} + u_{3(k)} + u_{12(ij)} + u_{13(ik)} + u_{23(jk)}. \tag{29}$$

For this model we cannot derive an expression relating the cell probabilities comparable to Equations 22, 24, or 26. We will see in the next section that this lack of a closed form relationship will force us to use iterative methods when computing estimates of cell probabilities.

Building log-linear models for higher dimensional tables is straightforward now that we have examined the four types of models in three-dimensional tables. In higher dimensions we can always reduce the relationships among the cell probabilities to a sequence of relationships, each of one of the four types presented in Table 9.4. Before doing this we define a restricted class of models, called hierarchical, which eliminates certain models from consideration.

Definition: A log-linear model is called hierarchical if whenever a u-term involving a set of variables is 0 then all u-terms involving that set of variables are also 0.

In other words, a hierarchical model does not allow interactions between two variables if either variable has a zero main effect. Thus in a four-dimensional table whenever the parameters in $\{u_{123(ijk)}\}$ are 0 it must also be the case that $\{u_{1234(ijkl)}\}$ are all 0. There are some occasions when it is desirable to fit non-hierarchical models to contingency tables, but we omit them from our discussion

because they are usually difficult to interpret and their analysis does not coincide
with the methods that we present.

As a convenience, whenever we talk about a u-term being 0, we mean that all
parameters for that term are 0 (e.g., $u_{12} = 0$ means $u_{12(ij)} = 0$ for all i and j).
Keeping the hierarchy constraint in mind, setting $u_{12} = 0$ implies that for all
levels of all other variables the 2-dimensional tables corresponding to variables
and 2 exhibit independence between rows and columns. Setting $u_{123} = 0$ states
that at each level of the other variables (4, 5, etc.) the three-dimensional tables
involving variables 1, 2, and 3 exhibit no second order interaction. Analogous to
parameters in linear models for continuous data, any u-term involving one set of
variables is the value of the corresponding effect averaged over all levels of the
remaining set of variables. Thus in a $2 \times 2 \times 2 \times L$ table

$$u_{123(ijk)} = \frac{1}{L} \sum_{l=1}^{L} u^{(l)}_{123(ijk)} \qquad (30)$$

where $u^{(l)}_{123(ijk)}$ is the 3-way interaction for the $2 \times 2 \times 2$ table at the lth level of
variable 4.

It is important to realize that an interaction term being 0 does not necessarily
imply that the corresponding variables are independent if we ignore the other
variables in the classification. In Table 9.4e if we ignore the 2 levels of cancer
knowledge or *collapse* over variable 3 the probabilities corresponding to the
cross-classification of radio and newspaper habits are given in Table 9.5. The
rows and columns of this 2×2 table are not independent. Having $u_{12} = 0$ only
tells us that within each level of cancer knowledge there is independence; in the
marginal table there may not be. We present a theorem that tells us when we can
safely collapse a table without distorting the effects of interest. We collapse a
table over a set of variables, A, by forming the marginal table involving the
remaining variables. We say then that a table is collapsible with respect to a
parameter if the value of that parameter is unchanged in the collapsed table.

Theorem 1:   Suppose that we are interested in a u-term involving a set of
variables B. The table is collapsible over A with respect to that u-term if the
u-terms linking A and B are 0.

In Table 9.4e, u_{23} was changed when we collapsed over variable 1 because
both $u_{12} \neq 0$ and $u_{13} \neq 0$. If $u_{12} = 0$ then the table is collapsible with respect to
any u-term involving variable 2, and in particular with respect to u_{23}.

We have shown in this section, that by focusing on the logarithms of the cell
probabilities we can build models that are useful for exploring relationships
among categorical variables. These models involve u-terms that are similar to the
effect parameters in analysis of variance. The interpretation of interactions in
contingency tables is similar to those in analysis of variance but depend now on
how cross product ratios change across levels of variables. We also saw, in

TABLE 9.5
TABLE 9.4e Collapsed Over Variable 3

	R^+	R^-
N^+	.1565	.1335
N^-	.3735	.3365

Theorem 1, when we could collapse, or reduce, a table without losing information about effects of interest.

ESTIMATION OF PARAMETERS
IN LOG-LINEAR MODELS

In the previous section we saw how the log-linear model could be used to describe relationships between the underlying cell probabilities or cell expectations in a contingency table. In practice the contingency table that we observe is only a sample, and we want to make statistical inferences about the underlying probability structure. In this section we discuss the problem of estimating the expected cell counts assuming an underlying model, and in the next section we discuss methods of testing whether a model adequately describes the observed data.

We begin by finding the minimal sufficient statistics for the parameters in log-linear models. A set of statistics is sufficient if it provides a reduction of the original data but still contains all of the data that are needed to estimate the underlying parameters. Minimal sufficient statistics provide the maximum amount of reduction possible while still containing all of the data essential for estimation of the parameters. It is important to find the minimal sufficient statistics because they enable us to ignore the part of the data that is irrelevant for estimation purposes.

For log-linear models the minimal sufficient statistics always consist of sets of marginal totals. Which marginal totals are needed depends on the u-terms in the model and we now present the four steps used to determine which margins should be included:

1. The margins corresponding to all of the highest order u-terms are included.

2. Repeat step 1 for the next highest order u-terms.

3. Delete any marginal totals that are redundant. Thus if we know the two-way marginal totals $\{x_{ij+}\}$ for all values of i and j then we do not also need the one-way margins, $\{x_{i++}\}$, because they can be obtained from $\{x_{ij+}\}$ by summing over the levels of the second variable.

4. Repeat steps 1–3 beginning with the next highest order u-terms and repeat until all u-terms have been exhausted.

We use these rules for determining the minimal sufficient margins for the model

$$\log p_{ijkl} = u + u_{1(i)} + u_{2(j)} + u_{3(k)} + u_{4(l)} + u_{12(ij)} + u_{13(ik)}$$
$$+ u_{23(jk)} + u_{34(kl)} + u_{24(jl)} + u_{123(ijk)}. \tag{31}$$

Applying step 1 we write down $\{x_{ijk+}\}$ corresponding to u_{123}. Step 2 tells us to proceed to the two-way u-terms, so we include $\{x_{ij++}\}$, $\{x_{i+k+}\}$, $\{x_{+jk+}\}$, $\{x_{++kl}\}$, $\{x_{+j+l}\}$. The margins $\{x_{ij++}\}$, $\{x_{i+k+}\}$, and $\{x_{+jk+}\}$ are redundant when we know $\{x_{ijk+}\}$ so they are removed leaving $\{x_{ijk+}\}$, $\{x_{++kl}\}$, $\{x_{+j+l}\}$. These are the minimal sufficient statistics because applying steps 1 and 2 beginning with second order u-terms produces only redundant marginal totals. Note that this set of margins completely determines the log-linear model in Equation 31 in the sense that any other log-linear model would have a different set of minimal sufficient statistics.

It is true in general that there is a 1-1 correspondence between sets of minimal sufficient margins and hierarchical log-linear models. Using this fact we will henceforth define models by specifying marginal totals. We use the term *configuration* for a set of marginal totals including a set of variables. We denote the configuration by placing the variables in brackets. Thus the configuration [12] in a four-dimensional table is $\{x_{ij++}\}$, $i = 1, \ldots, I; j = 1 \ldots, J$. With this representation the model in Equation 31 is defined by the configurations [24], [34], and [123].

With the minimal sufficient statistics at hand we desire a unified method of estimating expected cell counts and the corresponding u-terms. The principle of maximum likelihood provides such a unified approach to estimation. Maximum likelihood estimates of parameters have desirable properties in general: They are functions of sufficient statistics and in large samples there are no other parameter estimates that have smaller variances. See Rao (1965) for a detailed discussion of maximum likelihood estimation. As we proceed, we will see that in contingency tables maximum likelihood estimates (MLE's) of cell expectations will have the added properties of being relatively easy to compute as well as being "intuitively reasonable." We briefly discuss alternatives to MLE's later.

We assume that the contingency tables we study are complete in the sense that all cell expectations are strictly positive (i.e., none is zero). In a later section we consider incomplete tables. The following theorem helps to determine when MLE's exist and suggests a method of computing them. The result is due originally to Birch (1963). Haberman (1974) presents a generalization of Birch's results.

Theorem 2:   Under Poisson or multinomial sampling there is at most one set of MLE's of the expected cell counts. A set of estimates $\hat{m}$, are the MLE's if and only if the minimal sufficient configurations of the $\hat{\mathbf{m}}$ are equal to the corresponding minimal sufficient configurations of the cell counts $\mathbf{x}$ and the $\hat{\mathbf{m}}$ satisfy the constraints of the model.

For the model of independence in a two-dimensional table, Theorem 2 tells us that the MLE's must satisfy the following:

$$\hat{m}_{i+} = x_{i+}, i = 1, \ldots, I$$
$$\hat{m}_{+j} = x_{+j}, j = 1, \ldots, J. \tag{32}$$

Furthermore, any solution to Equations 32 is the unique MLE. As long as no marginal totals are 0, the estimates are

$$\hat{m}_{ij} = \frac{x_{i+} x_{+j}}{x_{++}}. \tag{33}$$

These estimates are "intuitively reasonable" since the cell estimate is the grand total multiplied by the estimates of, respectively, the probability of being in the ith row and the probability of being in the jth column.

If any of the observed margins corresponding to the minimal configuration are 0 then some cell estimates will be 0. In this case we cannot estimate all of the u-terms in the model. This is because a count of 0 transforms to $-\infty$ when we take logarithms. Thus when we say that MLE's exist we mean that all cell estimates are positive. If some cell estimates are 0 then we say that MLE's don't exist. Theorem 2 tells us that if any of the minimal configurations has a 0 margin then MLE's do not exist. The converse is not true as there are some pathological cases where MLE's don't exist even though all minimal configurations are positive. Haberman (1974) presents results useful for detecting these situations. In practice these problems are detected by watching for cell estimates that appear to be converging to 0.

To find MLE's we have to find positive cell estimates which satisfy the conditions of Theorem 2. For some models it is possible to write down an explicit formula for the cell estimates as we did in Equation 33. These are called direct estimates. For other models we can only obtain estimates by an iterative method. It is useful to know when a model yields direct estimates. Large sample (asymptotic) variances are easily computed for direct models but not for models that require iteration. See Lee (1977) for a discussion of this problem. There are also relationships between chi-square statistics that hold only for direct models.

For the 2^3 tables we divided the possible log-linear models into three types: those where one set of variables is completely independent of the remaining set of variables, those where some variables are conditionally independent given the levels of the remaining variable, and a model described as having no second-order interaction. For the models in the first two categories we could find relationships between cell probabilities and some marginal probabilities. In these cases we can find direct cell estimates by substituting observed margins for expected margins. Thus from Equation 26 we obtain MLE's under the model defined by Equation 27

$$\hat{m}_{ijk} = \frac{x_{i+k} x_{+jk}}{x_{++k}}. \tag{34}$$

We cannot find direct estimates for the no second-order interaction model. In larger tables the same principle applies: If some sets of variables are independent or if some are conditionally independent of others then we may be able to find direct estimates. Bishop, Fienberg, and Holland (1975) present the following steps for formally determining whether direct estimates exist:

1. Combine into a single variable those variables that always appear together.
2. Erase any variables that appear in all configurations.
3. Erase any variables that appear in only one configuration.
4. Remove any redundant configurations.
5. Repeat steps 1–4 as often as you can.

If at the end of these steps there are two or less configurations remaining then direct estimates exist; otherwise there are not direct estimates. As an example consider the model in six dimensions defined by [36], [46], [56], [123], and [345]. Using steps 1–4 we reduce the configurations to [36], [46], [56], and [345] but we cannot eliminate any other configurations, so direct estimates do not exist. If we had started with [36], [46], [56], [123] we could remove all configurations and the direct estimates are

$$\hat{m}_{ijklmn} = \frac{(x_{++k++n})(x_{+++l+n})(x_{++++mn})(x_{ijk+++})}{(x_{+++++n})^2(x_{++k+++})}. \tag{35}$$

The iterative scheme needed to obtain estimates for indirect models is based on the result of Theorem 2, which says that the estimated or fitted margins must equal the observed margins for all margins comprising the set of minimal configurations. The scheme, referred to as *iterative proportional fitting* (IPF), was first introduced by Deming and Stephan (1940) to adjust the entries of a table to fit prespecified marginal totals.

Let $C_1, \ldots, C_k$ be the configuration that we want to fit. Let $\hat{m}^{(0)}$ be an initial set of cell estimates. Let $\hat{m}^{(0)}$ and $\hat{m}^{(1)}$ be the initial and final estimates in a given cell after adjusting the table to fit C_1. Let $x_{(a)+}$ be the desired marginal total in C corresponding to the given cell and let $\hat{m}^{(0)}_{(a)+}$ be the corresponding marginal total computed from the initial cell estimates. The following equation defines the way to get $\hat{m}^{(1)}$ from $\hat{m}^{(0)}$:

$$\hat{m}^{(1)} = \hat{m}^{(0)} \frac{x_{(a)+}}{\hat{m}^{(0)}_{(a)+}}. \tag{36}$$

he table with counts $\hat{\mathbf{m}}^{(1)}$ now has margins that match the desired margins in $^-_1$. The next step in IPF would set $\hat{m}^{(1)}$ to be the initial estimates and use in elationship in Equation 36 to fit C_2. At the kth step C_k is fitted. The set of k steps ill be called a cycle. After a complete cycle the cell estimates agree with the esired margins in configuration C_k but may not agree with any of the previous onfigurations.

The simplicity of the IPF algorithm is best illustrated with an example. Table .6(a) presents the initial counts in a 2×2 table and the row and column margins at are to be fitted. Table 9.6(b) gives the cell estimates after the first step. These ere obtained via Equation 36,

$$\hat{m}_{ij}^{(1)} = \hat{m}_{ij}^{(0)} \frac{x_{i+}}{\hat{m}_{i+}^{(0)}} . \tag{37}$$

he $m_{ij}^{(1)}$ are the estimates in Table 19.6(b). The estimates in Table 9.6(c), $m_{ij}^{(2)}$, re obtained after the second step

$$\hat{m}_{ij}^{(2)} = \hat{m}_{ij}^{(1)} \frac{x_{+j}}{\hat{m}_{+j}^{(1)}} . \tag{38}$$

n this case we have fitted the configurations exactly after one cycle. In general e would repeat the cycles until a desired degree of accuracy is attained.

The following facts suggest how to use IPF to obtain MLE's:

1. If the initial cell estimates exhibit only the interactions specified by the inimal configurations then the estimates at the end of a cycle exhibit only the iteractions specified by the configuration.

2. If the initial estimates have nonzero interactions not specified by the onfigurations fitted then the estimates at the end of a cycle exhibit these same onzero interactions.

TABLE 9.6(a)
Initial Counts in a 2 × 2 Table

1	1	2	(9)	Numbers in parentheses are
				the configurations C_1, C_2
1	1	2	(30)	to be fitted
2	2			
(17)	(22)			

TABLE 9.6(b)
Cell Estimates After Fitting Row Totals

4.5	4.5	9
15	15	30
19.5	19.5	

TABLE 9.6(c)
Cell Estimates After Fitting Column Totals

3.92	5.08	9
13.08	16.92	30
17	22	

Justification for these two points lies in the fact, noted previously, that cros‹ product ratios are unaffected by multiplication of a row or column by a constan‹ We are also ensured of convergence of IPF. For a proof of its convergenc‹ properties see Fienberg (1970). Thus if our initial estimates do not exhibit an‹ interactions other than those specified by the model to be fitted, then the IP‹ scheme will converge to cell estimates that match the minimal configurations an‹ Theorem 2 ensures that these are the unique MLE's.

The first example of IPF illustrates how it can be used to "adjust" cell coun‹ to fit any marginal constraints. In Table 9.7 we adjust a table originally analyze‹ by Deming and Stephen (1940). The cell counts are a sample of students in Ne‹ England. If the marginal proportions of students are known one would want ‹ adjust the original table so that it fit these margins and still had exactly the sam‹ interaction pattern as the original sample. The italicized counts are the cell coun‹ after five-cycles of IPF with the original counts used as initial estimates. Con‹ vergence was quite rapid as the maximum difference between the fourth and fif‹ cycle cell estimates was 10^{-5}. Because we are using IPF to fit the margin‹

TABLE 9.7
Using IPF to Adjust a Table to Fit Known Margins

| State | Age | | | | |
	7 to 13	14 to 15	16 and 17	18 to 20	
Maine	3623	781	557	313	
	3612.98	781.23	549.43	308.35	5252
New Hampshire	1570	395	251	155	
	1588.16	400.80	251.15	154.89	2395
Vermont	1553	419	264	116	
	1607.86	435.14	270.36	118.64	2432
Massachusetts	10538	2455	1706	1160	
	10492.08	2451.82	1680.14	1140.96	1576‹
Rhode Island	1681	353	171	154	
	1661.48	349.97	167.18	150.37	2329
Connecticut	3882	857	544	339	
	3915.44	867.04	542.73	337.78	5663
	22878	5286	3461	2211	3383‹

The table is an artificial 5% sample of New England students in 1930. The know‹ marginal totals are in italics as are the adjusted counts. (From Deming & Stephan 1940.)

tals, $\{x_{i+}\}$ and $\{x_{+j}\}$, the interactions, as measured by the cross product ratios, re the same as in the original table. For example, the cross product ratio for the × 2 table consisting of the first two states and first two age categories is 1.167 oth before and after applying IPF. In effect what we have done here is to ombine the *known* marginal totals with the *sampled* interactions to get better stimates of the true cell counts.

To use IPF to obtain MLE's we only need to choose initial estimates that xhibit interactions included in the minimal configurations. If we take all initial stimates to be one then all interactions are 0, so this condition is met. Starting ith all ones and fitting the appropriate configurations will always produce 1LE's if they exist and most computer programs take these to be initial esti-ates. If we use IPF to find MLE's for a direct model we obtain the estimates xactly after one cycle, except in some unusual cases where two cycles are equired. See Bishop, Fienberg, and Holland (1975) for a discussion of con-ergence properties of IPF.

Table 9.8 presents data that were previously analyzed by Fienberg (1977). The ariables are aptitude (1), education (2), and occupation (3). We present a de-iled analysis of the data in the next two sections but here we only fit the model efined by [12], [23]. This is a direct model so we could have found MLE's vithout iteration but we used IPF and started with all cell estimates being one. 'onvergence was achieved after one cycle and the estimates are given in Table .9 along with Freeman–Tukey deviates which are discussed in the next section. Iaving these estimates we want to see what they say about the relationship

TABLE 9.8
Cross-Classification of Individuals by Aptitude, Education,
and Employment (Fienberg, 1977)

	E_1 (less than 13 years)							E_2 (between 13 and 15 years)					
	A_1	A_2	A_3	A_4	A_5			A_1	A_2	A_3	A_4	A_5	
O_1	42	72	90	27	8	239	O_1	55	82	106	48	18	309
O_2	1	1	2	2	0	6	O_2	2	2	5	2	0	11
O_3	0	0	1	0	0	1	O_3	0	3	4	0	0	7
O_4	172	208	279	99	36	794	O_4	151	198	271	126	35	781
	215	281	372	128	44	1040		208	285	386	176	53	1108

	E_3 (16 years)							E_4 (17 or more years)					
	A_1	A_2	A_3	A_4	A_5			A_1	A_2	A_3	A_4	A_5	
O_1	22	60	85	47	19	233	O_1	3	12	25	8	5	53
O_2	8	15	25	10	12	70	O_2	19	33	83	45	19	199
O_3	1	3	5	2	1	12	O_3	19	60	86	36	14	215
O_4	107	206	331	179	99	922	O_4	42	92	191	97	79	501
	183	284	446	238	131	1237		83	197	385	186	117	968

TABLE 9.9
Expected Values for the Model of Conditional Independence of Occupation and Aptitude Given Level of Education

E_1

	A_1	A_2	A_3	A_4	A_5
O_1	49.4	64.6	85.5	29.4	10.1
	(-1.1)*	(.9)	(.5)	(-.4)	(-.6)
O_2	1.2	1.6	2.1	0.7	0.3
	(-.0)	(-.3)	(.1)	(1.2)*	(-.4)
O_3	0.2	0.3	0.4	0.1	0.0
	(-.4)	(-.4)	(.9)	(-.2)	(-.1)
O_4	164.1	214.5	284.0	97.7	33.6
	(.6)	(-.4)	(-.3)	(.2)	(.4)

E_2

	A_1	A_2	A_3	A_4	A_5
O_1	58.0	79.5	107.6	49.1	14.8
	(-.4)	(.3)	(-.1)	(-.1)	(.8)
O_2	2.1	2.8	3.8	1.7	0.5
	(.1)	(-.4)	(.6)	(.3)	(-.8)
O_3	1.3	1.8	2.4	1.1	0.3
	(-1.5)*	(.9)	(1.0)*	(-1.3)*	(-.5)
O_4	146.6	200.9	272.1	124.1	37.4
	(.4)	(-.2)	(-.1)	(.2)	(-.3)

E_3

	A_1	A_2	A_3	A_4	A_5
O_1	26.0	53.5	84.0	44.8	24.7
	(-.8)	(.9)	(.1)	(.4)	(-1.2)*
O_2	7.8	16.1	25.2	13.5	7.4
	(.2)	(-.2)	(.0)	(-.9)	(1.5)*
O_3	1.3	2.8	4.3	2.3	1.3
	(-.1)	(.3)	(.4)	(-.1)	(-.1)
O_4	102.9	211.7	332.4	177.4	97.6
	(.4)	(-.4)	(-.1)	(.1)	(.2)

E_4

	A_1	A_2	A_3	A_4	A_5
O_1	4.5	10.8	21.1	10.2	6.4
	(-.6)	(.4)	(.9)	(-.6)	(-.5)
O_2	17.1	40.5	79.1	38.2	24.1
	(.5)	(-1.1)*	(.5)	(1.1)*	(-1.0)*
O_3	18.4	43.8	85.5	41.3	26.0
	(.2)	(2.3)*	(.1)	(-.8)	(-2.6)*
O_4	43.0	102.0	199.3	96.3	60.6
	(-.1)	(-1.0)*	(-.6)	(.1)	(2.2)*

Numbers in parentheses are Freeman–Tukey Deviates
*deviates larger than .90

etween aptitude, education, and occupation. We also want to determine whether
the data are in accordance with the fitted model. This leads us to consider
goodness-of-fit tests.

GOODNESS OF FIT TESTS

After one hypothesizes a structure for a contingency table it is important to ask
whether the observed table is in accord with the hypothesized model. We thus
test how well the observed counts are fitted by the estimated (or expected) cell
counts under the model. Although there are a number of different testing methods, some of which have advantages in special tables (e.g., Fisher's "exact" test
is given in Fisher, 1925), we seek a unified method compatible with testing in
log-linear structures. We use two tests based on the likelihood ratio statistic.

$$G^2 = 2 \sum_i 0_i \log(0_i/E_i) \tag{39}$$

and the more familiar Pearson statistic

$$X^2 = \sum_i \frac{(0_i - E_i)^2}{E_i} \tag{40}$$

where 0_i are the observed counts and E_i are the expected counts under the model
being tested and the summation is over all cells in the table. These statistics
provide convenient ways of testing a variety of hypotheses in contingency tables.
We use the following result about G^2 and X^2 to construct tests.

Theorem 3: Let 0_i be the observed counts generated by either Poisson or multinomial sampling, and let E_i be the MLE's of cell expectations under a parametric
model. Let t be the number of cells in the table, and let q be the number of
independent parameters in the model. If the model satisfies certain smoothness
criteria then both G^2 and X^2 are distributed approximately as chi-square random
variables with $(t - q)$ degrees of freedom (denoted by χ^2_{t-q}).

For a description of the smoothness criteria, see Birch (1964). These criteria
are satisfied for all hierarchical log-linear models and, in fact, for all models
considered in this chapter. It is important to realize that if the estimates are found
by a method other than maximum likelihood this result might not hold. See
Chernoff and Lehmann (1954) or Murthy and Gafarian (1970) for examples.
In a 2×2 table, under the hypothesis of independence of rows and columns,
there are four cells and three independent parameters: u, $u_{1(1)}$, and $u_{2(1)}$. Thus X^2
and G^2 are approximately distributed as χ^2_1 if the hypothesis is true. The 95th
percentile of χ^2_1 is $\chi^2_{1,.95} = 3.84$, so a test of level $\alpha = .05$ based on X^2 would

reject the hypothesis of independence when $X^2 > 3.84$. Similarly a test could be made using G^2. In large samples, X^2 and G^2 will be approximately equal but in small samples there may be larger differences. We discuss the small sample properties of these statistics below.

Because the degrees of freedom associated with the model being tested are $t - q$ we must make some adjustments when MLE's of all parameters do not exist. Adjustments are made whenever estimated counts are 0. As an example, consider a 3×2 table under the model of independence of rows and columns. The degrees of freedom are two if all MLE's exist. Suppose that the observed total for the first row is 0. MLE's for all cells don't exist because $\hat{m}_{11}$ and $\hat{m}_{12}$ are 0 using Equation 33. We can only test the fit of the model of independence if we eliminate these two cells from consideration. If we do that we are left with a 2×2 table and thus have one degree of freedom. In general we count the number of cells with 0 expected values, t_e, and the number of parameters, q_e, for which MLE's do not exist. The appropriate degrees of freedom are

$$DF = (t - t_e) - (q - q_e) = t - q + q_e - t_e. \tag{41}$$

We can usually determine q_e by looking at the minimal configurations and counting one parameter for each marginal total which is 0. This will not always give the correct degrees of freedom in the "pathological" situations alluded to earlier. In these cases care must be taken in counting q_e. One is alerted to these situations when IPF converges to a 0 cell estimate and none of the configuration totals including this cell are 0.

The likelihood ratio statistic G^2 has an advantage over X^2 in that it can be partitioned to test nested hypotheses. We now give an example of a nested set of hypotheses. Consider a three-dimensional table and let the first model be

$$\log m_{ijk} = u + u_{1(i)} + u_{2(j)} + u_{3(k)} + u_{12(ij)} + u_{13(ik)} \tag{42}$$

and the second model is

$$\log m_{ijk} = u + u_{1(i)} + u_{2(j)} + u_{3(k)} + u_{12(ij)}. \tag{43}$$

Note that model 2 is a special case of model 1 because all of the parameters in model 2 are also included in model 1. We say that model 2 is nested within model 1. Let df_1 and df_2 be the degrees of freedom associated with models 1 and 2 respectively. Let G_1^2 and G_2^2 be the likelihood ratio statistics for testing models 1 and 2. Define

$$G_{2|1}^2 = G_2^2 - G_1^2. \tag{44}$$

If model 2 is correct (implying model 1 is also correct) then $G_{2|1}^2$ is approximately distributed as $\chi^2(df_2 - df_1)$. We can express $G_{2|1}^2$ as

$$G_{2|1}^2 = 2 \sum_i \hat{m}_i^{(1)} \log \frac{\hat{m}_i^{(1)}}{\hat{m}_i^{(2)}}, \tag{45}$$

TABLE 9.10
Chi-square Values for the Data
Presented in Table 9.8

Model	DF	X^2	G^2
[12],[13],[23]	36	23.6	25.1
[12],[23]	48	48.0	50.9
[12],[13]	45	1301.1	1142.2
[13],[23]	48	184.6	190.8
[12],[3]	57	1336.8	1179.6
[13],[2]	57	1424.1	1319.7
[23],[1]	60	226.7	228.2
[1],[2],[3]	69	1519.8	1357.0

where $\hat{m}_i^{(j)}$ is the MLE in cell i under model j for $j = 1, 2$. A test based on $G^2_{2|1}$ gives an answer to the question "is model 2 tenable given that we believe model 1 is true?"

We now illustrate the use of goodness-of-fit tests in an analysis of the data given in Table 9.8. Table 9.10 gives results of all hierarchical models of interest. Note that there are some large discrepancies between X^2 and G^2, but these are only in cases where both statistics are large. With the exception of the first two models both X^2 and G^2 are larger than the 99.5 percentile of the respective chi-square distributions. Thus using either statistic leads us to reject these models as candidates for the underlying structure of the model. The chi-square values for the first two models are all less than the 75th quartiles of the corresponding chi-square distributions, which indicates a very good fit. Because the model {[12], [23]} is a subset of {[12], [13], [23]}, we can look at the difference of G^2 values to measure the difference in fit between the two models. $G^2_{2|1} = 25.8$ which is not quite significant at the .01 level, using χ^2_{12} as the appropriate distribution. This tells us that, assuming the model of no second order interaction holds, there is some evidence that aptitude and occupation are not independent given level of education. At this point in the analysis we would consider the no second order interaction model to provide the best fit. The conditional independence model also fits well and because it has twelve fewer parameters it may provide a more parsimonious description of the data.

The analysis up to this point has been based upon goodness-of-fit statistics to measure the overall fit of a model. It may be that a model provides a good fit to most of the cells in the table but a small number of poorly fitted cells inflate the values of X^2 and G^2. A study of the fit of the model in individual cells may give us an understanding of the structure well beyond that which is obtained only by a comparison of X^2 or G^2 values. The most obvious measure of fit in a cell is the cell residual

$$r_i = x_i - \hat{m}_i. \qquad (46)$$

This is not very helpful because we have no yardstick for deciding how large cell residual should be. There are two "standardized" cell residuals we conside components of X^2

$$s_i = \frac{x_i - \hat{m}_i}{\sqrt{\hat{m}_i}} \tag{4}$$

and Freeman–Tukey deviates

$$t_i = \sqrt{x_i} + \sqrt{x_i + 1} - \sqrt{4\hat{m}_i + 1}. \tag{4}$$

If the model is the true model, then both s_i and t_i are normally distributed in larg samples. Both Σs_i^2 and Σt_i^2 are approximately distributed as chi-squares wit degrees of freedom appropriate for the model being fitted. Although residuals i different cells are not independent we can get a rough means of detecting larg residuals by taking, let us say, the 95th percentile of the chi-square distributic and dividing it by the number of cells in the table, as suggested by Bishop Fienberg, and Holland (1975). A cell may be considered an outlier if t_i^2 or s_i^2 larger than this number. We prefer to use t_i instead of s_i because they have bette properties in small samples. See Freeman and Tukey (1950) for a comparison c different transformations of counts.

We return now to Table 9.9 and focus on the Freeman–Tukey deviates for th model that postulates the independence of occupation and aptitude given a pe sons' educational level. Since the model has 48 degrees of freedom and $\chi^2_{48,.95}$ 65.4, a deviate may be considered large if it exceeds .90 in absolute value. Now .90 = $\sqrt{65.4/80}$. We will declare too many cells to be outliers using th procedure because we ignored the problem of selection bias (picking the large residuals to test) but, nevertheless, we have a means of seeing where the mod fits well and where it doesn't. An asterisk marks the cells with deviates large than .90. It is apparent now that the model fits well in the first three education levels but not in the fourth. This is reasonable since a person in this categor consisting of people with graduate education, would have chosen his occupatic to fit his aptitude. If we only consider the other three levels of education then th conditional independence model has a G^2 of 25.2 with 36 degrees of freedo whereas the no second order interaction model has a G^2 of 14.3 with 24 degree of freedom. Now the difference in G^2 for the two models is 10.9 with 12 degree of freedom. Occupation and aptitude do appear to be independent for each of th first three levels of education. We have seen that by eliminating certain cells w can consider different models for different parts of the table. In the next sectic we will consider other ways of fitting models to parts of a table.

We conclude with a brief discussion of the validity of the chi-square appro: imation to the distributions of X^2 and G^2. As a general rule the approximation good when all cell expectations are "large," but there has been conflicting ev dence as to what constitutes a large expectation. Many authors (e.g., Cochra 1952), consider five to be a large expected value. Many researchers consid ive to be the smallest cell expectation allowable in a table if the approximation is to be good.

New evidence by Larntz (1978) shows that this restriction is much too conservative. Larntz's main findings are:

1. The true significance level using X^2 is well approximated by the chi-square distribution when all cell expectations are greater than one.

2. When cell expectations are small (less than 1.5), using chi-square to approximate the distribution of G^2 yields a conservative test.

3. For moderate cell expectations, between 1.5 and 4.0, using G^2 and the chi-square distribution yields a test with a much higher significance level than that desired (i.e., too many results are declared significant).

Larntz shows that the large values of G^2 result mainly from cells with small counts but moderate expected values. In these cases one should be careful about using G^2.

As far as yielding the proper significance levels, X^2 agrees with the chi-square approximation much more closely as does G^2, so for tables with many cell expectations smaller than four one should be cautious about using G^2. When most cells have larger expected values, G^2 behaves well and also has the advantage of yielding conditional tests of nested hypotheses as outlined in this section.

ANALYZING INCOMPLETE TABLES

Up until this point our analysis of contingency tables has assumed that all cells have positive expected counts. There are often situations in which there is a zero probability of observing responses in certain cells. For example, in a cross-classification of people by ethnic group and organizational membership one would assume the expected number of Black Ku Klux Klan members to be zero. We refer to such cells as *structural zeros* and tables containing such cells are called *incomplete tables*. Goodman (1968) also refers to them as *truncated tables*.

The class of hierarchical models that we have defined was developed to describe complete tables but can easily be generalized to incomplete tables. The essential points can be illustrated in a two-dimensional table. Let ℓ be the set of cells that are structural zeros. The saturated model for the cells with positive expectations is

$$\log m_{ij} = u + u_{1(i)} + u_{2(j)} + u_{12(ij)}. \tag{49}$$

If we define $u_{12(ij)} = 0$ if $(i, j) \in \mathcal{I}$ the u-terms satisfy the usual constraints

$$\sum_i u_{1(i)} = \sum_j u_{2(j)} = \sum_i u_{12(ij)} = \sum_j u_{12(ij)} = 0. \tag{50}$$

Goodman (1968) defines the model of quasi-independence as the multiplicative model

$$m_{ij} = a_i b_j, \text{ for } (i, j) \in \mathcal{I}. \tag{5}$$

Thus for the cells with positive expectations the cell probabilities are the product of a row effect and a column effect. This model can also be expressed by the log linear model

$$\log m_{ij} = u + u_{1(i)} + u_{2(j)}, \text{ for } (i, j) \in \mathcal{I} \tag{5}$$

(i.e., for the complete part of the table we have the usual log-linear model). Table 9.11(a) presents a data set previously analyzed by Goodman (1968) and Kastenbaum (1958). There are two structural zeros which are denoted by the "lethal" cells. The structure of the table is more easily understood by reordering the columns to obtain Table 9.11(b). The two columns on the right form a complete × 2 table while the first two columns form a 2 × 2 table with 0 probability of being on the diagonal. We see below that a test for quasi-independence is based on only the "complete" part of the table.

MLE's under quasi-independence and other quasi log-linear models in contingency tables can be obtained by a simple modification of IPF. Instead of taking initial cell estimates to be all ones, we start with zeros in the structural zero cells and ones in the remaining cells. If MLE's exist, the IPF scheme will always converge to the correct estimates but the speed of convergence is generally slower than in complete tables. Table 9.12 gives MLE's for the quasi-independence model fit to the data of Table 9.11(b). It took eight cycles of IPF reach these estimates. Note that for the two left columns the fitted values equal

TABLE 9.11(a)
Numbers of Progeny From Mating Translocation-Bearing Males
to Attached-X Females (Goodman, 1968)

Female Type	Male Sperm Type			
	AB	A'B'	A'B	AB
Female with Y chromosome	1413	1029	lethal	22
Female with a proximal segment of the translocation	lethal	548	346	12

TABLE 9.11(b)
A Reordering of the Columns of Table 9.11(a)

Female Type	Male Sperm Type			
	A'B	AB	A'B'	A
Female with Y chromosome	lethal	1413	1029	22
Female with a proximal segment of the translocation	346	lethal	548	12

TABLE 9.12
Maximum Likelihood Estimates Under Quasi-Independence
in Table 9.11(b)

		Male Sperm Type		
?male Type	A'B	AB	A'B'	AB'
?male with Y chromosome	—	1413	1010.03	2258.97
?male with a proximal segment of the translocation	346	—	566.97	1268.03

?e observed counts while the remaining MLE's are the MLE's for the model of ?dependence fit to the 2×2 table in the right two columns.

In order to test the fit of quasi log-linear models we can again appeal to the ?ct that X^2 and G^2 have approximately chi-square distributions if the model is ?rrect. The structural zeros contribute nothing to X^2 or G^2. It remains to com-?te the degrees of freedom associated with a quasi log-linear model. The basic ?le still holds: Count the number of fitted cells and subtract the number of ?rameters estimated. Thus we take the number of degrees of freedom for the ?rresponding complete table and subtract t_e, the number of structural zeros. If ?y margins corresponding to the minimal configurations are structural zeros we ?d these to get q_e, the number of inestimable parameters. With these definitions ?e degrees of freedom are given by Equation 41. When there are also sampling ?ros that produce zero marginal totals then we must also include them in ?justing the degrees of freedom. In Table 9.12 t_e is 2 so the adjusted degrees of ?eedom are $3 - 2 = 1$, which corresponds to the 2×2 subtable used to test ?dependence.

Rules for detecting when MLE's exist are given by Fienberg (1970). These ?les, as well as those for counting degrees of freedom, are based on the assump-?n that the table is inseparable. Inseparability means basically that the table ?nnot be split apart. Table 9.13(a) is an example of a separable table and Table ?.13(b) illustrates exactly why it is separable. The table is actually two individual ?bles, one 2×4 table and one 2×5 table. With this arrangement we see that, ?r testing quasi-independence, there are three degrees of freedom from one table ?d four degrees of freedom from the other. Hence the correct degrees of free-?m for the quasi-independence model is seven. If we use Expression 41 without ?alizing that the table is separable we take the usual degrees of freedom, 27, and ?btract $t_e = 18$, which leaves nine degrees of freedom. This example serves as a ?arning that care must be taken in counting degrees of freedom in incomplete ?bles. See Bishop, Fienberg, and Holland (1975) for a complete discussion of ?parability and degrees of freedom.

Incomplete tables are useful even when certain cells have nonzero expecta-?ns but we wish to fit a log-linear model only to the portion of the table which ?cludes certain cells. We illustrate an application of this idea to the data in Table

TABLE 9.13(a)
Relationship Between Radial Asymmetry and Locular Composition
in Staphylea (Bishop, Fienberg, & Holland, 1975)

Locular	Coefficient of Radial Asymmetry								
Composition	0.00	0.47	0.82	0.94	1.25	1.41	1.63	1.70	1.8
3 even, 0 odd	462	—	—	130	—	—	2	—	1
2 even, 1 odd	—	614	138	—	21	14	—	1	—
1 even, 2 odd	—	443	95	—	22	8	—	5	—
0 even, 3 odd	103	—	—	35	—	—	1	—	0

TABLE 9.13(b)
Rearrangement of Table 9.13(a)

Locular	Coefficient of Radial Asymmetry								
Composition	0.00	0.94	1.63	1.89	0.47	0.82	1.25	1.41	1.7
3 even, 0 odd	462	130	2	1	—	—	—	—	—
0 even, 3 odd	103	35	11	0	—	—	—	—	—
2 even, 1 odd	—	—	—	—	614	138	21	14	1
1 even, 2 odd	—	—	—	—	443	95	22	8	5

9.8. For the data in Table 9.8 it is reasonable to consider the 10 cells correspond
ing to E_1, E_2, and 0_3 to be structural zeros. People in these cells are teachers wh
are not college graduates. Despite the fact that there are observed counts in som
of these 10 cells we want to consider models that ignore them.

Table 9.14 gives the values of G^2 for all hierarchical models fitted to thi
modification of Table 9.8. We are led to the same two models as before. A
before, after looking at residuals, the model of quasi-independence of occupatio
and aptitude given education is seen to fit well. One could analyze the dat

TABLE 9.14
Values of G^2 for the Data of Table 9.8
with Cells in E_1, E_2, O_3
Considered Structural Zeros

Model	DF	G^2
[12],[13],[23]	28	17.3
[12],[23]	40	41.8
[12],[13]	35	867.3
[13],[23]	40	183.7
[12],[3]	47	904.2
[13],[2]	47	1046.1
[23],[1]	52	219.1
[1],[2],[3]	59	1081.6

urther by treating some of the poorly fitted cells at level E_4 as structural zeros out we do not pursue this here.

Another example of using the ideas of incomplete tables to ignore certain cells arises in the analysis of social mobility tables. If we cross-classify people according to the person's status and his father's status, we may choose to ignore people who have the same status as their father. Goodman (1968) provides an example of the analysis of such a table.

PATH ANALYSIS IN CONTINGENCY TABLES

Social science researchers have been very interested in developing multiple-equation models to describe systems in which variables have simultaneous effects on each other. These models are usually referred to as *structural equations models* and the attendant analysis is called *path analysis* because it seeks to determine the direction of any causal relationships. Duncan (1975) provides an excellent reference for this subject.

Until very recently, path analysis has been restricted to situations where the response variables were continuous. In order to form structural equation models we need a way to describe the relationship between explanatory variables and a response variable when the variables are discrete. For convenience we assume that the response variable is dichotomous. Suppose that variables 1 and 2 are the explanatory variables (or independent variables) and variable 3 is the response (or dependent variable). We define the logit for the (i, j)th level of variables 1 and 2 by

$$\text{logit}(i,j) = \log \frac{m_{ij1}}{m_{ij2}}. \tag{53}$$

The most general model for the effect of variables 1 and 2 is

$$\text{logit}(i, j) = v + v_{1(i)} + v_{2(j)} + v_{12(ij)} \tag{54}$$

where the v-terms satisfy the usual constraints of summing to zero over any of their indices. The relationship in Equation 54 says that the conditional probability of being in level 1 of variable 3 is affected by variable 1, variable 2, and by a joint effect of both variables.

A logit model can always be derived from a log-linear model for the full contingency table. Thus in the three-dimensional table we are considering, the saturated model

$$\log m_{ijk} = u + u_{1(i)} + u_{2(j)} + u_{3(k)} + u_{12(ij)} + u_{13(ik)}$$
$$+ u_{23(jk)} + u_{123(ijk)} \tag{55}$$

leads directly to the logit model in Equation 54 if we express $(\log m_{ij1} - \log m_{ij})$ as a function of u-terms. The relationship between the u-terms and v-terms is

$$v = 2u_{3(1)}; \quad v_{1(1)} = 2u_{13(11)}; \quad v_{2(1)} = 2u_{23(11)}; \quad v_{12(11)} = 2u_{123(111)}. \quad (5\text{6})$$

The relationship between the log-linear model and the logit model is comparable to the relationship between the joint distribution of two continuous variables and the regression model for the response variable. Note that there may be more than one possible log-linear model yielding the same logit model because the logit model does not put any restrictions on the relationship between variables 1 and 2.

Goodman (1973) uses logit models to describe causal relationships when certain variables can be considered as posterior to others. Table 9.15 contains an example of Coleman (1964) which was analyzed by Goodman (1973). School boys were interviewed at two points in time and were asked about their conception of the "leading crowd" ($+$ in, $-$ out) and their attitude toward the "leading crowd" ($+$, $-$). Variables A and B measure membership and attitude toward the leading crowd, respectively, at the time of the first interview, while C and D measure these attributes at the time of the second interview.

Variables A and B precede variable C and, if we assume that membership determines attitude, we can assume that C precedes D. We thus have a recursive model. We begin by looking at logit models for the effect of A and B on C. We do this by fitting log-linear models to the marginal table consisting of variables A, B, and C. Because we treat A and B as joint explanatory variables we only consider models which contain an AB interaction. The only model that fits well is $[AB]$, $[AC]$, $[BC]$ which has $G^2 = .02$ with one degree of freedom. This corresponds to the logit model

$$\text{logit}_C(i, j) = v + v_{1(i)} + v_{2(j)}. \quad (5\text{7})$$

We next model the effect of ABC on D. To do this we consider models for the four-dimensional table that include the ABC interaction. There are two models that fit well. The model with configurations $[ABC]$, $[AD]$, $[BD]$, $[CD]$ has $G^2 = 1.19$ while the model with configurations $[ABC]$, $[BD]$, $[CD]$ has $G^2 = 4.04$. We

TABLE 9.15
Cross-Classification of 3398 Schoolboys with Respect to Membership
in and Attitude Toward the "Leading Crowd" (Coleman, 1964)

First Interview		Membership	Second Interview			
			+	+	−	−
Membership	Attitude	Attitude	+	−	+	−
+	+		458	140	110	4█
+	−		171	182	56	8█
−	+		184	75	531	28█
−	−		85	97	338	55█

TABLE 9.16
Expected Values for the Logit Model in Expression

Membership	Attitude	Membership (2nd interview) +	−
+	+	598.87	158.13
+	−	352.13	143.87
−	+	258.13	812.87
−	−	182.87	891.13

:fer to these as models 1 and 2, respectively. Since $G_2^2 - G_1^2 = 2.85$ is not
gnificant with one degree of freedom, Goodman chooses model 2 as the best
tting model. We agree with his choice but consider model 1 further. Note that
ie logit model defined by model 1 is

$$\text{logit}_D(i, j, k) = w + w_{1(i)} + w_{2(j)} + w_{3(k)}. \tag{58}$$

We now combine the relationships of Equations 57 and 58 to get expected
alues for the original table. Table 9.16 gives the expected values in the marginal
ible ABC given by Equation 57. Table 9.17 gives the conditional probability of
aving a positive attitude towards the "leading crowd" given the levels of ABC as
efined by the fitted model in Equation 58. Combining the marginal and condi-
onal probabilities we obtain the expected counts under the recursive model.
his type of modeling is of interest because the expected counts in Table 9.18 do
ot correspond to any single log-linear model fitted to Table 9.15. Note that the
kelihood ratio statistic, G^2, for the fit of Table 9.18 is $G^2 = 1.21$ which is the
im of the respective G^2 for each of the logit models in Equations 57 and 58.

The path diagram for this pair of logit models is given in Table 9.19(a). A and
each have an effect on C, and D is related to each of A, B, and C. Table 9.19(b)
 the path diagram for the model selected by Goodman. It differs only in that A
oes not have a direct effect on D.

We did not encounter any problems in separating causal effects for the data of
able 9.15 because we postulated a recursive model. By assuming C preceded D
/e could estimate the effect of C on D. If one assumed that C and D were
imultaneously endogenous variables then it would not be possible to separate
ie effect of C on D from the effect of D on C. This is because the relationship

TABLE 9.17
Conditional Probabilities of Positive Attitude Using Expression

		Membership +	+	−	−
		Attitude +	−	+	−
1embership at	+	.756	.494	.727	.456
2nd interview)	−	.689	.411	.656	.374

TABLE 9.18
Expected Counts for the Recursive System Defined by Equations 57 and 58

First Interview		Membership	Second Interview			
Membership	Attitude	Attitude	+ +	+ −	− +	− −
+	+		453.02	145.85	109.02	49.11
+	−		173.86	178.27	59.09	279.67
−	+		187.73	70.39	533.20	279.67
−	−		83.36	99.51	333.66	557.47

TABLE 9.19
Path Diagrams for Two Recursive Models
for Table 9.15

between C and D is a function of a cross-product ratio, which is symmetric in both variables. Brier (1978) discusses the problems arising from structural equation models in contingency tables. Although it is not possible to use logit models in exactly the same fashion as regression models they are very useful in interpreting relationships, as exhibited here.

OTHER APPLICATIONS OF THE METHODOLOGY OF LOG-LINEAR MODELS

In the preceding sections we have developed the basic techniques for using log-linear models to analyze complete or incomplete contingency tables. It would be impossible here to describe all of the possible uses of log-linear models but we briefly describe some interesting and important applications that indicate the power and flexibility of the methods.

There are often situations in which the row and column variables have the same categorization. We have seen one example already in the previous section where we classified students according to their attitude during the first interview and their attitude during the second interview. We refer to these as *square tables*. When the number of categories of each variable is three or more there are interesting models that we can use to describe the table.

TABLE 9.20
Unaided Distance Vision of 7477 Women Aged 30–39

Right Eye Grade	Left Eye Grade			
	(1)	*(2)*	*(3)*	*(4)*
(1)	1520	266	124	66
(2)	234	1512	432	78
(3)	117	362	1772	205
(4)	36	82	179	492

Note: (1) is highest rating.

The data in Table 9.20 was studied by Stuart (1953) and further analyzed by Bishop, Fienberg, and Holland (1975). The model of symmetry states that

$$m_{ij} = m_{ji} \text{ for all } i, j \qquad (59)$$

(i.e., the cell expectations are symmetric about the diagonal of the table). Note that symmetry puts no restriction on the diagonal cell expectations. This model implies that the right and left eyes are interchangeable as far as vision properties go. Symmetry can be defined by the log-linear model

$$\log m_{ij} = u + u_{1(i)} + u_{1(j)} + u_{12(ij)} \qquad (60)$$

where

$$u_{12(ij)} = u_{12(ji)}. \qquad (61)$$

Another hypothesis of interest is that the marginal probabilities are the same for both right and left eyes, that is,

$$m_{i+} = m_{+i} \text{ for all } i. \qquad (62)$$

This hypothesis, called *marginal homogeneity*, cannot be defined in terms of a log-linear model for a square table. We can, however, define the model of quasi-symmetry in terms of a log-liner model, and then quasi-symmetry together with marginal homogeneity implies complete symmetry in the table. *Quasi-symmetry* is defined by

$$\log m_{ij} = u + u_{1(i)} + u_{2(j)} + u_{12(ij)} \qquad (63)$$

where

$$u_{12(ij)} = u_{12(ji)}. \qquad (64)$$

Thus the interaction terms are symmetric in the quasi-symmetry model.

For the data in Table 9.20, Bishop, Fienberg, and Holland conclude that quasi-symmetry holds but that neither symmetry nor marginal homogeneity do. They also consider some generalizations, which they call adjusted symmetry and adjusted quasi-symmetry, which provide interesting ways of interpreting the vision data.

Log-linear models can also be used to analyze paired comparison experiments. In these experiments t items are to be compared in pairs by a set of judges. Bradley and Terry (1952) formulated a model for this situation which bears their name. The Bradley–Terry model states that the probability of item i being rated better than item j is given by

$$P(i \geq j) = \frac{\pi_i}{\pi_i + \pi_j}, \; i \neq j \tag{65}$$

where $\pi_i \geq 0$ for all i and the π_i sum to one over the t items. The model also assumes that all ratings, whether by the same or different judges, are independent. Bradley and Terry use their model without appealing to log-linear methodology.

Fienberg and Larntz (1976) show that the Bradley–Terry model can be viewed as either a quasi-symmetry model or as a quasi-independence model, depending on which way we arrange the counts. Let x_{ij} be the number of times item i is preferred to item j and let n_{ij} be the number of times items i and j are compared. Note that

$$x_{ij} + x_{ji} = n_{ij}. \tag{66}$$

For the arrangement in Table 9.21(a), Fienberg and Larntz show that the Bradley–Terry model is equivalent to quasi-symmetry. In Table 9.21(b) the columns correspond to the three possible comparisons among the three items. In general this arrangement would have $\binom{t}{2}$ columns. Quasi-independence this table is also equivalent to the Bradley–Terry model.

Because the Bradley–Terry model is equivalent to a log-linear model we can appeal to the general theory regarding existence and uniqueness of MLE's. We can also use iterative proportional fitting to obtain the MLE's. Fienberg and Larntz also show how to build log-linear models for extensions of the simple paired comparison model. Davidson and Farquhar (1976) give a bibliography of paired comparison methods.

TABLE 9.21
Two Possible Arrangements of Paired Comparison Data
with Three Items

		(a) Against					(b) Comparison		
		I_1	I_2	I_3			1	2	3
For	I_1	—	X_{12}	X_{13}	Pre-	I_1	X_{12}	X_{13}	—
	I_2	X_{21}	—	X_{23}	ferred	I_2	X_{21}	—	X_{23}
	I_3	X_{31}	X_{32}	—	Item	I_3	—	X_{31}	X_{32}

Larntz and Weisberg (1976) use log-linear models to study the formation of dyads. A *dyad* consists of two individuals pairing in such a way that the pair (i, j) cannot be distinguished from the pair (j, i). A dyad cannot consist of an individual paired with itself. The dyad counts can thus be given as a t × t upper triangular contingency table. Table 9.22, reproduced from Larntz and Weisberg (1976), gives the number of times that dyads were formed among $t = 6$ U.S. Navy recruits. An observer in the bunkhouse recorded the formation of dyad (i, j) whenever the ith recruit was seen talking to the jth recruit.

Larntz and Weisberg first fit a model that assumes that dyads are formed independently and at random. They show that this is equivalent to quasi-independence fit to Table 9.22. Using IPF, MLE's are obtained for Table 9.22 and, not surprisingly, the independence model does not fit well. They found that by fitting one extra parameter to account for the racial composition of the recruits and two extra parameters for the proximity of bunks they could adequately describe the dyad formation. These models were also log-linear in nature and were estimated via IPF.

FURTHER READINGS REFERENCES

Because we have only been able to present an introduction to the analysis of discrete data we list a number of general sources as well as references for some specific topics that we have not mentioned.

For a comprehensive treatment of categorical data analysis the text by Bishop, Fienberg, and Holland (1975) is strongly recommended. An extensive bibliography can also be found there. Cox (1970) emphasizes models for dichotomous variables. For those with a strong mathematical background, Haberman (1974) presents a rigorous theoretical development of the log-linear model. Gokhale and Kullback (1978) present an information-theoretic approach. Other general references are Fienberg (1977) and Plackett (1974). The recently collected papers of Goodman (1978), *Analyzing Qualitative/Categorical Data,* would be of special interest to social scientists.

TABLE 9.22
Dyads Formed Between Six Naval Recruits
(Larntz & Weisberg, 1976)

Subject Number	1	2	3	4	5	6
1		41	10	5	6	3
2			9	6	6	3
3				42	13	5
4					15	7
5						14
6						

One approach to the analysis of categorical data that we have not discussed is the method of weighted least squares, as developed by Grizzle, Starmer, and Koch (1969). In this methodology, a transformation of the cell probabilities is made so that the "usual" linear model, as applied to continuous data, holds, approximately, for this transformed data. This methodology has the advantage of being very flexible but has some shortcomings in comparison with maximum likelihood techniques.

We have not talked at all about defining or making inferences about measures of association in contingency tables. The series of papers by Goodman and Kruskal (1954, 1959, 1963, 1972) should be referred to here. For material on the related topic of measures of agreement see Cohen (1960) or Lin (1974). We have not discussed tables where there is an ordering of the categories of certain variables. Haberman (1974a) and Williams and Grizzle (1972) discuss this from the log-linear and weighted least squares approaches, respectively. There has recently been interest in the analysis of contingency tables arising from cluster or stratified sampling schemes. Altham (1976), Brier (1979), and Cohen (1976) discuss some aspects of this problem.

REFERENCES

Altham, P. M. E. (1976). Discrete variable analysis for individuals grouped into families. *Biometrika, 63*, 263–269.

Birch, M. W. (1963). Maximum likelihood in three-way contingency tables. *Journal of the Royal Statistical Society*, Series B, *25*, 220–233.

Birch, M. W. (1964). A new proof of the Pearson-Fisher theorem. *Annals of Mathematical Statistics, 35*, 718–724.

Bishop, Y. M. M., Fienberg, S. E., & Holland, P. W. (1975). *Discrete multivariate analysis: Theory and practice*. Cambridge, MA: MIT Press.

Bradley, R. A., & Terry, M. E. (1952). Rank analysis of incomplete block designs. I. The method of paired comparisons. *Biometrika, 39*, 324–345.

Brier, S. S. (1979). The utility of systems of simultaneous logistic response equations. In K. F. Schuessler (Ed.), *Sociological methodology*. San Francisco: Jossey-Bass.

Brier, S. S. (1979). *Categorical data models for complex sampling schemes*. Unpublished doctoral dissertation, School of Statistics, University of Minnesota.

Chernoff, H., & Lehmann, E. L. (1954). The use of maximum likelihood estimates in χ^2 tests for goodness of fit. *Annals of Mathematical Statistics, 25*, 579–586.

Cochran, W. (1952). The χ^2 test of goodness of fit. *Annals of Mathematical Statistics, 23*, 315–345.

Cohen, J. (1960). A coefficient of agreement for nominal scales. *Educational and Psychological Measurement, 20*, 37–46.

Cohen, J. (1976). The distribution of the chi-squared statistic under clustered sampling from contingency tables. *Journal of the American Statistical Association, 71*, 665–670.

Coleman, J. S. (1964). *Introduction to mathematical sociology*. New York: Free Press.

Cox, D. R. (1970). *The analysis of binary data*. London: Methuen.

Davidson, R. R., & Farquhar, P. H. (1976). A bibliography on the method of paired comparisons. *Biometrics, 32*, 233–240.

Deming, W. E., & Stephan, F. F. (1940). On a least squares adjustment of a sampled frequency table when the expected marginal totals are known. *Annals of Mathematical Statistics, 11,* 427–444.

Duncan, O. D. (1975). *Structural equations models.* New York: Academic Press.

Dyke, G. V., & Patterson, H. D. (1952). Analysis of factorial arrangements when the data are proportions. *Biometrics, 8,* 1–12.

Fienberg, S. E. (1970). An iterative procedure for estimation in contingency tables. *Annals of Mathematical Statistices, 41,* 907–917.

Fienberg, S. E. (1977). *The analysis of cross-classified categorical data.* Cambridge, MA: MIT Press.

Fienberg, S. E., & Larntz, K. (1976). Log linear representation for paired and multiple comparison models. *Biometrika, 63,* 245–254.

Fisher, R. A. (1925). *Statistical methods for research workers.* New York: Macmillan.

Freeman, M. F., & Tukey, J. W. (1950). Transformations related to the angular and the square root. *Annals of Mathematical Statistics, 21,* 607–611.

Gokhale, D. V., & Kullback, S. (1978). *The information in contingency tables.* New York: Marcel Dekker.

Goodman, L. A. (1968). The analysis of cross-classified data: independence, quasi-independence, and interaction in contingency tables with or without missing cells. *Journal of the American Statistical Association, 63,* 1091–1131.

Goodman, L. A. (1973). The analysis of multidimensional contingency tables when some variables are posterior to others: A modified path analysis approach. *Biometrika, 60,* 179–192.

Goodman, L. A. (1978). *Analyzing qualitative/categorical data: Log-linear models and latent structure analysis* (J. Magidson, Ed.). Cambridge, MA: Abt Books.

Goodman, L. A., & Kruskal, W. H. (1954). Measures of association for cross-classifications. *Journal of the American Statistical Association, 49,* 732–764.

Goodman, L. A., & Kruskal, W. H. (1959). Measures of association for cross-classifications. II: Further discussion and references. *Journal of the American Statistical Association, 54,* 123–163.

Goodman, L. A., & Kruskal, W. H. (1963). Measures of association for cross-classifications, III: Approximate sampling theory. *Journal of the American Statistical Association, 58,* 310–364.

Goodman, L. A., & Kruskal, W. H. (1972). Measures of association for cross-classifications, IV: Simplification of asymptotic variances. *Journal of the American Statistical Association, 67,* 415–421.

Grizzle, J. E., Starmer, C. F., & Koch, G. G. (1969). Analysis of categorical data by linear models. *Biometrics, 25,* 489–504.

Haberman, S. J. (1974). *The analysis of frequency data.* Chicago: University of Chicago Press.

Haberman, S. J. (1974a). Loglinear models for frequency tables with ordered classifications. *Biometrics, 30,* 589–600.

Johnson, N. L., & Kotz, S. (1969). *Discrete distributions.* New York: Wiley.

Kastenbaum, M. A. (1958). Estimation of relative frequencies of four sperm types in Drosophila melanogaster. *Biometrics, 14,* 223–228.

Larntz, K. (1978). Small sample comparisons of exact levels for chi-squared goodness-of-fit statistics. *Journal of the American Statistical Association, 73,* 253–263.

Larntz, K., & Weisberg, S. (1976). Multiplicative models for dyad formation. *Journal of the American Statistical Association, 71,* 455–461.

Lee, S. K. (1977). On the asymptotic variances of $\hat{u}$ terms in log linear models of multidimensional contingency tables. *Journal of the American Statistical Association, 72,* 412–419.

Lin, Y. S. (1974). *Statistical measurements of agreement.* Unpublished doctoral dissertation, School of Statistics, University of Minnesota.

Murthy, V. K., & Gafarian, A. V. (1970). Limiting distributions of some variations of the chi-square statistics. *Annals of Mathematical Statistics, 41,* 188–194.

Nerlove, M., & Press, S. J. (1976). *Multivariate log-linear probability models for the analysis qualitative data*. Discussion paper no. 1, Center for Statistics and Probability, Northweste University.

Plackett, R. L. (1974). *The analysis of categorical data*. London: Griffin.

Rao, C. R. (1965). *Linear statistical inference and its applications*. New York: Wiley.

Stuart, A. (1953). The estimation and comparison of strengths of association in contingency table *Biometrika, 40,* 105–110.

Williams, O. D., & Grizzle, J. E. (1972). Contingency tables having ordered response categorie *Journal of the American Statistical Association, 67,* 55–63.

10 On the Use and Misuse of Chi-Square

Kevin L. Delucchi
Developmental Studies Center, San Ramon, California

One of the most useful tools available to any data analyst—especially one who deals with social science data—is Pearson's statistic known as chi-square. Its usefulness stems primarily from the fact that much of the data collected by social scientists is categorical in nature—whether ordered or unordered. Not only are variables such as sex, school, ethnicity, and experimental group categorical, but one can argue that many other measures are best, that is, conservatively, analyzed by being treated as categorical variables. This would include, for example, the ubiquitous Likert-type item often found in questionnaires and other measures.

As well as being applicable in many common analysis situations, the chi-square statistic is also quite widely known, relatively easy to compute, and available on most computer packages of statistical software. Like the good-natured nextdoor neighbor who always lends a hand without complaining, however, the chi-square statistic is easy to take for granted and easy to misuse.

The title of this chapter comes from a 1949 landmark article by Lewis and Burke entitled "The Use and Misuse of the Chi-Square Test," which appeared in *Psychological Bulletin*. The purpose of their article was to counteract the improper use of this statistic by researchers in the behavioral sciences. It addressed nine major sources of error, cited examples from the literature to illustrate these points, and caused a stir among practicing researchers. The Lewis and Burke paper was followed by several responses (Edwards, 1950; Pastore, 1950; Peters, 1950) and a rejoinder by Lewis and Burke (1950).

Since then, use of the chi-square statistic among social scientists has increased, a great deal of research has been conducted on its behavior under a variety of conditions, and several methods have been developed to handle some

of the problems cited by Lewis and Burke. Several years ago I reviewed developments since Lewis and Burke's original paper (Delucchi, 1983). In this chapter, I
provide a further update, reviewing those common errors, providing examples of
some of them, and discussing supplementary and complementary procedures for
the analysis of data commonly analyzed with Pearson's chi-square statistic.

THE USE OF CHI-SQUARE

To begin, let me remind the reader that there is a distinction between Pearson's
chi-square statistic (Pearson, 1900) and the chi-square distribution. The former is
a number calculated from data, which is compared to the latter, a family of
theoretical distributions defined by their degrees of freedom. Unless stated otherwise, the phrase *chi-square* refers here to the computed statistic, symbolized by
X^2, as opposed to the Greek letter chi (χ), which is used to denote the distribution.

As originally proposed by Pearson, the statistic is based on comparing the
observed frequencies in a contingency table with those frequencies that would be
expected under the hypothesis of no association when testing for independence
between two variables in the single sample model, or with those expected under
the hypothesis of homogeneity of distributions in the multiple sample model.

Table 10.1 illustrates the case of a 2 × 3 contingency table.[1] In this example
we have the responses of 79 teachers from two groups of schools. Teachers at one
group of schools are involved in an educational intervention, whereas those in
the other school are serving as a control group. As part of an effort to determine
the effects of the intervention on the teachers' perceptions of school climate, the
teachers filled out a questionnaire that included a section asking them to indicate
how typical a series of descriptions were of their school. The item used in Table
10.1 read, "The principal determines the educational program and philosophy."
Their responses were classified into one of three categories: not typical, somewhat typical, and typical. We wish to know if there is evidence that teachers from
the two groups view this aspect of school climate differently. Pearson's statistic is
defined as:

$$X_\nu^2 = \sum_{i=1}^{I} \sum_{j=1}^{J} \frac{[(f_{ij} - E(f_{ij})]^2}{E(f_{ij})} \tag{1}$$

---

[1]These data, as are most of the other examples in this chapter, were collected as part of the
evaluation of the Child Development Project (CDP), a multiyear demonstration program that is
attempting to promote the prosocial development of elementary-age children. Interested readers are
referred to Solomon, Watson, Delucchi, Schaps, and Battistich (1988) and Watson, Solomon, Battistich, Schaps, and Solomon (1989) for additional information.

TABLE 10.1
Contingency Table of School by Principal's Perceived Role

SCHOOL by PDETER

Principal determines the educational program and philosophy

	Count	not typical 1	somewhat 2	typical 3	Row Total
SCHOOL Control	1	7	14	24	45 57.0
Program	2	12	16	6	34 43.0
	Column Total	19 24.1	30 38.0	30 38.0	79 100.0

Chi-Square	Value	DF	Significance
Pearson	10.92937	2	.00423
Likelihood Ratio	11.49290	2	.00319

Minimum Expected Frequency—8.177

Where:

I = number of rows
J = number of columns
ν = degrees of freedom
$= (I - 1)(J - 1)$
f_{ij} = observed frequency in ith row, jth column
$E(f_{ij})$ = expected value of the observed frequency
$= \dfrac{(F_{i.})(F_{.j})}{F_{..}}$

Computing the expected values gives us the following:

$$X^2_{(2-1)(3-1)} = [(7 - 10.8)^2 + (14 - 17.1)^2 + (24 - 17.1)^2$$

$$\frac{(12 - 8.2)^2 + (16 - 12.9)^2 + (6 - 12.9)^2]}{10.8 + 17.1 + 17.1 + 8.2 + 12.9 + 12.9}$$

$$= \frac{863.42}{79}$$

$$= 10.9, \tag{2}$$

which we then compare to a tabled value for $\alpha = .05$ from the chi-square distribution with two degrees of freedom, $X^2 = 5.99$. Our computed value is greater than the tabled value, so we have evidence to reject the hypothesis under study, which is the null hypothesis of no group differences.

The Misuse of Chi-Square

Lewis and Burke centered their 1949 article around nine principle sources of error they found in their review of published research. Those nine sources, in the order Lewis and Burke listed them, are:

1. lack of independence among single events or measures;
2. small theoretical frequencies;
3. neglect of frequencies of non-occurrence;
4. failure to equalize the sum of the observed frequencies and the sum of the theoretical frequencies;
5. indeterminant theoretical frequencies;
6. incorrect or questionable categorizing;
7. use of nonfrequency data;
8. incorrect determination of the number of degrees of freedom; and
9. incorrect computations.

Two of these errors, (8) incorrect determination of the number of degrees of freedom and (9) incorrect computations, are largely obsolete thanks to the widespread use of computer packages of statistical software. Nevertheless, it does no harm to remind the reader that errors in computation, program coding, data entry, and so forth are easy to make. A very good habit to acquire is to doubt your results and check the integrity of your data all the way back to the original raw data file. This is especially important in small-sample data sets where each data point carries substantial weight in the final results.

The seventh error, the use of nonfrequency data, is also an error that is not often encountered in the current research literature. This is probably the result of greater familiarity with chi-square among practitioners and journal reviewers. Suffice it to note the data entered into Equation 1 must be frequencies, not percentages, means, or any number that is not a count.

Lewis and Burke cited the first error in their list, lack of independence among single events or measures, as the error they found most frequently in their brief review of articles that used the chi-square statistic to analyze data. This is also probably the most likely cause of the fifth source of misuse, indeterminant theoretical frequencies, which they noted, "commonly arises from a lack of independence between measures" (p. 478).

It is interesting to note that one of the examples Lewis and Burke used to illustrate this error, in which a set of die are thrown repeatedly, is actually a poor, if not incorrect, example (Pastore, 1950). One of the basic assumptions under which the statistic is derived is that of independence of the data. Just as one should not compute a two-sample t test on matched-pair data, so also one must not compute Pearson's chi-square on dependent measures. This is true regardless of what produces the interdependence; repeated measurement of the same person, sample matching, or correlation inherent in the subjects themselves such as data from spouses, siblings, parent and child combinations, and so on. The proper statistic for correlated data is McNemars's measure in the 2×2 table, and either Stuart's or Bowker's test in the $K \times K$ table (Marascuilo & McSweeny, 1977).

Small Theoretical Frequencies

Lewis and Burke (1949) labeled the second error in their list, the use of expected frequencies that are too small, as the most common weakness in the use of chi-square (p. 460). They took the position that expected values of 5 were probably too low and stated a preference for a minimum expected value of 10, with 5 as the absolute lowest limit. As examples they cited two published studies that used chi-square tests with expected values below 10. It appears today that their position, a popular one among researchers, may be overly conservative.

This problem of small expected values has been examined from the perspectives of two different applications. In testing goodness-of-fit hypotheses, the categories are chosen arbitrarily, permitting control over the size of the expected values by choice of category sizes. In contrast, the categories of contingency tables used for testing association hypotheses are relatively fixed, and one is forced to increase the expected values by increasing the sample size and/or collapsing rows and/or columns. Research taken from the perspective of this latter case are considered first.

Tests of Association Hypotheses in Contingency Tables.   Based on Monte Carlo and empirical studies, recommendations with respect to minimum expected cell frequencies in testing hypotheses of association have included recommended minimum values of 1 (Jeffreys, 1961; Kempthorne, 1966; Slakter, 1965), 5 (Fisher, 1938), 10 (Cramer, 1946), and 20 (Kendall, 1952). Cochran (1952) first proposed the oft-cited rule-of-thumb that chi-square may be applied if no more than 20% of the cells have expected values between one and five. Wise (1963) suggested that small (i.e., less than five) but equal expected frequencies were preferable to unequal frequencies where a few expected values are small, and the remaining frequencies are well above most criteria. Good, Grover, and Mitchell (1970) concluded that if the expected values are equal, they may be as low as 0.33 (p. 275).

This view of the statistic as being robust with respect to minimum expected values is also supported by the findings of Lewontin and Felsenstein (1965), who used Monte Carlo methods to examine $2 \times N$ tables with fixed marginals. With small expected values in each cell and degrees of freedom greater than five, they concluded that the test tends to be conservative. Even the occurrence of expected values below one generally does not invalidate the procedure. Bradely, Bradely, McGrath, and Cutcomb (1979) conducted a series of sampling experiments to examine the Type I error rates of chi-square in the presence of small expected values in tables as large as 4×4. Their results offer strong support for the robustness of the statistic in meeting preassigned Type I error rates. Additional support comes from Camilli and Hopkins (1978) study of chi-square in 2×2 tables. They found that expected values as low as one or two were acceptable when the total sample size was greater than 20.

Testing Goodness-of-Fit Hypotheses. In testing goodness-of-fit hypotheses Kendall and Stuart (1969), following suggestions by Mann and Wald (1942) and Gumbel (1943), recommended that one choose the boundaries of categories so that each has an expected frequency equal to the reciprocal of the number of categories. They preferred a minimum value of five categories. Slakter (1965, 1966), Good (1961), and Wise (1963) found that in testing goodness of fit expected values may be as low as one or two for an alpha of .05 when expected values are equal. For unequal expected values or an alpha of .01, the expected frequencies should be at least four.

Yarnold (1970) numerically examined the accuracy of the approximation of the chi-square goodness-of-fit statistic. He proposed that "if the number of classes, s, is three or more, and if r denotes the number of expectations less than five, then the minimum expectation may be as small as $5r/s$" (p. 865). He concluded that "the upper one and five percentage points of the X^2 approximation can be used with much smaller expectations than previously considered possible" (p. 882).

After considering earlier work, Roscoe and Byars (1971) concluded that one should be concerned primarily with the average expected value when considering the goodness-of-fit statistic with more than one degree of freedom. In the case of equal expected cell frequencies, they suggested an average value of 2 or more for an alpha equal to .05 and 4 or more for an alpha equal to .01. In the nonuniform case, they recommend average expected values of 6 and 10, respectively. They urged the use of this average-expected-value rule in the test for independence as well, even when the sample sizes are not equal. As Horn (1977) noted, this average-expected-value rule is in agreement with Slakter's (1965, 1966) suggestion that what may be most important is the average of the expected frequencies and also subsumes Cochran's rule that 20% of the expected frequencies should be greater than one.

Summarizing this work on minimum expected values for both association and goodness-of-fit hypotheses, as a general rule, the chi-square statistic may be properly used in cases where the expected values are much lower than previously considered permissible. In the presence of small expected values, the statistic is quite robust with respect to controlling Type I error rate, especially under the following conditions: (a) the total N is at least five times the number of cells; (b) the average expected value is five or more; (c) the expected values tend toward homogeneity; and (d) the distribution of the margins is not skewed. Additional references on this matter that may be of interest to readers can be found in Hutchinson (1979).

For most applications, Cochran's rule, which states that all expected values be greater than one and not more than 20% be less than five, offers a fair balance between practicality and precision. An alternative to consider, especially in the case of small or sparse tables, is the computation of an exact test (Agresti & Wackerly, 1977; Baker, 1977; Mehat & Patel, 1980; Mehat and Patel, 1983; Mehat, Patel, & Gray, 1985). In recent years, these procedures have become more accessible due to the availability of increased computer power and efficient algorithms. A comprehensive implementation can be found in the *Statxact* software (Cytel Software, 1991). In spite of its name, however, the use of an "exact test" is not without controversy. As is discussed in a later section, debate still continues over the appropriate use of both exact tests and continuity corrections. Berkson (1978), Kempthorne (1979), Upton (1982) and D'Agostino, Chase, and Belanger (1988) offered the opposition to its use in 2 × 2 tables.

Power Considerations.   An important point that is easily overlooked concerns the effect of small expected values on the power of the chi-square test. Overall (1980) examined the effect of low expected frequencies in one row or column of a 2 × 2 design on the power of the chi-square statistic. (This most often results from the analysis of infrequently occurring events). Setting $(1 - \alpha)$ = .70 as a minimally acceptable level, Overall concluded that when expected values are quite low, the power of the chi-square test drops to a level that produces a statistic that, in his view, is almost useless because low power means the inability to detect an existing difference.

Specific advice as to the selection of sample size is difficult to provide as the requirements and standards of researchers vary. In general, following Cochran's rule will provide sufficient power in most cases. Tables for computing power in the use of chi-square are given in Cohen (1988, chap. 7). The point here is to remind the reader that Type II error rates go up as sample size goes down.

Neglect of Frequencies of Nonoccurrence

Omitting frequencies of nonoccurrence from contingency tables is a surprisingly easy error to make, and examples can still occasionally be found. Consider, for example, the case of some of the early work on the detection of item bias. In

1979, Scheuneman proposed a method of detecting potentially biased items in an otherwise unbiased test analogous to the more demanding item-response theory approach by categorizing test-takers based on the total test score to equate for ability differences. To test an item for evidence of bias against some subgroup based on, say, sex or ethnicity of the test-taker, she proposed classifying each person in the sample on three dimensions: their group membership, total test score, and whether or not they passed the item.

But the contingency table she formed for calculating chi-square on was not this three-dimensional table, but rather a two-dimensional table defined by total-score grouping and group membership—counting only the numbers of each group that passed the item in question. As noted by several critics (Baker, 1981; Marascuilo & Slaughter, 1981), the resulting statistic is not distributed as chi-square because she neglected to count the frequency of the group members who did not pass the item. For an example of the statistically correct approach the reader is referred to Zwick and Ericikan (1989).

By neglecting the frequencies of nonoccurrence one usually commits the fourth error, failure to equalize the sum of the observed frequencies and the sum of the theoretical frequencies. Although relatively rare, this will result directly from the error discussed earlier—neglecting the frequency of nonoccurrence. One quick check of the validity of a contingency table for computing chi-square is to see if the sum of the observed frequencies is equal to the sum of the expected. If they are not equal, something is wrong.

Incorrect or Questionable Categorizing

This problem, more an issue of methodology than of mathematical statistics, is found in situations where the data need to be categorized in some arbitrary form in the absence of naturally occurring categories such as group membership. The distribution of frequencies within a set of categories is at the heart of the statistic, so the selection of those categories obviously will have a great deal of influence on the obtained value. The conservative data analyst will define categories before collecting data (preferably as a result of collecting and analyzing pilot data). The categories should be mutually exclusive so that each outcome belongs in one, and only one, category, and they must be as well-defined as possible so that there is no question about what constitutes membership in a given category. The categories themselves should cover the full range of possible responses, yet not be so narrowly defined that the resulting frequencies produce very low expected values.

While on this subject of classification, a comment on the matter of mis-classification is appropriate. One issue of categorical analysis that has received little attention in social science research is the effect of misclassification on the power and Type I error rate of the chi-square test. Most of the relevant literature is found in the biostatistics literature (e.g., Mote & Anderson, 1965). One exception to this in the area of educational research is an article by Katz and McSweeny (1979), who discussed the effects of classification errors on the significance level and power of the test for equality or proportions. They developed and discussed a correction procedure based on estimates of the probability of false negatives and false positives and noted that the detrimental effects of misclassification can be marked, including a loss in power. This problem is especially likely to occur when one of the proportions being tested is small, and the probability of misclassification is not equivalent across groups. Any researcher who suspects the presence of misclassified data should consult the Katz and McSweeny (1979) article and the references they cited. The key to using their procedure, and its major drawback, is the need for estimates of the rate of misclassification that often may be unobtainable.

Correction for Continuity

As part of their discussion on the proper use of the chi-square statistic, Lewis and Burke presented the Yates correction for continuity, noting that it is justified only in the case of a 2×2 table. Since the time of their writing, questions have arisen regarding the appropriateness of the use of a correction for continuity.

Categorical variables are discrete and the chi-square distribution is continuous, thus a correction to improve the approximation can be made. The most well-known correction was proposed by Yates (1934) and is formed by adding or subtracting $\frac{1}{2}$ to each observed frequency so as to move the observed value closer to the expected value. Thus it becomes more difficult to reject the hypothesis being tested. Symbolically, the corrected chi-square, X_c^2, is written as

$$X_c^2 = \sum_{i=1}^{I} \sum_{j=1}^{J} \frac{\left[\left(f_{ij} + \frac{1}{2} - E(f_{ij}) \right) \right]^2}{E(f_{ij})} \tag{3}$$

The analytical derivation of the correction expressed in Equation 3 is given by Cox (1970).

The disagreement over the use of this correction is based not on its theoretical grounding but on its applicability. Plackett (1964), confirming empirical results of Pearson (1947), argued that the correction is inappropriate if the data come from independent binomial samples. Grizzle (1967) extended Plackett's results to the general case and concluded that the correction is so conservative as to render it useless for practical purposes.

The consensus of several investigators (Camilli & Hopkins, 1978; Conover, 1974a, 1974b; D'Agostino, Chase, & Belanger, 1988; Mantel, 1974; Mantel & Greenhouse, 1968; Miettinin, 1974; Starmer, Grizzle, & Sen, 1974; Upton,

1982) is that the correction for continuity becomes overly conservative when either or both of the marginals in a table are random. As this is often the case in social science research, the use of the correction should not be given the blanket recommendation that often accompanies it.

These critics are not without critics of their own. In a paper read to the Royal Statistical Society, Yates (1984, followed by comments from several noteworthy statisticians) held that the correction for continuity is misunderstood due to strict adherence to Neyman–Pearson critical levels, the use of strict nominal levels and a refusal by investigators to accept his arguments for conditioning on the marginals. In any event, as a couple of the discussants following Yates noted, even the simple 2×2 table contains a great deal of potential information and the analysis of even such a simple case cannot be taken lightly.

So the debate continues after 50 years. If strong conservatism is desired and/or the marginal totals in the contingency table being analyzed are fixed values, then the Yates correction should be applied. In all other cases, however, one must be cautious in its use because the correction for continuity will produce very conservative probability estimates.

Having reviewed common sources of misuse, let us move on to supplementary and alternative procedures that can aid in the exploration of data appropriate to a chi-square–based analysis.

SUPPLEMENTARY
AND ALTERNATIVE PROCEDURES

Whereas a properly executed chi-square statistic may well be a thing of beauty to behold—at least to some of us—in many ways it is only the simplest of forms of statistical analysis. There are at least three major shortcomings to its use: (a) it is an omnibus test, (b) it does not necessarily utilize all of the information available in a contingency table such as the ordering of categories, and (c) its significance level is partly a function of sample size. So by itself a significant chi-square statistic may not provide all of the information contained in the table. The researcher should keep in mind several procedures that supplement or serve as an alternative to a chi-square test. A comprehensive treatment of these and other methods may be found in Agresti (1990).

One way to understand why a contingency table produces a statistically significant test statistic is to examine the cell entries expressed as more than just counts. Table 10.2 is a table produced by SPSSX from the data shown in Table 10.1. The difference in these two tables results from the information requested of the software.

In addition to cell counts, Table 10.2 displays the cell information in terms of each cell's expected value, its count as a percentage of the row, column, and

TABLE 10.2
Expanded Display of Table 10.1

SCHOOL by PDETER

Principal determines the educational program and philosophy

Count Exp Val Row Pct Col Pct Tot Pct Residual Std Res Adj Res		not typical 1	somewhat 2	typical 3	Row Total
SCHOOL					
Control	1	7 10.8 15.6% 36.8% 8.9% −3.8 −1.2 −2.0	14 17.1 31.1% 46.7% 17.7% −3.1 −.7 −1.4	24 17.1 53.3% 80.0% 30.4% 6.9 1.7 3.2	45 57.0%
Program	2	12 8.2 35.3% 63.2% 15.2% 3.8 1.3 2.0	16 12.9 47.1% 53.3% 20.3% 3.1 .9 1.4	6 12.9 17.6% 20.0% 7.6% −6.9 −1.9 −3.2	34 43.0%
	Column Total	19 24.1	30 38.0%	30 38.0%	79 100.0%

Chi-Square	Value	DF	Significance
Pearson	10.92937	2	.00423
Likelihood Ratio	11.49290	2	.00319

Minimum Expected Frequency—8.177

total N, and as a residual from the expected value in "raw," Studentized, and adjusted forms. Note that the largest residuals are found in the column marked "typical" where 53.3% (24 out of 45) Control teachers chose this response versus 17.6% (6 out of 34) of the Program teachers. By re-expressing the cell entries in each of these forms the data analyst may begin to see more of the information contained in the table that the basic cell counts alone cannot provide.

Comparison of Individual Proportions

The chi-square procedure, as Berkson noted in 1938, is an omnibus test.[2] In the case of a test for homogeneity among K groups classified by J levels of the dependent variable A, the hypothesis under test is expressed as

$$H_0: \begin{bmatrix} P(A_1|G_1) \\ P(A_2|G_1) \\ \cdot \\ \cdot \\ \cdot \\ P(A_J|G_1) \end{bmatrix} = \begin{bmatrix} P(A_1|G_2) \\ P(A_2|G_2) \\ \cdot \\ \cdot \\ \cdot \\ P(A_J|G_2) \end{bmatrix} = \dots = \begin{bmatrix} P(A_1|G_K) \\ P(A_2|G_K) \\ \cdot \\ \cdot \\ \cdot \\ P(A_J|G_K) \end{bmatrix} = \begin{bmatrix} P(A_1) \\ P(A_2) \\ \cdot \\ \cdot \\ \cdot \\ P(A_J) \end{bmatrix} \quad (4$$

against the alternative that H_0 is false. If the hypothesis is rejected, one would like to be able to find the contrasts among the proportions that are significantly different from zero. This may be accomplished by a well-known procedure that allows one to construct simultaneous confidence intervals for all contrasts of the proportions in the design, across groups, while maintaining the specified Type error probability. The method is an extension of Scheffe's (1953) theorum, which is used for the construction of contrasts in the analysis of variance. Scheffe's work was extended by Dunn (1961) and applied to qualitative variables by Goodman (1964) in the 1960s.

If a linear contrast in the population proportions in a contingency table is denoted as Ψ, the sample estimate is $\hat{\Psi}$ and is defined as

$$\hat{\Psi} = \Sigma a_k \hat{p}_k, \quad (5$$

where $\hat{p}_k$ is the proportion in Group k and $\Sigma a_k = 0$. The limiting probability is ($- \alpha$) that, for all contrasts,

$$\hat{\Psi} - SE_{\hat{\Psi}} \sqrt{\chi^2_{k-1:1-\alpha}} < \psi < \hat{\Psi} + SE_{\hat{\Psi}} \sqrt{\chi^2_{k-1:1-\alpha}} \quad (6$$

where

$$SE^2_{\hat{\Psi}} = \sum a_k^2 \frac{\hat{p}_k \hat{q}_k}{n_k}, \hat{q}_k = 1 - \hat{p}_k \quad (7$$

and $\sqrt{\chi^2}$ is the $(1 - \alpha)$th percent value from the chi-square distribution with $K - 1$ degrees of freedom. Some of the earlier work with this procedure may be found in Gart (1962), Gold (1963), and Goodman (1964).

Table 10.3 contains an example of such a contrast. Here, the proportion of teachers from each group who chose "very typical" as their answer are compared.

---

[2]It is intriguing that in spite continuing criticism of omnibus tests as not providing specific answers to research questions, they are still widely used. See Rosnow and Rosenthal (1989) for further discussion including their rule of thumb which states that whenever we use a chi-square or F test with greater than one degree of freedom, we have probably tested a question in which we are not interested.

TABLE 10.3
Computing a Confidence Interval for the Difference
Between Proportions

$$\hat{\psi} = (1)\,\frac{24}{45} + (-1)\,\frac{6}{34}$$

$$= .5333 - .1765$$

$$= .3568$$

$$SE^2_{\hat{\psi}} = (1)^2\,\frac{(.5333)(.4667)}{45} + (-1)^2\,\frac{(.1765)(.8235)}{34}$$

$$= \frac{.2489}{45} + \frac{1453}{34}$$

$$= .0055 + .00427$$

$$= .0098$$

$$SE^2_{\hat{\psi}} = \sqrt{SE^2_{\hat{\psi}}} = \sqrt{.0098} = .09902$$

$$.3568 - \sqrt{.0098}\,\sqrt{5.99} < \psi < .3568 + \sqrt{.0098}\,\sqrt{5.99}$$

$$.114 < \psi < .599$$

The only drawback to this post hoc application is its lack of power relative to a planned set of contrasts. A generally more powerful procedure results from the use of a Bonferroni-type critical value where the Type I error probability is spread over just the contrasts of interest. Such a value may be found in the table given originally by Dunn (1961) and included in many tests (cf. Marascuilo & Serlin, 1988). The value $\sqrt{\chi^2}$ in the confidence interval is replaced by the value taken from Dunn's table based on Q, which equals the number of planned contrasts and the degrees of freedom, which equals infinity.

Measures of Association

The value of a chi-square statistic is difficult to evaluate as it is both a function of the truth of the hypothesis under test and the sample size. To double the size of a sample, barring sample-to-sample fluctuations, will double the size of the computed chi-square statistic. To compensate for this, the data analyst should always calculate an appropriate measure of association in order to assess the practical, that is, the meaningful significance of the findings.

Bishop, Fienberg, and Holland (1975, chap. 11) provided an overview of various measures of association for two-dimensional tables. They made an important point when they noted that the issue today is not to develop an appropriate measure of association for a given problem, but rather "to choose wisely from among the variety of existing measures" (p. 373). For example, SPSSX and BMDP both offer over 12 measures of association to choose from. Table 10.4 is a

TABLE 10.4
Measures of Association for the Data of Table 10.1

Statistic	Value	ASE1	T value	Approximate Significance
Phi	.37195			.00423 *1
Cramer's V	.37195			.00423 *1
Contingency Coefficient	.34862			.00423 *1
Lambda :				
symmetric	.20482	.11844	1.61109	
with SCHOOL dependent	.20588	.18347	1.00639	
with PDETER dependent	.20408	.11224	1.64993	
Goodman & Kruskal Tau :				
with SCHOOL dependent	.13835	.07330		.00454 *2
with PDETER dependent	.07190	.03956		.00367 *2
Uncertainty Coefficient :				
symmetric	.08259	.04599	1.79391	.00319 *3
with SCHOOL dependent	.10643	.05921	1.79391	.00319 *3
with PDETER dependent	.06747	.03762	1.79391	.00319 *3
Kendall's Tau-b	−.34075	.09591	−3.53772	
Kendall's Tau-c	−.38584	.10906	−3.53772	
Gamma	−.55844	.13738	−3.53772	
Somers's D :				
symmetric	−.33725	.09492	−3.53772	
with SCHOOL dependent	−.29510	.08352	−3.53772	
with PDETER dependent	−.39346	.11052	−3.53772	
Pearson's R	−.35403	.10173	−3.32169	.00069
Spearman Correlation	−.36041	.10141	−3.39041	.00055
Eta :				
with SCHOOL dependent	.37195			
with PDETER dependent	.35403			

*1 Pearson chi-square probability
*2 Based on chi-square approximation
*3 Likelihood ratio chi-square probability

copy of the measures of association produced by SPSSX for the example in Table 10.1.

If the data are generated from a single sample, then the proper test is one of independence and a measure of association is the mean square contingency coefficient. Designated as ϕ^2, its sample estimate is calculated as

$$\phi^2 = \sum_{i=1}^{I} \sum_{j=1}^{J} \frac{f_{ij}^2}{f_{i\cdot} - f_{\cdot j}} - 1. \qquad (8)$$

It can be shown that the maximum value that ϕ^2 can attain is $\phi^2_{max} =$ the minimum of $(I - 1)$ or $(J - 1)$. To correct for this compute

$$\phi^{2'} = \frac{\phi^2}{\phi^2_{max}}, \tag{9}$$

which is referred to as Cramer's measure of association (Cramer, 1946).

If both variables are ordered, one is presented with a variety of choices including the standard product-moment correlation coefficient (Kendall & Stuart, 1969), tau-a and tau-b (Kendall, 1970; Kendall & Stuart, 1979), Goodman and Kruskal's tau, and gamma (Goodman & Kruskal, 1954, 1959, 1963). Comparison of these methods is given by Gans and Robertson (1981) and Cesa (1982). Tau is generally recommended as it approaches the normal distribution faster than Spearman's rho (Kendall, 1970) and is not inflated by the exclusion of tied values as gamma is.

When the frequencies of the K groups are cross-classified by a dependent variable that is ordered, Serlin, Carr, and Marascuilo (1982) proposed a measure that is the ratio of the calculated test statistic to the maximum the statistic can reach. Their measure ranges from zero to unity, and it is interpreted just as η^2 is in the parametric analysis of variance (ANOVA). For Table 10.2, $\eta = .37$.

In the case of a 2×2 table, the well-known measure of association based on x^2 is ϕ^2 and is calculated as

$$\phi^2 = \frac{X^2}{N}. \tag{10}$$

If Kendall's tau is calculated for the same table, it will be seen that phi = tau.

An alternative to the use of phi is to employ the odds ratio (Fienberg, 1980). For a 2×2 table the categories defining the table may be labeled as A, not-A, B, and not-B. The probability of observing B, given the presence of A, can be expressed as

$$\frac{P(B|A)}{P(\bar{B}|A)}. \tag{11}$$

Alternatively, the probability of observing B, given the absence of A, is

$$\frac{P(B|\bar{A})}{P(\bar{B}|\bar{A})}. \tag{12}$$

A simple measure of association, apparently first proposed by Cornfield (1951), is the ratio of these two odds. In the sample, the measure is calculated as

$$\hat{\gamma} = \frac{f_{11} f_{22}}{f_{12} f_{21}} \tag{13}$$

with a standard error estimated as

$$SE_{\hat{\gamma}} = \sqrt{\frac{1}{f_{11}} + \frac{1}{f_{22}} + \frac{1}{f_{12}} + \frac{1}{f_{21}}}. \tag{14}$$

A useful discussion of this measure, which is widely used in bio-medical research, including additional references may be found in Fleiss (1973). The choice between the two coefficients, tau and phi, for the 2×2 table is not clear-cut, and the reader is referred to Fleiss for further discussion.

Analysis of Ordered Categories

In spite of its usefulness, there are conditions under which the use of Pearson's chi-square, although appropriate, is not the optimum procedure. Such a situation occurs when the categories forming a table have a natural ordering. The value of the statistic expressed in Equation 5 will not be altered if the rows and/or columns in a table are permuted. However, if ordering of the rows or columns exists, their order cannot meaningfully be changed. This is information to which chi-square is not sensitive. Instead, the researcher may choose among several alternatives.

If both rows and columns contain a natural ordering, two methods are available. The first is a procedure taken from Maxwell (1961) as modified by Marascuilo and McSweeny (1977). It is used to test for a monotonic trend in the responses across categories.

The first step is to quantify the categories using any arbitrary numbering system. As the method is independent of the numbers chosen, both Maxwell and Marascuilo and McSweeny recommended numbers that simplify the calculations such as the linear coefficients in a table of orthogonal polynomials. These coefficients are then applied to the marginal frequencies, the $Y_{i.}$ and $Y_{.j}$, to produce the sums and sums of squares for use in calculating a slope coefficient by the usual equation:

$$\hat{\beta} = \frac{N(\Sigma\Sigma Y_i Y_j - (\Sigma Y_i)(\Sigma Y_j))}{N(\Sigma Y_i^2) - (\Sigma Y_j^2)} . \tag{15}$$

Under the assumption that $B = 0$, the standard error of $\hat{\beta}$ is calculated as

$$SE_\beta = \frac{S_{Y_j}^2}{N - 1(S_{Y_j}^2)} . \tag{16}$$

Then the hypothesis of no linear trend may be tested by

$$X^2 = \frac{\hat{\beta}^2}{SE^2\hat{\beta}^2} \sim \chi^2_{\nu-1}. \tag{17}$$

A second procedure for examining tables with ordered marginal categories involves the use of Kendall's (1970) rank tau, corrected for ties. If the observed tau is statistically significant, the hypothesis of no association is rejected. In addition, the statistic itself is a measure of association or array of the data, as discussed in the previous section.

When one of the two variables defining a table is ordered, Kruskal and Wallis's (1952) nonparametric one-way analysis-of-variance procedure may be utilized to test for equality of distributions. This procedure is described by Marascuilo and Dagenais (1982). Consider the case of an $I \times J$ contingency table, where the dimension I is defined by mutually exclusive ordered categories. The Kruskal–Wallis statistic is based on a simultaneous comparison of the sum of the ranks for the K groups. To apply the statistic in the case of an $I \times K$ table, the frequencies within a category along dimension I are considered to be tied and, therefore, are assigned a midrank value. One then sums the ranks across I, within Group k, to obtain the summed ranks used in calculating the statistic.

Log- and Logit-Linear Models

This versatile statistic of Pearson's can also be extended to three-dimensional tables as well (Agresti, 1990; Fienberg, 1980). Given the expected frequencies derived from a model, one computes the statistic as shown in Equation 1. The degrees of freedom are computed as the number of cells in the table minus the number of parameters fitted. As Fienberg (p. 40) noted, Equation 1 is asymptotically equivalent to G^2 which is -2 times the log of the likelihood ratio statistic. The choice between these two statistics is discussed in the next section.

The derivation of the expected values in multidimensional tables are, of course, at the heart of log-linear and logit-liner models. Many articles and texts are now available for these procedures, including the works of Bishop et al. (1975), Goodman (1978), Haberman (1978), and Fienberg (1980). These procedures are implemented through several packaged computer programs including LOGLINEAR in SPSSX, SAS CATMOD, Goodman's ECTA, BMDP 4F, Nelder's GLIM, and Bock's Multiqual, which are familiar to many researchers.

Although most applicable for analyzing multidimensional tables, it should be pointed out that these models can be used on two-dimensional tables as well. It is likely that log-linear models will eventually supersede the use of Pearson's chi-square in the future because of their similarity to ANOVA procedures and their extension to higher-order tables. Discussion of this methodology, however, is beyond the scope of this chapter.

Log-Likelihood Ratio

An alternative procedure to calculating Pearson's chi-square to test a hypothesis concerning a multinomial is the use of the likelihood ratio statistic. It is a maximum likelihood estimate labeled G^2 and defined as

$$G^2 = 2 \sum_{i=1}^{I} \sum_{j=1}^{J} f_{ij} \log_e \frac{f_{ij}}{E(f_{ij})}. \tag{18}$$

In their text on discrete multivariate analysis, Bishop et al. (1975) used log-linear models, as opposed to additive models, for contingency table analysis. As a summary statistic they stated a preference for maximum likelihood estimators (MLEs) on theoretical grounds. Additionally, practical reasons for the use of this procedure were given:

1. Ease of computation for linear models.
2. MLEs satisfy certain marginal constraints they called intuitive.
3. "The method of maximum likelihood can be applied directly to multi nomial data with several observed cell values of zero, and almost always produces non-zero estimates for such cells (an extremely valuable property in small samples)" (p. 58).

They further stated, "MLEs necessarily give minimum values of G^2, it is appropriate to use G^2 as a summary statistic . . . although the reader will observe that, in the samples where we compute both X^2 and G^2, the difference in numerical value of the two is seldom large enough to be of practical importance" (p. 126).

There are cases where the likelihood-ratio statistic may be preferred over chi square. Such may occur when some expected values are quite small or when the contingency table contains a structural zero.

Several investigators have compared X^2 and G^2 in a variety of research situations. Chapman (1976) provided an overview of much of this research, including the work of Neyman and Pearson (1931), Cochran (1936), Fisher (1950), Good et al. (1970), and West and Kempthorne (1972). From these comparisons, neither of the two procedures emerges a clear favorite. When one method is better in some respect than the other, it seems to result from a particular configuration of sample size, number of categories, expected values, and the alternative hypothesis. An exception to the general equivalence of these two statistics can be found in the literature on partitioning of contingency tables, which is discussed following the next section.

Comparison of Two Independent Chi-Squares

It is conceivable that situations may occur in which one may want to test the equality of two independent chi-square values. One direct method to accomplish this would be to compute the same measure of association for each table and visually compare their values. If a test is required, Knepp and Entwisle (1969) presented, in tabular form, the 1% and 5% critical values for this comparison for degrees of freedom that equal 1 to 100. They also provided a normal approximation calculated as

$$Z = \frac{\frac{1}{2}(X_1^2) - \frac{1}{2}(X_2^2)}{\sqrt{\nu}}, \tag{19}$$

where X_{21} and X_{22} are two independent sample chi-square values, each with ν degrees of freedom. The statistic Z is approximately distributed as a unit normal variable.

D'Agostino and Rosman (1971) offered another simple normal approximation for comparing two chi-square value in the form of

$$\frac{\sqrt{x_1^2} - \sqrt{x_2^2}}{\sqrt{1 - \frac{1}{4\nu}}}. \tag{20}$$

This approximation was tested by Monte Carlo methods and found to be quite good for cases with degrees of freedom greater than two. With one degree of freedom the researcher must use Knepp and Entwistle's tabled values, which are 3.19 for $\alpha = .05$ and 3.66 for $\alpha = .01$. D'Agostino and Rosman also noted that for df's greater than 20, the denominator in Equation 20 makes little difference and

$$\sqrt{X_1^2} - \sqrt{X_2^2} \tag{21}$$

may be used in place of Equation 19.

The same question that produced the data in Table 10.1 was asked of 68 teachers from two groups in a different school district. Pearson's chi-square for this second sample equaled 5.106 compared to a value of 10.929 in Table 10.1. With only two degrees of freedom we can use Equation 19 to obtain a z statistic of 2.05, leading us to conclude that the two sample statistics are different from each other. In other words, the lack of homogeneity between groups is not the same for our two samples.

As noted by Serlin (personal communication, 1990) one should be able to extend this same approach to tables with different degrees of freedom. Using the relatively accurate cube-root approximation one should be able to compute a z statistic as

$$Z = \frac{\sqrt[3]{\frac{X_1^2}{\nu_1}} - \sqrt[3]{\frac{X_2^2}{\nu_2}}}{\sqrt{\frac{2}{9\nu_1} + \frac{2}{9\nu_2}}}. \tag{22}$$

Although this approximation is quite good for even two or three degrees of freedom, this is still a large-sample approximation.

One should note that these procedures should be used with extreme caution

for at least two reasons. It is possible for very different configurations within tw
tables to produce the same chi-square values. It is also possible to obtain differe
chi-square values from tables with identical internal patterns if the sample siz
differ between tables.

Partitioning

At about the same time that Lewis and Burke were writing, the first extensi
work on the partitioning of an $I \times J$ contingency table into components w
being conducted by Lancaster (1949, 1950, 1951), who demonstrated that
general term of a multinomial can be reduced to a series of binomial terms, ea
with one degree of freedom. This work along with the work of Irwin (1949
Kimbal (1954), Kastenbaun (1960), Castellan (1965), and Bresnahan a
Shapiro (1966) allows one to decompose a contingency table into a set of small
tables whose individual chi-square statistics sum to the total chi-square.

The partitioning of contingency tables is not often seen in the literatur
however, for two primary reasons. First, log-linear analysis, the examination
residuals, and the use of contrasts permit one to examine the sources of variatic
as easily. Second, Shaffer (1973) demonstrated that to test one partition f
statistical significance is actually to test the hypothesis that no partition is signif
cant against the alternative that one is significant and the remaining partitions a
not. The interested reader is referred to the references cited earlier.

Several procedures that supplement or provide an alternative to partitioni
are available. Graphical analysis is discussed and exemplified by Boardm
(1977), Cohen (1980), Cox and Laugh (1967), Fienberg (1969), and Snee (1974
One version of graphical analysis, based on Brown's work (1974, 1976),
implemented by BMDP's 2F procedure (Dixon, 1983).

CONCLUSIONS

Ninety years after its original development, Pearson's chi-square statistic r
mains a useful and powerful tool in our attempts to account for variation in dat
Its ready availability makes for widespread use while research into its vario
properties and over its appropriate applications continues. In addition to remin
ing the researcher to pay heed to all of the usual issues and warnings applicable
any inferential statistic, such as being aware of its assumptions and what preci
hypothesis it tests, a few points bear repetition.

Under certain conditions, expected cell frequencies less than five do n
substantially alter the Type I error rate of the chi-square statistic. The decrease
power that accompanies these small expected values, though, should encoura
one to use large sample sizes.

The debate over the use of the Yates correction for continuity is unresolve

here is general agreement, however, that the correction often results in an
verly conservative test when the margins in a table are generated from random
ariables. There are a number of supplementary and alternative approaches to the use of
'earson's chi-square that the researcher should know. Often the questions one
sks of data may be more directly or efficiently answered by planned contrasts of
roportions, partitioning of the total chi-square, or the use of log-linear models.
A useful paper on this subject was written by Cochran (1954). He presented
methods for dealing with some specific contingency table designs and probability
istributions. In addition to the previously mentioned recommendations regard-
ng minimum expected values, he discussed testing goodness-of-fit hypotheses in
ifferent distributions, degrees of freedom in $2 \times N$ tables, and combining 2×2
ables.

ACKNOWLEDGMENTS

his chapter was written while the author was a research associate at the Devel-
pmental Studies Center. He is now senior statistician at the Treatment Research
Jnit, University of California, San Francisco.

The author would like to acknowledge and thank Drs. Patricia Busk and Ron
erlin for helpful discussions, Drs. Daniel Solomon, Victor Battistich, and an
nonymous reviewer for many helpful suggestions and the late Dr. Leonard
Marascuilo who suggested this topic to the author many years ago.

REFERENCES

Agresti, A. (1990). *Categorical data analysis*. New York: John Wiley & Sons.

Agresti, A., & Wackerly, D. (1977). Some exact conditional tests of independence for R × C cross-
classification tables. *Psychometrika, 42*, 111–125.

Baker, R. J. (1977). Algorithm AS 112. Exact distributions derived from two-way tables. *Applied
Statistics, 26*, 199–206.

Baker, F. B. (1981). A criticism of Scheuneman's item bias technique. *Journal of Educational
Measurement, 18*, 59–62.

Berkson, J. (1938). Some difficulties in interpretation of the chi-square test. *Journal of the American Statistical Association, 33*, 526–536.

Berkson, J. (1978). In dispraise of exact tests. *Journal of Statistical Planning and Inference, 2*, 27–
42.

Bishop, Y. M. M., Fienberg, S. E., & Holland, P. W. (1975). *Discrete multivariate analysis:
Theory and practice*. Cambridge, MA: MIT Press.

Boardman, T. J. (1977). Graphical contributions to the X^2 statistics for two-way contingency tables.
Communications in Statistics: Theory and Methods, A6, 1437–1451.

Bradely, D. R., Bradely, T. D., McGrath, S. G., & Cutcomb, S. D. (1979). Type I error rate of the
chi-square test of independence in R × C tables that have small expected frequencies. *Psychological Bulletin, 86*, 1920–1927.

Bresnahan, J. L., & Shapiro, M. M. (1966). A general equation and technique for the exac partitioning of chi-square contingency tables. *Psychological Bulletin, 66,* 252–262.

Brown, M. B. (1974). The identification of sources of significance in two-way contingency tables *Applied Statistics, 23,* 405–413.

Brown, M. B. (1976). Screening effects in multidimensional contingency tables. *Applied Statistics 25,* 37–46.

Camilli, G., & Hopkins, K. D. (1978). Applicability of chi-square to 2-×-2 contingency table with small expected cell frequencies. *Psychological Bulletin, 85,* 163–167.

Castellan, N. J. Jr. (1965). On the partitioning of contingency tables. *Psychological Bulletin, 64* 330–338.

Cesa, T. (1982). *Comparisons among methods of analysis for ordered contingency tables in psy chology and education.* Unpublished doctoral dissertation, University of California, Berkeley

Chapman, J. A. W. A. (1976). A comparison of the chi-square, -2 Log R, and multinomia probability criteria for significance tests when expected frequencies are small. *Journal of the American Statistical Association, 71,* 854–863.

Cochran, W. G. (1936). The chi-square distribution for the binomial and Poisson series with small expectations. *Annals of Eugenics, 2,* 207–217.

Cochran, W. G. (1952). The chi-square test of goodness-of-fit. *Annals of Mathematical Statistics 23,* 315–345.

Cochran, W. G. (1954). Some methods for strengthening the common chi-square tests. *Biometrics 10,* 417–451.

Cohen, A. (1980). On the graphical display of the significant components in two-way contingency tables. *Communications in Statistics: Theory and Methods, A9,* 1025–1041.

Cohen, J. (1988). *Statistical power analysis for the behavioral sciences.* Hillsdale, NJ: Lawrence Erlbaum Associates.

Conover, W. J. (1974a). Rejoinder. *Journal of the American Statistical Association, 69,* 382.

Conover, W. J. (1974b). Some reasons for not using the Yates continuity correction on 2-×-2 contingency tables. *Journal of the American Statistical Association, 69,* 374–382.

Cornfield, J. (1951). A method of estimating comparative rates from clinical data: Applications t cancer of the lung, breast, and cervix. *Journal of the National Cancer Institute, 11,* 1269–1275

Cox, D. R. (1970). The continuity correction. *Biometrics, 57,* 217–219.

Cox, D. R., & Laugh, E. (1967). A note on the graphical analysis of multidimensional contingency tables. *Technometrics, 9,* 481–488.

Cramer, H. (1946). *Mathematical methods of statistics.* Princeton, NJ: Princeton University Press

CYTEL Software. (1991). *User manual, version 2.* Cambridge, MA: Author.

D'Agostino, R. B., & Rosman, B. (1971). A normal approximation for testing the equality of two independent chi-square values. *Psychometrika, 36,* 251–252.

D'Agostino, R. B., Chase, W., & Belanger, A. (1988). The appropriateness of some common procedures for testing the equality of two independent binomial populations. *The American Statistician, 42*(2), 198–203.

Delucchi, K. L. (1983). The use and misuse of chi-square: Lewis and Burke revisited. *Psychological Bulletin, 94,* 166–176.

Dixon, W. J. (Ed.) (1983). *BMDP statistical software.* Berkeley: University of California Press

Dunn, O. J. (1961). Multiple comparison among means. *Journal of the American Statistical Association, 56,* 52–64.

Edwards, A. E. (1950). On "The use and misuse of the chi-square test": The case of the 2-×-2 contingency table. *Psychological Bulletin, 47,* 341–346.

Fienberg, S. E. (1969). Preliminary graphical analysis and quasi-independence for two-way contingency tables. *Applied Statistics, 18,* 153–168.

Fienberg, S. E. (1980). *The analysis of cross-classified categorical data* (2nd ed.). Cambridge MA: MIT Press.

Fisher, R. A. (1938). *Statistical methods for research workers* (7th ed.). London: Oliver & Boyd.

Fisher, R. A. (1950). The significance of deviations from expectations in a Poisson series. *Biometrics, 6*, 17–34.

Fleiss, J. L. (1973). *Statistical methods for rates and proportions.* New York: Wiley.

Gans, L., & Robertson, C. A. (1981). The behavior of estimated measures of association in small and moderate sample sizes for 2-×-3 tables. *Communications in Statistics: Theory and Methods, A10*, 1673–1686.

Gart, J. J. (1962). Approximate confidence limits for the relative risk. *Journal of the Royal Statistical Society, Series B, 24*, 454–463.

Gold, R. Z. (1963). Tests auxiliary of chi-square tests in a markov chain. *Annals of Mathematical Statistics, 34*, 56–74.

Good, I. J. (1961). The multivariate saddlepoint method and chi-squared for the multinomial distribution. *Annals of Mathematical Statistics, 32*, 535–548.

Good, I. J., Grover, T. N., & Mitchell, G. J. (1970). Exact distributions for chi-squared and for the likelihood-ratio statistic for the equiprobable multinomial distribution. *Journal of the American Statistical Association, 65*, 267–283.

Goodman, L. A. (1964). Simultaneous confidence intervals for cross-products ratios in contingency tables. *Journal of the Royal Statistical Society, Series B, 26*, 86–102.

Goodman, L. A. (1978). *Analyzing qualitative/categorical data.* Cambridge, MA: Abt Books.

Goodman, L. A., & Kruskal, W. H. (1954). Measures of association for cross classifications. *Journal of the American Statistical Association, 49*, 732–764.

Goodman, L. A., & Kruskal, W. H. (1959). Measures of association for cross classifications II: Further discussion and references. *Journal of the American Statistical Association, 54*, 123–163.

Goodman, L. A., & Kruskal, W. H. (1963). Measures of association for cross classifications III: Approximate sampling theory. *Journal of the American Statistical Association, 58*, 310–364.

Grizzle, J. E. (1967). Continuity correction in the chi-square test for 2-×-2 tables. *American Statistician, 21*(4), 28–32.

Gumbel, E. J. (1943). On the reliability of the classical chi-square test. *Annals of Mathematical Statistics, 14*, 255–263.

Haberman, S. J. (1978). *Analysis of qualitative data. Volume I: Introductory topics.* New York: Academic Press.

Horn, S. D. (1977). Goodness-of-fit tests for discrete data: A review and an application to a health impairment scale. *Biometrics, 33*, 237–248.

Hutchinson, T. P. (1979). The validity of the chi-squared test when expected frequencies are small: A list of recent research references. *Communications in Statistics: Theory and Methods, A8*, 327–335.

Irwin, J. O. (1949). A note on the subdivision of chi-square into components. *Biometrics, 36*, 130–134.

Jeffreys, H. (1961). *Theory of probability* (3rd ed.). Oxford: Clarendon Press.

Kastenbaum, M. A. (1960). A note on the additive partitioning of chi-square in contingency tables. *Biometrics, 16*, 416–422.

Katz, B. M., & McSweeney, M. (1979). Misclassification errors and data analysis. *Journal of Experimental Education, 47*, 331–338.

Kempthorne, O. (1966). The classical problem of inference: Goodness-of-fit. In J. Neyman (Ed.), *Fifth Berkeley symposium on mathematical statistics and probability* (pp. 235–249). Berkeley: University of California Press.

Kempthorne, O. (1979). In dispraise of the exact test: Reactions. *Journal of Statistical Planning and Inference, 3*, 199–213.

Kendall, M. G. (1952). *The advanced theory of statistics* (Vol 1, 5th ed.). London: Griffin.

Kendall, M. G. (1970). *Rank correlation methods* (4th ed.). London: Griffin.

Kendall, M. G., & Stuart, A. (1969). *The advanced theory of statistics* (Vol. 3, 3rd ed.). London: Griffin.

Kendall, M. G., & Stuart, A. (1979). *The advanced theory of statistics* (Vol. 2, 4th ed.). London: Griffin.

Kimball, A. W. (1954). Short cut formulas for the exact partitioning of chi-square in contingency tables. *Biometrics, 10,* 452–458.

Knepp, D. L., & Entwisle, D. R. (1969). Testing significance of differences between two chi squares. *Psychometrika, 34,* 331–333.

Kruskal, W. H., & Wallis, W. A. (1952). Use of rank in one-criterion variance analysis. *Journal of the American Statistical Association, 47,* 401–412.

Lancaster, H. O. (1949). The derivation and partition of chi-square in certain discrete distributions. *Biometrika, 36,* 117–129.

Lancaster, H. O. (1950). The exact partitioning of chi-square and its application to the problem of pooling of small expectations. *Biometrika, 37,* 267–270.

Lancaster, H. O. (1951). Complex contingency tables treated by the partition of chi-square. *Journal of the Royal Statistical Society, Series B, 13,* 242–249.

Lewis, D., & Burke, C. J. (1949). The use and misuse of the chi-square test. *Psychological Bulletin, 46,* 433–489.

Lewis, D., & Burke, C. J. (1950). Further discussion of the use and misuse of the chi-square test. *Psychological Bulletin, 47,* 347–355.

Lewontin, R. C., & Felsenstein, J. (1965). The robustness of homogeneity tests in 2-$\times$-n tables. *Biometrics, 21,* 19–33.

Mann, H. B., & Wald, A. (1942). On the choice of the number of intervals in the application of the chi-square test. *Annals of Mathematical Statistics, 13,* 306–317.

Mantel, N. (1974). Comment and a suggestion. *Journal of the American Statistical Association, 69,* 378–380.

Mantel, N., & Greenhouse, S. W. (1968). What is the continuity correction? *The American Statistician, 22*(5), 27–30.

Marascuilo, L. A., & Dagenais, F. (1982). Planned and post hoc comparisons for tests of homogeneity where the dependent variable is categorical and ordered. *Educational and Psychological Measurement, 42,* 777–781.

Marascuilo, L. A., & McSweeney, M. (1977). *Nonparametric and distribution-free methods for the social sciences.* Monterey, CA: Brooks/Cole.

Marascuilo, L. A., & Serlin, R. C. (1988). *Statistical methods for the social and behavioral sciences.* New York: W. H. Freeman.

Marascuilo, L. A., & Slaughter, R. E. (1981). Statistical procedures for identifying possible sources of item bias based on chi-square statistics. *Journal of Educational Measurement, 18,* 229–248.

Maxwell, A. E. (1961). *Analysing qualitative data.* London: Methuen.

Mehat, C. R., & Patel, N. R. (1980). A network algorithm for the exact treatment of the 2-$\times$-k contingency table. *Communication in Statistics: Simmulation and Computation, B9,* 649–664.

Mehat, C. R., & Patel, N. R. (1983). A network algorithm for performing Fisher's exact test in r $\times$ c contingency tables. *Journal of the American Statistical Association, 78,* 427–434.

Mehat, C. R., Patel, N. R., & Gray, R. (1985). On computing an exact confidence interval for the common odds ratio in several 2-$\times$-2 contingency tables. *Journal of the American Statistical Association, 80,* 969–973.

Miettinen, O. S. (1974). Comment. *Journal of the American Statistical Association, 69,* 380–382.

Mote, V. L., & Anderson, R. L. (1965). An investigation of the effect of misclassification on the properties of chi-square tests in the analysis of categorical data. *Biometrika, 52,* 95–109.

eyman, J., & Pearson, E. S. (1931). Further notes on the chi-square distribution. *Biometrika, 22,* 298–305.

verall, J. E. (1980). Power of the chi-square tests for 2-×-2 contingency tables with small expected frequencies. *Psychological Bulletin, 87,* 132–135.

astore, N. (1950). Some comments on "The use and misuse of the chi-square test." *Psychological Bulletin, 47,* 338–340.

earson, K. (1900). On the criterion that a given system of deviations from the probable in the case of a correlated system of variables is such that it can be reasonably supposed to have arisen from random sampling. *Philosophical Magazine,* July, 157–175. In E. S. Pearson (Ed.), (1947), *Karl Pearson's early statistical papers.* Cambridge: Cambridge University Press.

eters, C. C. (1950). The misuse of chi-square: A reply to Lewis and Burke. *Psychological Bulletin, 47,* 331–337.

lackett, R. L. (1964). The continuity correction for 2-×-2 tables. *Biometrika, 51,* 327–337.

oscoe, J. T., & Byars, J. A. (1971). An investigation of the restraints with respect to sample size commonly imposed on the use of the chi-square statistic. *Journal of the American Statistical Association, 66,* 755–759.

osnow, R. L., & Rosenthal, R. (1989). Statistical procedures and the justification of knowledge in psychological science. *American Psychologist, 44,* 1276–1284.

cheffe, H. A. (1953). A method for judging all contrasts in the analysis of variance. *Biometrika, 40,* 87–104.

cheuneman, J. (1979). A method of assessing bias in test items. *Journal of Educational Measurement, 16,* 143–152.

erlin, R. C., Carr, J. C., & Marasucilo, L. A. (1982). A measure of association for selected nonparametric procedures. *Psychological Bulletin, 92,* 786–790.

haffer, J. P. (1973). Testing specific hypotheses in contingency tables: Chi-square partitioning and other methods. *Psychological Reports, 33*(2), 343–348.

lakter, M. J. (1965). A comparison of the Pearson chi-square and Kolmogorov goodness of fit tests with respect to validity. *Journal of the American Statistical Association, 60,* 854–858.

lakter, M. J. (1966). Comparative validity of the chi-square and two modified chi-square goodness of fit tests for small but equal frequencies. *Biometrika, 53,* 619–622.

nee, R. D. (1974). Graphical display of two-way contingency tables. *American Statistician, 28,* 9–12.

olomon, D., Watson, M. S., Delucchi, K. L., Schaps, E., & Battistich, V. (1988). Enhancing children's prosocial behavior in the classroom. *American Educational Research Journal, 25,* 527–554.

tarmer, C. F., Grizzle, J. E., & Sen, P. K. (1974). Comment. *Journal of the American Statistical Association, 69,* 376–378.

pton, G. J. G. (1982). A comparison of alternative tests for the 2-×-2 comparative trial. *Journal of the Royal Statistical Society, Series B, 145,* 86–105.

Vatson, M., Solomon, D., Battistich, V., Schaps, E., & Solomon, J. (1989). The child development project: Combining traditional and developmental approaches to values education. In L. P. Nucci (Ed.), *Moral development and character education* (pp. 51–92). Berkeley: McCutchan.

Vest, E. N., & Kempthorne, O. A. (1972). A comparison of the chi-square and likelihood ratio tests for composite alternatives. *Journal of Statistical Computation and Simulation, 1,* 1–33.

Vise, M. E. (1963). Multinomial probabilities and the X^2 and chi-square distributions. *Biometrika, 50,* 145–154.

arnold, J. K. (1970). The minimum expectation in chi-square goodness-of-fit tests and the accuracy of approximation for the null distribution. *Journal of the American Statistical Association, 65,* 864–886.

Yates, F. (1934). Contingency tables involving small numbers and the chi-square test. *Journal of the Royal Statistical Society Supplement, 1,* 217–235.

Yates, F. (1984). Tests of significance for 2-×-2 contingency tables. *Journal of the Royal Statistical Society, Series A, 147,* 426.

Zwick, R., & Ericikan, K. (1989). Analysis of differential item functioning in the NAEP History Assessment. *Journal of Educational Measurement, 26,* 55–66.

11 Some Aspects of the Analysis of Categorical Data

B. S. Everitt
Institute of Psychiatry, University of London

INTRODUCTION

This chapter is primarily concerned with methods for the analysis of data arising in the form of *counts* or *frequencies*. Such *categorical data* are common particularly in the social and behavioral sciences. Table 11.1, for example shows the results of recording hair color for a number of individuals and Table 11.2 the results of recording eye color for the same sample of people. Of far more interest, of course, is Table 11.3, which gives the *cross-classification* of hair and eye color for these individuals. Table 11.3 is a simple example of a *contingency table*.

The numbers appearing in Tables 11.1, 11.2, and 11.3 are counts of individuals falling into particular categories of the categorical variable (*s*) forming the table. These numbers might be transformed into proportions or percentages but it is important to note that, in whatever form they are presented, the data were originally frequencies or counts rather than continuous measurements. Of course, continuous data is often put into discrete form by the use of intervals on a continuous scale. Age, for example, is a continuous variable, but if people are classified into different age groups, the intervals corresponding to these groups can be treated as if they were discrete units.

The questions we might wish to ask about categorical data are similar in many respects to those usually of concern for continuous data. For example, we may wish to investigate whether two categorical variables are related, or how a categorical response variable is related to a number of explanatory variables (which may or may not themselves be categorical). So why should the analysis of categorical data need separate consideration? Of course, the distributional as-

TABLE 11.1
Hair Color Data

Fair	Red	Medium	Dark	Black
(FH)	(RH)	(MA)	(DH)	(BH)
1455	286	2137	1391	114

sumptions made for continuous measurements (usually involving normality), are not justified for categorical random variables; different assumptions are needed and these lead to different methods of analysis. The distinction between the types of analysis technique used for continuous, normally distributed observations and those used for categorical and other nonnormally distributed data, is often made specific by referring to members of the former class as *parametric* and to the latter as *nonparametric*. To introduce some of the concepts and issues involved we begin by looking in detail at one of the most commonly occurring examples of categorical data, namely that involving a 2 × 2 contingency table.

THE 2 × 2 CONTINGENCY TABLE

Data in the form of 2 × 2 tables occur very frequently in the social sciences, education and medical investigations. Such data may arise in several ways. For instance, when N subjects are sampled from some population and each individual is classified according to two dichotomous variables, or when a *predetermined* number of individuals in each of the categories of one of the variables are sampled, and for each sample, the number of individuals in each of the categories of the second variable assessed. An example of the former is seen in Table 11.4, which arises from sampling 100 individuals and classifying them with respect to age, above and below 40 and with respect to amount of smoking, above and below 20 cigarettes a day. An example where a predetermined number of subjects in each category of one of the variables is sampled is shown in Table 11.5. In this investigation of the frequency of the side effect, nausea, with a particular drug, 50 subjects were given the drug and 50 a placebo.

TABLE 11.2
Eye Color Data

Light	Blue	Medium	Dark
(LE)	(BE)	(ME)	(DE)
1580	718	1774	1311

TABLE 11.3
Hair Color and Eye Color Data

Eye Color	| Hair Color					| Total
	FH	RH	MH	DH	BH	Total
LF	688	116	584	188	4	1580
BE	326	38	241	110	3	718
ME	343	84	909	412	26	1774
DE	98	48	403	681	81	1311
Total	1455	286	2137	1391	114	5383

The general form of a 2×2 table can be written as shown in Table 11.6. The questions of interest for such tables depend essentially on how the data in the table arise. For example in Table 11.4, interest would center on whether an *association* exists between the two classifying variables, age and smoking behavior, or whether they are *independent*. In Table 11.5 the equality or otherwise of the proportion of people given drug treatment who suffer nausea, and the corresponding proportion for those people given the placebo, would be of concern. However, although the substantive questions may differ, the test employed in each situation is the same, namely the *chi-squared test* proposed originally by Pearson (1900) and Yule (1911). The most convenient form of this test is

$$X^2 = \frac{(ad - bc)^2 N}{m_1 m_2 n_1 n_2}. \tag{1}$$

When the two variables forming the table are independent or the two binomial proportions of interest are equal, the test statistic, X^2 has in large samples, a χ^2 distribution with one degree of freedom. Applying the test to the data on the side effect nausea shown in Table 11.5 gives

$$X^2 = \frac{(15 \times 46 - 35 \times 4)^2 \times 100}{50 \times 50 \times 19 \times 81} = 7.86. \tag{2}$$

The associated p value is less than .01, and we are led to suspect the truth of our hypothesis that the frequency of nausea is independent of the treatment involved.

TABLE 11.4
Smoking and Age Data

Amount of Smoking	| Age		Total
	Under 40	Over 40	Total
<20/day	50	15	65
>20/day	10	25	35
Total	60	40	100

TABLE 11.5
Side Effects and Drug Data

| Treatment | Nausea | | Total |
	Present	Absent	
Drug given	15	35	50
Placebo given	4	46	50
Total	19	81	100

The proportion of people suffering from nausea when treated with the drug ($\hat{p}_1 = .30$) appears to be considerably higher than the proportion of placebo treated patients experiencing nausea ($\hat{p}_2 = .08$).

An estimate of the standard error of the observed difference, $\hat{p}_1 - \hat{p}_2$ of the two proportions is given by

$$\left(\frac{\hat{p}_1 \hat{q}_1}{n_1} + \frac{\hat{p}_2 \hat{q}_2}{n_2} \right)^{1/2}. \tag{3}$$

This expression in Equation 3 enables us to find an approximate, normal-based confidence interval for the difference in the two proportions; because the standard error in Equation 3 takes the value 0.0753, this leads to an approximate 95% interval, (0.0684, 0.3716).

Performing the same test for the smoking/age data in Table 11.4 gives the result, $X^2 = 22.16$, a value that is clearly highly significant. Here the explanation of the significant finding is in terms of a positive association between age and smoking; this might be quantified by a coefficient analogous to the correlation coefficient for two continuous variables (see Everitt, 1992, chap. 3).

This chi-square test is approximate and will not hold exactly when the *expected values* of the cells of the table are small. These values are estimates of the values to be expected in the various cells of the contingency table when there is no association between the variables. They can be calculated simply from the *marginal totals* of the table as shown in Table 11.7; their values for Table 11.5 are shown in Table 11.8.

Fisher (1925) advanced a rule of thumb that the expected number in any one cell should not be less than five and this has found its way into the "folklore" of

TABLE 11.6
General 2 × 2 Contingency Table

| Variable B | Variable A | | Total |
	Category 1	Category 2	
Category 1	a	b	a + b
Category 2	c	d	c + d
Total	a + c	b + d	N = a + b + c + d

TABLE 11.7
Estimation of Expected Values

	A_1	A_2	Total
B_1	$\dfrac{n_1 m_1}{N}$	$\dfrac{n_1 m_2}{N}$	n_1
B_2	$\dfrac{n_2 m_1}{N}$	$\dfrac{n_2 m_2}{N}$	n_2
Total	m_1	m_2	N

statistical testing, although it is well known to be conservative particularly for tables larger than 2×2 (see the next section).

In an attempt to overcome this problem Yates (1934) suggested a correction involving deducting $\frac{1}{2}$ from the observed deviations of observed values from expectations when calculating the chi-squared test statistic. This correction, which Yates termed the *continuity correction,* alters the statistic in Equation 1 to

$$X_c^2 = \frac{\left(|ad - bc| - \frac{1}{2}N\right)^2 N}{m_1 m_2 n_1 n_2}. \tag{4}$$

For Table 11.5 this gives $X_c^2 = 6.50$, a value that still indicates a considerable association between side effect and treatment.

An alternative testing procedure that is often used in the case of 2×2 tables with small expected frequencies is *Fisher's exact test,* which involves the use of the actual probability distribution of the observed frequencies. For fixed marginal totals the required distribution is easily shown to be the *hypergeometric* given by

$$P(a,b,c,d,m_1,m_2,n_1,n_2) = \frac{n_1! n_2! m_1! m_2!}{a! b! c! d! N!}. \tag{5}$$

Fisher's exact test involves the use of Equation 5 to find the probability of the observed table and that of every other arrangement of cell frequencies giving as much as more evidence of an association, always keeping in mind that the

TABLE 11.8
Expected Values Under Independence for Table 11.5

Treatment	Nausea		Total
	Present	Absent	
Drug given	9.5	40.5	50
Placebo given	9.5	40.5	50
Total	19	81	100

TABLE 11.9
The Incidence of Suicidal Feelings in Psychotic and Neurotic Patients

| | Type of Patient | | |
	Psychotics	Neurotics	Total
Suicidal feelings	2(4)	6(4)	8
No suicidal feelings	18(16)	14(16)	32
Total	20	20	40

marginal totals are to be regarded as fixed. The sum of these probabilities is use to judge the hypothesis of no association.

To illustrate the use of Fisher's exact test we apply it to Table 11.9, whic shows the number of patients having suicidal feelings amongst 20 diagnosed a psychotic and 20 diagnosed as neurotic. (The expected frequencies under th hypothesis of independence are shown in parentheses in Table 11.9; two of the are below 5). First we find the probability of the observed table, P_0

$$P_0 = \frac{8!32!20!20!}{2!6!18!14!20!} = 0.095760.$$

Returning to Table 11.9 and keeping in mind that the marginal frequencies are t be taken as fixed, the frequencies in the body of the table can be arranged in tw ways both of which would represent, had they been observed, more extrem discrepancies between the diagnostic groups with respect to suicidal feeling These arrangements are shown in Table 11.10.

The probabilities associated with these two tables, P_a and P_b are given by

$$P_a = 0.020160$$
$$P_b = 0.001638.$$

The required probability, P is consequently, given by

$$P = P_0 + P_a + P_b$$
$$= 0.095760 + 0.020160 + 0.001638$$
$$= 0.117558.$$

TABLE 11.10
More Extreme Cell Frequencies than Those Observed

(a)			(b)		
P	N	Total	P	N	Total
1	7	8	0	8	8
19	13	32	20	12	32
20	20	40	20	20	40

o the data gives no evidence that psychotic and neurotic patients differ in their equency of suicidal feelings.

It is important to note that Fisher's exact test indicates departure from the null ypothesis in a *specific direction* in contrast to the chi-squared test that assesses epartures in either direction. In the case where the sample sizes in each group e the same (as they are in our example), the probability obtained from applying isher's test may be doubled to give the equivalent of a two-tailed test, giving for able 11.9, $P = 0.23512$. It is of considerable interest to compare this value with e corresponding probabilities obtained from the Pearson chi-square test .11385) and its Yates's corrected version (0.23572). These values reflect a umber of general points about these three tests when applied to small or moder- e sized samples

1. The Yates's corrected chi-square gives a probability value similar to that obtained from Fisher's exact test.

2. Yates's corrected chi-square and Fisher's exact test give p values that are more conservative (that is, larger) than those obtained from the Pearson test.

(In large samples, it is well known that all three methods are equivalent). Fisher's test is apparently conservative, so his exact test has often been the bject of severe criticism. (A recent example is D'Agostino, Chase, & elanger, 1988). Much of this criticism centers around the conditional nature of isher's test, assuming as it does, that both sets of marginal totals are fixed. The guments are of a subtle and technical nature but primarily involve whether or ot the marginal totals in a table (however generated), provide any information n the existence of an association. Yates (1984) argued strongly that they do not nd consequently concluded that Fisher's exact test is appropriate for the analysis f 2 × 2 tables. Cox (1984), Barnard (1984), and Little (1989) provided further ipport for this view. The most recent paper criticizing Fisher's test (D'Agostino al., 1988) concentrates on illustrating the apparent conservative nature of the est, while failing to confront the arguments for conditioning on the margins. In e author's opinion the balance of evidence is strongly in favor of the exact test. lore recent work on exact tests for contingency tables is described in Mehta and atel (1986).

Up to this point we have confined our attention almost exclusively to tests of gnificance for the hypothesis of no association in 2 × 2 tables. However, nportant questions of *estimation* may also arise particularly when the null ypothesis is discarded. This is particularly true of certain types of study; for xample, in studying the aetiology of a disease it is often useful to estimate the ncreased risk (if any) of incurring a particular disease if a certain factor is resent. If in the *population* from which our sample is taken the relevant propor- ons of people with the disease and with the factor and so forth, are as in Table

TABLE 11.11
Population Values for Disease Data

Factor	Disease		
	Present	Absent	
Present	P_1	P_3	$P_1 + P_3$
Absent	P_2	P_4	$P_2 + P_4$
	$P_1 + P_2$	$P_3 + P_4$	1

11.11, then the risk of having the disease present for those individuals having the factor present is

$$\frac{P_1}{(P_1 + P_3)} \tag{7}$$

and for those individuals not having the factor present it is

$$\frac{P_2}{(P_2 + P_4)}. \tag{8}$$

In many situations involving this type of example the proportion of subject having the disease will be small; consequently P_1 will be small compared with P and P_2 will be small compared with P_4; the *ratio* of the risks given by Equation 7 and 8 then very nearly becomes

$$\frac{P_1 P_4}{P_2 P_2}. \tag{9}$$

This quantity is properly known as the *approximate relative risk* but is often referred to simply as *relative risk* and denoted by ψ. An estimate of ψ can be obtained from the sample frequencies shown in Table 11.12 as

$$\hat{\psi} = \frac{ad}{bc}. \tag{10}$$

A confidence interval for ψ can be obtained by considering ln $\hat{\psi}$ and its variance estimated as

$$\mathrm{var}(\ln \hat{\psi}) = \frac{1}{a} + \frac{1}{b} + \frac{1}{c} + \frac{1}{d}. \tag{11}$$

As an example of the procedure we consider a population, the members of which have been equally exposed to a viral infection; a proportion of the population have been inoculated against the infection. After the epidemic has passed, a random sample of people is selected and the numbers of inoculated and uninoculated that have escaped infection are recorded with the results shown in Table 11.13.

TABLE 11.12
Sample Values for Disease Data

| | Disease | | |
Factor	Present	Absent	Total
Present	a	b	a + b
Absent	c	d	c + d
	a + c	b + d	a + b + c + d

It is clear from these data that the proportion of uninoculated people infected by the virus is considerably larger than the proportion of inoculated so affected. In other words the risk of being infected had a person been inoculated is less than the risk had the person not been inoculated. To quantify this difference we use Equations 10 and 11 to derive a confidence interval for relative risk. First we find $\hat{\psi}$ and the variance of $\ln \hat{\psi}$:

$$\hat{\psi} = 0.201$$

$$\ln \hat{\psi} = -1.60$$

$$\text{var}(\ln \hat{\psi}) = 0.401.$$

A 95% confidence interval for $\ln \psi$ is given by

$$-1.60 \pm 1.96 \times 0.63$$

$$= -2.83 \text{ to } -0.37.$$

Taking exponentials of the two limits gives the required 95% confidence interval for ψ as 0.06 to 0.69. Consequently the risk that an inoculated person will be infected by the virus could be as high as 69% of that of an uninoculated person, or it might be as low as 6%.

$r \times c$ CONTINGENCY TABLES

In this section we discuss the analysis of contingency tables arising from the cross-classification of two categorical variables when the number of rows or

TABLE 11.13
Incidence of Virus Infection

	Not Infected	Infected	Total
Not Inoculated	130(d)	20(c)	150
Inoculated	97(b)	3(a)	100
Total	227	23	250

number of columns of the table, or both, are greater than two. A general nomenclature for such tables is shown in Table 11.14. The hypothesis of the independence of the two variables forming the table can now be formulated as

$$H_0 : p_{ij} = p_{i.} p_{.j}, \tag{12}$$

where p_{ij} is the probability of an observation belonging to the ith category of the row variable and the jth category of the column variable, $p_{i.}$ is the probability of an observation belonging to the ith category of the row variable (without reference to the column variable) and $p_{.j}$ represents the corresponding probability for the jth category of the column variable. The maximum likelihood estimates of $p_{i.}$ and $p_{.j}$ are obtained from the appropriate marginal totals as

$$\hat{p}_{i.} = \frac{n_{i.}}{N} \tag{13}$$

and

$$\hat{p}_{.j} = \frac{n_{.j}}{N}. \tag{14}$$

The estimated expected value under the hypothesis of independence is therefore

$$E_{ij} = N\hat{p}_{i.}\hat{p}_{.j} = \frac{n_{i.} n_{.j}}{N}. \tag{15}$$

The well-known chi-squared statistic for testing independence is then given by

$$X^2 = \sum_{i=1}^{r} \sum_{j=1}^{c} \frac{(n_{ij} - E_{ij})^2}{E_{ij}}. \tag{16}$$

Under H_0 this statistic has a chi-squared distribution with $(r - 1)(c - 1)$ degrees of freedom.

TABLE 11.14
The r by c Contingency Table

Rows—Variable 1	Columns—Variable 2				
	1	2	. . .	c	Total
1	n_{11}	n_{12}	. . .	n_{ic}	$n_{1.}$
2	n_{21}	n_{22}	. . .	n_{2c}	$n_{2.}$
.				.	
.	.	.	.	.	
.		.	.	.	
r	n_{r1}	n_{r2}	. . .	n_{rc}	$n_{r.}$
Total	$n_{.1}$	$n_{.2}$	. . .	$n_{.c}$	$n_{..} = N$

To illustrate the chi-squared test we return to the data given in Table 11.3, which shows a sample of individuals cross-classified with respect to eye and hair color. The estimated expected values under the hypothesis of independence are shown in Table 11.15, and the chi-square statistic takes the value 1,240 with 12 degrees of freedom. Clearly this indicates that the hypothesis of independence is not supportable. Given the nature of the two variables forming the table this is, of course, not surprising.

A point that was briefly mentioned in the previous sections was that the derivation of the chi-square distribution as an approximation for the distribution of the test statistic given in Equation 16 is made under the assumption that the expected values are not too small. This vague term has, following Fisher's comment, generally been interpreted as meaning that all expected values in the table should be greater than five for the chi-square test to be valid. Cochran (1954) pointed out that this rule is too stringent, and suggested that if relatively few expectations are less than five (say, one cell out of five) a minimum expectation of unity is allowable. Even this suggestion may be to restrictive, because work by Lewontin and Felsenstein (1965) and Slakter (1966) shows that many of the expected values may be as low as unity without affecting the test greatly. Lewontin and Felsenstein gave the following conservative rule for tables in which $r = 2$.

The $2 \times c$ table can be tested by the conventional chi-square criterion if all the expectations are 1 or greater

The authors point that even this rule is extremely conservative and in the majority of cases the chi-square criterion may be used for tables with expectations in excess of 0.5 in the smallest cell.

Although contingency tables formed from two categorical variables are those most commonly encountered, more complex tables involving three or more variables are frequently of concern. An example involving four variables is shown in Table 11.16. For such tables a richer variety of hypotheses than that of

TABLE 11.15
Estimated Expected Values Under Independence for Hair Color, Eye Color Data

	Hair Color					
Eye Color	FH	RH	MH	DH	BH	Total
LE	127.1	83.9	627.2	408.3	33.5	1580
BE	194.1	38.1	285.0	185.5	15.2	718
ME	479.5	94.3	704.3	458.4	37.6	1774
DE	354.4	69.7	520.5	338.8	27.8	1311
Total	1455	286	2137	1391	114	5383

TABLE 11.16
Voting Behavior: Vote by Sex by Class by Age

Age Group	Men		Women	
	Conservative	Labor	Conservative	Labor
	Upper Middle Class			
>73	4	0	10	0
51–73	27	8	26	9
41–50	27	4	25	9
26–40	17	12	28	9
<26	7	6	7	3
	Lower Middle Class			
>73	8	4	9	2
51–73	21	13	33	8
41–50	27	12	29	4
26–40	14	15	17	13
<26	9	9	13	7
	Working Class			
>73	8	15	17	4
51–73	35	62	52	53
41–50	29	75	32	70
26–40	32	56	36	67
<26	14	34	18	33

simple independence become of interest. For example in Table 11.16 we may wish to assess whether voting behavior is independent of age conditional on sex and class, or whether any association between voting intention and class is the same for males and females. The approach taken to the analysis of such tables is the application of what are known as *log-linear models;* such models are described in detail in chapter 9 of this volume.

A significant overall chi-square test for an $r \times c$ contingency table indicates the lack of independence of the two variables involved, but provides no information as to whether this lack of independence occurs throughout or only in a specific part of the table. An extremely useful addition to the chi-square test is provided by the technique of *correspondence analysis,* which allows a graphical display of departures from independence that can be extremely helpful in gaining insight into the structure of the table.

CORRESPONDENCE ANALYSIS

Correspondence analysis attempts to display graphically the relationships present in a two-way table of counts (such as Table 11.3), by deriving *coordinates* representing the row categories and column categories of the table. The correpondence analysis coordinates are analogous to those derived in *principal components analysis* (see Everitt & Dunn, 1992) of continuous data, except that they partition the total chi-square value rather than the total variance.

Correspondence analysis consists essentially of finding the *singular value decomposition* of the matrix C containing the individual components of the chi-square statistic in Equation 16, that is, the values

$$c_{ij} = \frac{n_{ij} - E_{ij}}{\sqrt{E_{ij}}}. \tag{17}$$

The singular value decomposition of C consists of finding matrices U, V, and Δ (diagonal) such that

$$C = U\Delta V', \tag{18}$$

where U contains the *eigenvectors* of CC' and V the eigenvectors of $C'C$. Δ contains the *eigenvalues* of CC' on its main diagonal. Such a decomposition leads to

$$c_{ij} = \sum_{k=1}^{R} \delta_k^{1/2} u_{ik} v_{jk}, \qquad i = 1 \ldots, r, \qquad j = 1 \ldots, c \tag{19}$$

where $R = \min(r - 1, c - 1)$ is the *rank* of the matrix C and u_{ik} and v_{jk}, $k = 1 \ldots, R$ are the elements of the kth column of U and the kth column of V respectively: $\delta_1 \ldots, \delta_R$ are the nonzero eigenvalues of CC', so that

$$\text{trace}(CC') = \sum_{k=1}^{R} \delta_k = \sum_{i=1}^{r} \sum_{j=1}^{c} c_{ij}^2 = X^2. \tag{20}$$

Most applications of correspondence analysis use the first two columns of U, u_1, and u_2 and the first two columns of V, v_1, and v_2 to provide a graphical display of the c_{ij}, that is, the *residuals* from the independence model. The entries in u_1 and u_2 give the two-dimensional coordinates of points representing the row categories of the contingency table, those in v_1, and v_2 give the corresponding coordinates for the column categories. How well the two-dimensional coordinates represent the residuals can be judged by the size of the first two eigenvalues of CC' relative to the remainder.

An explanation of how to interpret the derived coordinates is made simpler if we consider the situation where the first eigenvalue is dominant so that the residuals from the independence model can be well represented by the one-dimensional coordinates given in u_1 and v_1. In this case we see from Equation 19 that

$$c_{ij} \approx \delta_1^{1/2} u_{i1} v_{j1}. \tag{21}$$

From Equation 21 we see that when u_{i1} and v_{j1} are both large and positive (or both large and negative), then c_{ij} will be large and positive indicating a large positive association for the ith row and jth column of the table. Similarly, when u_{i1} and v_{j1} are large but have different signs, c_{ij} will be large and negative indicating that row i and column j have a negative association. Finally, when the product $u_{i1}v_{j1}$ is near zero, the association between the ith row and the jth column is low.

An important point that must be stressed is that it is not the closeness of a row point to a column point that determines their degree of association but the *comparison* of their respective distances from the origin.

To illustrate how correspondence analysis works in practice we use the eye color, hair color data given in Table 11.3. The results from applying correspondence analysis are shown in Table 11.17. Plotting the two-dimensional coordinates gives Fig. 11.1. It is this graphical display that is the quintessential feature of correspondence analysis. It allows a direct visualization of how eye colors are associated with hair colors. For example, it is clear from Fig. 11.1 that there is a large positive association between dark eyes and black or dark hair, and a large negative association between dark eyes and fair hair.

LOGISTIC REGRESSION

Table 11.18 shows a set of data on psychotropic drug consumption amongst a sample of individuals in a part of London (Data taken from Murray, Dunn, Williams, & Tarnopsky, 1981). Each individuals original response would have been yes or no to the question of whether they took such drugs. Table 11.18 resembles a contingency table, but the questions of most interest would now involve asking how the variables sex, age, and caseness affect psychotropic drug

TABLE 11.17
Results from Applying Correspondence Analysis to Hair Color-Eye Color Data

Eye Color	u_1	u_2	Hair Color	v_1	v_2
LE	−0.535	−0.276	FH	−0.633	−0.521
BE	−0.327	−0.348	RH	−0.120	−0.064
ME	0.043	0.810	MH	−0.059	0.756
DE	0.778	−0.381	DH	0.670	−0.304
			BH	0.362	−0.245
Eigenvalues	δ_1	δ'_2	δ_3	δ_4	
	1077.3	162.12	4.6	0.0	

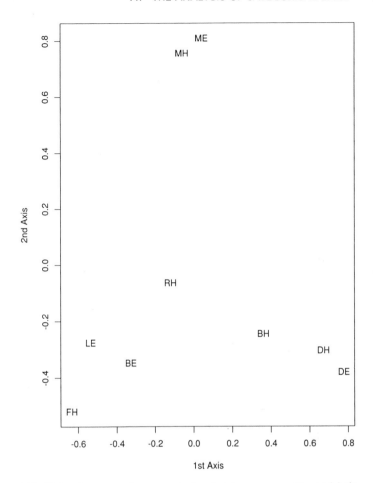

FIG. 11.1. Correspondence analysis of data on eye color and hair color (labels as in Table 11.17)

taking. An obvious approach would be to postulate a *linear model* for the probability, p, that an individual takes drugs, that is, a model such as

$$p = \text{Prob. of taking drugs} = \beta_0 + \beta_1\text{Sex} + \beta_2\text{Age} + \beta_3\text{Caseness}, \tag{22}$$

where sex and caseness are dummy variables. Such a model for p has however several drawbacks.

1. The probability, p, is constrained to be between zero and one. Estimating the parameters in Equation 22 by the usual methods (for example, *least squares*) might lead to fitted values of p outside this range.

TABLE 11.18
Patterns of Psychotropic Drug Consumption

Sex	Mean Age	Probable Case	N Taking Drugs	Total
Male	23.2	No	9	531
Male	36.5	No	16	500
Male	54.3	No	38	644
Male	69.2	No	26	275
Male	79.5	No	9	90
Male	23.5	Yes	12	171
Male	36.5	Yes	16	125
Male	54.3	Yes	31	121
Male	69.2	Yes	16	56
Male	79.5	Yes	10	26
Female	23.2	No	12	568
Female	36.5	No	42	596
Female	54.3	No	96	765
Female	69.2	No	52	327
Female	79.5	No	30	179
Female	23.2	Yes	33	210
Female	36.5	Yes	47	189
Female	54.3	Yes	71	242
Female	69.2	Yes	45	98
Female	79.2	Yes	21	60

2. Linear models such as Equation 22 assume error terms with equal variance, which is unlikely for this type of response.

A more useful approach is to apply to linear model to the probability *after* applying a transformation; here the most appropriate is to take

$$\lambda = \ln \frac{p}{1 - p}. \tag{23}$$

This is known as the *logistic transformation*. As p varies from 0 to 1, λ varies between $-\infty$ and ∞. The model of interest now becomes

$$\lambda = \beta_0 + \beta_1 \text{Sex} + \beta_2 \text{Age} + \beta_3 \text{Caseness}. \tag{24}$$

In general, where there were k explanatory variables, $x_1, x_2, \ldots, x_k$, some of which could be categorical and some continuous, the model would have the form

$$\lambda = \beta_0 + \beta_1 x_1 \ldots + \beta_k x_k. \tag{25}$$

To use the model we clearly first have to estimate the parameters β_0, $\beta_1, \ldots, \beta_k$ which we can do using *maximum likelihood*. From Equation 25 we and that p, the probability that the binary response variable takes the value one, is given by

$$p = \frac{\exp\left(\beta_0 + \sum_{i=1}^{k} \beta_i x_i\right)}{1 + \exp\left(\beta_0 + \sum_{i=1}^{k} \beta_i x_i\right)}. \tag{26}$$

If we now represent the observed values of our binary response variable as y_1, $y_2 \ldots, y_n$ the likelihood is given by

$$L = \prod_{i=1}^{n} p^{y_i}(1 - p)^{(1-y_i)}, \tag{27}$$

which using Equation 26 can be written as

$$L = \prod_{i=1}^{n} \frac{\exp\left[y_i\left(\beta_0 + \sum_{i=1}^{k} \beta_i x_i\right)\right]}{1 + \exp\left(\beta_0 + \sum_{i=1}^{k} \beta_i x_i\right)} \tag{28}$$

Various algorithms may be used to find the values of $\beta_0, \beta_1 \ldots, \beta_k$, which maximize L, but details need not concern us here. Instead we return to the psychotropic drug data of Table 11.18. For these data the relevant estimates and their standard errors are given in Table 11.19. The interpretation of the regression coefficients is essentially the same as in the *multiple regression* situation for continuous response variables although it has to be remembered that we are now dealing with the transformed response; so, for example, being considered a likely psychiatric case increases the logistic transformed response by 0.7 compared to

TABLE 11.19
Estimates of Regression Coefficients and their Standard Errors
for the Logistic Model Fitted to the Data in Table 11.18

Variable	Regression Coefficient	Standard Error
Sex (Males = 1, Female = 2)	0.31	0.05
Age	0.03	0.002
Prob. Case (1 = No, 2 = Yes)	0.70	0.04

Note: Chi-square test that all regression coefficients are zero; $X^2 = 467.2$, $df = 19$, $p < .001$

not being considered a case. A more appealing interpretation is available if w
consider the transformed response in a little more detail. The term $p/(1 - $
gives the *odds* of drug taking compared to not taking drugs; if this ratio is great
than one then the odds are in favor of drug taking. Consequently the logist
transformation is simply ln(odds). From Table 11.19 we see that for individua
not regarded as likely psychiatric cases

$$\ln(\text{odds}) = -3.4 + 0.7 + 0.3\text{Sex} + 0.03\text{Age} \tag{2}$$

and for those regarded as likely psychiatric cases

$$\ln(\text{odds}) = -3.4 + 1.4 + 0.3\text{Sex} + 0.03\text{Age}. \tag{3}$$

The difference between these is 0.7 and so exp(0.7), that is, 2.0 gives th
estimated ratio of the odds for likely psychiatric patients against those regarde
as unlikely psychiatric patients. The odds in favor of taking psychotropic drugs
approximately twice as high for the former than for the latter. A test that all th
regression coefficients are zero is provided by a chi-square test, which for th
psychotropic drug data takes the value 467.2 with 19*df*, indicating clearly tha
some, at least, of the coefficients differ from zero.

A number of stepwise procedures are available for choosing subsets of var
ables most important for determining the response variable. Details are given i
Everitt (1989).

CASE-CONTROL STUDIES

One-to-one matching is frequently used by research workers to increase th
precision of a comparison. The matching is usually done on variables such a
age, sex, weight, IQ, and the like, information that can be obtained relativel
easily. Two samples matched in this way must be thought of as *correlated* rathe
then independent, which makes the usual chi-square test for assessing the diffe
ence between frequencies, invalid. Fortunately, for comparing the matched case
and controls on a single variable, an appropriate test, due to McNemar (1955), i
available. The general form for matched data for a categorical variable with tw
categories is shown in Table 11.20. As we are concerned with the differenc
between the two samples, the entries in the N-E and S-W cells of the table are c
no interest, because *b* refers to matched pairs both of whom possess the attribute
whereas the frequency *c* refers to pairs both of whom do not possess the attribute
Consequently a comparison of cases and controls is based on *a* and *d*. Under th
hypothesis that cases and controls do not differ with respect to possession o
otherwise of the attribute we would expect the entries in the main diagonal o
Table 11.20 to each equal $(a + d)/2$. Now if the observed frequencies *a* and *d*
and their expected values $(a + d)/2$ are substituted in the usual formula for chi
square, we obtain

$$X^2 = \frac{(a - d)^2}{(a + d)} \tag{31}$$

our test statistic. If a correction for continuity is applied, this expression becomes:

$$X^2 = \frac{(|a - d| - 1)^2}{(a + d)}. \tag{32}$$

nder the hypothesis of no difference between cases and controls with respect to he attribute this test statistic has a chi-square distribution with one degree of eedom.

To illustrate the use of McNemar's test we use the data shown in Table 11.21, hich arises from testing the serum cholesterol levels of 110 *pairs* of first-year edical students; one member of each pair was male and the other female and embers of each pair were matched on age.

To test whether the proportion of students with high cholesterol is the same for hen, and women, we use McNemar's test as outlined earlier. Note again that nly the information in the two cells of the table relating to untied pairs is used. The test statistic given in Equation 31 takes the value

$$X^2 = \frac{(20 - 15)^2}{(20 + 15)} = 0.71,$$

value that clearly gives no evidence of any difference in the two proportions of nterest.

For the matched pair case-control study in which p risk variables are under nvestigation, Woolson and Lachenbruch (1982) suggested a method of analysis ased on the linear-logistic model described earlier. The data from such a study vould take the general form shown in Table 11.22. For a person with risk factor alues $x_{i1}, x_{i2}, \ldots, x_{ip}$, the probability of disease is modeled by the linear ogistic function given in Equation 26. For matched pair case control data, the onditional likelihood is determined by computing the product of n *conditional robabilities,* one for each pair. For each pair i one considers the observed values

TABLE 11.20
Frequencies in Matched Samples

		Sample 1	
		A absent	A present
	A present	a	b
ple 2	A absent	c	d

TABLE 11.21
Serum Cholesterol Level
(Above and Below 210 mg/ml)
for 110 Matched Pairs

	Females		
Males	Normal	High	Total
Normal	60	15	75
High	20	15	35
Total	80	30	110

TABLE 11.22
Notation for Matched Pair Case-Control Data
p risk variables

Pair	Case	Control
1	$(x_{11}, \ldots, x_{1p})$	$(y_{11}, \ldots, y_{1p})$
2	$(x_{21}, \ldots, x_{2p})$	$(y_{21}, \ldots, y_{2p})$
.	.	.
.	.	.
.	.	.
i	$(x_{i1}, \ldots, x_{ip})$	$(y_{i1}, \ldots, y_{ip})$
.	.	.
.	.	.
.	.	.
n	$(x_{n1}, \ldots, x_{np})$	$(y_{n1}, \ldots, y_{np})$

of the risk variables for case and control as fixed, then computes the probability that the vector **x** corresponds to the case and the vector **y** to the control, given that either this correspondence or the exact reverse correspondence occurs, that is, **y** to case and **x** to control. The product of these n probabilities, the conditional likelihood is then given by

$$\prod_{i=1}^{n} \frac{\exp \sum_{j=1}^{p} \beta_j (x_{ij} - y_{ij})}{1 + \exp \sum_{j=1}^{p} \beta_j (x_{ij} - y_{ij})}. \tag{33}$$

To estimate the β's we can use the same approach described in an earlier section by noting that the function in Equation 33 is identical to that in Equation 28, when all values of the dichotomous dependent variable are set at unity, the independent variables are the intra-pair differences of the p risk variates and the intercept term, β_0, is excluded.

To illustrate this approach to case-control studies we use the data shown in Table 11.23, which arises from a study designed to test the hypothesis that known risk factors for the development of schizophrenia would be more common in schizophrenics with a low age of onset compared to those with age of onset in the commonly occurring range. The risk factors considered were "complications during pregnancy and birth," and "family history of psychosis," both rated as simple dichotomies, present or absent. Thirty-six people with a strict adult diagnosis of schizophrenia who had been seen for any reason by a child psychiatrist before the age of 16 were identified as the low age of onset cases. Controls who also had adult schizophrenia, but who had not been seen by the psychiatric

TABLE 11.23
Case-Control Study-Risk Factors
for Schizophrenia

Pair	Case		Control	
1	0	1	0	0
2	1	0	1	0
3	0	0	0	0
4	1	1	1	0
5	0	0	1	0
6	0	0	0	0
7	0	0	0	0
8	1	0	1	0
9	0	1	0	0
10	0	0	0	0
11	0	0	1	0
12	1	0	1	0
13	0	0	1	0
14	0	0	0	0
15	0	1	0	0
16	0	0	0	0
17	1	0	0	0
18	0	0	0	1
19	0	0	0	1
20	0	0	1	0
21	1	1	0	0
22	0	0	0	0
23	0	0	0	1
24	1	1	0	0
25	0	1	0	0
26	0	0	1	1
27	0	1	1	0
28	1	0	0	0
29	0	0	0	0
30	1	0	0	0
31	0	0	0	0
32	0	1	0	0
33	1	0	0	0
34	0	0	0	0
35	1	0	0	0
36	0	0	0	0

ervice until after the age of 21 were matched one-for-one with the cases on sex, ace, and socioeconomic class.

The estimated coefficients for the logistic model and their standard errors are hown in Table 11.24. For these data, the coefficients are not significantly ifferent from zero and consequently there is no evidence that patients with early nset of schizophrenia differ from those with late onset with respect to the two sk factors considered.

TABLE 11.24
Parmeter Estimates and Standard Errors
for Logistic Model on Case-Control Data

Variable	Coefficient	Standard Error	Coefficient/Standard Error
Birth complications	0.805	0.607	1.326
History	0.038	0.574	0.066

LATENT CLASS MODELS

An alternative approach to describing and modeling the associations between a set of categorical variables, than those discussed in this chapter or the log-linear models considered in Vol. 2, chap. 2, is the *latent class model* a full account of which is given in Lazarsfeld and Henry (1968). This model, which is analogous in some respects to the factor analysis model for continuous variables (see Everitt & Dunn, 1992), postulates the existence of an underlying categorical *latent variable,* with say c classes; within any category of the latent variable the manifest or observed categorical variables are assumed independent of one another (the axiom of *conditional independence*). Observed associations between the manifest variables are thus assumed to result from the underlying grouping of the data produced by the categorical latent variable.

The latent class model may be formulated as a *finite mixture density* (see Everitt & Hand, 1981) as follows.

Suppose $\mathbf{x}' = [x_1, x_2 \ldots, x_p]$ is a vector containing the values of the p manifest dichotomous variables, so that x_j is either zero or one. The latent class model implies that $\mathbf{x}$ has a probability density function given by

$$f(\mathbf{x};\boldsymbol{\alpha},\Theta) = \sum_{i=1}^{c} \alpha_i f_i(\mathbf{x};\boldsymbol{\theta}_i) \tag{34}$$

where

$$f_i(\mathbf{x};\boldsymbol{\theta}_i) = \prod_{j=1}^{p} \theta_{ij}^{x_j}(1 - \theta_{ij})^{(1-x_j)} \tag{35}$$

and $\boldsymbol{\alpha}' = [\alpha_1, \alpha_2 \ldots, \alpha_c]$, $\Sigma_{i=1}^{c} \alpha_i = 1$, $\Theta = [\boldsymbol{\theta}_1 \ldots, \boldsymbol{\theta}_c]$.

The elements of $\boldsymbol{\theta}_i' = [\theta_{i1} \ldots, \theta_{ip}]$ give the probability of variables in the ith category of the latent variable taking the value unity. The density function, f, is a finite mixture density in which the component densities, $f_1 \ldots, f_c$ are *multivariate Bernoulli* densities arising from the local independence requirement. Formulating the latent class model in this way allows estimation of the parameters, $\boldsymbol{\alpha}$ and $\boldsymbol{\Theta}$, by maximum likelihood, the details of the estimation procedure being as follows:

Given a sample of n independent vectors $\mathbf{x}_1 \ldots, \mathbf{x}_n$, the likelihood function assuming the latent class model is given by

$$L = \prod_{k=1}^{n} f(\mathbf{x}_k;\boldsymbol{\alpha},\boldsymbol{\Theta}) \qquad (36)$$

so that the log-likelihood, L, is given by

$$L = \sum_{k=1}^{n} \ln \sum_{i=1}^{c} \alpha_i f_i(\mathbf{x}_k;\boldsymbol{\theta}_i). \qquad (37)$$

Remembering that $\sum_{i=1}^{c} \alpha_i = 1$, we can differentiate L with respect to the parameters and this leads, after a little algebra to the following estimation equations

$$\hat{\alpha}_i = \frac{1}{n} \sum_{k=1}^{n} \hat{P}(i/\mathbf{x}_k) \qquad (38)$$

$$\boldsymbol{\theta}_i = \frac{1}{n\hat{\alpha}_i} \sum_{k=1}^{n} \mathbf{x}_k \hat{P}(i/\mathbf{x}_k), \qquad (39)$$

where $\hat{P}(i/\mathbf{x}_k)$ is the estimated value of the posterior probability that observation $\mathbf{x}_k$ arises from class i of the latent variable, and is given by

$$\hat{P}(i/\mathbf{x}_k) = \frac{\hat{\alpha}_i f_i(\mathbf{x}_k;\hat{\boldsymbol{\theta}}_i)}{f(\mathbf{x}_k;\hat{\boldsymbol{\alpha}},\hat{\boldsymbol{\Theta}})}. \qquad (40)$$

Equations 38 and 39 do not of course, give the parameter estimates explicitly because $\hat{P}(i/\mathbf{x}_k)$ involves the parameters in a complex way. Given however, initial values for the elements of $\boldsymbol{\alpha}$ and of the $\boldsymbol{\theta}_1 \ldots, \boldsymbol{\theta}_c$, initial values of the posterior probabilities can be obtained that can be used in the right-hand side of Equations 38 and 39 to give revised estimates of the parameters and the procedure repeated until some appropriate convergence criterion is satisfied. The procedure is generally known as the Expectation Maximization (EM) algorithm, and is described in detail in Dempster, Laird, and Rubin (1977).

As an illustration of the application of the latent class model we use the data in Table 11.25. These data arise from asking long-term psychiatric patients to list the names of all acquaintances they could remember and for each name to indicate whether or not the person was regarded as a friend, whether or not the relationship was active, whether or not the person was missed, and whether or

TABLE 11.25
Acquaintance of Long-Term Psychiatric Patients

4. Type	3. Status	2. Loss	1. Intimate	n
Active	Friend	Missed	Confides	529
			Doesn't Confide	424
		Not Missed	Confides	51
			Doesn't Confide	193
	Not friend	Missed	Confides	185
			Doesn't Confide	274
		Not Missed	Confides	46
			Doesn't Confide	311
Not Active	Friend	Missed	Confides	81
			Doesn't Confide	279
		Not missed	Confides	13
			Doesn't Confide	228
	Not Friend	Missed	Confides	25
			Doesn't Confide	256
		Not Missed	Confides	18
			Doesn't Confide	1893

not they thought they could confide in the person. Consequently each name was described by a four-component vector of dichotomous variables.

Two and three class models were fitted to these data with the results shown in Tables 11.26 and 11.27.

A chi-square statistic measuring the goodness-of-fit of each model can be calculated; for the two-class model this takes the value 179.0 with 6 df, and for the three-class model the value 16.2 with 1 df. Although neither model is a

TABLE 11.26
Latent Class Analysis Results
for "Acquaintances" Data,
Two Class Solution

Parameter	Class 1	Class 2
α_i	0.56	0.44
θ_{i1}	0.00	0.44
θ_{i2}	0.10	0.84
θ_{i3}	0.11	0.71
θ_{i4}	0.13	0.78

Note: α_i = Prob (observation in class i); θ_{i1} = Prob (Being able to confide in name/class i); θ_{i2} = Prob (Name being missed/class i); θ_{i3} = Prob (Name being regarded as a friend/class i); θ_{i4} = Prob (Name being an active acquaintance/class i)

TABLE 11.27
Latent Class Analysis Results for "Acquaintances" Data,
Three Class Solution

Parameter	Class 1	Class 2	Class 3
α_i	0.41	0.25	0.34
θ_{i1}	0.01	0.73	0.03
θ_{i2}	0.00	0.90	0.58
θ_{i3}	0.02	0.73	0.53
θ_{i4}	0.09	0.89	0.48

Note: α_i = Prob (observation in class i); θ_{i1} = Prob
(Being able to confide in name/class i); θ_{i2} = Prob (Name
being missed/class i); θ_{i3} = Prob (Name being regarded
as a friend/class i); θ_{i4} = Prob (Name being an active
acquaintance/class i)

particular good as judged by their chi-square values, the interpretation of the
classes found is relatively straightforward and intuitively sensible. In the two-
class solution the division is clearly into "close friends" and perhaps "just
names"; in the three-class solution this division is again clear, and the additional
class might be described as "friends whom one could not confide in." A full
description of the example is given in Leff et al. (1990).

CONCLUSIONS

The analysis of categorical data is an important topic in many scientific disciplines and particularly in the behavioral and social sciences and medicine. In this
chapter a number of useful methods have been discussed but the coverage has of
course, been less than comprehensive. An area not covered at all is that of
ordinal categorical data and readers are referred to Agresti (1984) for details.
Again nothing has been said about *measures of association* for contingency
tables; such measures are discussed in the series of papers by Goodman and
Kruskal (1954, 1959, 1963, 1972).

REFERENCES

Agresti, A. (1984). *Analysis of ordinal categorical data.* New York: Wiley.
Barnard, G. A. (1984). Discussion of Yates (1984). *Journal of the Royal Statistical Society, Series A, 147,* 449–450.
Cochran, W. G. (1954). Some methods for strengthening the common χ^2 tests. *Biometrics, 10,* 417–451.
Cox, D. R. (1984). Discussion of Yates (1984). *Journal of the Royal Statistical Society, Series A, 147,* 451.

D'Agostino, R. B., Chase, W., & Belanger, A. (1988). The appropriateness of some commc procedures for testing equality of two independent binomial proportions. *The American Statisi cian, 2,* 198–202.

Dempster, A. P., Laird, N. M., & Rubin, D. B. (1977). Maximum likelihood from incomplete da via the EM algorithm. *Journal of the Royal Statistical Society, Series B, 39,* 1–38.

Everitt, B. S. (1992). *The analysis of contingency tables* (2nd ed.). London: Chapman and Ha

Everitt, B. S. (1989). *Statistical methods for medical investigations.* London: Edward Arnol

Everitt, B. S., & Dunn, G. (1992). *Applied multivariate data analysis.* London, Edward Arnol

Everitt, B. S., & Hand, D. J. (1981). *Finite mixture distributions.* London: Chapman & Ha

Fisher, R. A. (1925). *Statistical methods for research workers.* Edinburgh: Oliver & Boyd.

Goodman, L. A., & Kruskal, W. H. (1954). Measures of association for cross-classificaiton *Journal of the American Statistical Association, 49,* 732–764.

Goodman, L. A., & Kruskal, W. H. (1959). Measures of association for cross-classifications, Further discussions and references. *Journal of the American Statistical Association, 54,* 123 163.

Goodman, L. A., & Kruskal, W. H. (1963). Measures of association for cross-classifications, I Approximate sampling theory. *Journal of the American Statistical Association, 58,* 310–36

Goodman, L. A., & Kruskal, W. H. (1972). Measures of association for cross-classifications, I Simplification of asymptotic variances. *Journal of the American Statistical Association, 67,* 41 421.

Lazarsfeld, P. L., & Henry, N. W. (1968). *Latent structure analysis.* Boston: Houghton Miffli

Lewontin, R. C., & Felsenstein, J. (1965). The robustness of homogeneity tests in 2 × N table *Biometrics, 21,* 19–33.

Little, R. J. A. (1989). Testing the equality of two independent binomial proportions. *The Americ Statistician, 43,* 283–288.

McNemar, Q. (1955). *Psychological statistics.* New York: Wiley.

Mehta, C. R., & Patel, N. R. (1986). A hybrid algorithm for Fisher's exact test on unordered r × tables. *Communications in Statistics, 15,* 387–403.

Murray, J., Dunn, G., Williams, P., & Tarnopsky, A. (1981). Factors affecting the consumption psychotropic drugs. *Psychological Medicine, 11,* 551–556.

Pearson, K. (1900). On the criticism that a given system of deviations from the probable in the ca of a correlated system of variables is such that it can be reasonably supposed to have arisen fro random sampling. *Philosophical Magazine, 50,* 157–175.

Slakter, M. J. (1966). Comparative validity of the chi-square and two modified chi-squa goodness-of-fit tests for small but equal expected frequencies. *Biometrika, 53,* 619–623.

Woolson, R. F., & Lachenbruch, P. (1982). Regression analysis of matched case-control dat *American Journal of Epidemiology, 115,* 444–452.

Yates, F. (1934). Contingency tables involving small numbers and the χ^2 test. *Journal of the Roy Statistical Society Supplement, 1,* 217–235.

Yates, F. (1984). Tests of significance for 2 × 2 tables (with discussion). *Journal of the Roy Statistical Society, Series A, 147* 426–463.

Yule, G. U. (1911). *An introduction to the theory of statistics.* London: Griffin.

IV
OTHER TOPICS

This last section incorporates several chapters that deal with important topics but cannot be classified under a single heading.

It is remarkable how little attention exploratory data analysis (EDA) has received in conventional statistic books of the social sciences. The orthodox emphasis on hypothesis testing (especially by psychologists, as noted in chapter 11 of the first volume) has often diverted researchers from essential and important issues. Data should be perceived as more than just the necessary input for testing a hypothesis; they may often contain new and unexpected insights into the phenomenon under investigation. EDA provides simple and systematic procedures for initial processing of the data. Some of the fundamentals of EDA are presented in chapter 12 by Smith and Prentice.

Chapter 13, by Wainer and Thissen, presents graphical data analysis. One possibility, though not the only one, is to view it as elaborating specific aspects of EDA. Another important fact concerns the compatibility between the graphical presentation of the data and the processing strategies that it invokes. This is an important area for more collaboration between statisticians and cognitive psychologists.

Rapid growth in the use of computers and corresponding statistical packages has had a marked impact on developments in all scientific branches. A comprehensive review of computer use in psychological research is presented by Church in chapter 14.

While the opportunities offered by the introduction of computers should not be undervalued, their utilization is not without cost. Besides an inevitable financial burden, computers and corresponding software packages often lead to mechanical analyses and reasoning procedures that may result in unwarranted conclusions. At least for the time being, computers cannot replace the human mind; at best, if appropriately used, they can assist it. This point is brought home in an elegant and stimulating manner by Loftus in chapter 15.

Research in the social sciences is often conducted to identify influences of specific interventions. Time series methodology, discussed in chapter 16 by Rushe and Gottman, enables the scientist to describe data sets over time and provides powerful methods to evaluate change. Time series has been primarily applied in physiological psychology, but the authors show that it may have much broader application.

12 Exploratory Data Analysis

Albert F. Smith
State University of New York at Binghamton

Deborah A. Prentice
Princeton University

Top professional athletes are paid lavish sums of money for their services as members of sports teams. As each professional sports season begins, the headline sports story is frequently about the salary that has been negotiated between a star player and a team. Given the enormous financial investment a team makes in its players, it is reasonable to ask whether the investment pays off—that is, whether team success is related to the earnings of team members. As part of an inconclusive article that addressed this question, the *New York Times* published a display, from which Fig. 12.1 is adapted, as one-third of its front sports page (Bondy, 1991). For each of three professional leagues, teams are rank-ordered by number of salary dollars per victory achieved during the 1990–1991 seasons. This display is sadly uninformative in several respects, and we begin this chapter on the exploratory analysis of data by pursuing the question of how players' salaries relate to team success.

The most obvious shortcoming of Fig. 12.1 as a source of information about the relationship of salaries and team success is that it provides no information about team success. Although a committed fan may remember how many victories were achieved by each National Football League team during the 1990 regular season, most readers of the newspaper will not. If the price per victory for a team is high, but the team won many games, the team's management may consider the money to have been well spent. If the price per victory is low and the team won many games, the management has gotten a great deal (and perhaps exploited its players). Clearly, information about number of victories is essential.

The second shortcoming of Fig. 12.1 is the salary measure it provides. Dollars per victory would be an informative measure about the relationship between salaries and team success if every team in a league had the same salary budget.

349

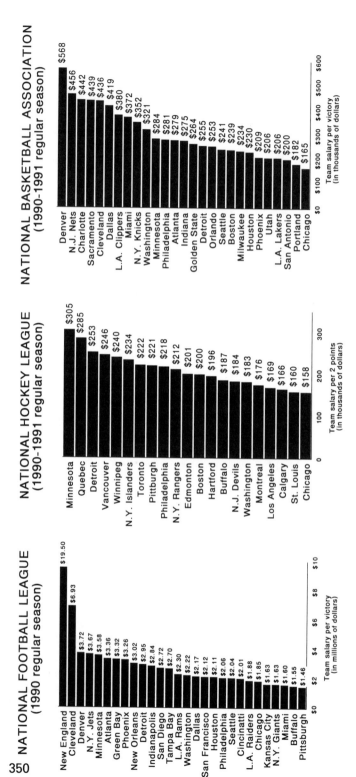

NATIONAL FOOTBALL LEAGUE
(1990 regular season)

New England	$19.50
Cleveland	$6.93
Denver	$3.72
N.Y. Jets	$3.67
Minnesota	$3.58
Atlanta	$3.36
Green Bay	$3.32
Phoenix	$3.26
New Orleans	$3.02
Detroit	$2.95
Indianapolis	$2.84
San Diego	$2.72
Tampa Bay	$2.70
L.A. Rams	$2.30
Washington	$2.22
Dallas	$2.17
San Francisco	$2.12
Houston	$2.11
Philadelphia	$2.06
Seattle	$2.04
Cincinatti	$2.01
Chicago	$1.88
L.A. Raiders	$1.85
Kansas City	$1.63
N.Y. Giants	$1.63
Miami	$1.60
Buffalo	$1.55
Pittsburgh	$1.46

Team salary per victory
(in millions of dollars)

NATIONAL HOCKEY LEAGUE
(1990–1991 regular season)

Minnesota	$305
Quebec	$285
Detroit	$253
Vancouver	$246
Winnipeg	$240
N.Y. Islanders	$234
Toronto	$222
Pittsburgh	$221
Philadelphia	$218
N.Y. Rangers	$212
Edmonton	$201
Boston	$200
Hartford	$196
Buffalo	$187
N.J. Devils	$184
Washington	$183
Montreal	$176
Los Angeles	$169
Calgary	$166
St. Louis	$160
Chicago	$158

Team salary per 2 points
(in thousands of dollars)

NATIONAL BASKETBALL ASSOCIATION
(1990-1991 regular season)

Denver	$568
N.J. Nets	$456
Charlotte	$442
Sacramento	$439
Cleveland	$436
Dallas	$419
L.A. Clippers	$380
Miami	$372
N.Y. Knicks	$352
Washington	$321
Minnesota	$284
Philadelphia	$281
Atlanta	$279
Indiana	$275
Golden State	$264
Detroit	$255
Orlando	$253
Seattle	$241
Boston	$239
Milwaukee	$234
Houston	$230
Phoenix	$209
Utah	$206
L.A. Lakers	$206
San Antonio	$200
Portland	$182
Chicago	$165

Team salary per victory
(in thousands of dollars)

FIG. 12.1. Salary expenditures per victory during 1990–1991 regular season in each of three professional sports leagues: (a) National Football League; (b) National Hockey League; and (c) National Basketball Association. (Copyright © 1991 by The New York Times Company. Reprinted by permission.)

TABLE 12.1
Total Salary and Success Statistics
for Professional Sports Teams, 1990–1991

Team	Salary Total ($ Millions)	Games Won
(a) National Football League		
Rams	11.500	5
Pittsburgh	13.140	9
Dallas	15.190	7
Tampa Bay	16.200	6
Phoenix	26.300	5
San Diego	16.320	6
Atlanta	16.800	5
Detroit	17.700	6
Kansas City	17.930	11
Cincinnati	18.090	9
Seattle	18.360	9
Denver	18.600	5
Houston	18.990	9
Miami	19.200	12
New England	19.500	1
Indianapolis	19.880	7
Green Bay	19.920	6
Buffalo	20.150	13
Chicago	20.350	11
Philadelphia	20.600	10
Cleveland	20.790	3
Giants	21.190	13
Minnesota	21.480	6
Jets	22.020	6
Washington	22.200	10
Raiders	22.560	12
New Orleans	24.160	8
San Francisco	29.680	14

Team	Salary Total ($ Millions)	Points Earned
(b) National Hockey League		
Toronto	6.327	57
Quebec	6.555	46
Islanders	7.020	60
Hartford	7.154	73
Devils	7.268	79
Washington	7.411	81
Winnepeg	7.560	63
Buffalo	7.573	81
Montreal	7.832	89
Vancouver	7.995	65

(continued)

TABLE 12.1   (*Continued*)

Team	Salary Total ($ Millions)	Games Won
Edmonton	8.040	80
Philadelphia	8.284	76
Calgary	8.300	100
Chicago	8.374	106
St. Louis	8.400	105
Los Angeles	8.619	102
Rangers	9.010	85
Detroit	9.614	76
Pittsburgh	9.724	88
Boston	10.000	100
Minnesota	10.370	68

Team	Salary Total ($ Millions)	Games Won
(c) National Basketball Association		
Orlando	7.843	31
Minnesota	8.236	29
Miami	8.928	24
Washington	9.630	30
Seattle	9.881	41
Chicago	10.065	61
Scaramento	10.975	25
San Antonio	11.000	55
Utah	11.124	54
Milwaukee	11.232	48
Indiana	11.275	41
Denver	11.360	20
Portland	11.466	63
Charlotte	11.492	26
Phoenix	11.495	55
Golden State	11.616	44
Dallas	11.732	28
LA Clippers	11.780	31
New Jersey	11.856	26
Houston	11.960	52
Atlanta	11.997	43
LA Lakers	12.064	58
Philadelphia	12.364	44
Detroit	12.750	50
Boston	13.384	56
New York	13.728	39
Cleveland	14.388	30

(Each team does play the same number of games.) But in none of the professional sports leagues for which data are provided in Fig. 12.1 is there true salary parity over teams. Investigating the relationship between player salaries and team success requires information about both variables. Table 12.1 shows the number of victories and the total salary budget for teams in each of the three leagues. Figure 12.2 plots victories as a function of salary budget. Inspection of Table 12.1 and Fig. 12.2 permit both preliminary statements about the relationship of these variables and some interpretation of the most salient aspects of Fig. 12.1.

In no panel of Fig. 12.2 do the plotted points fall on a straight line or on any sort of monotonic curve. Thus, there is clearly no simple relationship between player salaries and team success. It is also clear, however, that in each league, there is a tendency for higher salary budgets to be associated with greater success. For football and hockey, there appears to be a genuine positive relationship between salaries and success, although, at every level of salary budget, there is a great deal of variability in team success. In addition, in both leagues, there appear to be points that depart dramatically from the remaining points, and we consider the reasons for their departure and their impact on our assessment of the salary–success relationship later in the chapter. For basketball, on the other hand, there appears to be little relationship between salaries and success, largely because the salary budgets of most teams fall within a very narrow range. In fact, unlike football and hockey, basketball has a team salary cap that places an upper limit on the salaries that organizations can pay their players. Thus, the data analyst with knowledge of basketball might be surprised to find a strong relationship between total team salary and team success (although this does not preclude other salary indices from being related to basketball team success).

PHILOSOPHY
OF EXPLORATORY DATA ANALYSIS

Exploratory data analysis (EDA) is both a philosophy of the investigation of data and a recommended set of tools and techniques. The fundamental tenet of the philosophy is that data should be *explored:* Although a set of data can be analyzed according to a plan devised prior to its collection, the data should nevertheless be studied carefully as they may reveal more, or other, than anticipated. Thus, EDA stresses the importance of making every datum available for study at the beginning of an investigation and of avoiding premature or woodenheaded application of a program of analysis devised prior to data collection.

Consistent with this philosophy, proponents of EDA have developed a set of analytic strategies that preserve the information contained in the data and present it in a useful and meaningful way. In particular, EDA recommends the use of summary measures that are relatively insensitive to various sorts of contamina-

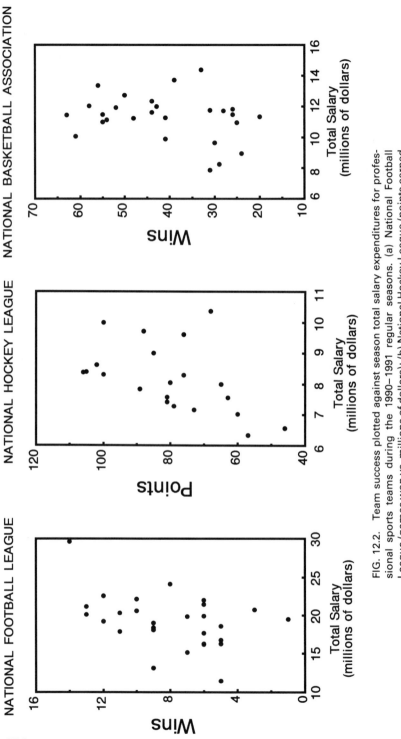

FIG. 12.2. Team success plotted against season total salary expenditures for professional sports teams during the 1990–1991 regular seasons. (a) National Football League (games won vs. millions of dollars); (b) National Hockey League (points earned vs. millions of dollars); and (c) National Basketball Association (games won vs. mil-

tion of the data and that do not involve strong assumptions about the distributional form of the data. Although EDA techniques are particularly suited to the analysis of data from exploratory investigations, the summary measures provide a good description of any set of data.

Exploration of data can be carried out in a variety of ways; proponents of the EDA approach recommend extensive use of graphical displays (see Wainer & Thissen, chap. 13 in this vol.). Studying graphical displays of data—particularly scatterplots to examine the relationship between two variables—is a standard recommendation in courses on data analysis and statistics. But it is a recommendation that is often ignored. EDA emphasizes the study of an *appropriate* display of any set of data as the first step in developing a strategy for its analysis.

In the remainder of this chapter, we survey some of the principal techniques of exploratory data analysis, emphasizing their application to sample sets of data, many of which are drawn from various subfields of psychology. Some attention is given to the relationship between EDA and the data-analytic techniques with which psychologists are more familiar; we show that EDA techniques can be particularly helpful in guiding more customary analyses.

The philosophy of exploratory data analysis and the formal techniques that are the standards of EDA were articulated and demonstrated in books by Tukey (1977) and by Mosteller and Tukey (1977). The theoretical foundations of these exploratory techniques are detailed in two volumes edited by Hoaglin, Mosteller, and Tukey (1983, 1985); we refer frequently to chapters in these volumes. In addition, several summary chapters are available (e.g., Hartwig & Dearing, 1979; Leinhardt & Wasserman, 1979). Velleman and Hoaglin (1981) summarized many of the techniques and presented computer algorithms for some EDA procedures. It is not the purpose of this chapter to retread the well-worn paths of exploratory data analysis, although some such retreading is inevitable. Rather, our goal is to illustrate the value of the EDA techniques and to suggest how these techniques can serve as an important initial step in the investigation of psychological data.

NONPARAMETRIC PROCEDURES, ROBUST STATISTICS, AND EDA

Before discussing the techniques of exploratory data analysis, we attempt to clarify the relationship of EDA to related classes of analytic procedures. EDA is concerned primarily with exploration and description of data, not with inference. The techniques are designed to identify fundamental, conceptually meaningful patterns and relationships in data and to call attention to observations that deviate greatly from those fundamental patterns. Thus, EDA consists primarily of *resistant* techniques and summary statistics (e.g., Besag & Seheult, 1988; Hoaglin, Mosteller, & Tukey, 1983; Mosteller & Tukey, 1977)—that is, techniques that are insensitive both to gross perturbations in a few data points and to small perturbations in many data points. Many of these resistant procedures involve the selection and examination of cases on the basis of their ranks. For example, in EDA, the median, a rank-based sample statistic, is preferred to the mean as a measure of location: The insensitivity of the median, but not the mean, to these sorts of perturbations is easily demonstrated.

A family of rank-based procedures with which psychologists are more familiar is *nonparametric* or, more properly, distribution-free methods (e.g., Lehmann, 1975; see Gibbons, 1982). Nonparametric methods, like many EDA techniques, are based on ranks. However, in contrast to EDA, nonparametric methods are concerned principally with inferences from samples to populations when the nature of the population distribution is unknown or when no assumptions are made about its detailed form (see Huber, 1981; Mood, Graybill, & Boes, 1974). For example, using nonparametric methods, quantitative statements about the likelihood that a null hypothesis is being rejected falsely will not overstate the true probability, regardless of the nature of the population distribution.

A third set of related techniques is *robust* procedures. Robust procedures, like nonparametric methods, are concerned primarily with inference rather than with exploration and description. A statistic is defined as robust if it is efficient—that is, if its variance is not markedly increased—over a variety of situations that deviate from theoretical assumptions (Huber, 1981; Wu, 1985). Consider, for example, the contrast between the mean (a nonrobust statistic) and the median (a robust statistic). The mean is a relatively efficient estimate of central tendency if the population distribution is normal (i.e., the variance of the sample mean for samples from a normal distribution is smaller than the variance of the sample median for samples of the same size; see Mosteller & Rourke, 1973, p. 252; Mosteller & Tukey, 1977, p. 17). However, the mean is much less robust than the median: Even slight departures of the population distribution from normal alter the variance of the sample mean quite substantially. The variance of the sample median, on the other hand, is relatively unaffected by departures from normality (Huber, 1981, p. 3; Mosteller & Tukey, 1977, p. 17; Rosenberger & Gasko, 1983). Thus, the median and other robust procedures are designed to be relatively insensitive to deviations of empirical distributions from those assumed by classical procedures.

TECHNIQUES FOR THE EXAMINATION
OF A SAMPLE MEASURED ON ONE VARIABLE

In a set of data that consists of a measurement of each of a sample of research units (e.g., people, places, or even responses) on a single variable, one is typically interested in obtaining a representative value of that variable and in appreciating not only quantitatively, but qualitatively as well, the nature of the variability among the research units. Examination of the entire distribution of observations can reveal important characteristics of the data that might otherwise go undetected.

Visual Inspection of a Sample of Counts

We begin our discussion of the analysis of a single variable by illustrating the basic importance of simply looking at data. A vivid example of the benefits of careful inspection of data comes from Stellman (1989), who discovered a data-processing error in an epidemiological study by visually inspecting a complete distribution of observations. Survey respondents had been asked to rate the frequency with which they ate each of 28 food items. As part of a quality control check, Stellman examined the frequency distribution of number of items (of 28) to which no response had been made. Figure 12.3 shows how many respondents, of 25,000, failed to respond to each possible number of items, from 0 to 26. Stellman's report does not permit a distinction between 27 items missing and all 28 items missing.) Inspection of Fig. 12.3 reveals a peculiar functional form— holes in the histogram at exactly 8 and exactly 18 missing items. This finding led

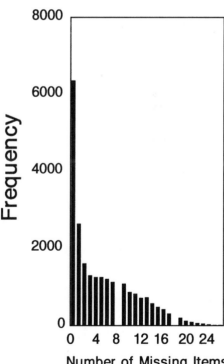

FIG. 12.3. Number of respondents who failed to respond to particular numbers of items (after Stellman, 1989).

Stellman to a thorough investigation of the data-processing procedures because as he noted, "distributions of real data do not contain giant holes" (p. 859).

Stellman unraveled the mystery: An error had been made in the program tha coded the questionnaires. From the perspective of exploratory data analysis, th lesson here is that inspection of the data prior to further analysis revealed potentially significant problem.

Studying the Shapes of Samples of Data: Stem-and-Leaf Displays

The EDA approach maintains that data should be studied without preconception about their distributional form. Therefore, proponents of EDA call into questio the convention of describing a set of data by its mean and variance. Wherea these summary statistics are sufficient descriptors for normally distributed data they may be inappropriate to describe data encountered in practice. For example Fig. 12.4 shows the density functions of three distributions—a uniform distribu tion, an exponential distribution, and a normal (Gaussian) distribution. Each ha mean 10 and variance 100. Clearly the mean and variance alone provide insuff cient information about the properties of a dataset: The shape of the set is als important.

Tukey (1977) proposed the stem-and-leaf display as an effective means t diagram a sample of data. A stem-and-leaf display is a frequency histogram tha retains numeric information about the data that are tabulated; thus, the displa can be constructed directly from the data. Like a histogram, a stem-and-lea display conveys information about the shape of a sample of data. (For detaile advice concerning the construction of stem-and-leaf displays, see Emerson & Hoaglin, 1983c; Tukey, 1977, pp. 7–16; Velleman & Hoaglin, 1981, provid algorithms for computer-aided construction of stem-and-leaf displays.)

A stem-and-leaf display not only provides information about the shape of sample of data; it also facilitates the extraction from the data of summary statis tics. Tukey (1977) suggested that a sample of data could be adequately an generally characterized by a subset of its order statistics. The order statistics of sample are simply the observed values of the sample ordered by increasin magnitude (see, e.g., Mood et al., 1974, pp. 251ff.; Rosenberger & Gaske 1983). Thus, a sample of size N has N order statistics: The first order statistic i the lowest value, the second is the next-to-lowest value, and the Nth orde statistic is the highest value. The complete set of order statistics would ex haustively describe a sample on some variable; Tukey proposed that a subset c the order statistics provides sufficient information about the data for most pu poses.

According to Tukey, the order statistics that summarize a sample mo usefully are the median, the extremes, and the hinges—values that are ordinall halfway between the median and the extremes. (Hoaglin, 1983, uses the ter

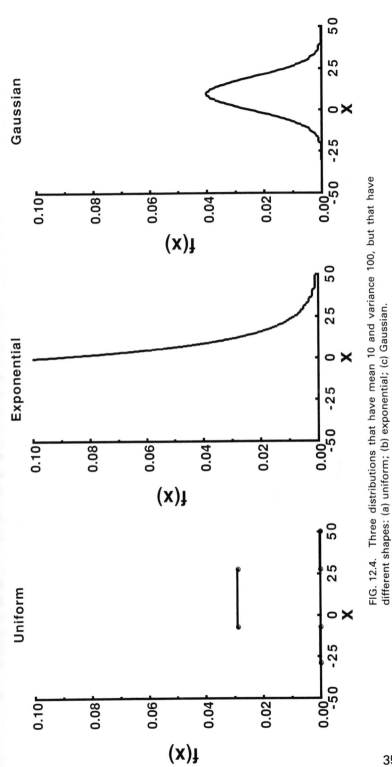

FIG. 12.4. Three distributions that have mean 10 and variance 100, but that have different shapes: (a) uniform; (b) exponential; (c) Gaussian.

359

fourths for the hinges.) In exploratory data analysis, the median serves as the measure of the location of a set of values, and the hingespread—the difference between the hinges—serves as the measure of dispersion. The values of the median, extremes, and hinges are conveniently obtained from the stem-and-leaf display, which acts as a sorting procedure as well as a visual representation of the sample's shape. These five summary order statistics are frequently arranged in table called the letter-value display (Hoaglin, 1983) or five-number summary (Tukey, 1977). When additional detail about the structure of the tails of a sample is required, the five-number summary can be supplemented with additional order statistics from the tails (e.g., the values that cut off one-eighth of the values in each tail, the values that cut off one-sixteenth in each tail, etc.).

We illustrate the analysis of a set of values on a single variable with some data on the classification of causes of death. Data on cause of death, as recorded on death certificates, are a principal measure of the health status of the citizens of locality. Investigators often wish to compare mortality data across countries, thus causes of death, as abstracted from death certificates, are transcribed into numerical International Classification of Diseases (ICD) code. The ICD is revised periodically to take account of advances in medical knowledge, and following the implementation of an ICD revision, the impact of the revision on mortality data is assessed.

Deaths that occurred during 1979 were the first to be coded according to the ninth revision of the ICD. To evaluate the impact of this revision on U.S. mortality statistics, Sorlie and Gold (1987) calculated, for each of the 50 states and the District of Columbia, the ratio of the number of 1979 deaths coded as chronic ischemic heart disease to the number of 1978 deaths so coded. Their results are shown in Table 12.2. Inspection of these values shows, first, that in every state, the ratio was less than 1, and second, there was considerable variation over states in the ratio of deaths attributed to chronic ischemic heart disease during the 2 years.

Figure 12.5 shows a stem-and-leaf plot of these ratios: We have used two stem lines for each leading digit (which represents tenths), and have used the number of hundredths in the ratio as the leaves. Forty-nine of the 51 values appear to constitute an orderly, symmetric group of values, but the set of values is decidedly skewed: Two values—those of Maryland and Delaware—are very much displaced from the remainder of the set of ratios.

By counting through the stem-and-leaf plot, the median, hinges, and extremes can be identified; these are shown in the five-number summary in Table 12.3. This summary provides the information required for a quick diagnosis of the symmetry of the sample. In a symmetric distribution, the median is equidistant from the two hinges and is also centered between the two extremes. The distribution of ICD ratios is clearly asymmetric—the left side is longer than the right side.

TABLE 12.2
Ratio of 1979 Chronic IHD Deaths to 1978 Chronic IHD Deaths, by State

State	Ratio	State	Ratio	State	Ratio
Alabama	0.687	Kentucky	0.618	North Dakota	0.821
Alaska	0.846	Louisiana	0.721	Ohio	0.758
Arizona	0.807	Maine	0.964	Oklahoma	0.792
Arkansas	0.791	Maryland	0.340	Oregon	0.876
California	0.693	Massachusetts	0.895	Pennsylvania	0.658
Colorado	0.768	Michigan	0.716	Rhode Island	0.737
Connecticut	0.821	Minnesota	0.821	South Carolina	0.642
Delaware	0.329	Mississippi	0.636	South Dakota	0.826
Dist. of Columbia	0.688	Missouri	0.796	Tennessee	0.664
Florida	0.789	Montana	0.807	Texas	0.622
Georgia	0.647	Nebraska	0.829	Utah	0.780
Hawaii	0.876	Nevada	0.614	Vermont	0.577
Idaho	0.753	New Hampshire	0.816	Virginia	0.656
Illinois	0.681	New Jersey	0.748	Washington	0.711
Indiana	0.788	New Mexico	0.960	West Virginia	0.700
Iowa	0.734	New York	0.854	Wisconsin	0.774
Kansas	0.757	North Carolina	0.648	Wyoming	0.777

Note: These data are from Sorlie & Gold (1987).

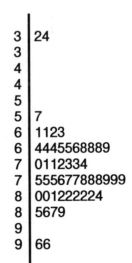

Unit = .01

```
3 | 24
3 |
4 |
4 |
5 |
5 | 7
6 | 1123
6 | 4445568889
7 | 0112334
7 | 555677888999
8 | 001222224
8 | 5679
9 |
9 | 66
```

FIG. 12.5. Stem-and-leaf display of ratios of number of 1979 ischemic heart disease deaths to number of 1978 ischemic heart disease deaths for 51 vital registration areas. (The data are from Sorlie & Gold, 1987.)

TABLE 12.3
Five-Number Summary for Ratios
of Coded Deaths for Two Years

$N = 51$		
Median		0.757
Hinges	0.664	0.816
Extremes	0.329	0.964

At this point, either of two paths might be pursued in the exploration of this set of data. As a precursor to analysis by procedures that assume normally (or, at least, symmetrically) distributed data, one might attempt to symmetrize the distribution by applying a transformation to the data. The transformation of data to improve the shape of its distribution is a customary technique of EDA, and we consider this strategy later in the chapter. Alternatively, one might proceed directly to the identification of outliers.

Treatment of Outliers

An important goal of exploratory data analysis is to identify outlying values in a set of data—that is, values that seem extreme and inconsistent with the other observed values. Once outliers have been identified, thoughtful decisions can be made about them. Outlying values might be present due to some error in data collection or processing. Or they might arise through some process distinctly different from the process that generated the other values in the data set. In any case, they are of sufficient interest to warrant special study.

Tukey (1977) recommended the hingespread—the difference of the upper and lower hinges—as the sample measure of dispersion on the basis of which values may be classified as outliers. The hinges and their spread, like the median, are *resistant*—they are essentially independent of the actual values of any outliers. Whereas the variance of a sample will increase greatly if one observation in a sample is changed to a value markedly different from the sample mean, this operation has no effect on the hingespread. For the hinges (and their spread) to change at all would require that some value outside the hinges be changed to a value inside the hinges or vice versa.

Values that fall more than one and one-half hingespreads outside a hinge are classified as outliers (see Hoaglin, 1983; Tukey, 1977, pp. 43–45); values that are more than 3 hingespreads outside hinge are sometimes classified as *severe* outliers. In the heart disease ratios data, the hingespread is 0.152, so values that fall below 0.436 or above 1.044 merit attention as outliers. There are no high outliers, but two low ones—Delaware and Maryland.

Sorlie and Gold (1987) investigated the certification of chronic ischemic heart disease deaths in Maryland to determine why cause of death codings under the two versions of the ICD were so discrepant. Most prominent among the explanations were that the preferences of physicians for certain medical terms in specifying cause of death led to different classifications under the two versions of the ICD, and that characteristics of physicians themselves, rather than of the decedents, influenced choice of terms in death certifications. For our purposes it is important that the careful analysis of the discrepancy in classifications was prompted by the observation that Maryland and Delaware were outliers. Identification of outliers, followed by an investigation of what makes them outliers, can offer clues to the normal processes that are responsible for the main body of the data.

Boxplots

Much of the location and dispersion information in a five-number summary can be displayed graphically in a *box-and-whisker plot* or *boxplot* (Emerson & Strenio, 1983; Tukey, 1977, pp. 39–41; see also Tukey, 1977, pp. 47–48, concerning schematic plots; Wainer & Thissen, chap. 13 in this vol.). Adjacent to a numerical scale for the plotted variable (e.g., the ratio of numbers of chronic ischemic heart disease deaths in 1979 and 1978), a box is drawn that extends from the lower hinge to the upper hinge, with a crossbar at the median. A whisker extends from each end of the box to the most extreme value that is not an outlier. Each outlier is marked separately, and the values at the ends of the whiskers and outlying values are identified. Figure 12.6 shows a boxplot of the sample of ratios from Sorlie and Gold (1987).

TECHNIQUES FOR THE COMPARISON OF SEVERAL SAMPLES MEASURED ON ONE VARIABLE

Psychologists are often interested in comparing several samples measured on a single variable, rather than in simply evaluating a single sample of numbers. For example, a psychologist might wish to compare the data of subjects who have served in several different conditions of an experiment. After the essential location and dispersion information described in the preceding section is determined for each condition, a graphical display of this information can be constructed. Parallel boxplots provide a convenient way to compare a single variable over multiple samples (see Emerson & Strenio, 1983; Wainer & Thissen, chap. 13 in this vol.). The next several examples illustrate this use of boxplots.

Data from a Questionnaire Concerning Attributions. Gyato (1991) administered an instrument to several groups of children to assess their attributions of personal responsibility in achievement situations. Some of these children had been classified by their schools either as gifted or as learning disabled, whereas

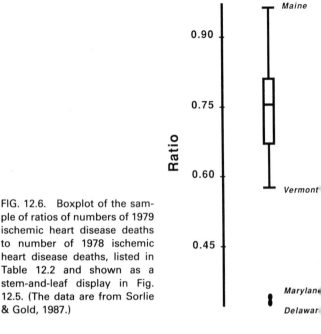

FIG. 12.6. Boxplot of the sample of ratios of numbers of 1979 ischemic heart disease deaths to number of 1978 ischemic heart disease deaths, listed in Table 12.2 and shown as a stem-and-leaf display in Fig. 12.5. (The data are from Sorlie & Gold, 1987.)

others had not been given any special label. The top panel of Fig. 12.7 shows parallel boxplots of the scores on the attribution scale for subjects in the three labeling groups. Several features of these plots suggest issues that merit further investigation. First, the center of the distribution of scores (indicated by the median crossbar) for children in the unlabeled (control) group is higher than that for children in either of the labeled groups. Second, the middle portions of the distributions of scores for children in the labeled groups are more dispersed than those for children in the unlabeled group. In addition, the distributions of scores in the labeled groups are asymmetric, whereas the distribution of scores in the unlabeled group is essentially symmetric. It may be of interest that the nature of the asymmetry differs for the gifted and learning-disabled groups: The former is skewed toward higher scores, whereas the latter is skewed toward lower scores.

Some additional insight into the differences among the groups is afforded by studying separately the distributions of scores on two different subsets of questions on the scale—questions that concern responsibility for positive experiences (e.g., doing well on a test) and those that concern responsibility for negative experiences (e.g., having trouble understanding something in school). The center and bottom panels of Fig. 12.7 show parallel boxplots of the scores on these two subscales for the three groups of children. These boxplots reveal different patterns of performance on positive and negative questions. For positive experiences, assertion of personal responsibility declines systematically from children labeled as gifted through unlabeled children to children labeled as learning dis-

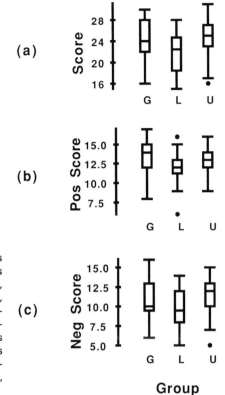

(a)

(b)

(c)

FIG. 12.7. (a) Parallel boxplots display scores of three groups of children labeled as gifted (G), labeled as learning disabled (L), and unlabeled (U) on an attributional measure. (b) Parallel boxplots for the positive events subscale. (c) Parallel boxplots for the negative events subscale. (The data are from Gyato, 1991.)

Group

abled. In contrast, for negative experiences, the pattern resembles the overall pattern—unlabeled children tend to affirm more responsibility for negative experiences than do children in either of the labeled groups. (One should interpret these patterns with caution, however, because the data from the subscales are not independent, but were collected from the same subjects.)

This example illustrates how EDA can be used to guide subsequent analyses. Indeed, our examination of these data has revealed patterns that might otherwise have gone unnoticed. For example, Gyato's plan of analysis of her data called for a comparison of unlabeled and labeled groups, followed by a comparison of the two labeled groups. Although the former difference is likely present in the data, we have identified the added complication of the different patterns on the two subscales of the instrument and the different asymmetries in the distributions of total scores in the two labeled groups.

Data from an Experiment on Memory. Parallel boxplots are equally effective for displaying the results of experiments in which several variables have been manipulated. For example, Smith (1991; Smith, Jobe, & Mingay, 1991b) investigated the correspondence of individuals' reports about what they had eaten during a specified period and records they had kept of their dietary intake during that period. Eight groups of subjects were defined by the crossing of two reference period durations (2 weeks and 4 weeks) with four retention intervals (0, 2, 4, and 6 weeks). Each subject's report was scored against his or her diary record to obtain a match rate—the proportion of recorded items that was reported. Figure 12.8 shows a boxplot for the match rates of each of the eight conditions of the experiment. These plots have been organized to reveal how the experimental manipulations influenced the performance measure. Specifically, the abscissa shows retention interval in weeks, and the boxplots have been ordered according to this variable. At each retention interval, the outlines of the boxes for the two different reference periods have been shaded differently. Altogether, the eight boxplots serve as an effective way to visualize the results of the experiment and to formulate (or, more typically, to modify) an analytic strategy.

Inspecting the boxplots, we find approximate equality among the eight experimental conditions in the amount of dispersion among match rates, although the hingespreads in the immediate test (0-week retention interval) conditions tend to be smaller than those in the delayed test conditions. The only outliers are in the condition that involved immediate test following a 4-week recording period.

Additional study of the boxplots reveals that retention interval had a potent effect on performance: As retention interval lengthens, match rates tend to decline, but the rate of decline slows as the retention interval becomes longer. This

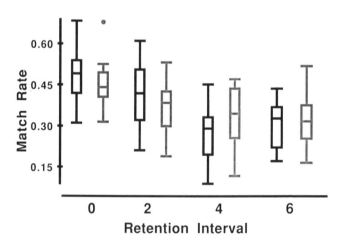

FIG. 12.8.   Parallel boxplots for the eight conditions of a factorial experiment reported by Smith (1991; Smith et al., 1991b). For one experimental factor, retention interval, boxplots are ordered according to the scale on the abscissa. The second experimental factor, reference period length, is represented by the shading of the outlines of the boxplots: darker = 2 weeks; lighter = 4 weeks.

observation suggests that the pattern of decline in performance over retention intervals might be captured by an exponential function: Smith (1991; Smith et al., 1991b), in conducting an analysis of variance on these data applied a contrast that represented such a function and found that it adequately represented the pattern in the data. The boxplots further suggest that the decrease in match rate over retention intervals of increasing length is more precipitous following a 2-week recording period than following a 4-week recording period, and this difference also was confirmed (for a complete account of these data, see Smith & Jobe, in press).

Transformations

In each of these examples, the data have been well behaved, and no special measures have been required for their analysis. However, some of the techniques of exploratory data analysis can be particularly effective for identifying organized structure in data that appear to be a hopeless mess. Specifically, transformations can be applied to symmetrize samples of data, to equate the dispersions of samples, and to bring in outliers (see Emerson & Stoto, 1983; Mosteller & Tukey, 1977, pp. 79–118; Tukey, 1977, p. 57ff.). Recommendations concerning transformations are not unique to EDA; most texts on the analysis of variance and on regression discuss the situations in which transformations are useful and prescribe appropriate methods (e.g., Fleiss, 1986, pp. 59–68, 110; Myers & Well, 1991, pp. 109–110; Neter, Wasserman, & Kutner, 1989, pp. 142–151; Winer, Brown, & Michels, pp. 354–358, 442–445).

When comparing several samples that have been measured on one variable, it is desirable that measurements in the samples be symmetric around their respective middle values and the dispersions of the different samples be approximately equal. These conditions characterized the sets of data in the examples of the preceding section. When data are not characterized by these properties, application of a transformation may yield transformed data that are. When transformation is potentially useful, the EDA approach to data analysis recommends that an appropriate transformation be selected from the family of power transformations. Using the power transformation of power p, for every score y_i there is a transformed score z_i, $z_i = y_i^p$ for p not 0, or $z_i = \log y_i$, for situations in which one might like p to be 0 (Emerson & Stoto, 1983; Stoto & Emerson, 1983; Tukey, 1977, p. 89). (By convention, for p less than zero, the transformation used is $z_i = -y_i^p$, so that for any p, Z increases with Y.) Power transformations have different compressive and expansive effects at different points on numerical scales. In this section, we demonstrate the use of power transformations to equalize dispersions of several samples of data and summarize a procedure for choosing an appropriate value of p.

Poorly behaved raw data were collected by Smith, Jobe, and Mingay (1991a) in a study of the effects of thought instructions on frequency estimates. Prior to indicating how often they had eaten a particular food during a specific period, subjects were asked either to think about all of the different types of occasions on which they ate a particular food or to think about the most recent occasion on which they had eaten the food. Subjects made their frequency judgments about either 1-month or 1-year periods. Each subject in the experiment answered just one frequency question; approximately 20 responses were obtained for each question. We consider here the responses to the four questions for a single food item.

Figure 12.9 shows boxplots for the responses to these four questions. They represent a striking contrast to the orderly pictures of Figs. 12.7 and 12.8. Variation in reference period length made it likely—indeed, almost certain—that the dispersion of responses would vary dramatically among conditions. The dispersion among frequency estimates in the 1-year conditions is greater than the dispersion in the 1-month conditions. From Fig. 12.9, it is difficult to discern any orderly effects of the variable of interest—the type of thoughts in which subjects engaged prior to making their frequency estimates. It is also clear that the data, in their raw form, violate some of the assumptions of analysis of variance, the

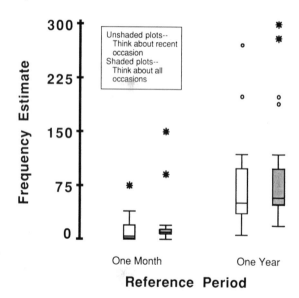

FIG. 12.9. Parallel boxplots for four conditions of Smith et al.'s (1991a) study of the effects of prior thoughts on frequency judgments. Each boxplot represents one combination of reference period and prior thought instruction. Reference period lengths are indicated on the abscissa; prior thought conditions are distinguished by the shading of the boxplot. (Outliers are indicated with circles; severe outliers are denoted by asterisks.)

statistical procedure that a psychologist would be inclined to carry out on these data.

Smith and associates performed a logarithmic transformation on the data (after adding a small constant to each response to eliminate zeroes). Figure 12.10 shows boxplots of the transformed data for the four questions. It is clear from these boxplots that the transformation improved the orderliness of the data considerably. Moreover, the transformed data reveal that the context manipulation had a systematic effect on frequency estimates.

Why did Smith and associates choose the logarithmic transformation ($p = 0$)? To find the power transformation that will eliminate the dependence of dispersion on level, a spread-versus-level plot may be constructed (Stoto & Emerson, 1983; Tukey, 1977, pp. 100–110). If, over samples, hingespread is a power function of median, then log hingespread is a linear function of log median. Subtracting the slope of this linear function from 1 yields the power p that will "undo" the dependence of dispersion on level. For the four samples of frequency estimates plotted in Fig. 12.9, the ordered pairs of log median and log hingespread are 0.7, 1.2), (1, 0.9), (1.7, 1.8), and (1.8, 1.7). The slope of a line fit to these points is 0.67 (although the last three are essentially on a line with slope 1). Subtracting 0.67 from 1 yields the value 0.33—between 0 that suggests the use of the log transformation and 0.5 that suggests the use of the square root transformation. (Tukey recommended the use of powers that are integer multiples of one

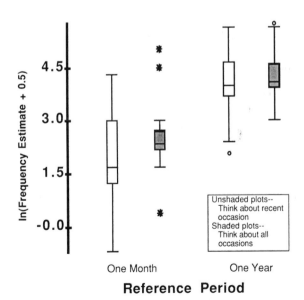

FIG. 12.10. Parallel boxplots of the data shown in Fig. 12.9 after applying a logarithmic transformation.

half.) Smith and associates' choice of the log transformation was appropriate, b
the square root transformation might have been useful instead. When the poin
that represent ordered pairs of log medians and log hingespreads are approx
mately linear, the spread-versus-level plot may be used to estimate an appropriat
value of p.

For each type of data structure discussed in this chapter, strategies are avai
able for assessing whether a power transformation will endow a set of observa
tions with desirable properties (e.g., symmetry for a single sample; equal disper
sions for several samples; a linear relationship between two variables). I
particular, for each type of data, a plot that is analogous to the spread-versus
level plot may be constructed and used to determine which power transforma
tion, if any, is appropriate. These are reviewed by Emerson and Stoto (1983) an
by Stoto and Emerson (1983); a theoretical analysis is presented by Emerso
(1983).

THE ANALYSIS OF THE RELATIONSHIP
BETWEEN TWO ORDERED VARIABLES

Many psychological studies examine the relationship between two ordered var
ables (that can often be treated as continuous). Linear regression methods ar
frequently used to characterize the relationship between such variables, an
correlation indices are used to describe the degree of association between th
variables. Elementary statistics texts, as well as advanced books on regressior
recommend routinely that any analysis of the relationship between two variable
include the construction and study of a scatterplot of the data, in which eac
matched pair of values on the variables of interest is plotted as a single poin
Such a scatterplot can help determine the appropriateness of a linear model an
bring to the attention of the investigator any pronounced or systematic departure
from linearity. This approach is certainly consistent with the spirit of EDA. ED
goes further, however, by attempting to describe the relationship between vari
ables using techniques that are highly insensitive to outliers (see Emerson
Hoaglin, 1983b; Mosteller & Tukey, 1977).

The first parts of this section discuss one procedure for fitting resistant lines
describe several examples in detail, and discuss the relationship of the results t
those that would be obtained by using ordinary regression procedures. The las
part of this section covers another aspect of the analysis of relationships betwee
ordered variables—smoothing. Not all relationships between ordered variable
are linear, and EDA includes tools for assessing and describing nonlinear rela
tionships. These smoothing techniques are particularly valuable in analyses c
sequential data.

esistant Lines

ordinary least squares regression, one identifies that line through a set of
ints around which the sum of squared distances of points from the line (on the
sponse variable) is a minimum. For the same reason that variance is not a
sistant sample statistic, ordinary least squares regression does not yield resis-
nt estimates of the parameters of the best-fitting line. The procedure is highly
nsitive to outliers; a markedly deviant point may dramatically influence the
tted line.

As an alternative to least squares regression, one can use any of several
ocedures to fit a resistant three-group line (see Emerson & Hoaglin, 1983b,
c. 5A). We describe here a procedure that is guaranteed to converge on a
lution for the coefficients of the line within a small number of iterations
Emerson & Hoaglin, 1983b, 1985). (Some other procedures, although concep-
ally simpler, fail to converge.)

Let the two variables be labeled X, the predictor, and Y, the response. The first
ep is to divide the data points into three groups of equal size according to their
alues on X—these are called the left, middle, and right groups. Within each
roup, a summary point is determined, the coordinates of which are the median
the x values within the group and the median of the y values within the group.
he form of the line to be fit is

$$y_i = a + b(x_i - x_M),$$

here b is the slope, x_M is the value on X of the summary point of the middle
roup, and a is the predicted value of Y at x_M.

An initial estimate of the slope of the resistant line, b^0, is the slope of the line
at connects the left and right summary points; an initial estimate of the level of
e line, a^0, the fitted value of Y at $X = x_M$, is the average of the residuals of the y
alues of the summary points after subtraction of the products of b and the
ifference of the summary x from x_M. Next, the procedure is repeated using sets
f pairs (x_i, r_i), in which r_i, the residual of the ith point, is given by

$$r_i = y_i - [a^0 + b^0(x_i - x_M)].$$

The slope of the originally fit line and the sum of that slope and the slope of the
ne fit to the residuals serve as preliminary bounds on the solution for the slope,
nd successive iterations then hone in on the actual slope. The goal of the pro-
edure is to find the slope of a line that will make the medians of the y-residuals in
he left and right groups equal, in which case the slope of the resistant line fit to
hem will be zero. On successive iterations, one narrows the boundaries on the
orrect solution. It is impractical to carry out this procedure by hand: Velleman and
Ioaglin (1981) presented a computer algorithm for the procedure, or an algorithm

NATIONAL FOOTBALL LEAGUE

NATIONAL HOCKEY LEAGUE

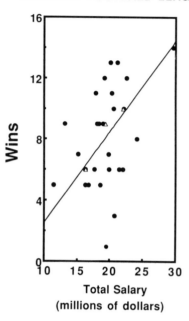

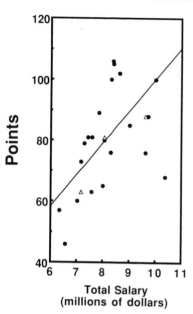

NATIONAL BASKETBALL ASSOCIATION

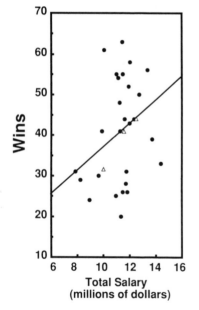

FIG. 12.11. Resistant lines fit to the team salary and success data of Table 12.1: (a) National Football League; (b) National Hockey League; and (c) National Basketball Association. In each panel, the solid points represent teams and the three open triangles represent the summary points for the left, middle, and right groups.

an be programmed with little difficulty from Emerson and Hoaglin's (1985) description of the procedure.

We used this procedure to fit resistant lines to the player salary and team success data for each of the three professional sports. The results are shown in Figure 12.11. Several aspects of the data deserve comment. First, for all three professional sports, there appears to be some relationship between the total salaries paid by a team and the team's success: In each case, the resistant line fit to the data has a positive slope. Note, however, that for none of these leagues is the relationship perfectly linear—some data points deviate markedly from the lines that we have fit. It is advisable to investigate the deviations of points from these lines for they may contain stories of interest.

For each of the three leagues, we calculated the residuals of the points from the line (by subtracting from each y_i the value of the fitted y at x_i). These residuals are plotted in Fig. 12.12 as a function of team total salary (which, of course, has a perfect linear relationship with predicted team success). In no case do the residuals have any sort of systematic association with total salary, and in each case, there is at least one extreme point. In Fig. 12.13, stem-and-leaf plots display the distributions of residuals.

Outliers are teams that exhibited performance that differed sharply from predictions based on their total salaries, given the relationship between salaries and success. In both football and basketball, none of the teams is an outlier according to the technical definition presented earlier, although several teams in each league are distinguished by outstandingly poor or excellent performance given their salaries. In hockey, on the other hand, even though the residuals are highly dispersed, the point that represents the Minnesota North Stars is an outlier. During the regular National Hockey League (NHL) season, the North Stars total salary was the highest in the league, but the team earned only 68 points. (In hockey, two points are awarded for a win, and one point is awarded for a tie.) It is of some interest to note that, in postseason play, the North Stars nevertheless reached the Stanley Cup finals, where they lost to the Pittsburgh Penguins in the seventh game. Thus, despite their poor performance in the regular season, it would be incorrect to conclude that the North Stars were not worth their salaries. To summarize, we answer directly the question raised, but clumsily addressed, by the *New York Times* concerning the relationship of team salaries and success. There is, in every league, a positive relationship between these variables. In none of the leagues that we have studied is the relationship perfect, but in each case, teams that have higher salary budgets tend to be more successful.

Emerson and Hoaglin (1983b) described additional procedures for fitting resistant lines to the relationship between two variables, and Emerson and Hoaglin (1985) extended these procedures to the case of the relationship between a variable and each of a set of predictors (i.e., the resistant analog of multiple regression).

NATIONAL FOOTBALL LEAGUE

NATIONAL HOCKEY LEAGUE

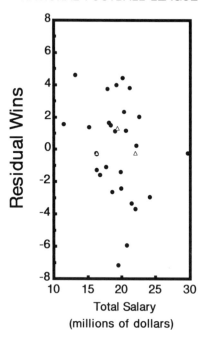

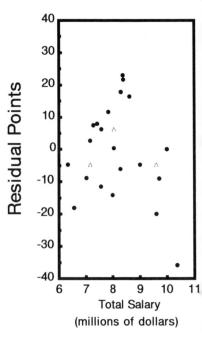

NATIONAL BASKETBALL ASSOCIATION

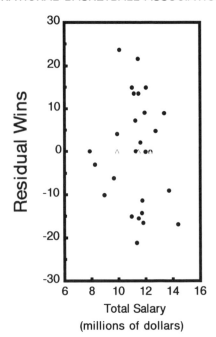

FIG. 12.12. Plots of residuals after the fit of the resistant lines shown in Fig. 12.11 versus team total salary. The open triangles represent summary points for the left, middle, and right groups of residuals.

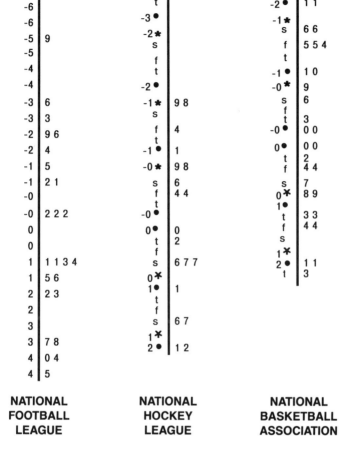

NATIONAL	NATIONAL	NATIONAL
FOOTBALL	HOCKEY	BASKETBALL
LEAGUE	LEAGUE	ASSOCIATION

FIG. 12.13. Stem-and-leaf displays of the residuals following fits of resistant lines to the team salary and success data for three professional sports.

Relationship of Resistant Lines to Least Squares Regression

The major benefit of resistant lines over more conventional regression techniques is that no single data point has a special influence on how the line projects through the bivariate space defined by the variables. The resistant line technique, like most of the techniques described in this chapter, permits the identification of general trends in data; observations that deviate from the general pattern appear as large residuals and do not influence the overall fit disproportionately. Consider, for example, the hockey data discussed in the previous section. We noted that given the underlying relationship between player salaries and team success the Minnesota North Stars' regular season performance was unusually poor given their total salaries. The resistant line is relatively unaffected by this outlier Indeed, if we consider perturbing only the point that represents the North Stars, i could occupy any position in the bivariate space below and to the right of the triangle that represents the summary point for the right group without having any impact on the resistant line (see Fig. 12.12).

Such is not the case with conventional least squares techniques. We carried out ordinary regression analyses on each of the three data sets; Table 12.4 shows the slopes of each of the resistant and least-squares lines. In all three comparisons, the resistant line is substantially steeper than the least squares line Inspection of Fig. 12.12 shows that each dataset contains either a highly paid team that performed poorly or a poorly paid team that performed well. Whereas such observations do not influence the resistant line, they have a major impact on the least squares line.

Concerning the Advisability of Fitting Resistant Lines

We conclude this section with a comment on the most appropriate cases for fitting resistant lines. Because carrying out resistant line procedures is somewhat ar duous, one might wish to do some preliminary assessment of whether these pro cedures will be beneficial. Some helpful clues can be obtained from conventional least-squares regression analyses (although see Wu, 1985, pp. 319–322, for some cautions concerning unusual situations). Most statistical packages (e.g., SAS BMDP, SPSS) include, in their procedures for regression analysis, provisions for computing diagnostic measures to evaluate the adequacy of a regression model These diagnostics include measures of the potential influence of each case on the estimated regression function (leverage), the actual influence of each case on the regression function (Cook's distance), and the discrepancy between a case's value on the response variable and its value predicted by the function (the residual). The last of these measures is quite familiar; we discuss the first two in greater detail

TABLE 12.4
Slopes of Resistant and Least-Squares Lines
for the Professional Sports Data Sets

League	Resistant	Least Squares	Ratio
Football	0.594	0.390	1.522
Hockey	10.4	7.4	1.399
Basketball	2.9	2.2	1.340

Note: For football and basketball, slopes are wins/$1 million. For hockey, slopes are points/$1 million.

The mechanism of least squares regression is such that cases that are relatively extreme in their values on the predictor variable (i.e., that have high leverage) may exert disproportionate influence on the fitted line (see Darlington, 1990, chap. 14; Neter et al., 1989, chap. 11). In other words, these cases will tend to draw the fitted line toward themselves. If a case with high leverage has an extreme value on the response variable, then a distorted conclusion about the relationship between the variables may be drawn from the regression analysis. The residual for the case with high leverage will be too small, for example, and the residuals of other cases will be too large.

Whereas leverage is a measure of the potential influence of a case, Cook's distance is a measure of a case's actual influence. It is an index of the amount of change that would be observed in the predicted values of the response variable for the entire set of data were the case in question to be removed from consideration. Cook's distance depends on both a case's leverage and the size of its residual; the largest Cook's distances are obtained when both are large. If a preliminary least squares regression reveals cases with large Cook's distances—Cook's distances with values that deviate strikingly from the other values—then a resistant line will improve understanding of the relationship between the variables under study. For example, in fitting the least-squares line to the hockey data, we computed the value of Cook's distance for each of the 21 teams. These values ranged from 0.0001 to 0.7907, with a median of 0.025 and hinges of 0.005 and 0.055. The largest Cook's distance was that of the North Stars, and it greatly exceeded the second-highest value. High Cook's distances indicate that a single point has had a major influence on the regression model estimated using least-squares and that the relationship between the variables will be better characterized by resistant methods.

Smoothing

If one assumes that the relationship between two variables is essentially continuous, but nonlinear, a representation of the relationship may be extracted from data by smoothing. The fundamental idea of smoothing is that to plot the y value associated with any x value, y values associated with nearby x values may be aggregated with the observed y into a more stable value. The performance of a variety of smoothers that are resistant to seemingly erratic observations has been evaluated (see Tukey, 1977, pp. 204–236, 523–542; Velleman, 1982). Smoothing may be particularly appropriate for the analysis of sequences of observations that are ordered in time or in space (e.g., learning performance over trials).

The simplest smoothing procedure involves taking running medians of three observations repeatedly until the sequence of y values is unchanged by further application of the smoother. Specifically, one takes the sequence of y values (ordered according to their corresponding x values) and substitutes for each value the median y value for that x and the two adjacent x's. (Special treatment is give to end values.)

The first row of Table 12.5 shows performance (proportion of correct re sponses) by a single subject in the first 10 of 52 400-trial sessions of a probabili tic category learning experiment (Smith, 1990). On each trial, the subjec classified a letter string as belonging to one of two categories and receive feedback. The second row shows running medians of three: For example, th value assigned to the second session is the median of the values from the firs second, and third sessions in the top row. The third row shows the result o applying the same running median smoother to the second row. The last row o the table shows that further application of the smoother does not result in an additional change in the sequence.

Although this example is particularly undramatic, the potential value o smoothing is evident in Figs. 12.14 and 12.15, which show additional analyse of data from this experiment. The symbols connected by lines in Fig. 12.1 represent raw proportion correct, by session, for each of 52 sessions complete by the single subject in this learning study; the bold solid curve was yielded b smoothing this sequence using repeated running medians of three. The smoothe curve conveys more clearly than does the raw data how performance change over sessions. Panel a of Fig. 12.15 shows performance during the first 13 an last 13 sessions of the experiment as a function of the degree to which stimu were members of one category rather than the other. (The stimulus propert represented on the abscissa is absolute value of log likelihood ratio; larger value characterize stimulus strings that are substantially more likely to have bee sampled from one category rather than the other.) Panel b shows the results o smoothing these curves using repeated running medians of three. The learnin that occurs during this task clearly results in vastly improved performance o stimuli that are potentially distinguishable according to their categories of origin

Each of the smoothed curves that we have shown is somewhat ragged and ca be smoothed further. These examples indicate that substantial benefits can b achieved with the very simplest of resistant smoothers. Additional technique

TABLE 12.5
Running Medians for 10 Sessions of Probabilistic Category Learning

	Session									
	1	2	3	4	5	6	7	8	9	1
Raw data	0.54	0.50	0.51	0.52	0.53	0.51	0.55	0.51	0.50	0.
Running medians	0.54	0.51	0.51	0.52	0.52	0.53	0.51	0.51	0.51	. .
Running medians	0.54	0.51	0.51	0.52	0.52	0.52	0.51	0.51	0.51	. .
Running medians	0.54	0.51	0.51	0.52	0.52	0.52	0.51	0.51	0.51	. .

Note: The data are from Smith (1990).

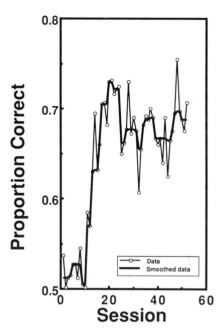

FIG. 12.14. Performance, by session, of a single subject in a probabilistic category learning study. The raw data are represented by the connected points; the bold line shows the result of smoothing by repeated running medians of three. The data are from Smith (1990).

hat could be applied after repeated running medians, including treatment of end-values, are discussed by Tukey (1977, chap. 16) and Velleman (1982).

ANALYSIS OF TWO-WAY TABLES

n the preceding section, we discussed the analysis of relationships between a esponse variable Y and a predictor variable X. Often, one is interested in the elationship between a response variable and several predictors. For predictor variables that are many-leveled and inherently ordered, Emerson and Hoaglin 1985) discussed the resistant analog of multiple regression. In this section, we discuss procedures for the analysis of two-way factorial tables (of the sort that night represent condition means in an experiment in which two variables have been manipulated).

The entries in any two-way table can be expressed as a set of coefficients that epresent the overall level of the table, and the row, column, and cell (or residual) effects. For example, consider a table that contains condition means X_{ij} from a 3 × 3 factorial experiment, in which rows represent the levels of predictor variable A and columns represent the levels of predictor variable B. Letting i index rows and j index columns, each X_{ij} can be written as

$$X_{ij} = m + a_i + b_j + r_{ij},$$

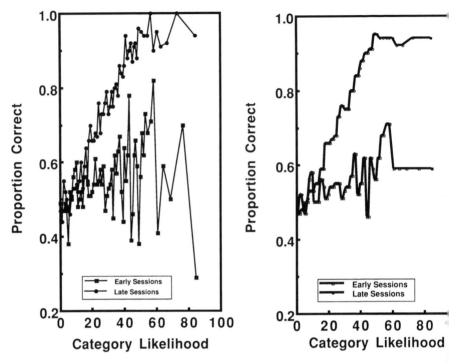

FIG. 12.15. (a) Performance as a function of relative likelihood of category membership by stimulus strings during the first 13 sessions (squares) and last 13 sessions (circles) of the probabilistic category learning experiment. (b) The functions of Panel a, smoothed. The data are from Smith (1990).

where m is the overall level of the table, the a_i are the row effects, the b_j are the column effects, and the r_{ij} are residuals. In the analysis of variance, in which the decomposition of a table of means is based on means, the overall level is the grand mean, the row effects are deviations of row means from the grand mean, the column effects are the deviations of column means from the grand mean, and the residuals are the deviations of cell means from the grand mean after removal of the row and column effects. Residuals, of course, are not part of a model of the data represented in such a table, and the most parsimonious representation of a two-way table would be one with no residuals. To the extent that residuals are large, an additive model that contains only row and column effects is a poor representation of the data.

Panel a of Table 12.6 shows a two-way table of the sort that we have been discussing. Panel b shows a decomposition of the table based on means: The grand mean is in the lower right corner of the table; the row and column effects are shown to the right of the rows and below the columns, respectively; and the

TABLE 12.6
A Two-Way Table of Numbers
and Its Decomposition by Means

(a) The Two-Way Table

		B		
A	1	2	3	Mean
1	1.0	10.0	100.0	37.00
2	0.1	1.0	10.0	3.70
3	0.01	0.1	1.0	0.37
Mean	0.37	3.7	37.0	13.69

(b) Grand Mean, Row, Column, and Cell Effects

		B		
A	1	2	3	Effect
1	−22.68	−17.01	39.69	23.31
2	9.72	7.29	−17.01	−9.99
3	12.96	9.72	−22.68	−13.32
Effect	−13.32	−9.99	23.31	13.69

cells contain the residuals. Notice that the sum of the row effects is zero and the sum of the column effects is zero. Furthermore, the sum of the residuals in each row and column is zero, and so, necessarily, the overall sum of the residuals is zero. We can recover any cell value of Panel a by adding the grand mean, row and column effects, and the residual for that cell. The set of residuals is clearly unwieldy, and indeed, we have deliberately constructed an example in which the results of a decomposition based on means are unsatisfactory.

An objective in the analysis of two-way tables is to achieve, if possible, a simple additive model, so one possible simplification of this table might involve a transformation of the data (see the section on transformations; Emerson & Stoto, 1983; Stoto & Emerson, 1983). Table 12.7 shows the logarithms (using base 10) of the entries in Panel a of Table 12.6. Panel b of Table 12.7 shows the decomposition by means of the entries in Panel a. All of the residuals in Panel b are 0; taking logarithms permits a much simpler description of the relationship of the response variable Y to the predictors A and B. Thus, transforming the entries in two-way tables may improve the parsimony of a modeled relationship.

Returning to the original data (Panel a of Table 12.6), we note that the only entry in the table that exceeds the mean—the 100 in the rightmost cell of the top row—is very much an outlier. (Incidentally, note that this outlier status was "cured" by symmetrizing the numbers with the application of the logarithmic transformation.) To illustrate the effect of this outlier on the decomposition of the table, we replace the 100 with the largest number that is not an outlier (24.85,

TABLE 12.7
Logarithms of the Numbers in Table 12.6
and Decomposition by Means of the New Table

(a) The Two-Way Table

		B		
A	1	2	3	Mean
1	0.0	1.0	2.0	1.00
2	−1.0	0.0	1.0	0.00
3	−2.0	−1.0	0.0	−1.00
Mean	−1.0	0.0	1.0	0.00

(b) Grand Mean, Row, Column, and Cell Effects

		B		
A	1	2	3	Effect
1	0.00	0.00	0.00	1.00
2	0.00	0.00	0.00	0.00
3	0.00	0.00	0.00	−1.00
Effect	−1.00	0.00	1.00	0.00

TABLE 12.8
The Numbers in Table 12.6 with One Substitution,
and Decomposition by Means of the New Table

(a) The Two-Way Table

		B		
A	1	2	3	Mean
1	1.00	10.00	24.85	11.95
2	0.10	1.00	10.00	3.70
3	0.01	0.10	1.00	0.37
Mean	0.37	3.7	11.95	5.34

(b) Grand Mean, Row, Column, and Cell Effects

		B		
A	1	2	3	Effect
1	−5.98	−0.31	6.29	6.61
2	1.37	−1.06	−0.31	−1.64
3	4.61	1.37	−5.98	−4.97
Effect	−4.97	−1.64	6.61	5.34

which is 1.5 hingespreads above the upper hinge). Panel a of Table 12.8 shows the new table, and Panel b shows its decomposition by means. A comparison of Panels b of Tables 12.6 and 12.8 demonstrates that the change in one cell entry has wrought profound changes on the row and column effects and on the table of residuals. An understanding of the original data clearly requires a decomposition technique that does not allow the value of a single cell entry to diffuse throughout the two-way table.

Tukey (1977, pp. 363–371) suggested such a technique based on medians. Median polish is an iterative procedure: On each iteration, one finds row medians, column medians, and the median of these medians, which accumulate into row effects, column effects, and an overall level effect. The procedure is continued until all row and column medians are as close as possible to zero. The algebra of the procedure is presented formally by Emerson and Hoaglin (1983a), who also discussed various mathematical issues associated with this technique. We first demonstrate median polish and its potential advantages with the artificial example we have been discussing and then carry out the procedure on a table of real data.

Successive panels of Table 12.9 show median polish for the two-way array of Table 12.6. A single iteration of median polish involves working through the rows and then the columns of a table (or alternatively, through the columns and then the rows). The original two-way table is shown in Panel a. We first find the median of each row; these are indicated to the right of the respective rows (Panel b). New cell entries are calculated by subtracting the row median from the cells in each row (Panel c). Then, the value for the overall level of the table, which was initially zero, is adjusted by finding the median of the row medians, recording it at the lower right, and subtracting it from each of the row medians to yield adjusted row effects (Panel d). Note that as each adjustment is made (Panels c and d), the original values for any cell of the data array can be recovered by adding the overall level, the row effect, and the cell effect.

Next, we perform the same operations on columns. We find the median of the cell entries in each column, write it below the column (Panel e), and then subtract it from the cell entries in its column (Panel f). We then find the median of the column effects, add it to the overall level in the lower right, and subtract it from the column effect entries (in this case, the median of the column medians is zero). Returning to the rows, we find that all row medians are zero, and checking back with the columns, we find that all column medians are zero. Thus, no additional iterations are needed. A check by addition shows that each entry of the original table can be reconstructed by adding the overall level, the row effect, the column effect, and the cell residual. Note that although the median row, column, and cell effects are zero, the means of these sets of effects are not. A comparison of the row, column, and cell effects in Panel f of Table 12.9 with those of Panel b of Table 12.6 illuminates the difference between decomposition by means (mean polish) and by medians (median polish).

TABLE 12.9
Median Polish of the Data Array from Table 12.6

(a) Data Array

	B		
A	1	2	3
1	1	10	100
2	0.1	1	10
3	0.01	0.1	1

(b) Identification of Row Medians

	B			
A	1	2	3	Median
1	1	10	100	10
2	0.1	1	10	1
3	0.01	0.1	1	0.1
Median	0	0	0	0

(c) Subtraction of Row Medians from Row Entries

	B			
A	1	2	3	Median
1	−9	0	90	10
2	−0.9	0	9	1
3	−0.09	0	0.9	0.1
Median	0	0	0	0

(d) Adjustment of Overall Table Level

	B			
A	1	2	3	Median
1	−9	0	90	9
2	−0.9	0	9	0
3	−0.09	0	0.9	−0.9
Median	0	0	0	1

(e) Identification of Column Medians

	B			
A	1	2	3	Median
1	−9	0	90	9
2	−0.9	0	9	0
3	−0.09	0	0.9	−0.9
Median	−0.9	0	9	1

(continued)

TABLE 12.9   (*Continued*)

(f) Subtraction of Column Medians from Column Entries

A	B			
	1	*2*	*3*	*Median*
1	−8.1	0	81	9
2	0	0	0	0
3	0.81	0	−8.1	−0.9
Median	−0.9	0	9	1

Table 12.10 shows the results of median polish of the data in Table 12.8. (Recall that, save for the alteration of the largest value, these data are identical to those of Table 12.6.) A comparison of Tables 12.9 and 12.10 shows that the effect of altering one extreme value appears only in the residual for the changed cell; everything else remains the same. This comparison is strikingly different from the parallel results using mean polish (see Tables 12.6 and 12.8). Again, mean polish of a two-way table results in the diffusion of the value in each cell over the entire table, whereas median polish confines extreme values to their own cells.

We conclude this discussion of two-way tables and median polish with a more complex example that requires multiple iterations of polish. Abelson, Kinder, Peters, and Fiske (1982) conducted a prestudy in which they asked survey respondents in 1979 whether each of four potential candidates for the U.S. presidency in 1980 had ever elicited each of a set of emotions. The rows of Table 12.11 list the emotions; the columns indicate the candidates; and the cells contain percentages of respondents who answered affirmatively. In the decomposition of this table, a row effect indicates the tendency of the political candidates collectively to elicit the row emotion, and a column effect indicates the tendency of the column candidate to elicit any emotion at all. Of principal interest in the analysis of this table is the extent to which cells exhibit dramatic departures from a simple additive structure—that is, the extent to which cells have big residuals after the overall level, row, and column effects have been removed.

TABLE 12.10
Median Polish of the Data Array from Table 12.8

A	B			
	1	*2*	*3*	*Median*
1	−8.1	0	5.85	9
2	0	0	0	0
3	0.81	0	−8.1	−0.9
Median	−0.9	0	9	1

TABLE 12.11
Emotional Responses to Candidates

	Candidate			
Emotion	Carter	Ford	Kennedy	Reagan
Hopeful	79	55	54	26
Frustrated	59	49	39	25
Happy	49	42	35	19
Angry	47	42	52	28
Proud	47	32	37	15
Disgusted	47	41	43	29
Relieved	41	37	22	14
Afraid	32	15	24	27
Sad	31	38	54	17
Ashamed	12	21	42	11

Note: Each point represents the percentage of people who said that the particular candidate elicited the particular emotion. The data were collected in a pilot study for the investigation reported by Abelson et al. (1982).

Table 12.12 shows the results of median polish of the data in Table 12.11. These results, which were achieved in four iterations, reveal systematic overall differences between emotions and between politicians. (Note that the rows and columns have been arranged by effect size.) The row effects indicate that as a group, the candidates tended to elicit hope and frustration but not fear. The column effects indicate that Carter, who was president at the time, elicited more responses than the other candidates, perhaps because he was best known. Reagan, on the other hand, elicited few emotions and (ironically) appears to have been relatively unknown.

TABLE 12.12
Median Polish of the Emotional Responses to Candidates Data

	Carter	Kennedy	Ford	Reagan	Row Effect
Hopeful	16.5	−1.0	1.0	−8.5	15.5
Frustrated	2.0	−10.5	0.5	−4.0	10.0
Angry	−8.0	4.5	−4.5	1.0	8.0
Disgusted	−3.0	0.5	−0.5	7.0	3.0
Happy	1.0	−5.5	2.5	−1.0	1.0
Sad	−14.5	16.0	1.0	−0.5	−1.5
Proud	3.5	1.0	3.0	−0.5	−3.5
Relieved	−0.5	−12.0	4.0	0.5	−5.5
Ashamed	−26.0	11.5	−8.5	1.0	−9.0
Afraid	0.0	−0.5	−8.5	23.0	−15.0
Column Effect	8.0	0.5	−0.5	−20.0	39.0

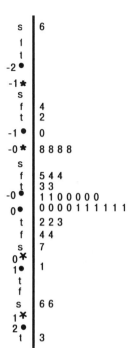

```
s │ 6
↑ │
t │
-2 ● │
-1 ✱ │
 s │
 f │ 4
 t │ 2
-1 ● │ 0
-0 ✱ │ 8 8 8 8
 s │
 f │ 5 4 4
 t │ 3 3
-0 ● │ 1 1 0 0 0 0 0
 0 ● │ 0 0 0 0 1 1 1 1 1 1
 t │ 2 2 3
 f │ 4 4
 s │ 7
 0 ✱ │
 1 ● │ 1
 t │
 f │
 s │ 6 6
 1 ✱ │
 2 ● │
 t │ 3
```

FIG. 12.16. Stem-and-leaf display of the residuals following median polish of the emotional responses to candidates data (see Table 12.10).

The residuals tell the most interesting story. Figure 12.16 shows a stem-and-leaf plot of the residuals. Most of the residuals have values around 0. The median of the residuals is 0, and the upper and lower hinges are 1.0 and −4.5, respectively. Five of the residuals in the table are outliers and are quite distinct from the rest of the entries. These outliers reveal distinctive patterns of emotions elicited by each of the candidates. Carter made people feel hopeful and decidedly not ashamed or sad. By contrast, Kennedy made people feel both ashamed and sad. And although these candidates generally did not elicit fear in the surveyed public, Reagan made people feel decidedly fearful.

Finally, Table 12.13 shows the results of a decomposition by means of this table. Although the cells in Table 12.13 that contain the biggest residuals are analogous to those yielded by median polish, we call attention to a major difference. The biggest residuals in the means analysis are substantially smaller than the biggest residuals after median polish. The table of residuals from a means analysis must sum to zero across both rows and columns, so a big residual must be offset in its row and column by other residuals of at least modest size. Again, we see how this nonresistant procedure leads to a diffusion of extreme values throughout the table.

Additional techniques for resistant analysis of two-way tables are presented by Godfrey (1985) and by Emerson and Wong (1985); Cook (1985) extended these procedures to the analysis of tables with three or more predictor variables.

TABLE 12.13
Means Polish of the Emotional Responses to Candidates Data

	Carter	Kennedy	Ford	Reagan	Row Effect
Hopeful	16.8	−4.0	0.0	−12.9	17.8
Frustrated	7.3	−8.5	4.5	−3.4	7.3
Angry	−3.9	5.3	−1.7	0.4	6.5
Disgusted	−1.7	−1.5	−0.5	3.6	4.3
Happy	4.1	−5.7	4.3	−2.6	0.5
Sad	−12.7	14.5	1.5	−3.4	−0.7
Proud	5.6	−0.2	−2.2	−3.1	−3.0
Relieved	3.8	−11.0	7.0	0.1	−7.2
Afraid	−1.2	−5.0	−11.0	17.1	−11.2
Ashamed	−18.2	16.0	−2.0	4.1	−14.2
Column Effect	8.7	4.5	1.5	−14.6	35.7

CONCLUSIONS

In summary, exploratory data analysis is both a philosophy of and a strategy for the investigation of samples of data. The techniques emphasize resistance and robustness—insensitivity to outliers and to contamination of data, and indifference to the nature of the distribution from which the sample observations originate. Our brief and incomplete overview of the techniques has focused on those that are especially suited to the types of data that psychologists study. We have sought both to convey the potential value of these procedures for illuminating the structure of a set of data and to provide enough operational information to encourage their use.

As instructors of graduate-level courses in statistics, we have found that our students appreciate the techniques of EDA in principle but often fail to put them into practice. The major obstacle seems to be the time and effort required to carry out these procedures by hand. On these grounds, there is cause for optimism: EDA techniques are appearing with increasing frequency in standard statistical packages, making them easy and painless to use. (Indeed, stem-and-leaf diagrams and boxplots are now available in both mainframe—SAS, SPSS, BMDP—and PC packages—Systat, Datadesk; additional techniques are available in selected PC packages.) We hope this chapter contributes to the application of these procedures to psychological data.

REFERENCES

Abelson, R. P., Kinder, D. R., Peters, M. D., & Fiske, S. T. (1982). Affective and semantic components in political person perception. *Journal of Personality and Social Psychology, 42,* 619–630.

Besag, J., & Seheult, A. (1988). Resistant techniques. In S. Kotz & N. Johnson (Eds.), *Encyclopedia of statistical sciences* (Vol. 8, pp. 98–101). New York: Wiley.

Bondy, F. (1991, May 14). Does royal treatment pay off? Sure, sometimes. *New York Times,* pp. B9, B12.

Cook, N. R. (1985). Three-way analyses. In D. C. Hoaglin, F. Mosteller, & J. W. Tukey (Eds.), *Exploring data tables, trends, and shapes* (pp. 125–188). New York: Wiley.

Darlington, R. B. (1990). *Regression and linear models.* New York: McGraw-Hill.

Emerson, J. D. (1983). Mathematical aspects of transformation. In D. C. Hoaglin, F. Mosteller, & J. W. Tukey (Eds.), *Understanding robust and exploratory data analysis* (pp. 247–282). New York: Wiley.

Emerson, J. D., & Hoaglin, D. C. (1983a). Analysis of two-way tables by medians. In D. C. Hoaglin, F. Mosteller, & J. W. Tukey (Eds.), *Understanding robust and exploratory data analysis* (pp. 166–210). New York: Wiley.

Emerson, J. D., & Hoaglin, D. C. (1983b). Resistant lines for y versus x. In D. C. Hoaglin, F. Mosteller, & J. W. Tukey (Eds.), *Understanding robust and exploratory data analysis* (pp. 129–165). New York: Wiley.

Emerson, J. D., & Hoaglin, D. C. (1983c). Stem-and-leaf displays. In D. C. Hoaglin, F. Mosteller, & J. W. Tukey (Eds.), *Understanding robust and exploratory data analysis* (pp. 7–32). New York: Wiley.

Emerson, J. D., & Hoaglin, D. C. (1985). Resistant multiple regression, one variable at a time. In D. C. Hoaglin, F. Mosteller, & J. W. Tukey (Eds.), *Exploring data tables, trends, and shapes* (pp. 241–279). New York: Wiley.

Emerson, J. D., & Stoto, M. A. (1983). Transforming data. In D. C. Hoaglin, F. Mosteller, & J. W. Tukey (Eds.), *Understanding robust and exploratory data analysis* (pp. 97–128). New York: Wiley.

Emerson, J. D., & Strenio, J. (1983). Boxplots and batch comparison. In D. C. Hoaglin, F. Mosteller, & J. W. Tukey (Eds.), *Understanding robust and exploratory data analysis* (pp. 58–96). New York: Wiley.

Emerson, J. D., & Wong, G. Y. (1985). Resistant nonadditive fits for two-way tables. In D. C. Hoaglin, F. Mosteller, & J. W. Tukey (Eds.), *Exploring data tables, trends, and shapes* (pp. 67–124). New York: Wiley.

Fleiss, J. L. (1986). *The design and analysis of clinical experiments.* New York: Wiley.

Gibbons, J. D. (1982). Distribution-free methods. In S. Kotz & N. Johnson (Eds.), *Encyclopedia of statistical sciences* (Vol. 2, pp. 400–408). New York: Wiley.

Godfrey, K. (1985). Fitting by organized comparisons: The square combining table. In D. C. Hoaglin, F. Mosteller, & J. W. Tukey (Eds.), *Exploring data tables, trends, and shapes* (pp. 37–66). New York: Wiley.

Gyato, K. P. (1991). *The perceived attributions and behavior of children in achievement situations.* Unpublished master's thesis, State University of New York, Binghamton, NY.

Hartwig, F., & Dearing, B. E. (1979). *Exploratory data analysis* (Sage University Paper Series on Quantitative Applications in the Social Sciences, Series No. 07-016). Beverly Hills, CA: Sage Publications.

Hoaglin, D. C. (1983). Letter values: A set of selected order statistics. In D. C. Hoaglin, F. Mosteller, & J. W. Tukey (Eds.), *Understanding robust and exploratory data analysis* (pp. 33–57). New York: Wiley.

Hoaglin, D. C., Mosteller, F., & Tukey, J. W. (Eds.). (1983). *Understanding robust and exploratory data analysis.* New York: Wiley.

Hoaglin, D. C., Mosteller, F., & Tukey, J. W. (Eds.). (1985). *Exploring data tables, trends, and shapes.* New York: Wiley.

Huber, P. J. (1981). *Robust statistics.* New York: Wiley.

Lehmann, E. L. (1975). *Nonparametrics: Statistical methods based on ranks.* San Francisco: Holden-Day.

Leinhardt, S., & Wasserman, S. S. (1979). Exploratory data analysis: An introduction to selected methods. *Sociological Methodology, 1979,* 311–365.

Mood, A. M., Graybill, F. A., & Boes, D. C. (1974). *Introduction to the theory of statistics.* New York: McGraw-Hill.

Mosteller, F., & Rourke, R. E. K. (1973). *Sturdy statistics: Nonparametrics and order statistics.* Reading, MA: Addison-Wesley.

Mosteller, F., & Tukey, J. W. (1977). *Data analysis and regression: A second course in statistics.* Reading, MA: Addison-Wesley.

Myers, J. L., & Well, A. D. (1991). *Research design and statistical analysis.* New York: Harper Collins.

Neter, J., Wasserman, W., & Kutner, M. H. (1989). *Applied linear regression models* (2nd ed.). Homewood, IL: Irwin.

Rosenberger, J. L., & Gasko, M. (1983). Comparing location estimators: Trimmed means, medians, and trimean. In D. C. Hoaglin, F. Mosteller, & J. W. Tukey (Eds.), *Understanding robust and exploratory data analysis* (pp. 297–338). New York: Wiley.

Smith, A. F. (1990, November). *Sensitivity to frequency in probabilistic category learning.* Paper presented at the 31st Annual Meeting of the Psychonomic Society, New Orleans.

Smith, A. F. (1991). Cognitive processes in long-term dietary recall. *Vital and Health Statistics,* Series 6, No. 4 (DHHS Publication No. 92-1079). Washington, DC: U.S. Government Printing Office.

Smith, A. F., & Jobe, J. B. (in press). Reports of long-term dietary memories: Data and a model. In N. Schwarz & S. Sudman (Eds.), *Autobiographical memory and the validity of retrospective reports.* New York: Springer.

Smith, A. F., Jobe, J. B., & Mingay, D. J. (1991a). Question-induced cognitive biases in reports of health-related behaviors. *Health Psychology, 10,* 244–251.

Smith, A. F., Jobe, J. B., & Mingay, D. J. (1991b). Retrieval from memory of dietary information. *Applied Cognitive Psychology, 5,* 269–296.

Sorlie, P. D., & Gold, E. B. (1987). The effect of physician terminology preference on coronary heart disease mortality: An artifact uncovered by the 9th revision ICD. *American Journal of Public Health, 77,* 148–152.

Stellman, S. D. (1989). The case of the missing eights: An object lesson in data quality assurance. *American Journal of Epidemiology, 129,* 857–860.

Stoto, M. A., & Emerson, J. D. (1983). Power transformations for data analysis. *Sociological Methodology, 1983–1984,* 126–268.

Tukey, J. W. (1977). *Exploratory data analysis.* Reading, MA: Addison-Wesley.

Velleman, P. F. (1982). Applied nonlinear smoothing. *Sociological Methodology, 1982,* 141–177.

Velleman, P. F., & Hoaglin, D. C. (1981). *Applications, basics, and computing of exploratory data analysis.* Boston, MA: Duxbury Press.

Winer, B. J., Brown, D. R., & Michels, K. M. (1991). *Statistical principles in experimental design* (3rd ed.). New York: McGraw-Hill.

Wu, L. L. (1985). Robust M-estimation of location and regression. *Sociological Methodology, 1985,* 316–388.

Note added in proofs. After we completed this chapter, a new book edited by Hoaglin, Mosteller, and Tukey, *Fundamentals of Exploratory Analysis of Variance* (1991, New York: Wiley), was published. This volume applies, explicitly within the context of analysis of variance, many of the techniques discussed in this chapter and by Hoaglin and associates (1983, 1985). Because analysis of variance plays a central role in the analysis of psychological data, this book may be of interest to psychologists who wish to increase their use of exploratory techniques in data analysis and interpretation.

13 Graphical Data Analysis

Howard Wainer
Educational Testing Service

David Thissen
University of North Carolina at Chapel Hill

INTRODUCTION

Psychology is full of an easy complexity. Physical sciences gain in truth when most quantitative, whereas psychology, when most quantitative has been of least scope, though the sweetness of elegance lingers on. Over the century since Wundt's laboratory started modern experimental psychology, its characteristic paradigms have emerged in fits and starts. In an attempt to deal with its frequently crude data, psychology has adopted, adapted, and polished a set of statistical procedures and models that are second in sophistication and complexity only to those employed by Carlyle's "dismal science." The often self-conscious attempt to make paradigms statistically rigorous when experimental controls lacked rigor was in keeping with comments of statisticians such as Wallis (1949), who argued that "So-called 'high-powered,' 'refined,' or 'elaborate' statistical techniques are generally called for when the data are crude and inadequate—exactly the opposite, if I may be permitted an *obiter dictum,* of what crude and inadequate statisticians usually think" p. 471.

Of course, there were many reasons other than self-conscious defensiveness for the development and use of high-powered statistical techniques. Often such techniques were desperately required. This need provided the impetus for the development of rigorous, formal statistical models, but de-emphasized the need for descriptive methods: Methods whose aims were exploratory rather than confirmatory.

The past 30 years have seen a vigorous development of methods, by the foremost of statisticians, that have as their very nature an informality that was unheard of in the social sciences for a half century. These techniques are primarily graphical in form, flexible and robust in character, and informative in a wide variety of problems and so are of general applicability. It is toward a review of these techniques that this chapter is directed.

The signal event in this area was the 1977 publication of Tukey's *Exploratory Data Analysis* (EDA). Prepublication versions of this document abounded, and so dating the start of the movement of informal data analysis by that book's publication is a bit misleading. Consequently we refer to Tukey as the modern progenitor of the movement that dates back at least to 1962 and the publication of Tukey's prophetic "Future of data analysis." Other recent works of importance on this topic include: Bertin (1973), Chambers, Cleveland, Kleiner, and Tukey (1983), Cleveland (1985), Cleveland and McGill (1988), Everitt (1978), Gnanadesikan (1977), Monkhouse and Wilkinson (1971), Mosteller and Tukey (1968, 1977), Tufte (1983), Wainer (1984, 1990a, 1992), Wainer and Thissen (1981, 1986), and Wang (1978).

Limits of this Chapter

It is the purpose of a review article to start where the last review article left off and to contain as much of the intervening work as space permits. This allows the researcher to read the most recent review and be more or less current with the work done at the time that review was written. This review is an update of one we prepared about a decade ago (Wainer & Thissen, 1981); we include here the same material in instances where it is still relevant as well as newer developments as they have taken place. We attempt to increase the depth of coverage as the work becomes more current.

We do not directly discuss robust statistics, although robust data analysis is one aim of many of the procedures that are discussed. The reader interested in robustness is referred to any of the standard sources (e.g., Rousseuw & Leroy, 1987; Wainer, 1982). Sometimes graphical methods allow the easy computation of a statistical test (e.g., binomial paper, Mosteller & Tukey 1949) or a statistic (computing a robust correlation graphically, Sandiford 1932; or model parameters, Bock & Jones 1968); we generally do not discuss this aspect, although occasional reference to such things are made. Furthermore, although we recognize that graphics have many uses, we generally limit ourselves to graphics for data analysis. Graphs for communicative purposes or nomographs for computational ones we leave to other accounts. Occasionally some rules for good exploratory graphs carry over into presentational rules, and when this occurs we make mention of it.

We view this chapter as didactic, and so it contains many examples of the sorts of plots we discuss. This avoids the anomalous situation of a chapter on graphs describing its subject in prose. We intend to "show" rather than "tell" whenever possible. We exclude color for purely economic reasons. Dynamic displays, graphs that allow a high degree of interaction between the display and the user, are excluded for the obvious reason.

The role of graphs in theory development is often misunderstood. Tilling 1975), in his history of experimental graphs, restated this misconception:

Clearly an ability to plot an experimental graph necessarily precedes an ability to analyze it. However, although any map may be considered as a graph, and carefully constructed maps had been in use long before the eighteenth century, we do not expect the shape of a coast-line to follow a mathematical law. Further, although there are a great many physical phenomena that we do expect to follow mathematical laws, they are in general so complex in nature that direct plotting will reveal little about the nature of those laws. (p. 193)

Attitudes like these have hindered appropriately serious regard for such theories as that of continental drift, the initial evidence for which (noticed by every chool child) is solely graphical.[1]

The point of this chapter is to introduce to psychology many of the recent levelopments in graphical data analysis, as well as to aid in their legitimization or theory construction within a scholarly context. This is done in the ardent elief that graphs can aid us in the discovery and understanding of psychological henomena. Although science (following Chamberlain) may be the "holding of multiple working hypotheses," the picturing of data allows us to be sensitive "not nly to the multiple hypotheses we hold, but to the many more we have not yet hought of, regard as unlikely or think impossible" (Tukey, 1974, p. 526).

HISTORY

"he use of visual displays to present quantitative material is very old indeed. As hakespeare noted (*Henry VI,* Act IV), "Our forefathers had no other books but he score and tally." Both score and tally represented an advance to the concept of bstract number from more literally iconic predecessors. Our use of "graphic" ere is the opposite of "graphic" in the sense of literal life-likeness. Historical levelopment displays both the replacement of iconic aspects of representation by progressively more abstract (and potentially more logically elaborate) forms as vell as the development of signs and sign systems progressively stripped of their conic features and adapted instead to the grammar and syntax of linearly configured, written counterparts to spoken language. For most human purposes, the lphanumerical system proved infinitely more useful and largely displaced raphic devices as means of recording, reordering, manipulating, comprehending, and analyzing symbolic representations of quantitative aspects of phenomena. The principal exception to the preponderant alphanumerical form uses the calar representation of space, and objects concretely located in space, on a

---

[1]And, not to be argumentative, but see Mandelbrot (1982, chap. 5) for an extended discussion of he (fractal) mathematics of coastlines.

graphic plane. The earlier-to-evolve form of schematic spatial representation is the map; the more highly abstract form is the geometric diagram. Cartography and geometry, in both their terrestrial and astronomical applications, have been the most important areas of graphic development. Geometry also evolved to treat space as pure abstraction equivalent to number. The movement of objectives in space made for ready extension to include time in the graphic spatial plane. Certain other graphic systems, including mechanical and architectural drawing, musical notation, astrological and alchemical or scientific chemical symbol systems, were all partially diagrammatic in character. The systemization of the spatial diagrammatic forms by Descartes in 1637 in the Cartesian coordinate system and his integration of the geometric and the algebraic systems established what until the present day remains the most intellectually important and useful of diagrammatic graphic systems.

As Biderman (1978) noted, the Cartesian system so dominated intellectual conceptions of what graphs were and what they were for—that is, the depiction of the mathematical functions governing the behavior of objects in space and time—that it took more than a century and a half before it occurred to anyone that graphs could be used for anything else. Furthermore, as Biderman also noted, the Cartesian tradition was so strong that it misled those who were using graphs in altogether different ways for altogether different intellectual tasks into the belief that they were doing Cartesian geometric analysis. In truth, they were engaged in something quite different, involving no geometry more complex than that well known even in pre-classical antiquity. What they were doing was, however, an important intellectual departure from Cartesianism—that is, graphic methods were being applied to exploratory analysis of empirical statistics. Eventually, with d'Alembert, Gauss et al., a method of joining the Cartesian and the statistical graphic approaches developed, but, in application, curve-fitting remained on an intellectually separate track until very late in the 19th century. Cartesian curve-fitting uses data to determine (comprehend) the structure (curves = laws) governing the universe. The statistical orientation uses curves (regularities) to determine (comprehend) the structure of concrete sets of data—data about phenomena that are important to understand in their own right.

A major conceptual breakthrough in graphical presentation came in 1786 with the publication of Playfair's *Political Atlas* in which spatial dimensions were used to represent nonspatial, quantitative, idiographic, empirical data. Although it now seems natural to represent, for example, rising and falling imports over time as a rising and falling line, it does not seem to have been done before that time and was quite an accomplishment. Notably, in addition to the statistical line chart, Playfair at one fell swoop single-handedly invented most of the remaining forms of the statistical graphic repertoire used today—the bar chart and histogram, the surface chart, and the circle diagram or "pie chart."

An extensive history of graphical developments is provided by Funkhouser (1937), who reviewed the use of graphic display in the physical and social sciences from early picture writing to uses during the 1930s. It contains many examples, but, because of economic and technical reasons, spends many pages describing color graphs rather than reproducing them. A similar problem confronts the authors of this review, as is evident in the section on multivariate display. More recent histories have appeared that contain careful analyses of Playfair's contribution to the development of the graphical form (Costigan-Eaves & Macdonald-Ross, 1990a, 1990b.) The interested reader is referred to Tufte's (1983) wonderful *The Visual Display of Quantitative Information* for a presentation of historical graphs in all of their colorful glory.

A useful tool for the study of the history, development, and applications of the graphical method is the annotated bibliography prepared by B. M. Fienberg and Franklin (1975).

GRAPHICS FOR DATA ANALYSIS

In the sections to follow, we describe a variety of procedures judged useful for data analysis. These methods display the data and thus in a real sense describe them. They aid in analysis and interpretation, summarize what we know about the data, and expose what we do not know. The usefulness of any particular display is determined by comparison with the following list of desirable characteristics (proposed by Gnanadesikan, 1980):

1. *descriptive capacity*—the ability to provide a full description of the data set under consideration

2. *versatility*—"The greatest value of a graph is when it forces us to see what we were not expecting" (Tukey, 1977). To fulfil this a graph must be versatile to show us aspects of the data that we were not expecting to look at (e.g., We wanted to look at level, but it also shows us spread).

3. *data orientation*—The first reaction one ought to have on looking at a good graph is not "What a beautiful graph" but rather "What interesting data." A good graph ought to be modest and stand in the background. Thus of good data displays it may be said what Mark Van Doren observed about brilliant conversationalists: *"In their presence others speak well."*

4. *potential for internal comparisons*—An important use of graphical displays is to make comparisons between different data series. Some graphical forms allow this, others (e.g., the double *y*-axis graph do not, and ought to be avoided; see Wainer, 1991a, 1992).

5. *aid in focussing attention*—Note the emphasis in Tukey's famous epigram quoted in 2.

6. *degree to which they are self-critical of assumptions*—When building a graph one must make a variety of decisions/assumptions about the data structure

in advance of plotting them (i.e., their scale). A good graph will tell you loud and clear if you have chosen unwisely (e.g., if all data points cluster near zero but one point huddles in an upper extreme a transformation is called for).

7. *adaptability to large volumes of data*—If one has 3 or fewer points to display a sentence is a plausible first choice; between 4 and 20 numbers are often communicated well in a table, but with more than 20 points a graph is the first choice. Any graphical form (e.g., pie charts; Wainer, 1991b) that cannot accomplish this ought to be avoided.

We do not go through this list of desiderata for each display technique, but the reader should remember these and compare each technique with the others on these bases. Furthermore, this list forms a basis of comparisons for other techniques that we do not mention but that the reader might find available. For many purposes some of these desiderata are not crucial, and so a method that is not say, versatile, may be very useful for a narrow purpose of a particular investigation. These criteria are general ones, meant for the overall evaluation of a data analytic technique.

One-Way Displays of One-Way Data

Such is the current renaissance of the development of statistical graphics that even the graphics associated with counting are being altered. Although numerals are useful for the storage of numbers and their presentation in tabular form, the act of counting may be aided by other graphic devices; and entirely graphic displays are often superior to tables for data-analytic purposes.

Even now, when calculating machines as powerful as the room-sized computers of past decades are pocket-sized, and when general-purpose computers cost less than color televisions, much counting is still done by hand. A prerequisite to efficient data analysis is the ability to count quickly and accurately. Tukey (1977) complained that the traditional tallying procedure,

$$/ \quad // \quad /// \quad //// \quad \cancel{||||} /$$

is slow and "treacherous" because one can accidently make completed figures of 4 or 6 ($\cancel{||||}$ or $\cancel{|||||}$). He suggested another tallying procedure, using dots and lines to form a square figure, as in Fig. 13.1. Successive dots (representing the counts 1 to 4) form a square; lines connecting the dots represent 5 to 8, and the diagonals are 9 and 10. A series of such figures is easy to total: Completed figures are multiplied by 10, and the rest are added (i.e., there are 22 sophomore boys in the two-way example in part C of Fig. 13.1).

The square figures are so easily read as numbers that it is frequently unnecessary to translate them into numerals; see, for example, part B of Fig. 13.1, which gives a kind of bar chart for scores from 0 to 10, and part C of Fig. 13.1, which is a two-way table. Whereas the new figures are not universally praised, they have

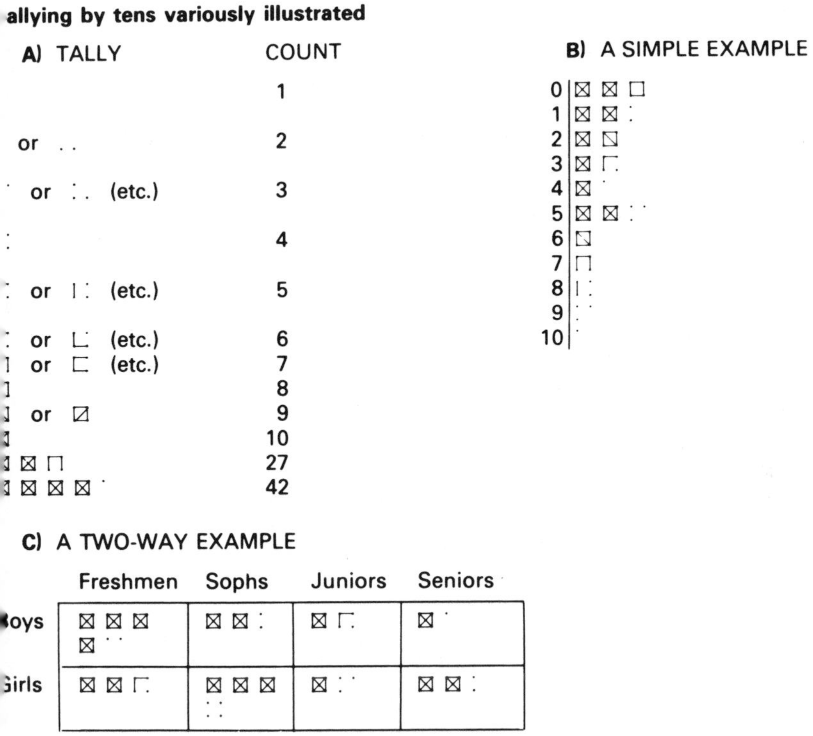

allying by tens variously illustrated

A) TALLY			COUNT
			1
or	..		2
˙ or	∴	(etc.)	3
∷			4
∷ or	⌐∷	(etc.)	5
∷ or	⌐∷	(etc.)	6
⌐ or	⊏	(etc.)	7
⌐			8
⌐ or	⊠		9
⊠			10
⊠ ⊠ ⌐			27
⊠ ⊠ ⊠ ⊠ ˙			42

B) A SIMPLE EXAMPLE

```
 0 | ⊠ ⊠ ▢
 1 | ⊠ ⊠ ∶
 2 | ⊠ ◹
 3 | ⊠ ⌐
 4 | ⊠ ˙
 5 | ⊠ ⊠ ∴
 6 | ◹
 7 | ⌐
 8 | ⎪∶
 9 | ∷
10 | ˙
```

C) A TWO-WAY EXAMPLE

	Freshmen	Sophs	Juniors	Seniors
Boys	⊠ ⊠ ⊠ ⊠ ∴	⊠ ⊠ ∶	⊠ ⌐	⊠ ˙
Girls	⊠ ⊠ ⌐	⊠ ⊠ ⊠ ∷	⊠ ∴	⊠ ⊠ ∶

FIG. 13.1. Tallying by tens variously illustrated, from Tukey (1977). used by permission.

come into fairly widespread use since they were introduced 20 years ago in the preliminary edition of EDA because they have been found useful by many in practical data analysis.

It turns out that the "traditional tally mark" is traditional only in Western cultures. For millennia, the tally mark used in Eastern cultures (in conjunction with character-based writing) is based on the character 正, transliterated *cheng* from the Chinese. Hsieh (1981) illustrated its use as an alternative to the Western tally mark and the Tukey dots-and-lines system. The character (meaning "unbiased, or possessing integrity" according to Hsieh, p. 174) has five strokes, and in its use as a tally mark the strokes are added sequentially until the character is complete. There is no room for extra strokes, and, at least for some linguistic groups, the character forms a *gestalt* that fails if it is incomplete; thus it avoids the pitfalls of the Western lines-and-slash tally. This mark is commonly used in many Oriental cultures both for the usual purposes of counting and for public display of such numbers as election tallies.

While Tukey has been improving the way people represent counts when a

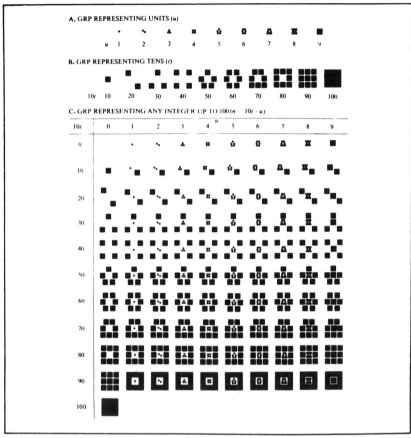

FIG. 13.2.   The basic scale of graphic rational patterns (GRP) showing
integers from 1 to 100, from Bachi (1978). Used by permission.

computer is not doing the work, Bachi (1968, 1976, 1978a, 1978b) had been
improving the way computers represent numbers to people. Bachi's work makes
heavy use of variations on a theme he called the *graphic rational pattern* (GRP).
The basic square GRP is shown in Fig. 13.2; patterns of small squares represent
the units and larger squares represent the tens—the result is a system that graphically represents amount (the more, the darker) and precisely represent numbers
at the same time (each figure can be read as an exact count). The figures must,
for practical purposes, be computer-generated, of course; but currently available
computer graphic systems can easily produce patterns like those in Fig. 13.2, or
the various circular variants Bachi designed for use in a wide variety of contexts.
The displays in Fig. 13.3 show one use for the GRP: A traditional bar chart is
replaced by a dot of the little clusters of square. Display by the GRP method of

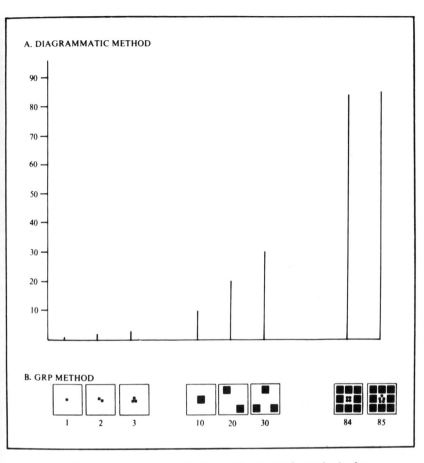

FIG. 13.3.   A comparison of GRP and diagrammatic methods, from Bachi (1978). Used by permission.

the seven counts requires much less space and is probably as informative as the "diagrammatic" representation, or bar chart, given earlier. Bachi's GRP method also may be used in bivariate and multivariate displays; these are discussed in later sections of this review.

Two-Way Displays of One-Way Data

Stem-and-Leaf Diagrams.   The stem-and-leaf display is the most important device for the analysis of small batches of numbers to appear since the *t* test. The stem-and-leaf display permits the data analyst to examine the distributional properties of a batch of data, check for outliers, and compute a collection of useful order statistics, all for the price of writing down the data (once) and counting a bit.

```
↓      1*
2      2  | 3,9
4      3  | 9,3               Alaska, Nevada
5      4  | 5,               Vermont, Wyoming
       5*                     Delaware
11     6  | 3,7,7,1,3,8
       7  | 6,
13     8  | 9,
15     9* | 7,5

21     1** | 30,79,74,41,77,86
√(7)   2   | 54,76,18,18,33,38,85
22     3   | 27,94,04,26,10,41,57,97,95
13     4   | 95,66,32,56          Massachusetts
9      5** | 15,
8      6   | 07,                  New Jersey
7      7   | 82,                  Michigan
       8
6      9** | 71,58                Ohio, Texas

4      1*** | 572,008,678,132     Calif, Ill, NY, Pa
↑      2    |
```

50 populations in tens of thousands   50 populations in millions

```
M25h |   246                      M25h |   2.5
H13  | 89      432                H13  | 0.89    4.3
  1  | 23    1678                   1  | 0.23    17
```

FIG. 13.4.   A stem-and-leaf display of the 1960 populations of the 50 states, from Tukey (1977). Used by permission.

The horticulture associated with stem-and-leaf diagrams is described most completely in Tukey's (1977) volume, but abridged treatments are included in Tukey (1972), Andrews (1978), and Leinhardt and Wasserman (1979). A set of tips for prospective gardeners is also included here. A robust and healthy stem-and-leaf diagram, plucked from Tukey's (1977) greenhouse, is shown in Fig. 13.4. The data displayed are the populations of the 50 states as determined by the 1960 census, in units of 10,000 people.

The numbers in boldface on the left side of the vertical bar are the "stems" (the top one is 1*; the bottom one is 2), and the numbers on the right side of the vertical bar are the "leaves." Each state is represented by a leaf, which is made up of the trailing digits of that state's 1960 population in units of 10,000; each leaf is attached to a stem, which is the first digit of that state's population. Thus, the least populated state has one stem 2, has leaf 3, and had a population in 1960 of 23 × 10,000 = 230,000. For convenience, some states of special interest (the most and least populous, and the lead author's home state) are named at the right of the display, providing us with the information that the least populated state is

Alaska. Nevada is clearly next, with 290,000. At the other end of the distribution, New York was most populous, with 16,780,000 inhabitants (its stem was 1 *** and its leaf 678).

The asterisks to the right of the stems and to the left of the bar might be called "buds"; they are place-holders, indicating the number of digits in each leaf. In this essentially logarithmic stem-and-leaf display, the states with populations between 100,000 and 990,000 are represented by one-digit stems in the upper segment; states that had populations in the millions are represented (with equal precision) by two-digit or three-digit leaves in the lower segments of the plot. The asterisks are reminders of the scale-shifts associated with increasing values of the stems, and the corresponding increase in the size of the leaves. (There could be asterisks next to each stem; some are omitted in Fig. 13.4 for typographical clarity.)

To the left of the stems in Fig. 13.4 are numbers—the cumulative counts from the top to the middle and from the bottom to the middle. Once a stem-and-leaf display has been made, the data have been partially ordered and a number of useful order statistics may be computed. There are 50 states, thus the median is the average of the 25th and the 26th states, or the 25h (for 25-and-a-half) entry on the plot. So the median is computed by counting in (either from the top or the bottom) to 25 and 26 and averaging those entries. The median is 246 (10,000s) and is recorded next to the code "M25h" in the box at the bottom of the stem-and-leaf.

Stem-and-leaf displays are now included in many introductory statistics texts (see, e.g., Moore & McCabe, 1989), and they are commonly used for the presentation of research results in the empirical literature. Such displays are produced, at least in their most elementary form, by many widely distributed packages of data-analysis software (e.g., SPSS-X, Minitab, SYSTAT).[2]

Tukey (1977) called the 25th and 75th percentiles of the distribution "hinges."[3] The hinges, that is, 25th and 75th percentiles or quartiles, are the 13th

---

[2]Significant progress has been made in the past decade in the inclusion of sophisticated graphics for data analysis in software for both large and small computers. Ten years ago, when we first reviewed this area, many of the techniques we described were only available in uncommon or difficult-to-use computer implementations; now the more popular graphic forms have been integrated in many standard statistical packages. We occasionally mention specific computer programs that do particular graphics, by way of illustration of this trend. However, we do not attempt to make the lists exhaustive; we could not, in any event, because new statistical software is released monthly.

[3]Tukey (1970), in the widely circulated (mimeographed?) "Limited Preliminary Edition" (Vol. I) of *Exploratory Data Analysis,* wrote a long and picturesque story about the name "hinges," that went like this: Referring to the quartiles, Tukey (1970, pp. 2–8) wrote, "We need a name for the end quarters thus formed. Germans sometimes call them 'die fliegende Viertel'—the flying quarters. For shortness we will call them wings. We will refer to the points that mark off the wings . . . very frequently. If the wings are thought of as flapping, the points ought to be hinges. Hinges we shall call them, and 'H' we shall mark them." This entire bit was suppressed before the publication of Tukey 1977), in which it would have been on page 33.

numbers counting in—have a "depth" of 13. In the present example they are 8 and 432 (10,000s), and are recorded next to "H13" in the box below the stem and-leaf. That box is filled by including the numbers whose depth is one (the extremes). The numbers in the box make up what Tukey called a "five-number summary" of the batch. A number of Tukey's (1977) robust procedures for estimating the location and width of the distribution, as well as for identifying outliers, are based on the information in the five-number summary.

One strength of the five-number summary is its ability to show outliers and fringeliers. An outlier is a very unusual data point that occurs; a fringelier is a rare point that occurs more often than seldom. To detect such points we need both a sense of usual and a sense of location for a particular point. The location of the hinges as well as the distance between them provides us with a sense of both usual level and usual spread. Points that are far away from the hinges (measured in terms of the distance between the hinges) are candidates for separate treatment. Outliers are sometimes called *contaminants* (as in a "contaminated normal distribution"). This is an unfortunate term, in that it suggests that we would be better off trimming them off and discarding them. In South Africa good building stone is sometimes "contaminated by diamonds." Finding outliers may be the point of our investigation (in the middle-ages the rare individuals who survived plagues then became immune—the beginning of our understanding of what led to inoculation against disease). Hence our emphasis on outliers being separated from the rest of the data and treated separately.

Tukey also made heavy use of five-number summaries when considering transformation, or "re-expressions," of batches of data, especially when it is desirable to achieve symmetry in the distribution for some further analysis. It is clear that the population data of Fig. 13.4 are markedly asymmetrical. If the larger populations were not compressed by changing the stems from 100,000s to millions and then to tens of millions, the stem-and-leaf display would be more than 200 lines long, and there would be only four states in the last 100 lines. So the data were (implicitly) log-transformed in Fig. 13.4.

Figure 13.5 includes two stem-and-leaf displays of the population data after they have actually been transformed to be log(population in 10,000s). The stem-and-leaf display on the left gives the log data with three-significant-digit accuracy "for storage"; but it is too spread out to show the form of the distribution well. The stem-and-leaf on the right "squeezes" the leaves onto shorthand stems (* for zero or one, "t" for two or three, "f" for four or five, "s" for six or seven, and ". for eight or nine); the form of the distribution is clarified. The distribution of the logs is fairly symmetrical, with no extreme values; we use log population data for other examples later in the chapter. The log transformation is often useful for examining data sets in which the variability is proportional to the size of the data point. Many analytic procedures assume homogeneous variance while attempting to detect differences in means (e.g., ANOVA). This is rarely true (consider the variance in nose lengths versus the variance in the length of telephone poles).

1	**13***	6			**1***		
2	**14**	6		1	**t**	3	Alaska
4	**15**	29		4	**f**	455	
5	**16**	5		6	**s**	67	
6	**17***	9		15	**1·**	888888999	
12	**18**	003338		17	**2***	11	Ariz, Nebr
15	**19**	589		√ 25̲̲	**t**	22223333	
	20			25	**f**	444445555	
17	**21***	15		16	**s**	666666677	
21	**22**	4557		7	**2·**	899	
25̲̲	**23**	4478		4	**3***	00	Ill, Pa
√ 25	**24**	04589		2	**t**	22	Cal, NY
20	**25***	1135					
16	**26**	0004679					
9	**27**	18					
7	**28**	9					
6	**29***	89					
4	**30**	05					
	31						
2	**32**	02					
	33*						

FIG. 13.5. Stem-and-leaf displays of the log-transformed populations of the 50 states, from Tukey (1977). Used by permission.

t is more plausible to believe that variance is proportional to mean, and so a log transformation makes the resulting data more amenable to traditional confirmatory procedures. More technically it relates to the fact that in many situations the error distribution is more likely to be well approximated by a lognormal distribution than a normal one.

Stem-and-leaf displays may be made with one-, two-, or more-digit stems, or leaves, or both, or the leaves may be labels rather than digits; they may be made with or without asterisks or commas or upside-down or rightside-up by a computer or by hand. The distributions of data from two groups may be compared with "back-to-back" stem-and-leaf displays; these have a common set of stems in the middle of the page and leaves on both sides—showing one group on the left and the other on the right. Or several may use a common stem on the left, for an even more elaborate plot (see later section on Inside-Out plots). This short discussion is meant to indicate that there are many ways to look at data as a stem-and-leaf display. Some of those ways may be useful.

Box Plots.   The five-number summary associated with the stem-and-leaf display provides the seeds for Tukey's next-most-useful display, the box plot. A set of basic box plots is shown in Fig. 13.6, giving the distribution of telephone bills (in $) for groups with varying lengths of residence in Chicago. For each of

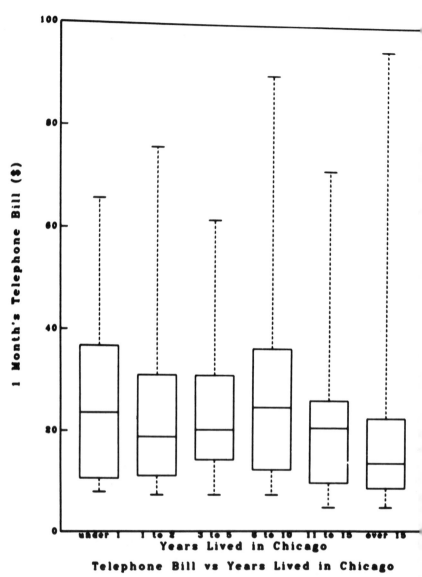

FIG. 13.6.   A regular box plot of monthly telephone bills versus number of years lived in Chicago, from McGill et al. (1978). Used by permission.

the six groups, the box encloses the middle 50% of the data: the top of the box i at the upper hinge (75th percentile) and the bottom of the box is at the lowe hinge (25th percentile). The line across the middle of the box is the median, and the dotted lines (frequently called whiskers) extend to the extremes.

The regular box plots of Fig. 13.6 give an informative display of six distribu-
ions. They are all skewed upward (note the long upper whiskers), and the "under
" and "6 to 10" year groups receive high phone bills while the "over 15" year
group receives lower ones. Some obvious interpretations are that new arrivals
make more long distance calls back to their former home town, and long-time resi-
dents are making more long distance calls to their children who have moved away.
McGill, Tukey, and Larsen (1978) provided a number of intriguing elabora-
ions on the basic box plot. These include the plots in Fig. 13.7, which show the
ame data as displayed in Fig. 13.6. The data have been log-transformed to
approximate symmetry; the width of each box is proportional to root group size;
and a lack of overlap of the obvious "notches" indicates a significant difference at
a "rough 95% level." Formulas for the size of the notches and other technical
details are given in McGill et al. (1978); this example represents one of the few
expressions of hypotheses-testing ideas in the new graphics. Figure 13.7, showing the entire distributions, represents a marked improvement over the classical
"mean with standard error bars." These plots follow in the tradition of "range
harts" (Schmid, 1954).

Tukey (1977) distinguished between *schematic plots* for which he provided
precise rules about the treatment of outliers and such, and regular box plots that
may be drawn quite flexibly. Tufte (1979) proposed yet another class of box-plot
variants called mid-gap plots: They are box plots with the top, bottom, and sides
of the box omitted. Mid-gap plots increase the comprehensible density of such
displays for multiple group comparisons; but the sides of the box can no longer
be used to convey information.

The psychologist interested in comparing groups will undoubtedly find a
favorite graph in the box plot or a variant. But the statisticians who have been
designing data-analytic graphics betray their own concerns with the detailed
analysis of single distributions (instead of the gross analysis of several distribu-
ions) by providing a plethora of distributional displays. Tukey, of course, is an
innovator and adaptor in the area of distributional display, with a variety of
contributions besides the essential, all-purpose stem-and-leaf display.

Dot Charts.   Cleveland (1985, p. 144ff.) introduced the idea of the *dot
chart;* his introductory example is shown in Fig. 13.8. Cleveland (1985) wrote
that the dot chart was invented "in response to the standard ways of displaying
labeled data—bar charts, divided bar charts, and pie charts—which usually
convey quantitative information less well to the viewer than dot charts" (p. 144).
In this example we can readily see that graphs play a more important role in the
communication of information in the natural sciences than in the social sciences.
That data may be more important in the natural sciences is one possible conclusion from this display. A major advantage of this type of display is that it allows
the inclusion of much more data than would be possible with a bar chart (its
predecessor).

Cleveland (1985, chap. 4) and Cleveland and McGill (1985) developed a

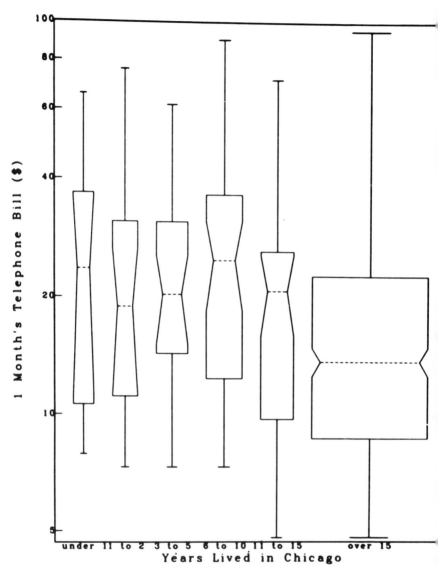

FIG. 13.7. A variable width notched box plot of the data in Fig. 13.6, from McGill et al. (1978). Used by permission.

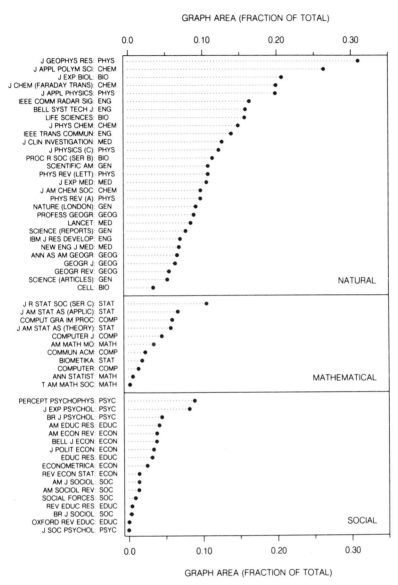

FIG. 13.8. Dot chart showing the fraction of space devoted to graphs in 57 scientific journals, from Cleveland (1985). Used by permission.

heory of the elements of graphical perception; dot plots were designed using that heory, to minimize various sources of error in graphical interpretation. Cleveand presented a number of variants of the basic dot chart intended to serve a variety of purposes.

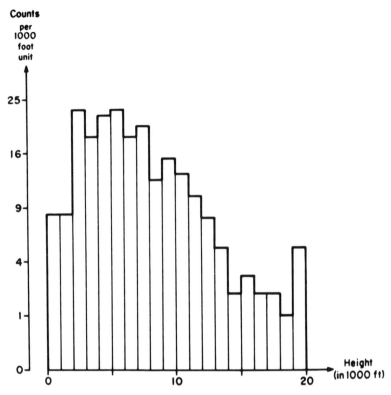

FIG. 13.9.   A rootogram of the heights of 218 volcanoes, from Tukey (1972). Used by permission.

Suspended Rootograms.   In his pioneering comments on graphics in data analysis, Tukey (1972) questioned a number of assumptions implicit in the traditional use of the histogram to compare empirical and theoretical distributions. Tukey argued that histograms need not be drawn with area proportional to count; he also argued (following Jevons, 1884) that comparisons are best made between data and fitted straight lines. An example of a better "-gram" following Tukey's first argument is his proposed *rootogram*, in which area is proportional to the square root of the count—on the grounds that the roots of counts are usually better behaved statistically than are the counts themselves. A traditional histogram of the height of some 218 volcanos is shown is Fig. 13.9; in Fig. 13.10, the same data are displayed as a rootogram of the square roots of the heights.

Figure 13.10, of course, suggests a normal distribution. That distribution could be superimposed on Fig. 13.10, and the goodness-of-fit examined by comparing the curve to the tops of the histobars; but using a curve as a standard of comparison is always poor graphical practice. Instead, Tukey provided the

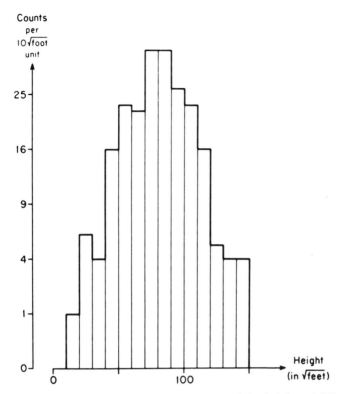

FIG. 13.10. A rootogram of the square roots of the heights of 218 volcanoes, from Tukey (1972). Used by permission.

ianging rootogram shown in Fig. 13.11, in which the rootobars of Fig. 13.10 have been hung from the fitted normal distribution, leaving the discrepancies at he bottoms as deviations around a horizontal line. An even better display might be the *suspended rootogram* of Fig. 13.12 in which the hanging rootogram is urned upside-down, suspending the normal curve from the axis; and the devia-ions, not the data, are plotted as excess or deficit root counts. In this example, Tukey concluded that the "fit of the normal curve to the square roots of these volcano heights is very good indeed"; that conclusion was not strongly suggested by the traditional display in Fig. 13.9. Wainer (1974), in an early experimental evaluation of the new graphics, validated the usefulness of hanging rootograms.

P-P and Q-Q Plots. The classical alternative to the histogram for distribu-ional display, at least since the invention of normal probability paper, has been he probability plot suggested by Galton in 1899 and created by Hazen a decade ater (Funkhouser, 1937). Normal probability paper is ruled with the quantiles of

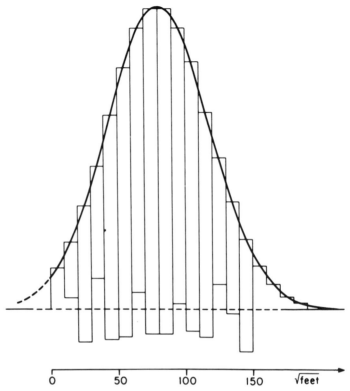

FIG. 13.11. A hanging rootogram of the heights of 218 volcanoes, from Tukey 1972). Used by permission.

the normal distribution (usually in z-score units) on the abscissa, with the inter vals chosen so that a plot of a cumulative normal distribution is a straight line Thus, when a scatterplot is made on such a grid, with the ordered data on the outline and the quantiles associated with each observation's percentile on the abscissa, the plot resembles a straight line to the extent that the data are normall distributed. Deviations from linearity are diagnostic of nonnormality. The plot once made, provides an easy way to make a detailed analysis of the shape of the distribution. However, because normal probability paper has always been a b hard to find (and paper ruled for any other distributions even harder), and proba bility plots have been tedious to make even when the paper is at hand, such plot have not been used often. The computer has changed all of that. Probability plot made by computer graphic systems, or even line printers, are now as easily mad as any two-way plot; and the scale may be set to be appropriate for any distribu tion: A gamma plot is no more difficult to make than a normal one.

Wilk and Gnanadesikan (1968) and Gnanadesikan (1977) offered a number c

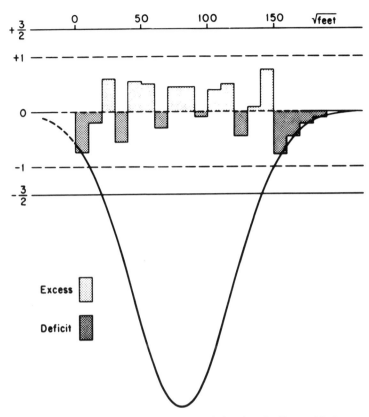

FIG. 13.12. A suspended rootogram of the data in Figure 10, from Tukey (1972). Used by permission.

suggestions for the use of both *quantile* (Q-Q) and *percentile* (P-P) plots. The name *Q-Q plot* refers to all possible elaborations of the traditional probability plot: The ordered data may be plotted against the quantiles of a theoretical distribution, or the quantiles of one empirical distribution may be plotted against another, or two theoretical distributions may be displayed together. The goal is always to compare two distributions; "the same" is always a straight line. An example of a Q-Q plot taken from Wilk and Gnanadesikan (1968) is shown in Fig. 13.13. The data plotted make up a distribution of log energies associated with an individual repeatedly speaking a single word. The display is far superior to a list of the several hundred data points; from it, it is clear that the distribution is bimodal with one made at the lower extreme and another around 1.0 on the normal quantile (*z* score) scale. Both modes are represented by positive deviations from the (imaginary) straight line that would appear if the data were normal. The plot begins high (in the lower left-hand corner), indicating that the

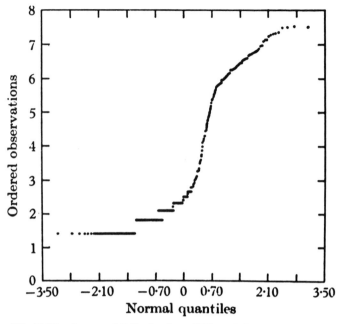

FIG. 13.13.   A normal Q-Q plot from Wilk and Gnanadesikan (1968).
Used by permission.

distribution of the data does not have a tail, as a normal distribution should, but
rather has a large number of tied values at the lower extreme. The second mode is
indicated by the "hump" above the imaginary 45 line about two-thirds of the way
up the plot. Such displays can be more useful than histograms, as there are no
potential artifacts of categorization. They do require some practice to read skill-
fully, but Wilk and Gnanadesikan provided much helpful advice, and Daniel and
Wood (1971) provided a large section of computer-generated examples of Q-Q
plots, as an aid in acquiring skills in interpretation. P-P plots are plots of percentiles rather than quantiles, but are otherwise similar to Q-Q plots; P-P plots
emphasize difference in the middles of distributions, whereas Q-Q plots emphasize the tails. And P-P plots are affected by linear transformations of the data,
whereas Q-Q plots are not. This occurs because if two distributions are different
only in location and/or scale a Q-Q plot will still be linear (although its slope will
reflect differences in the scales and its intercept differences in their locations).
P-P plots will only be linear if the two distributions are identical in all respects,
including location and scale. P-P plots have been studied relatively little.

Wilk and Gnanadesikan discussed in detail the different virtues of Q-Q and
P-P plots, and offered several original suggestions for their use. Two of the most
interesting proposals in Gnanadesikan's (1977) book, from Gnanadesikan (1973,

and Wilk and Gnanadesikan (1968), are the use of Q-Q plots as an aid in the evaluation of dimensionality in principal component analysis and the use of normal and gamma Q-Q plots to analyze effects and variance components in experimental data. Although those techniques are too complex to be reviewed in detail here, the investigator confronted with complex multidimensional data or complex experimental designs would do well to consider those procedures. Daniel and Wood (1971) also make heavy use of Q-Q plots in their treatment of regression as a data-analytic tool; Q-Q plots of residuals are an important part of their analyses. Easton and McCulloch (1990) suggested a multivariate generalization of Q-Q plots, using "matching" concepts to overcome the difficulties inherent in ordering multivariate data. But much of this work is concerned with plots of two or more variables, which brings us to the next topic.

Two-Way Display of (Mostly) Two-Way Data

In the April 1963 issue of *The American Statistician,* Bradley (1963) described an early procedure for producing a scatterplot with the assistance of computational machinery. It worked like this: beginning with a computer card deck on which are punched the values of X and Y, use a card-sorter to order the cards on X; then draw a diagonal line across the top of the deck and reorder the cards, this time on Y. The result was a scatterplot of the order statistics of X and Y, made of the (reordered) pieces of the diagonal line on top of the cards. The plot could be photographed for permanent storage.

Bertin (1977, 1980) used a similar but much more general scheme for the graphical analysis of data matrices using an array in which the entries are shaded proportionally to the observation in the cell. The rows and columns were then permuted in his "domino" apparatus to yield a visual cluster structure. The obtained structure was then interpreted. In Fig. 13.14 there are three versions of the same data with the one on the right being the preferred display indicating the structure of meat production in Western Europe. Figure 13.15 shows the similarity of Bertin's "graphical matrix" to Bradley's scatterplot in its method of construction. Such displays, reminiscent of Guttman scalograms, are useful for multivariate data and are discussed in the next section. In his review of this work, Kosslyn (1985) noted that the mechanical processes involved in Bertin's procedures could well be replaced by computerized algorithms and display; we look forward to software implementations of Bertin's ideas.

Fortunately, considering the love affair of psychologists with both correlational analysis and the scatterplot, techniques for mechanically producing such plots have matured considerably in the past three decades. Ten years ago, when we first reviewed data-analysis graphics, we felt compelled to discuss regression lines on line-printer scatterplots. Such plots were always ugly; fortunately, they are now superfluous. There are currently many large and small computer programs for large and small computers that use a so-called *graphical user interface*

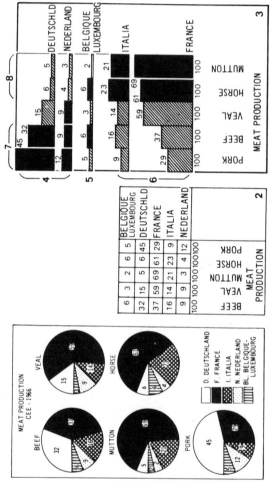

FIG. 13.14. A comparison of three methods of displaying meat production in Western Europe, from Bertin (1980). The pie chart is included as an example of poor practice, with the profile (3) preferred. Used by permission.

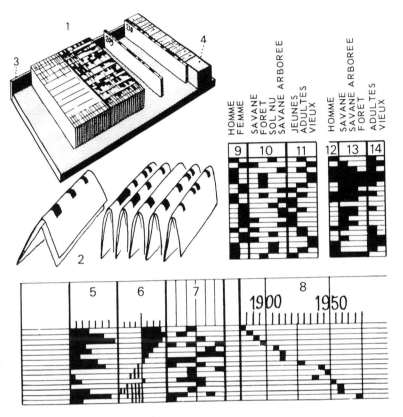

FIG. 13.15. A simplified version of Bertin's 'Domino Apparatus' for the manipulation of a graphical data matrix (Bertin, 1977). Used by permission.

GUI) to produce such plots. Many of these programs will produce a high-quality scatterplot on the screen (or on paper) with the click of a mouse-button, and superimpose on it the regression line and/or the regression equation. Some of the more sophisticated software (e.g., SPSS Graphics for large systems, SYSTAT, JMP) will add such niceties as the 95% confidence envelope for the regression line. In the more extensive statistical packages, a large number of variables ancillary to the regression are also available for plotting. So, because the machine is doing the work, the question is no longer "Shall we plot?" but rather it is "What shall we plot?"

Diagnostic Plots. In the context of regression analysis, the answer given by Daniel and Wood (1971; Wood, 1973) to that question is "Plot everything." Besides advocating quantile plots of residuals from regression equations, they discussed the usefulness and interpretation of plots of residuals against the fitted dependent variable, the residuals against independent variables (both those included and excluded from the equation), and "component-plus-residual plots."

The data, fit, and residuals are no longer the only candidates for plotting regression analysis. Recent advances in regression methods make use of a number of different kinds of "diagnostic plots" that are designed to assist the data analyst in fitting the model. The choice of the best regression equation in "all possible subsets" regression, as performed by some computer programs (e.g., BMDP9R; Dixon, 1988, is usually made with the help of the "C_p plot" (Daniel & Wood 1971; Furnival & Wilson 1974; Gorman & Toman 1966). Such plots use Colin Mallow's C_p statistic to compare the goodness-of-fit of large numbers of regression equations, considering simultaneously the number of predictors in the equation and the residual variance. These plots are extremely useful indeed, without them, all possible subsets regression might be an algebraic nightmare rather than a practical tool in data analysis.

Although one major advance of the past decade in multiple regression has been the replacement of so-called stepwise procedures with all possible subset searches for model selection, served by the C_p plot, another has been a proliferation of procedures for robust regression analysis. Denby and Mallows (1977) suggested a solution to the problem of selecting the "trimming" parameter for Huber's (1972) extremely robust "trimmed M-estimators" of multiple regression weights; that solution is based on a series of diagnostic plots. Basically, the residuals and all of the weights are plotted against the trimming parameter; then the data analyst picks the result that makes sense.

Gnanadesikan (1977) suggested yet another variety of diagnostic plotting, based on a creative choice of variables to be placed on a scatterplot. The idea is to detect multivariate outliers in data sets containing several variables. It is done by plotting the values of the several variables on the last two principal components (those associated with the smallest eigenvalues), the opposite of the usual procedure in principal components analysis. Variation on those components is usually essentially random, so any outliers on such a scatterplot probably consist of highly unusual data and should be inspected closely.

Enhanced Scatterplots. In addition to these sophisticated procedures, there have been numerous suggestions to improve the performance of the traditional bivariate scatterplot by enhancing it. One of the easiest ways to enhance a scatterplot is to mark the points with something more informative than dots, or at least to use the GUI to let the user obtain identifying information. In an approach that started with the computer program MacSpin, but is now becoming commonplace, the data analyst is permitted to "click on" a point or set or points on the scatterplot and have the data identified, either on the plot or in another window. It is nice to be able to figure out which point is which, but some data analysts have done much better than that.

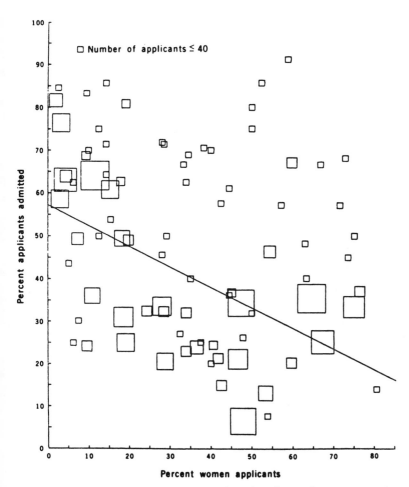

FIG. 13.16.   Scatter plot of the proportion of applicants that are women plotted against the proportion of applicants admitted for 85 departments at the University of California, Berkeley; from Bickel et al. (1976). Used by permission.

Bickel, Hammel, and O'Connell (1975) analyzed the relationship between admission rate and the proportion of women that apply to the various academic departments at the University of California at Berkeley. When those data are plotted, as they are in Fig. 13.16, with the relative number of applicants determining the size of the box plotted for each department, there is clearly a negative correlation. That negative correlation is due almost exclusively to a trend for the large departments. Whereas group size does not always merit such prominence in data display, in this case the enhanced plot provides vital information about the

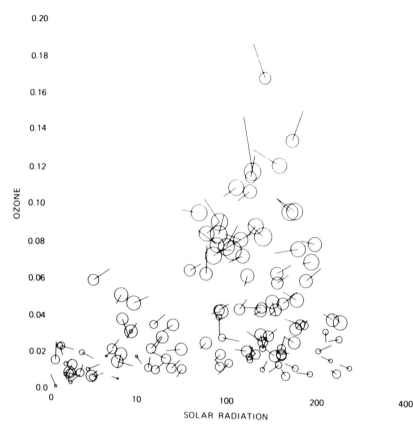

FIG. 13.17. Scatter plot of ozone concentration against solar radiation, from Bruntz et al. (1974). Used by permission.

relationship in question. A simpler scatterplot, with identical points for each
department, would not show the substantively crucial trend.

Even more elaborate enhancements in the form of informative plotting charac-
ters are now easy to find. The scatterplot in Fig. 13.17 appears to be a plot of
ozone concentration against solar radiation (each point represents one day's
weather and pollution data). But the "weathervanes" plotted instead of points by
Bruntz, Cleveland, Kleiner, & Warner (1974) actually reflect three more variables. The size of the circle is temperature, the angle of the line is wind direction,
and its length is inversely proportional to wind speed. High ozone levels are
associated with hot, calm days with lots of sunshine. Bachi (1978b) provided a
number of similar graphics; many of them depend on color for their effect and
cannot be reproduced effectively here.

But the graphic rational pattern joins the scatterplot (or the two-way table) in

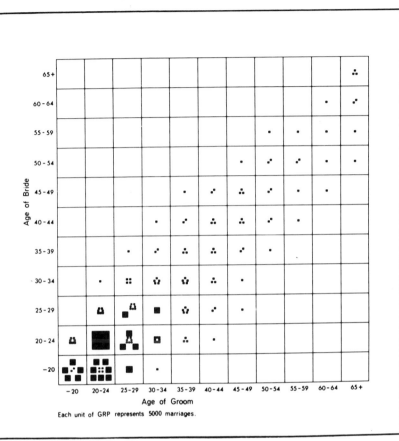

FIG. 13.18.   A display of the frequency distribution of marriages in the United States by age of brides and grooms, from Bachi (1978). Used by permission.

Fig. 13.18, which is an unusually precise presentation of data on ages at marriage in the United States. The data were categorized on both the X and Y variables to begin with, thus the GRPs provide a highly informative way to plot the relationship; the graphic is as precise as a table about the counts and as informative as a scatterplot about the relationship. Any scatterplot that would be more useful if information about counts were added for each data point may be enhanced by plotting GRPs instead of dots. (Imagine Fig. 13.16, the Berkeley data, with the appropriate GRP in place of each square. Is it better?)

The points need not be the entire content of a scatterplot; there are also lines, and some enhancements add more lines. It is possible that the simplest enhanced scatterplot to date is the "rangefinder box plot" suggested by Becketti and Gould

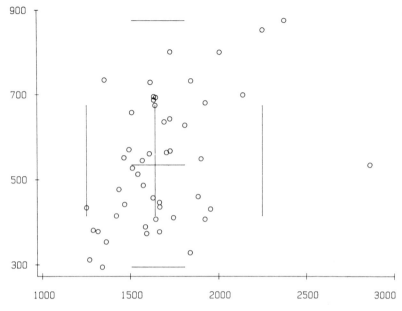

FIG. 13.19. Rangefinder box plot of 1980 divorce rates against birth-rates in the 49 states other than Nevada, from Becketti and Gould (1987). Used by permission.

(1987). Figure 13.19 shows Becketti and Gould's example, plotting 1980 divorce rates against birthrates for 49 of the 50 states.[4] The idea is that the content of two box plots (for X and Y) are superimposed on the graph, giving the appearance of a camera's bright-line rangefinder—hence the name. Becketti and Gould (1987) described the enhancements as follows:

> The rangefinder box plot contains precisely the same information as the box plots for both of the variables displayed. The two central line segments intersect at the cross-median values. The vertical line segments cover the interquartile range of the divorce rate, the variable measured along the vertical axis. The horizontal line segments cover the interquartile range of the birth rate. The upper and lower horizontal line segments are drawn at the upper and lower adjacent values of the divorce rate—that is, at the points where the whiskers of the box plot would terminate. [See Chambers, Cleveland, Kleiner, & Tukey, 1983, for formulas for the adjacent value.] The right and left vertical line segments mark the upper and lower adjacent values for birth rate. (p. 149)

Earlier, Tukey (1972, 1977) suggested a different generalization of his concept of the box plot into two dimensions to derive a "schematic (x, y) plot" that may also be used to detect outliers and describe the general form of a two-way

---

[4]Nevada is omitted.

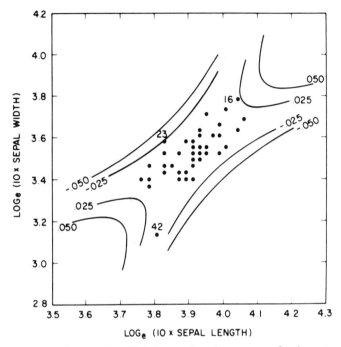

FIG. 13.20. Scatter plot with influence function contours for the natural logarithms of sepal length and width of 50 *iris setosa,* from Gnanadesikan (1977). Used by permission.

relationship with few assumptions about the distributional behavior of the data. Cleveland (1979) proposed the use of robust locally weighted regression lines to enhance the visual impression of the overall trend in a bivariate plot.

Devlin, Gnanadesikan, and Kettenring (1975) and Gnanadesikan (1977) suggested the addition of "influence function[5] contours" to scatterplots as an aid in the interpretation of correlations and as a technique for spotting outliers. Thissen, Baker, & Wainer (1981) illustrated several alternative methods for showing influence. Some software for data analysis, for example, SYSTAT, now includes an option to plot influence contours. Figure 13.20 shows such an enhanced

---

[5]The influence of a data point y on a parameter θ, can be obtained by estimating θ with y and again without it. The weighted difference of these two estimates is the influence of y on θ. An influence function depicts the influence as a function of both y and θ. More formally (from Gnanadesikan, 1977, after Hampel, 1974), for a general parameter $\theta = T(F)$, expressed as a functional of the distribution function, F, the influence function $I(y;\theta)$ at y is defined as

$$I(y;\theta) = \lim_{\epsilon \to 0} \left(\frac{\bar{\theta} - \theta}{\epsilon} \right),$$

where $\bar{\theta} = T(\bar{F})$ and $\bar{F} = (1 - \epsilon)F + \epsilon\delta_y$ is a "perturbation" of F by δ_y, the distribution function for a point mass of 1 at y.

scatterplot from Gnanadesikan (1977), with several points identified. The "influence contours" are, numerically, the "effect" of any point on that line on th
correlation: The number associated with each line is the amount the correlatio
would change if a point on that line were deleted from the data. In the figure
points numbered 16 and 23 have substantial (opposite) effects on the value of th
correlation, which would be more or less unchanged if both were removed bu
would change by about 0.025 if only one were deleted. The point marked 42
however much it may seem to be an outlier, is an inconsequential one, havin
only a negligible effect on the correlation.

There are special techniques—scatterplots that actually represent time serie
or trend data; both Tukey (1977) and Cleveland and Kleiner (1975) emphasize
the usefulness of lines drawn through moving statistics of one sort or another
Figure 13.21 uses some of those techniques to show that some of the ozon

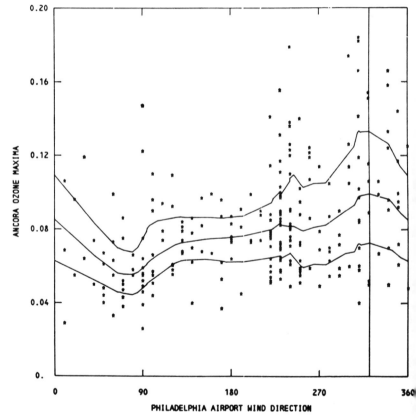

FIG. 13.21.   Scatter plot of ozone concentration at Ancora, NJ, against
wind direction at Philadelphia, enhanced with moving averages, from
Cleveland and Kleiner (1975). Used by permission.

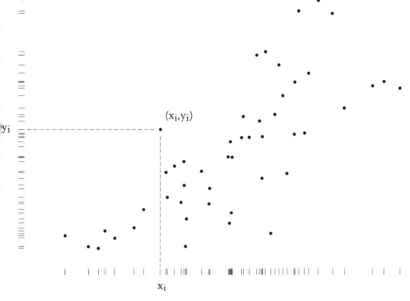

FIG. 13.22. Dot-dash-plot, from Tufte (1983). Used by permission.

pollution in Ancora, NJ, comes from Philadelphia. Although the unadorned scatterplot of ozone concentrations at Ancora against wind direction in Philadelphia shows only a few high points near the vertical line that marks the Philadelphia–Ancora wind direction, the superimposed moving averages show a clear peak and place the blame for the bad air on Philadelphia. Tukey (1972) suggested that sometimes this plot should be extended to two cycles (of 360) so that any effect can be seen in context. Chambers et al. (1983, pp. 91–104) and Cleveland (1985, pp. 167–186) provided extensive discussions of new, alternative smoothing procedures.

Finally, an elegant display for data analysis (if not for public presentation) is Tufte's (1983, p. 133) minimalist *dot-dash-plot* shown in Fig. 13.22. In keeping with his goal of maximizing what he called the "data-ink ratio," Tufte suggested eliminating all nondata elements of the scatterplot (including the axes and labels, not to mention such superfluous elements as grid lines and the frame), leaving only the point cloud. Then, where the axes would be, Tufte plotted dashes at the position of each datum in the two marginal distributions; the density of the dashes provides univariate plots of the distribution of each variable. The complete absence of identifying information probably makes the dot-dash-plot unacceptable for public presentation; but for the data analyst who (presumably) already knows what the variables are and what values they may take, the plot conveys exactly what bivariate data analysis requires: the joint and marginal distributions, with no wasted ink or effort.

More can be done with scatterplots than was discussed here. But some situations are too complex for even the most enhanced scatterplot, or are not organized well for presentation on coordinate axes. The next section deals with those situations.

TWO-WAY DISPLAYS
OF MULTIVARIATE DATA

Until recently, most common display methodologies had to confine themselves to the two dimensions of the plane. Attempts to represent three or more dimensions on a surface involved such devices as multiple-bar charts, subdivided bilateral frequency diagrams, perspective drawings, contour plots, shading variations, and so forth. These schemes are well known in cartography and their advantages and disadvantages are fully described in Bertin's classic treatise (Bertin, 1973). Depiction of more than three dimensions by these techniques was difficult, and the results of some attempts left much to be desired. For example, one attempt to display four dimensions is the Two-Variable Color Map (U.S. Bureau of the Census, 1976). In this display, two statistical variables are represented on top of two geographic ones. One variable is represented on the geographic background by increasing saturations of blue, with the lowest level yellow; the second, with increasing saturations of red, the lowest level again being yellow. Bivariate events are represented by overlaying one color scheme on the other, thus yielding various color mixtures of yellow, green, orange, and purple in different saturations.

This sort of map, though difficult to describe, is still more difficult to comprehend when viewed. This criticism was leveled by S. E. Fienberg (1979) and shown experimentally to be valid by Wainer and Francolini (1980). They reported that a similar conception was provided a century earlier by Mayr (1874), who obtained a more evocative image by using the more natural visual metaphor of white (maximally unsaturated) instead of yellow. A further problem with the Two-Variable Color Map was suggested by Cleveland and McGill (1983), in a small psychophysical experiment in which they determined that colors induced size-illusions when used on maps.

Nevertheless, the search for effective multivariate displays was not exhausted by this discovery; not even for just four variables. The last 20 years has seen increased interest in this area by statisticians concomitant with the development and use of multivariate statistical procedures, and a number of interesting suggestions have been made. What follows are some brief descriptions of some of these suggestions, after which we illustrate them on a sample data set.

Tables

The initial collection, and hence display, of most data sets begins with a data table. Thus any discussion of multivariate display should start with the table as the most basic construction. Rules for table construction are often misguided, aimed at the use of a table for data storage rather than data exploration or communication. The computer revolution of the past 20 years has reduced the need for archiving of data in tables, but rules for table preparation have not been revised apace with this change in purpose.

Ehrenberg (1977) suggested some very specific preparation rules to allow tables to serve as an effective multivariate display. Among them are: (a) rounding heavily, (b) ordering rows and columns by some aspect of the data, (c) spacing to aid perception, and (d) flanking the display with suitable summary statistics. Chakrapani and Ehrenberg (1976) illustrated this advice on correlation matrices and such matrices as are usually found in factor analysis output. They provided convincing evidence of the efficacy of one-digit correlation matrices, omitting values that are sufficiently small. Ramsay (1980) noted that the structure of correlation matrices is exposed better by omitting as much visual clutter as possible (omit decimal points). He generated a series of such matrices, omitting all correlations below a particular size, and then increasing the allowable appearance threshold in each generation. Not only does this increase the readability of the correlation matrix, but often more accurately reflects the precision of the correlation as well. McGill (1978) described other changes that can be made in tables when they are printed to increase their ability to expose structure. His suggestions center around the notion of making the physical size and/or darkness of the numbers displayed relate to their importance. In some circumstances he emphasized the especially large ones, in others, the small ones. For example schemes for looking at correlation matrices see Taguri, Hiramatsu, Kittaka, and Wakimoto (1976). Wainer, Groves, & Lono (1980) showed that in certain kinds of tasks, for data sets of only modest size and complexity, tables do very well indeed in comparison to other graphical forms. Wainer (1980a) showed that tables are quite effective with young children as well.

The most recent work on effective tabular presentation (Wainer, 1992) provides three simple rules for designing effective tables. Driving these rules is the orienting attitude that a table is for communication, not data storage. Modern data storage is accomplished well on magnetic disks or tapes, optical disks, or some other mechanical device. Paper and print are meant for human eyes and human minds.

We begin with Table 13.1; Table 5/19 in the Bureau of the Census' well-known book *Social Indicators III*.

Any redesign task must first try to develop an understanding of purpose. The presentation of this data set must have been intended to help the reader answer such questions as:

TABLE 13.1

Deaths Due to Unexpected Events, by Type of Event, Selected Countries: Mid-1970's

Table 5/19. Deaths Due to Unexpected Events, by Type of Event, Selected Countries: Mid-1970's

(Rate per 100,000 population)

Country	Year[1]	Deaths due to all causes	Deaths due to unexpected events					
			Total	Transport accidents	Natural factors[2]	Accidents occurring mainly in industry[3]	Homicides and injuries caused intentionally[4]	Other causes[5]
Austria..............	1975	1,277.2	75.2	34.8	29.7	4.3	1.6	4.8
Belgium..............	1975	1,218.5	62.6	25.0	25.8	1.5	.9	9.4
Canada..............	1974	742.0	62.1	30.9	18.0	3.9	2.5	6.8
Denmark..............	1976	1,059.5	41.1	18.3	15.6	1.0	.7	5.5
Finland..............	1974	952.5	62.3	23.7	26.0	2.9	2.6	7.1
France..............	1974	1,049.5	77.8	23.8	31.0	1.0	.9	21.1
Germany (Fed. Rep.).	1975	1,211.8	66.4	24.8	31.6	1.8	1.2	7.0
Ireland..............	1975	1,060.7	48.6	19.8	20.1	1.9	1.0	5.8
Italy..............	1974	957.8	47.2	22.8	19.2	1.9	1.1	2.2
Japan..............	1976	625.6	30.5	13.2	9.7	2.1	1.3	4.2
Netherlands..........	1975	832.2	40.3	17.8	18.2	1.0	.7	2.6
Norway..............	1976	998.9	48.4	17.3	25.1	1.9	.7	3.4
Sweden..............	1975	1,076.6	55.8	17.2	27.9	1.3	1.1	8.3
Switzerland..........	1976	904.1	48.4	20.6	20.4	2.1	.9	4.4
United Kingdom.......	1976	1,217.9	34.8	13.0	13.9	1.3	1.1	5.5
United States.......	1975	888.5	60.6	23.4	15.8	2.6	10.0	8.8

[1]Most current year data available.
[2]Includes fatal accidents due to poisoning, falls, fire, and drowning.
[3]For some countries data relate to accidents caused by machines only.
[4]By another person, including police.
[5]Includes accidents caused by firearms, war injuries, injuries of undetermined causes, and all other accidental causes.

426

1. What is the general level (per 100,000 population) of accidental death in the countries chosen?
2. How do the countries differ with respect to their respective rates of accidental death?
3. What are the principal causes of accidental death? Which are the most frequent? The least frequent?
4. Are there any unusual interactions between country and cause of accidental death?

These are obviously parallel to the questions that are ordinarily addressed in the analysis of any multifactorial table—overall level, row, column, and interaction effects.

Before going further we invite you read Table 13.1 carefully and see to what extent you can answer these four questions. But don't peek ahead!

The first rule of table construction is to:

I. Order the rows and columns in a way that makes sense. We are almost never interested in "Austria First." Two useful ways to order the data are:
   i. Size places—Put the largest first. Often we look most carefully at what is on top and less carefully further down. Put the biggest thing first! Also, ordering by some aspect of the data often reflects ordering by some hidden variable that can be inferred.
   ii. Naturally—Time is ordered from the past to the future. Showing data in that order melds well with what the viewer might expect. This is always a good idea.

Table 13.2 is a redone version of Table 13.1. A few typos have been corrected, some uninformative columns removed and the rows ordered by the total death rate. The columns were already ordered in a reasonable way and so were left unaltered. Now we can begin to answer questions 1 and 2. (We see that France is the most dangerous place, having an accidental death rate of about 78 per 100,000, that is more than twice that of Japan (about 30 per 100,000), which, at least by this measure, appears to be the safest country. Now that the rows are ordered the overall death rate (taken as an unweighted median) can be easily calculated—count down eight countries—and is around 50 per 100,000.

Note that when we referred to the actual rates we rounded. This is very important. The second rule of table construction is to:

II. Round—a lot! This is for three reasons:
   i. Humans cannot understand more than two digits very easily.
   ii. We can almost never justify more than two digits of accuracy statistically.
   iii. We almost never care about accuracy of more than two digits.

TABLE 13.2
Table 13.1 with Rows Ordered by Overall Death Rate, Typographical
Errors Corrected, and Uninformative Columns Removed

Deaths Due to Unexpected Events, by Type of Event,
Selected Countries: Mid-1970s
(Rate per 100,000 population)

Country	Total Unexpected Deaths	Transport Accidents	Natural Factors	Industrial Accidents	Homicides	Other Causes
France	77.8	23.8	31.0	1.0	0.9	21.1
Austria	75.2	34.8	29.7	4.3	1.6	4.8
Germany	66.4	24.8	31.6	1.8	1.2	7.0
Belgium	62.6	25.0	25.8	1.5	0.9	9.4
Finland	62.3	23.7	26.0	2.9	2.6	7.1
Canada	62.1	30.9	18.0	3.9	2.5	6.8
United States	60.6	23.4	15.8	2.6	10.0	8.8
Sweden	55.8	17.2	27.9	1.3	1.1	8.3
Ireland	48.6	19.8	20.1	1.9	1.0	5.8
Norway	48.4	17.3	25.1	1.9	0.7	3.4
Switzerland	48.4	20.6	20.4	2.1	0.9	4.4
Italy	47.2	22.8	19.2	1.9	1.1	2.2
Denmark	41.1	18.3	15.6	1.0	0.7	5.5
Netherlands	40.3	17.8	18.2	1.0	0.7	2.6
United Kingdom	34.8	13.0	13.9	1.3	1.1	5.5
Japan	30.5	13.2	9.7	2.1	1.3	4.2

Let us take each of these reasons separately.

Understanding.   Consider the statement that "This year's school budget is $27,329,681." Who can comprehend or remember that? If we remember anything, it is almost surely the translation, "This year's school budget is about 27 million dollars."

Statistical justification.   The standard error of any statistic is proportional to one over the square root of the sample size. God did this and there is nothing we can do to change it. Thus suppose we would like to report a correlation is .25. If we do not want to report something that is inaccurate, we must be sure that the second digit is reasonably likely to be 5 and not 6 or 4. To accomplish this we need the standard error to be less than .005. But because the standard error is proportional to $1/\sqrt{n}$, the obvious algebra $(1/\sqrt{n} \sim .005 \Rightarrow \sqrt{n} \sim 1/.005 = 200)$ yields the inexorable conclusion that a sample size of the order of 200^2 or 40,000 is required to justify the presentation of more than a two-digit correlation. A similar argument can be made for all other statistics.

Who cares?   We recently ran across a table of average life expectancies.[6] It proudly reported that the mean life expectancy of a male at birth in Australia was

---

[6]*UN Demographic Yearbook*, 1962.

TABLE 13.3
Table 13.2 with Entries Rounded to Integers

**Deaths Due to Unexpected Events, by Type of Event,
Selected Countries: Mid-1970s**
(Rate per 100,000 population)

Country	Total Unexpected Deaths	Transport Accidents	Natural Factors	Industrial Accidents	Homicides	Other Causes
France	78	24	31	1	1	21
Austria	75	35	30	4	2	5
Germany	66	25	32	2	1	7
Belgium	63	25	26	2	1	9
Finland	62	24	26	3	3	7
Canada	62	31	18	4	3	7
United States	61	23	16	3	10	9
Sweden	56	17	28	1	1	8
Ireland	49	20	20	2	1	6
Norway	48	17	25	2	1	3
Switzerland	48	21	20	2	1	4
Italy	47	23	19	2	1	2
Denmark	41	18	16	1	1	6
Netherlands	40	18	18	1	1	3
United Kingdom	35	13	14	1	1	6
Japan	31	13	10	2	1	4

67.14 years. What does the '4' mean? Each unit in the hundredth's digit of this overzealous reportage represents 4 days. What purpose is served in knowing a life expectancy to this accuracy? For most communicative (not archival) purposes '67' would have been enough.

Table 13.3 contains a revision of Table 13.2 in which each entry is rounded to the nearest integer. The original entries had only one extra digit, thus the clarifying effect of rounding is modest. In this version of the table the unusual homicide rate of the United States jumps out at us. At a glance we can see that it is an order of magnitude greater than that found in any civilized nation. We also see an unusual entry for France under "other causes" that raises questions about definitions.

The effects of too many decimal places is sufficiently pernicious that we would like to emphasize the importance of rounding with another short example. Equation 1 is taken from *State Court Caseload Statistics: 1976:*

$$Ln(DIAC) = -.10729131 + 1.00716993 \times Ln(FIAC), \tag{1}$$

where DIAC is the annual number of case dispositions, and FIAC is the annual number of case filings. This is obviously the result of a regression analysis with an overgenerous output format. Using the standard error justification for rounding we see that to justify the eight digits shown we would need a standard error that is of the order of .000000005, or a sample size of the order of 4×10^{16}. This is a very large number of cases—the population of China does not put a dent in it. The actual n is the number of states, which allows one digit of accuracy at most. If we round to one digit and transform out of the log metric we arrive at the more statistically defensible equation

$$DIAC = .9 \; FIAC. \tag{2}$$

This can be translated into English as

"There are about 90% as many dispositions as filings."

Obviously the equation that is more defensible statistically is also much easier to understand. A colleague, who knows more about courts than we do, suggested that we needed to round further, to the nearest integer (DIAC = FIAC), and so a more correct statement would be

"There are about as many dispositions as filings."

A minute's thought about the court process reminds one that it is a pipeline with filings at one end and dispositions at the other. They must equal one another and any variation in annual statistics reflects only the vagaries of the calender. The sort of numerical sophistry demonstrated in Equation 1 can give statisticians a bad name.[7]

III. ALL is different and important. Summaries of rows and columns are important as a standard for comparison—they provide a measure of usualness. What summary we use to characterize ALL depends on the purpose. Sometimes a sum is suitable, more often a median. But whatever is chosen it should be visually different than the individual entries and set spatially apart.

Table 13.4 makes it clearer how unusual the U.S. homicide rate is. The column medians allow us to compare the relative danger of the various factors. We note that although "transport accidents" is the worst threat, it is closely followed by "natural factors." Looking at the entries for the United States we can see that "natural factors" are under somewhat better control than in most other countries.

Can we go further? Sure. To see how requires that we consider what distinguishes between a table and a graph. A graph uses space to convey information. A table uses a specific iconic representation. We have made tables more understandable by using space—making a table more like a graph. We can improve

---

[7]We sometimes hear from colleagues that our ideas about rounding are too radical. That such extreme rounding would be "ok if we knew that a particular result was final. But our final results may be used by someone else as intermediate in further calculations. Too early rounding would result in unnecessary propagation of error." Keep in mind that tables are for communication not archiving. Round the numbers and, if you must, insert a footnote proclaiming that the unrounded details are available from the author. Then sit back and wait for the deluge of requests.

TABLE 13.4
Table 13.3 with Column Medians Calculated and Total Isolated

**Deaths Due to Unexpected Events, by Type of Event,
Selected Countries: Mid-1970s**
(Rate per 100,000 population)

Country	Total Unexpected Deaths	Transport Accidents	Natural Factors	Industrial Accidents	Homicides	Other Causes
France	78	24	31	1	1	21
Austria	75	35	30	4	2	5
Germany	66	25	32	2	1	7
Belgium	63	25	26	2	1	9
Finland	62	24	26	3	3	7
Canada	62	31	18	4	3	7
United States	61	23	16	3	10	9
Sweden	56	17	28	1	1	8
Ireland	49	20	20	2	1	6
Norway	48	17	25	2	1	3
Switzerland	48	21	20	2	1	4
Italy	47	23	19	2	1	2
Denmark	41	18	16	1	1	6
Netherlands	40	18	18	1	1	3
United Kingdom	35	13	14	1	1	6
Japan	31	13	10	2	1	4
Median	53	22	20	2	1	6

tables further by making them more graphical still. A semigraphical display like the stem-and-leaf diagram (Tukey, 1977) is merely a table in which the entries are not only ordered but are also spaced according to their size. To put this notion into practice, consider the last version of Table 13.1 shown as Table 13.5.

The rows have been spaced according to what appear to be significant gaps (Wainer & Schacht, 1978) in the total death rate, dividing the countries into five groups. Further investigation is required to understand why they seem to group that way, but the table has provided the impetus.

The highlighting of single entries points out the unusually high rate of transport accidents in Canada and Austria as well as the unusually low rates of death due to natural factors in the United States and Canada. The determination that these values are indeed unusual was done by additional calculations in support of the display (subtract out row and column effects and look at what sticks out). But the viewer can appreciate the result without being aware of the calculations. Spacing tables commensurate with the values of their entries and highlighting unusual values are often useful techniques but are not as universally important as the three rules mentioned previously.

The version of Table 13.1 shown as Table 13.5 is about as far as we can go. It may be that for special purposes other modifications might help, but Table 13.5

TABLE 13.5
Table 13.4 with Rows Spaced by Total Death Rate
and Unusual Values Highlighted

Deaths Due to Unexpected Events, by Type of Event,
Selected Countries: Mid-1970s
(Rate per 100,000 population)

Country	Total Unexpected Deaths	Transport Accidents	Natural Factors	Industrial Accidents	Homicides	Other Causes
France	78	24	31	1	1	21
Austria	75	35	30	4	2	5
Germany	66	25	32	2	1	7
Belgium	63	25	26	2	1	9
Finland	62	24	26	3	3	7
Canada	62	31	18	4	3	7
United States	61	23	16	3	10	9
Sweden	56	17	28	1	1	8
Ireland	49	20	20	2	1	6
Norway	48	17	25	2	1	3
Switzerland	48	21	20	2	1	4
Italy	47	23	19	2	1	2
Denmark	41	18	16	1	1	6
Netherlands	40	18	18	1	1	3
United Kingdom	35	13	14	1	1	6
Japan	31	13	10	2	1	4
Median	53	22	20	2	1	6

☐ = an unusual data value

does allow us to answer readily the four questions about these data phrased earlier. Some aspects are memorable. Who can forget the discovery of the gigantic disparity between the homicide rate in the United States and that of the other 15 nations reported.[8]

Bertin (1977) suggested the use of a *graphical matrix* in which the cells of a matrix representing the observations-by-variables are shaded in by amounts that vary as a function of the size of that cell's data. The rows and columns are then permuted until a simple structure is obtained.

---

[8]These data are more than 15 years old, but their message certainly stayed with us enough so that when a newspaper article in the *New York Times* on August 13, 1989 reported that Detroit and Washington, DC had annual homicide rates of about 60 per 100,000 we knew enough to be horrified. Tables with memorable content can be memorable.

Draftsman's Displays. Tukey and Tukey (1981, 1983), Chambers et al. 1983) and Cleveland (1985) encouraged the use of the *draftsman's display* for essentially) bivariate analysis of more-than-two variables. A draftsman's display s an array of scatterplots; the entire display has the physical form of a correlation matrix among the variables, so it is either a lower triangle or a square matrix with he diagonal omitted. In place of (numerical) correlations, however, the draftsman's display has a conventional scatterplot for each pair of variables. Put imply, that is (often) a lot of plots! However, the draftsman's display has the advantage that it shows any distributional peculiarities that might be obscured by he numerical value of the correlation coefficient. The creation of draftsman's displays is labor intensive; in practice, they are created only by a computer. A number of statistical software packages (e.g., Data Desk, SYSTAT, JMP, STATGRAPHICS) produce draftsman's displays (sometimes called scatterplot matrices).

Glyphs. Anderson (1960) suggested the use of a starlike glyph consisting of a central circle with rays coming out of it, in which each ray corresponded to a variable to be displayed, and the length of the ray to the value of that variable. Variations on this theme abound. For example, one could connect the ends of each of the rays, omitting the rays themselves, preserving only the outline and compare the shapes of the resulting polygons (Siegel, Goldwyn, & Friedman, 1971). These polygons were used extensively to communicate multivariate health and demographic information for the state of Arkansas (Walls & Epley, 1975). Another adaptation of this sort of procedure, the "weathervane" plot mentioned earlier), was used (with the wind speed represented somewhat backward) by Bruntz et al. (1974) to try to depict the complex dependence of ambient atmosphere ozone on a variety of meteorological variables. We used glyphs with shapes reminiscent of Christmas trees to display bias and random variance in a simulation study of the performance of various robust statistical estimators Thissen & Wainer, 1986).

Kleiner and Hartigan (1981) pieced together line segments, proportional in length to the variables they represent, to form variable size tree diagrams much like those so commonly used in hierarchical cluster analysis (Gruvaeus & Wainer, 1972) to depict multivariate data. This technique capitalizes on the correlational structure among the variables to yield the background against which to display the values of each variable. This technique shows explicitly what the others only suggest. Wakimoto (1977) proposed another variation on the use of tree diagrams for display, as well (in Wakimoto & Taguri, 1978) as other sorts of special schemes for different purposes.

Inside-Out Plots. Ramsay (1980) used multiple stem-and-leaf diagrams in his *Inside-Out* plots to yield another interesting technique. In an Inside-Out plot one arranges the data in a matrix so that the rows are the observations and the columns are the variables (much as is done in Bertin's and Ehrenberg's methods. Next the columns are robustly centered and scaled. This matrix is examined "Inside-Out".

Inside-Out plotting of the residual matrix is Ramsay's principal contribution. We first note that the rows are labeled OUTSIDE the matrix, and the standardized and doubly centered data are INSIDE. We turn this inside-out by preparing stem representing the data on the outside, and next to the stem (under the appropriate variable name) we plot the label inside. The observations of interest are those that are extreme in one or more of the columns that indicate an unusual interaction between variable and observation.

The contention is that one may be interested, superficially, in the column effects and scales, but they only reflect on the scaling of the variable and are frequently of no more than secondary importance. The row effects reflect the overall level of each observation and again are not of primary interest, especially because such things are easily examined with traditional display methods (e.g., stem-and-leaf diagrams). The data matrix must, of course, be transformed initially to be reasonably symmetric and all the variables should be oriented so that as much as possible, they form a positive manifold. If this is not done, the row summaries are not very meaningful. What is of interest is the structure of the residuals; that is difficult to see in the ordinary tabular representation. Tukey (1977, chaps. 11–12) presented alternative plots for two-way tables.

Faces. An ingenious method of display, relying on human ability to perceive and remember even small variations in the structure of human faces, was developed and tested by Chernoff (1973; Chernoff & Rizvi 1975). This scheme involves letting the size, shape, or orientation of each feature of a cartoon face represent a particular variable. Thus one might let the size of the eye represent one variable, the width of the mouth another, the length of the nose a third, and so on. A number of years ago, computer programs were developed that will allow the representation of up to 18 variables; such algorithms are now available in statistical packages (e.g., SYSTAT). How well this scheme performs is not fully explored, although Jacob, Egeth, and Bevan (1976) and Wainer (1979a) found that human judgment of relative distance between faces is rather good. That is, the cluster of faces produced perceptually correspond closely to those of formal analyses.

FACES have been criticized because the effect associated with a particular variable configuration may work against the message the data structure is trying to convey. For example, if each aspect of the face was being used to represent a subscore on some personality inventory, it would be indeed unfortunate if depressive was represented by a happy smiling face. Of course, a wisely chosen featural representation restricts this possibility, but care must be taken. Jacob (1976) utilized a careful scaling experiment to allow experts to assign features to variables in such a way so as to optimize the extent to which the hypothetical face escribed earlier resembled the personality condition it depicted. Alternative eta-iconic displays based on Chernoff faces have been proposed for special urposes that do not have this particular problem; Wainer (1983) proposed the se of a cartoon rabbit.

Other Suggestions. Andrews (1972) suggested representing each variable as Fourier component of a periodic function, and thus one could then group ariables by the similarity of the observed cyclic function.

There have also been some special purpose displays devised for multivariate ontingency tables. One such method, the "floating fourfold circular display" (or FCD for short) was described by S. E. Fienberg (1975), and is reminiscent of coxcombs" used by Florence Nightingale (1858). 3FCDs are often helpful for he examination of those discrete multivariate models describes in Bishop, S. E. ienberg, & Holland (1975). Bachi's (1968) GRPs (mentioned earlier) can also e adapted for such use, as can Wainer and Reiser's (1978) "Cartesian rectan-les." Other approaches are described and discussed in Barnett (1981), Cleve-ind and McGill (1988), Cox and Laub (1967), S. E. Fienberg (1969), and Snee 1974).

A MULTIVARIATE EXAMPLE:
THE WORST AMERICAN STATE REVISITED

Just what such words as progress and civilization mean is often disputed, but no one doubts that such things exist. Holland is obviously a more progressive country than Portugal, and equally obviously France is more civilized than Albania. It is when concrete criteria are set up that dispute begins, for every man tries to measure the level of a given culture by his own yardstick

(Angoff & Mencken, 1931, p. 1)

ixty years ago Angoff and Mencken began their comparative study of social ndicators in search of "The Worst American State." Having started out with the asic premise that some places are better to live in than others, they went on to uote Todd that,

We shall have to agree that life on the whole is better than death, that health is better than sickness, that freedom is better than slavery, that control over fate is better than ignorance, that moderate provision for human need is better than chronic lack, that broad interest and moderate desires are better than narrowness and enforced asceticism. (p. 1)

In an effort to reexamine Angoff and Mencken's conclusions half a century ter, and to illustrate some of the multivariate display techniques described reviously, we gathered data for seven of the same variables (from the *Statistical bstract of the United States: 1977*).

TABLE 13.6
Excerpted from "Worst American State: Revisited" Data

State	Population (1,000s)	Average per Capita Income ($)	Illiteracy Rate (% popul.)	Life Expectancy	Homicide Rate (1,000)[a]	Percent High School Graduates	Average No. Days Per Year Below Freezing
Alabama	3,615	3,624	2.1	69.05	15.1	41.3	20
California	21,198	5,114	1.1	71.71	10.3	62.6	20
Iowa	2,861	4,628	.5	72.56	2.3	59.0	140
Mississippi	2,341	3,098	2.4	68.09	12.5	41.0	50
New Hampshire	812	4,281	.7	71.23	3.3	57.6	174
Ohio	10,735	4,561	.8	70.82	7.4	53.2	124
Oregon	2,284	4,660	.6	72.13	4.2	60.0	44
Pennsylvania	11,860	4,449	1.0	70.43	6.1	50.2	126
South Dakota	681	4,167	.5	72.08	1.7	53.3	172
Vermont	472	3,907	.6	71.64	5.5	57.1	168

[a] "Homicide rate per 1,000" is actually combined murders and nonnegligent manslaughter per 1,000 population.

Table 13.6 shows data on 10 states for the 7 variables indicated. The form of he table is not a recommended one, but is done in a manner that is probably most ommon. The states are ordered alphabetically; the numbers are given in varying accuracy (population is given to the nearest thousand, life expectancy to the hundredth of a year, or 4 days). It is clear that although the accuracy represented may be justified by the data, it is not the most useful way to show the data for communicative nor exploratory purposes.

Following Ehrenberg's (1977) suggestions, the data were rounded, states were reordered by an aspect of the data (life expectancy), the variables were reordered, and column medians were calculated and shown. In addition, space was used to demarcate Alabama and Mississippi from the rest, which an examination of the data indicates is justified.

Viewing Table 13.7 tells us much more than was immediately evident for the original data table—that the two southern states are substantially inferior to the other eight on the first five social indicators. We see that California seems to have a relatively high homicide rate and per capita income. Furthermore, we get an impression of the overall levels of each of these indicators from the summaries at the bottom of the table, thus adding meaning to any state, which does not seem too important in a short list, but that may become more important with larger tables. Ehrenberg (1977) argued that most tables are looked at by individuals who are not naive with respect to their contents, and so have a reasonably good idea about the approximate position of each member. Thus if one looked at the bottom of a list for a state one expected to find there, and only later discovered that it was somewhere else, this would be useful and surprising information. He claimed that the losses associated with not having the table in alphabetical order are modest (for most applications) compared to the gains in potential for internal comparisons. The Statistical Atlases of the United States published in the latter part of the 19th century presented the data ordered by some meaningful ranking along with some indexing device.

To apply Ramsay's inside-out procedure we rescaled the data in Table 13.7 so that all variables "pointed in the same direction." Thus illiteracy rate was transformed (by an inverse square root) to a measure of literacy rate, homicide rate became [through -logit(homicide rate)] a function of its complement. Population became log (population) and the square root of income was used. Then we standardized by columns robustly and obtained row effects, which are shown in Fig. 13.23. These are only the main effects, which reaffirm our original observation (from the revamped table) that the two Southern states are different. The matrix of residuals was then examined "inside-out" to yield the picture in Fig. 3.24.

We note that despite Iowa's generally high showing in this competition it has a still higher position on life expectancy than anticipated; and the Southern states and Pennsylvania seem to have lower life expectancies than would be predicted from their overall showing. In addition, we see that California has a higher

TABLE 13.7
Table 13.6 with Rows and Columns Reordered

State	Life Expectancy	Homicide Rate	Income (100s)	High School Grads (%)	Illiteracy Rate	Population (100,000s)	No Days of Freezing
Iowa	73	2	46	59	.5	29	140
Oregon	72	4	47	60	.6	23	44
South Dakota	72	2	42	53	.5	7	172
California	72	10	51	63	1.1	212	20
Vermont	72	6	39	57	.6	5	168
New Hampshire	71	3	43	57	.7	8	174
Ohio	71	7	46	53	.8	107	124
Pennsylvania	70	6	44	50	1.0	119	126
Alabama	69	15	36	41	2.1	36	20
Mississippi	68	12	31	41	2.4	23	50
Medians	68	6	44	55	2.4	26	125

Stem and leaf display of state effects

IOWA, OREGON, CALIFORNIA	1.5	IA OR CA
SOUTH DAKOTA	1.0	SD
VERMONT, NEW HAMPSHIRE, PENNSYLVANIA	0.5	VT NH PA
OHIO	0.0	OH
	-0.5	
	-1.0	
	-1.5	
	-2.0	
ALABAMA	-2.5	AL
MISSISSIPPI	-3.0	MS

FIG. 13.23. Stem-and-leaf display of state effects using the data in table 13.6 after column standardizing.

homicide rate than would be expected as well as a higher income and lower literacy rate. These latter findings are also visible in Table 13.7, now that we know to look for them. The low literacy rate in California suggest an interpretation based on its large Spanish-speaking population. The reader is invited to further pore over this display for additional information. The stem (scale) is in robust z scores, and can be approximately interpreted that way. This display has the added advantage of getting better as the data set (number of observations) gets larger. We are typically only interested in observations with large residuals, and so when data bunch up in the middle (as would be the case with a larger data set) we can safely ignore them. Moreover, this display method works well when data are not scored in the same way, though it does take some preprocessing to get the data ready for plotting. That includes a variety of two-way scatter plots to determine the best orientation of each variable. In this instance we ordered "number of days below freezing" in the same direction as literacy, not because of

	Life Expectancy	Non-Homicide Rate	Income	%HS grads	Literacy Rate	Population	# Days Below 0° C
4.0							
3.6							
3.2						AL	
2.8						MS	
2.4	IA		CA				
2.0		MS					
1.6		AL	OH				
1.2		SD				OH	MS
0.8	VT	IA NH	PA			PA	AL
0.4	SD CA OR	PA OH	IA OR AL	CA	SD IA VT	CA	NH VT
0.0		OR		NH OR MS VT	AL OH NH OR		OH PA SD
-0.4	OH	VT		AL OH IA			
-0.8			NH		MS		IA
-1.2	NH		SD	PA	PA	IA OR	
-1.6	AL	CA	MS VT	SD		NH	
-2.0					CA	VT	
-2.4						SD	
-2.8	PA						OR
-3.2							CA
-3.6	MS						
-4.0							

FIG. 13.24. Inside-out plot of the residuals after row and column effects have been removed from the data in Table 13.6.

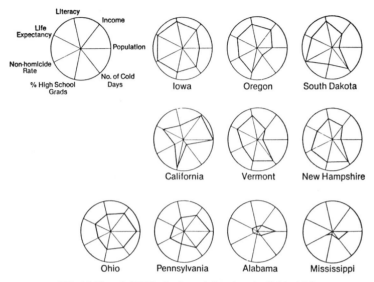

FIG. 13.25.   A STAR display of the data in Table 13.6.

any love for cold weather, but rather because it was in this direction that it relate
to all the variables that are easily oriented. (Angoff and Mencken ordered "num
ber of Baptists" as "more = worse" partially because of its high correlation wit
"number of lynchings" in that orientation).

Shown in Figs. 13.25 and 13.26 are STARs and Andrews' curves of thes
same data. Once again we see much the same structure. Both STARS an
Andrews' curves show the similarity and isolation of Mississippi and Alabama
STARS seems to show other distinctive features more clearly than do the An
drews' curves. They also allow easier identification of the variables that caus
the display to take one particular shape. Andrews' curves could have accommo
dated many more variables but not too many more states, whereas STARS coul
easily have accommodated more states, albeit one would have needed a mor
clever display format to keep them all identifiable. Also the STAR glyph canno
handle many variables, for even with seven it is hard to remember which i
which and thus be able to interpret why a particular state looks as it does. Both o
these techniques may be helpful in allowing a visual clustering of the data
although they do not necessarily provide a memorable picture. Both technique
present some difficulties to the observer in the relating of visual features t
variables.

As the last example of multivariate display let us consider the use of Chernof
FACES. Before doing this we must assign each variable to a facial feature. Thi
is not always easy, nor is it unimportant. After several tries we arrived at th
following scheme.

1. *Population → the number of faces/state*—The number of faces is proportional to the log of the population. We used one large face in each state for easier identification and as many identical small faces as required. The size of these latter faces was kept small so as to allow us to fit them within the confines of the state boundaries.

2. *Literacy rate → size of the eyes* (bigger = higher).

3. *% HS graduates → slant of the eyes* (the more slanted the better).

4. *Life expectancy → the length of the mouth* (the longer the better).

5. *Homicide rate → the width of the nose* (the wider the nose the lower the homicide rate).

6. *Income → the curvature of the mouth* (the bigger the smile the higher the income).

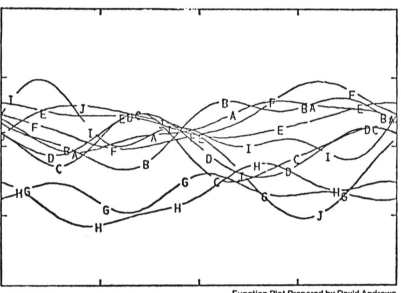

Function Plot Prepared by David Andrews

Legend

A New Hampshire
B Vermont
C Pennsylvania
D Ohio
E Iowa
F South Dakota
G Alabama
H Mississippi
I Oregon
J California

FIG. 13.26. A 'function plot' of the data in Table 13.6.

FIG. 13.27. Facing the nation: Yet another display of the data in Table 13.6, plus the data for the rest of the United States, using Chernoff's (1973) faces.

7. *Temperature* → *the shape of the face* (the more like a peanut the warmer the more like a football the colder).

8,9. *Longitude and latitude* → *The X and Y position of the face* on the coordinate axes of the paper represented the position of the state.

Thus we tried to use sensible visual metaphors for representing each variable "bigger" was the general rule when normative direction was clear. In the case of a variable (such as weather) where desirability could not be determined easily we used an aspect of the face that is not ordered. To show the adaptability of the FACE scheme to larger data sets, we prepared a plot involving all 50 states Similar plots could have been prepared for most other meta-iconic schemes (STARs, TREEs, etc.). The resulting plot is shown in Fig. 13.27.

A viewing of the map reveals many things. First, we can see the relative density of population in the East at a glance. Next note the temperature gradient as one goes south from North Dakota to Texas. The Pacific current is also evident. Looking more closely we see that the Deep South looks very homogeneous and low on all variables of quality of life used. Thus we can see that Angoff and Mencken's findings of Mississippi as the "Worst American State," followed closely by Alabama, South Carolina, Georgia, Arkansas, Tennessee North Carolina, and Louisiana, is still essentially valid almost a half century later at least with these variables). Note further that New England states (Vermont, New Hampshire, and Maine) look the same: They are generally high on education variables, as well as having low homicide rates, but seem to have low incomes. Massachusetts seems to have a somewhat lower literacy rate but a higher per capita income. Connecticut and New Jersey seem remarkably similar with higher incomes still. We also see a clustering of Mideastern states on all variables (Pennsylvania, Ohio, Michigan, and Indiana) with the border states of Virginia, West Virginia, and Kentucky falling somewhere between their rural southern neighbors and their more industrial northern ones.

The Midwest looks homogeneous with the rather surprising difference between North and South Dakota in income. A check back to the original data indicates that this is not a data entry mistake, and there is a substantial difference between these two neighbors. We also note that except for the cold weather, North Dakota seems a pleasant place to live. Utah has an interesting structure, being very high on all variables except income, which may reflect the influence of the Mormon church on the state. There are many other interesting similarities that might be noted, and the reader is invited to study the map more closely. As a last comment we draw the reader's attention to the similarity between California and Hawaii. We see benign weather, long-life, a high income, low homicide rate, high proportion of high school graduates, but a low literacy rate. This reflects either their high proportion of non-English-speaking inhabitants, or a propensity for lotus eating so common in paradise.

Three-and-More-Way Displays of Multivariate Data

Thus far we have restricted ourselves to the description of display methodologies confined to two dimensions of the plotting medium. This was due primarily to the widespread availability of paper and blackboards, and because of the restraints imposed on us by publication media. Technology is changing, so that in the near future other display modes will be common and will allow the use of more general techniques. There have been advances in the display of data in three-or-more-way displays.

Capturing of complex data structures by adapting dynamic media to the needs of data presentation has been called *kinostatistics* (Biderman, 1971). Biderman argued that the communication of such things as changes in rates through time, multidimensional relationships, statistical variance, measures of association, and other complex functions of data can be more efficiently done in a dynamic medium. This was illustrated in a film by B. M. Fienberg (1973).

The differences between a display technique designed to communicate with others and one done for communication with oneself (data exploration) are small. Thus perhaps Biderman's notion of kinostatistics was formed partially by exploratory suggestions like that of Barnard (1969), who proposed a dynamic four-dimensional display in which one starts with two-dimensional perspective drawing of a surface y as a function of variables x_1 and x_2, then by moving the display one can introduce a third variable, x_3. He hypothesized further that if one changes with respect to x_3 slowly, one might be able to add another variable x_4 on a much faster cycle. This would present the viewer with, in Kruskal's (1975) words, "pictured surface that heaves (for x_3) and quivers (for x_4)" (p. 32).

A realization of such a scheme was devised by Friedman, Tukey, and Tukey (1979) under the general name of PRIM-9. PRIM-9 was a computer-based display system that would take a multivariate data set and allowed the user to display a scatter plot of any two variables in a traditional way and then rotate, in real time, that plot through any third dimension. To gain some understanding of what this did for the data explorer, consider a three-dimensional set of points in the shape of a donut projected into two-space from the side. A rotation around the X-axis shows the appearance and disappearance of the hole and gives the viewer a strong impression of the shape of the data distribution. With similar kinds of manipulations the experienced PRIM-9 analyst could explore complex data efficiently. PRIM-9 had other features that allowed the isolation of certain areas, changes in scale, and so forth. Huber (1987) told interesting stories about what the developers decided not to do in the course of the development of three-dimensional scatterplots.

What was high-end and experimental a decade ago is now broadly available for some varieties of desk-top computers. MacSpin, DataDesk, JMP, and SYSTAT are computer programs for the Apple Macintosh that will spin three-dimensional points and perform a variety of highly interactive graphical data analyses. Details about the capacity of such technology can easily take up an entire book (e.g., Cleveland & McGill, 1988). Moreover much of what dynamic display does is poorly conveyed statically—the instamatic in Yosemite syndrome (Wainer, 1987). However a good introduction is provided by Becker, Cleveland and Wilks (1987).

Dynamic Displays.   An extraordinary tour de force of 20th-century display technology was developed by Geoffry Dutton of Harvard, and discussed and displayed at the First Conference on Social Graphics. This display was a four-dimensional statistical graphic called "Manifested Destiny." The data being displayed were the population distributions of the United States from 1790 until 1970. This was done by generating a contour map of the United States in which the heights of the mountains were proportional to the population at that point. One can look at a map of the United States for any point of view; usually it is from below Texas, but that is merely convention. In his map Dutton generated one view (from off the coast of Massachusetts) that reflects the 1790 population distribution; another from, say New Jersey, from the 1800 census, and so around the country, until the 1970 census is seen from off the California coast. He then interpolated both geographically and in time to yield many, many views in a relatively smooth set of changes across time and around the country. Next these many pictures were put together into a film strip (one picture/frame), and the film made into a hologram. The hologram image floats inside of what looks like a lampshade and turns before the viewer. As it turns one sees the mountains of population grow westward. The effect is very dramatic indeed.

A useful bibliography of dynamic graphical aids had been compiled by Posten (1976, 1977), and more recently by Cleveland and McGill (1988).

EVERYTHING ELSE

In the foregoing sections of this review we tried to give the reader a flavor of the exciting developments in the field of graphical data analysis, with an eye toward both the future and the past. In doing so the chapter reads like Stephen Leacock's young man who ran out of his house, jumped on his horse, and galloped off in all directions at once. The sketchy nature of this review is due principally to the vast nature of the topic and the sensible space restrictions under which the authors labored. There are many areas left unmentioned. In this section we try to touch a few of these, but discuss them in far less detail than they merit.

Complexity versus Simplicity

There is a substantial difference in epistemology between the multihued multidimensional graphs favored by such organizations as census (Barabba, 1980) and the mass media (Wainer, 1980c) and the simple diagrams suggested by the sophisticated statisticians at Bell Labs (Cleveland, 1985; Gnanadesikan, 1977, 1980). In the former case, an important role of the graphic is to attract attention as well as to inform. The latter assumes that the analyst is already interested, and the motivations are well described by the desiderata at the beginning of the third section. The determination of what display methodology should be used must be made by a careful examination of the displayer's purpose. Often a plot will have several purposes and so the displayer must order priorities. Tufte (1983) and Wainer (1984) warned against trying to do too much; trying to make an exploratory graph a data archive can destroy much of the graph's effectiveness in its primary role.

Tufte (1983) tried to provide a theoretical basis for the development of graphical standards. His basic tenet (although by no means universally accepted) is the same as the architectural one of "less is more." Tufte stated (and illustrated) that if a particular piece of a graph can be removed without losing information, then the resulting graph is better than the original. This rule bodes ill for pseudo-perspectival plots often found in newspapers. Tufte called such extra stuff "chart-junk." From this point of view he defined a measure of the quality of a graph by its "data-ink ratio." This is the ratio of the amount of ink used to depict the data divided by the total amount of ink in the graph. As this ratio approaches unity, so the graph's quality increases. Graphs with a low D-I ratio Tufte dubbed "boutiqu graphics" suitable only for the purpose of decoration.

Much of what Tufte discovered has its basis in the work of Bertin (1973 1977), who provided a thorough if idiosyncratic theory of graphic display. Ber tin's work has remained largely inaccessible to English reading audiences but i now available in translation (Bertin 1980, 1983). Wainer (1992) extended an specialized Bertin's theory to facilitate the measurement of graphicacy.

Standards

We have not dealt with the complex issues of graphical standards, although muc has been written about them. Graphical standards were a concern in the mid-19t century, and several abortive attempts to develop rules and standards were mad in sessions of the International Statistical Institute and the beginning of the 20t century. In 1914 a joint committee of a number of national associations presente their preliminary report. These rules were published in the *Journal of the Ameri can Statistical Association* in 1915 (Joint Committee on Standards for Graphi Presentation, 1915). More recent versions were published in 1979 by the Ameri can National Standards Institute, as well as another version by the U.S. Arm (1966).

Even though there have been several attempts to revise these rules and stan dards, for the most part they have stood the test of time rather well. This i partially due to the wisdom of those who originally formulated them and partiall because the necessary empirical evidence to challenge these standards has no been gathered. A carefully prepared description of graphical standards and thei application was prepared by Schmid and Schmid (1979), which is a revision o Schmid's (1954) first *Handbook*. Although an excellent effort in most regards even the revision spends a great deal of time (as the 1915 Standards) talkin about T-squares and pen nibs and relatively little about Raster scans, refresl tubes, and other output devices of modern technology. This field is vast, but brief introduction is provided by Teicholz (1976).

Advice about how to prepare graphics is plentiful, but often conflicting. Fo instance, Schmid (1983, pp. 15–16) included axes and grid lines (!) as obligator features of a scatterplot, in the same year that Tufte (1983) suggested the dot dash-plot in Fig. 13.22.

Experimental Evidence

[Paraphrasing Margerison 1965; quoted by Kruskal (1975)], "Drawing graphs like motor-car driving and love-making, is one of those activities which almos every Psychologist thinks he can do well without instruction. The results are o course usually abominable." How do we know that the rules specified by th experts are in fact correct? Bertin provided the rudiments of a theory, as di

owman (1968), but there is no large body of cohesive evidence to support them.
he beginnings of a theory have been proposed by Cleveland and McGill (1985;
leveland, 1985, chap. 4) in which they propose an ordering of what they called
e elementary graphical perception tasks (e.g., judgments of position on a
ommon scale, length, angles, slopes, areas, and so on); they found, in a series
f experiments, that judgment of position along a common scale is least error-
one, whereas judgment of areas and angles are more error-inducing. Keeping
ese results in mind, they proposed such graphic devices as the dot chart,
eveloped to use the most effective kinds of perceptual processing. Kosslyn
1985) observed that there is a large body of research on more general perceptual
nd cognitive topics that could be brought to bear on questions of graphical
isplay; but to date little of that theory has been applied. Simkin and Hastie
1987) described a series of experiments integrating a cognitive theory of graphi-
al perception into the evaluation of very simple displays (bar charts, divided bar
harts, and pie charts).

Most early work was done piecemeal on one small problem or other without
ny careful attempt to integrate the findings within the broader context of percep-
al and cognitive psychology. In the late 1920s and early 1930s a series of
apers explored the relative merits of bar charts, pie charts, and so forth (Croxton
z Stein 1932; Croxton & Stryker 1927; Eells 1926; Huhn 1927). More recently
Vainer, Groves, and Lono (1978) continued this in a somewhat broader sense.
Vainer (1974) tested some of Tukey's notions about hanging histograms, and
hernoff and Rizvi (1975) conducted some experiments on the stability of the
erceptual clusters of faces when the variable-feature assignments were per-
uted. Freni-Titulaer and Louv (1984) compared Kleiner and Hartigan's (1981)
ees and castles; they found that trees usually performed better. In cartography
ere is a more widespread tradition of the testing of new ideas (see for example
astner & Robinson 1969; Crawford 1976; Wainer & Biderman 1977, 1978;
Vainer & Francolini 1980). A very extensive and thoughtful review of this area
repared by Macdonald-Ross (1977) is a sensible place for the interested reader
o start.

Little formal work has been done on the perceptual efficacy of the techniques
escribed here. For example, there have been some experiments on the use of the
catter plot to visually estimate a correlation (e.g., Strahan & Hansen 1978), but
xcept for Wainer and Thissen's (1979) paper, the bivariate distributions were
lways Gaussian, and so the Pearson r is always better. In Wainer and Thissen
1979) we showed that when the data were not Gaussian the scatter plot allowed
ven naive viewers to disregard the outliers to some extent and still accurately
stimate the underlying correlation. It is hypothesized that the augmentations
nentioned earlier would aid still more, but these were not tested. Relles and
Rogers (1977) also looked into the use of a graphical aid for the discovery of
utliers. Despite the very poor quality of their graphs, they concluded that their
ubjects became "fairly robust estimators of location." However, the estimation

of statistics from graphics depends, at least to some extent, on the graphics themselves; Cleveland, Diaconis, and McGill (1982) found that the addition o empty space around the point cloud in a scatterplot increased the perceived correlation.

Ehrenberg did some experiments testing his own recommendations, but the results would be more persuasive coming from an independent source. Wainer (1980c) found that children do well with good tables (confirming Ehrenberg's findings), and Wainer, Groves, and Lono (1978) found similar results with adults. Yet none of these answers the fundamental question of data graphics. A good graph "forces us to notice what we never expected to see" (Tukey 1977, p vi.). Yet how do we test the extent to which a graph does this? This aspect of graphics research seems to be a perfect question for psychologists—an area that requires a deep knowledge of perception and its associated experimental para- digms. Perhaps this area is one where psychometricians can usefully contribute Certainly the need of this area is well expressed by the late labor leader John L Lewis, who when asked what the labor movement wanted replied "More."

We need more experimentation with the innovations developed, we need more careful training in the use of graphs for our students, more integration of results from a variety of disciplines, more flexible software to utilize the astonishing variety of new equipment being produced, and greater acceptance of graphical presentation of data in professional publications.

It is on this last note that we wish to conclude. We began this review noting that the use of graphics by psychologists has lagged far behind their use of elegant statistical procedures. Part of the blame for this appears to be peer pressure suggesting that it is not the work of the scientist to draw little pictures. A second part is economic, which forces journals to warn authors to "limit their use of figures to only those essential for presentation." (Note "essential" not "use- ful.") We are warned that the publication of figures is expensive, yet who is to say that for the conveyance of ideas a figure in not "em for em" (Biderman, 1980b) cheaper than the requisite prose?

Are things changing? This chapter represents one change, but it seems clear that the changes were in the wind well before we were invited to prepare this chapter. S. E. Fienberg (1979) surveyed the statistical literature for graphs in the course of preparing his excellent paper. He found that the use of graphs in the journal *Biometrika* for the display of data hit a peak in the early 1930s and had dropped substantially to remain essentially constant thereafter. The same was true for the *Journal of the American Statistical Association*. We did a similar survey of several psychology journals 10 years ago and found quite a different picture. A smoothed summary of some of what we found is shown in Fig. 13.28, and it is clear that whereas the use of graphs to communicate data has undergone a sharp renaissance over the past 30 years, there was evidence of a recent decline. We hope that the renewal of interest among statisticians will spark a

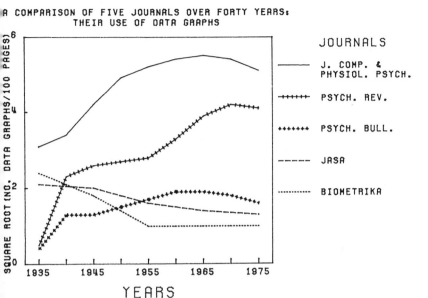

FIG. 13.28. Plot of the trends in the use of graphs for data display by psychological and statistical journals over a period of forty years reproduced from Wainer and Thissen (1981).

similar revival in the use of graphs in psychology, for we strongly support Yogi Berra's observation that: "You can see a lot just by lookin." This chapter has been an attempt to review some new ways to look.

Postscript: Line Quality

Figure 13.28 was prepared with some of the finest computer software and hardware available for the production of statistical graphics when the original version of this review was written, circa 1980. The system involved a room-size time-sharing computer, a pen plotter, and a good deal of command-language and trial and error. Figure 13.29 shows the same data plotted in minutes using contemporary graphics software (DeltaGraph) running on a desktop computer (an Apple Macintosh), and printed on a laser printer. Although the quality of the circa-1980 plot was barely acceptable for some purposes, the quality of the circa-1990 plot is easily up to the standards of any scientific presentation. Certainly the greatest advance in statistical graphics in the decade of the 1980s has been the improvements in computer software and hardware that have brought graphic artist quality to the productions of the scientists' desktop. It is now up to the scientist to decide what to plot.

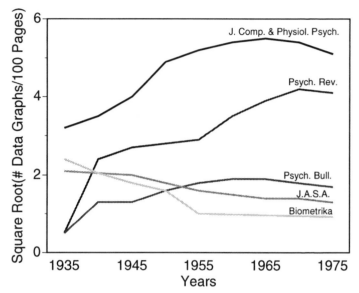

FIG. 13.29.   A contemporary re-drawing of Fig. 13.28, using circa-1990 hardware and software.

CONCLUSIONS

Getting information from a table is like extracting sunlight from a cucumber
(Farquhar & Farquhar, 1891)

The disdain shown by these two 19th-century economists reflected a minority opinion at that time. Since then the use of graphs for data analysis and communication has increased in fits and starts. Strangely, we find that the quality of graphs used has not increased since the time of Playfair's invention, and the tables, spoken of so disparagingly by the Farquhars, remain, to a large extent, worthy of contempt. This chapter has been a review of methods new and old, that improve the way that graphs and tables can be used to aid in the depiction, exploration, summarization, and communication of data.

ACKNOWLEDGMENTS

The initial version of this chapter owed a great deal of its substance and thought to the help provided by the many colleagues who responded to our initial letter with bibliographies, reprints, preprints, advice, and criticism. We thank you all. Of special help were Albert D. Biderman, William H. Kruskal, Frederick Mosteller, and John W. Tukey, who provided help and advice and supported the notion that research on graphics is a proper pursuit for a scholar, and is not merely the drawing of pictures. This version was aided by the many who commented on the chapter after it first appeared. We would like to single out Gideon Keren for his careful reading of the manuscript and his thoughtful suggestions for improvement. In addition we would like to thank Edward R. Tufte, whose graphical scholarship informed and inspired. He also provided a set of rules for writing that we have violated almost as often as he has. To wit use:

1. no more than three first-person singulars,
2. no more than three self-citations,
3. no more than two exclamation points,
4. no more than two boldface,
5. no more than one language, and
6. no more than one philosopher.

Sorry Edward.

REFERENCES

American National Standards Institute (1979a). *American national standard illustrations for publications and projection* (ANSI Y15.1M). New York: American Society Mechanical Engineers.

American National Standards Institute (1979b). *American national standards time-series charts* (ANSI Y15.2M). New York: American Society Mechanical Engineers.

Anderson, E. (1960). A semi-graphical method for the analysis of complex problems. *Technometrics, 2,* 387–92.

Andrews, D. F. (1972). Plots of high-dimensional data. *Biometrics, 28,* 125–36.

Andrews, D. F. (1978). Exploratory data analysis. *International encyclopedia of statistics* (pp. 97–101). New York: Free Press.

Angoff, C., & Mencken, H. L. (1931). The worst American state. *American Mercury, 31,* 1–16, 175–188, 355–371.

Bachi, R. (1968). *Graphical rational patterns.* Jerusalem: Israeli University.

Bachi, R. (1976). Graphical methods for presenting statistical data: Chairman's comments. *The American Statistical Association Proceedings, Social Statistics Section* (pp. 72–73). Washington, DC: American Statisticial Association.

Bachi, R. (1978a). *Graphical statistical methodology in the automation era: Graphic Presentation of Statistical Information.* Paper presented at 136th Annual Meeting American Statistical Association Social Statistics Section, Session on Graphical Methods for Statistical Data, Boston, 1976. (Tech. Rep. No. 43, pp. 4–6). Washington, DC: Census Bureau.

Bachi, R. (1978b August). *Proposals for the development of selected graphical methods.* Paper presented at 136th Annual Meeting American Statistical Association Social Statistics Section, Session on Graphical Methods for Statistical Data, Boston, 1976. (Tech. Rep. No. 43 pp. 23–68). Washington, DC: Census Bureau.

Barabba, V. (1980). *The revolution in graphic technology*. Paper presented at Annual Meeting American Association Advancement of Science, San Francisco.

Barnard, G. (1969). Summary remarks. In N. L. Johnson & H. Smith (Eds.), *New Developments in Survey Sampling* (pp. 696–711). New York: Wiley Interscience.

Barnett, V. (1981). *Interpreting multivariate data*. New York: Wiley.

Becker, R. A., Cleveland, W. S., & Wilks, A. R. (1987). Dynamic graphics for data analysis. *Statistical Science, 2,* 355–395.

Becketti, S. & Gould, W. (1987). Rangefinder box plots. American Statistician, 41, 149.

Bertin, J. (1973). *Semiologie graphique* (2nd ed.). The Hague: Mouton-Gautier. (English translation done by W. Berg & H. Wainer and published as *Semiology of graphics*. Madison, WI: University of Wisconsin Press, 1983.)

Bertin, J. (1977). *La graphique et Le Traitement Graphique de L'Information*. Paris: Flammarion.

Bertin, J. (1980). Graphics and the graphical analysis of data (W. Berg & H. Wainer, Trans.). Berlin: De Gruyter.

Bickel, P. J., Hammel, E. A., O'Connell, J. W. (1975). Sex bias in graduate admissions: Data from Berkeley. *Science, 187,* 398–404.

Biderman, A. D. (1971). Kinostatistics for social indicators. *Educational Broadcast Review, 5,* 13–19.

Biderman, A. D. (1978 June). *Intellectual impediments to the development and diffusion of statistical graphics, 1637–1980*. Paper presented at 1st General Conference Social Graphics, Leesburg, VA.

Biderman, A. D. (1980 February). *The Playfair Enigma: Toward understanding the development of the schematic representation of statistics from origins to the present day*. Paper presented at Annual Meeting American Association for the Advancement of Science., San Francisco.

Bishop, Y., Fienberg, S. E., & Holland P. (1975). *Discrete multivariate analysis*. Boston: MIT Press.

Bock, R. D., & Jones, L. V. (1968). *The measurement and prediction of judgement and choice*. San Francisco: Holden-Day.

Bowman, W. J. (1968). *Graphic communication*. New York: Wiley.

Bradley, J. V. (1963). Rank-order correlation scatter diagrams without plotting points. *The American Statistician, 17,* 14–15.

Bruntz, S. M., Cleveland, W. S., Kleiner, B., & Warner, J. L. (1974). The dependence of ambient ozone on solar radiation, wind, temperature, and mixing height. In Preprint vol: Symposium Atmospheric Diffusion and Air Pollution Santa Barbara, California pp. 9–13. Boston: American Meteorol. Society.

Castner, H. W., & Robinson, A. H. (1969). *Dot area symbols in cartography: The influence of pattern on their perception*. American Congress of Survey and Mapping. Cartography Division (Tech. Monog. No. CA-4.

Chakrapani, T. K., & Ehrenberg, A. S. C. (1976). *Factor analysis or BGA?* Unpublished manuscript, Multivariate Study Group of Royal Statistical Society.

Chambers, J. M., Cleveland, W. S., Kleiner, B., & Tukey, P. A. (1983). *Graphical methods for data analysis*. Boston: Duxbury.

Chernoff, H. (1973). The use of faces to represent points in *k*-dimensional space graphically. *Journal of the American Statistical Association, 68,* 361–368.

Chernoff, H., & Rizvi, H. M. (1975). Effect on classification error of random permutations of features in representing multivariate data by faces. *Journal of the American Statistical Association, 70,* 548–554.

Cleveland, W. (1979). Robust locally weighted regression and smoothing scatterplots. *Journal of the American Statistical Association, 74,* 829–836.

Cleveland, W. S. (1985). *The elements of graphing data*. Boston: Duxbury.

Cleveland, W. S., Diaconis, P. & McGill, R. (1982). Variables on scatterplots look more highly correlated when the scales are increased. *Science, 216,* 1138–1141.

Cleveland, W. S. & McGill, R. (1983). A color-caused optical illusion on a statistical graph. *American Statistician, 37,* 101–105.

Cleveland, W. S. & McGill, R. (1985). Graphical perception and graphical methods for analyzing scientific data. *Science, 229,* 828–833.

Cleveland, W., & Kleiner, B. (1975). A graphic technique for enhancing scatter plots with moving statistics. *Technometrics, 17,* 447–454.

Cleveland, W. S., & McGill, M. E. (Eds.). (1988). *Dynamic graphics for statistics.* Belmont, CA: Wadsworth.

Costigan-Eaves, P., & Macdonald-Ross, M. (1990a). *The method of curves: A brief history to the early nineteenth century.* London.

Costigan-Eaves, P., & Macdonald-Ross, M. (1990b). William Playfair (1759–1823). *Statistical Science, 5,* 330–339.

Cox, D. R., & Laub, E. (1967). A note on the graphical analysis of multidimensional contingency tables. *Technometrics, 9,* 481–488.

Crawford, P. V. (1976). Optimal spatial design for thematic maps. *Cartographic Journal, 13,* 145–155.

Croxton, F. E., & Stein, H. (1932). Graphic comparisons by bars, squares, circles and cubes. *Journal of the American Statistical Association, 27,* 54–60.

Croxton, F. E., & Stryker, R. E. (1927). Bar charts versus circle diagrams. *Journal of the American Statistical Association, 22,* 473–482.

Daniel, C., & Wood, F. S. (1971). *Fitting equations to data.* New York: Wiley.

Denby, L., & Mallows, C. L. (1977). Two diagnostic displays for robust regression analysis. *Technometrics, 19,* 1–13.

Devlin, S., Gnanadesikan, R., & Kettenring, J. (1975). Robust estimation and outlier detection with correlation coefficients. *Biometrika, 62,* 531–545.

Dixon, W. J. (1988). *BMDP Statistical Software Manual: 1988 Edition.* Berkeley: University California Press.

Dutton, G. (1978). *Manifest destiny: A graphic account of the settlement and growth of America 1790–1970.* Paper presented at 1st General Conference Social Graphics, Leesburg, VA.

Easton, G. S. & McCulloch, R. E. (1990). A multivariate generalization of quantile-quantile plots. *Journal of the American Statistical Association, 85,* 376–386.

Eells, W. C. (1926). The relative merits of circles and bars for representing component parts. *Journal of the American Statistical Association, 21,* 119–132.

Ehrenberg, A. S. C. (1977). Rudiments of numeracy. *Journal of the Royal Statistical Society, Series A, 140,* 277–297.

Everitt, B. (1978). *Graphical techniques for multivariate data.* London: Heinemann.

Farquhar, A. B., & Farquhar, H. (1891). *Economic and industrial delusions: A discourse of the case for protection.* New York: Putnam.

Fienberg, B. M. (1973). *Approaches to kinostatistics* [Film]. Washington, DC: Bureau of Social Science Research.

Fienberg, B. M. & Franklin, C. A. (1975). *Social graphics bibliography.* Washington, DC: Bureau of Social Science Research.

Fienberg, S. E. (1969). Graphical analysis of contingency tables. *Applied Statistics, 18,* 153–168.

Fienberg, S. E. (1975). Perspective Canada as a social report. *Social Indicators Research, 2,* 153–174.

Fienberg, S. E. (1979). Graphical methods in statistics. *The American Statistician, 33,* 165–178.

Freni-Titulaer, L. W. J. & Louv, W. C. (1984). Comparisons of some graphical methods for exploratory multivariate data analysis. *American Statistician, 38,* 184–188.

Friedman, J., Tukey, J. W., & Tukey, P. A. (1979). Approaches to analysis of data that concentrate near higher-dimensional manifolds. *Proceedings of the 2nd IRIA Symposium Data Anal. Informatics.* Versailles, France.

Funkhouser, H. G. (1937). Historical development of the graphical representation of statistical data. *Osiris, 3,* 269–404.

Furnival, G. M., & Wilson, R. W. (1974). Regression by leaps and bounds. *Technometrics, 16,* 499–511.

Gnanadesikan, R. (1973). Graphical methods for informal inference in multivariate data analysis. *Proceedings of the International Statistical Institute Bulletin, 45,* 195–206.

Gnanadesikan, R. (1977). *Methods for statistical data analysis of multivariate observations.* New York: Wiley.

Gnanadesikan, R. (1980 February). *Graphical data analysis: Issues, tools, and examples.* Paper presented at Annual Meeting American Association Advancement of Science, San Francisco.

Gorman, J. W., & Toman, R. J. (1966). Selection of variables for fitting equations to data. *Technometrics, 8,* 27–51.

Gruvaeus, G. T., & Wainer, H. (1972). Two additions to hierarchical cluster analysis. *British Journal Mathematical Statistical Psychol, 25,* 200–206.

Hampel, F. R. (1974). The influence curve and its role in robust estimation. *Journal of the American Statistical Association, 69,* 383–393.

Hsieh, H. (1981). Chinese tally mark. *American Statistician, 35,* 174.

Huber, P. (1972). Robust statistics: A review. *Annals of Mathematical Statistics, 43,* 1041–1067.

Huber, P. J. (1987). Experiences with three-dimensional scatterplots. *Journal of the American Statistical Association, 82,* 448–453.

Huhn, R. von (1927). Further studies in the graphic use of circles and bars: A discussion of the Eell's experiment. *Journal of the American Statistical Association, 22,* 31–36.

Jacob, R. J. K. (1976). *Computer-produced faces as an iconic display for complex data.* Doctoral dissertation, Johns Hopkins University, Baltimore, MD.

Jacob, R. J. K., Egeth, H. E., & Bevan, W. (1976). The face as a data display. *Human Factors, 18,* 189–200.

Jevons, W. S. (1884). *Investigations in currency and finance.* London: Macmillan.

Joint Committee on Standards for Graphics Presentation. (1915). Preliminary Report. *Journal of the American Statistical Association, 14,* 790–797.

Kleiner, B., & Hartigan, J. (1981). Representing points in many discussions by trees and castles. *Journal of the American Statistical Association, 75,* 260–269.

Kosslyn, S. M. (1985). Graphics and human information processing. *Journal of the American Statistical Association, 80,* 499–512.

Kruskal, W. H. (1975). Visions of maps and graphs. In *Auto Carto II: Proceedings of the International Symposium Computer-assisted Cartography.* Washington, DC: Census Bureau.

Leinhardt, S., & Wasserman, S. S. (1979). Exploratory data analysis: An introduction to selected methods. In K. Schussler (Ed.), *Sociological methodology.* San Francisco: Jossey-Bass.

Macdonald-Ross, M. (1978). Research in graphic communication (IET Monogr. 7). United Kingdom: Institute of Education Technology, Open University.

Mandelbrot, B. B. (1982). The fractal geometry of nature. San Francisco: W. H. Freeman & Co.

Mayr, G. von. (1874). *Gutachten uber die Anwendung der graphischen and geographischen Methods in der Statistik.* Munich.

McGill, R. (1978). *Printing tables to expose structure.* Paper presented at Annual Meeting of the American Statistical Association, San Diego.

McGill, R., Tukey, J. W., & Larsen, W. (1978). Variations of box plots. *The American Statistician, 32*(1), 12–16.

Monkhouse, F. J., & Wilkinson, H. R. (1971). *Maps and diagrams.* London: Methuen.

Moore, D. S. & McCabe, G. P. (1989). *Introduction to the practice of statistics.* San Francisco: W. H. Freeman.

Mosteller, F., & Tukey, J. W. (1949). The uses and usefulness of binomial probability paper. *Journal of the American Statistical Association, 44,* 174–212.

Mosteller, F., & Tukey, J. W. (1968). Data analysis: Including statistics. In G. Lindsey & E.

Aronson (Eds.), *The handbook of social psychology* (pp. 80–203). Reading, MA: Addison-Wesley.

Mosteller, F., & Tukey, J. W. (1977). *Data analysis and regression*. Reading, MA: Addison-Wesley.

Nightingale, F. (1858). *Notes on matters affecting health, efficiency and hospital administration of the British army, founded chiefly on the experiences of the late war*. London: Harrison.

Playfair, W. (1786). *The commercial and political atlas*. London: Corry.

Posten, H. O. (1976). A bibliography on audio-visual materials for statistical education. *The American Statistician, 30*, 91–96.

Posten, H. O. (1977). Supplement to a bibliography on audiovisual materials for statistical education. *The American Statistician, 31*, 163–165.

Ramsay, J. O. (1980). *Inside-out displays and more*. Paper presented at a Symposium on Multivariate Data Display, Psychometric Society Meeting Iowa City.

Relles, D., & Rogers, W. (1977). Statisticians are fairly robust estimators of location. *Journal of the American Statistical Association, 72*, 107–11.

Rousseuw, P. J., & Leroy, A. M. (1987). *Robust regression and outlier detection*. New York: Wiley.

Sandiford, P. (1932). *Educational psychology* (Appendix A). London: Longman's Green.

Schmid, C. F. (1954). *Handbook of graphic presentation*. New York: Ronald.

Schmid, C. F. (1983). *Statistical graphics: Design principles and practices*. New York: Wiley.

Schmid, C. F., & Schmid, S. E. (1979). *Handbook of graphic presentation* (2nd Ed.). New York: Wiley.

Siegel, J. H., Goldwyn, R. M., & Friedman, H. P. (1971). Pattern and process in the evolution of human septic shock. *Surgery, 70*, 232–245.

Simkin, D. & Hastie, R. (1987). An information-processing analysis of graph perception. *Journal of the American Statistical Association, 82*, 454–465.

Snee, R. D. (1974). Graphical display of two-way contingency tables. *The American Statistician, 28*, 9–12.

Social Indicators III (1980). Washington, DC: U.S. Bureau of the Census.

State court caseload statistics: 1976 (1976). Williamsburg, VA: National Center for State Courts.

Strahan, R. F., & Hansen, C. J. (1978). Underestimating correlation from scatterplots. *Applied Psychological Measurement, 2*, 543–550.

Taguri, M., Hiramatsu, M., Kittaka, T., Wakimoto, K. (1976). Graphical representation of correlation analysis of ordered data by linked vector patterns. *Journal Japanese Statistical Society, 6*, 17–25.

Teicholz, E. (1976). Computer graphics: A perspective. Reprint from *Biosciences Communications*. Basel, Switzerland: Karger.

Thissen, D., Baker, L., & Wainer, H. (1981). Influence enhanced scatter plots. *Psychological Bulletin, 90*, 179–184.

Thissen, D., & Wainer, H. (1986). XTREE: A multivariate graphical icon applicable in the evaluation of statistical estimators. *The American Statistician, 40*, 149–153.

Tilling, L. (1975). Early experimental graphs. *British Journal Historical Science, 8*, 193–213.

Tufte, E. R. (1979). Personal communication.

Tufte, E. R. (1983). *The visual display of quantitative information*. Cheshire, CT: Graphics Press.

Tukey, J. W. (1962). The future of data analysis. *Annals of Mathematical Statistics, 33*, 1–67.

Tukey. (1970). *Exploratory Data Analysis (Limitied Preliminary Edition)*. Reading, Mass: Addison-Wesley.

Tukey, J. W. (1972). Some graphics and semi-graphic displays. In T. A. Bancroft (Ed.), *Statistical papers in honor of George W. Snedecor* (pp. 293–316). Ames: Iowa State University Press.

Tukey, J. W. (1974). *Mathematics and the picturing of data*. Proceedings of the International Congress of Mathematics, Vancouver.

Tukey, J. W. (1977). *Exploratory data analysis*. Reading, MA: Addison-Wesley.

Tukey, J. W. & Tukey, P. A. (1983). Some graphics for studying four-dimensional data. *Computer science and statistics: Proceedings of the 14th symposium on the interface* (pp. 60–66). New York: Springer-Verlag.

Tukey, P. A., & Tukey, J. W. (1981). Graphical display of datasets in 3 or more dimensions. In V. Barnett, Ed.) *Interpreting multivariate data* (chp. 10–12). Chichester, U.K.: Wiley.

U.S. Bureau of the Census. (1976, August). *STATUS. A monthly chartbook of social and economic trends*. Washington, DC: author.

U.S. Department of the Army. (1966). *Standards of statistical presentation*. Washington, DC: Government Printing Office.

Wainer, H. (1974). The suspended rootogram and other visual displays: An empirical validation *The American Statistician, 28,* 143–145.

Wainer, H. (1977). *Data display-graphical and tabular*. Hackensack, NJ: NCCD.

Wainer, H. (1979a). *About faces in factor analysis* (Tech. Rep. No. 547-791). Bureau of Social Science Research.

Wainer, H. (1980a). A test of graphicacy in children. *Applied Psychological Measurement, 5,* 331–340.

Wainer, H. (1980b). A timely error. *Royal Statistical Society News and Notes, 7,* 6.

Wainer, H. (1980c). Making newspaper graphs fit to print. In P. Kolers, M. E. Wrolstad, & H. Bouma (Eds.), *Processing of visible language* (Vol. 2, pp. 125–142). New York: Plenum.

Wainer, H. (1982). Robust statistics: A survey and some prescriptions. In G. Keren (Ed.), *Statistical and methodological issues in psychology and social sciences research*. (pp. 187–216). Hillsdale, NJ: Lawrence Erlbaum Associates.

Wainer, H. (1983). Multivariate displays. In M. H. Rizvi, J. Rustagi & D. Siegmund (Eds.), *Recent advances in statistics* (pp. 469–508). New York: Academic Press.

Wainer, H. (1984). How to display data badly. *The American Statistician, 38,* 137–147.

Wainer, H. (1987). Deja view: A discussion of dynamic graphics for data analysis. *Statistical Science, 2,* 388–389.

Wainer, H. (1990a). Graphical visions from William Playfair to John Tukey. *Statistical Science, 5,* 340–346.

Wainer, H. (1990b). Measuring graphicacy. *Chance, 3*(4), 52, 58.

Wainer, H. (1991a). Double X-axis graphs.*Chance, 4*(1), 50–51.

Wainer, H. (1991b). Pie Charts. *Chance, 4*(2), 52–53.

Wainer, H. (1992). Understanding graphs and tables. *Educational Researcher, 21,* 14–23.

Wainer, H., & Biderman, A. D. (1977). Some methodological comments on evaluating maps *Cartographic Journal, 14,* 109–114.

Wainer, H., & Biderman, A. D. (1978). Reply to Noyes. *Cartographic Journal, 15,* 104–105.

Wainer, H., & Francolini, C. (1980). An empirical inquiry into human understanding of "two variable color maps." *The American Statistician, 34,* 81–93.

Wainer, H., Groves, C., & Lono, M. (1978, August). *Some experiments in graphical comprehension*. Paper presented at Annual Meeting American Statistical Association, San Diego.

Wainer, H., & Reiser, M. (1978). Assessing the efficacy of visual displays.

Wainer, H., & Schacht, S. (1978). Gapping. *Psychometrika, 43,* 203–212.

Wainer, H., & Thissen, D. (1981). Graphical data analysis. In M. R. Rosenzweig & L. W. Porter (Eds.), *Annual review of psychology* (pp. 191–241). Palo Alto, CA: Annual Reviews.

Wainer, H., & Thissen, D. (1986). Computer graphics for the scholar. *Scholarly Communication, 6,*1, 11–16.

Wainer, H., & Thissen, D. (1979). On the robustness of a class of naive estimators. *Applied Psychological Measurements, 3*(4), 543–551.

Wakimoto, K. & Taguri, M. (1978). Constellation graphical method for representing multidimensional data. *Annuals of the Institute of Mathematical Statistics. 30,* 97–104.

Wallis, W. A. (1949). Statistics of the Kinsey Report. *Journal of the American Statistical Association, 44,* 463–484.

Walls, R. C. & Epley, E. A. (1975). *Arkansas health graphics.* Little Rock: University of Arkansas.

Wang, P. C. C. (1978). Graphical representation of multivariate data. New York: Academic Press.

Wilk, M. B. & Gnanadesikan, R. (1968). Probability plotting methods for the analysis of data. *Biometrika, 55,* 1–17.

Wood, F. S. (1973). The use of individual effects and residuals in fitting equations to data. *Technometrics, 15,* 677–695.

14 Uses of Computers in Psychological Research

Russell M. Church
Brown University

A computer is a general-purpose device that can do the jobs of many special-purpose devices, and do them better. In the past, different special-purpose devices were required in each stage of the research process; now computers are often used instead. This use of a single device to do many qualitatively different tasks has greatly facilitated research in psychology. This chapter can only give a brief overview of the uses psychologists have made of computers, but much more detail can be found in a journal of the Psychonomic Society, *Behavior Research Methods, Instruments, & Computers.*

The stages of research include literature search, experimental design, experimental control, data acquisition, data retention, data analysis, development of theory, comparison of data with theory, drafting of figures, preparation of manuscripts, and communication. This chapter describes the uses of computers in a single experimental study of repetitive timing. The computer methods used are compared with other methods currently available, and some speculations are made about changes in the use of computers in psychological research in the next five years.

In research reports, investigators rarely report the details of the computer techniques employed. A single sentence might be included in the apparatus section, such as "An IBM-AT computer controlled the experimental equipment and recorded the responses." Occasionally a software package might be named, but the reader normally has little basis for knowing whether or not computers were used extensively in each stage of the research reported. This is appropriate for a report on the substance of the research. For this purpose, one wants to know the background of the research (the introduction), what was done (the method), what was found (the results), and how the results might be explained (the discus-

TABLE 14.1
Examples of Special-Purpose Devices
for Various Research Activities

Activity	Device
Literature search	Reference books
Experimental design	Book of random numbers
Experimental control	Relay circuits
Data acquisition	Counters
Data retention	File cabinets
Data analysis	Calculator
Development of theory	Books of tables
Comparison of data with theory	Graph paper
Drafting of figures	Lettering sets
Preparation of manuscript	Typewriter
Communication	Telephone

sion). For a reader interested in the substance of the research, it is not important to know how the procedure was implemented, what equipment was used to analyze the data, and so on. For those concerned with research methods, however, it may be important to know the computer hardware and software, and how they were used.

The left column of Table 14.1 lists 11 distinct research activities, and the right column gives an example of a special-purpose device to assist an investigator in conducting each of these activities. Now computers are often used for each of these 11 research activities, replacing the special-purpose devices.

LITERATURE SEARCH

One method of finding previous research on a particular subject is to conduct a year-by-year examination of certain reference books, such as *Science Citation Index, Indicus Medicus,* and *Psychological Abstracts.* The investigator writes down the references and makes notes about them. This has been the standard process, but it is time consuming and prone to error.

For a numbers of years, libraries have been able to offer facilities for key-word searching of journal titles and abstracts from data bases located elsewhere. With this method, because charges are based primarily on the time that the terminal is connected to the data base, browsing is discouraged. Instead people carefully plan a search strategy with keywords selected from a thesaurus, and then execute the search rapidly. If the number of references uncovered are not excessive, request is made for a printed list to be made at the vender's location (because printing locally requires much longer connection time). The printed list normally arrives in a few days by mail. This is an improvement over the use of reference ooks because the search is rapid and the printed report is neat and accurate. But t does not arrive immediately and it is not in computer-readable form so that it annot be easily searched or sorted.

Recently several data bases have become available on compact disc (CD) ead-only optical storage devices. A single removable compact disc may contain 00 megabytes of information, equivalent to about 230,000 typewritten pages. One of the databases (PsychINFO) contains journal references to the psychologi-al literature since 1974. These data are available on disks (PsychLIT) from the American Psychological Association and can be searched with a program such as SilverPlatter. Many libraries subscribe to this service so that, in the library, an nvestigator may use a personal computer (such as an IBM-AT or Macintosh) connected to a CD reader to examine a large number of potentially relevant bstracts. Other databases are also available on compact discs, and Medline is particularly valuable for biological and medical topics. These facilities encour-ge browsing by searching and sorting on various keywords. Eventually, one can elect a reasonable subset of references (and abstracts) to print or download onto loppy disks for further analysis. Each CD ROM/computer station is a single-ser system so as it becomes more popular, competition for the computers in the ibrary makes the system less readily available.

At present it is possible to download a large set of references and then examine it in more detail on another personal computer with database manage-ment software such as PROCITE (for the IBM-AT and Macintosh) or END-NOTE and ENDLINK (for the Macintosh). The main problem is to handle the somewhat idiosyncratic field structures that exist in various data bases. These are ll standard text files, so the format can always be examined (and changed as eeded) with a word-processing program.

Improvements in computer access to the psychological research literature can mprove scholarship in the field. With the rapid increase in the number of ournals and the volume of relevant articles, many researchers are concerned that hey are unable to keep up with the literature. If access is difficult, costly, time consuming, or incomplete, many investigators will proceed without a clear knowledge about what is already known. If access is easy, inexpensive, rapid, nd complete, good scholarship will become routine. Literature searches proba-ly will be greatly improved in the next few years. With local area networks, ppropriate communication software, and a CD-ROM carousel, in many organi-ations it is possible to conduct literature searches from one's desk, not just at the ibrary. The ideal is for entire articles (not just references and abstracts) to be vailable. This poses no particular technical difficulties, but it would require najor cooperation between government agencies, research libraries, and scien-ific societies to organize such an effort.

Although the journal literature is generally much more important than mono-graphs to most psychological investigators, on-line catalogs of books are becom-ng standard in many libraries so that an investigator may readily obtain information about the availability and location of a book either in one's own library or in other libraries.

EXPERIMENTAL DESIGN

The design of an experiment consists of the selection of variables of interest and a decision of what to do about each of them. Some variables may be controlled (that is, held constant), whereas others may be varied. With respect to any pair of variables that are varied, there are three possibilities: They may be counterbalanced, randomized, or confounded. Confounding may be partial or complete.

The main value of a computer in experimental design is in the implementation of randomization. For small problems, such as the random partition of 20 subjects into two groups of 10 subjects each, the use of a standard table of random numbers is suitable (Rand Corporation, 1955). But for large problems, such as the presentation of the opportunity for food at random waiting times with a mean of 1 minute during a 3-hour session of 10 rats, the use of a computer is a major convenience. The essence of the use of computers for this purpose is the pseudorandom number generator, an iterative equation that generates a sequence of numbers that appear to be equally probable and independent with a very long period between repetitions of the sequence (Knuth, 1973). Such a particular uniform distribution can be readily transformed into other uniform distributions and distributions of different shapes. (The normal and exponential are especially useful.)

Some random number generators supplied with application programs are easily shown to have systematic biases by standard chi-square tests of goodness of fit. For research purposes, investigators should use only random number generators that have been thoroughly tested. The investigator probably should perform some additional checks to verify that the implementation is correct and, if necessary, a defective random generator should be replaced with one that meets various tests for systematic biases. Standard textbooks on algorithms and books with algorithms implemented in various languages provide the necessary information (Press, Flannery, Teukolsky, & Vetterling, 1986). When a random generator is selected, its output should be used as is. There is no way to know either the direction or the amount of bias if an investigator sometimes changes the assignment of subjects or the time of occurrence of an event in an attempt to make it subjectively "more random."

EXPERIMENTAL CONTROL

Prior to the mid-1960s, the computer was primarily used by psychologists for data analysis. The development of the LINC computer provided a new perspective (Clark & Molnar, 1964). The computer was seen as a laboratory instrument, primarily for control of experiments and data acquisition, but also for data storage, data analysis, development of theory, and comparison of data with theory.

In the 1970s and 1980s the minicomputer became more and more widely used as a laboratory computer. Many of these were from Digital Equipment Corporation (particularly the PDP-8 and PDP-11 series). The microcomputers, especially IBM and clones, have now largely replaced minicomputers in many laboratories. They provide adequate power for most applications and both hardware and software are less expensive and easily available.

Figure 14.1 shows the procedure of a repetitive tapping task. A tone occurs at a regular interstimulus interval (ISI), and a person attempts to tap in synchrony with the stimulus. The interresponse intervals (IRI) are recorded to the nearest millisecond. In one experiment, a subject pressed a microswitch in synchrony with a 50-ms tone that occurred at an interstimulus interval of 500 ms (Fig. 14.1). There were 12 2-m periods with the periodic tones, separated by 30-s periods of rest. (These data and the analysis of them come from Church, Broadbent, & Gibbon, in press.).

This is a simple procedure to implement either with special purpose equipment or a computer. We used an IBM-AT computer with a Metrobyte board to control an oscillator output (the tone), to record input (the response), and for timing. A short Pascal program controlled the experimental procedure. For more complex stimuli, such as speech or pictures, the use of computer-generated stimuli has permitted far greater specification and control than would be possible with special-purpose devices (such as a tape recorder, tachistoscope, or slide projector).

Many experimental procedures are much more complex than the one used for

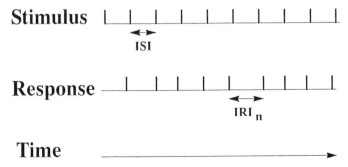

FIG. 14.1.   Procedure for repetitive tapping experiment. Stimuli were presented at a fixed interstimulus interval (ISI) and the subject attempted to tap synchonously. The successive interresponse intervals (IRI_n) are recorded.

repetitive tapping. For example, we often need to test 10 subjects simultaneously and asynchronously and to modify the conditions on the basis of the performance of a subject. For this we have prepared a general-purpose control language that automatically handles all processes that are always done (such as storing time marked input and output events) but permits the user to specify the experimental procedure itself. It is an analyzable system that provides any degree of temporal accuracy within the capabilities of the hardware (Maksik & Church, 1992). Various commercial applications are also available for experimental control, usually combined with hardware and data analysis programs.

There are several advantages of a computer over specialized hardware circuits for control of experiments:

1. Ease of modification. It takes substantial time to set up and check a special purpose control apparatus that is set up for a particular experiment. Thus, there is justifiable reluctance to change the apparatus to conduct another experiment if there may be some further use of the present configuration. With a computer, all data acquisition programs can be saved indefinitely so that the procedure used in a previous experiment can be repeated whenever it is scientifically desirable to do so. Thus, different experiments can be performed in the same day using the computer control apparatus.

2. Reliability. After a computer program has been properly checked, failures are exceedingly rare. With special-purpose equipment, a contact can fail, a wire can be dislodged, and so on. The computer program itself serves as a permanent and accurate record of the procedure actually implemented (and appropriate documentation facilitates the reading of this record). Although a wiring diagram of a relay circuit can be kept permanently, the wiring diagram may not accurately represent where the wires are located.

3. Space. The necessary computer equipment to control experiments normally occupies much less space than that required by alternative devices.

4. Necessity. For some purposes, such as rapid interactive control, complex stimulus displays, very accurate timing of multiple events, a computer may be the only reasonable equipment that can accomplish the task.

In the next 5 years, the standard microprocessor used in the psychological laboratory will probably be faster, more powerful, and cheaper. A single microprocessor can be used for many subjects independently with any time-critical event providing an interrupt signal to the computer. Alternatively, separate microprocessors can be devoted to each subject, perhaps networked to a central computer with more capacity for program development and data storage. A standard experimental control and data acquisition application may be developed that is hardware independent and separate from data analysis applications. This would provide the investigator with the flexibility to choose an appropriate combination of programs for experimental control, data acquisition, and data analysis.

Portable computers will undoubtedly be more widely used because they have adequate power for most purposes, their prices are decreasing, and they permit a laboratory to be set up temporarily where it is convenient for the subjects to be (at a hospital, home, or wherever).

DATA ACQUISITION

The raw data from a psychological experiment consists of a description of which input or output line was activated (and, in the case of analog variables, the value on this line), and the time of its activation. For most purposes, millisecond accuracy is sufficient, and the raw data can be recorded as a list of time-coded events. It is also highly desirable to document, with these data, the date and time of the experiment, the subject, the experimenter, and the program used to implement the procedure.

In the experiment shown in Fig. 14.1, a record was required of the time of occurrence of each stimulus and each response. With a standard interfacing board on an IBM-AT computer, it is straightforward to write a program to record a code for each event (stimulus or response) and its time of occurrence to the nearest millisecond. If electromechanical devices had been used instead, the times might be recorded by a printing counter. But this would be somewhat less accurate and, most critically, the data would be in an inconvenient form for subsequent analysis because the printed times cannot be directly used by a computer for data analysis.

Many experiments require the acquisition of data at very fast rates, the data may come from many sources (subjects or devices), and there may be a great deal of data in a single experiment. It is rare that these requirements strain the capacity of a standard laboratory computer.

DATA RETENTION

The raw data from an experiment can easily be retained for long periods of time. The standard media for long-term storage are magnetic tapes on reels and cartridges, floppy disks, and removable hard disks. Floppy disks are used most frequently; removable optical disks are becoming a reasonable choice for inexpensive, secure storage of large amounts of data. There is always the possibility of loss of data through accident, theft, media defect, normal wear, and so forth, thus it is essential that a backup copy be maintained in a different location. Considerable space can be saved by some data compression scheme, but many investigators save data in standard text form because it can be immediately read by most applications programs. Some investigators also keep a printed copy of the raw data, because this is a form that is particularly easy to browse.

The major purpose of data retention is to be able to perform subsequent analyses, but occasionally the data collected in one laboratory may be particularly useful to an investigator in another laboratory. For such archiving purposes considerable attention must be made to thorough documentation. This effort should be undertaken when a standard experimental format is used for a long period of time, the value of the data to others is considerable, and the cost of replication is excessive. The major test of the quality of the data is the ability of others to replicate the results independently following the recipes in the method section of a published report.

The standard amount of storage will undoubtedly continue to increase. Psychologists will increasingly use very large data bases, share data with others, and perform much more thorough data analyses on large data bases.

DATA ANALYSIS

In the 1950s psychologists used computers primarily for data analysis. A large organization, such as a university, would support a mainframe computer for many purposes (such as research, accounting, and education) and investigators could bring data and programs to be run in batch mode. A printout of the results would be available at the computer center in a few hours, but the analysis would have to be redone if there were any errors in the program, even a single misspelled word. In the 1960s the availability of the timeshared mainframe greatly facilitated data analysis. The investigator could work at a terminal in the psychological laboratory remote from the computer, get immediate feedback from program errors so that they could be corrected quickly, and the results of the analysis would be available at the terminal.

Now the general availability of personal computers and statistical packages has made it unnecessary for investigators to depend on central computer facilities. Figure 14.2 shows the probability of a response in the tapping experiment in each 5-ms interresponse interval as a function of the interresponse interval. The probability is near zero until about 450 ms, rises to a maximum near the interstimulus interval (500 ms), and then falls in a fairly symmetrical manner to near zero at about 550 ms. The calculation of such a frequency distribution is straightforward with a computer and an appropriate language or application program. The raw data consists of a list of times, so the interresponse intervals are differences between successive response times. A programming language (such as C, Pascal, or BASIC) can be used to count the number of interresponse intervals within successive 5-ms blocks. Alternatively, the successive response times (in text format) can be transferred to an application program for the same purpose. Spreadsheets (such as EXCEL, LOTUS, and QUATTRO), statistics programs

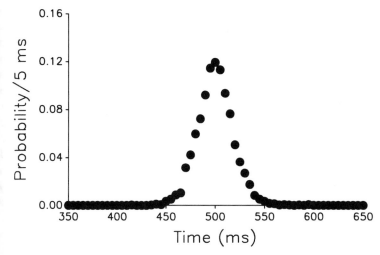

FIG. 14.2. Results of a repetitive tapping experiment with a 500 ms ISI. The probability of a response (in 5-ms bins) for one subject as a function of time since the last stimulus.

uch as STATVIEW+, SYSTAT), or calculation programs (such as MATLAB) e all useful. A mathematics programing system (such as Mathematica) can be ;ed effectively for data analysis, theory development, and other stages of the search process. Unless speed of analysis is a primary consideration, an applica-on program should normally be used for data analysis. The program is less kely to be in error, and the attached graphics permit the investigator to visualize e results. For exploratory purposes, a spreadsheet is particularly useful because requires that the investigator examine each of the steps of a complex calcula-on that later can be compared to the output of a statistical program.

Of course, for the repetitive tapping data, a simple histogram could have been llculated without a computer, although it would have taken much longer to mplete because there were over 2,500 data points. Modern electronic calcula-rs are superior to the mechanical rotary calculators used previously, but any alysis is tedious and prone to error if extensive data must be entered by hand, pecially if data must be entered several times. With analysis application pro-ams, it is possible to explore the data much more deeply, examining the effect various transformations and combinations of variables.

In some cases, the best computer to use for the analysis of data may not be the me one used for the acquisition and retention of data. This is not a problem if e data are in a format that can readily be transferred between computers and terpreted by the applications program. At present, ASCII text format is the ost general and serves the purpose of providing compatibility of data between mputer systems.

In the next 5 years, data analysis programs are likely to improve with respec to ease of use and versatility but, already, they are among the most evolved of th programs available for various stages of the research process.

DEVELOPMENT OF THEORY

In the development of general theories of performance, the computer has becom the major metaphor. One task for investigators of artificial intelligence is t program computers to act in a manner that, if done by a person, would be calle "intelligent." Many of these investigators have taken an engineering approach t the problem and attempt to develop optimal designs to accomplish well-specifie goals even if the methods employed are very different from those used by people The very successful chess-playing programs are good examples because they us massive, rapid search techniques beyond the capability of human subjects wh achieve similar levels of performance by pattern analyses currently beyond th capability of the computer programs. Some investigators, impressed by the abili ty of humans to perform some tasks that are still quite difficult for computers such as complex visual pattern recognition, attempt to design computer program that may duplicate the processes used by humans. This approach enriches psy chological theory by making it explicit and testable.

Beginning with the influential analysis of Broadbent (1958), it has becom conventional to consider the organism as a series of interconnected, intervenin; variables with a physical stimulus as input and a motor response (or othe physiological response) output. The intervening variables consist of sensory perceptual, and memory storage units, and the transformation rules consist c filters and other devices. This kind of information-processing model has becom very useful and it is directly related to the standard serial computer.

More recently it is becoming conventional to consider the organism as a set o converging parallel connections with a physical stimulus as input and a moto response (or other physiological response) output. The intervening variable consist of the representation of the stimulus and the representation of the memo ry, and the transformation rules consist of those involved in the modification an utilization of connection weights between various processing nodes. This kind c connectionist model (Rumelhart, McClelland, & the PDP Group, 1986) ha become very useful and is directly related to developments in parallel computer in which many independent computations can be simultaneously performed

In addition to these general theoretical orientations, it is necessary to specif in any particular experiment, the specific theory that transforms the measure input stimulus into the measured output response. One proposal for repetitiv tapping that has received considerable empirical support is the Wing Kristofferson (Wing, 1980) proposal that there are two independent processe (clock and motor), and the clock drives the motor process. In order to fit the forr

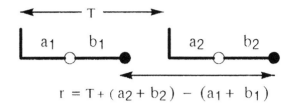

$$r = T + (a_2 + b_2) - (a_1 + b_1)$$

FIG. 14.3. Theoretical process model. An internal clock is assumed to have a fixed interval (T) between pulses, and each pulse is assumed to generate an event (open circle) at the end of an exponentially distributed waiting time (a) that generates a response (solid circle) at the end of a second exponentially distributed waiting time. If each of these times is independent, the interval between successive responses (r) is distributed as the difference between two generalized gamma distributions of order two.

of the interresponse interval distribution, the Tau-Gamma hypothesis, was proposed.

Figure 14.3 shows a process that might generate the observed interresponse intervals. It assumes that there is an oscillator with a fixed time interval (T) between pulses. Each pulse of the oscillator is assumed to generate a random waiting time, an exponentially distributed variable with single constant (a) that defines the instantaneous probability of occurrence of an internal event (the open circle). This internal event is assumed to generate a second random waiting time, another exponentially distributed variable with a single constant (b) that defines the instantaneous probability of a response (the closed circles). Each of the times is assumed to be independent of the others.

The simple model diagrammed in Fig. 14.3 provides explicit predictions about the form of the expected probability of interresponse times. This is shown in Fig. 14.4. The parameters of the distribution are the mean (which will be equal to T), and the decay constant for the two exponential functions (corresponding to a and b). The values of the parameters used in this figure are just one of many that could have been used—they are the values that subsequently were found to best fit the data.

There are two ways to derive the consequences of the process shown in Fig. 14.3: simulation and explicit solution. Simulation normally requires so many calculations that a computer is essential, and most simulations are written in a programming language, such as C, Pascal, or BASIC. For the process shown in Fig. 14.3, one writes a short program to choose a random waiting time with one mean (a) and then a second random waiting time with another mean (b), calculates the sum of these two times plus T and stores this value. After a large number of these values have been calculated and recorded (at least a thousand) the distribution can be examined graphically. Replication of the process, with a

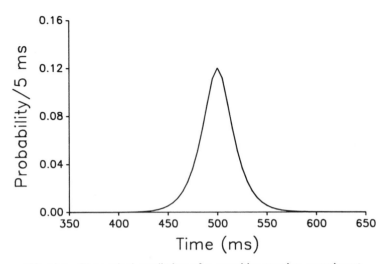

FIG. 14.4. Theoretical prediction of a repetitive tapping experiment
with 500 ms ISI. The probability of a response (in 5-ms bins) is shown
as a function of time since the last stimulus.

different starting seed for the random number generator, can be conducted to
determine the reliability of the result. For more complicated theories, efficient
subprograms that implement well-established algorithms are available (Press,
Flannery, Teukolsky, & Vetterling, 1986). As an alternative to a general programming language, applications specifically designed for simulation (such as
STELLA or EXTEND on the Macintosh) may be used.

Simulation provides an excellent approximation of the correct distribution,
but it is not completely satisfying because it is not exact, the fitting of models
with many parameters is very time consuming because a separate simulation
must be done for each combination of parameter values, and the way that each
parameter affects the outcome may not be clear. The explicit solution may be
guided by the simulated result but, at present, the process of deriving it has not
received other help from computers.

COMPARISON OF THEORY TO DATA

For the comparison of theory and data, it is necessary to search the values of the
parameters of the theory to maximize the correspondence of theory and data.
Figure 14.5 shows the comparison of the best Tau-Gamma function to the data.

For such a comparison, it is necessary to specify the range of parameter values
to be considered, the resolution to be considered and the measure of goodness of
fit. Normally, the analyst seeks to minimize the sum of squares of the deviation

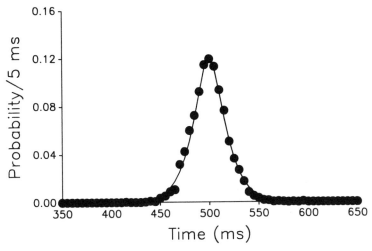

FIG. 14.5. Comparison of data and theory. The results of a repetitive tapping experiment with 500 ms ISI (Fig. 14.2) are compared with the theoretical prediction (Fig. 14.4).

of the data from the theory (the least squares criterion). Finally, the search method must be specified. When feasible, exhaustive searches probably should be employed, but thoughtful use of hill-climbing techniques usually produce equivalent results. Especially when theory accounts for a high percentage of the variance in the data, as in the present case, it is desirable to examine the residuals (differences between data and theory) for indications of further structure that may reveal a need to modify the model. The theory can be considered complete only if the residuals are random (Tukey, 1977). The probability that a given residual is above the median should be independent of the probability that the previous residual was above the median. If there is evidence of systematic deviations in the residuals, the theory does not fit the data, regardless of the percentage of variance accounted for.

The comparison of theory and data can either be done with a programming language or with a spreadsheet. The use of a spreadsheet for this purpose is particularly convenient. The first column contains the time values, the second contains the data, the third column contains the equation for the theory, and the fourth contains the squared residuals. The sum of squared residuals can serve as a measure of goodness of fit, and the aim is to minimize this value. If the parameters of the equation refer to a few specific cells, the analyst merely needs to type values into these cells and observe the measure of goodness of fit and/or observe the pair of functions (data and theory) that can be automatically redrawn on the screen whenever a value is changed.

PREPARATION OF FIGURES

Figures are used for two very different purposes: for discovery and for communication. When the purpose is discovery, figures are closely related to data analysis, theory development, and comparison of data with theory; when the purpose is communication, they are closely related to manuscript preparation.

Figures for Discovery

The major value of graphs in psychological research is as an aide to discovery of regularities (Chambers, Cleveland, Kleiner, & Tukey, 1983). The graphs associated with spreadsheets and statistics applications are often satisfactory for this purpose, but the graphical features of programs for exploratory data analysis facilitate the generation of many useful plots. The main aim is to get rapid visualization of measures of each variable singly and of the relationships among measures. Speed and ease of use are critical, but details of appearance are not.

Figures for Communication

In the preparation of a results section of a manuscript, it is often useful to start with rough drafts of the figures. They provide an outline of the story to be told. Spreadsheet programs (such as EXCEL, LOTUS, and QUATTRO) provide easy to-use business graphics that are directly connected to the values in the spreadsheet. If a standard format is used, templates can be saved on which to put new data. If a particularly complex sequence of commands is necessary to obtain a particular format, a Macro sheet can be prepared that can be run when the format is required.

For final figures to be used in publications, a graphics program designed to produce publication quality graphics (such as SigmaPlot) should be used that produces graphics on a pen plotter or laser printer. The data can be transferred directly from the values (in text mode) used for the graphs from the spreadsheet program. The format of the final figure should be carefully selected for appearance, legibility, consistency and, most importantly, for the information conveyed (Tufte, 1983).

For graphical representation of procedures (such as Fig. 14.1) and models (such as Fig. 14.3), various application programs are available. These figures were drawn with the graphical section of the word processor used in the preparation of this manuscript (INTERLEAF on an IBM-RT), but there are many alternatives such as the popular MACDRAW for Macintosh computers. Laser printers provide excellent printed output, but high-density dot matrix printers now also produce satisfactory output.

Previously, two methods for preparing final drafts of figures were available: pen and ink, or letters and symbols that can be pasted. With pen and ink there was increasing concern of making an error as the figure neared completion, but he use of paste-down letters was slow. With either method, minor adjustments, such as a change of the symbols used for the data points or a rescaling of one of he axes, often required that the entire figure be redone. In contrast, computer-generated graphs can be revised over and over until their format is perfected.

PREPARATION OF MANUSCRIPT

The original idea of hackers that a mainframe computer could serve as the world's most expensive typewriter may have started out as an amusement, but it has become the dominant use of computers on college campuses, businesses, and elsewhere. The first major use of computers by psychologists was for the analysis of data, and the second major use was for writing. This was not possible when the mainframe computers were used in batch mode, but when timesharing became generally available, computers were used extensively for writing. The main problem was that response time was often poor, so that one had to learn to type slowly. When minicomputers became available in psychological laboratories, word-processing programs were used on them for the preparation of manuscripts, as well as for editing programs. Now the use of microcomputers for word processing is routine. For this purpose there are many excellent programs, such as WORD for the IBM-AT and Macintosh, and the basis for choice should be primarily availability or familiarity rather than inherent superiority. Most word processors come with various additional utilities, such as outlining facilities and spelling checkers.

The superiority of word processors over previous methods is enormous. In the preparation of a manuscript, some individuals use pen and ink; others use dictating machines, and others use typewriters. By using a word-processing system that permits numerous revisions, manuscripts may be prepared more quickly, they contain fewer typographical errors, and they are clearer. The final output device may be a dot matrix printer, and these can now have excellent resolution. But the office standard has become the laser printer.

COMMUNICATION

When different computer systems are used in the same laboratory, it is highly desirable that they be able to communicate with each other. The results of a literature search should be available to the word processor used for the preparation of the manuscript; the stored data must be available to the data analysis programs, and so forth. Text data can be readily transferred between computers with direct connections or by moderns and appropriate communication software (such as KERMIT or RED RYDER), or by use of a storage medium that several different computers can use.

Local area networks are becoming increasingly available for communication between computers in one laboratory and in nearby facilities. Such network make it possible to share expensive devices (such as laser printers on a pri server) and infrequently used software (with a file server). Interconnections the local area networks into institutionwide networks are also becoming increa ingly available and provide additional benefits. It provides the investigator wi many mainframe capabilities from the office or laboratory, and electronic ma provides a simple, rapid, inexpensive, and nonobtrusive means of communica tion with colleagues anywhere in the world. Although electronic mail now co sists mostly of messages typed on a keyboard of a computer or terminal ar messages read on a screen, large text documents can be sent from one comput to another for manipulation by various application programs (such as wo processors and spreadsheets).

Although some journals are prepared to accept manuscripts in computer read able form, the possibilities of electronic publishing are now under active discu sion (Gardner, 1990).

CONCLUSIONS AND SPECULATIONS

In this case study, and in most of my research, computers served in place special-purpose devices. They served as effective substitutes for reference book books of random numbers, relay circuits, banks of counters, file cabinet calculators, books of tables, graph paper, lettering sets, typewriters, and tel phones. Computers were used at every stage of the project: introduction, meth od, results, and discussion, and in the preparation of the research report.

All of the applications of computers to the research process that have bee described are used widely and routinely; none of them was required for th success of the research. Still, the impact of the computer on the research w enormous. Our experience is not atypical. In this case study and, perhaps in all my research, the computer facilitated the work on some quantitative dimensio (e.g., increase in speed, decrease in errors). A sufficiently large quantitativ improvement, however, leads to a qualitative change, because some projects th would not have been undertaken were successfully completed.

Although it might be desirable for a single computer to handle all stages of th research process, for various reasons different computers are often used. Som decisions are made by the library, others by a departmental users group, an others by a single laboratory so that uniformity cannot be guaranteed. It mig not even be desirable given that a particular computer or software applicatio may be especially appropriate for a particular stage of the research process.

Computer hardware has been becoming cheaper, faster, and more powerf and this trend will undoubtedly continue. The power of the standard IBM an Macintosh office computers now approximates the power expected of advance workstations only a few years ago. They have ample power, and extensive wel written software is readily available at low prices, thus IBM and Macintosh microcomputers (and equivalents from other manufacturers) will probably remain the standard computers in psychological research. Certain specialized research topics may require some of the special features of more expensive computers, but this should be explicitly justified. Less expensive computers may occasionally be used for specific tasks because they, too, have enormous power, but the huge software base for the IBM and Macintosh computers will undoubtedly keep them (and equivalents) as the typical ones in psychological laboratories. The major features that distinguished IBM computers (with an open architecture) from Macintosh computers (with a friendly graphical interface) are no longer major factors because each is adopting the successful features of the other. The lower price, somewhat easier interfacing standards, and greater familiarity will undoubtedly maintain the IBM computers and clones as the most frequent ones in psychological laboratories; the excellent graphics capabilities, fine routines available on the read-only memory (ROM), consistent user interface, and some applications programs available only on the Macintosh will continue to make it the computer of choice for many psychologists.

Although a few applications have become very standard, such as the word processor and the spreadsheet, most applications will remain specialized. This reflects the different needs of various people for types of graphics and types of data analysis. Whether or not new types of applications will be identified is impossible to predict, but it is likely that some creative use will be made of symbolic processing (such as programs like Mathematica).

A comparison of the uses of computers in psychology described in 1983 with those described here indicates that: (a) Computers were used in all aspects of the research process in 1982 and continue to be so used now; (b) the typical computer hardware has changed from minicomputers to microprocessors, with substantial increases in power, speed, and capacity and substantial decrease in cost and frequency of repair; and (c) the development of excellent software applications for many stages of the research process (particularly data analysis, preparation of figures, and preparation of manuscripts) has greatly facilitated the research process.

ACKNOWLEDGMENTS

This chapter is based on a Presidential Address to the Society for Computers in Psychology in 1982 that was published as R. M. Church (1983). The influence of computers on psychological research: A case study, *Behavior Research Methods & Instrumentation, 15,* 117–126. Many sections of that article are reproduced here by permission of Psychonomic Society, Inc. Other sections of this chapter have been revised as necessary to reflect changes in usage since that time.

REFERENCES

Broadbent, D. E. (1958). *Perception and communication.* New York: Pergamon.

Chambers, J. M., Cleveland, W. S., Kleiner, B., & Tukey, P. A. (1983). *Graphical methods fo data analysis.* Belmont, CA: Wadsworth.

Church, R. M. (1983). The influence of computers on psychological research: A case study. *Be havior Research Methods & Instrumentation, 15,* 117–126.

Church, R. M., Broadbent, H. A., & Gibbon, J. (in press). Biological and psychological descrip tion of an internal clock. In I. A. Gormezano & E. A. Wasserman (Eds.), *Learning and memory The behavioral and biological substrates.* Hillsdale NJ: Lawrence Erlbaum Associates.

Clark, W. A., & Molnar, C. E. (1964). The LINC: A description of the laboratory instrumer computer. *Annals of the New York Academy of Science, 115,* 653–668.

Gardner, W. (1990). The electronic archive: Scientific publishing for the 1990s. *Psychologica Science, 1,* 333–341.

Knuth, D. (1973). *The art of computer programming. Vol. 2: Seminumerical algorithms* (2nd ed. Reading, MA: Addison-Wesley.

Maksik, Y., & Church, R. M. (1992). A system for automatically analyzing and connecting real-tim experiment control programs. *Behavior Research Methods, Instruments & Computers, 24,* 140–14€

Press, W. H., Flannery, B. P., Teukolsky, S. A., & Vetterling, W. T. (1986). *Numerical recipes The art of scientific computing.* Cambridge: Cambridge University Press.

Rand Corporation (1955). *A million random digits with 100,000 normal deviates.* New York: Fre Press.

Rumelhart, D. E., McClelland, J. L., & the PDP Group (1986). *Parallel distributed processing Vol. 1: Foundations.* Cambridge, MA: MIT Press.

Tufte, E. R. (1983). *The visual display of quantitative information.* Chesire, CT: Graphics Press

Tukey, J. W. (1977). *Exploratory data analysis.* Reading, MA: Addison-Wesley.

Wing, A. M. (1980). The long and short of timing in response sequences. In G. E. Stelmach & J Requin (Eds.), *Tutorials in motor behaviour.* Amsterdam: North-Holland.

15

Computer Simulation: Some Remarks on Theory in Psychology[1]

Geoffrey R. Loftus
University of Washington

Almost a decade ago, Russell Church delivered the Presidential Address to the Society for Computers in Psychology (Church, 1983). In this address, Church presented an excellent summary of the usefulness and pervasiveness of computers in all phases of psychological research. He started with the literature search, proceeded through the phases of experimental control, recording of results, storage of data, analysis of results, development of theory, comparison of theory with data, preparation of figures, and ended with the processing of the manuscript. For each of these phases, Church compared the tedium of the precomputer technique with the ease and efficiency of the corresponding postcomputer technique. Presented in this way, the enormous facilitative impact of the computer on our research endeavors was breathtaking: Indeed, as Church's arguments unfolded, it became difficult to imagine how scientific research ever got done in those bygone days before there were computers.

Today, as the computer revolution accelerates, this general view has become yet more ingrained, and it is virtually impossible to envision scientific research carried out in any sort of computerless environment. My own laboratory, for example, is computerized to a degree that far exceeds Church's fantasies (Stoddard & Loftus, 1988).

Does this mean, however, that more computerization is always better in all phases of research in the social sciences? I argue in this chapter that the answer is, "not necessarily." In particular, there is a danger that letting the computer do our thinking—as opposed to our busy work—for us can potentially deprive the scientific enterprise of the creative and insightful thinking that is the sine qua non of scientific progress.

Consider, as an example, the use of the computer in statistical analysis of

---

[1]This chapter is a slight revision of Loftus (1985).

data. Over years of reviewing manuscripts, I have developed the nervous conviction that there is too much emphasis on pouring raw data into statistical packages such as SPSS or BMD, and simply accepting whatever numbers emerged—chisquares, F ratios, whatever—as the conclusion, without further ado. This problem (described in greater detail by Loftus, 1991) issues, in my opinion, from researchers adopting an ultracookbook approach to statistical analysis wherein they make binary conclusions (reject H_0 or do not reject H_0) without understanding the subtleties of the mathematical models that underlie the conclusions (or even that the conclusions depend on a model to begin with). This does not seem like a very imaginative or fruitful way to go about trying to figure out what our data are trying to say to us. To paraphrase Freedman (1983), it seems that off-the-shelf statistical analysis programs produce off-the-shelf conclusions.

In this chapter, I wish to pick up on this theme. I focus on the use of the computer as a theoretical tool—in particular, on the use of computers in the construction of simulation models of mind and behavior. Computer simulation models, along with their close cousins, artificial intelligence programs, are becoming an increasingly popular way instantiating theory in the social sciences, especially in psychology and in economics. I believe that sometimes in the social sciences, as in the natural sciences, computer simulation is an endeavor that is entirely appropriate and scientifically productive. Later, I return to describe one such simulation. But often, I believe that computer simulation in the social sciences is not so useful.

Computer simulation is undeniably lots of fun—but I argue that it has at least three drawbacks. First, computer simulation promotes the building of complex theories, which are really no more than restatements of the complex behavior that the simulation is designed to simulate. Second, computer simulation removes the incentive to do the hard conceptual work necessary to produce simple, elegant theories. Third, computer simulation promotes accounting for data rather than searching for truth. Indeed, it may promote the belief that I find scientifically distasteful and unesthetic, that there is really no truth to be found at all.

THE HISTORICAL APPROACH

I want to illustrate these points using an example from one of the oldest of the natural sciences, astronomy. In so doing, I provide a little nutshell history of theory in astronomy.

I have chosen a historical approach because I believe it provides perspective. It allows us to draw back—to pull ourselves out of the day-to-day activities involved in the research enterprise and to view a scientific problem through a wide-angle lens. Psychology is, as the cliché goes, a young science. This youth provides us with a convenient excuse when we confront the occasional confusion and seeming directionlessness of the field. But because psychology is young we, as psychologists, can perhaps learn some lessons by using this historical approach. We can look at what happened to other sciences when they were in the same developmental stage as psychology is now, and we can see how they dealt with similar problems. We can see not only what the solutions to these problems turned out to be—but we can imagine what the solutions might have been, had circumstances been a little different. Perhaps with this perspective, we can anticipate some of the potential traps and cul-de-sacs that our discipline is headed for before it's too late to avoid them.

Observational Origins of Astronomy

So let's first turn the clock back to prebiblical times, when people first started trying to figure out the heavenly system. In hindsight, it all seems so simple. Most of us have a pretty good image in our heads at least of the nine planets revolving around the sun, set against some backdrop of fixed stars. But in the beginning, it must have seemed unbelievably complex. Freedman (1983) made this point very nicely:

> Some problems in the natural sciences now look very clean and simple, but only because of the analytic work that has been done. To appreciate this point, imagine trying to figure out the orbit of Mars for yourself. You go out on a clear night, look up in the sky, and see thousands of points of light. Which one is Mars? To start closer to the beginning, which one are planets and which are stars? Continuing to watch for several hours might only confuse matters further: for the pattern of stars will gradually change as the night wears on. Even recognizing this change depends on prior knowledge; for it is hard to see the shifting pattern of the stars without using the constellations. (p. 11)

That was the beginning. Things must have seemed pretty complicated. Over the centuries, however, theories began to emerge that, in one way or another, began to impose some order on this celestial confusion. Some of these theories were simple and fanciful, and they accounted for the data only in the crudest, qualitative ways. Other theories—notably that of the Egyptian astronomer Ptolemy—were much more complex, but represented serious attempts to account for what was observed. Indeed, Ptolemy's system, although belittled now for being earth-centered rather than sun-centered, accounted for the extant astronomical data quite well. It encapsulated the general view of the universe at the time, and it also served tolerably for practical applications such as compilation of the planetary position tables that were used by generations of seafarers as they navigated the ancient Mediterranean trade routes.

Epicycle Madness

We now move forward several millennia to the mid-1500s, by which time enormous strides had been made in cosmological theory development. The major conceptual achievement of the era was the heliocentric model, conceived by the

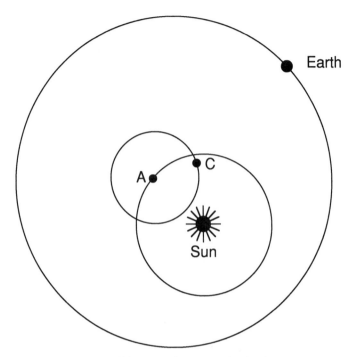

FIG. 15.1.   A system of epicycles.

Polish cleric, Nicholas Copernicus, and published in 1543. In Copernican theory
the sun was placed more or less in the center of the solar system. This innova-
tion, of course, represented quite a radical departure from the Ptolemaic system
according to which everything revolved around the earth.

That was the good news. The bad news was that, despite the conceptual
advance represented by Copernicus's model, the state of knowledge and theory in
cosmology was still pretty much of a mess. Much of the problem derived from
Copernicus's (and everybody else's) refusal to abandon the ancient Platonic
dictum that any celestial orbit must assume the form of a perfect circle. In
hindsight, we know that this constraint was bound to cause problems, because
planetary orbits are, in fact, ellipses, not circles. But if you were a 16th-century
astronomer, you didn't know that, and you were committed to circles. This
meant that you had to come up with some rather exotic system in order to fit the
data. The system of choice, for both the Ptolemaic and Copernican systems, was
based on epicycles, an example of which is illustrated in Fig. 15.1. Figure 15.1
shows a simplified version of the earth's orbit, according to the Copernican
system. As is evident, the center of the earth's orbit is actually not the sun.
Rather, it is an imaginary point in space (labeled C) somewhere in the general
vicinity of the sun. But this point was not stationary. Instead, it revolved, in

perfect circle, around yet another imaginary point in space (point A), which itself revolved in a perfect circle centered, at last, on the sun. By appropriately arranging these circles, along with their periods of revolution and their phases, it was possible to work things out so that the earth, considered in isolation, wobbled around the sun in more or less of an elliptical orbit.

Of course, this was not the whole story. Copernicus actually needed a few more epicycles for the earth, plus other epicyclical systems for all the other known planets, including the moon. Indeed, Copernicus actually wound up with a system that incorporated 48 epicycles. In contrast Ptolemy's earth-centered systems incorporated, when all was said and done, only 40 epicycles. Copernicus had achieved his conceptual advance at the cost of decreased parsimony. Figure 15.2 shows a partial depiction of the system.

As a psychologist, it's fascinating to read accounts of this period. There is an eerie similarity between the state of cosmology in the 1500s and the state of psychology today. There were lots of isolated bits and pieces of theory to describe various phenomena, all relatively unconnected to one another. The data were haphazard, and were fit by theory in only the loosest kind of way. Discre-

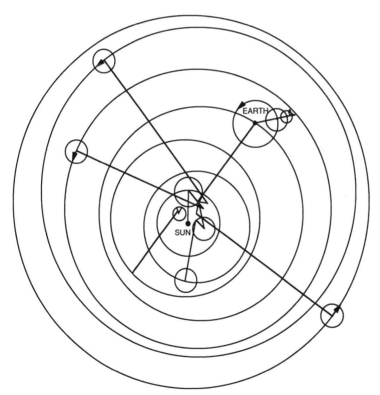

FIG. 15.2.   Part of the Copernican sun-centered model.

pant data presented no problem. Either they were ignored, or the theory could b
tuned and expanded until the offending observations were forced into submis
sion. Epicycles could be moved around, added here, and deleted there. Distance
and angular speeds could be modified. In short, there were lots of parameters i
the system. Substitute "memory" for "universe" and "strength of association" fc
"epicycles" and the resemblance of cosmology to at least one area of psycholog
becomes disconcertingly striking.

There was a kind of angst among 16th-century astronomers about the prospec
of ever coming up with a simple elegant theory of the universe. The genera
notion seemed to prevail that the structure of the universe was just awfull
complicated, and it was hopeless and arrogant to think that it could be describe
in any simple way. An episode involving Georg Rheticus, who was a contempo
rary and disciple of Copernicus, dramatically illustrates the frustration engen
dered by this state of mind.

> When on one occasion he [Rheticus] became perplexed and got stuck in the theory
> of Mars and could no longer see his way out he appealed as a resort to his guardian
> angle as an oracle. The ungracious spirit thereupon seized Rheticus by the hair and
> alternately banged his head against the ceiling then let his body down and crashed it
> against the floor, to which treatment he added the following oracular pronounce-
> ment "These are the motions of Mars." (quoted in Koestler, 1959, p. 160)

As this vignette illustrates, it did not seem that scientists were at all optimistic

And finally, theory was not taken seriously as a reflection of truth. Rather,
was viewed as merely a means of accounting for data. One Andreas Osiander
another of Copernicus's colleagues, forcefully expressed this view on a numbe
of occasions. He wrote, for example, to Copernicus, "For my part I've alway
felt about hypotheses [by which Osiander meant astronomical theory] that the
are not articles of faith but bases of computation, even so if they are false it doe
not matter, provided that they exactly represent the phenomena" (Koestler, 195⁹
p. 167). Osiander wrote in a similar vein to the bedeviled Rheticus, offerin
advice about how to deal with opponents of the Copernican view: "The Aristc
telians and theologians will be easily placated if they are told that several hypotI
eses can be used to explain the same apparent motions; and that the prese
hypotheses are not proposed because they are in reality true, but because they ar
the most convenient to calculate the apparent composite motions" (Koestle
1959, p. 167). And finally, Osiander took it upon himself to write an anonymou
preface to Copernicus's book in which he made his position quite clear: "So far a
hypotheses are concerned, let no one expect anything certain from astronom
which cannot furnish it, lest he accept as the truth ideas conceived for anothe
purpose (i.e., as mere calculating aids) and depart from this study a greater foc
than when he entered it" (Koestler, 1959, p. 167).

Arthur Koestler (1959), in his superb history of cosmology, *The Sleepwalker*

oted that Copernicus himself seemed quite satisfied with this general philoso-
hy of cosmological theory. Koestler wrote,

> He [Copernicus] did believe that the Earth really moved but was impossible for him
> to believe that either the Earth or the planets moved in the matter described in his
> system of epicycles and deferents, which were geometrical fictions. And so long as
> the why and the how of the heavenly motions rested on a purely fictional basis with
> wheels on wheels which the astronomer manipulated with happy unconcern for
> physical reality, he could not object to Osiander's correct statement about the purely
> formal nature of his hypotheses. (Koestler, 1959, p. 171)

In other words, Copernicus did believe in a rough, qualitative version of his
heory. But he didn't believe the details—rather, the details were just inserted
rbitrarily for the purpose of fitting the data.

Later Koestler continued, "The physical nature of the motions, the forces of
ature behind them, were not the astronomer's concern. Whenever necessary, a
ew epicycles were added to the existing machinery of wheels—which did not
1atter much since they were fictional anyway and nobody believed in their
hysical reality" (Koestler, 1959, p. 274).

Kepler's Laws

o this was the state of affairs when Kepler entered the picture. However, Kepler
vas unique in that he could not accept the idea that the purpose of a cosmological
heory was just to account for data. On the contrary, he believed that the uni-
erse, complex though it appeared to be, really and truly operated according to
ome simple scheme. And Kepler took it upon himself to figure that scheme out.
Ie spent 40 years of his life immersed in this endeavor, in the process producing
1e three laws of planetary motion for which he is famous. These laws are:

1. The planets have elliptical orbits with the sun at one focus.
2. A line, connecting a planet to the sun, sweeps out equal areas in equal
   amounts of time.
3. The square of a planet's period of revolution is proportional to the cube of
   its mean distance from the sun.

'hey're really true, these laws—they describe what really goes on.

Kepler's working out of these simple laws was, relative to the theoretical
acophony that preceded them, a monumental achievement. But it was not
rrived at lightly. In the process of formulating his laws, Kepler spent uncount-
ble hours, both in thinking and in tedious computation. He went through enor-
1ous amounts of frustration and lost years exploring blind alleys. But in the end,
: all paid off. As Freedman (1983) succinctly pointed out, "Astronomers still use
Kepler's model. He got it right."

What motivated Kepler in his fanatical search for simple laws? I think two major factors were responsible. First, Kepler had an unyielding belief that the laws were there to be found. I mentioned this earlier and I return to it later. But there was a second factor, not quite as romantic as the first, perhaps, but nonetheless important. This is that the sheer amount of boring computation involved in making predictions from any kind of complex astronomical theory was enough to put almost anyone off. Consider the Copernican system with its 48 epicycles. As one might expect, it was awfully cumbersome to actually use. From a scientific point of view, simply churning out the computations involved in making predictions from theory was impossibly tedious. From a practical point of view, the navigational tables and other practical devices that issued from the theory were filled with errors. Moreover, the theory wasn't stable. It kept getting modified in response to new data and new ideas. And every time it was modified, all the computations had to be cranked out all over again.

So it is not surprising that there would be plenty of motivation to seek simple accurate, and endurable laws. Kepler seemed especially absorbed by this motivation. He did the work and he won the big prize.

Kepler's Computer Simulation

So that's what really happened. Kepler started with a mess and, after 40 years of work, managed to turn it into something simple and elegant.

But as I noted earlier, an advantage of the historical approach is that, in addition to illuminating what really happened, it allows you to speculate about what might have been. So let's now depart into a fantasy world. Suppose Kepler had a computer at his disposal. In this case, the situation might have been a lot different. Kepler could have instantiated any model of the universe that he wanted as a computer simulation, and, as a result, his life could have been a lot easier—he could have had much more time for fun and relaxation. Cranking out the computations necessary to derive predictions and test models would no longer have been a problem, no matter how complex the model. So Mars is not working out quite right according to some new data just in from the observatory. It's necessary to add a new epicycle to Mars' orbit and recompute the predictions? No problem. All Kepler needed to do is to add another loop in the Mars subroutine, let the revised simulation chug away overnight, and there would be the fresh new predictions waiting for him the next morning along with the least squares fit to the data.

The danger that lurks in this situation is, I hope, evident. With a computer Kepler might not have had the incentive to search for simple laws, and they might never have been found. If Kepler had a computer, we might now have a universe in which all the extant data are accounted for almost perfectly—but a universe that is awfully complex. Moreover, it would not occur to us that there might be nything better. Our very conception of the universe, now so simple, would have been much different. We would think of it instead as a set of complicated motions of mysterious points of light in the sky that scientists account for and deal with using some complicated model. The model, in fact, would probably seem more real than the universe itself to anybody who worried about such things.

It turns out that I am not the only person who has these kinds of fantasies. In a paper called "Statistics and the scientific method," Freedman (1983), dealt with specifically with the problems and misuse of regression models and structural equation models in the social sciences. He demonstrated the disadvantages of these models relative to the classic theories of the natural sciences, including Kepler's. Freedman concluded with the following:

> I sometimes have a nightmare about Kepler. Suppose a few of us were transported back in time to the year 1600 and were invited by the emperor Rudolph II to set up an Empirical Department of Statistics in the Court at Prague. Despairing of those circular orbits, Kepler enrolls in our department. We teach him the general linear model, least squares, dummy variables, everything. He goes back to work, fits the best circular orbit for Mars by least squares, puts in a dummy variable for the exceptional observation—and publishes. And that's the end, right there in Prague at the beginning of the 17th century. (p. 23)

It's a chilling thought.

PSYCHOLOGY AND COSMOLOGY

Why have I been writing about Copernicus and Kepler and cosmological theory? I believe that much of today's psychology is, in many respects, similar to the cosmology of the 1500s. Let me review what I consider to be some of the relevant shortcomings of theory in psychology.

Chaos

First, nobody seems to agree on theory. There are different theories for different phenomena, and, in many instances, there are different theories to account for the same phenomena. As Watkins (1981; 1984) pointed out, every psychologist worth his salt has to have a theory of something, and theories have become so personal that they are like toothbrushes. A given theory is used and explored by its owner, and, although occasionally acknowledged, it is not actively used by anyone else. When the owner disappears or loses interest in the theory, the theory dies.

What concurrent theory, instantiated as a computer simulation, will still be in psychology textbooks, centuries down the road?

Complexity

Second, theories are often designed not to explain simple behavior but rather to describe complex behavior. There seems to be an increasing tendency toward the belief that human beings and their behavior are fundamentally complex and there is no way around it. This is seen, for example, in current movement toward ecological validity, wherein it is argued that a psychological phenomenon is not a suitable topic of scientific investigation unless that phenomenon is demonstrated to be an obvious and pervasive part of everyday behavior (e.g., Haber, 1983; Neisser, 1976; but see Banaji & Crowder, 1989; Loftus, 1983, and Uttal, 198. for opposing views). If theories are designed initially to account for complex behavior, it is no wonder that the theories themselves are complex.

A brief clarification may be in order here. No one will deny that complex everyday behavior is interesting and important. However, I would like to emphasize that there is an important difference between (a) designing theories that, from the start, are meant to account for complex behavior and (b) searching for simple laws that can be extended (quite likely using computer simulation) to account for complex behavior. The former (somewhat defeatist) strategy entail abandoning the proposition that there are simple laws to begin with, whereas the latter strategy is a time-honored one that has proved remarkably fruitful in the natural sciences. Later in this chapter, I return to this issue.

Instability

Third, theories in psychology are constantly in flux. It is exceedingly rare that a theory will last long without encountering discrepant data. But it is rarer still that a theory will be abandoned in the face of such adversity. Rather, discrepant data generally lead to a returning or an extension of the theory—to the modern-day equivalent of adding another epicycle or two.

It is disquieting to compare this state of affairs in the social sciences with what happens to theories in the natural sciences when they are faced with discrepant data. Theories in the natural sciences are generally quite stable, and the consequences of discrepant data are pretty dramatic. Kepler himself rejected a theory based on several years of work when new observations showed a discrepancy of 8 minutes of arc between the observed and the predicted orbit of Mars. Eight minutes of arc is not much—about the apparent size of a penny at a distance of 10 yards—but it was clearly greater than the error in the state-of-the-art measuring instruments and, as such, was sufficient to force rejection of the entire theory. Many years later, in the mid-1800s, the French astronomer Leverrier discovered some small anomalies in the predicted orbital path of the planet Uranus. These discrepancies could not be explained unless there was another, as yet undiscovered, planet out there in the void beyond Uranus. There was. It was Neptune. The postulation of another planet might, of course, be viewed as a "returning of the theory." But it was a returning that turned out to be firmly based on reality.

Accounting for Data

And finally, there is typically not the assumption of an underlying truth, an underlying reality in the construction of psychological theory. Instead, like the Copernican model of the solar system, psychological theories seem to be endowed with the implicit understanding that a theory or model is just a device to account for the data. The goal is 99% of the variance.

To illustrate this point a fortiori, I cannot resist relating an anecdote about a computer simulation of short-term memory that I carried out many years ago with a computer science undergraduate whom I call Kim. Kim seemed relatively indifferent to most of her academic work, but for some reason became fanatically interested and involved in this simulation. She would spend night after night at the computer center, poring over her Pascal code, and would appear in my office the next morning to discuss her findings. One day, we were discussing some data from the literature on intrusion and omission errors in a Brown–Peterson task. We had discovered that our simulation logically could not predict data correctly, even qualitatively. Kim's reaction was to announce that the data could not be correct. When I asked her why not, she said, "Because the way short-term memory works is . . . ," and went on to describe the workings of our model. I was amazed. It was not just that Kim had ceased to believe in an underlying reality that our model was simulating. For her, the model itself had become reality.

COMPUTER SIMULATION
IN THE SOCIAL SCIENCES

I talked about the similarities between 20th-century psychology and 16th-century cosmology. However, there is a difference between the two disciplines. We 20th-century psychologists are now equipped with some extremely sophisticated 20th-century research tools for collecting data and constructing theory. Foremost among the theory construction tools is the computer simulation. As should be evident at this point, I believe that computer simulation leads to a potentially serious problem: By making it so easy to construct and test extremely complex models, computer simulation removes much of the motivation to find simple and elegant theories—or even to search for simple kinds of behaviors to make theories of. Adding the degree of theoretical power allowed by computer simulation to a model that is only vaguely conceptualized to begin with is like equipping a covered wagon with a turbojet engine. The fit is just entirely inappropriate.

The other side of the coin is, as I mentioned earlier, that it is great fun to make computer simulation models. You can endow the model with anything you feel like, and you can get the data and the theoretical fit appearing in front of you on the computer screen almost instantaneously. As with video games, you get immediate feedback, and it is incredibly reinforcing. With a little work, the model can always be made to fit the extant data, thereby producing the illusion of success, at least for the moment (cf. Freedman, 1983; Keil, 1984). The whole enterprise becomes an almost irresistible game.

As pointed out to me by my colleague, Walter Schneider, good examples of computer simulation run amuck are found in the field of econometrics. Econometric models combine economic theory with a host of assumptions, along with various types of economic data, in order to forecast some important economic phenomenon, say, energy usage. These models have been criticized for a variety of reasons, ranging from the validity of the assumptions on which they are based, to the quality of the data that go into them, to the ability of their users—often governmental agencies—to mold them in such a way as to obtain predictions that are favorable to their policies, instead of the other way around (e.g., Commoner, 1979; Freedman, Rothberg, & Sutch, 1983).

Most of the criticism that is leveled against economic models can be boiled down to the problem that the models are simply too large, unwieldy and ad hoc to allow unambiguous, trustworthy predictions. They are sufficiently malleable to be able to fit extent data rather well, but they fall apart when asked to forecast the future. I think the reason for this is clear: The models have been constructed more with the idea of accounting for data than of reflecting economic reality.

SHOULD COMPUTERS BE BANNED?

It may seem thus far as if I have painted an unnecessarily gloomy picture of the role of computer simulation in science. Am I being like the ancient naysayers who decried the invention paper as evil because it would eliminate any motivation to memorize, and who then later bemoaned the invention of the printing press because it would spell doom to the art of calligraphy? Do I believe that computer simulation has no legitimate place in the scientific enterprise? Of course not. Despite the dangers I have tried to illustrate, I think there are several very valuable roles that computer simulation can and should play in the social sciences or in any other branch of science. Let me just mention a couple.

Extension of Theory to the Real World

Computer simulation is a superb technique for extending a well-established, durable theory from the domain of the laboratory to the domain of the uncontrolled, disorganized, external world. Wolfram (1984) provided some interesting illustrations. Consider, for example, the path of an electron in a uniform magnetic field. The behavior of an electron is such a situation is well understood and can be well predicted from fundamental principles. However, the path of the electron in some complex, nonuniform field cannot be solved analytically and cannot be predicted at all, except by computer simulation.

I want to reemphasize at this point that the laws governing behavior of electrons in general and electrons in magnetic fields in particular are already well understood. A computer simulation whose purpose is to extend a well-established theory from simple to complex situations is very different from a computer simulation whose purpose is to model the complex situation to begin with without having the theory as a starting point.

Are the examples of these kinds of situations in psychology? I believe that, indeed, there are some very nice examples, particularly in the area of visual science. Consider, to briefly illustrate, an article by Wandell (1984) on the topic of color constancy. The problem that Wandell addressed was: How is it that objects continue to appear to be the same color independently of the spectral composition of the ambient illumination? That is, how is it that an object in two different lighting situations (say, daylight and fluorescent light) reflects light to our eyes consisting of two entirely different spectral compositions and yet is perceived and reported to be the same color.

Wandell began with a very well worked out, very well tested, and very precise theory of visual information processing. This theory dealt with the relationships among entities that are firmly rooted in optics and physiology, such as spectral distributions, number of quanta arriving at the retina, and size of retinal ganglion cell fields. It was only after the theory itself was well worked out, well tested, and widely accepted that it was applied, via computer simulation, to actual scenes whose complexity exceeded the laboratory situations of uniform ambient lighting and sine-wave gratings.

Practical Applications

Sometimes, there is a need for information that ideally requires a theory, but for which no good theory exists. In pre-Keplerian times, for example, maritime navigators needed tables of planetary positions. Such tables were generated by the Ptolemaic or Copernican theories. Tedious to generate, and error-filled though they were, these tables were certainly better than nothing.

Similar situations exist in the domain of psychology. For example, there is a need (or, at any rate, a market) these days for expert systems. An expert system is, of course, a computer program that simulates an expert in some technical field, say, aeronautical engineering. In principal, interested parties can seek advice from the expert system in the same way that they could seek advice from the expert. The initial cost of the expert system is more than that of a human expert, but the subsequent salary is presumably lower.

Ideally, one would produce an expert system by combining a simple, durable theory of human cognition with a suitable knowledge base.[2] That is not possible, of course, because a simple, durable theory of human cognition is not available. But from the standpoint of those who would like to use an expert system, a system based on a mishmash of theory is better than no system at all. Expert systems users are, like the ancient mariners, relatively indifferent to the sources of their practical devices.

CONCLUSIONS

I want to end this chapter with an optimistic note by returning to the mind and motivation of Kepler. Aficionados of Kepler and his work might raise an objection to Kepler's behavior as I portrayed in my fantasy. They might challenge the supposition that Kepler would capitulate to the computer's seductive powers. Such an objection might well be justified. As I said earlier, Kepler was a fanatical believer in the existence of underlying truths. He believed that the simple laws were there to be found if you were just willing to do the work required to find them. Much of what we know about Kepler, his motivations, and his personality leads us to believe that he would have resisted the temptation to build an enormously complex theory designed solely to account for data, computer or no computer. I would like to hope that social scientists will similarly come to resist the temptation to build complex computer simulation models designed with the purpose of accounting for complex data derived from complex situations. We can call that enterprise fun, we can call it a game, we can even call it a rough shortcut to the solution of practical problems. But we should not think of it as the ultimate goal.

REFERENCES

Banaji, M. R., & Crowder, R. G. (1989). The bankruptcy of everyday memory. *American Psychologist, 44,* 1185–1193.

Commoner, B. (1979). *The politics of energy.* New York: Knopf.

Church, R. M. (1983). The influence fo computers on psychological research: A case study. *Behavior Research Methods & Instrumentation, 15,* 117–126.

---

[2]At least this is my opinion. Workers in artificial intelligence who construct expert system models may well argue that a theory of cognition is irrelevant to their purposes.

Freedman, D. A. (1983). *Statistics and the scientific method* (Tech. Rep. No. 19). Berkeley, CA: University of California, Department of Statistics.

Freedman, D. A., Rothenberg, T., & Sutch, R. (1983). On energy policy models. *Journal of Business and Economic Statistics, 1*, 24–36.

Haber, R. N. (1983). The impending demise of the icon: A critique of the concept of iconic storage in visual information processing. *Behavioral and Brain Sciences, 6*, 1–10.

Keil, F. (1984). Transition mechanisims in cognitive development and the structure of knowledge. In R. Sternberg (Ed.), *Mechanisms of cognitive developments*. San Francisco: W. H. Freeman.

Koestler, A. (1959). *The sleepwalkers*. New York: Universal.

Loftus, G. R. (1983). The continuing persistence of the icon. *Behavioral and Brain Sciences, 6*, 28.

Loftus, G. R. (1985). Johannes Kepler's computer simulation of the universe: Some remarks about theory in psychology. *Behavioral Research Methods, Instruments, and Computers, 17*, 149–156.

Loftus, G. R. (1990). On the tyranny of hypothesis testing in the social sciences. *Contemporary Psychology 36*, 102–105.

Neisser, U. (1976). *Cognition and reality*. San Francisco: W. H. Freeman.

Stoddard, P. K., & Loftus, G. R. (1988). An IBM XT-Compatible, computer-based slide-projector laboratory. *Behavior Research Methods, Instrumentation, and Computers, 20*, 541–551.

Uttal, W. R. (1983). Don't exterminate perceptual fruit flies! *Behavioral and Brain Sciences, 6*, 39–40.

Wandell, B. A. (1984). Visual sensing by human and computers. *Behavior Research Methods, Instruments, & Computers, 16*, 88–95.

Watkins, M. J. (1981). Human memory and the information-processing metaphor. *Cognition, 10*, 331–336.

Watkins, M. J. (1984). Models as toothbrushes. *Behavioral and Brain Sciences, 7*, 86.

Wolfram, S. (1984). Computer software in science and mathematics. *Scientific American, 251*(3), 188–203.

16

Essentials in the Design and Analysis of Time-Series Experiments

Regina H. Rushe and John M. Gottman
University of Washington

HOW TO DESIGN TIME-SERIES EXPERIMENTS

The purpose of this chapter is to provide a very broad overview of the design and analysis of time-series experiments. Social scientists find time-series methodology a highly sensitive and specific tool to detect subtle, but important, changes over time. Psychologists find it particularly appropriate for research in education, psychotherapy, psychophysiology, and other areas where interventions are assessed in imperfectly controlled settings.

The emphasis is on concepts and design, as well as a limited amount of statistical methodology. We believe social scientists must be well grounded in both statistical and substantive issues in order to make valid decisions about specific issues in time-series analysis.

Time-series data require statistical analyses that will maximize the information available in many, dependent observations that change in important ways over time. Most statistical tests taught in introductory courses have assumptions that are violated or have limited ability to retrieve important information in such circumstances. Fortunately, statisticians have been challenged by time-series data and continue to develop statistical theory and applied techniques to make time-series analysis a fruitful and reliable endeavor.

It is useful to think of time-series methodology as an outgrowth of the observation process used in the physical sciences. Campbell and Stanley (1963) gave a "pre-experimental" example from 19th-century science where a bar of iron that has remained unchanged for many months is dipped in a bath of nitric acid. Should the bar then lose weight, the change would be attributed to the nitric acid bath. The physical sciences have had much success with experimental designs

based on a process of pretest observation—intervention—posttest observatio
and then reasoning that any change concomitant with the intervention must b
due to the intervention. By repeating the number of observations made bot
before and after an intervention, the pretest–posttest pre-experimental design ca
be considerably strengthened and becomes a time-series experiment.

Levels of Causal Inference in Time-Series Designs

Scientific reasoning begins with observation and has the goal of explaining wh
things happen. Progress is made through systematic and progressive inference
about causes from observations. Different levels of valid causal inference diffe
entiate three types of time-series designs. The three designs discussed here ar
from Glass, Willson, and Gottman (1975): detecting a pattern of concomitan
variation, ex post facto hypothesis generation, and the planned experiment.

The most primitive time-series experiment involves passively observing
system over time until a pattern of concomitant variation is detected. Co
occurrence and parallel statistical behavior can be observed frequently: On ho
sunny days a great deal of ice cream is sold; people who weigh less consum
fewer calories; and unhappy couples bicker frequently. Although concomitan
variation may be considered necessary, it is not sufficient to justify causal argu
ments. Hot weather may not be the one cause of ice cream sales, calories may no
be the sole determinant of weight, and complaining may not inevitably lead to
lower marital satisfaction. Nonetheless, concomitant variation is an exceller
starting point for exploratory data analysis and hypothesis generation. Ice crear
sales could also be influenced by advertising, weight can be affected by exercise
and what is seen by an outsider as complaining might be perceived by a spouse a
caring, constructive criticism. Other time-series designs will have fewer threat
to valid inductive reasoning.

A stronger level of causal inference can be made from passive observation i
concomitant variation is observed after a dramatic event. Generating post ho
hypotheses to account for fluctuations in a system has been called an ex pos
facto time-series experiment. The Dow Jones Industrial Average is a favorit
target of post hoc speculation. Changes in the status of wars, industrial strikes
and fiscal policies have all been observed to shift stock prices. Archival record
are a common source of data for ex post facto time-series designs and can be use
to evaluate the impact of changing social policies. The effectiveness of change
in laws regulating liquor sales or penalties for drunk driving on actual highwa
safety can be evaluated in this manner.

Glass et al. (1975) noted similar indices do not always reflect a similar shi
after an important event. In a high-risk high school dropout program, teacher
believed a major breakthrough occurred after a long, individual, emotional, tal
with each of three students. Behavioral indices revealed that each of the studen
significantly avoided the teacher subsequent to the talk, did not improve i

:ademic performance and significantly increased disruptive classroom par-
cipation. Clearly, generating hypotheses after critical incidents does not always
:ad to strong causal inferences. Planned experiments, with some amount of
ontrol over relevant variables, remains the best experimental design for using
:ientific reasoning to select between competing hypotheses.

It is important to recall that scientific reasoning is unable to prove that a
ypothesis is correct. Instead, support for one hypothesis is gained by disproving
competing hypothesis. This makes the development of clever and theoretically
iteresting competing hypotheses very important in thinking through a planned
xperiment. Unlike conditions in the physical sciences, observations in the social
:iences occur in a context of constant change. For these and other reasons, no
ne design for a planned experiment can be used all the time.

lanned Time-Series Experiments

lass et al. (1975) proposed at least eight distinct designs that are variations on
ie basic time-series experiment identified by Campbell and Stanley (1963).
nly three of these will be reviewed here with their original examples: multiple-
roup-multiple-intervention, operant, and interaction designs. These designs
ere selected to give a sense of the range of possibilities and for their similarity
 other designs frequently used in psychology but not referred to as a time
:ries. It is important to emphasize that no one design is inherently any more
alid than another. It is the actual application of a design, in conjunction with all
ie other decisions of a planned experiment, that is more or less valid.

In the Campbell and Stanley notation, (where O = an observation and I = an
itervention) the process involved in the basic experiment is: O O O I O O O. In
ie *multiple-group-multiple-intervention* design, each group has its own inter-
ention. In this notation:

$$\frac{0\ 0\ 0\ I_1\ 0\ 0\ 0}{\frac{0\ 0\ 0\ I_2\ 0\ 0\ 0}{0\ 0\ 0\ I_3\ 0\ 0\ 0}}$$

he example given in Glass et al. described the state-by-state crackdown on
)eeding. In January 1956, the state of Connecticut began to suspend licenses for
)eeding offenses. Thirty days for the first offense, 60 days for the second
ffense, and an indefinite period of time at the third offense. Data on Connecticut
affic fatalities before and after the crackdown in speeding was supplemented
ith similar data from nearby states (Massachusetts, Rhode Island, New York,
nd New Jersey) where no such crackdown on speeding was in effect. In this
pplication, I_1 was the implementation of license suspension in Connecticut and
. was the "no crackdown" control (see Fig. 16.1).

The *multiple-group-multiple-intervention* design avoids the interactions of
iultiple interventions that would be present in a *one-group-multiple-intervention*

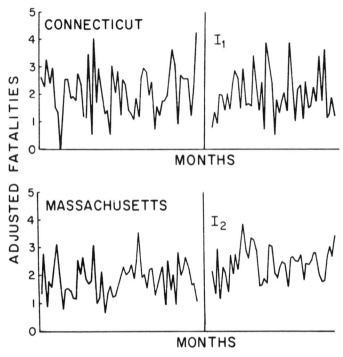

FIG. 16.1.   Fatalities/100,000,000 Driver Miles Minus Monthly Average
Plus 2 for Connecticut (upper) and Massachusetts (lower) before and
after the January 1956 crackdown on speeding in Connecticut.
(Source: Glass et al., 1975, page 27.)

design. Random assignment to groups or matching groups to control for some
variables (matching is preferable when there are few groups or units) is possible
with this design, although that did not occur in the example given here. Indeed
the selection bias obscures the apparent finding that the Connecticut crackdown
reduced traffic fatalities.

In the *operant* design, a return to baseline condition occurs that adds support
to the hypothesis that changes away from the first baseline were indeed due to the
intervention. The design notation is:

$$O\ O\ O\ I_1\ O\ O\ O\ O\ O\ O\ I_1\ O\ O\ O.$$

The operant design is most frequently seen in applied behavior analysis. Kazden
(1982), Hersen and Barlow (1976), and others presented elaborations of the
operant design and made popular the phrase *A-B-A design* as an alternative
notation for the operant design previously presented. Glass et al. presented the
example from Broden, Hall, and Mitts (1971) on the effects of self-monitoring
on the study behavior of an eighth-grade girl. She was observed for 7 days under

baseline conditions. On the eighth day she was instructed to record her own study behavior for 5 days. Five more days of observation followed for a second baseline, and finally a second 9-day phase of self-monitoring (See Fig. 16.2).

There are two important drawbacks to the operant design as presented. The intervention effect is presumed to be reversible and some interventions (although somewhat reversible) may not return to baseline (e.g. learning to drive a car). Glass et al. argued that the return to baseline as a criterion for intervention effect is too stringent and should be replaced with a definition of significant change from baseline.

The *interaction* design is the time-series counterpart to a factorial experimental design. Two interventions are presented in four combinations: neither I_1 nor I_2 (baseline), I_1 alone, I_2 alone, and finally with I_1 and I_2 together. This results in a design with four stages:

$$O\ O\ O\ I_1\ O\ O\ O\ I_2\ O\ O\ O\ I_1 I_2\ O\ O\ O$$

Essentially, this design is a 2×2 factorial strung out sequentially. Unlike the factorial experiment where interventions occur simultaneously, the "interaction" design has the potential problem of order effects. When more than one group can be used, the order of the interventions can be randomized over time. For exam-

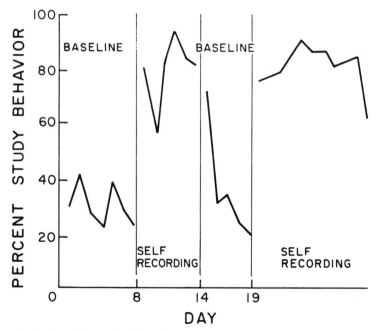

FIG. 16.2. Effects of self-monitoring on the study behavior of a single student (after Broden et al. 1971). (Source: Glass et al., 1975, page 34.)

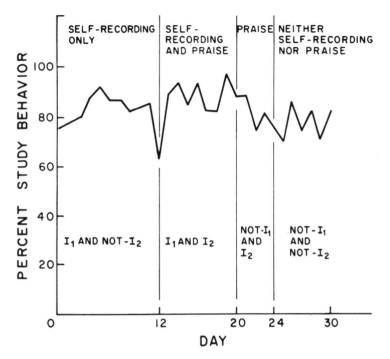

FIG. 16.3. Effects of combined and separate self-monitoring and teacher praise on the study behavior of a single student (after Broden et al. 1971). (Source: Glass et al., 1975, page 36.)

ple, the experiment might be conducted with three groups or three subjects as follows:

$$0\ 0\ 0\ I_1\ 0\ 0\ 0\ I_2\ 0\ 0\ 0\ I_1\ I_2\ 0\ 0\ 0$$
$$0\ 0\ 0\ I_2\ 0\ 0\ 0\ I_1\ 0\ 0\ 0\ I_1\ I_2\ 0\ 0\ 0$$
$$0\ 0\ 0\ I_1\ I_2\ 0\ 0\ 0\ I_1\ 0\ 0\ 0\ I_2\ 0\ 0\ 0$$

It is important to make clear predictions on how each of the interventions should affect the observed series (i.e., increase mean or variability). In the statistical analysis of this time series, each of the predicted intervention effects will be assessed or modeled.

Using the Broden et al. (1971) data again, the eighth-grade girl was now going through the interventions of self-recording only (I_1 only), self-recording and teacher praise simultaneously ($I_1 I_2$ together), teacher praise only (I_2 only), and neither self-recording nor teacher praise (See Fig. 16.3).

A time-series analysis must demonstrate that the perturbations of a system are not uncontrolled variations, that is, noise in the system. This problem of partitioning noise from "effect" in the social sciences is particularly challenging, because experimental effects are often surpassed by nonexperimental variation. Time-series designs are in a unique position relative to many other experimental designs because rival hypotheses *about* history, maturation, and intervention effect can be evaluated.

Patterns of Interventions and Intervention Effects

Time-series analysis is most sensitive when used to confirm hypotheses about a specific, anticipated intervention effect. Unless a specific hypothesis is tested, the researcher is at risk for confusing random fluctuations in the data with true experimental effects. Intervention effects can be sudden or slow, change level or slope, be fleeting or permanent. Glass et al. (1975) listed 10 different effects of intervention in order to assist the experimenter in developing specific statistical models to test in time-series analyses (See Fig. 16.4).

The simplest intervention effect is an abrupt change in level that will occur when an intervention is quickly and easily implemented. Another simple effect is

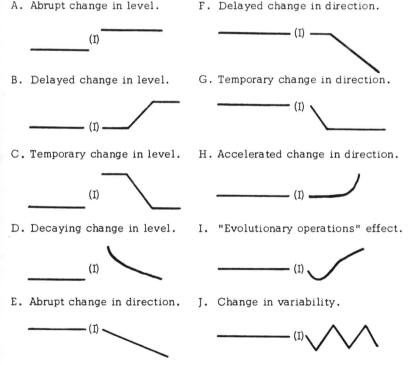

A. Abrupt change in level.

B. Delayed change in level.

C. Temporary change in level.

D. Decaying change in level.

E. Abrupt change in direction.

F. Delayed change in direction.

G. Temporary change in direction.

H. Accelerated change in direction.

I. "Evolutionary operations" effect.

J. Change in variability.

FIG. 16.4.   Varieties of intervention effects in the time-series experiment. (Source: Glass et al., 1975, page 44.)

when there is a clear, perhaps delayed, change in slope, or direction. This ca happen when the intervention is highly effective, but requires some incubatio period. Immunization programs, or changes in safety laws that "grandfather" ol preexisting units would be examples where the change would not be expected i the level of a series but a delayed change in direction. The other interventio effects are variations on either changes in level or changes in slope.

Thus, across the wide range of experimental control options available to socia scientists, a variety of time-series methods exist that can detect patterns in dat collected over time. The design of time-series experiments and the interpretatio of time-series analyses become even more flexible and sophisticated when th investigator explicitly considers the nature of the data. This includes not only a understanding of potential limitations due to the number of observations, but th nature of the observations themselves. Observations can vary in terms of thei numerical properties and the selected unit of analysis.

Numerical Properties of Time-Series Data

Time-series data must have the properties of real numbers and therefore b interval data. However noninterval, polychotomous data can be modified so tha some quality of the category can be observed as a univariate time series. Gottma (1979) proposed several methods to convert the categorical data used to describ social interactions into an interval time series. One method involves creating numerical variable that is used to rescale the codes on some common dimension such as activity, positiveness, or tension. Alternatively, proportion scores fc each category can be computed by noting the percent of standardized interval (not necessarily time) that contain at least one occurrence of the coding category

All coding systems do some work that can be reduced to one or severa dimensions that can be recorded along a numerical continuum. Social interactio coding systems are developed to discriminate various groups or specific types c communication patterns. Weights can be assigned to optimize the discriminatior For example, Wills, Weiss, and Patterson (1974) used a regression equation t discriminate love days and regular days for distressed marriages. In the origina work, husbands were told by the experimenters to be particularly affectionate t their wives during love days. The amount of discrimination each code perform is reflected in the regression weights and can be used to further elaborate th computation of a numerical coding system from a categorical coding system.

Sampling Rate

The rate at which the behavior stream is sampled is also known as the interobse vation interval or rate of observation. The sampling rate of a time series is ofte arbitrary but can have important implications for the description and interpreta tion of a statistical model. Most systems are quite complex, and any one model of the data may not detect the same pattern across all sampling intervals. Glass et al. (1975) gave the problem of detecting the effect of a new incentive program on absenteeism. Should the workplace be observed each day, each week, or each month? Sampling on a Monday or Friday (when absenteeism is greatest) is more likely to detect the change due to the new program than sampling on a Wednesday. Oversampling can partially obscure the effects of an intervention, if that effect was strong only at intermittent points on the time continuum. If absenteeism measurements were taken every day, the changes in absenteeism on Mondays and Fridays would not be as profound. The effects of sampling time units can be difficult to anticipate and therefore emphasize the importance of replicating research results.

The term *aliasing* is used to describe the condition where a pattern remains undetected or incorrectly detected because the true pattern was imbedded in another pattern. Aliasing is sometimes observed in moving pictures of the spokes of a moving wheel. At slower speeds the spokes clearly move in the same direction as the rim. As the speed increases, a frequency will eventually be achieved where the spokes appear to move in the opposite direction of the rest of the wheel. A psychological example of aliasing might be seen in the activity level of a depressed individual. If the actual activity were highest in the morning and lowest in the evening, a very different pattern would be detected depending on the sampling rate. If an observation were taken every morning, the pattern could be one of normal activity. If observations were taken in the morning and the evening, the atypical diurnal pattern could be documented.

Number of Observation Points Over Time

If there were a general rule of thumb regarding the number of observations needed in a time-series design, it would consider the complexity of the patterns to be discovered in the data. The more complex the pattern (and therefore the more parameters to be fit in the model) the greater the number of points needed. If a cyclical pattern is to be detected by the statistical model, many occurrences of the same pattern or cycle must appear in the raw data. Also the less noise, the fewer the points needed. The magnitude of the phenomenon or effect also determines the number of observations needed to adequately model the data. A large effect requires fewer points to model than a small effect.

The trick here is to know how complex a model is required to describe a phenomenon before the data are collected. Under optimal conditions (very little signal noise, a simple pattern with a clear effect), a minimum of two cycles might suffice. Textbooks on time series vary in their recommendations from a minimum of 50–100 points (Chatfield, 1975; Glass, Wilson, & Gottman, 1975; McCleary & Hay, 1980; Nazam, 1988). Monte Carlo studies are underway to see when sample size can be decreased even further (Crosbie, 1991).

Unit-repetitive versus Unit-replicative Designs

In a *unit-repetitive design,* the same single, intact body is observed at successive points in time. For example, a single child may be observed interacting with classmates each day for 60 days. In contrast, a *unit-replicative design* replicate measurements on different individuals over time. For example, student achievement in the second grade may be measured for 20 years. In a unit-replicative design the experimental unit is a concept, such as second graders, rather than a group of particular individuals.

The concept of unit-repetitive versus unit-replicative time-series designs has important implications for design validity, measurement, and statistical analysis. In a unit-repetitive design, attributing shifts in a time-series to a change in composition of the experimental unit is illogical. Unit-replicative designs are more prone to invalidity due to an alteration in the nature of the individual(s) comprising the experimental unit that is coincident with the intervention. However, unit-repetitive designs may be far more subject to a type of "Hawthorne" (reactive) or practice effects than unit-replicative designs.

In summary, although the difference between repetitive and replicative units is rarely made explicit in time-series texts, this distinction may be crucial for judging the validity of an interpretation of a time-series design (Glass, Wilson, & Gottman, 1975).

HOW TO DESCRIBE TIME-SERIES DATA

Descriptive statistical models of raw data are the essence of time-series analysis because they are used to describe structure, or patterns, in the data. Patterns may be detected by examining the series on a point-by-point basis or by examining the series as a whole. Point-by-point variability is described in terms of how the covariance (or, equivalent for purposes here, correlation) structure changes over time. Patterns across the series as a whole are best described in terms of rhythmic functions, such as a sum of sinusoidal waves. It should not be assumed that either covariance or sinusoidal patterns are invariant throughout a time series. Indeed it is very important for statistical analysis for the patterns in the series to be stable over time, a character called *stationarity.*

In summary, the basic building blocks in descriptive time-series analysis are the covariance function and the sums of sine and cosine waves function— assuming these patterns are stable across time in the series (i.e., stationary). These same building blocks are used to model time series in many different statistical and mathematical approaches.

At the most general level, there are two approaches to modeling time-series data. In the social sciences, Autoregressive Integrated Moving Average (ARIMA) models are preferred because they are powerful and simple to use. In the physical sciences, decomposition models are preferred because they describe mathematical functions in the series with more precision. Although this chapter is written for social scientists who are more likely to be familiar with ARIMA models, our goal is to broaden this perspective and encourage the use of the more flexible and descriptive decomposition models.

Autocovariance and Autocorrelation Functions

When a single series is examined for point-to-point changes, the covariance structure is more correctly referred to as Autocovariance. In most statistical applications, *covariance* refers to how two variables literally covary. But in time-series analysis, a single univariate series is compared to itself over time. Recall from basic statistics that the covariance for any two variables (x and y) is:

$$\text{cov}(x, y) = 1/(N - 1) * \Sigma[(x - \bar{x}) * (y - \bar{y})].$$

The autocovariance of an entire series could be calculated by comparing every point in the series with every other point. In practice, this is rarely done because the autocovariance deteriorates quickly. Specific data points are most highly related when they are in close proximity. The proximity of any two points in the series is described as a lag relationship. When there is only one time unit separating the two points (sometimes it is helpful to think of two identical series that are parallel and then shifted by one unit), it is called a lag 1 relationship. Separation by two time units is called a lag 2 relationship, and so forth. The equation used to describe autocovariance across the entire series is called the *autocovariance function* and for 1 lag is expressed as:

$$\text{autocov}_1 = 1/N * \sum_{t=1}^{N-1} (x_t - \bar{x})(x_{t+1} - \bar{x}).$$

Alternatively, variation in the series can be described using covariance with standardized units of deviation. Recall from basic statistics that the correlation (x, y) is equal to the covariance, with an adjustment (division by the standard deviations of x and y) to keep x and y in a common metric. Covariance and correlation are often used interchangeably in statistics when merely describing the degree of patterning:

$$r = \frac{\Sigma(x - \bar{x})(y - \bar{y})}{\sqrt{\Sigma(x - \bar{x})^2 * \Sigma(y - \bar{y})^2}}.$$

Analogous to autocovariance, the correlation between any two points in a time series is called an autocorrelation and can be computed at any lag between points. The autocorrelation function for all adjacent points in an entire series can be conceptualized as superimposing the series onto itself with a slight shift in

time. By assigning different lead or lag values, it is possible to compute autoco
relations between different lags. The autocorrelation function at a lead of tw
points is defined as:

$$r = \frac{\sum\limits_{t=1}^{N-2} (x_t - \bar{x})(x_{t+2} - \bar{x})}{\sum\limits_{t=1}^{N} (x_t - \bar{x})^2}.$$

A graph composed of many autocorrelations at different leads or lags (order
is called a *correllogram*. Correllograms can be used to begin to fit a model to th
stationary time series. Usually points that are close together in the sequence wi
be autocorrelated to some degree.

The *order* of a time series refers to the number of lags required to describ
most of the autocovariance or autocorrelation in a series. In descriptive tim
series, the autocovariance is usually determined for one lag because most serie
are found to be of order one. That is, most of the structure in covariance i
between adjacent points in the series. Longer, more complicated patterns, requir
longer lag autocorrelations, also called higher-order models. Simpler patterns ar
adequately described in lower-order models.

To determine the order of a series, the partial autocorrelation is calculated. I
general statistics, partial correlations measure the true relationship between tw
variables exclusive of indirect influence from a third variable. When a time serie
has an autocorrelation greater than one, it is useful to know the partial autoco
relations of the series at lag 1 (independent of lag 2) and lag 2 (independent of la
1). In time-series analysis, partials of the lower-order models are of little interes
to us.

Cyclicity and the Spectral Density Function

An alternative to describing point-by-point variation in a time series is to describ
rhythms in the series as a whole through the use of sine waves. Patterns that ar
repeated frequently can only be described through the use of superimposed sin
and cosine waves of different cycles per unit time (called frequencies).

Much as a prism breaks sunlight into all the colors of the spectrum (each wit
different frequencies of electromagnetic oscillation) with different brightness,
spectral decomposition breaks a time series into its basic frequency component
each with a different amount of energy or variance accounted for. It is the
possible to graph the relative contribution of all detected frequencies. Histo
ically, graphs of relative frequency strength did not represent cycles as frequer
cies (cycles per unit time). Instead, early graphs of relative frequency strengt
represented cycles as periods (time per unit cycle $= 1/f$). These early graph

were therefore called *periodograms* (which represented periodic, or repeating, functions).

The irregularities in a periodogram may provide additional theoretical information to the investigator and we encourage its use for visual exploratory analysis in our lab. However, the periodogram fails to meet important statistical properties (such as decreasing variance as the number of observations increases) and its use beyond visual examination is inappropriate. For data analytic purposes, an averaged or smoothed periodogram, called the *spectral density function,* is required.

A graph of the spectral density function lists all observed sine waves from the larger spectrum and their corresponding probability weights (from zero to one) assigned to describe the relative contribution, or density, of each period to the rhythmic process.

Stationarity

Stationarity is a statistical property that refers to the condition of relatively constant mean and variance throughout the time series. Stationarity is important because most time-series models assume the data are independent of any one historical starting point. Without some assumption of stability it would be impossible to make any reasonable inferences about the data. Many data sets do not meet the conditions of stationarity but can be mathematically transformed until they do. The two alternatives to transform a nonstationary series are (a) modeling deterministic processes and (b) differencing.

A deterministic process can be accurately *modeled* with a mathematical function. Examples of deterministic components are mean, slope, and regularly repeating cycles. The identification of trends (i.e., systematic changes in mean, slope, or cyclicity over time) should not be done through visual examination of the data alone, because the eyeball may confuse trend with stochastic drift (McCleary & Hay, 1980). Fortunately, software programs that enable the identification of specific deterministic trends, provide empirical tests for these functions. Once deterministic components have been identified, they can be subtracted from the data until the series becomes stationary.

If deterministic components are systematically subtracted from a series, they may be examined using more traditional experimental statistics, such as repeated measure ANOVA, which were designed to compare deterministic constants over time. If deterministic processes were the only patterns of interest, we could stop our analysis here. The most common motivation for time-series analysis is to describe nondeterministic, or stochastic, patterns in the data. The point to remember is, the decision to use time-series analysis does not exclude traditional hypothesis testing.

Time-series data can also be made stationary with a procedure known as *differencing.* Differencing a series once (also called first differencing) merely

TABLE 16.1
Second Differences
Eliminate a Quadratic Trend

t	x_t	∇x_t	$\nabla(\nabla x_t) = \nabla^2 x_t$
1	1.20	—	—
2	4.30	3.10	—
3	8.70	4.40	1.30
4	15.80	7.10	2.70
5	25.00	9.20	2.10

Note: The symbol ∇ denotes the differenced series.

takes the "difference" between, or subtracts, every two adjacent points in series:

$$z_t = Y_t - Y_{t-1}, \text{ where } d = 1.$$

Differencing the data once is said to remove both local and overall linear tren and to result in a function that is an estimate of the rate of change (slope) of th original series. If you are more interested in the way a variable changes than the variable's absolute magnitude, then a first-differencing transformation is a attractive modeling alternative to determine linear trend. Differencing a secon time removes a quadratic trend and estimates changes in the rate of change. general, to remove an nth degree polynomial, differencing is required n time (See Table 16.1 and Fig. 16.5).

Although differencing is simple and easy to use, we believe it is a powerf procedure that is best used with caution. In addition to removing deterministi

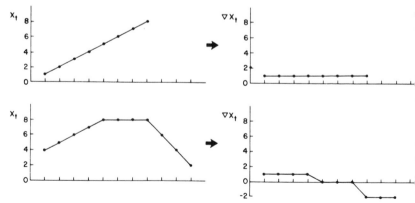

FIG. 16.5. How first differencing eliminates local as well as overall trend. (Source: Gottman, 1981, page 94.)

ends from the series, differencing alters the character of the raw data (Gottman, 1981). By acting as a "bandpass filter," differencing increases the intensity of faster, erratic frequencies. When the relative contribution of the high-frequency components has been increased, the net effect is a decrease in the contribution of lower or lower frequencies. This means one might inadvertently eliminate low-frequency cycles of interest and amplify high-frequency cycles not of interest. But if differencing is done by an informed user, it could also amplify high-frequency signal and dampen low-frequency noise. This is the power of differencing.

Determining the amount of differencing required to make a series stationary is also necessary; both overdifferencing and underdifferencing are to be avoided. Underdifferencing leaves deterministic processes, or dependence, in the series that should have been removed. Overdifferencing introduces dependence into the data that should not be there. Typically, only one or two differencing steps are necessary.

The Wold Decomposition Theorem

Even an intuitive explanation of the essentials of time-series analysis must mention the Wold decomposition theorem (Wold, 1938) because it provides the outline for all examples in this chapter. The terms used in the theorem are explained after the theorem is stated. The theorem states that any stationary process (including those processes made stationary through differencing or removing deterministic components) can be modeled as the sum of two uncorrelated processes, one purely deterministic and one nondeterministic (also called stochastic or probabilistic). This means that the goal of a time-series analysis is to account for all deterministic and stochastic trends until the series is reduced to white-noise, that is, a completely random mix of a wide range of frequencies with no meaningful signals, or patterns. Alternatively, any real data time series can be approximated by starting with white-noise and "adding" deterministic and stochastic patterns. This idea can also be expressed in an equation:

Real data = [deterministic patterns] + [stochastic patterns] + [random error, also called white noise].

Autoregressive and Moving Average Models

Once the series is stationary, modeling the stochastic components with time series may begin. In most social science work, this has been done with *moving average* (MA) and *autoregressive* (AR) models. Although the two models are theoretically parallel, their interpretations differ dramatically. In a Moving Average, a model of the stochastic series is created by summing weighted values of white noise. If only one weight (or parameter) were needed to duplicate the stationary time series the model would be:

$$y_t = a_t - \theta_1 a_{t-1}.$$

The general form of an MA process of order q, that is, with q parameters for the stochastic series is:

$$y_t = a_t - \theta_1 a_{t-1} - \theta_2 a_{t-2} - \ldots \theta_q a_{t-q}.$$

An autoregressive model of the stochastic series is created by decomposing the observed series into white noise by summing weighted lagged observations. If only one lag is required to describe the stochastic component, the series is said to be an AR of order 1:

$$y_t = \phi_1 y_{t-1} + a_t, \text{ for lag } 1.$$

The general form of an AR process of order p, that is, with p lags and autoregressive parameters is:

$$y_t = \phi_1 y_{t-1} + \phi_2 y_{t-2} + \ldots + \phi_p y_{t-p} + a_t, \text{ for lag } p.$$

In summary, the number of parameters in an AR, MA or, ARMA model is called the *order of the series* because (as in using autocovariance/autocorrelation to describe a series) the order of a series is an estimate of the complexity of the patterns. In a MA process, order is the number of weighted white noise elements needed to model the data. In an AR process, order is the number of lags between observations points weighted to reduce the series to white noise.

The order of an AR or MA process is determined by examining the autocorrelation and partial autocorrelation functions. If the autocorrelation function is elevated at only one lag and dies off to approximately zero, this is evidence for a first-order process. Usually more than just the autocorrelation function is needed to identify the order of a time series. This is because the first-order autocorrelation inflates the second-order autocorrelation, which in turn inflates the third-order autocorrelation. To look at autocorrelations beyond the first order (or lag), without the artificial boost from previous autocorrelations, it is necessary to compute and plot the partial autocorrelation function for the higher-order model. Once again, the partial autocorrelation function is inspected for sudden drop-off (See Table 16.2).

The decision to use either an MA or AR model (or both) is made by calculating many models and selecting the best one. If the goal of the time-series analysis is to assess intervention effects, AR models are better at describing smooth exponential change over time, whereas MA models are better at describing sudden intervention changes. Criteria for selecting the best model are controversial and range from ease of interpretation to parsimony in the number of parameters. For most time-series applications, autoregressive models are recommended over moving average (MA) models because they are computed with closed solution estimates. Estimation of the parameters in MA models require solving nonlinear equations by numerical iterations; these equations rarely have unique

TABLE 16.2
Identification of the Autoregressive and Moving Averages
Components of an ARIMA (*p*, 0, *q*) Series

Model	Autocorrelation	Partial Autocorrelation
ARIMA (*p*, 0, 0)	Dies out slowly	Cuts off after lag *p*
ARIMA (0, 0, *q*)	Cuts off after lag *q*	Dies out slowly
ARIMA (*p*, 0, *q*)	Dies out slowly	Dies out slowly

solutions and even more rarely have easy interpretations. This makes the AR models easier to identify and understand (Durbin, 1970; Gottman, 1981).

ARIMA (*p*,*d*,*q*) Models

Autoregressive Integrated Moving Average (ARIMA) modeling allows any of a very large class of models to be fit to the data to describe both the deterministic and nondeterministic patterns in the data. First developed by Box and Jenkins (1970), ARIMA models have done a great deal to popularize the use of time-series analysis in the social sciences because they appear simpler and easier to use than other modeling procedures. Consequently, most software packages offer Box–Jenkins models and too many social scientists equate Box–Jenkins models with time-series analysis.

The three parameters of ARIMA models describe: *p* (the number of past observations in the autoregressive relationship), *d* (the number of times the series had to be differenced to achieve stationarity in the mean and variance of the series), and *q* (the number of moving averages).

The differencing (*d*) parameter is the first to be fit in an ARIMA model. This is because, even in ARIMA modeling, all series must first be stationary. The previous discussion on using differencing to make a series stationary is most appropriate here. In fact, outside of ARIMA models, we have rarely seen differencing used in the scientific literature.

Once the series has been made stationary, that is, the residual series has no remaining linear or nonlinear trend, the stochastic portion of the series can be modeled. This is most often accomplished by fitting *p* autoregressive parameters to the stochastic series and modeling the residuals with *q* moving average parameters. Alternatively, and less frequently, a moving average of order (*q*) could be fit to the stochastic portion of the series and the residuals modeled with *p* autoregressive parameters. Through the joint use of both AR and MA parameters, the Box and Jenkins goal of parsimony (lowest possible order) is achieved. If no differencing was required to make the series stationary (i.e., the *d* parameter in the ARIMA model was 0), this should be equivalent to an ARMA model in non-ARIMA approaches.

ARIMA models can also describe certain types of cyclical patterns. McCleary and Hay (1980) defined seasonality as "any cyclical or periodic fluctuation in a time series that recurs or repeats itself at the same phase of the cycle or period" (p. 80). Many cycles in nature are not deterministic, that is, they do not repeat at strictly regular intervals. Instead, these cycles can be thought of as probabilistic, or as repeating at approximately regular intervals. Box–Jenkins models cannot describe probabilistic cycles, only deterministic ones. However, many social phenomena are adequately described as strict cycles and the use of ARIMA models in these circumstances is very appropriate.

The seasonal ARIMA model notation is $(p, d, q)(P, D, Q)_s$ where P, D, and Q describe the differencing, AR and MA components of the cyclical patterns, respectively. The s parameter denotes the length of the season in units of the original time series. So, if the time series was measured in months, an $s = 12$ parameter would indicate an annual cycle.

Rather than the routine use of ARIMA models, we recommend each deterministic process be examined and modeled separately. This is the only way the investigator can become aware of the dynamics in the raw data. Differencing transformations tell the user little about structural changes and are often difficult to interpret in terms of the raw data. When a complete model of the series is built with known deterministic and stochastic elements, each parameter can be examined and interpreted independently. Furthermore, the examination of independent contributions to the series can be done both before and after inferential procedures to better describe the original series and interpret statistical inferences.

Selecting the Best Model

Whether the investigator chooses an AR, MA, ARMA, or ARIMA model, the question of when to stop parametrizing the model is always a good one. There are a host of test statistics to use, and the wise investigator will become familiar with several. Tests of fit for models are usually in terms of variance of the original series accounted for and whether the residuals contain patterns. There are three general approaches to comparing models.

One is used by Box–Jenkins: Fit one model to the stochastic component of the series and a second model to the residuals. If the series was stationary before the stochastic component was modeled, then the residual should have no remaining patterns. The conjoint AR-MA (or MA-AR) models are often more parsimonious than AR or MA models alone. This is the primary advantage of the Box–Jenkins approach. However, the advantage of AR models, with statistics in the same metric as the original process, is lost.

In Box–Jenkins modeling, residuals must be equivalent to white noise. Unfortunately, there is no satisfactory test for white noise. A reasonable first approximation might be to check if the autocorrelations fall within ± 2 standard deviations, but because we do not know the true parameters of the model, this test is not valid. The Box–Pierce test of white noise is the one test most commonly used. However, many theorists (Anderson, 1971; Chatfield, 1975; Pandit & Wu, 1983) question whether the Box–Pierce test can detect systematic deviations from white noise. Most software packages offer several alternative tests of white noise, in addition to the Box–Pierce. The conservative approach would be to use several tests as well as examining the data, because every test has severe limitations. For example, the spectral density of the residuals could also be examined for important (i.e., theoretically interpretable) frequencies.

A second alternative to model selection is a modification of the Box–Jenkins method developed by Wu and Pandit (1983). Rather than assume the data were generated by an ARMA (p, q) model and then try to find p and q by trial and error, a better strategy is to approximate the dependence in the data more and more closely by fitting a sequence of ARMA models of increasing order. They stop at the point when there is no longer significant improvement in the approximation, as judged by the residual sum of squares. No empirical examination of autocovariance functions, spectra, residuals, and so forth is required. In special cases, this approach is equal to the one used in ARIMA models.

To test the residuals for patterns when several models of increasing order were fit, the Quenouille test is often used, although it assumes a certain distribution (asymptotically normal with variance $1/T$) for the residuals. Nonetheless, the Q test is a rough asymptotic test of the order of an AR process. The null hypothesis that a pth autoregressive coefficient is zero is tested by comparing the pth partial autocorrelation coefficient to a normal distribution with zero mean and variance $1/T$.

A third approach to selecting the best model was originally derived in a proof by Mann and Wald in 1943 and is the approach recommended by Gottman 1981). As long as the residual series after AR model fitting is normal and independently distributed, the model is asymptotically (i.e., under large sample theory) valid. A test statistic, based on a t distribution with $(T - p)$ degrees of freedom should be used instead of the usual tests of normality. It is recommended that several AR models be fit—even overshooting the first small autoregressive parameter (p)—before the best fit model can be selected. This approach does not lend itself to parsimony, so the smallest possible order should be selected if there is any doubt.

Model fitting is part science and part art, but there are guidelines. Model fitting is an iterative process of identification, estimation, and diagnostic checking. Usually, several models fit the data and the difference in terms of their ability to account for variability in series is similar. The best model is a simple model: few parameters, statistical fit, easy interpretation in terms of the raw data, and answers a question about the original time series. This combination of statistical and aesthetic skills may explain why psychologists have been slow to master time-series methodology. Examples of the decision-making process when modeling time-series data are included later in this chapter.

Example 1: A Descriptive Model
of New England Traffic Fatalities

The data set used to demonstrate the preferred approach to modeling time-series data is from Glass et al. (1975). The first 60 observations from the New England traffic fatalities data used in earlier examples are presented again. There are several interesting patterns that coincide in these data. These patterns occur in the form of trends, cycles, and stochastic processes. First, the deterministic processes of trends and cycles will be detected and modeled. When no additional important deterministic patterns can be found in the series, the data will be stationary and additional modeling of the nondeterministic process will proceed.

Modeling Individual Deterministic Components. The first step is to detect and remove trend. Begin with a visual examination of a graph and descriptive statistics of the raw data (See Fig. 16.6). Note the downward linear trend in these data. To discover the details of this downward linear trend a spectral analysis is run (in this case using the Gottman–Williams program called SPEC) and the periodogram examined. In our lab the periodogram is preferred over the spectral density function for visual inspection because the periodogram does not have weighted window estimates that smooth over sharp peaks. These sharp peaks should be retained when inspecting the data for trends and cycles.

The periodogram shows some elevation at zero, which indicates some variability is accounted for in linear trend. An alternative to the frequency domain inspection using the periodogram is a time domain inspection using the correlo-

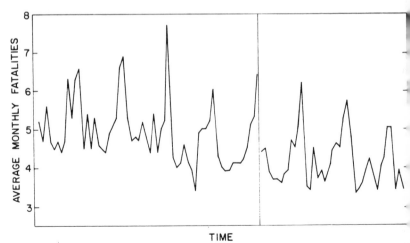

FIG. 16.6. Average monthly traffic fatalities in four Northeast control states. (Source: Gottman, 1981, page 17.)

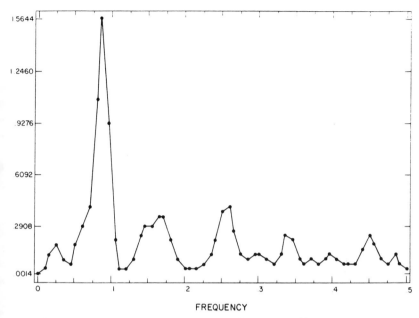

FIG. 16.7.   Periodogram of detrended traffic fatalities. (Source: Gottman, 1981, page 279.)

ram. Linear trend in the correlogram is indicated by a function that dies off
nearly.

Linear trend is usually removed by calculating a least-squares fit to the data in
rder to obtain a linear equation and residuals. This example used the Gottman–
Villiams program called DETREND. Alternatively, first-order differencing
ould be used, but differencing yields no equation of specific mathematical
inctions about how the series was transformed. The residual variance is .617
nd an additional search for nonlinear trends is indicated.

After linear trend has been detected and removed, the next step is to detect
nd remove nonlinear, deterministic cycles. The Gottman–Williams program
ESINE has been run on the detrended data and the periodogram is presented
See Fig. 16.7). An inspection of this periodogram indicates an important cycle
a frequency slightly greater than .075. A frequency of .075 ($f = .075$)
anslates into a period (period $= t = 1/f$) of 13.3 months or an approximately
nnual trend. The DESINE software estimated a function for a 12-month deter-
inistic cycle using least-squares criteria and calculated the residual variance for
is model as .371. So far, we have reduced the residual variance from .617 for
e detrended data to almost half that amount after removing one deterministic
ycle (See Fig. 16.8).

In Fig. 16.8 the behavior of the detrended, desined series is examined to see

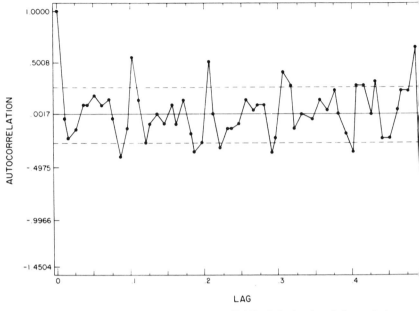

FIG. 16.8.   Autocovariance function (ACF) of desined and detrended
traffic fatalities data. (Source: Gottman, 1981, page 280.)

whether variability will be captured within the 95% confidence intervals (
$\pm 2/(\sqrt{N})$ by calculating a revised autocovariance function (ACF). Figure 16.
indicates ongoing variability and a spectral density function of these data sugge
6-month and 4-month periods. To continue to remove cycles is questionab.
because there is no obvious reason for traffic fatalities to repeat a 4- or 6-mon
cycle. For now, the more elaborate model is computed in order to compare i
performance against the alternative 12-month cycle model (See Table 16.3). On
criteria for selecting the best model are reviewed here.

Many software packages model each of these deterministic processes sep.
rately and remove that determinism from the data so that an inspection of tl
residuals should reveal a stochastic process. There are several statistical tests
help the investigator decide whether to search for even more determinism. Tl
Box–Pierce and Quenouille tests are two found most often in computer pacl
ages.

Modeling the Nondeterministic Component.   After all the deterministic pr
cesses have been modeled and accounted for in the data, that which remai
should be nondeterministic with relative stationarity over time.

There are two mathematically equivalent models used to model stationa

TABLE 16.3
Results of Various Options in Modeling the Traffic Fatalities Data

Components of Model	Residual Variance	Autoregressive Parameters						Sinusoidal Parameters					
		ϕ_1	ϕ_2	ϕ_3	ϕ_4	ϕ_5	ϕ_6	$T=12$		$T=6$		$T=4$	
								$\hat{A}$	$\hat{B}$	$\hat{A}$	$\hat{B}$	$\hat{A}$	$\hat{B}$
Trend	.617												
De-sine $T=12$	.371							-.276	.674				
AR(1)	.371	-.023											
AR(2)	.350	-.029	-.234										
AR(3)	.342	-.064	-.239	-.150									
AR(4)	.342	-.063	-.237	-.150	.008								
AR(5)	.342	-.063	-.234	-.145	.009	.017							
AR(6)	.330	-.066	-.236	-.118	.053	.029	.187						
Trend	.617												
De-sine $T=12$, $T=6$, $T=4$	.237							-.276	.674	-.249	.262	-.340	.369
AR(1)	.227	-.200											
AR(2)	.227	-.209	-.041										
AR(3)	.225	-.204	-.020	.100									
AR(4)	.224	-.211	-.019	.113	.064								
AR(5)	.224	-.211	-.019	.113	.065	.006							
AR(6)	.206	-.213	-.038	.081	.070	.066	.283						

time-series data: time domain and frequency domain models. The basic question asked by the two kinds of models are different, although they are really mathematically equivalent, linked by a theorem that uses Fast Fourier Transfer functions. In time domain analysis, questions are formulated directly in terms of time. In frequency domain time-series, questions are formulated in terms of cycles or waveforms in the data. ARIMA models are time domain models and like all time domain models, have the two subtypes to choose from: autoregressive (AR) and moving averages (MA) models. Time domain and frequency domain models are equivalent, so it really does not matter which is selected. But some problems are comprehended more readily in one domain or the other.

In this example time domain models were chosen to model the stochastic portion of the data. Within the time domain, six autoregressive models were fit to each alternative model of the deterministic components of the series. (A discussion of the selection of AR versus MA models was in the ARIMA section earlier.)

Selecting the Best Model.   Modeling a data set is completed when a comparison of several alternative models yields a model that both fits and is readily interpretable. Both models are computed in order to compare a detrended, 12 month desined model (Model 1) against a detrended 4-, 6-, and 12-month desined model (Model 2), both models will be computed.

If parsimony and explanatory power were the only criteria, the best model would still be difficult to choose. Model 1 has fewer parameters but accounts for less variance. Model 2 accounts for more variance but has more parameters. This is a common dilemma when building purely statistical models. In addition to parsimony and explanatory power, the best model has an interesting interpretation that can be used to build theory. Model 1, with only a 12-month cyclical determinism, can be interpreted as the impact of an annual increase in traffic perhaps summer vacations. In Model 2 the 6-month cycle could be the effects of weather in terms of adjusting to wet roads (snow in the late fall and rain in the spring). The 4-month cycle must be interpreted as reoccurring three times a year and is more difficult to interpret. However, there is a 3-month cycle of major holidays where traffic increases every season: Memorial Day, Labor Day, Thanksgiving, and Easter. A third model is created with a 3-month cycle to reflect the four major holidays (See Table 16.4).

Model 3 is selected as the best of the three models because it is the most interesting. It has as many parameters as Model 2 but accounts for slightly more variance. Model 1 still has fewer parameters but accounts for less variance and is less interesting than Model 3. The criteria of parsimony, explanatory power, and interest are usually not simultaneously met by any one model. We recommend that interest and potential for theory construction be the most important of the three criteria.

TABLE 16.4
Reanalysis of the Traffic Fatalities Data with Cycles at 12, 6, and 3 Months

Components of Model	Residual Variance	Autoregressive Parameters						Sinusoidal Parameters					
								$T = 12$		$T = 6$		$T = 4$	
		ϕ_1	ϕ_2	ϕ_3	ϕ_4	ϕ_5	ϕ_6	$\hat{A}$	$\hat{B}$	$\hat{A}$	$\hat{B}$	$\hat{A}$	$\hat{B}$
Trend	.617												
De-sine T = 12, 6, 3	.250							-.276	.674	-.249	.262	-.151	.294
AR(1)	.249	-.087											
AR(2)	.243	-.101	-.153										
AR(3)	.237	-.125	-.170	-.160									
AR(4)	.210	-.072	-.112	-.118	.337								
AR(5)	.203	-.131	-.092	-.098	.350	.176							
AR(6)	.201	-.110	-.051	-.109	.339	.161	-.117						

Note: The sinusoidal parameters, $\hat{A}$ and $\hat{B}$ are the estimated weights for the sum of sine and cosine waves.

Example 2: An Inferential Procedure
to Evaluate Intervention Effects Using
the Interrupted Time-Series Experiment

The concepts of interrupted time-series analysis are illustrated before the statisti cal analysis. The basic strategy is to fit a model to the preintervention data and then fit a model to the postintervention series. If the intervention has had some effect, then the pre- and postintervention models will not be equivalent. This can be verified using a test statistic (e.g., χ^2) comparing the pre- and postintervention models. This is the approach taken in the example that follows.

It is also possible to test a priori hypotheses about specific intervention effects by planning specific comparisons. Each planned comparison could be tested by fitting a model specific to that comparison and the model with the best fit indicates the intervention effect that best describes the change in the data. Mc Cleary and Hay (1980) and McDowall, McCleary, Meidinger, and Hay (1980) advocated this approach because they believed that testing a limited range of intervention effects avoids confusing the investigator and enhances inter pretability. For example, a zero-order intervention effect (also known as a trans fer function in engineering contexts) has an abrupt, permanent shift after the intervention. A first-order transfer function describes steady, gradual change Other transfer functions test for abrupt temporary changes and gradual temporary changes. More complex effects are possible, but advocates of this perspective believe most effects are sufficiently described by these models.

The Ireland data set (Glass et al., 1975) is used to illustrate how to detect intervention effects by using the interrupted time-series quasi-experiment. The percentage of students who passed intermediate and senior-level exams was monitored before and after a change in funding. From 1879–1924 funding was contingent on student performance that may have produced irregularities in the scoring of examinations in order to economize fees. After 1925 there were no longer limitations in funding based on student performance and the examinations were standardized. Did the change in fiscal policy and subsequent standardiza tion effect the percent of students who passed their exams? The time series of the percent of students passing exams from 1879–1971 are presented in Fig. 16.9. The 1925 intervention, or change in social policy, is noted in the graph (See Fig. 16.9).

Both ARIMA and mathematical decomposition models can be used to detect change in an interrupted time-series experiment. The Ireland data presented here is analyzed with decomposition models. It would be a serious omission not to note that a great deal of interrupted time-series work has been done using ARIMA models (where it is called "impact assessment"). Although several mod els may be fit to the data, the researcher may not simply choose the model that confirms a favorite hypothesis. The chosen model is the best fit by other criteria too.

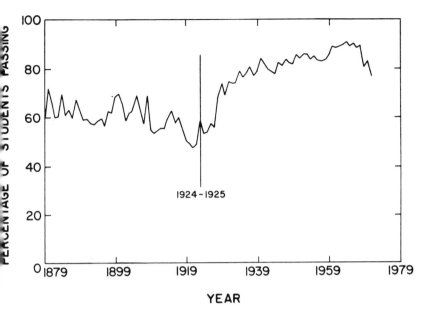

FIG. 16.9.   Time series of percent of students passing exams from 1879–1971, with 1925 intervention noted. (Source: Gottman, 1981, page 339.)

Gottman (1981) used an AR(1) model to analyze the Ireland data set and was able to detect linear changes. An examination of the partial autocorrelation function (PACF) for the series revealed truncation after the first lag and supported selection of an AR(1) model (See Table 16.5). Rather than computing the exact AR(1) model, we can think it through conceptually. It is reasonable to assume the slope of the regression line would be equal to the first autocorrelation coefficient ($\gamma_1 = .536$) and the intercept would be equal to the mean level of the

TABLE 16.5
ACF and PACF for the Ireland Data

Lag	Autocorrelations (ACF)	Partial Autocorrelations (PACF)
1	.536	.536
2	.390	.143
3	.316	.059
4	.230	.092
5	.086	.088
6	.052	.042

Note: Based on Glass et al., 1975, p. 105.

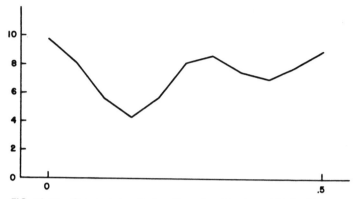

FIG. 16.10.   Spectral density function of residuals to AR1 fit. (Source: Gottman, 1981, page 342.)

series ($L = 59.97$). If this model was worth considering for the preintervention data, the residuals should look like white noise. The Box–Pierce test of white noise was used:

$$Q = n \sum_{j=1}^{k=6} r^2_{(j)} = 45(.536)^2 = 1.99.$$

(Only 6 lags were used to illustrative this conceptual example, however, in statistical model building, the Box–Pierce test should be used on a minimum of 20 lags.) Q was compared to a $\chi^2(k - p - q) = \chi^2(lags - AR - MA) = \chi^2(5)$ and was not significant. Recall that in the earlier discussion on model building it was noted that there is no sensitive test of white noise and we encourage the use of several tests (both statistical and examination of the data) The Box–Pierce test is more likely to decide the model fits (i.e., give false positives). As a further check on the adequacy of this model, the spectral density function of the residuals was also examined for peaks. If the residuals were white noise, the spectral density function should have no peaks or distinguishing characteristics. The spectral density function in Fig. 16.10 was found to be consistent with these characteristics of white noise.

When the AR(1) model from the preintervention series was applied to the postintervention data, a crude but useful analysis was performed by plotting the residuals on a graph with a band marking ±2 standard deviations. As shown in Fig. 16.11, the intervention effect appears to be significant because the residuals were outside the two standard deviation band.

In order to conclude the intervention effect was significant, evidence of change consistent with an AR(1) model must be found. To test the assumption of linear change, the autocorrelations were computed for the residuals (of the lin-

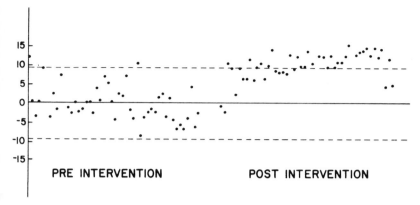

FIG. 16.11.   Plotted residuals of an autoregressive fit. (Source: Gottman, 1981, page 341.)

early detrended postintervention series). The Box–Pierce test of white noise
residuals was used again:

$$Q = n \sum_{j=1}^{k=6} r_{(j)}^2 = 46(.041)^2 = 1.89.$$

The lack of statistical significance supported the chart's evidence that the postintervention series was different from the preintervention series in a linear deterministic fashion.

In the actual practice of interrupted time-series analysis, we recommend that
the preintervention and postintervention series each be modeled separately and
then compared. The advantage of this later approach is a more precise description of intervention effects. The Ireland data is used again to illustrate the comparison of two models approach.

Once again we begin by selecting a model for the series, but this time the pre-
and postintervention series are modeled independently. The two different AR(p)
models are of the form:

Y_t = [deterministic trend] + [stochastic trend] + [residual error]

$$Y_t = [m_1 t + b_1] + \left[\sum_{i=1}^{p} \phi_i Y_{t-i} \right] + [e_t] \quad \text{for } t < 1924$$

$$Y_t = [m_2 t + b_2] + \left[\sum_{i=1}^{p} \phi_i Y_{t-i} \right] + [e_t] \quad \text{for t} > 1924$$

TABLE 16.6
AR Terms for Model Building with the Ireland Data

Number of Terms	Parameter Estimates	t Values	Significance
$p = 1$	$\phi_1 = .60$	7.10	$p < .001$
$p = 2$	$\phi_1 = .53$	5.27	$p < .001$
	$\phi_2 = .16$	1.57	$p \approx .12$
$p = 3$	$\phi_1 = .51$	4.74	$p < .001$
	$\phi_2 = .092$	.77	—
	$\phi_3 = .14$	1.32	$p \approx .19$
$p = 4$	$\phi_1 = .51$	4.66	$p < .001$
	$\phi_2 = .13$	1.08	$p \approx .28$
	$\phi_3 = .096$	.79	—
	$\phi_4 = -.011$	-.01	—
$p = 5$	$\phi_1 = .50$	4.48	$p < .001$
	$\phi_2 = .13$	1.04	$p \approx .30$
	$\phi_3 = .12$	.94	$p \approx .34$
	$\phi_4 = -.043$	-.34	—
	$\phi_5 = .039$	.35	—

Earlier we estimated an AR(1) because the partial autocorrelation function (PACF) truncated after one lag. This selection of the order of an AR model can be done more carefully by examining the statistical significance of several models. In Table 16.6, the parameter estimates and significance for five different AR models are presented.

Model building is the exact opposite of the usual ANOVA hypothesis-testing situation, where terms are assumed to be zero until proven otherwise. Terms should be included if there is any suggestion that they contribute to a better model. Strict adherence to significance levels is not encouraged and both the AR(2) or AR(3) model deserve further attention. Both models are used to test for intervention effects.

To develop a statistical test for intervention effects, we return to the usual hypothesis-testing situation. Let the null hypothesis be the situation where there is no intervention effect and the pre- and postmodels are equivalent. Let the alternative hypothesis be the situation where there is an intervention effect and the pre- and postmodels are different. An ordinary F test can test where $m_1 = m_2$ and $b_1 = b_2$ (See Gottman, 1981 for the details on calculating SS_0 and SS_1):

$$F = \frac{(SS_0 - SS_1)/2}{(SS_1)/\nu}.$$

The error degrees of freedom, ν, are equal to the number of observations (93) minus the number of "start-up" observations [2 in the AR(2) model or 3 in the

AR(3)] minus the number of parameters fit [6 in the AR(2), 7 in the AR(3)]. The error degrees of freedom is given by the formula $v = 89 - 2p$ (where p = parameters).

In the AR(2) model $F = 5.74$ with $v = 85$ and probability $<.005$. The AR(3) model gave an $F = 5.99$ with $v = 83$ and probability $<.005$. Both models support the conclusions of significant intervention effects. In Fig. 16.12, the statistical models were superimposed onto the data set. (The estimates of m_1, b_1, m_2, and b_2 were adjusted to reflect the weighting of the number of parameter estimates in the model.) The AR(3) fit is slightly tighter than the AR(2) and therefore the AR(3) might be the preferred model.

It is interesting to note what would have happened to the F statistic had the autocorrelation between observations not been modeled. The significance would have been spuriously high with $F = 53.89$. Although the F statistic has been robust in the face of other violations, the assumption of independent observations is not so forgiving.

It can be concluded that the change in social policy that occurred in 1924 was a significant event that changed the number of students passing the exams.

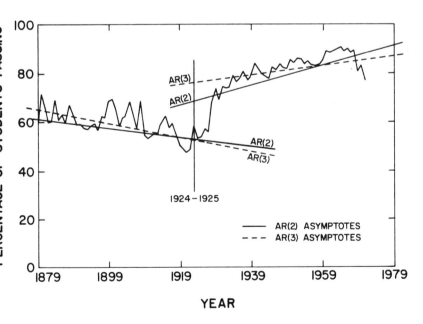

FIG. 16.12. Two autoregressive models fitted to the Ireland data. (Source: Gottman, 1981, page 364.)

RECENT INNOVATIONS
IN TIME-SERIES ANALYSIS

Autoregressive, moving average, and ARMA models assume that the data have been generated by stationary processes that are *linear in the parameters* of the model (as opposed to linear in the data values over time). Recent work has involved extension of time-series methods to models that are not stationary and not linear in the model parameters.

Many estimation techniques are based on the assumption of local linearity, with time-varying model parameters. Priestley (1988; 1989) described these new models. ARMA models of any order can be represented in *state-space* in which the model is a first-order model of a vector-valued processes. This representation is similar to the representation of a finite-order differential equation as a vector-valued first-order differential equation. This approach is based on the work of Akaike (1974). The approach and its advantages over the standard methods of ARMA estimation are summarized in Aoki (1987).

Nonlinear models of various types have been the *bi-linear models,* the *threshold autoregressive models,* and *exponential autoregressive models.*

A bilinear model adds to an ARMA model terms in which the past of the series is multiplied by the white noise process. For example,

$$X_t + 0.3X_{t-1} = e_t + .2e_{t-1} + .8X_{t-1}e_{t-1},$$

contains one bi-linear term $.8X_{t-1}e_{t-1}$. Priestly (1989) noted that this model type is more powerful than adding powers of X_t and e_t (Priestly, 1989, p. 52). The reasons have to do with a general expansion of a time series called a Volterra series.

Threshold autoregressive models (Tong, 1983) are AR models in which the parameters switch once a parameter threshold is reached. For example,

$$X_t = .3X_{t-1} + e_t \quad \text{if } X_t < 5, \text{ but}$$

$$X_t = .6X_t + e_t^* \quad \text{if } X_t \geq 5.$$

It turns out to be the case that threshold models are good for representing periodic phenomena, known as *limit cycles.*

Exponential autoregressive models (Ozaki, 1982) have features taken from nonlinear differential equations representing forced oscillations, such as Duffings or Van der Pol's equations. These models can represent catastrophe theory jumps as well as limit cycles. They have the potential for being chaotic solutions to nonlinear systems.

Priestley (1989) developed a general approach to estimating nonlinear models, called *state-dependent* models. He employed a sequential type of algorithm similar to the Kalman filter algorithm and applied the method to data simulated by known nonlinear models, with reasonable results (Priestley, 1988).

Generalizations to nonstationary processes have also been developed in which he spectral representation of a time series has been expanded to the concept of an *volutionary spectrum*. In an evolutionary spectral representation, the amplitudes ›f the sine and cosine components are time-varying functions (see Priestley, 989, chap. 6). Again, the generalization is that the series is *locally* stationary, ust as the generalization to nonlinearity involved local linearity.

RESOURCES FOR TIME-SERIES ANALYSIS

[he *Journal of Applied Time Series Analysis* publishes advances in methodology. Many of the technical advances come from applications in econometrics, engi‑ neering, and geology, but are relevant to problems in psychology. Recent issues ›f this journal have debated how to handle missing data, statistical tests of model dentification, and how to enhance true patterns in the data while reducing noise hrough statistical transformations and filtering.

Software for time-series analysis has become much more available, flexible, nd simple to use in the past 10 years. Nazam (1988) listed the names and ddresses of almost 20 different software programs for time-series analysis. Although some of this information is no longer current, it is a good starting point ›or a comprehensive review of software alternatives.

This review was limited by what was obtainable through the University of Washington computing centers and the authors' preferred software. The univer‑ ity supports four packages that perform some form of time-series analyses: SAS/ETS, SHAZAM, SPSS, and TSP. The Williams–Gottman time-series pro‑ ;rams were written specifically for our developmental social psychophysiology ab and are available to others on request. The most frequent users of time-series oftware are econometricians and most software programs were written to fulfill heir demands. Consequently, the majority of software programs (including all hose reviewed here) permit the calculations of ARIMA and forecasting (or xtrapolation into the future) models.

The SAS Institute offers a package called Econometric Time Series (ETS), vhich appears to be reasonably comprehensive. The 1984 version 5 has several nteresting features. SPECTRA computes the spectral density and coherence tatistic for two time series, including the phase shift. This information can tell he user about the similarity of two time series. STATESPACE offers multivari‑ .te time domain modeling using stationary vectors and first-order processing. We lave not used this package, but are excited by the advances into multivariate pplications.

SHAZAM is the popular econometrics program from the department of Eco‑ iomics at the University of British Columbia. Autoregressive models with miss‑ ng data are offered (a problem not often handled in commercial software for ime-series analysis). An approach to time-series analysis using least squares regression techniques (not covered in this chapter) is emphasized and higher-order AR and MA models are offered with appropriate higher-order statistical tests. One of the distinctions of SHAZAM is a user's manual valued as entertaining reading.

SPSS/PC+ announced a time-series package in 1987 called Trends. Each procedure is illustrated with a sample problem and explanations are simple and clear. Trends permits ARIMA, regression and individual components modeling. In addition to a full frequency component analysis, you may search for multiplicative or seasonal factors with a separate SEASON command. The number of alternative statistical tests of model fit is more limited than other software packages, but this may be less confusing to the novice. Missing data can be handled in a variety of ways. An interrupted time-series analysis is offered through the use of ARIMA models.

Quantitative Micro Software in Irvine, California offers a flexible package called Time Series Programs (TSP). Version 6 has been available since 1988 and can handle "a few thousand observations." The manual claims to assume nothing about the users knowledge of computers or time-series analysis. Clear explanations of alternatives in test statistics are provided and interpretive guidelines are offered. Data can be entered directly or as Loftus 1-2-3 files. This package does not offer modeling of individual (deterministic and stochastic) components but ARIMA models are computed. Advanced statistical techniques (not discussed in this chapter) include nonlinear least squares, estimation of probit and logit binary choice models and vector autoregression.

The Williams–Gottman programs are of special interest to psychologists who want to use the mathematical decomposition approach to time-series modeling but do not have a strong mathematical or engineering background. Programs available from the International Mathematical and Statistical Library (IMSL) require the user to be very explicit about modeling decisions, whereas our programs were written to maximize exploration before specific modeling decisions are made. Frequency and time domain models are available for both univariate and bivariate applications. Analyses for interrupted time series are simple to compute. Confidence intervals for statistical tests are included and graphical displays are automatic. In addition to mathematical decomposition, these programs also offer ARIMA models and forecasting.

TIMEID is a useful public domain package available free of charge. It is limited to the ARIMA approach, but allows for model exploration as well as direct identification. A sample data set identical to one discussed in McCleary and Hay (1980) makes this a particularly useful tool for self-tutoring in the ARIMA tradition. Autocorrelation and partial autocorrelation functions are graphed with confidence intervals and Box–Pierce Q statistic.

This chapter has presented only the most fundamental concepts at an intuitive level. We recommend the reader continue learning by actually doing time-series analyses and reading more when problems arise. The reference section of this hapter lists many excellent sources. The book by Gottman (1981) is especially ood for explanations that begin at an intuitive level and progress to some :atistical sophistication.

REFERENCES

kaike, H. (1974). Markovian representations of stochastic processes and its application to the analysis of autoregressive moving average processes. *Annals of the Institute of Statistical Mathematics, 26,* 363–387.

nderson, T. W. (1971). *The statistical analysis of time-series.* New York: Wiley.

oki, M. (1987). *State space modeling of time series.* Berlin: Springer-Verlag.

ox, G. E. P., & Jenkins, G. M. (1970). *Time-series analysis: forcasting and control.* San Francisco: Holden-Day.

roden, M., Hall, R. V., & Mitts, B. (1971). The effect of self-recording on the classroom behavior of two eighth-grade students. *Journal of Applied Behavior Analysis, 4,* 191–199.

ampbell, D. T., & Stanley, J. C. (1963). *Experimental and quasi-experimental designs for research.* Boston: Houghton Mifflin.

hatfield, C. (1975). *The analysis of time-series: theory and practice.* London: Chapman and Hall.

rosbie, J. (1991). Interrupted Time-Series Analysis with Short Series: Why it is Problematic; How it can be Improved. *Behavioral Assessment 4* 181–220.

urbin, J. (1970). Testing for serial correlation in least-squares regression when some of the regressors are lagged dependent variables. *Econometrica, 38,* 410–421.

lass, G. V., Willson, V. L., & Gottman, J. M. (1975). *Design and analysis of time series experiments.* Boulder: Colorado Associated University Press.

ottman, J. M. (1981). *Time-series analysis: A comprehensive introduction for social scientists.* Cambridge: Cambridge University Press.

ottman, J. M. (1979). Time-series analysis of continuous data in dyads. In M. Lamb, S. Suomi, & G. Stephenson (Eds.), *Social interaction analysis: Methodological issues* (pp. 207–230). Madison: University of Wisconsin Press.

lersen, M., & Barlow, D. (1976). *Single-case experimental designs: Strategies for studying behavior change.* New York: Pergamon.

azden, A. E. (1982). *Single-case research designs: Methods for clinical and applied settings.* New York: Oxford University Press.

1ann, H. B., & Wald, A. (1943). On the statistical treatment of linear stochastic difference equations. *Econonometrica 11* 173–220.

1cCleary, R., & Hay, R. A., Jr. (1980). *Applied time series analysis for the social sciences.* Beverly Hills, CA: Sage Publications.

1cDowall, D., McCleary, R., Meidinger, E. E., & Hay, R. A. (1980). *Interrupted time series analysis* Beverly Hills, CA: Sage Publications.

azem, S. M. (1988). *Applied time series analysis for business and economic forecasting.* New York: Marcel Dekker.

zaki, T. (1982). The statistical analysis of perturbed limit cycle processes using nonlinear time series models. *Journal of Time Series, 3,* 29–41.

andit, S., & Wu, S. (1983). *Time series and system analysis with applications.* New York: Wiley.

riestley, M. B. (1988). Current developments in time series modeling. *Journal of Econometrics, 37,* 67–86.

riestley, M. B. (1989). *Nonlinear and non-stationary time series analysis.* London: Academic Press.

ong, H. (1983). *Threshold models in non-linear time series analysis.* New York: Springer-Verlag.

Wills, T. A., Weiss, R. L., & Patterson, G. R. (1974). A behavioral analysis of the determinants of marital satisfaction. *Journal of Consulting and Clinical Psychology 42* 802–811.

Wold, H. (1938). *A study in the analysis of stationary time-series*. Uppsala: Almquist and Wiksell

Wu, S., & Pandit, S. M. (1983). *Time series and system analysis*. New York: Wiley.

Author Index

A

Abelson, R. P., 385, 386, *388*
Agresti, A., 301, 304, 311, *315*, 345, *345*
Akaike, H., 524, *527*
Altham, P. M. E., 292, *292*
American National Standards Institute, 446, *451*
Anderson, E., 433, *451*
Anderson, R. L., 303, *318*
Anderson, T. W., 170, *196*, 511, *527*
Andrews, D. F., 400, 435, *451*
Angoff, C., 435, *451*
Aoki, M., 524, *527*
Appelbaum, M. I., 64, *70*, 75, *94*, 95, 108, 113, 114, 121, *125*, *126*
Arnold, S., 4, *41*

B

Bachi, R., 398, 399, 418, 419, 435, *451*
Bakan, D., 202, *231*
Baker, F. B., 302, *315*
Baker, R. J., 301, *315*
Banaji, M. R., 486, *490*
Barabba, V., 445, *452*
Barcikowski, R. S., 64, *68*, 75, 93
Barlow, D., 496, *527*

Barnard, G., 443, *452*
Barnard, G. A., 327, *345*
Barnett, V., 221, *231*, 435, *452*
Battistich, V., 296n, *319*
Bayes, T., 202, *231*
Becker, R. A., 444, *452*
Becketti, S., 419, 420, *452*
Belanger, A., 301, 303, *316*, 327, *346*
Bell, D. E., 229, *231*
Berger, J. O., 210, 218, 221, 225, *231*
Berhardson, C. S., 44, *69*
Berkson, J., 301, 306, *315*
Bernardo, J. M., 230, *231*
Bertin, J., 392, 413, 414, 415, 424, 432, 446, *452*
Besag, J., 355, *389*
Bevan, W., 434, *454*
Bickel, P. J., 417, *452*
Biderman, A. D., 394, 443, 447, 448, *452*, *456*
Birch, M. W., 270, 277, *292*
Bishop, Y. M. M., 262, 264, 272, 275, 280, 283, 284, 289, 291, *292*, 307, 311, 312, *315*, 435, *452*
Blair, R. C., 113, *125*
Boardman, T. J., 314, *315*
Bock, R. D., 246, 249, 250, *256*, 392, *452*
Boes, D. C., 356, 358, *390*

Bogartz, W., 108, *125*
Boik, R. J., 66, 66*n*, 69, 86, *93*
Bondy, F., 349, *389*
Bose, R. C., 66, *70*
Bowman, W. J., 447, *452*
Box, G. E. P., 73, 74, 77, 78, *93*, 218, *231*, 233, 254, *256*, 509, *527*
Bradely, D. R., 300, *315*
Bradely, T. D., 300, *315*
Bradley, J. V., 413, *452*
Bradley, R. A., 290, *292*
Bresnahan, J. L., 314, *316*
Brier, S. S., 288, 292, *292*
Broadbent, D. E., 468, *476*
Broadbent, H. A., 463, *476*
Broden, M., 496, 497, 498, *527*
Brook, J., 184, *197*
Brown, D. R., 75, *94*, 367, *390*
Brown, M. B., 56, 60, *69*, 314, *316*
Brunswik, E., 115, *126*
Bruntz, S. M., 418, 433, *452*
Burke, C. J., 295, 298, 299, *318*
Byars, J. A., 300, *319*

C

Camilli, G., 300, 303, *316*
Campbell, D. T., 493, 495, *527*
Carlson, J. E., 111, 114, *126*, 129, *163*, 167, 168, *197*
Carmer, S. G., 53, 54, *69*
Carr, J. C., 309, *319*
Cartwright, B., 108, *127*
Castellan, N. J., Jr., 314, *316*
Castner, H. W., 447, *452*
Cesa, T., 309, *316*
Chakrapani, T. K., 425, *452*
Chambers, J. M., 392, 420, 423, 433, *452*, 472, *476*
Chapman, J. A. W. A., 312, *316*
Chase, W., 301, 303, *316*, 327, *346*
Chatfield, C., 501, 511, *527*
Chen, J. J., 244, *256*
Chernoff, H., 277, *292*, 434, 442, 447, *452*
Chilag, N., 122, *126*
Christ, D. E., 215, *231*
Church, R. M., 463, 464, 475, *476*, 477, *490*
Clark, W. A., 463, *476*
Clemen, R. T., 229, *231*

Cleveland, W., 421, 422, *452, 453*
Cleveland, W. S., 392, 405, 407, 418, 420, 423, 424, 433, 435, 444, 445, 447, 448, *452, 453*, 472, *476*
Cliff, N., 168, *196*
Cochran, W., 280, *292*
Cochran, W. G., 299, 312, 315, *316*, 331, *345*
Cohen, A., 314, *316*
Cohen, J., 53, *69*, 95, 96, 97, 108, 121, *126*, 165, 166, 169, 170, 172, 173, 175, 175*n*, 176, 177, 178, 179, 180, 181, 182, 183, 185, 187, 190, 193, 196, *196, 197*, 259, 292, *292, 301, 316*
Cohen, M. J., 75, 76, 79, *94*
Cohen, P., 53, 67, 69, 95, 96, 97, *126*, 165, 169, 170, 172, 179, 181, 182, 183, 184, 185, 187, 190, 196, *197*
Coleman, J. S., 286, *292*
Commoner, B., 488, *490*
Conover, W. J., 303, *316*
Cook, N. R., 387, *389*
Cornfield, J., 309, *316*
Costigan-Eaves, P., 395, *453*
Cox, D. R., 291, *292*, 303, 314, *316*, 327, *345*, 435, *453*
Cramer, E. M., 95, 108, 113, 114, 121, *125*, *126*, 168, 193, *197, 198*
Cramer, H., 299, 309, *316*
Crawford, P. V., 447, *453*
Crosbie, J., 501, *527*
Crowder, R. G., 486, *490*
Croxton, F. E., 447, *453*
Cutcomb, S. D., 300, *315*
CYTEL Software, 301, *316*

D

Dachler, H. P., 96, 115, *126*
Dagenais, F., 311, *318*
D'Agostino, R. B., 301, 303, 313, *316*, 327, *346*
Delucchi, K. L., 296*n, 319*
Daniel, C., 412, 413, 415, 416, *453*
Darlington, R. B., 95, *126*, 377, *389*
Davidson, M. L., 83, *93*
Davidson, R. R., 290, *292*
Dayton, C. M., 53, *69*, 75, *93*
Dearing, B. E., 355, *389*

de Finetti, B., 202, 219, *231*
DeGroot, M. H., 211, 230, *231*
Delucchi, K. L., 296, *316*
Deming, W. E., 272, 274, *293*
Dempster, A. P., 343, *346*
Denby, L., 416, *453*
Devlin, S., 421, *453*
Diaconis, P., 448, *452*
Dickey, J. M., 221, *231*
Dixon, W. J., 56, 60, *69*, 314, *316*, 416, *453*
Duncan, D. B., 55, *69*
Duncan, O. D., 285, *293*
Dunn, G., 333, 334, 342, *346*
Dunn, O. J., 44, 48, 52, 62, 63, *69*, 241, *256*, 306, 307, *316*
Dunnett, C. W., 59, 60, 64, *69*
Durbin, J., 509, *527*
Dutton, G., 444, *453*
Dyke, G. V., 265, *293*

E

Easton, G. S., 413, *453*
Eber, H. W., 180, *197*
Edwards, A. E., 295, *316*
Edwards, A. L., 75, *93*
Edwards, W., 202, 220, 225, *231, 232,* 234, *256*
Eells, W. C., 447, *453*
Egeth, H. E., 434, *454*
Ehrenberg, A. S. C., 425, 437, 448, *452, 453*
Einot, I., 46, *69*
Eircikan, K., 302, *320*
Ekstrom, D., 75, *93*
Emerson, J. D., 358, 363, 367, 369, 370, 371, 373, 379, 381, 383, 387, *389, 390*
Engelman, L., 56, 60, *69*
Entwisle, D. R., 312, *318*
Epley, E. A., 433, *457*
Everitt, B. S., 324, 333, 338, 342, *346,* 392, *453*

F

Farquhar, A. B., 450, *453*
Farquhar, H., 450, *453*
Farquhar, P. H., 290, *292*

Feldt, L. S., 64, *70, 77n,* 78, 79, *93, 94*
Felsenstein, J., 300, *318,* 331, *346*
Fienberg, B. M., 395, 443, *453*
Fienberg, S. E., 262, 264, 272, 274, 275, 280, 283, 284, 289, 290, 291, *292, 293,* 307, 309, 311, 312, 314, *315, 316,* 424, 435, 448, *452, 453*
Finn, J. D., 4, 35, *41,* 64, *69,* 250, *256*
Fisher, R. A., 48, 52, *69,* 129, *163,* 277, *293,* 299, 312, *317,* 324, *346*
Fiske, S. T., 385, 386, *388*
Flannery, B. P., 462, 470, *476*
Fleishman, A., 96, 115, *126*
Fleiss, J. L., 310, *317,* 367, *389*
Forsythe, A. B., 60, *69*
Francolini, C., 424, 447, *456*
Franklin, C. A., 395, *453*
Freedman, D. A., 478, 479, 483, 485, 488, *491*
Freeman, M. F., 280, *293*
Freni-Titulaer, L. W. J., 447, *453*
Fridlund, A. J., 75, 76, 79, *94*
Friedman, H. P., 433, *455*
Friedman, J., 444, *453*
Friedman, M., 67, *69*
Funkhouser, H. G., 394, 409, *454*
Furnival, G. M., 416, *454*

G

Gaba, A., 218, *232*
Gabriel, K. R., 46, *69*
Gaebelein, J., 95, 109, 110, 111, 112, 113, 114, *126*
Gafarian, A. V., 277, *293*
Games, P. A., 54, 59, 60, *69*
Gans, L., 309, *317*
Gardner, W., 474, *476*
Gart, J. J., 306, *317*
Gasko, M., 356, 358, *390*
Geisser, S., 74, 77, 78, 79, *93*
Gibbon, J., 463, *476*
Gibbons, J. D., 356, *389*
Glass, G. V., 96, *126,* 494, 496, 497, 498, 499, 501, 502, 512, 518, 519, *527*
Gnanadesikan, R., 392, 395, 410, 411, 412, 413, 421, 421. 416. 412. 421*n*, 422, 445, *453, 454, 457*
Gocka, E. F., 105*n*, 107, *126*

Godfrey, K., 387, *389*
Gokhale, D. V., 291, *293*
Gold, E. B., 360, 361, 362, 363, 364, *390*
Gold, R. Z., 306, *317*
Golden, R. N., 75, *93*
Goldwyn, R. M., 433, *455*
Good, I. J., 299, 300, 312, *317*
Goodman, L. A., 281, 282, 285, 286, 291, 292, *293,* 306, 309, 311, *317,* 345, *346*
Gorman, J. W., 416, *454*
Gottman, J. M., 494, 496, 497, 498, 499, 500, 501, 502, 506, 507, 509, 511, 512, 513, 514, 518, 519, 520, 521, 522, 523, 527, *527*
Gould, W., 419, 420, *452*
Gray, R., 301, *318*
Graybill, F. A., 356, 358, *390*
Greenhouse, S. W., 74, 77, 78, 79, *93,* 303, *318*
Grizzle, J. E., 292, *293,* 303, *317, 319*
Grover, T. N., 299, 312, *317*
Groves, C., 425, 447, 448, *456*
Gruvaeus, G. T., 433, *454*
Gumbel, E. J., 300, *317*
Gyato, K. P., 363, 365, *389*

Hertzog, C., 75, 84, *93*
Higgins, J. J., 113, *125*
Hill, M. A., 56, 60, *69*
Hiramatsu, M., 425, *455*
Hoaglin, D. C., 355, 358, 360, 362, 370, 371, 373, 379, 383, *389, 390*
Hochberg, Y., 48, 52, 54n, 59, 63, 64, 68, 69
Hocking, R. R., 95, *127,* 129, *163*
Hogarth, R., 219, *231*
Holland, P. W., 262, 264, 272, 275, 280, 283, 284, 289, 291, *292,* 307, 311, 312, *315,* 435, *452*
Hollander, M., 63, *69*
Hooper, J. W., 167, 168, *197*
Hopkins, K. D., 300, 303, *316*
Horn, S. D., 300, *317*
Hotelling, H., 64, *69,* 167, *197*
Howell, D. C., 108, 111, 112, 121, *126*
Howell, J. F., 60, *69*
Hsieh, H., 397, *454*
Huber, P. J., 356, *389,* 416, 444, *454*
Huhn, R. von, 447, *454*
Huitema, B. E., 87, *93*
Humphreys, L. G., 96, 115, *126*
Hutchinson, T. P., 301, *317*
Huynh, H., 64, *70,* 77n, 78, 79, *93, 94*

H

Haber, R. N., 486, *491*
Haberman, S. J., 270, 271, 291, 292, *293, 294,* 311, *317*
Hall, R. V., 496, 497, 498, *527*
Hamer, R. M., 244, *256*
Hammel, E. A., 417, *452*
Hampel, F. R., 421n, *454*
Hand, D. J., 342, *346*
Hansen, C. J., 447, *455*
Harrison, P. J., 218, *232*
Hartigan, J., 433, 447, *454*
Hartwig, F., 355, *389*
Hastie, R., 447, *455*
Hay, R. A., Jr., 501, 505, 510, 518, *527*
Hays, W. L., 4, 5, *41*
Hayter, A. J., 52, 54, 54n, *69*
Henry, N. W., 342, *346*
Herr, D. G., 95, 109, 110, 111, 112, 113, 114, *126*
Herr, O. G., 129, *163*
Hersen, M., 496, *527*

I

Imhof, J. P., 74, 83, *94*
Irwin, J. O., 314, *317*
Isaacs, G. L., 215, *231*

J

Jackson, P. H., 212, 215, *231, 232,* 234, 248, *256*
Jacob, R. J. K., 434, *454*
Jeffreys, H., 299, *317*
Jenkins, G. M., 509, *527*
Jennings, J. R., 75, 76, 79, *94*
Jennrich, R. I., 56, 60, *69*
Jevons, W. S., 408, *454*
Jobe, J. B., 365, 366, 367, 368, *390*
Joe, G. W., 108, *126*
Johnson, N. L., 262, *293*
Joint Committee on Standards for Graphic Presentation, 446, *454*
Jones, L. V., 392, *452*

K

adane, J. B., 221, *231*
ahneman, D., 202, *231*
aiser, M. K., 75, *94*
astenbaum, M. A., 282, *293,* 314, *317*
atz, B. M., 303, *317*
azden, A. E., 496, *527*
eeney, R. L., 229, *231*
eil, F., 488, *491*
empthorne, O. A., 299, 301, 312, *317, 319*
endall, M. G., 299, 300, 309, 310, *317, 318*
eppel, G., 75, *94,* 243, 245, *256*
eren, G., 95, 96, 97, 102n, 108, 109, 111, 114, 115, 118, 120, 121, *126,* 175n, *197*
erlinger, F. N., 95, 96, 97, *126*
eselman, H. J., 59, *69,* 83, 84, 88, *94*
eselman, J. C., 88, *94*
ettenring, J., 421, *453*
euls, M., 48, *70*
imball, A. W., 314, *318*
inder, D. R., 385, 386, *388*
irk, R. E., 48, 51, 52, *70,* 75, 77n, 79, *94,* 237, 241, *256*
ittaka, T., 425, *455*
leinbaum, D. G., 163, *163*
leiner, B., 392, 418, 420, 422, 423, 433, 447, *452, 453, 454,* 472, *476*
nepp, D. L., 312, *318*
nuth, D., 462, *476*
och, G. G., 292, *293*
oestler, A., 482, 483, *491*
osslyn, S. M., 413, 447, *454*
otz, S., 262, *293*
ramer, C. Y., 48, *70*
rus, D. J., 168, *196*
ruskal, W. H., 60, *70,* 292, *293,* 309, 311, *317, 318,* 345, *346,* 444, 446, *454*
ullback, S., 291, *293*
utner, M. H., 367, 377, *390*

L

achenbruch, P., 339, *346*
aird, N. M., 343, *346*
ana, R. E., 75, *94*
ancaster, H. O., 314, *318*
arntz, K., 281, 290, 291, *293*

Larsen, W., 404, 405, 406, *454*
Laub, E., 435, *453*
Laugh, E., 314, *316*
La Valle, I. H., 211, *231*
Lazarsfeld, P. L., 342, *346*
Lee, S. K., 271, *293*
Leff et al., 345
Lehmann, E. L., 163, *163,* 277, *292,* 356, *389*
Leinhardt, S., 355, *390,* 400, *454*
Lepine, D., 64, *70*
Leroy, A. M., 392, *455*
Levy, K. J., 62, 67, *70*
Lewis, C., 95, 96, 97, 102n, 108, 109, 111, 114, 115, 118, 120, 121, *126,* 168, 170, 175n, 196, *197, 198*
Lewis, D., 295, 298, 299, *318*
Lewontin, R. C., 300, *318,* 331, *346*
Libby, D. L., 244, *256*
Lichtenstein, S., 202, *232*
Lin, Y. S., 292, *293*
Lindley, D. V., 218, 229, 230, *231, 232*
Lindman, H., 202, 220, 225, *231,* 234, *256*
Lipscomb, K., 203, 204, *232*
Little, R. J. A., 327, *346*
Loftus, G. R., 477, 478, 486, 490, *491*
Lono M., 425, 447, 448, *456*
Louv, W. C., 447, *453*
Lowerr, J. S., 202, *232*
Lubin, A., 75, *94*

M

Macdonald-Ross, M., 395, 447, *453, 454*
Maksik, Y., 464, *476*
Mallows, C. L., 416, *453*
Mandelbrot, B. B., 393, *454*
Mann, H. B., 300, *318,* 511, *527*
Mantel, N., 303, *318*
Marascuilo, L. A., 44, 46, 54, 61, 62, 63, 67, *70, 71,* 299, 302, 307, 309, 310, 311, *318, 319*
Mattson, I., 64, *69,* 250, *256*
Maxwell, A. E., 310, *318*
Maxwell, S. E., 67, *70*
Mayr, G. von, 424, *454*
McCabe, G. P., 401, *454*
McCall, R. B., 64, *70,* 75, *94*
McCleary, R., 501, 505, 510, 518, *527*
McClelland, J. L., 468, *476*

McConaughy, S. H., 108, 111, 112, 121, *126*
McCullagh, P., 4, *41*
McCulloch, R. E., 413, *453*
McDonald, L. L., 163, *163*
McDowall, D., 518, *527*
McGill, M. E., 392, 435, 444, 445, *453*
McGill, R., 404, 405, 406, 424, 425, 447, 448, *452, 453, 454*
McGrath, S. G., 300, *315*
McNemar, Q., 338, *346*
McSweeney, M., 61, 62, 63, 67, *70*, 229, 303, 310, *317, 318*
Meehl, P. E., 202, *232*
Mehat, C. R., 301, *318*
Mehta, C. R., 327, *346*
Meidinger, E. E., 518, *527*
Mencken, H. L., 435, *451*
Mendoza, J. L., 83, 84, *94*
Michels, K. M., 75, *94*, 367, *390*
Miettinen, O. S., 303, *318*
Miller, H. L., 202, *232*
Miller, R. G., 46*n*, 48, 51, 52, 58, 61, 62, 63, 67, 68, *70*
Milligan, G. W., 122, *126*
Mingay, D. J., 365, 366, 367, 368, *390*
Mitchell, G. J., 299, 312, *317*
Mitts, D., 496, 497, 498, *527*
Molnar, C. E., 463, *476*
Monkhouse, F. J., 392, *454*
Mood, A. M., 356, 358, *390*
Moore, D. S., 401, *454*
Morrison, D. F., 64, *70*
Mosteller, F., 255, *256*, 355, 356, 367, 370, *389, 390*, 392, *454, 455*
Mote, V. L., 303, *318*
Mudholkar, G. S., 163, *163*
Murray, J., 334, *346*
Murthy, V. K., 277, *293*
Myers, J. L., 65, *70*, 75, 84, *94*, 96, 97, *126*, 367, *390*

N

Nazem, S. M., 501, 525, *527*
Nee, J. C. M., 175, 176, 180, 193, 196, *197*
Neisser, U., 486, *491*
Nemenyi, P., 61, 62, *70*
Nerlove, M., 259, *294*

Neter, J., 367, 377, *390*
Newman, D., 48, *70*
Neyman, J., 312, *319*
Nicewander, W. A., 168, *197*
Nightingale, F., 435, *455*
Novick, M. R., 212, 215, *231, 232,* 234, 244, 248, *256*

O

O'Brien, R. G., 75, *94*
O'Connell, J. W., 417, *452*
Olson, C. L., 37, *41,* 175, 180, *197*
Oude Voshaar, J. H., 62, *70*
Overall, J. E., 5, 95, 100, 101, 103, 108, 109, 110, 111, 113, 121, 122, *126,* 301, *319*
Ozaki, T., 524, *527*

P

Pandit, S., 511, *527*
Pastore, N., 295, 299, *319*
Patel, N. R., 301, *318,* 327, *346*
Patterson, H. D., 265, *293*
PDP Group, the, 468, *476*
Pearson, E. S., 312, *319*
Pearson, K., 296, 303, *319,* 323, *346*
Pedhazur, E. J., 95, 96, 97, *126,* 165, 182, *197*
Peters, C. C., 295, *319*
Peters, M. D., 385, 386, *388*
Peters, S. C., 221, *231*
Phillips, L. D., 202, *232*
Pillai, K. C. S., 170, 176, *197*
Pitz, G. F., 202, *232*
Plackett, R. L., 291, *294,* 303, *319*
Playfair, W., 394, *455*
Posten, H. O., 445, *455*
Press, S. J., 216, 218, *232,* 259, *294*
Press, W. H., 462, 470, *476*
Priestley, M. B., 524, 525, *527*
Puri, M. L., 162, *163*

Q

Quade, D., 75, *93*

R

Raiffa, H., 202, 211, 229, *231, 232*
Ramsay, J. O., 425, 433, *455*
Ramsy, P. H., 46, 55, *70*
Rand Corporation, 462, *476*
Rao, C. R., 79, 80, *94, 129, 163,* 167, 168, 175, *197,* 270, *294*
Rawlings, R. R., Jr., 108, *126*
Reiser, M., 435, *456*
Relles, D., 447, *455*
Rizvi, H. M., 434, 447, *452*
Robertson, C. A., 309, *317*
Robey, R. R., 64, *68*
Robinson, A. H., 447, *452*
Rogan, J. C., 59, *69,* 83, 84, *94*
Rogers, W., 447, *455*
Roscoe, J. T., 300, *319*
Rosenberger, J. L., 356, 358, *390*
Rosenthal, R., 306*n, 319*
Rosman, E., 313, *316*
Rosnow, R. L., 306*n, 319*
Rothenberg, T., 488, *491*
Rouanet, H., 64, *70*
Rourke, R. E. K., 356, *390*
Rousseuw, P. J., 392, *455*
Rovine, M., 75, 84, *93*
Roy, S. N., 66, *70,* 161, *163,* 167, 168, *197*
Rozeboom, W. W., 167, 168, *197*
Rubin, A. S., 60, 61, *70*
Rubin, D. B., 343, *346*
Ruchkin, D. S., 75, 76, 79, *94*
Rumelhart, D. E., 468, *476*
Ryan, T. A., 54, *70*

S

Samuel, A. G., 73, *94*
Sandiford, P., 392, *455*
SAS Institute, Inc., 56, 60, *70*
Satterthwaite, F. E., 88, *94*
Savage, L. J., 202, 219, 220, 225, *231, 232,* 234, *256*
Schacht, S., 431, *456*
Schafer, W. D., 53, *69*
Schaps, E., 296*n, 319*
Scheffé, H., 48, 52, *70,* 109, 111, 112, 114, 120, *127,* 129, 138, 142, 149, *163,* 306, *319*

Scheuneman, J., 302, *319*
Schlaifer, R., 202, 211, 212, *232*
Schmid, C. F., 405, 446, *455*
Schmid, S. E., 446, *455*
Searle, S. R., 18*n,* 37, *41,* 129, *163*
Seber, 140
Seheult, A., 355, *389*
Sellke, T., 225, *231*
Sen, P. K., 162, *163,* 303, *319*
Serlin, R. C., 307, 309, *318, 319*
Shaffer, J. P., 54*n,* 59, *70,* 88, *94,* 314, *319*
Shapiro, M. M., 314, *316*
Šidák, Z., 44, *71*
Siegel, J. H., 433, *455*
Simkin, D., 447, *455*
Slakter, M. J., 299, 300, *319,* 331, *346*
Slaughter, R. E., 302, *318*
Slovic, P., 202, *231, 232*
Smith, A. F., 365, 366, 367, 368, 378, 379, 380, *390*
Smith, A. F. M., 230, *231*
Smith J. Q., 229, *232*
Smith, W. S., 221, *231*
Snee, R. D., 314, *319,* 435, *455*
Social Indicators III, 425, *455*
Solomon, D., 296*n, 319*
Solomon, J., 296*n, 319*
Sorlie, P. D., 360, 361, 362, 363, 364, *390*
Speed, F. M., 95, *127,* 129, *163*
Spetzler, C. A., 219, *232*
Spiegel, D. K., 5, 95, 100, 101, 103, 108, 109, 110, 111, 113, 121, 122, *126*
SPSS, Inc., 56, 59, *71*
Srikantan, K. S., 170, *197*
Staël von Holstein, C. -A. S., 219, *232*
Stanley, J. C., 96, *126,* 493, 495, *527*
Starmer, C. F., 292, *293,* 303, *319*
State court caseload statistics: 1976, 429, *455*
Statistical Abstract of the United States, 435
Stein, H., 447, *453*
Stellman, S. D., 357, *390*
Stephan, F. F., 272, 274, *293*
Stevens, J. P., 37, *41*
Stoddard, P. K., 477, *491*
Stoline, M. R., 58, *71*
Stoto, M. A., 367, 369, 370, 381, *389, 390*
Strahan, R. F., 447, *455*
Strenio, M. A., 363, *389*
Stryker, R. E., 447, *453*

Stuart, A., 289, *294*, 300, 309, *318*
Subbaiah, P., 163, *163*
Sutch, R., 488, *491*
Swanson, M. R., 53, 54, *69*

T

Taguri, M., 425, 433, *455, 456*
Tamhane, A., 48, 52, 54*n*, 59, 63, 64, 68, *69*
Tamhane, A. C., 60, *71*
Tarnopsky, A., 334, *346*
Tatsuoka, M. M., 11, 14*n*, 16*n*, 35, 37, *41*
Teicholz, E., 446, *455*
Terry, M. E., 290, *292*
Teukolsky, S. A., 462, 470, *476*
Thayer, J. F., 75, 76, 79, *94*
Thissen, D., 392, 421, 447, 449, *455, 456*
Thompson, P. A., 122, *126*
Thiao, G. C., 218, *231*, 233, 254, *256*
Tilling, L., 393, *455*
Timm, N. H., 111, 114, *126*, 129, 134, 137, 144, 145, 149, 151, 158, 160, 162, *163*, 167, 168, *197*
Toman, R. J., 416, *454*
Tong, H., 524, *527*
Tufte, E. R., 392, 395, 405, 423, 445, 446, *455*, 472, *476*
Tukey, J. W., 48, *71*, 255, *256*, 280, *293*, 355, 356, 358, 360, 362, 363, 367, 369, 370, 377, 379, 383, *389*, *390*, 392, 393, 395, 396, 397, 400, 401, 401*n*, 402, 403, 404, 405, 406, 408, 409, 410, 411, 420, 422, 423, 431, 433, 434, 444, 448, *453, 454, 455, 456*, 471, *476*
Tukey, P. A., 392, 420, 423, 433, 444, *452, 453, 455, 456*, 472, *476*
Tversky, A., 202, 229, *231*

U

Upton, G. J. G., 301, 303, *319*
Ury, H. K., 59, *71*
U. S. Bureau of the Census, 424, *456*
U. S. Department of the Army, 446, *456*
Uttal, W. R., 486, *491*

V

van den Burg, W., 168, 170, 175*n*, 196, *197*, *198*
Van der Vaart, H. R., 63, *71*
Vasey, M. W., 75, 76, 79, *94*
Velleman, P. F., 355, 358, 371, 377, 379, *390*
Vetterling, W. T., 462, 470, *476*
Vitaliano, P. P., 64, *71*
von Winterfeldt, D., 202, *232*

W

Wackerly, D., 301, *315*
Wainer, H., 97*n*, *127*, 392, 395, 396, 409, 421, 424, 425, 431, 433, 434, 435, 444, 445, 446, 447, 448, 449, *454, 455, 456*
Wakimoto, 433
Wakimoto, K., 425, 433, *455, 456*
Wald, A., 300, *318*, 511, *527*
Wallis, W. A., 61, *70*, 311, *318*, 391, *457*
Walls, R. C., 433, *457*
Wandell, B. A., 489, *491*
Wang, P. C. C., 392, *457*
Warner, J. L., 418, 433, *452*
Wasserman, S. S., 355, *390*, 400, *454*
Wasserman, W., 367, 377, *390*
Watkins, M. J., 485, *491*
Watson, M. S., 296*n*, *319*
Weisberg, S., 291, *293*
Welch, B. L., 59, 61, *71*, 88, *94*
Welder, J. A., 4, *41*
Well, A. D., 367, *390*
West, E. N., 312, *319*
West, M., 218, *232*
Wherry, R. J., 176, 177, *198*
Wiggins, A. D., 59, *71*
Wilk, M. B., 410, 411, 412, 413, *457*
Wilkinson, H. R., 392, *454*
Wilkinson, L., 180, *198*
Wilks, A. R., 444, *452*
Wilks, S. S., 161, *163*, 168, 169, *198*
Williams, O. D., 292, *294*
Williams, P., 334, *346*
Willson, V. L., 494, 496, 497, 498, 499, 50[1], 502, 512, 518, 519, *527*

ilson, R. W., 416, *454*
ilson, W., 202, *232*
iner, B. J., 52, *71, 75, 94,* 96, 122, *127,*
    367, *390*
ing, A. M., 468, *476*
inkler, R. L., 218, 219, 221, *231, 232*
ise, M. E., 299, 300, *319*
olf, G., 108, *127*
olfe, D. A., 63, *69*
olfram, S., 488, *491*
ong, D. S., 122, *126*
ong, G. Y., 387, *389*
ood, F. S., 412, 413, 415, 416, *453,*
    457
oodworth, G. C., 233, 244, *256*
oolson, R. F., 339, *346*

Wu, L. L., 356, 376, *390*
Wu, S., 511, *527*

Y

Yarnold, J. K., 300, *319*
Yates, F., 303, 304, *320,* 325, 327, *346*
Yule, G. U., 323, *346*

Z

Zellner, A., 218, *232*
Zwick, R., 44, 46, 54, 62, *71,* 193, *198,* 302,
    320

Subject Index

A

ANOVA, 3, 16, 43
  Unbalanced designs, 95–125
  Bayesian methods, 234–256
ANCOVA, 3, 16, 37–39
Autocorrelation, *see* time series
Autocovariance, *see* time series

B

Bayesian statistics, 201–293
  ANOVA, 234–256
  Bayes theorem, 203–216
  hypothesis testing, 221–225
  likelihoods, 201–204, 216–221, 223–225, 270–272 (*see also* maximum likelihood estimates)
  predictions, 225–228
  priors/posteriors, 204–216, 233–234
Bonferroni inequality, 44, 83–84, 240–245

C

Canonical analysis, 167–168
Chi-square, 277–278, 280, 295–315, 323–327, 330–331
  comparing of, 312–314
  correction for continuity, 303–304, 325
  partitioning, 314
Coding, 4–6, 10–11, 97–100, 103–104, 118–120, 122–125
Comparisons
  Bayesian, 237–239, 248–254
  for categorical data, 306–307
  Dunn-Benferoni, 52–53, 56–59
  Fisher's protected t-tests, 53–54, 56–59
  Newman-Keuls, 54–55
  for repeated measures, 64–67, 83–89
  Scheffe's, 49–51, 56–59
  Tukey's, 51–52, 56–59
Computer
  applications to psychology, 459–476
  simulations, 469–470, 487–490
Conjugate prior distributions, 210–215
Contingency tables, 193–196, 259–262, 295–315, 322–332
Contrasts, *see* comparisons
Correlation, 165–197
Correspondence analysis, 332–334

E

EDA (Exploratory Data Analysis), 179, 349–390, 392
  box plots, 364–367, 403–405
  percentile and quantile plots, 409–413

EDA (Exploratory Data Analysis) (*cont.*)
  resistant lines, 371–377
  stem-and-leaf displays, 358–362, 399–403
  transformations, 367–370

F

Fisher's exact test, 325–327
Freeman-Tukey deviates, 280

G

Geisser-Greenhouse *F* test, 77–78
General linear model, 3–41, 129–163
  rank, 12, 17, 114, 130–156
Goodness of fit, 277–281, 300–301
Graphical Data Analysis, 355, 391–455, 472–
  473 (*see also* EDA)

H, I

Hypothesis testing, *see* significance testing
Iterative Proportional Fitting, 272–275

L

Latent models, 342–345
Linear model, *see* General linear model
Log-linear models, 262–292
  hierarchical, 267–268

M

Maximum likelihood estimates, 270, 274–279,
  282–283, 311–312
McNemar's test, 338–339
Multivariate analysis, 129–163
  association measures, 168–171
  MANCOVA, 31, 129–130, 149–156, 161–
    163, 180–185
  MANOVA, 3, 31, 35–37, 129–149, 161–
    163, 180–185
  repeated measures, 79–83
  significance testing, 174–180
  graphical presentation, 435–455

O, P

Outliers, 280, 362–363, 371–373
Path analysis, 285–288
Power, 46–47, 50, 78, 301
  for multivariate analysis, 82–83
  for set correlation, 174–178

R

Regression, 4–9, 11, 99–114, 165–166, 16●
  170
  graphical plots, 413–424
  logistic, 334–338
  resistant lines, 371–372
Reparamaterization, 18–20, 147–149
Repeated measures, 73–94
  degrees of freedom, 77–79
  multiple comparisons, 64–67, 248–254
  multivariate analysis, 79–83

S

Sampling schemes, 260–262
Significance testing, 26–31, 74, 174–180,
  223–225
Stationarity, 505–507
Sufficient statistics, 269–270

T

Time series, 493–527
  autocorrelations and autoregression, 503–
    504, 507–512, 514–516
  interventions, 495–500, 518–523
  moving averages, 507–512, 514–516
Type I error, 43–47, 53–54, 73–74, 76, 83,
  179–180, 300–301

U

Unbalanced designs, *see* unequal frequencies
Unequal frequencies, 95–125
  proportional, 102–108
  regression solution, 97–114
  sources of, 96–97